American Inventors, Entrepreneurs, and Business Visionaries

REVISED EDITION

CHARLES W. CAREY, JR.

Revised by IAN C. FRIEDMAN

Facts On File
An imprint of Infobase Publishing

American Inventors, Entrepreneurs, and Business Visionaries, Revised Edition

Copyright 2011, 2002 by Charles W. Carey, Jr.

Facts On File, Inc.
An imprint of Infobase Publishing
132 West 31st Street
New York NY 10001

Library of Congress Cataloging-in-Publication Data
Carey, Charles W.
  American inventors, entrepreneurs, and business visionaries / Charles W. Carey, Jr. —
  Rev. ed. / rev. by Ian C. Friedman.
      p. cm.
  Includes bibliographical references and indexes.
  ISBN 978-0-8160-8146-2 (hc : acid-free paper)
  1. Inventors—United States—Biography. 2. Businesspeople—United States—Biography.
  3. United States—Biography. I. Friedman, Ian C. II. Title.
  CT214.C29 2010
  609.2'273—dc22   2009054269

Text design by Joan M. McEvoy
Composition by Newgen Publishing
Cover printed by Sheridan Books, Ann Arbor, Mich.
Book printed and bound by Sheridan Books, Ann Arbor, Mich.
Date printed: October 2010
Printed in the United States of America

10 9 8 7 6 5 4 3 2 1

CONTENTS

NOTE ON PHOTOS

Many of the illustrations and photographs used in this book are old, historical images. The quality of the prints is not always up to modern standards, and in some cases the originals are from glass negatives or are damaged. The content of the illustrations, however, made their inclusion important despite problems in reproduction.

LIST OF ENTRIES

AUTHOR'S NOTE

Any compilation of important people, no matter how many are included, is sure to leave out someone who somebody else thinks should have been included. Trying to capture the history of American invention and entrepreneurialism in less than 300 individual essays necessitates leaving out lots of people who probably should have been included. Therefore, let me explain my rationale for who was included in this book and who was not.

A few people are so famous that they would have been included in anyone's book about American inventors, entrepreneurs, and business visionaries. These people include Thomas Edison, Henry Ford, Bill Gates, Andrew Carnegie, J. P. Morgan, Oprah Winfrey, John Jacob Astor, and a few others. Beyond these individuals, it becomes necessary to pick those people who allow the author to tell a story about the nature of invention and entrepreneurialism in America. To this end I wanted to include people from all categories of American life—men, women, blacks, whites, Hispanics, Asians, the old, the young, the native-born, and the immigrants. If this book has one message, it is that anyone can be, because all kinds of people

have been, successful innovators and visionaries in the realm of American business.

If this book has two messages, the second is that you do not have to be famous to have been an important contributor to the growth of business activity in the United States. To this end I have included a number of lesser-known, one might say obscure, people who serve as representatives of the vast body of small inventors and local businesspeople who have made their communities better places to live. And if this book has three messages, the third is that inventors and entrepreneurs are a colorful lot. To this end I have included people who became involved in invention and business in unusual ways, who succeeded (or failed) because of unusual circumstances, or who simply had a good story to tell. It is my opinion that success in business—indeed, any endeavor—is one part hard work and brains and one part luck, and so I have included as many people as I could who succeeded because they were both good and lucky.

I hope you enjoy learning about all of the inventors, entrepreneurs, and business visionaries featured in this book.

ACKNOWLEDGMENTS

We offer deep gratitude to many people who played key roles in helping us write this book, including: Owen Lancer, Nicole Bowen, Matt Speliotis, Jim Pollack, Vickie Budge, Ariel Myers, Sarah DeCapua, Gene Springs, Seth Pauley, and Melissa Cullen-Du Pont.

INTRODUCTION

The American economy has changed dramatically over the last four centuries. What was primarily an agrarian society has been transformed into an industrial one that depends on products and services that were once inconceivable. These changes came about as a direct result of the efforts of inventors, entrepreneurs, and business visionaries who dreamed of better ways to do or to make things and then made their dreams into reality. The following is a discussion of how the economy changed from one century to the next and the individuals who brought about these changes.

SEVENTEENTH AND EIGHTEENTH CENTURIES

The colonial period was marked by a general economic dependence on Great Britain. The Navigation Acts prohibited Americans from trading directly with anyone other than British merchants, and various other measures such as the Iron Act and the Hat Act prohibited Americans from manufacturing anything that could be made in the home country. As a result, most inventions developed by colonial Americans pertained to agriculture. For example, the first American invention to receive a patent of any sort was SYBILLA RIGHTON MASTERS's corn-refining machine. Patented in 1715, this machine basically duplicated an old American Indian process for grinding corn. Likewise, there was little entrepreneurial activity in colonial America that was not related to agriculture. Most Americans in New England and the Mid-Atlantic colonies (New York, New Jersey, Pennsylvania, and Delaware) lived and worked on family-owned farms, which for the most part produced what the family needed to survive. A few larger holdings in New York, Pennsylvania, and Maryland produced wheat for the international market, while farmers living around the coastal towns raised vegetables and dairy products for urban dwellers. The South was dominated by plantations, which generally produced a staple crop for the international market. One such crop was indigo, which was introduced from the Caribbean to South Carolina by ELIZABETH LUCAS PINCKNEY. Most free southerners, however, earned their living as subsistence farmers.

Outside of being a planter, entrepreneurial activity in colonial America was generally restricted to four areas. A young man between the ages of 14 and 21 could apprentice himself to an artisan and learn a trade, after which he could start his own business. The classic example is BENJAMIN FRANKLIN, who rose from printer's apprentice to prominent publisher. Although most small businessmen made only a modest living, some, like WILLIAM FLORA, were able to prosper to the point that they could engage in land speculation toward the end of their career. Women were generally discouraged from working outside the home; however, widows, like SARAH KEMBLE KNIGHT, were permitted to operate taverns, inns, and boardinghouses as a means of supporting themselves. And since land was the basis of agriculture, land speculation was generally open to men and women alike. But the most lucrative activity was being a merchant, and it was thus that nonplanters attained positions of wealth and prestige.

Although the Navigation Acts forced Americans to ship their goods in British vessels, it also defined American ships as British vessels. Barred from manufacturing, the shrewdest colonial Americans bought or built ships and became merchants. By the beginning of the American Revolution, Americans constituted a major part of Great Britain's merchant fleet. Most merchants, like ROBERT MORRIS, JOHN BROWN, and THOMAS HANDASYD PERKINS, got their start by joining the family mercantile firm and then forming a partnership with an older merchant. During the colonial period American merchants dominated the carrying trade between the 13 colonies and Great Britain, but they also engaged in extensive if illegal trade with French, Spanish, and Dutch traders in the West Indies, Africa, and Europe. After the war, Morris, Brown, and Perkins opened the China trade to American merchants and further extended American mercantile contacts around the globe. Meanwhile, other American merchants, like JOHN JACOB ASTOR and RENÉ AUGUSTE CHOUTEAU, gradually took over the North American fur trade from their British and French competitors, while others, like JOHN WESLEY HUNT, began establishing commercial connections between the Atlantic coast and the trans-Appalachian West.

Nonagricultural invention in the colonial and early national period before 1785 revolved mostly around the carrying trade. In 1731 THOMAS GODFREY invented the octant, which enabled seamen to gauge their latitude, and in the mid-1780s JAMES FORTEN invented a device for handling sails that greatly simplified the process of rigging a merchant ship. Also in the mid-1780s, several inventors, like JOHN FITCH, had begun the process of replacing sailing vessels on America's rivers and lakes with steamboats.

The successful conclusion of the American Revolution freed U.S. entrepreneurs from the restrictions against manufacturing. After 1785 inventors and entrepreneurs began devoting more and more attention and energy to industrialization. That same year, OLIVER EVANS built a fully automated flour mill in Delaware, the first of its kind in North America. Five years later SAMUEL SLATER built the first American factory in Rhode Island, which revolutionized the production of cotton textiles in the United States. ELI WHITNEY's cotton gin encouraged the spread of cotton cultivation,

thus providing mills like Slater's with plenty of raw materials. By the middle of the next century, the cotton gin had enriched thousands of people, including planters like WILLIAM ELLISON and slave traders like ZIBA B. OAKES.

NINETEENTH CENTURY

The trend toward self-sufficiency that began in the late 18th century carried over into the early 19th century. The nascent Industrial Revolution demanded more sophisticated machinery for making things, and American inventors responded. THOMAS BLANCHARD's irregular turning lathe proved to be an invaluable machine for manufacturing other machines, while JOHN THORP's ring spinning machine greatly sped up the process of spinning cotton fibers into yarn. The trend toward self-sufficiency can also be seen in everything from the manufacture of soap and rubber, industries initiated by WILLIAM COLGATE and CHARLES GOODYEAR, respectively, to the increased popularity of home medicine, made popular by botanic physicians like SAMUEL THOMSON. Like the textile industry, the shoe industry was transformed by the introduction of machines, especially the shoe-stitching and shoe-lasting machines of LYMAN REED BLAKE and JAN ERNST MATZELIGER, respectively. Other industry-transforming materials, machines, and processes invented during the century include sandblasting, developed by BENJAMIN CHEW TILGHMAN and RICHARD ALBERT TILGHMAN; celluloid, a plasticlike substance invented by JOHN WESLEY HYATT that led LEO HENDRIK BAEKELAND to invent modern plastic; and MARGARET KNIGHT's machine for making paper bags.

As manufacturing activity increased, the need for better transportation and communication increased also. CORNELIUS VANDERBILT is best known for his activities as a railroadman, but the "Commodore" began his entrepreneurial career as a ferryman and later created the East Coast's dominant steamboat line. PETER COOPER invented the *Tom Thumb* locomotive, and ROBERT LIVINGSTON STEVENS connected New York City and Philadelphia via railroad; Stevens also designed the modern T-rail for railroad tracks. To facilitate the handling of freight on railroads and steamboat lines, expressmen like HENRY WELLS created Wells

Fargo and American Express, the forerunners of United Parcel Service (UPS) and FedEx, while private law enforcement officials like ALLAN PINKERTON established private detective agencies to police the rails and bring train robbers to justice.

While transportation services were improving, so were communications. To make it easier for people to keep in touch with one another, SAMUEL F. B. MORSE invented the telegraph and EZRA CORNELL established Western Union, the country's first national communications network. By mid-century, ROYAL EARL HOUSE had transformed Morse's invention into the printing telegraph, and CYRUS WEST FIELD had laid the first transatlantic telegraph cable. And ship-to-ship and ship-to-shore communications were greatly enhanced by MARTHA HUNT COSTON's signal flares.

As the railroads crept farther and farther from the Atlantic seaboard, the demand for more iron and steel and better ways to produce both increased dramatically. The work of foundrymen like JOSEPH REID ANDERSON was made much easier by the American Bessemer process and the dry-air furnace, invented by WILLIAM KELLY and JAMES GAYLEY, respectively. Steel also played an important role in the taming of the Midwest. Farmers arriving in these areas in mid-century needed plows and farm implements unlike anything easterners had ever devised, but thanks to steel, inventors like JOHN DEERE, CYRUS HALL McCORMICK, J. I. CASE, and CHARLES WESLEY MARSH developed the steel plow, the mechanical reaper, the thresher-separator, and the harvester, respectively.

As farmers moved farther west, they benefited greatly from such inventions as JOSEPH FARWELL GLIDDEN's barbed wire, which protected their fields from wandering animals, and SAMUEL COLT's revolver, which offered them personal protection where the law had yet to reach. They also benefited from the rise of mail-order merchandising as initiated by MONTGOMERY WARD and perfected by RICHARD WARREN SEARS. And in the West, Anglos like RICHARD KING and HARRIET STRONG created ranches and commercial farms that were plugged into the national economy, while earlier settlers of foreign birth, like JOHN SUTTER and ESTEBAN OCHOA, lost their land and mercantile empires in the flood of settlers from the East.

As mercantile activity increased throughout the country, cities grew at a rapid pace. To keep up with the demand for new buildings, JAMES BOGARDUS made use of new foundry techniques to invent cast-iron architecture, while ELISHA GRAVES OTIS invented the elevator to safely transport people and goods to all levels of a building. The one-cent newspaper, brainchild of BENJAMIN HENRY DAY, served as a medium for advertising a bewildering array of products, from the sewing machine, invented by ELIAS HOWE and perfected by ISAAC MERRITT SINGER, to LYDIA ESTES PINKHAM's patent medicine for women. By century's end, newspaper and magazine publishing had grown into a major industry, thanks largely to the publications of MIRIAM LESLIE, JOSEPH PULITZER, FRANK ANDREW MUNSEY, WILLIAM RANDOLPH HEARST, and EDWARD WILLIAM BOK, the advertising techniques of J. WALTER THOMPSON, and the Linotype typesetting machine invented by OTTMAR MERGENTHALER. Business owners were provided with a faster way to write letters and reports by CHRISTOPHER LATHAM SHOLES's typewriter, a better way to secure their places of business by LINUS YALE, JR.'s padlocks, a faster way to deliver packages, at least in New York City, by ALFRED ELY BEACH's pneumatic mail delivery system, and a more accurate way to tabulate accounts by WILLIAM SEWARD BURROUGHS's adding machine. Respite from the hustle and bustle of city life was provided by ALEXANDER JOY CARTWRIGHT, JR., who popularized the modern game of baseball, traveling acting companies and circuses such as SAMUEL DRAKE's and P. T. BARNUM's, respectively, and vaudeville routines performing in theaters such as those controlled by B. F. KEITH and E. F. ALBEE.

By the end of the century, residents in most urban areas could shop in department stores, like those of JOHN WANAMAKER and MARSHALL FIELD, and discount stores, like those of F. W. WOOLWORTH. Among other items, these stores offered ready-to-wear garments made by LEVI STRAUSS and other manufactures from cloth produced by MOSES HERMAN CONE and CEASAR CONE, among others. They could also patronize grocery stores that carried prepackaged food and beverage items like GAIL BORDEN's condensed milk, CHARLES LOUIS FLEISCHMANN's baker's yeast, GUSTAVUS FRANKLIN SWIFT's packaged beef, ADOLPHUS BUSCH's bottled beer, flaked grain products invented by JOHN HARVEY KELLOGG and W. K. KELLOGG as well as C. W. POST, and a variety of fruits and vegetables preserved via AMANDA THEODOSIA JONES's vacuum canning process. Rather than heat their homes with coal, they could use kerosene refined by the Standard Oil Company, the brainchild of JOHN DAVISON ROCKEFELLER and HENRY MORRISON FLAGLER, using a desulfurization process invented by HERMAN FRASCH. They could even smoke ready-made cigarettes made by JAMES BUCHANAN DUKE's American Tobacco Company.

The latter half of the century witnessed the amazing proliferation of railroads across the country. Led by entrepreneurs like JAMES JEROME HILL, JAY GOULD, E. H. HARRIMAN, and MINOR COOPER KEITH, railroad companies laid thousands of miles of railroad in the western United States and Central America, all as a means to bring agricultural produce to market in the eastern United States. The money to build these lines was provided by bankers like J. P. MORGAN and individual investors like HETTY GREEN. The lines ran on rails of steel, produced by mills like ANDREW CARNEGIE's, that were anchored by wooden ties from the forests of FREDERICK WEYERHAEUSER and other lumbermen. Railroads hauled freight and passengers in railcars manufactured by GEORGE MORTIMER PULLMAN, among others. They lubricated their locomotives with oil from Pennsylvania, where GEORGE HENRY BISSELL and EDWIN LAURENTIDE DRAKE had drilled the first oil well in North America, via lubricators designed by ELIJAH MCCOY.

If the mid-19th century was the age of the railroad, the century's last two decades were the age of electricity. Although THOMAS ALVA EDISON's interests were amazingly broad, it was in the field of electricity that he made his major contribution. Among other things, his work led directly to SAMUEL INSULL's development of the central power station. This development, coupled with GEORGE WESTINGHOUSE's invention of several electrical transmission devices, made possible home lighting via the incandescent lightbulb as perfected by LEWIS HOWARD LATIMER and WILLIAM DAVID COOLIDGE, street lighting via CHARLES FRANCIS BRUSH's arc lamp, and home entertainment via EMILE BERLINER's gramophone. Electricity transformed industry via the alternating-current electric motor invented by NIKOLA TESLA and industrial shop lighting via PETER COOPER HEWITT's mercury-vapor lamp. It also made possible a number of industrial applications such as EDWARD GOODRICH ACHESON's method for making abrasive material and synthetic graphite and CHARLES HALL's method for extracting aluminum from bauxite. It transformed public transportation via the electric streetcar, pioneered by CHARLES TYSON YERKES, that was powered by THOMAS DAVENPORT's electromagnetic motor and GRANVILLE T. WOODS's modified troller. It transformed communications by providing a strong and reliable power source for the telephone, invented (in various incarnations) by ALEXANDER GRAHAM BELL and ELISHA GRAY; the telephone replaced the telegraph shortly after MICHAEL IDVORSKY PUPIN invented the inductance coil, thus making possible long-distance telephony. And electricity stimulated the mining industry by creating a huge demand for copper wiring, thus making millionaires out of western copper magnates like MARCUS DALY.

As industrial activity became increasingly important in the late 19th century, many industrialists and financiers sought to corner markets, thereby eliminating competition and improving profits. Rockefeller was the most successful at creating a trust, as Standard Oil eventually controlled about 90 percent of the petroleum business in America. Morgan played a major role in arranging the financing for the establishment of U.S. Steel, a number of lesser-known trusts, and the consolidation of several railroads. Another important trustmaker was JOHN WARNE GATES, who engineered four different trusts related to the manufacture of steel products.

TWENTIETH CENTURY

During the 19th century, the U.S. economy made the transition from agrarian-centered to industrial-centered. Nonetheless, by 1900 the majority of Americans still labored on farms rather than in factories. This situation would change in the 20th century; by the end of World War II, farming had ceased to be the number-one occupation in the United States. Between 1900 and 1950, factory jobs increased as a result of the establishment of new industries that revolved around the automobile, the airplane, and electronics. But by the end of the 20th century, the manufacturing sector had given way to the service sector as the primary mode of generating income for the greatest number of Americans.

Prior to 1870 most new products and processes came from tinkerers who may or may not have understood the physical principles involved in their discoveries. This situation changed as a result of Edison's tremendous success with a scientific approach to invention. Edison inspired many 20th-century imitators, including ARTHUR DEHON LITTLE, founder of the first independent industrial research firm in the country. Few companies made better use of industrial research than Du Pont, which was founded in the 18th century by ÉLEUTHÉRE IRÉNÉE DU PONT DE NEMOURS to manufacture gunpowder. By 1900, the company had expanded its horizons, and its laboratories produced neoprene and nylon, invented by WALLACE HUME CAROTHERS, and Kevlar, invented by STEPHANIE LOUISE KWOLEK. Another Du Pont researcher, FREDERICK GARDNER COTTRELL, invented the electrostatic precipitator as a way to reduce air pollution. By the end of the century, industrial research was the rule, not the exception, as a number of scientifically trained researchers were making important discoveries. PERCY LAVON JULIAN pioneered the production of synthetic hormones for a variety of applications, EDITH MARIE FLANIGEN invented the synthetic emerald and the molecular sieve, KATHERINE BURR BLODGETT developed nonreflective glass, and RACHEL FULLER BROWN, ELIZABETH LEE HAZEN, and GERTRUDE BELLE ELION developed important antibiotic and pharmaceutical drugs.

The most important new industry to arise during the century's first half was the automobile industry. Although the automobile was invented in Europe, it was perfected in the United States. The first American-made automobile was produced by CHARLES EDGAR DURYEA and JAMES FRANK DURYEA, but within a few years they had attracted a number of competitors. Perhaps the most interesting one was the Stanley Steamer, a steam-powered car designed and manufactured by FRANCIS EDGAR STANLEY and FREELAN OSCAR STANLEY. Stiffer competition was provided by RANSOM ELI OLDS and DAVID DUNBAR BUICK; both of their companies would later become part of General Motors, which was founded by WILLIAM CRAPO DURANT, a wagon maker turned car manufacturer. The toughest competitor of all, however, was HENRY FORD, who perfected the modern assembly line and churned out automobiles almost as fast as people could buy them. By mid-century, the price of entering the automobile industry had become prohibitive, as HENRY JOHN KAISER, who made millions in the heavy construction industry, discovered to his sorrow.

The rise of the U.S. auto industry stimulated a number of developments ancillary to the mass production and design of automobiles. First came new tools, such as CHARLES HOTCHKISS NORTON's cylindrical grinder for manufacturing crankshafts. Second came a wave of new features for autos, including MARY ANDERSON's windshield wiper, VINCENT HUGO BENDIX's electric starter motor and shoe brakes, CHARLES FRANKLIN KETTERING's yearly model change and V-8 engine, and EUGENE JULES HOUDRY's high-octane gasoline.

The need for gasoline led to major developments in the petroleum industry. Previously, it had been centered in western Pennsylvania, but in the 20th century Americans began looking for it in the Southwest and around the world. HOWARD ROBARD HUGHES, SR., gave the industry a shot in the arm when he invented a special drill bit capable of punching through the granite shelves that protected much of the oil in Texas, Louisiana, and Oklahoma. By 1930, oilmen like H. L. HUNT and J. PAUL GETTY were bringing up millions of barrels of crude oil from these three states. Three decades later, ARMAND HAMMER struck it rich in the oilfields of California.

Next to automobiles, the biggest consumer of petroleum products was airplanes. WILBUR and ORVILLE WRIGHT pioneered this industry in 1903, when they successfully flew the first self-propelled aircraft. Other aviation pioneers were GLENN HAMMOND CURTISS, inventor of the seaplane; MALCOLM and ALLAN LOCKHEED, founders of one of the most successful commercial aircraft manufacturers; JUAN TERRY TRIPPE, founder of Pan American Airways, the first airline to offer around-the-globe service; ELMER AMBROSE SPERRY, whose innovative use of the gyroscope resulted in the development of autopilots for aircraft; WILLIAM POWELL LEAR, who developed the first successful private jet; and HOWARD ROBARD HUGHES, JR., who built two of the largest airplanes ever constructed.

Several major industries that arose in the 20th century were centered around electronics. The pioneer in this area was LEE DE FOREST, inventor of the Audion vacuum tube. EDWIN HOWARD ARMSTRONG used the Audion to vastly improve radio reception in the century's first two decades. De Forest's and Armstrong's inventions contributed directly to the development of radio as a major form of entertainment, especially after businessmen like HUGO GERNSBACK began selling inexpensive kits so that anyone could build his own radio.

Radio was soon dwarfed by the rise of television, the most popular entertainment media of all time. Like the automobile, television was not invented in America, but it was perfected here. Two major developments came in the 1930s, when PHILO TAYLOR FARNSWORTH invented the image dissector, which transmitted moving images to a receiver, and VLADIMIR KOSMA ZWORYKIN invented the electronic picture tube for receiving and projecting moving images. Other television pioneers include EDWARD JOHN NOBLE, the candy manufacturer who established the American Broadcasting Companies (ABC) as one of the earliest television networks, and PETER CARL GOLDMARK, inventor of color television. As the new medium became increasingly popular, audiences demanded innovative programming, and they received it. Between 1960 and 2000, MERV GRIFFIN created two of the most popular game shows of all time, JIM HENSON used puppetry to create one of the most popular variety shows of all time, ROBERT WARREN PITTMAN invented Music Television (MTV) as alternative viewing for the younger generation, OPRAH WINFREY established herself as the queen of the talk show, and JOHN WERNER KLUGE and TED TURNER established networks that changed the nature of television programming via

their innovative approaches to broadcasting movies, sports, and news.

The most important industry to arise in the second half of the 20th century was the computer industry. Once again, U.S. inventors and entrepreneurs led the way in the discovery and application of electronic data processing. The industry grew out of the successful efforts of HERMAN HOLLERITH to build an electromechanical tabulator for the U.S. Census Bureau in the 1880s. Major developments involving electronics, especially de Forest's invention of the vacuum tube, led JOHN WILLIAM MAUCHLY and JOHN PRESPER ECKERT, JR., to build the first all-electronic computers in the 1940s. Their efforts were greatly enhanced by those of GRACE HOPPER, who developed the first computer language compiler, also known as software, so that nonprofessional users could get a computer to do what they wanted it to do. Before long, entrepreneurs such as ROSS PEROT were custom-designing software to do a variety of jobs for a multitude of customers. AN WANG and ROBERT NORTON NOYCE made major contributions to computer technology by inventing magnetic core memory and the integrated circuit, or computer chip, respectively. STEPHEN GARY WOZNIAK and STEVEN PAUL JOBS used the technology of Wang and Noyce as well as money raised by venture capitalists like ARTHUR ROCK to build the first personal computer (PC). The PC's incredible popularity led BILL GATES to develop several different software packages to further enhance their usability. STEVE CASE's America Online made it easier for PC users to access the World Wide Web, and KIM POLESE established Java as the computer language of choice for accessing individual web sites.

As Americans made the gradual shift from an agrarian-centered society to an industrial-centered one, the number of items intended for personal consumption increased, as did the average worker's ability to afford such items. These items fall roughly into four main categories: food, fashion, convenience, and entertainment. The trend toward ready-packaged foods that had begun in the 19th century was carried forward in the 20th. The most noticeable aspect of this trend, and one that demonstrates clearly the nation's growing prosperity, is the popularity of nonessential food items such as ASA GRIGGS CANDLER's Coca-Cola, MILTON SNAVELY HERSHEY's chocolate bars, WILLIAM WRIGLEY, JR.'s chewing gum, WALLACE J. AMOS's chocolate chip cookies, and BEN COHEN and JERRY GREENFIELD's ice cream. Other food items supplied homemakers with the means to provide their families with more variety without sacrificing nutrition, such as GEORGE WASHINGTON CARVER's peanut butter, JOHN THOMPSON DORRANCE's condensed soup, JAMES LEWIS KRAFT's cheese, CLARENCE BIRDSEYE's frozen foods, MARGARET FOGARTY RUDKIN's Pepperidge Farm bread, and ROMANA ACOSTA BAÑUELOS's Mexican foods. The latter decades of the century saw the emergence of fast food, carry-out, and delivery food services, the pioneers in these activities being RAY KROC's McDonald's, HARLAND DAVID SANDERS's Kentucky Fried Chicken, and TOM MONAGHAN's Domino's Pizza.

Another excellent indicator of the growing prosperity of U.S. society is the increased importance 20th-century Americans placed on beauty and fashion. MADAME C. J. WALKER, EDNA WALLACE HOPPER, GARRETT AUGUSTUS MORGAN, ELIZABETH ARDEN, and MARY KAY ASH all became wealthy by selling cosmetics, hair treatments, and other beauty aids; unfortunately, MARJORIE STEWART JOYNER's invention of the permanent wave machine did little to enhance her income. The heightened fashion consciousness of the 1920s led women to abandon the corset for IDA ROSENTHAL's brassiere, and, if they could afford to, buy one of LILLY DACHÉ's custom-designed hats. After World War II, LIZ CLAIBORNE designed practical but attractive garments for working women, LINDA JOY WACHNER turned Warnaco into the largest manufacturer of brand-name apparel, and WILLI SMITH designed street-smart clothing for the young and hip.

Twentieth-century Americans spent money on a number of items that earlier generations would have regarded as luxuries. WILLIS HAVILAND CARRIER's air conditioner, which he seems to have invented without any knowledge of the work of JOHN GORRIE, made life in the country's hotter climes much more bearable. KING CAMP GILLETTE struck paydirt when he invented the disposable razor blade. Steadily rising incomes led a number of post–World War II Americans to move into their own home in the suburbs, which were pioneered by ABRAHAM LEVITT, or to buy a condominium in a fancy building like the ones controlled by HARRY and LEONA HELMSLEY. GERTRUDE AGNES MULLER invented a toilet seat and a car seat for young children, SYLVAN NATHAN GOLDMAN made grocery shopping much easier by inventing the folding shopping cart, RICHARD GURLEY DREW made it possible to repair a number of items by inventing Scotch tape, CANDIDO JACUZZI eased aching muscles by inventing the hot tub, EDWIN HERBERT LAND modified GEORGE EASTMAN's simple camera and ready-to-use film to make instant photography possible, FRANCES GABE performed a tremendous service for the elderly and infirm by designing the first self-cleaning house, MARION O'BRIEN DONOVAN made life simpler for the parents of young children by inventing the disposable diaper, EARL SILAS TUPPER made "leftovers" a favorite meal among Americans by inventing Tupperware, MARTHA STEWART made an art form out of gracious but casual living, and TEMPLE GRANDIN designed livestock handling equipment that reduced much of the trauma experienced by animals being led to slaughter.

During the 20th century, entertainment became one of the biggest industries in the country. Critics of the lack of wholesomeness of present-day entertainment would do well to consider some earlier forms that were highly profitable as well as believed by most to be highly immoral. Before the law ran them out of business, ADA EVERLEIGH and MINNA EVERLEIGH, ALPHONSE CAPONE, and VITO GENOVESE made millions from prostitution, bootleg liquor, and narcotics, respectively. Movies were invented around the turn of the century and generally provided wholesome entertainment for the entire family. An early movie pioneer was JAMES STUART BLACKTON, one of the first animators, who also produced the first movie to use special effects. Over the years, FREDERIC WALLER made a visit to the movies more realistic by inventing the widescreen system known as Cinerama, WALT DISNEY pioneered methods of animation and cinematography and introduced Mickey Mouse and a host of animated characters to viewers around the country, and HARRY WAYNE HUIZENGA made it possible to view movies in the privacy of the home via video rental.

Reading continued to provide the dual benefits of entertainment and education to wide audiences, and to this end regional newspaper publishers like BENJAMIN JEFFERSON DAVIS, self-help authors like DALE CARNEGIE, news agents like KENT COOPER, and literary agents like MARIE DUTTON BROWN played important roles. Magazines, which first became popular forms of entertainment in the 19th century, benefited from new technology such as HAROLD EUGENE EDGERTON's stroboscopic flash to provide readers with high-quality pictures. Among the most popular magazines were HENRY ROBINSON LUCE's *Time, Life, Fortune,* and *Sports Illustrated,* MALCOLM STEVENSON FORBES's *Forbes,* and HUGH MARSTON HEFNER and CHRISTIE ANN HEFNER's *Playboy.*

Athletic contests, many of which were held in areas covered by R. BUCKMINSTER FULLER's geodesic domes, captured the interest of millions of fans and led to the enrichment of boxing promoter DON KING and wrestling promoter VINCE MCMAHON; unfortunately, JAMES A. NAISMITH profited little from his inventions, basketball and volleyball.

The recording industry became a multimillion-dollar business in itself, thanks in no small part to the efforts of COLONEL TOM PARKER, manager of the legendary Elvis Presley, and BERRY GORDY, JR., founder of Motown Records. Modern materials and manufacturing methods helped create the toy industry, and one would be hard-pressed to think of a toy that has been a bigger seller than RUTH HANDLER's Barbie doll.

As automobiles and airplane fares became more affordable, people began taking longer trips and staying in hotels and motels such as the ones operated by CONRAD NICHOLSON HILTON, JOHN WILLARD MARRIOTT, and KEMMONS WILSON, and they began using credit cards such as ALFRED SCHIFFER BLOOMINGDALE's Diners Club to pay for meals and lodging.

The expansion of the U.S. economy in so many new directions led naturally to the expansion of the entrepreneur's ability to manage a business. A number of inventions made it easier to do many of the little things that have to be done around an office; JOHN ROBERT GREGG's shorthand allowed secretaries to take dictation faster and with greater accuracy, CHESTER FLOYD CARLSON's photocopier eliminated much of the drudgery and duplication in recordkeeping, BETTE NESMITH GRAHAM's Liquid Paper allowed secretaries to cover up their typos without having to retype an entire page.

New ways to market items were also developed. Rather than wait for customers to come to a store, ALFRED CARL FULLER sold his brushes door-to-door, the same way Madame C. J. Walker sold her beauty aids. Neither Mary Kay Ash nor Earl Silas Tupper invented the home party as a marketing technique, but both gave their own unique twists to it in the process of making it a powerful sales tool. JAY VAN ANDEL and RICH DEVOS perfected the techniques of multilevel marketing and made Amway into a multibillion-dollar corporation. SAM WALTON located "big-city" stores in small towns, and in the process sold more merchandise to residents of rural areas than anyone other than he had dreamed possible. Meanwhile, more traditional retailers enlisted the services of "mystery shoppers," like VICKIE LEA HENRY, to ascertain what sort of sales training their employees needed.

Early in the 20th century, the establishment of community-based banks, like MAGGIE WALKER's, provided funds for small, community-based businesses like EARTHA MARY MAGDALENE WHITE's. As the century progressed, the stock market became even more important as a vehicle for raising funds for corporate growth or acquisition and enabled successful stockbrokers such as JOSEPH P. KENNEDY to become millionaires. The advent of discount brokerages such as MURIEL SIEBERT's provided small investors with a good way to earn more income from their savings. But the most controversial business finance technique to arise during the century was the use of so-called junk bonds. Junk bonds were touted by MICHAEL ROBERT MILKEN in the 1970s as high-yielding investments, and for a while they performed just as he had predicted. Unfortunately, in the 1980s they were grossly abused and became a source of embarrassment for the investment community and the cause of economic ruin for many investors.

The most interesting business management techniques to arise during the century was the conglomerate. The conglomerate was a major departure from the trust, the business organization of choice of the previous century. Whereas a trust sought to dominate its industry either by gaining control of its competitors or by acquiring control over raw materials, transportation, and marketing in order to keep down the costs of manufacturing and selling its products, conglomerates sought to diversify by acquiring industries that had nothing to do with one another. The idea was to offset the sort of catastrophic losses that periodically befall a particular industry with the profits of a company in a totally unrelated industry. Although ABRAM NICHOLAS PRITZKER pioneered this technique in the 1940s, ROYAL LITTLE and CHARLES G. BLUHDORN are more commonly remembered as the founding fathers of the conglomerate. But while some entrepreneurs were combining disparate industries into one corporation, other entrepreneurs, the so-called corporate raiders like CARL CELIAN ICAHN, were buying large corporations and selling off their various divisions to the highest bidders.

TWENTY-FIRST CENTURY

In this first part of our new century, the impact of businesspeople and the pace of their influence have only accelerated. This is particularly seen in the realm of computer technology and Internet development. Computer company heads such as MICHAEL DELL have benefited from the technical and management innovation of people such as Oracle's LARRY ELLISON, Intel's ANDREW GROVE, which in turn has helped foster the creation of Internet pioneers, including Amazon's JEFFREY BEZOS, Yahoo's DAVID FILO and JERRY YANG, Google's SERGEY BRIN and LARRY PAGE, America Online's STEVE CASE, and Facebook's MARK ZUCKERBERG. As has been the case in the past, men and women are seeking and finding ways to innovate and create businesses that anticipate and meet the needs of others. Recently, this group of people has grown increasingly diverse, including JAY-Z and RUSSELL SIMMONS, two men who made their name in the music industry but have extended their impact to other realms of business including fashion.

The leading inventors, entrepreneurs, and business visionaries of our young century have, like all the others featured in this book, changed the landscape of the American economy. The farmer of the 17th century has become the computer programmer of the 21st, the head of a family mercantile firm of the colonial period has become the chief executive officer of a 21st-century conglomerate, and the semiliterate tinkerer of the early Industrial Revolution has become the researcher with a Ph.D. in a corporate laboratory. Whether one rues or revels in these changes, it should be obvious to the casual observer that inventors, entrepreneurs, and business visionaries have changed the United States and the world forever.

A

Acheson, Edward Goodrich

(1856–1931) *inventor of carborundum and synthetic graphite*

In 1926 the United States Patent Office published a list of 22 "Important Patents That Have Influenced the World's Progress." One of these patents was for carborundum, invented by Edward Acheson. From 1891 to 1929, when boron carbide was invented, carborundum was the hardest human-made compound in the world and was widely used in a number of industrial applications. Less celebrated was Acheson's invention of synthetic graphite, which eventually replaced the lead in lead pencils.

Acheson was born on March 9, 1856, in Washington, Pennsylvania. His father, William, was manager of an ironworks, and his mother, Sarah, was a homemaker. At age 16, Acheson completed his formal education and went to work for his father. The ironworks closed in 1874, and for the next six years Acheson worked as a railway ticket clerk, a surveyor's assistant, and a tank gauger. In 1880 he moved to Menlo Park, New Jersey, to work as a draftsman for THOMAS ALVA EDISON, the famous inventor.

Edison quickly discovered Acheson's inventive abilities (while working for his father, young Acheson had invented a primitive coal drilling machine). Soon Acheson was designing a graphite filament for the lightbulb and experimenting with the effects of electrical current on compounds of carbon and clay. In 1881 Edison promoted Acheson to assistant engineer and sent him to Europe where he supervised the construction of the first electric streetlight systems for Amsterdam, Antwerp, Brussels, Milan, and Paris. In 1883 he returned to Menlo Park; then in 1884 he went into the industrial research business on his own.

Unfortunately, Acheson was not another Edison. He quickly ran out of money and ideas, and in less than a year he was forced to go back to work for someone else, this time as an engineer for the Consolidated Electric Light Company in New York City. While with Con El, Acheson met and married Margaret Maher, with whom he had nine children. No longer having to invent under pressure, his creative juices began to flow again. In 1885 he invented a telephone wire that eliminated "cross talk," whereby two different conversations interfered with each other. In 1886 he sold the patent and the manufacturing rights to Standard Underground Cable Company. The money he received allowed him to return to independent industrial research on a part-time basis.

In 1890 Acheson moved to Monongahela, Pennsylvania, where he built an electrical power station. He used the profits from the sale of power to finance his return to full-time industrial research. Inspired by an earlier experiment he had done with Edison, in 1891 he mixed clay and coke (processed coal with a high carbon content) in an iron bowl, inserted an arc-light carbon electrode into the mixture, then heated the mixture to a high temperature via a powerful electrical current. The result was clear, green-tinged crystals that were almost as hard as diamonds. Acheson named the crystals "carborundum," thinking they were made from carbon and corundum (aluminum oxide). In fact, carborundum (also known as silicon carbide) contains carbon and silicon, two of the most abundant elements in nature.

Acheson knew from his ironworking days that fabricators desperately needed a tool for smoothing and deburring iron castings, and he believed that his discovery might be the very tool for these and similar grinding applications. He quickly organized the Carborundum Company with himself as president, built a shop near his power plant, and began producing small grinding wheels made from carborundum. In 1895 he moved his operations to Niagara Falls, New York, to take advantage of the tremendous supply of cheap hydroelectricity available there. His new factory, which included the world's largest electric furnace at the time, began producing a wide variety of abrasive products such as sandpaper, cloth belts, files, whetstones, and wheels of various shapes and sizes.

Acheson financed the move to Niagara Falls by selling some of his stock in the company, and in 1898 he lost controlling interest of Carborundum Company. Undeterred by this setback, in 1899 he founded Acheson Graphite Company to manufacture synthetic graphite. While experimenting with silicon carbide in 1895, Acheson had discovered that at 7500°F the silicon in carborundum vaporizes; what is left is graphite, a mineral composed of carbon. Synthetic graphite proved to be a superior substitute for natural graphite and lead in a variety of applications from lead pencils to paint. He spent most of his remaining years presiding over Acheson Graphite, and died on July 6, 1931, while visiting his daughter in New York City.

Further Reading

ME Stern Design and Communications. *The Carborundum Company: The First 100 Years, 1891–1991, a Commemorative History*. Niagara Falls, N.Y.: Flower City Printing, 1991.

Szymanowitz, Raymond. *Edward Goodrich Acheson: Inventor, Scientist, Industrialist; A Biography*. New York: Vantage Press, 1971.

Amos, Wally
(Wallace Amos, Jr.)
(1936–) *founder of Famous Amos cookies*

One of the most recognizable entrepreneurs of the 1970s was Wally Amos, founder and chief promoter of Famous Amos cookies. Amos's idea to open a store that sold nothing but chocolate chip cookies eventually led a host of imitators to open similar specialty stores in malls and shopping districts across the United States. Unfortunately, Amos was a better idea man than he was a businessman, and Famous Amos cookies ended up making more money for others than they made for him.

Amos was born Wallace Amos, Jr., on July 1, 1936, in Tallahassee, Florida. His father, Wallace, worked at the local gasworks, and his mother, Ruby, was a housekeeper. At age 12, young Wally's parents divorced, and he went to live with his mother's sister's family in New York City. Three years later, his mother and grandmother also moved to New York City, and he moved in with them. He attended the Food Trades Vocational High School with the intention of becoming a chef, but he dropped out to join the U.S. Air Force at age 17. Discharged in 1957, he spent the next four years studying at the Collegiate Secretarial Institute while working in the stockroom at Saks Fifth Avenue department store in New York City. In 1958 he married Maria La Forey with whom he had two children; they later divorced, and in 1966 he married Shirlee Ellis with whom he had one child.

In 1961 Amos went to work for the William Morris Agency, one of the country's top talent agencies, as a mailroom clerk, and within a year he had become the only black talent agent in the company. After six years of handling big-name acts such as Simon and Garfunkel, the Supremes, and Marvin Gaye, in 1967 he moved to Los Angeles, California, with the intention of becoming an independent record producer, music publisher, and personal manager. But Amos's company struggled for seven years, during which time he was almost always broke.

While living with his aunt and uncle in New York City, Amos had become enormously fond of his Aunt Della's homemade chocolate chip cookies. Although she never gave him the recipe, he never forgot how good they tasted, and whenever he needed to lift his spirits, he would bake a batch of his own. At first, he simply followed the directions on packages of Nestle's chocolate chip morsels, but later he began including pecans and a slight touch of coconut. Eventually, he began sharing his cookies with clients and friends, who always raved about how delicious they were. In 1974 B. J. Gilmore, a secretary for a musician whom Amos had called on, convinced him that his cookies were so good he should open a store and sell them. That same year, he borrowed $25,000 from various friends and opened a chocolate chip cookie store in downtown Hollywood. The cookies became an overnight hit, and soon he had people lining up to buy them. In 1975 Amos formed the Famous Amos Chocolate Chip Cookie Corporation, of which he owned 48 percent, and began selling his cookies to gourmet grocery stores and upscale department stores around the country. He promoted his cookies as if he were their personal manager and began making personal appearances on their behalf, casually attired in a Hawaiian shirt and a Panama hat. By 1977 his company owned several stores, and his two factories, one in Hollywood and one in Nutley, New Jersey, turned out about six tons of cookies per week.

In 1977 Amos made a fatal business mistake by moving to Honolulu, Hawaii, and leaving the day-to-day operations of Famous Amos in the hands of friends who meant well but had no business experience. By 1985 the company was losing money, despite annual sales of more than $10 million. Over the next four years, Amos was forced to reorganize the company four times, and each time his share of the company got smaller. Finally, in 1989, he sold out completely to a group of investors from Taiwan. Although he was retained at a salary to make public appearances and otherwise promote the company's cookies, it quickly became evident that Amos and his new employers had little in common, and that same year he left the company he had founded. Three years later, the company sold for $60 million, of which Amos received not a nickel.

During his last years with Famous Amos, Amos had given a series of public lectures at colleges and related venues about positive thinking and other motivational topics. Since his contract with the Taiwanese investors prohibited him from

entering the cookie business for two years after leaving Famous Amos, between 1989 and 1991 he made a living on the college lecture tour, charging thousands of dollars per appearance. This endeavor proved to be profitable enough that he continued to give lectures and motivational seminars even after he returned to the cookie business. In 1991 he formed Wally Amos Presents: Chip & Cookie. This business sold toys and books as well as cookies, but he closed it after a year when he was sued by the new owners of Famous Amos, who claimed the right to Amos's name, likeness, and voice when it came to marketing cookies. In 1992 he formed Uncle Noname Cookie Company and began selling a chocolate chip cookie very much like the one he made for Famous Amos, but after three years this company was still struggling to make a profit and he closed it shortly thereafter.

Amos eventually returned to work for Famous Amos after the Keebler Cookie Company acquired it, and in 2001 he was living in Kailua, Hawaii, with his third wife, Christine. He soon embarked on a new venture, Uncle Wally's Muffins, and he recently opened three cookie stores in Hawaii under the shortened and legally permissible name of Chip & Cookie. Amos continues his commitment to literacy programs, following his long tenure as spokesman for the Literacy Volunteers of America with his creation of the Read It Loud! Foundation, which promotes parents reading aloud to their children. He has written eight books on inspiration and motivation and remains active as a public speaker.

Further Reading

"About Wally," Wally Amos.com. Available online. URL: http://www.wallyamos.com. Downloaded on June 30, 2009.

Amos, Wally, and Leroy Robinson. *The Famous Amos Story: The Face That Launched a Thousand Chips.* Honolulu, Hi.: Pacific Printers, 1986.

Anderson, Joseph Reid
(1813–1892) *entrepreneur in ironworks*

Much is made of the Confederacy's lack of factories as a reason for its defeat in the Civil War. What few people realize, however, is that one of the United States' major foundries for the production of artillery pieces was located in Richmond, Virginia, and continued to manufacture cannons for the Confederate army for the duration of the war. This foundry, Tredegar Iron Works, was owned and operated by Joseph Anderson.

Anderson was born on February 16, 1813, in Botetourt County, Virginia. His parents, William and Anna, were farmers. After graduating from the U.S. Military Academy at West Point in 1836, he was commissioned a second lieutenant, assigned to the artillery, and sent to Fort Monroe, Virginia. In 1837 he married Sally Archer with whom he had five children. Later that year he resigned his commission to become the assistant state engineer for the Valley Turnpike in Virginia's Shenandoah Valley.

In 1841 Anderson took over management of the Tredegar Iron Works in Richmond. The company was one of the few major iron foundries in the South, and it had produced a considerable amount of iron for railroads until the panic of 1837 brought railroad construction to a virtual standstill. By 1841 the company had still not recovered, so Anderson was invited by Tredegar's officials to do what he could to revive the company. As a former artillery officer and graduate of West Point, he had a number of contacts in the War Department's ordnance division, the branch of the federal government that ordered cannon and other artillery pieces for the army and navy, and he used these contacts to win a number of government contracts.

Anderson also made Tredegar profitable by cutting costs. He resisted efforts by the government to make him modernize his equipment and procedures on the grounds that the costs of such modernization would make his operation unprofitable. On one occasion, he turned down a sizable contract that required him to make heavy cannons according to the Rodman method, whereby the barrel was cast around a hollow core and then cooled from the inside, the result being a stronger barrel. In 1847, he replaced many of the high-paid, skilled white workers in the foundry with hired slaves, which was easily done in Virginia owing to the decline of the plantation system in that state. When the remaining white workers walked off the job, Anderson fired the strikers and replaced them with more hired slaves. Arguing that the actions of the strikers were an attack on the slave system and therefore on the South itself, he won the support of the larger community, after which the strike came to a quick end. By 1848 the company was doing so well that Anderson was able to borrow enough money to buy out the owners and assume total control of Tredegar. From that time on, the company was also known as J. R. Anderson and Company.

Anderson continued to sell cannons to the federal government even after South Carolina seceded from the Union in 1860, although he also sold a considerable amount of ammunition to that state as well. However, when Virginia seceded in 1861, he became a full-fledged Confederate. He spent most of 1861 in the Confederate army as a brigadier general, and he was wounded during the Seven Days battles outside of Richmond. In 1862 he resigned his commission and returned to Tredegar, where he oversaw the production of cannons and ammunition for the Confederate army for the duration of the war. Tredegar was the largest producer of war materiel in the South during the Civil War, manufacturing more than one thousand cannons for the army, virtually all of the armor plate for the navy's ironclads such as the *Merrimac*, and countless rounds of artillery shells and cannonballs. Since the war also greatly stimulated the construction and repair of many miles of Southern railroads, the company also returned to the manufacture of iron rails.

When the Union army captured Richmond in 1865, it seized Tredegar Iron Works and closed it down. Anderson successfully petitioned the federal government to pardon him for his involvement in the war, thus winning the return of the confiscated ironworks. Although Tredegar had been damaged during the war, Anderson was able to repair the damage by using money he had made during the war from financing blockade-runners, which he had secreted in England for the war's duration. The company continued to thrive until 1873, when another panic seriously disrupted the national economy. In addition, improvements in the production of steel had allowed that commodity to replace iron in a number of construction and manufacturing applications. Nevertheless, Tredegar continued to serve as the principal manufacturer of iron in the Upper South for a number of years thereafter. Anderson's health failed toward the end of his life, and he died on September 7, 1892, in Isles of Shoals, New Hampshire, where he had gone to recuperate.

Further Reading

"Brigadier-General Joseph Reid Anderson." URL: http://www.patch.net/military/jra.html. Downloaded on June 30, 2009.

Dew, Charles B. *Ironmaker to the Confederacy: Joseph R. Anderson and the Tredegar Iron Works.* Richmond: Library of Virginia, 1999.

Anderson, Mary

(1866–1953) *inventor of the windshield wiper*

Mary Anderson invented the hand-operated windshield wiper. Although she received a patent for her idea, she never sold it to anyone. Shortly after her patent lapsed, her idea was copied and soon windshield wipers became standard equipment on cars and trucks. Today the motor-driven version of her invention makes it possible for millions of people to operate automobiles safely in inclement weather.

Few details are known about Anderson's life. She was born in Alabama in 1866, probably in Birmingham, where she spent most of her life in obscurity. Her parents' names and occupations are unknown, and she apparently never married.

Sometime around 1900 Anderson inherited a large sum of money from an aunt. She decided to celebrate her good fortune by visiting New York City, which she happened to do during the dead of winter. While riding an electric streetcar during a snowstorm, she noticed that the motorman operating the streetcar was shivering. Snow was sticking to the windshield, and he was constantly having to slide open the middle pane so he could wipe off the glass. In the process, he let in snow and cold air and made himself quite uncomfortable.

Upon returning to Alabama, Anderson gave much thought to the motorman's plight. She eventually came up with a way to wipe the windshield clean of snow and ice without having to open it. Her idea involved attaching a wiper blade to a swivel nut, which in turn was attached to a long handle. The swivel nut would be mounted through a hole in the metal frame above the windshield so that the wiper blade would be on the outside of the windshield and the long handle would be parallel to it but on the inside. When the handle was moved back and forth, a fan-shaped area on the windshield was wiped clean.

In 1903 Anderson patented her idea for a "window cleaning device for electric cars and other vehicles to remove snow, ice or sleet from the window" (*New York Times*). She got a Birmingham machinist to make a model, then offered to sell it to a manufacturing firm in Montreal, Canada. But the company declined her offer, and Anderson never tried to sell the idea to anyone else. Why she failed to do so is a mystery. There is evidence to suggest that she had been stung by the ridicule of her upper-class friends, who regarded tinkering with machines as something that only someone from the lower class would do. Or perhaps she simply did not know whom else to approach with her idea. Streetcars were not common in the South at that time, and the typical southern woman was neither trained nor encouraged to engage in business, but especially not in the North. In 1920 her patent lapsed. Shortly thereafter someone else patented a windshield wiper similar to Anderson's, and this is the one that was adopted for use on motor vehicles. Mary Anderson died on June 27, 1953, at her summer home in Monteagle, Tennessee.

Further Reading

Blashfield, Jean F. *Women Inventors 2: Amanda Jones, Mary Anderson, Bette Nesmith Graham, Ruth Benerito, Becky Schroeder.* Minneapolis, Minn.: Capstone Press, 1996.

Macdonald, Anne L. *Feminine Ingenuity: Women and Invention in America.* New York: Ballantine Books, 1994.

Arden, Elizabeth
(Florence Nightingale Graham)

(1878–1966) *founder of Elizabeth Arden Inc.*

One of the cultural changes brought about by World War I was the increased acceptance by society of women who used cosmetics other than skin cream. Prior to the war, just about the only women who painted their faces with lipstick, rouge, and the like were prostitutes, hence the euphemistic nickname "painted ladies." After the war, just about every woman who could afford cosmetics began using them. One of the top promoters of cosmetics in the United States was the woman who was known professionally as Elizabeth Arden. Like her archrival, Helena Rubinstein, Arden helped to popularize the use of cosmetics in the United States by teaching women how to apply them in a way that enhanced their natural feminine beauty.

Arden was born Florence Nightingale Graham on December 31, 1878, in Woodbridge, Ontario, Canada. Her parents, William and Susan, were tenant farmers. She dropped out of high school to become a nurse but quickly learned that, unlike her namesake, she could not stand to take care of sick people. After working successively in nearby Toronto as a dental assistant, stenographer, and cashier, she moved to New York City around 1908 to join her brother.

Arden got into the beauty business in 1908 while working as a cashier for Eleanor Adair, a beautician. That same year she persuaded Adair to teach her how to apply facials with skin cream, and before long she was doing an expert job. Within a year she had become partners with Elizabeth Hubbard, who was operating a beauty salon under her name on Fifth Avenue. When Hubbard insisted on ending the partnership after only a few months, in 1909 Arden borrowed $6,000 from her brother and bought Hubbard out. When it came time to name the new business, Arden simply removed "Hubbard" from the store's sign and substituted "Arden," from the title of an Alfred, Lord Tennyson poem, thus becoming known professionally (but not legally) as Elizabeth Arden. To give her salon that something extra, she decorated it with antiques and oriental carpets. She also painted the front door bright red, which became the trademark of her salons as they spread across the country.

Part of Arden's success was her complexion, which made her look 10 years younger than she really was. At first, she specialized in giving facial massages with skin cream to women who wanted a complexion like hers. On a trip to Paris, France,

in 1914 to see what Parisian salons were doing, she discovered they were using lots of cosmetics: mascara, eye shadow, rouge, and lipstick. Upon her return to New York City, she began promoting the use of cosmetics, and with her skillful touch she soon had her customers looking every bit as glamorous as the most sophisticated women in Paris. She contracted A. Fabian Swanson, a noted chemist, to develop the first nongreasy face cream, called Amoretta, which she also used as a foundation for the application of makeup. She also introduced the first lipstick shades that matched the different skin tones and fabric colors, and she taught her customers how to make their makeup part of their total fashion ensemble. Soon she was making as much money from the sale of cosmetics as she was from giving facials and other beauty treatments. She used the profits from the salon to open new salons, and by 1930 she owned more than one hundred beauty salons in the United States, Canada, and Europe. By 1947 she had opened health resorts in Mount Vernon, Maine, and Phoenix, Arizona.

Being successful in the beauty world meant maintaining a glamorous public image, and Arden spared no expense in this department. Although she spent large sums on magazine advertising, she always felt that her most effective promotion was her sponsorship of charity balls, which always attracted the cream of society and which were always featured prominently in the society pages of the newspapers. She loved breeding and training racehorses, as much for the fun as for the publicity, and in 1947 one of her horses, Jet Pilot, won the Kentucky Derby, the most prestigious horse race in the United States. Having divorced Thomas Lewis, her husband of 19 years, in 1934 (although he continued to work for her company for several years thereafter), in 1942 she married a Russian prince, Michael Evlanoff. Even though they were divorced two years later, the marriage established her as a fixture in high society and helped to keep her name before the cosmetic-buying public for many years.

Arden maintained strict control of her company until her death. By 1966, the Elizabeth Arden Company was doing annual sales of $60 million, and her personal fortune was estimated to be more than $10 million. After her death on October 18,

1966, in New York City, the company was sold to Eli Lilly & Company for $37.5 million.

Further Reading

Lewis, Alfred Allen, and Constance Woodworth. *Miss Elizabeth Arden.* New York: Pinnacle, 1974.

Shuker, Nancy. *Elizabeth Arden: Beauty Empire Builder.* Woodbridge, Conn.: Blackbirch Press, 2001.

Armstrong, Edwin Howard

(1890–1954) *inventor of radio circuitry and frequency modulation*

Although Americans did not invent radio communications, they developed most of the inventions that made radio and television into popular modern media. Edwin Armstrong, inventor of the regenerative and superheterodyne circuits as well as frequency modulation, is one of the most important but least known of the American radio pioneers.

Armstrong was born on December 18, 1890, in New York City. His father, John, was a publisher, and his mother, Emily, was a teacher. At age 10 Armstrong moved with his family to Yonkers, New York. Four years later he became fascinated with radio electronics, and he built a primitive electronics laboratory in his attic. In 1913 he received his B.S. in electrical engineering from Columbia University. Except for a brief stint with the U.S. Army Signal Corps in Paris, France, during World War I, he taught electrical engineering at Columbia from 1913 until his death. In 1923 he married Marion MacInnis with whom he had no children.

Early radios used crystals to receive signals. Unfortunately, they could not amplify these signals very well, so operators could hear them only by using earphones. In 1907 LEE DE FOREST invented the audion, a vacuum-tube receiver that amplified signals a little bit louder than the crystal could. However, not even De Forest knew why the audion worked. During his junior year at Columbia, Armstrong discovered that the audion's anode plate oscillated while receiving a radio signal. He then devised a circuit that fed this oscillating signal back into the audion's control grid, thereby amplifying the original signal so much that it could be heard across the room without earphones. Known

as the regenerative circuit, Armstrong's invention became and remained a standard feature of radio receivers into the 21st century.

While in Paris during the war, Armstrong and Harry W. Houck developed a way to amplify very high frequency (VHF) waves so they could be used in radio communications. VHF waves are perfectly suited to short-distance radio broadcasting because they are not affected by static, as lower frequency waves are; however, VHF waves are so weak they can barely be heard. By developing a circuit to generate and add a low-frequency signal to the VHF signal, they were able to transform the VHF signal into an intermediate signal that could be greatly amplified via a regenerative circuit. Known as the superheterodyne circuit, this invention became a basic feature of VHF wave reception.

Early commercial radio broadcasting impressed information on a carrier wave via amplitude modulation (AM), which varies the carrier wave's power. AM signals can be sent long distances and are perfectly suited for simple broadcasts such as talking or unaccompanied singing. However, AM is not well-suited for complex broadcasts such as a symphonic performance, and it is easily disrupted by static from electrical storms and random electric interference from machines. After the war, Armstrong drew on his work with VHF to develop a new way to modulate carrier waves. By 1933 he had fully developed frequency modulation (FM). This process varies the carrier wave's frequency, or how many individual waves are transmitted per second. This form of modulation eliminates static by producing a wider, higher frequency waveband, which also makes FM perfectly suited for the clear transmission of stereo broadcasts. Between 1950 and 2000, FM became the preferred modulation for radio and the required modulation for the audio channel in television.

Armstrong received several awards for his inventions, including the Institute of Radio Engineers' first Medal of Honor in 1918 and the Franklin Institute's Franklin Medal in 1941. He also became a wealthy man from the sale and licensing of his patents to the regenerative and superheterodyne circuits to such corporations as Telefunken, Westinghouse, and RCA. However, his adult life was marred by drawn-out lawsuits over patents.

In 1915 he was sued by De Forest, who claimed to have invented the regenerative circuit a year before Armstrong did. The suit dragged on until 1934 when the U.S. Supreme Court settled it in De Forest's favor; the radio community never accepted the validity of this ruling and generally considers Armstrong to be the inventor of the regenerative circuit. In 1948 he sued RCA and several other large companies for violating his patent rights to FM. Six years later—frustrated by the time and money the lawsuits were consuming and in ill health—on January 31, 1954, he committed suicide by leaping from his apartment window. Most of the suits were eventually settled in his favor.

Further Reading

Lessing, Lawrence P. *Man of High Fidelity: Edwin Howard Armstrong, A Biography.* New York: Bantam Books, 1985.

Lewis, Tom. *Empire of the Air: The Men Who Made Radio.* New York: HarperPerennial, 1993.

Ash, Mary Kay
(Mary Kathlyn Wagner)
(1918–2001) *founder of Mary Kay Cosmetics*

Surprising as it may seem, the single most popular brand of cosmetics in the United States cannot be bought in stores. The products of Mary Kay Cosmetics, which account for more than 8 percent of the nation's cosmetics sales, are available only from a self-employed Mary Kay Consultant, who demonstrates the products in customers' homes and teaches their proper application. The company was founded by Mary Kay Ash, who made herself wealthy while also providing an unprecedented moneymaking opportunity for women across America.

Ash was born Mary Kathlyn Wagner on May 12, 1918, in Hot Wells, Texas. Her parents, Edward and Lula, owned and operated a hotel. When she was three years old, her father developed tuberculosis and became an invalid; over the next four years her mother sold the hotel, moved the family to Houston, and went to work, first as a nurse and then as a restaurant manager. From the time she was seven, Ash went to school, cared for her father, and cooked and cleaned the house while her mother was at work. At age 17 she graduated from high school with the intention of becoming a doctor. However, her family could not afford college tuition, and that same year she married J. Ben Rogers with whom she had three children. They divorced in 1946, and in 1966 she married Melville Jerome Ash, who died in 1980.

After a few years of homemaking and motherhood, Ash found herself yearning for something more. About that time, a chance visit from a door-to-door saleswoman got her interested in selling child-care books on a part-time basis. Within nine months, Ash, who had excelled at public speaking and debating in high school, had sold $25,000 worth of the books, a significant amount given the fact that the Great Depression was still in full swing. This success led her to try her hand at selling pots and pans at "parties," evening get-togethers in prospective customers' homes of a dozen or so of their acquaintances. Although these items were of excellent quality, they were too expensive for most depression-era Houstonians, who evidently cared more about their children than their cookware. By 1939 she had moved on to another direct sales job, this time with the Stanley Home Products Company, which used parties to sell housecleaning supplies, tools, and gadgets. As part of its effort to train and motivate salespeople, Stanley sponsored an annual meeting during which the top salesperson was crowned "queen of sales." Ash was so impressed by the ceremony surrounding this award that she vowed to win it the following year, which she did.

By 1942 Ash was making enough money from selling Stanley products to afford to go to college, so she enrolled in the premed program at the University of Houston. She soon found out that her dream of becoming a doctor was no longer so strong, and after a year of juggling work, school, and home duties, she dropped out and recommitted herself to becoming a successful salesperson. Within 10 years she had become a sales manager with Stanley, and in 1952 she moved to Dallas to work for another direct sales organization, the World Gift Company, as national training manager in charge of sales. She quickly realized that at World Gift she was being overworked, underpaid, and not taken seriously because she was a woman. In 1963, when a man she had trained was made her boss at twice her salary, she decided she had had enough.

Too young, too broke, and too energetic to retire, Ash began making plans to start her own company. Angry and bitter over the treatment she had received because of her gender, she determined to create a company that prized rather than discounted the unique needs and talents of women. For more than 10 years she had been using homemade skin-care creams and lotions made and bottled by a woman who had once hosted a Stanley party; the woman's father had tanned raw cowhides into soft, supple leather, and she had simply added some fragrant scents to the chemicals he had used. In 1963 Ash paid the woman several thousand dollars for the formulas and rights to the skin-care products, and several thousand more to rent and outfit a small store in downtown Dallas. Calling her business Beauty by Mary Kay, she hired nine of her friends to give facials in the store and in customers' homes. Unlike other companies that sold cosmetics, Beauty by Mary Kay held classes in which customers were taught how to use the company's products to their best advantage. Customers were allowed to try products before buying them and were never pressured into buying anything. Ash's nine friends were called "consultants" and were trained to teach, not sell.

Women loved Ash's approach to the cosmetics business, and by the end of 1963 her company's sales had almost topped $200,000. In 1964 the company changed its name to Mary Kay Cosmetics, and by the end of the year its sales had risen to $800,000. This increase, as well as all future ones, was the direct result of the company turning to direct sales, Ash's strength. By 1965 she had recruited and trained almost 3,000 consultants to give classes at parties, a number that grew to more than 350,000 by 2000. Ash developed a special training program for her consultants by drawing on the sales and motivational methods she had learned with Stanley and by incorporating many of the positive thinking and personal motivation techniques espoused by DALE CARNEGIE, among others. She wrote a 200-page consultants' guidebook and implemented an awards program,

whereby hard-working consultants could earn more than $100,000 per year and win expensive prizes such as jewels, vacations, and automobiles. By emphasizing the "soft sell" over the "hard close," she made it possible for a great many women to sell as well as to buy her beauty products.

In 1968 Ash became a millionaire when Mary Kay Cosmetics became a public company, with herself as chairwoman of the board and chief executive officer. In 1985 the company went private after Ash and her family bought all outstanding shares, valued at $315 million. In 1987, she relinquished management of the company to her son, Richard Rogers, although she continued to play an active role in the company's affairs. By 2000, Mary Kay Cosmetics was doing annual sales of more than $1.5 billion, and the company employed more than 2,000 corporate employees in its office and manufacturing facilities in Dallas and five regional centers around the country. At the time of her death on November 22, 2001, in Dallas, Ash's personal fortune was estimated at more than $300 million.

Further Reading

Ash, Mary Kay. *Mary Kay*. New York: HarperPerennial, 1994.

Brands, H. W. *Masters of Enterprise: Giants of American Business from John Jacob Astor and J. P. Morgan to Bill Gates and Oprah Winfrey*. New York: Free Press, 1999.

Astor, John Jacob

(1763–1848) *entrepreneur in the fur trade*

One of the first self-made men in American history was John Jacob Astor. Astor rose from being a butcher in his father's shop to scion of one of the wealthiest families in the United States.

Astor was born on July 17, 1763, in Waldorf, in the duchy of Baden (modern Germany). His father, Jacob, was a butcher, and his mother, Maria, was a homemaker. At age 13 he went to work full time in his father's butcher shop. Two years later he left Waldorf for London, England, where he learned to make musical instruments in the shop of his brother George. When the American Revolution ended in 1783, he emigrated to the United States, where his brother Henry lived, and settled in New York City the following year. In 1785 he married Sarah Todd with whom he had eight children.

Astor saw America as the promised land, not because it was an untapped market for musical instruments but because of the incredible number of fur-bearing animals that lived there. He used the profits from his instrument business to buy furs from trappers, which at first he shipped back to London. The fur business proved to be so lucrative that by 1786 he was importing instruments from Europe, selling them in a shop run by his wife, and making trips to the regional fur market in Albany for furs to sell in his fur goods shop in New York City. In 1787 he made his first trip to Montreal, Canada, the center of the North American fur trade, where he established a warehouse. At the time, Canada was a British colony, and direct trade between it and any place other than England was prohibited. Although Astor continued to ship furs to London, he began smuggling furs across the U.S.-Canadian border, essentially along the same route traveled by General John Burgoyne's ill-fated expedition during the American Revolution. He also established a string of trading posts along this route and in other areas south of the Great Lakes where he entered into direct competition with the Montreal-based North West Company. His competitive position was greatly improved after 1794, when the Jay Treaty between the United States and Great Britain opened up large areas in the Canadian Great Lakes region to American fur traders. By 1800, Astor dominated the North American fur trade. This occurred partly because Astor, unlike the North West Company, did not depend on his own trappers, but instead bought from Indian, French Canadian, and American trappers indiscriminately, thus getting the best furs at the best prices. Also, Astor was able to circumvent British trade restrictions which his rivals were forced to obey.

In 1808 Astor, Ramsay Crooks, and several other partners chartered the American Fur Company, which set out to extend American domination of the North American fur trade into the Pacific Northwest. Astor hoped to establish trading posts along the route pioneered by the Lewis and Clark Expedition, as well as to establish a trading post on the Pacific Ocean from where he could more easily ship furs to China. His company succeeded in establishing Astoria near the mouth of the Columbia River in 1811, but the post was captured by the British during the War of 1812 and taken over by another Canadian rival, the South West Company. After the war ended, Astor concentrated his fur operation around the Great Lakes, making Mackinac Island in Lake Huron the center of his trading. He also expanded his operations into the Missouri River Valley where RENÉ AUGUSTE CHOUTEAU had done so well. In 1819 he turned over the day-to-day operation of American Fur to Crooks and Astor's son William and went on a 15-year tour of Europe. In 1834 he returned to New York City; that same year he sold the northern half of his share of American Fur to a syndicate headed by Crooks and the southern half to several descendants of Chouteau.

Along with René Auguste Chouteau, John Jacob Astor (shown here) was one of America's leading fur traders. *(Culver Pictures)*

Although the fur trade formed the basis of Astor's business enterprises, he also made large sums of money in other endeavors. In 1792 he became involved in the China trade, at first leasing space aboard other merchants' ships. He exchanged furs—which were worth twice as much in China as they were in the United States—for tea, silk, china, and lacquerware, all of which were in great demand in America. By 1805, he was using his own ships and specializing in the importation of ginseng, which was worth six times as much in the United States as it was in China. Between 1815 and 1827, when he ended his operations in the Far East, Astor's eight ships were frequent visitors to the ports of call of the North Pacific. In 1789 Astor began investing some of the profits from his fur business in Manhattan real estate, a practice which he continued until his death. By the mid-1820s he was collecting $100,000 in yearly rents, an astounding sum for the day. In 1834 he began construction of the Park Hotel, later renamed Astor House, which eventually became part of the Waldorf-Astoria, one of the most luxurious and well-known hotels in the United States. Astor's extensive property holdings in New York City formed the basis for the Astor family fortune, which increased substantially under the management of his son William and grandson John Jacob III.

Astor died on March 29, 1848, in New York City. At the time of his death, when his estate was worth approximately $10 million, he was generally considered to be the wealthiest person in the United States.

Further Reading

Brands, H. W. *Masters of Enterprise: Giants of American Business from John Jacob Astor and J. P. Morgan to Bill Gates and Oprah Winfrey.* New York: Free Press, 1999.

Porter, Kenneth W. *John Jacob Astor: Business Man.* Cambridge, Mass.: Harvard University Press, 1931.

Wilson, Derek A. *The Astors, 1763–1992: Landscape with Millionaires.* New York: St. Martin's Press, 1996.

B

Baekeland, Leo Hendrik
(1863–1944) *inventor of plastic*

One of the greatest inventions of the 20th century was plastic. Light yet strong, durable yet moldable, by the end of the century plastic had replaced iron and steel in a number of commercial applications, and it facilitated the development of a wide range of other applications. The father of modern plastic by virtue of having invented Bakelite, the first commercially successful plastic, was Leo Baekeland.

Baekeland was born on November 14, 1863, in St. Martens-Latem, Belgium. His father, Karel, was a shoemaker, and his mother, Rosalia, was a domestic worker. He was awarded a government scholarship to the University of Ghent, where he received a B.S. in chemistry in 1882 and a D.Sc. in organic chemistry in 1884. He spent the next five years at Ghent as an assistant to Theodore Swarts, a chemistry professor, then as a professor in his own right. In 1889 he married Swarts's daughter, Celine, with whom he had two children.

As a chemistry student and professor, Baekeland had become interested in photographic development. Dry plates had recently become popular as a way of capturing photographic images, and in 1889 there was a growing interest in the development of high-quality photographic paper for printing those images. He had also read BENJAMIN FRANKLIN's autobiography, which inspired him to come to America and become a successful inventor. During a trip to the United States in 1889, he was offered and accepted a research position with E. & H. T. Anthony and Company, a manufacturer of photographic supplies in New York City. Two years later, he became partners with Leonard Jacobi in an industrial research firm, which they opened in Yonkers, New York. In 1893 he invented Velox, a photographic paper coated with silver chloride that could be developed under artificial light. Velox became so popular that in 1899 GEORGE EASTMAN, founder of the Eastman Kodak Company, paid Baekeland and Jacobi $750,000 for the patent rights.

Baekeland also had a long-standing interest in developing an artificial thermoplastic resin that could be used as a fabrication material. At the time, the only thermoplastic material—one that is soft and pliable when heated but that stiffens at room temperature—was shellac, which was made from the secretions of a South Asian insect. Several attempts to make shellac chemically by reacting phenol with various aldehydes had resulted in the creation of either an amorphous gel or a hard, misshapen mass full of air bubbles, largely because the principles of reaction rates and molecular structure were virtually unknown. In 1902 Baekeland tried to make shellac by reacting phenol with formaldehyde. After five years of experiments, he discovered that catalyzing the reaction with an alkali caused the formation of the thermoplastic polymer resin he called Bakelite. Further experimentation showed that heating Bakelite for several hours at 300° Fahrenheit under pressure of from 50 to 100 pounds per square inch kept air bubbles from forming and produced a hard, strong, light, waterproof material. This material did not burn or conduct electricity, but it could be molded into virtually any shape while hot and stay in that shape after cooling. Best of all, unlike other "plastics"— so called because a shape or mold could be pressed into them—Bakelite did not soften when heated, did not get brittle when cooled, and did not react readily with most chemicals.

In 1909 Baekeland received a patent for Bakelite and opened a small manufacturing facility in Yonkers. The following year, he founded the General Bakelite Corporation and opened a larger facility in Perth Amboy, New Jersey. That same year Baekeland became embroiled in a patent lawsuit with THOMAS ALVA EDISON; Edison and Jonas W. Aylsworth had formed the Condensite Company, which made a Bakelite-like resin by using an acid catalyst. In 1914 Baekeland sued the Redmanol Chemical Products Company, which made a Bakelite-like resin by substituting formin for formaldehyde. After years of acrimonious contention, both disputes were settled in 1922 when General Bakelite acquired Condensite and Redmanol.

Meanwhile, General Bakelite was gradually becoming an important supplier to American manufacturers. In 1911 the company produced less than one and one-half tons of Bakelite. However, it quickly gained acceptance as a low-cost substitute for ivory in the manufacture of billiard balls. It also became popular as a replacement for hard rubber in a number of applications, as well as a primary material in the manufacture of electrical items. Bakelite was particularly important to the growing automobile industry, which prized light but strong materials. In 1913 production increased to 350 tons, in both powdered and liquid form. In 1922, the year the mergers with Condensite and Redmanol were effected, the company made 4,400 tons of Bakelite, and in 1939 General Bakelite sold more than 25,000 tons of plastic. At 65¢ per pound, this translated into annual sales of more than $33 million.

In 1939 Baekeland sold General Bakelite to Union Carbide and Carbon Corporation for stock valued at more than $16 million. He spent his retirement at his home in Yonkers and on his estate in Coconut Grove, Florida. He died on February 23, 1944, in a mental institution in Beacon, New York.

Further Reading

Amato, Ivan. "Leo Baekeland," Time 100. URL: http://www.time.com/time/time100/scientist/profile/baekeland.html. Downloaded on November 15, 2001.

Kaufmann, Morris. *The First Century of Plastics.* London: Chameleon Press, 1970.

"Leo Hendrik Baekeland." *Chemical Achievers: The Human Face of Chemical Science.* Available online. URL: http://www.chemheritage.org/classroom/chemach/plastics/baekeland.html. Downloaded on June 30, 2009.

Bañuelos, Romana Acosta

(1925–) *entrepreneur in Mexican food*

One of the more interesting Hispanic entrepreneurs in American history is Romana Bañuelos. An American citizen by birth, she rose from being a teenage mother of two who lived on an isolated ranch in Mexico to become the treasurer of the United States. Along the way, she founded one of the most successful ethnic food companies in the United States and served as president of the first bank owned and operated by Mexican Americans.

Bañuelos was born Romana Acosta on March 20, 1925, in Miami, Arizona. Her parents, Juan and Teresa, were undocumented Mexican immigrants. At age eight, she and her family were forced by U.S. immigration officials to leave the country, and they went to live with relatives on a ranch in the Mexican state of Sonora. As a young girl, she helped her parents raise chickens and bake pastries, which they sold in the local market. By age 19 she had married and divorced a Señor Torres with whom she had two children.

The rapid development of the American Pacific Coast that resulted from the United States' involvement against Japan in World War II created a tremendous demand for labor, and in 1944 Bañuelos moved with her children to Los Angeles, California, in search of opportunity. For the next five years, she worked as a common laborer in a laundry and a clothing factory. By 1949, the same year she married Alejandro Bañuelos with whom she had one child, she had managed to save $400, enough to open a small tortilla bakery in downtown Los Angeles. Called Ramona's Mexican Food Products, Inc. (the name was not a typo but in honor of Ramona, the young Mexican-American heroine of a Helen Hunt Jackson novel by the same name), the fledgling company filled an important niche in California's Chicano community. As Ramona's tortillas became increasingly popular, Bañuelos introduced new Mexican food products, until by 1980 the company was producing more than 20 different items. That same year, the company employed 400 workers and was grossing about $12 million. She later opened a plant in Gardena, which by 1990 was one of the largest food processing plants in California.

As Bañuelos's business grew, she experienced the frustration of dealing with financial institutions that were not always attuned to the needs of the Hispanic community or cognizant of the abilities of Hispanic entrepreneurs. In 1964 she and several other business leaders of Mexican descent attempted to redress this problem by cofounding the Pan American National Bank, which catered to East Los Angeles's Mexican-American residents. After serving on the bank's board of directors for five years, in 1969 she was elected the board's chairperson and was twice reelected unanimously.

In 1971 Bañuelos became the highest-ranking Mexican American in the federal government when she was sworn in as treasurer of the United States. In this position she performed a variety of duties, including the authorization of checks for funds spent by government agencies and the supervision of the destruction of worn-out bills. As treasurer, her signature appears on all new paper currency that was issued during her tenure in office. A member of the Republican Party, her name had been chosen from a list by then-President Richard M. Nixon. While her confirmation hearing was taking place in the U.S. Senate, her Gardena plant was raided by agents of the Immigration and Naturalization Service (INS), who arrested 36 undocumented workers. Although the hiring of illegal aliens was not illegal at the time, a great deal of negative publicity was generated by the incident, mostly by labor unions

complaining about her hiring practices. Bañuelos refused to withdraw her name from consideration, claiming that the raid had been an attempt to embarrass the president and the Mexican-American community. After the Senate confirmed her without dissent, Nixon ordered the INS to raid the newspaper that first published the story of Bañuelos's hiring practices. She served as treasurer until 1974, when she returned to southern California to manage her growing commercial activities as well as Ramona's Mexican Food Products Scholarship Foundation, which awards three full college scholarships each year to Mexican-American youths.

Further Reading

Martinez, Diana. "'The Strength Is in Money,' Says Romana Bañuelos," *Nuestro* 3, no. 5 (June/July 1979): 34.
National Women's History Project. *Las Mujeres: Mexican American/Chicana Women.* Windsor, Calif.: National Women's History Project, 1995.

Barnum, P. T.
(Phineas Taylor Barnum)
(1810–1891) *founder of Barnum & Bailey Circus*

"There's a sucker born every minute." Although no evidence exists to prove that P. T. Barnum actually said or wrote these words, they seem to fairly sum up his ethos during the early part of his show business career. For most of his later career, however, Barnum made sure his customers always got their money's worth, even if what they were seeing was not always what it was purported to be. What the self-titled "prince of humbug" did say, however, is instructive: "When all are kind and just and honest, want only what is fair and right, judge only on real and true evidence, and take nothing for granted, there will be no place for any humbug, harmless or hurtful."

Barnum was born Phineas Taylor Barnum on July 5, 1810, in Bethel, Connecticut. His parents, Philo and Irena, were farmers and storekeepers. At age 15, he went to work as a clerk in a general store not far from Bethel. A year later, he went to Brooklyn, New York, where he clerked for two years before returning to Bethel to open a fruit and confectionery store. In 1831, two years after he married Charity Hallett with whom he had four children, he started the *Herald of Freedom,* a newspaper in Danbury, Connecticut, that folded three years later. In 1834 he moved to New York City where he ran a boardinghouse and a grocery store.

In 1835 Barnum began his career as a showman by buying Joice Heth, reputedly the 161-year-old slave nurse of General George Washington. She was, of course, a fraud, but for a year Barnum made $750 per week exhibiting her to the credulous in New York City. In 1836 he and Aaron Turner put together a small circus, which they toured through the South. Over the next five years, Barnum tried to make it as a reputable businessman, but he lost all his money in a partnership to sell shoe blacking, bear's grease, and cologne water. In 1841 he returned to show business by buying John Scudder's American Museum in New York City, a five-story marble edifice that housed stuffed animals, wax figures, and the like. Barnum replaced such tame fare with theater, music, lectures, and freak shows featuring humans and animals, dead and alive. His most famous nonliving exhibit was the so-called Feejee Mermaid, a collection of hair, skin, and scales that looked like it might once have been a real mermaid (it had not).

In 1842 Barnum began a long partnership with Charles S. Stratton, a 10-year-old boy who stood 25 inches tall. Barnum christened him General Tom Thumb and put him on display at the museum. From 1844 to 1847, Barnum and Thumb toured the Continent and England, where they became favorites of the English in general and Queen Victoria in particular. Upon returning to the United States, Barnum used the money he had made in Europe to build Iranistan, a gaudy Persian-looking palace (it was actually modeled after the Royal Pavilion in Brighton, England) in Bridgeport, Connecticut.

In 1850 Barnum took on a tremendous challenge when he attempted to promote a legitimate talent, Jenny Lind. Known throughout Europe for her excellent soprano singing voice but virtually unheard of in the United States, Barnum contracted to have her tour the United States. The advance publicity generated by Barnum was tremendous, and by the time Lind arrived the American press were already referring to her as the "Swedish Nightingale," an epithet Barnum had coined. She sang to packed houses for virtually every performance, and both she and Barnum parted company much wealthier than they had been before.

In 1851, Barnum put together his second traveling circus, the Great Asiatic Caravan, Museum and Menagerie, featuring Tom Thumb, 10 elephants, and a collection of other "wild" beasts. The show's motto, "Can the Public Be Satisfied With Only 11 Camels?" packed them in. The caravan spent five years on the road, and made it all the way to California and back. Upon returning to New York City, Barnum worked hard to rejuvenate the American Museum's exhibits. He brought in the famed mountain man Grizzly Adams and a collection of bears, wolves, and buffalo. He also exhibited several real Indian chiefs, as well as the first hippopotamus ever seen in the United States. In 1863, he hosted and sold thousands of tickets to

Although he looks rather stern in this photograph, P. T. Barnum was one of the 19th century's leading purveyors of fun. *(Library of Congress)*

the social event of the year, the marriage of Tom Thumb to a dwarf named Lavinia Warren.

In 1870 Barnum began putting together the show that would make him famous. The Great Travelling World's Fair, as it was originally known, featured a circus, museum, menagerie, and horse show. In 1872, he expanded the circus to two rings, and the following year to three rings. In 1874, the same year he married Nancy Fish following the death the previous year of his first wife, the circus began playing under "the big top," a huge canvas tent. By 1877 the entire show was traveling on a train that consisted of 70 freight cars, six passenger cars, and a Magnificent Advertising Car, and it played in 140 towns coast to coast each year. In 1880 Barnum became partners with James A. Bailey and James L. Hutchinson, proprietors of the Great London Circus, Sanger's Royal British Menagerie and Grand International Allied Shows. The result was the Barnum & Bailey Circus or, as Barnum preferred to call it, "The Greatest Show on Earth." The highlight of the show was Jumbo, a seven-ton elephant who suffered an untimely death while rescuing a baby elephant from the path of a locomotive.

In 1891 Barnum became extremely ill. Knowing that death was imminent, he requested that the Bridgeport newspaper print his obituary before he died so he could enjoy reading it. They complied with his wish. He died on April 7, 1891, in Bridgeport.

Further Reading

Barnum, P. T. *The Life of P. T. Barnum.* Urbana: University of Illinois Press, 2001, reprint.

Fleming, Alice Mulcahey. *P. T. Barnum: The World's Greatest Showman.* New York: Walker and Co., 1993.

Floyd, E. Randall. *The Good, the Bad & the Mad: Weird People in American History.* Augusta, Ga.: Harbor House, 1999.

Harding, Les. *Elephant Story: Jumbo and P. T. Barnum under the Big Top.* Jefferson, N.C.: McFarland & Co., 2000.

Twitchell, James B. *20 Ads that Shook the World: The Century's Most Groundbreaking Advertising and How It Changed Us All.* New York: Crown Publishers, 2000.

Beach, Alfred Ely
(1826–1896) *inventor of the pneumatic subway*

The first subway in the United States was not powered by gasoline, steam, electricity, or cables, but by compressed air. The inventor of this short-lived innovation was Alfred Beach, better remembered today as a magazine editor.

Beach was born on September 1, 1826, in Springfield, Massachusetts. His father, Moses, was a newspaper publisher, and his mother, Nancy, was a homemaker. In 1838 he completed his private school education in Monson, Massachusetts, then moved with his family to New York City where his father had just purchased the *New York Sun.* In 1847 Beach married Harriet Eliza Holbrook with whom he had two children. In 1848 he and his brother assumed control of the *Sun* when their father retired. In 1852 Beach sold his share of the *Sun* to his brother in order to become coeditor and part owner of *Scientific American* magazine as well as supervisor of the Scientific American Patent Agency. Beach's life's work was devoted mainly to providing his readers with easy-to-read scientific information as well as researching and securing patents for his clients, who included THOMAS ALVA EDISON, CYRUS HALL McCORMICK, and SAMUEL F. B. MORSE.

Beach was also an inventor in his own right. His first invention was a typewriter that produced raised letters on a special strip that blind people could "read" with their fingertips. Beach's typewriter won a gold medal at the 1853 Crystal Palace Exposition in New York City. Around 1860 he invented a cable traction system for streetcars that was used for several years in New York City. And in 1865 he was granted a U.S. patent for improvements to the tunneling shield, a machine for driving tunnels in soft ground. The first shield, invented in the 1820s by Marc Isambard Brunel, was propelled by screw jacks through the soil; miners could then stand inside the shield, protected from cave-ins, while excavating the dirt encased by the shield. However, Brunel's shield was rectangular and thin, which made it difficult to shove through soil. Beach's shield was cylindrical, thicker, and powered by hydraulic jacks, thus making the shield easier and safer to use.

Beach's most impressive invention was the first operational subway in the United States. Originally, he set out to deliver mail quickly from one end of New York City to the other by using compressed air to force the mail through an underground tube. He soon realized that, given a proper vehicle in which to ride, people could be transported pneumatically as well. At the 1867 American Institute Fair in New York City, he demonstrated a prototype of his people-moving system. The all-metal, track-mounted car was cylindrical with flat ends and could seat 10 people. The metal tube through which the car traveled (which for demonstration purposes was mounted aboveground) had an inside diameter only slightly greater than the outside diameter of the car. Mounted at one end of the tube was a huge fan that blew against the flat end of the car with sufficient force to propel the car to the other end of the tube. When reversed, the fan generated enough vacuum to suck the car back to its starting point.

In 1868 Beach organized the Pneumatic Dispatch Company with himself as president, and he obtained a contract from the state government to construct an experimental pneumatic mail delivery tube under downtown New York. Beach then used this opportunity to construct a 300-foot-long pneumatic subway under Broadway using his tunneling shield; those members of the general public who were brave enough to test ride the subway were absolutely thrilled with the experience. At the time, the only other subway in existence was in London, England, and the passenger cars were pulled by steam locomotive. Although the London system was a success, sulfurous fumes from the locomotives often choked and irritated passengers, a problem Beach's subway would avoid. But when Beach applied to the governor of New York for a charter to construct an extended version of his pneumatic people mover under the entire city, he was turned down twice. In 1873 a new governor granted the charter, but the panic of 1873 prevented Beach from raising sufficient funds with which to build a city-wide system, and he abandoned the project.

Pneumatic subways never caught on. However, the idea resurfaced in the 1960s when engineers toyed with the idea of powering long-distance, high-speed trains via a combination of gravity and vacuum. Meanwhile, Beach devoted his remaining years to making the *Scientific American* one of the foremost scientific journals of the day. He died on New Year's Day, 1896, in New York City.

Further Reading

"Beach Pneumatic Subway." Available online. URL: http://www.shohola.com/AlfredBeach. Downloaded on June 30, 2009.

Daley, Robert. "Alfred Ely Beach and His Wonderful Pneumatic Underground Railway," *American Heritage* 12 (June 1961): 54–57.

Bechtel, Stephen
(1900–1989) *entrepreneur in major construction projects*

The grand scope and impressive success of the ambitious projects developed by the Bechtel Corporation under the leadership of Stephen Bechtel led him to frequently and proudly recite his favorite motto for his company: "We'll build anything for anybody, no matter what the location, type, or size." Though the motto could be interpreted as boastful, it was a fair reflection of his company's significant impact on large-scale construction and engineering projects in the United States and around the world throughout the 20th century and beyond.

Stephen Davison Bechtel was born on September 24, 1900, in Aurora, Indiana. He spent his early years growing up in various construction camps moving westward from Oklahoma that were built to support the railroad projects his father Warren was managing. His parents soon settled in Oakland, California. As a teenager, Bechtel spent his summers working as part of the construction crews. Following his graduation from high school, Bechtel spent 19 months serving in the U.S. Army as a motorcycle dispatch rider in France during World War I. Bechtel returned to the United States after the war and attended the University of California, Berkeley, but he dropped out before graduating, because as he later explained, "Dad needed us in the business."

Bechtel married his college sweetheart, Laura Peart, in 1923. Two years later they became parents to a son, Stephen Jr., and a few years later welcomed a daughter they named Barbara. Though only in his 20s, Bechtel became a vice president in his father's business, W. A. Bechtel and Co., and he played an important role in helping lead the company into what became the very lucrative business of pipeline construction. In 1933, Bechtel's father died suddenly while on a trip in Russia, and Stephen assumed leadership of the growing company.

At the time of his father's death and his subsequent ascension to the presidency of Bechtel, the company was already engaged in its greatest project: construction of the Hoover Dam. Working in a consortium with five other companies, Bechtel managed the administration, purchasing, and transportation for the Hoover Dam project. This five-year project was completed in 1936, and Bechtel soon formed a partnership, the Bechtel-McCone Corporation, which quickly became an industry leader in the construction of refineries and chemical plants. The company also was heavily involved in the creation of bridges, including the 8.2-mile San Francisco-Oakland Bay Bridge.

During World War II, Bechtel-McCone was instrumental in helping provide the U.S. military with ships and aircraft parts. This critically needed wartime production included 550 cargo carriers and oil tankers. In addition, Bechtel built a secret 1,600-mile pipeline through the rugged Canadian wilderness to Alaska.

Following World War II, Bechtel formed what is still the Bechtel Corporation. Also during this period, he made strategic choices to increase diversification of project types and international work that ultimately made the company enormously profitable and influential. A *Time* magazine profile of the 100 Most Important People of the Century listed Bechtel as one of the 20 key Builders and Titans and noted of his company, "It has been said, hyperbolically perhaps, that Bechtel engineers changed the physical contours of the planet more than any other humans." Among the massive projects in six continents and over 140 countries undertaken by the Bechtel Corporation during Stephen Bechtel's leadership were scores of airports, power plants, factories, bridges, hotels,

transit systems, and pipelines, including a nearly 1,100-mile pipeline in Saudi Arabia that was instrumental in building the burgeoning oil economy in that country.

Throughout his career, Bechtel was renowned for his visionary leadership style that emphasized personal visits to job sites around the world, where his well-dressed and soft-spoken manner often contrasted with the rough style of the projects and the men who worked on them. Bechtel viewed his role as the big-picture leader, who provided several trusted associates to handle the details and execution of the company's many complex projects. By any measure, he was extremely successful in realizing his goals. When Bechtel took over leadership in 1933, the company's revenues were about $20 million. By the time he retired in 1960, their revenues were $463 million and before the end of the 20th century they would rise to over $11 billion.

Bechtel remained the chief executive officer of Bechtel until 1960, when he relinquished that title and those duties to his son Stephen Bechtel, Jr. He then served briefly as chairman of Bechtel before assuming the largely ceremonial role of senior director. Bechtel lived for almost three decades in retirement, dying on March 14, 1989, in San Francisco.

Further Reading

Church, George J. "Stephen Bechtel," *Time* 100. Available online. URL: http://www.time.com/time/time100/builder/profile/bechtel.html. Downloaded on June 30, 2009.

McCartney, Laton. *Friends in High Places: The Most Secret Corporation and How It Engineered the World.* New York: Ballantine Books, 1989.

"Stephen D. Bechtel, Sr." Bechtel.com. Available online. URL: http://www.bechtel.com/BAC-Stephen-D-Bechtel-Sr.html. Downloaded on June 30, 2009.

Bell, Alexander Graham

(1847–1922) *inventor of the telephone*

Everyone knows that Alexander Graham Bell invented the telephone. What most people do not know, however, is that the experiments that led to its development grew out of his attempts to teach speech to the deaf. Despite his many contributions to the world of invention, all of his life Bell considered himself to be an inventor second and a teacher of the deaf first.

Bell was born Alexander Bell on March 3, 1847, in Edinburgh, Scotland; the middle name "Graham" was not added until 1858, and he was known as A. Graham Bell for most of the rest of his life. His father, Alexander, was a teacher of elocution and speech correction, and his mother, Eliza, was a pianist. He graduated from high school at age 14, then spent a year in London, England, studying the teaching of speech with his

Alexander Graham Bell's patent for the telephone is considered to be one of the most valuable patents of all time. *(Library of Congress)*

grandfather. Upon returning to Edinburgh in 1863, he spent the next five years teaching music and elocution in a succession of private schools. Meanwhile, his father had developed Visible Speech, a method for teaching deaf people how to speak, and in 1868 Bell went to London to serve as his father's assistant. Following an epidemic of tuberculosis that killed his two brothers and almost killed him, in 1870 he moved with his family to Brantford, Ontario, Canada. In 1871 Bell began teaching Visible Speech in Boston, Massachusetts. The following year he established his own school for the deaf, and in 1873 he became a professor of vocal physiology at Boston University. Four years later he married one of his deaf students, Mabel Hubbard, with whom he had two children. In 1882 he became an American citizen and moved to Washington, D.C., to establish a school for the deaf. In 1886, he arranged for Anne Sullivan to become the primary teacher of Helen Keller, who became legendary for surmounting the challenges of deafness, muteness, and blindness. Throughout his life, Bell remained intensely interested in teaching speech to the deaf, and he donated the royalties from the graphophone, an early recording device, to the American Association to Promote the Teaching of Speech to the Deaf, which in 1956 was renamed the Alexander Graham Bell Association for the Deaf.

Bell's work with the telephone began in Edinburgh in the 1860s, when he and his brothers tried to build a speaking machine. This device was a model of the human vocal organs; it was manipulated by levers to form the proper shapes for making speechlike sounds out of noise generated by blowing through a tube. This invention led Bell to experiment with tuning forks, which he sounded and held before his open mouth, then transformed the sound into various vowels and consonants by manipulating his mouth and tongue. Shortly thereafter he discovered that Hermann von Helmholtz, the great German scientist, had performed the same experiment, except that Helmholtz had sounded his tuning forks by means of electricity, the same motive power used to send messages by telegraph. This discovery eventually led Bell to the idea that tuning forks sounding at different frequencies could be used to send and receive multiple messages along the same telegraph line—and that speech and music could be transmitted telegraphically as well.

Bell did not return to this line of inquiry until 1874, when he received permission from the Massachusetts Institute of Technology to use its laboratories at night. He was assisted by Thomas A. Watson, a skilled mechanic, and financed by the parents of two students, including Gardiner Hubbard, his future father-in-law. At first Bell concentrated on sending multiple telegraph messages by causing electrical undulations similar to those caused by the vocal chords. In 1875 he received a patent for the harmonic telegraph, then turned his attention to developing the telephone. By 1876 he and Watson had constructed a simple version of the modern telephone. By shouting into a receiver, the person talking caused a diaphragm to vibrate, which varied the strength of an electric current. This current traveled along a wire to another receiver, where it caused an electromagnet to make a diaphragm vibrate in exactly the same way as the first diaphragm, thus reproducing the speech that had gone into the first receiver. That same year Bell received a patent for the telephone. In 1877 EMILE BERLINER invented a microphone that eliminated the need to shout, but otherwise the modern telephone remains little changed from Bell's first model. He and Watson spent the next year perfecting several of the telephone's features, then Bell departed for Scotland on his honeymoon. In his absence, Hubbard organized and ran the Bell Telephone Company, and when Bell returned after almost a year, he served primarily as a witness in the many patent lawsuits brought by ELISHA GRAY and his partners. For his invention, Bell received stock in the company named for him, most of which he sold within a few years.

After 1882 Bell took little interest in matters relating to the telephone. Instead, he joined his cousin, Chichester Bell, and Sumner Tainter in perfecting the graphophone. This device recorded sounds by cutting grooves in a rotating wax cylinder; when picked up by a stylus, these grooves were translated into sounds. The graphophone represented a major step forward in sound recording, and the Bell-Tainter patents were eventually sold for several hundred thousand dollars. In 1886 Bell used part of the proceeds from the stock sale to build Beinn Bhreagh, an estate near Baddeck on Cape Breton Island in Nova Scotia. The estate included a laboratory where he could continue to experiment. He spent the rest of his life between Washington and Beinn Bhreagh, and he alternated between teaching the deaf to speak and conducting research. Among the many projects he dabbled with were sonar detection, solar distillation, the tetrahedron as a structural unit, and hydrofoil craft. Meanwhile, he and his wife organized the Aerial Experiment Association, which supported research concerning manned flight. He died on August 2, 1922, at Beinn Bhreagh.

Further Reading

Evenson, Edward A. *The Telephone Patent Conspiracy of 1876: The Elisha Gray-Alexander Bell Controversy and Its Many Players.* Jefferson, N.C.: McFarland, 2000.

Grosvenor, Edwin S., and Morgan Wesson. *Alexander Graham Bell: The Life and Times of the Man Who Invented the Telephone.* New York: Harry Abrams, 1997.

Mackay, James A. *Alexander Graham Bell: A Life.* New York: J. Wiley, 1997.

Wren, Daniel A., and Ronald G. Greenwood. *Management Innovators: The People and Ideas that Have Shaped Modern Business.* New York: Oxford University Press, 1998.

Yenne, Bill. *100 Men Who Shaped World History.* San Francisco, Calif.: Bluewood Books, 1994.

Bendix, Vincent Hugo
(1881–1945) *inventor of automobile parts*

Starting a car today is as easy as turning a key in a switch. But when automobiles were first invented, starting one was almost literally a backbreaking feat. Two men revolutionized the automobile industry by making cars easier to start (and easier to sell), and one of them was Vincent Bendix. Because he also played a major role in supplying the American automotive industry with high-quality brakes, Bendix became known as "the king of stop and go."

Bendix was born on August 12, 1881, in Moline, Illinois. His father, Jan, was a Swedish Methodist Episcopal minister, and his mother, Alma, was a homemaker. When he was young, Bendix and his family moved to Chicago. He displayed an early aptitude for mechanical thinking by designing at age 13 a chainless bicycle. At age 16 he ran away to New York City. For the next three years he worked variously as an elevator operator, law clerk, and mechanic's assistant while attending engineering school at night. Between 1901 and 1907 he designed and built motorcycles for GLENN HAMMOND CURTISS, a small-engine manufacturer who later became an aviation pioneer. In 1907 he returned to Chicago to sell cars for Holmsman Automobile Company. That same year he designed and built an automobile known as the Bendix Motor Buggy, then organized the Bendix Company to manufacture it. He sold about 7,000 cars before going out of business in 1909.

Like all other automobiles at the time, the Bendix Motor Buggy was started by means of a giant hand crank mounted on the car's front. The crank was attached to the flywheel, a heavy disk connected to the engine by a shaft. One cranked until the flywheel developed enough momentum to "turn" the engine. This operation was both difficult—most women and many men simply were not strong enough to do it—and dangerous; the crank would often jam or "kick back," resulting occasionally in a sprained elbow or dislocated shoulder. Bendix became convinced that the general public would never accept automobiles unless someone invented a mechanical starter.

The Cadillac Company became the first manufacturer to address the problem by equipping their 1912 model with an electric starter motor invented by CHARLES KETTERING. However, this motor often failed to work because it was not linked securely to the flywheel. Bendix invented a suitable link between starter motor and flywheel, and in 1914 he contracted with the Eclipse Machine Company in Elmira, New York, to manufacture what became known as the Bendix starter drive. The device was hugely popular, and by 1919 Eclipse was filling orders for more than a million drives per year.

After spending several fruitless years trying to get into the fire engine manufacturing business, in 1923 Bendix founded Bendix Engineering Works in South Bend, Indiana. In 1924 he changed the company's name to Bendix Corporation, sold stock to the public, and built a new factory to manufacture a state-of-the-art shoe brake invented by the French engineer Henri Perrot, the U.S. rights to which Bendix had recently acquired. By 1928, the company was filling orders for more than three million brakes per year, most of which went to the General Motors Corporation. That same year Bendix Corporation began acquiring control of other automotive parts manufacturers, starting with Eclipse Machine. By the mid-1930s, the corporation controlled or owned outright more than 100 companies and held more than 5,000 patents.

In 1929 Bendix realized the growing potential of commercial aviation. He changed the company's name to Bendix Aviation Corporation and expanded the company's line of aircraft parts. To promote the development of airplane design, in 1931 he established the Bendix Transcontinental Air Races. In 1944 he founded Helicopter Inc. and began developing a four-passenger helicopter. Bendix hoped his helicopter would become a big seller once World War II ended, but he died before completing the design.

Bendix was a man of big ideas and expensive tastes. He enjoyed the extravagant lifestyle that was fairly typical for wealthy people during the 1920s. He was married and divorced twice; neither marriage resulted in children. He loved to invest in risky business ventures and real-estate deals, most of which went sour during the Great Depression. He was forced to declare personal bankruptcy in 1939, and all of his personal belongings were sold to pay his debts. All of these setbacks affected Bendix's ability to run his corporation, and in 1942 General Motors gained control of Bendix Aviation and forced Bendix to step down as president and chairman of the board. He died on March 27, 1945, in New York City.

Further Reading

Bendix: First Fifty Years in South Bend, 1923–1973. South Bend, Ind.: Bendix Management Club, 1973.

Fontaine, A. P. *Where Ideas Unlock the Future: The Story of the Bendix Corporation.* New York: Newcomen Society in North America, 1967.

"Vincent Bendix," National Aviation Hall of Fame. Available online. URL: http://nationalaviation.blade6.donet.com/components/content_manager_v02/view_nahf/htdocs/menu_ps.asp?NodeId=711021953&Group_ID=1134656385&Parent_ID=-1. Downloaded on June 30, 2009.

Berliner, Emile

(1851–1929) *inventor of the microphone and gramophone*

As an inventor, Emile Berliner never came close to achieving the same sort of lasting fame as ALEXANDER GRAHAM BELL, inventor of the telephone. Berliner did, however, design improvements to Bell's most memorable inventions, the telephone and the graphophone, an early version of the phonograph.

Berliner was born on May 20, 1851, in Hannover in the kingdom of Hanover, today part of Germany. His father, Samuel, was a merchant, and his mother, Sarah, was a homemaker. At age 14, he went to work as a printer's helper, and he later became a clerk in a dry goods store. By the time he was 19, he had designed an improvement to the weaving machine. In 1870 he emigrated to the United States and settled in Washington, D.C., where he worked as a store clerk. Over the next six years, he traveled back and forth among and worked in Washington, New York City, and Milwaukee, Wisconsin.

In 1876 Berliner began experimenting with the telephone, which Bell had just invented. The primary weakness of Bell's telephone was that it relied indirectly on the speaker's voice to generate the electric current that carried the spoken words to the receiver on the other end. This made it necessary for the speaker to shout in order to be heard. Berliner realized that current produced by a battery would eliminate the need to shout, and so he began looking for a way to superimpose spoken sound on a battery-powered electric current. In 1877 these experiments resulted in the development of the microphone. Like Bell's telephone

receiver, Berliner's microphone contained a diaphragm that vibrated when it was spoken into; unlike Bell's receiver, the microphone imposed these sounds on a current that was already being supplied to the receiver, so the speaker could speak very softly and still be heard at the other end. He also developed the continuous-current transformer, a device that produced the electrical current necessary to operate his telephone microphone. In 1877 Berliner filed for patents for both the microphone and the continuous-current transformer. He received a patent for the transformer that same year; meanwhile, other inventors, among them Bell and THOMAS ALVA EDISON, had also filed patents for microphone-like devices. A brouhaha ensued over who had the idea first, and it was not until 1897, 20 years later, that the U.S. Patent Office finally decided in Berliner's favor. Shortly thereafter, Bell Telephone bought Berliner's patents and put him on the company payroll as a consultant. Meanwhile, in 1881 Berliner had married Cora Adler with whom he had six children.

Having developed an improvement to Bell's great invention, Berliner set out to perfect another Bell invention, the graphophone. This device was itself an improvement on Edison's method for recording and playing sound, which was via an etched groove in a tinfoil disk. The graphophone substituted a rotating wax cylinder for the disk, and used a stylus to cut a deep groove rather than etch a shallow one. Unfortunately, the graphophone cut grooves in the cylinder vertically, which made it difficult to maintain a steady pressure on the stylus as it either cut the grooves or reproduced sounds from the cylinder, thus leading to distortions in the recording. Berliner replaced the cylinder with a hard-resin disk, or record, so that the grooves could be cut and played horizontally along a flat plane, the weight of the stylus head maintaining a constant pressure on the stylus. In 1887 he received a patent for this device, which he called the gramophone.

By 1891 Berliner had also developed the matrix method for making a master recording from which numerous copies could be made, something that was virtually impossible with either Bell's or Edison's machines. In 1894 he formed the Berliner Gramophone Company in Philadelphia,

Emile Berliner holds one of his many inventions.
(Library of Congress)

Pennsylvania, and began manufacturing the first commercially available record players. Because many homes were still without electricity at that time, his first models came with a hand crank with which to wind them up. By 1900 he had opened branch factories in England, France, and Germany, and his brother had built a record-pressing facility in Hamburg, Germany. In 1901 Berliner merged his company with Eldridge R. Johnson's, which produced a slightly different version of the gramophone, to form the Victor Talking Machine Company, which would later gain fame as RCA Victor.

Berliner loved to tinker with all sorts of devices, not just those related to sound. In 1908 he designed a lightweight engine for use in aircraft, and in 1919 he began experimenting with helicopters. In 1925, he invented the first acoustic tiles. He died on August 3, 1929, in Washington, D.C.

Further Reading

Read, Oliver, and Walter L. Welch. *From Tin Foil to Stereo: Evolution of the Phonograph.* H. W. Sams, 1976.

Shapiro, Michael. *The Jewish 100: A Ranking of the Most Influential Jews of All Time.* New York: Citadel Press, 2000.

Wile, Frederick W. *Emile Berliner, Maker of the Microphone.* New York: Arno Press, 1974.

Bezos, Jeffrey
(1964–   ) *founder of Amazon.com*

In 1999, *Time* magazine named Jeff Bezos the Person of the Year. At the age of only 35, Bezos had created the World Wide Web's greatest online shopping site, Amazon.com, and significantly changed the way people around the world shop for goods. In the more than a decade since—and unlike so many other young Internet success stories of the late 1990s—Bezos has solidified his place as one of the most prominent Internet entrepreneurs as well as his important role in the history of great American business leaders.

Jeffrey Preston Bezos was born on January 12, 1964, in Albuquerque, New Mexico. His last name at birth was Jorgensen, which was the surname of his biological father. Within a year and a half, Bezos's 18-year-old mother divorced Jorgensen. Three years later, Jackie married Mike Bezos, who adopted Jeff, legally changing his last name to Bezos. Bezos developed a strong relationship with his adoptive father, who had fled Cuba at the age of 15 and became a successful engineer.

When Bezos was a young child, his family lived in Houston, where he demonstrated unusual scientific aptitude and curiosity, became an avid fan of the television show *Star Trek*, and spent countless hours cajoling his parents to take him to Radio Shack so he could buy parts for personal projects. In the summers of his youth, Bezos spent extended periods of time at the large Cotulla, Texas, ranch of his maternal grandparents, where he tended cattle, dug ditches, laid pipe, and repaired pumps and windmills. Bezos later noted that these experiences taught him that "obstacles are only obstacles if you think they're obstacles. Otherwise they're opportunities."

Bezos moved with his family to Pensacola, Florida, and Miami as his father continued to rise while working with the large oil firm Exxon. Bezos graduated from Miami's Palmetto High School in 1982 and, as the valedictorian of his class, gave a speech that reflected his future ambition by expressing the need to colonize space. He then enrolled at Princeton University, intending to study physics, but he eventually found himself increasingly drawn to computer science, which became his major. Bezos graduated Phi Beta Kappa from Princeton in 1986 and then moved to New York City to work on Wall Street.

Working in quantitative hedge fund trading led Bezos to become increasingly interested in starting a company at what he later termed, "the intersection of computers and finance." While working at the financial firm D. E. Shaw in 1994, Bezos noticed a statistic that explained that the Internet was growing at a rate of 2,300 percent a year. This caused him to ask himself, "What kind of business plan might make sense in the context of that growth?" His search for the answer led to very disciplined research and analysis. Bezos determined that selling books online would provide the best opportunity for success in the burgeoning world of e-commerce. With the full support of his wife and relying on what he joked was a "regret minimization framework" that led him to believe that he would not regret his decision when he was 80 years old, Bezos decided to leave his lucrative job and move to Seattle to begin his new business venture.

Initially, Bezos planned to call his company Cadabra, as in the magic-related phrase abracadabra. However, confusion of his planned company name with the word cadaver led Bezos to change it to Amazon, after the South American river with a seemingly endless system of tributaries. Bezos's initial business plan underwent several revisions, and the company was not able to extend its funding far beyond the initial investment of $300,000 from Bezos's parents. Bezos set up an office in a two-bedroom Seattle home, had 300 friends and acquaintances test his new company's computer systems, and found them to be working perfectly. Amazon launched in July 1995, and within 30 days it received orders from all 50 states and 45 countries.

Still—in contrast to the vast amounts of venture capital flowing to even unproven firms a few years later—Amazon struggled to raise a million dollars in a second round of funding.

Amazon continued to excel and gained renown for such customer satisfaction innovations as one-click shopping, e-mail order verification, discount pricing, free shipping, and customer reviews. As Amazon expanded, it followed what Bezos called, "Six Core Values: customer obsession, ownership, bias for action, frugality, high hiring bar and innovation." He added that the vision of Amazon was to become, "the world's most customer-centric company. The place where people come to find and discover anything they might want to buy online." Supporting that vision has been Amazon's extension into other areas of commerce, including electronics, sporting goods, clothing, groceries, and more, which has changed Amazon from being the self-proclaimed "World's Biggest Bookstore" to being the "World's Biggest Anything Store."

Although Amazon was the leader of the Internet boom of the mid to late 1990s, it was able to avoid being among the casualties of the Internet bust of the early part of the 21st century. Much of the credit for this has gone to Bezos and his long-term strategic business philosophy. An example of this was Bezos's decision in the late 1990s to build an extra-giant automated warehouse in addition to the four most Amazon executives suggested, even though it piled another $60 million onto an investment that was nearly a quarter of a billion dollars in scope. The extra warehouse allowed Amazon to quickly meet all its orders at a time when many other online retailers were unable to do so, which improved the company's reputation and eventually its revenues and profits.

In 2009, Bezos was ranked 68th on *Forbes* magazine's list of the world's richest people with a net worth of almost $7 billion. In recent years, he has been active in developing and promoting the Kindle, Amazon's electronic book reader that has soared in popularity since its 2007 introduction. He is also the founder of Blue Origin, an aerospace company that is developing plans for commercial suborbital tourist service by 2013. Bezos lives with his wife MacKenzie and their four children north of Seattle.

Further Reading

Deutschman, Alan. "Inside the Mind of Jeff Bezos." *Fast Company.* Available online. URL: http://www.time.com/time/time100/builder/profile/bechtel.html. Downloaded on July 28, 2009.

"Jeffrey P. Bezos." Academy of Achievement. Available online. URL: http://www.achievement.org/autodoc/page/bez0bio-1. Downloaded on July 28, 2009.

Quittner, Josh. "The charmed life of Amazon's Jeff Bezos." *Fortune.* Available online. URL: http://money.cnn.com/2008/04/14/news/companies/quittner_bezos.fortune/index.htm. Downloaded on July 29, 2009.

Ramo, Joshua Cooper. "Jeffrey Preston Bezos." *Time.* Available online. URL: http://www.time.com/time/magazine/article/0,9171,992927,00.html. Downloaded on July 28, 2009.

Birdseye, Clarence

(1886–1956) *inventor of quick-frozen food*

Look in the frozen-foods section of just about any supermarket, and you will probably see Birds Eye brand of frozen vegetables. The brand name comes from the name of Clarence Birdseye, the person who invented the quick-freeze method. Although Birdseye did not invent frozen food—European companies had been selling whole frozen fish for at least a decade before he developed his process—he did invent the first practical method for freezing and packaging small portions of food.

Birdseye was born on December 9, 1886, in Brooklyn, New York. His father, Clarence, was an attorney, and his mother, Ada, was a homemaker. Shortly after the turn of the century he moved with his family to Montclair, New Jersey. He enrolled in Amherst College in 1908 but dropped out after two years because of financial difficulties. In 1910 he went to work as a naturalist for the U.S. Department of Agriculture's Biological Survey. In 1912, he went to Labrador, Canada, where he spent most of the next five years trapping and trading in furs. He soon discovered that fish caught from the ocean when the air temperature was very cold froze almost as soon as they were pulled out of the water and that, when they thawed out several months later, they still tasted pretty good. He

began experimenting with the meat of other creatures, such as rabbits and caribou, and found out that when meat is frozen quickly, it stays fresh as long as it is kept at a very low temperature. In 1915 he married Eleanor Gannett with whom he had four children.

In 1917 Birdseye moved to Washington, D.C., and for the next six years he worked as a purchasing agent for several companies. Meanwhile, he had been thinking about the freezing phenomenon he had discovered in Labrador, and in 1923 he decided to test its commercial applications. Borrowing space in a friend's New Jersey icehouse, he used a fan, some salt, and lots of ice to make fish freeze as quickly as he could, because he had also discovered that slow freezing spoils the taste. He eventually developed a method for quick-freezing food by pressing small portions between two very cold metal plates. Achieving the best success with fillets of haddock and other fish, in 1924 he and three partners formed the General Seafoods Company in Gloucester, Massachusetts. By 1929 the company was doing so well that Birdseye was able to sell his freezing process to what became the General Foods Corporation for more than $23 million.

That same year Birdseye turned his attention to quick-freezing vegetables. He and Charles F. Seabrook began experimenting at Seabrook's farm and packing plant near Bridgeton, New Jersey, and the following year, they formed Birds Eye Frosted Foods, with Birdseye as president. The company sold quick-frozen fruits and vegetables packaged in attractive cardboard containers that closely resembled those found in supermarkets today. Birds Eye also embarked on an aggressive educational and marketing campaign to help homemakers overcome their natural reluctance to the product. Once it became clear to the general public that frozen foods tasted just as good as fresh-picked or canned foods, sales increased astronomically. As a result of the company's success, Birdseye became a wealthy man.

In 1934 Birdseye stepped down as president of the company in order to explore his interests in electrical apparatus. From 1935 to 1938 he was president of the Birdseye Electric Company, which manufactured and marketed reflective and infrared heat lamps of his design. He went into semiretirement in 1938, and for the next 15 years he served in a number of technical societies, dabbled in horticulture, and invented things; during his lifetime he received almost 300 patents for devices such as the recoilless harpoon gun and a food dehydrator. In 1953 he went to Peru, where he developed a method for converting sugarcane stalks, straw, and similar farm products into paper pulp. He died on October 7, 1956, in New York City.

Further Reading

Campbell, H. "The Father of Frozen Food." *Country Living,* May 1989, p 162.

"Clarence Birdseye," Lemuelson-MIT Program. Available online. URL: http://www.web.mit.edu/invent/iow/birdseye.html. Downloaded on June 30, 2009.

Hess, John L., and Karen Hess. *The Taste of America.* Columbia: University of South Carolina Press, 1977.

Bissell, George Henry (1821–1884), and Edwin Laurentide Drake (1819–1880)
inventors of oil drilling techniques

One of the most interesting tales involving the relationship between invention and entrepreneurship is the drilling of the first American oil well. This epochal event resulted from the vision and genius of two very different men, George Bissell and Edwin Drake. While Bissell came up with the original idea of drilling for oil, it was Drake who figured out how to drill the first successful oil well. The contrast between their rewards for being successful in this endeavor could not have been more different. While Bissell went on to become one of the wealthiest men in New York City, Drake died in poverty.

Bissell was born on November 8, 1821, in Hanover, New Hampshire. His parents, Isaac and Nina, were farmers. He received his B.A. from Dartmouth College in 1845, then over the next eight years he taught foreign languages at the University of Norwich, worked as a reporter for the *Richmond* (Virginia) *Whig,* made a quick visit to Cuba, worked as an editor for the *New Orleans* (Louisiana) *Delta,* and served as a principal and superintendent in the New Orleans public school

system. In 1853 he moved to New York City where he opened a law partnership with Jonathan G. Eveleth.

Shortly after settling in New York, Bissell paid a visit to several of his former professors at Dartmouth College. While there, he discovered a sample of crude oil that had been collected in the Oil Creek region of northwest Pennsylvania. What captured his imagination about the sample is not exactly known. Perhaps he knew that people had been using petroleum for centuries in such varied applications as caulking ships and making medicines. At that time, kerosene was just becoming popular as a substitute for whale oil as a fuel for lamps, and Bissell may have suspected that it would be easier and cheaper to extract kerosene from petroleum than from coal tar or shale oil, its other sources. At any rate, he investigated the sample's source and found out that crude oil seeps naturally into several creeks in the vicinity of Titusville.

In 1854, the year before Bissell married Ophelia Griffin with whom he had two children, he and Eveleth bought and leased 200 acres adjoining Oil Creek for a total of $5,000. The partners also formed the Pennsylvania Rock Oil Company, the first petroleum company in the United States, and set out to extract oil from their property. For four years, the partners struggled, mostly because they had no better way to collect crude oil than by digging trenches and collecting the oil that puddled in them. The amount collected was not enough to make much more than a few dozen bottles of patent medicine, and the proceeds from this was not enough to cover the cost of the digging. Finally, in 1858 Bissell concluded that the only way to capture enough oil to make the operation profitable was to drill for it.

Drake was born on March 29, 1819, in Greenville, New York. His parents, whose names are not known, were farmers. At age eight he moved with his family to Castleton, Vermont, where he finished his basic education while helping out on the farm. At age 19 he left home, and over the next 19 years he worked successively as a night clerk on a Lake Erie steamboat; a hand on his uncle's farm near Ann Arbor, Michigan; a clerk in a Tecumseh, Michigan, hotel; a clerk in dry-goods stores in New Haven, Connecticut, and New York City; an express agent for the Boston & Albany Railroad in Springfield, Massachusetts; and a New Haven–based conductor on the New York & New Haven Railroad. In 1845 he married Philina Adams with whom he had one child; Philina died in 1854. In 1857, the same year he married Laura Dow with whom he had four children, Drake's health failed and he retired from the New York & New Haven Railroad.

At some point, Drake had purchased stock in Pennsylvania Rock Oil, and in 1858 Bissell recruited him to go to Titusville to handle a minor legal matter for the company. He also convinced Drake to travel to Titusville by way of Syracuse, New York, and Pittsburgh, Pennsylvania, so he could study salt-well drilling operations in those places to see if a similar operation might work to bring oil to the surface. Drake's visits to these operations and to Oil Creek convinced him that petroleum could indeed be procured by drilling.

In 1858 Drake and a fellow stockholder formed the Seneca Oil Company, leased the Pennsylvania Rock Oil Company's Oil Creek tract, and began probing for oil. For 19 months, Drake encountered one difficulty after another. First, he was unable to obtain a drill, so he employed men with shovels to begin digging the well by hand. Then, once drilling began, the drill hole kept filling up with clay and quicksand until it collapsed. He eventually solved this problem by driving cast-iron pipe through the drill hole, the first time pipe had ever been used in this application. Finally in 1859, at a depth of 69 feet, he struck oil, and the next day he began pumping 25 barrels of oil per day from the well. Word of his achievement quickly spread, and by 1865 Titusville was a boomtown in the center of the United States' first "oil rush."

Immediately upon hearing about Drake's success, Bissell moved to Franklin, Pennsylvania, not far from Titusville, and invested more than $300,000 belonging to him and several partners in land in the vicinity of Oil Creek. By 1863 he had acquired enough oil leases to ensure his fortune for life. That same year he returned to New York City where he continued to play an active role in the development of the infant petroleum industry. He was the major stockholder in the first railroad to reach the oil fields, and he later became president of the Peruvian Petroleum and Refining Companies, which for a while controlled most of the oil reserves on South America's Pacific coast. He invested much of the profits from his oil interests in commercial real estate, and at the time of his death in New York City on November 10, 1884, he was one of that city's largest property owners.

Drake, who proved to be a determined inventor, also proved to be a miserably inept entrepreneur. He failed to patent the use of pipe for drilling, and he lost untold millions as a result. And instead of exploiting his invention by sinking other wells and pumping them dry, he occupied himself primarily with buying and selling oil leases to other entrepreneurs, including Bissell. After four years in Titusville, he retired to New York City with about $16,000, still a sizable sum for the day. Hoping to finance a life of luxury for himself and his family, he invested the entire sum with a stockbroker who specialized in oil stocks. However, every project the broker invested in failed miserably, leaving Drake destitute. To make matters worse, his health deteriorated to the point that he could no longer work. He gave up his New York residence and moved, first to Vermont and then to Long Branch, New Jersey, where he and his family lived in abject poverty.

In 1870 the grateful citizens of Titusville learned of Drake's desperate situation and helped him relocate to Bethlehem, Pennsylvania, where they contributed to his upkeep. In 1873 the Pennsylvania state legislature voted him a modest annual pension. In 1900, 20 years after Drake's death on November 8, 1880, in Bethlehem, his body was exhumed and reburied in Woodlawn Cemetery in Titusville. In 1902 a monument to his memory was erected in Drake Well Memorial Park.

Further Reading

"Edwin L. Drake," *Virtual Vermont Internet Magazine.* Available online. URL: http://www.virtualvermont. com/history/edrake.html. Downloaded on June 30, 2009.

Hammerschmidt, Amy, et al. *Oil: The Power of Pennsylvania Petroleum.* Harrisburg, Pa.: Commonwealth Media Services, 1998, videorecording.

Miller, Ernest C. *An Investigation of North America's First Oil Well: Who Drilled It?* Rutland, Vt.: C. E. Tuttle Co., 1964.

Blackton, James Stuart

(1875–1941) *inventor of motion pictures special effects*

Before 1910, when movie producers discovered that southern California had a mild climate, lots of sunshine, varied terrain, and a large labor market, the cinematic capital of the United States was Brooklyn, New York. One of the first major motion picture companies to call Brooklyn home, and one of the largest of the early motion picture companies, was the Vitagraph Company. Vitagraph's chief producer, director, and cofounder, J. Stuart Blackton, was a pioneer in movie animation, and he produced the first American movie to use special effects.

Blackton was born James Stuart Blackton on January 5, 1875, in Sheffield, England. His father, Henry, was a carriage maker, and his mother, Jessie, was a homemaker. At age 11 he emigrated with his family to the United States, settling in New York City. As a teenager he worked as a carpenter while briefly attending the City College of New York at night. After leaving school, he became a vaudeville performer; his first act was "Mademoiselle Stuart and Her Lightning Sketches," in which he wore women's clothing while drawing rapid-fire caricatures to the accompaniment of the house band. Later, he created a routine with Alfred E. Smith in which Smith, the Komical Konjurer, performed amazing feats of ventriloquism and magic while Blackton, the Komical Kartoonist, put on slide shows (hand drawn and colored by Blackton) known as magic lantern presentations. By 1895 he had become a reporter and illustrator for the *New York Evening World*, and he was sent that same year to interview THOMAS ALVA EDISON, the famous inventor. Edison had recently built a movie studio for making short films for the kinetoscope, a hand-cranked, peep-show viewing device that could be found in penny arcades, hotel lobbies, amusement parks, and other such places. Impressed with Blackton's ability to draw quickly and well, Edison hired him to do the sketchwork for an animated motion picture he was planning to make, which was released in 1896 as *Enchanted Drawings*. It was the first animated movie in the history of American film.

That same year Blackton purchased one of Edison's kinetographs, an early motion-picture camera, so he could make movies of his own. By 1897, he, Smith, and William T. Rock had formed the Vitagraph Company. At first they just used the kinetoscope to make copies of Edison's films, which they exhibited during vaudeville performances between the live acts and as part of Blackton and Smith's own variety routine. Within a year they were also making movies of their own. One of their earliest films was *Tearing Down the Spanish Flag* (1898), which combined actual footage of the Spanish-American War with "reenactments" starring the partners and whomever else they could persuade to appear with them. Another early effort, *The Battle of Manila Bay* (1898), featured toy boats "attacking" each other in a bathtub, with explosions and smoke provided by several boxes of sparklers and cheap cigars. The movie, which was the first to use special effects, was a smash hit at the box office.

Predictably, Edison took offense at Vitagraph's film pirating, and until 1906 he took every legal action he could think of to put them out of business. Meanwhile, the partners expanded their repertoire by shooting newsreels, mostly of boxing events and gaudy public spectacles such as parades. Later they began making "trick films," in which stop-and-go photography creates the illusion that objects are rapidly appearing and disappearing, and a comedic series about "Happy Hooligan," a character played by Blackton. In 1906, having settled their legal differences with Edison, they began making movies in earnest. Most of their films were shot in an open-air studio on the roof of a commercial building in Brooklyn. Among the company's most popular offerings were productions of Shakespeare's dramas, movies about well-known fictional characters such as Sherlock Holmes and Oliver Twist, and a series about Old Testament figures such as Moses, David, Saul, and Salome. The company produced the first bonafide movie star, Florence Turner, the "Vitagraph Girl," and the first animal star, "Jean, the Vitagraph Dog." Four years later, Vitagraph was one of the largest movie companies in the United States, and Blackton had become a millionaire.

Vitagraph began to decline after 1910, when the major Hollywood producers started to take over the movie industry. Around 1920 Blackton went back to England where he produced several movies away from Hollywood's shadow. He had returned by 1926 when Vitagraph was sold to Warner Bros. He lost all the money he made from the sale in the stock market crash of 1929, and for a while he supported himself by showing his old movies at carnival sideshows. Later he drifted to Hollywood, where he became a minor functionary for a major production company. He was married four times, twice to actresses who appeared in his films, and had four children. He died on August 13, 1941, in Los Angeles, California.

Further Reading

"Biography: J. Stuart Blackton," ASIFA Hollywood Animation Archive. Available online. URL: http://www.animationarchive.org/2006/03/biography-j-stuart-blackton.html. Downloaded on June 30, 2009.

Trimble, Marian Blackton. *J. Stuart Blackton: A Personal Biography by His Daughter.* Metuchen, N.J.: Scarecrow Press, 1985.

Blake, Lyman Reed

(1835–1883) *inventor of the shoe-stitching machine*

Before 1850, shoes were made in the United States by hand, mostly by men working at home. By 1875, more than 150 million pairs of shoes had been made in the United States by machine, mostly by women working in factories. The person most responsible for this amazing transformation of the U.S. shoe-making industry was Lyman Blake, inventor of the shoe-stitching machine that became known as the McKay machine.

Blake was born on August 24, 1835, in South Abington, Massachusetts. The occupations of his parents, Samuel and Susannah, are unknown, but they were probably either millworkers or farmers. At age 16 Blake went into the shoe-making business with his older brother. The brother owned a leather shop, and his employees cut out the pieces of leather from which a pair of shoes would be made and assembled them into kit form. Blake took the kits to shoe stitchers who, in their own homes, sewed the uppers together and then nailed them to the soles. He also picked up the finished shoes and returned them to his brother, who sold them to wholesalers. By age 19 Blake was working for the I. M. Singer Company as a machine setup man. The company had just invented a sewing machine that could sew together uppers, and whenever one was sold in his territory, usually to a shop like his brother's, Blake would install the machine and teach the operators how to use it. In 1855 he married Susie Hollis with whom he had no children.

In 1856 Blake became a partner in the shoe manufacturing firm of Gurney, Mears, and Blake. He quickly realized that the company's shoe-stitching machines were of little value without a machine that could attach them to the soles; machine-stitched uppers simply piled up while waiting for someone to nail them to soles. This led him to redesign the shoe so that it could be made entirely by machine and to invent a machine that could do the job. Blake's shoe was made of leather pieces that were flexible enough to be molded around a horn. His machine made use of a curved sewing needle mounted above the horn that could stitch together the uppers, inner sole, and outer sole all in one operation.

In 1859 Blake's health failed, so he sold the rights to his patent for the shoe-stitching machine to Gordon McKay and moved to Staunton, Virginia, where he opened a retail shoe store. Two years later he returned to South Abington and became partners with McKay. After making the machine easier to use, mostly by making the horn movable and converting the machine so it could be powered by steam as well as a mechanically driven belt, they began selling what became known as the McKay stitching machine. They also developed an entire shoe factory system that revolved around the use of the McKay stitching machine, then sold the machine and the system to shoe manufacturers throughout New England. In 1874 Blake renewed his patent and then assigned it to the McKay Association, a consortium of New England shoe manufacturers that used the Blake-McKay factory system. By this time he had also invented at least 15 other machines for making shoes, such as a machine that waxed the thread used for shoe stitching, thus making it more durable; a machine for cutting channels into soles before stitching, thus making them easier to stitch; and a machine for stitching uppers together with lasting, a strong, durable, closely woven fabric.

In 1874 Blake retired from the shoe-making business, his skillful assignment of his several inventions having made him relatively wealthy. He spent his remaining years traveling the world. He died on October 5, 1883, in South Abington.

Further Reading

Blewett, Mary H. *Men, Women, and Work: Class, Gender, and Protest in the New England Shoe Industry, 1780–1910.* Urbana: University of Illinois Press, 1990.

"Lyman Reed Blake (1835–1883)," About Inventors. Available online. URL: http://inventors.about.com/library/inventors/blblake.htm. Downloaded on June 30, 2009.

Blanchard, Thomas

(1788–1864) *inventor of the irregular turning lathe*

The irregular turning lathe was one of the most important inventions of the early Industrial Revolution in the United States. This relatively simple (at least by modern standards) device, which was invented by Thomas Blanchard, made it possible to machine irregularly shaped items rather than make them by hand.

Blanchard was born on June 24, 1788, in Sutton Township, near Worcester, Massachusetts. His parents, Samuel and Susanna, were farmers. As a boy, Blanchard showed more interest in tinkering than in schoolwork, and at age 13 he invented an apple parer. Shortly thereafter he went to work in his brother's tack factory in nearby Millbury. Blanchard had two jobs: putting heads on tacks, and then counting the finished tacks. At the time, both jobs were done by hand, and Blanchard found them to be exceptionally monotonous. Seeking desperately for a way to make both tasks easier, he invented two machines: One put heads on tacks, and the other counted them. In his spare time he also invented a machine for shearing woolen cloth.

By the time he was 20, Blanchard had obtained enough money from the sale of the patent rights to the tack-header to open his own machine shop in West Millbury. By the time he was 30, he had gained a reputation as a first-rate machinist in the mill district south of Worcester. In 1818 Asa Waters II, proprietor of a Millbury gun factory that made muskets for the United States Army, asked Blanchard to help him redesign a new lathe for turning, or shaping, gun barrels. A lathe is a machine in which a length of unfinished material, usually either metal or wood, is fixed and rotated on its horizontal (long) axis against a cutting tool, which travels the length of the material and shapes it to the desired configuration. Waters's lathe did a fine job turning the symmetrical end of the gun barrel. Unfortunately, it did a poor job turning the asymmetrical features on the breech end of the barrel, the end closest to the trigger, so these features still had to be hand-filed.

Blanchard modified Waters's design by adding several cams to the end of the lathe where the barrel's breech end was turned. These irregularly shaped disks caused the cutting tool to move eccentrically, thus turning the breech end of the barrel in the desired pattern. Blanchard's barrel lathe quickly came to the attention of Roswell Lee, superintendent of the U.S. Armory in Springfield, Massachusetts. Lee ordered several barrel lathes for his armory, and influenced the superintendent of the armory in Harpers Ferry, Virginia, to order some as well.

Blanchard turned his attention next to designing for the two armories a lathe that could turn gunstocks, the wooden pieces upon which a gun's barrel, trigger, and magazine are mounted. The result was the Blanchard or irregular turning lathe, which Blanchard patented in 1820. Gunstocks are highly asymmetrical, so Blanchard invented a way to turn a piece of gunstock material by "copying" a finished gunstock. He mounted a finished gunstock next to the lathe, then connected the cutting tool to a tracer, a friction wheel that rolled along the outline of the finished gunstock. As the tracer bobbed in and out and up and down while moving along the gunstock's contour, the cutting tool duplicated the same motion on the piece of gunstock material being turned in the lathe. This resulted in the new gunstock being turned exactly like the traced gunstock. Over time, the irregular turning lathe, also known as the eccentric or Blanchard lathe, was adapted by a number of inventors so that virtually any item turned by hand could instead be mass produced.

Except for a brief stint as an armorer at the Springfield Armory from 1823 to 1827, Blanchard was self-employed throughout his adult life. Around 1830 he moved to New York City, and around 1840 he moved to Boston. He married three times and fathered six children. He supported himself and his dependents primarily by means of royalties paid on his various inventions, which total more than two dozen. Among them were machines for manufacturing firearms, bending wood, and copying sculptures, as well as a steam-powered carriage and a shallow-draft steamboat that could go upstream through rapids. None of these inventions, however, proved to be of the same importance as the irregular turning lathe, one of the machine tools that revolutionized American industry. He died on April 16, 1864, in Boston.

Further Reading

Cooper, Carolyn C. *Shaping Invention: Thomas Blanchard's Machinery and Patent Management in Nineteenth-Century America.* New York: Columbia University Press, 1991.

"Thomas Blanchard," National Park Service. Available online. URL: http://www.nps.gov/spar/historyculture/thomas-blanchard.htm. Downloaded on June 30, 2009.

Blodgett, Katharine Burr

(1898–1979) *inventor of nonreflective glass*

Katharine Blodgett did not discover monomolecular films; that honor belongs to her mentor, Irving Langmuir. Blodgett did, however, figure out what monomolecular films were good for and, in the process, invented a gauge for measuring very thin objects as well as a way to make glass "invisible."

Blodgett was born on January 10, 1898, in Schenectady, New York. Her father, George, was a patent attorney for the General Electric (GE) Company, and her mother, Katharine, was a child care worker. Her father was murdered before she was born, and while still a baby she moved with her mother and brother to New York City. Despite her father's untimely death, she led a privileged life, traveling extensively throughout France and Germany and receiving a private education. During her senior year at Bryn Mawr College, where she majored in physics, she traveled to Schenectady to see where she had been born and to learn about her father from the people he had worked with. Irving Langmuir, a future winner of the Nobel Prize in chemistry, showed her around the GE research laboratory. She impressed him with her intelligence and knowledge of physics, and he encouraged her to continue her studies in science.

After receiving her A.B. degree in 1917, Blodgett went to the University of Chicago to study chemistry. Her thesis dealt with the ability of carbon to absorb gases and contributed to the design of the first American-made gas mask just in time for American troops to be able to wear it during World War I. Upon receiving her M.S. degree in 1918, she returned to the GE laboratory in Schenectady, this time to be Langmuir's research assistant. From 1918 to 1933 she experimented with the flow of electrons in lightbulbs and vacuum tubes. This research was interrupted from 1924 to 1926 while, with Langmuir's urging and support, she earned her Ph.D. degree in physics at Cambridge University in England.

Meanwhile, Langmuir was experimenting with monomolecular films, so called because when an oily substance is placed on top of water it often spreads out until it is only one molecule thick. Because of their extreme thinness, monomolecular films behave as if they were two dimensional. For discovering monomolecular films, Langmuir was awarded the Nobel Prize in chemistry in 1932; however, he had never found any practical application for them. In 1933 he urged Blodgett to see what she could do with monomolecular films.

That same year Blodgett began experimenting with monomolecular films made from stearic acid, an oily ingredient in ordinary soap. By 1934 she had discovered how to transfer a stearic acid film to a metal plate and then how to stack up hundreds of individual layers of film on the plate. She noticed that as the layers stacked up, the color they reflected changed, but the color reflected by a certain number of layers was always the same. This meant that the thickness of the accumulated layers could easily be gauged by simply noting their color. Since each film is less than one-millionth of an inch thick, she was able to devise a color gauge that could measure the thickness of any transparent or semitransparent substance with much greater precision than had previously been possible. One simply noted the color of the substance in question and matched it up with a color in the gauge. Her gauge made it possible for the first time to measure the thickness of incredibly thin items such as blood corpuscles and antibodies.

Since each successive layer of film changed the color of the stack of films, and since color is simply a function of the amount of light reflected

Katharine Blodgett's experiments with monomolecular films led to the invention of nonreflective glass. *(Library of Congress)*

by a given surface, in 1938 it occurred to Blodgett that coating a transparent surface with monomolecular films might affect the amount of light that surface reflects. This thought led her to wonder if glass could be made nonreflective, or "invisible," by coating it with one or more monomolecular films. Over the next two years she discovered that when 44 film layers are put on a piece of glass, the light reflected from the glass is counter-reflected by the film layers in such a way that the two reflections cancel out each other. This completely eliminates all reflection or glare, thus making the glass invisible. The soapy films she used to make this discovery were so weak that they made glass nonreflective for only a short period of time, and although she obtained a patent for this coating process, she turned her attention to other uses for monomolecular films. However, just as her work with carbon inspired others to develop a better gas mask, her work with monomolecular films inspired others to develop stronger films that could permanently coat glass and other transparent surfaces. Today monomolecular films are used to reduce or eliminate glare in thousands of applications such as window glass, photographic lenses, picture frames, and automobile windshields.

During World War II Blodgett conducted war-related research. She helped find a reliable way to deice airplane wings and helped design a smoke-screen machine that could turn two quarts of oil into a field full of thick, white smoke. After the war she concentrated on developing materials with high electric resistance by coating them with low-conductivity monomolecular films.

In recognition of Blodgett's work with monomolecular films, these films eventually became known as Langmuir-Blodgett films. She was awarded the American Chemical Society's Francis Garvan Medal in 1951 and the Photographic Society of America's Progress Medal in 1972. In 1951 the mayor of Schenectady declared June 13 "Katharine Blodgett Day." She retired from GE in 1963. She died on October 12, 1979, having never married, in Schenectady.

Further Reading

Altman, Linda Jacobs. *Women Inventors*. New York: Facts On File, 1997.

Macdonald, Anne L. *Feminine Ingenuity: Women and Invention in America.* New York: Ballantine Books, 1994.

Yount, Lisa. *A to Z of Women in Science and Math.* New York: Facts On File, 1999.

Bloomberg, Michael

(1942–) *entrepreneur in financial media services*

From 2004–09, Michael Bloomberg made six dollars in salary, accepting one dollar a year to serve as mayor of New York City, while providing various charities with approximately $800 million. Bloomberg was able to achieve such unique financial feats because in previous decades he founded a financial services firm that successfully anticipated the expansion of technological and market needs. His transition from the pinnacle of business prosperity to the apex of civic leadership is unmatched in American history.

Michael Rubens Bloomberg was born in Boston on February 14, 1942. His father, William, was a bookkeeper for a dairy company who later sold mutual funds and died in 1963, and his mother, Charlotte, was a homemaker who celebrated her 100th birthday in 2009. The Bloomberg family moved to the Boston suburb of Brookline in 1945, but only after buying the house from a gentile lawyer because the original sellers refused to sell to Jews. They later moved to another town near Boston, Medford, where he lived until leaving for college at Johns Hopkins University in Baltimore. An Eagle Scout at the young age of 13, Bloomberg demonstrated similar diligence and ability to graduate from Johns Hopkins with a degree in electrical engineering and gain acceptance to the Harvard Business School.

Bloomberg graduated from Harvard and went to work on Wall Street for Salomon Brothers. He remained with Salomon from 1966 to 1981, during which time he rose to general partner and led the firm's efforts in equity trading and systems development. Known by both admirers and critics for his brash personality, Bloomberg became engaged in a power struggle with another Salomon partner and was released from the firm in 1981 with a $10 million severance.

Using much of this money, Bloomberg established Innovative Market Systems. The company, renamed Bloomberg L.P. in 1986, attracted large accounts with giant financial firms such as Merrill Lynch that valued its terminals that provided real-time financial news, market data, and analysis. The company also developed a syndicated news service, published books and magazines, and disseminated business information via television, radio, and the Web. As of 2009, the company had more than 250,000 terminals worldwide. Bloomberg L.P. was a leader in the technological revolution that affected the financial trading industry and Bloomberg himself became a billionaire.

In 2001, Bloomberg left his position as chief executive officer of Bloomberg L.P. to run for

Michael Bloomberg is the 108th mayor of New York City. *(Photo courtesy City of New York)*

mayor of New York City. Despite having no experience in elected office and changing his longtime party affiliation from Democrat to Republican, Bloomberg was able to gain a narrow victory by emphasizing the city's need for an effective business manager, particularly in the difficult wake of the September 11, 2001, attacks on New York City. He ran for reelection in 2005 and won in a landslide, defeating his nearest challenger by over 20 percentage points.

A change to New York City term limit law that would have prevented anyone from serving more than two terms as mayor was changed in 2008, which allowed Bloomberg to again run for mayor, in 2009. He was reelected by a surprisingly thin margin, which dampened speculation that he may eventually run for governor of New York, or perhaps president of the United States. Bloomberg has explained that when his political career concludes he will devote himself full time to his extensive philanthropy, which has provided hundreds of millions of dollars to various causes including Johns Hopkins University, the Centers for Disease Control and Prevention, and the Campaign for Tobacco-Free Kids.

Bloomberg married Susan Brown in 1975. Together they had two daughters before divorcing in 1993. Though he is mayor of New York City, he does not live in the traditional mayoral residence, Gracie Mansion, and instead remains in the house on the Upper East Side of Manhattan that he has lived in since before becoming the city's chief executive.

Further Reading

Bloomberg, Michael. *Bloomberg by Bloomberg.* New York: Wiley, 2001.

"#17. Michael Bloomberg." *Forbes.* Available online. URL: http://www.forbes.com/lists/2009/10/billionaires-2009-richest-people_Michael-Bloomberg_C610.html. Downloaded on July 28, 2009.

Murphy, Dean E. "Bloomberg a Man of Contradictions, but with a Single Focus." *New York Times.* Available online. URL: http://www.nytimes.com/2001/11/26/nyregion/bloomberg-a-man-of-contradictions-but-with-a-single-focus.html. Downloaded on July 28, 2009.

Bloomingdale, Alfred Schiffer
(1916–1982) *founder of Diners Club*

Alfred Bloomingdale did not invent the credit card, but he did play a major role in founding and expanding Diners Club. Before Diners Club, there were no credit cards that were honored universally by a broad range or number of business establishments. Under Bloomingdale's leadership, Diners Club became accepted by restaurants and hotels across the country, thus making it the first credit card that many businesspeople would not leave home without.

Bloomingdale was born on April 15, 1916, in New York City. His father, Hiram, was a department store executive, and his mother, Rosalind, was a homemaker. In 1938 he graduated from Brown University and went to work as a salesman at Bloomingdale Brothers (now Bloomingdale's), the retail establishment founded by his grandfather and great-uncle, in Manhattan. He quickly discovered that retailing was not in his blood, and three years later he became a theatrical agent, representing such stars as Judy Garland and Frank Sinatra. He also began producing and backing Broadway shows and motion pictures; one production was so unsuccessful that a critic advised Bloomingdale to "close the show and keep the store open nights." In 1946 he moved to Hollywood, California, to become an executive with Columbia Pictures. That same year he married Betty Newling with whom he had three children.

One day in 1949, Bloomingdale was having lunch in New York City with Frank McNamara, a friend whose finance company was in financial difficulty, and Ralph Schneider, McNamara's lawyer. Although the discussion was originally about McNamara's cash-flow problems, it ended up being about finding a better way to pay for business lunches when one of them (some sources say Bloomingdale, while others say McNamara) realized he had left his wallet and checkbook at home. At the time, there was no such thing as a universal credit card that could be used in a number of places. The credit cards that did exist were honored only in places of business operated by the issuing establishment, usually a department store, oil company, or hotel chain. Extending their lunch, the three men worked out the basic details for the first universal credit card, Diners Club. The idea was to charge members an annual fee, provide them with a credit card that would be honored at a number of eating establishments, then bill them once a month for their purchases. Participating restaurants would be guaranteed payment of Diners Club members' charges on a monthly basis minus a 4 percent discount.

To get the ball rolling, Bloomingdale agreed to put up $5,000 in cash, while McNamara put up the $35,000 owed to his finance company. After Bloomingdale returned to California, McNamara and Schneider contacted 5,000 New York City sales managers, most of whom took one or more business clients to lunch and/or dinner practically every working day, and found about 200 who thought a Diners Club membership at $75 per year was a great idea. McNamara and Schneider also found 14 restaurants, all of them in New York City, that thought Diners Club was a great idea. By the end of the year the company had 20,000 members. The company was overwhelmed by this response, especially since it found itself paying for its members' meals until the members paid their monthly statements. Since McNamara had yet to collect the money he had promised to put into the partnership, he and Schneider asked Bloomingdale to put up some more cash. Bloomingdale agreed, but only in return for a larger share of the company than the 15 percent he had received in exchange for his first $5,000. While McNamara and Schneider thought about his offer, Bloomingdale started a similar venture, Dine and Sign, in Los Angeles. In 1950 the two companies merged as Diners Club, with Bloomingdale becoming vice president.

In 1952 McNamara stepped down as president of Diners Club and sold his 70 percent interest to the other two partners for a total of $200,000. Although Schneider, the new president, took the card international by getting it accepted in establishments in Canada, Cuba, Great Britain, and Mexico, the company's growth was slow until 1955, when Bloomingdale assumed the presidency. Over the next 14 years, he managed to make Diners Club the most useful and prestigious credit card in America. He aggressively pursued campaigns to recruit more members as well as more participating establishments, since he knew that few people would pay a yearly fee for a card that was not honored in many places and that establishments would not participate if only a few customers used the card. To this end, he made heavy inroads into the lodging industry, and in 1959 he was responsible for implementing the first guaranteed hotel reservation program. A guest who planned to arrive late could hold his room by simply giving the hotel his Diners Club number, and the hotel was happy to hold the room because Diners Club would pay for the room even if the guest never arrived. In fact, by 1958 the card had become so successful that several competitors, including American Express and Carte Blanche, issued universal credit cards of their own. The following year the number of Diners Club members topped the 1-million mark and went public, becoming the first charge card to be listed on the New York Stock Exchange.

When Schneider died in 1964, Bloomingdale assumed his position as chairman of the board. By now Schneider's shares were worth so much that Bloomingdale could not afford to buy them, so he arranged for them to be acquired by the Continental Insurance Company. Ironically, Bloomingdale and Continental began battling almost immediately for control of Diners Club. Finally, in 1969, Bloomingdale resigned as chairman and president and left the company. At the time, there were 2 million Diners Club cardholders nationwide. He was given a lifetime contract as a consultant to keep him from going to work for American Express or Carte Blanche, the company's two biggest rivals.

After leaving Diners Club, Bloomingdale became involved in a number of land deals in California and was a partner in the Marina Bay Club and Hotel in Fort Lauderdale, Florida. He also served on a number of government advisory boards and as a trustee of Brown University and Loyola Marymount University. Six weeks before his death, he was sued for $5 million by Vicki Morgan, his longtime mistress, who claimed he had fathered her 15-year-old son, Todd. Although the suit was eventually dismissed, the details of his relationship with Morgan clouded his reputation. He died on August 20, 1982, in Santa Monica, California.

Further Reading

Evans, David, and Richard Schmalensee. *Paying with Plastic: The Digital Revolution in Buying and Borrowing.* Cambridge, Mass.: MIT Press, 1999.

Kohn, George C. *The New Encyclopedia of American Scandal.* New York: Facts On File, 2001.

Bluhdorn, Charles G.

(1926–1983) *founder of Gulf + Western Industries*

Charles Bluhdorn did not invent the corporate conglomerate. Both ROYAL LITTLE, founder of Textron Inc., and ABRAM NICHOLAS PRITZKER, founder of the Marmon Group, began building large corporations out of nonrelated companies before Bluhdorn. However, for many years Bluhdorn's Gulf + Western Industries served as the quintessential conglomerate, mostly because it attracted much more attention than either Textron or Marmon; in 1976 the comedy film *Silent Movie* satirized it as Engulf & Devour. In the process of building Gulf + Western, Bluhdorn made the business community and the general public aware of how diversified one corporation can get and still remain profitable. A consummate dealmaker, he also popularized the phrase, "What's the bottom line?"

Bluhdorn was born on September 20, 1926, in Vienna, Austria; his parents' names were Paul and Rose. At age 13 he went to school in England, and in 1942 he emigrated to the United States, settling in New York City. For the next three years he worked as a cotton broker while attending the City College of New York. In 1945 he went to work for an import-export firm and began taking night classes at Columbia University. Four years later he formed his own commodities importing firm, and by 1954 he had made $1 million. He married Yvette LeMarrec with whom he had two children.

Commodities trading is a very risky business, and Bluhdorn sought a way to avoid losing his fortune by investing some of his money in other types of businesses. In 1954 he bought Michigan Plating and Stamping, a small manufacturer that made bumpers for a Detroit automaker. The following year he acquired Beard and Stone Electric,

a Texas company that made electrical parts for automobiles. In 1958 he merged the two companies to form Gulf + Western Industries, with the plan of making replacement auto parts in the Gulf region where labor costs were relatively low, and then selling the parts to auto parts retailers in the West, where the demand for such parts was high. He acquired a number of other auto parts manufacturers over the next seven years, all of which he merged into Gulf + Western.

In 1966 Bluhdorn bought his first nonautomotive-related company when he acquired the New Jersey Zinc Company. A year later he bought Paramount Pictures, the Hollywood movie production company whose acquisition brought him and his corporation into the public eye. By 1979 Gulf + Western, with headquarters in New York City, had acquired companies that grew sugar, made cigars, rolled and stamped steel, manufactured paper products, produced television programs, made records, and printed sheet music, among other things, and was taking in several billion dollars per year. During the 1970s he acquired companies so fast that at one point he was buying about one every six weeks. Although many analysts were surprised by Gulf + Western's ability to keep tabs on all of its operations, much less keep them profitable, Bluhdorn's secret was simple: Instead of trying to run it all himself, he found good managers, put them in the right places, and then let them do their jobs. In essence, this is the same strategy followed by Little and Pritzker as they built their own conglomerates, although in a much quieter fashion. Bluhdorn also organized the conglomerate's hundreds of subsidiaries into seven divisions—automotive and building products, consumer products, financial services, food products, leisure time, manufacturing, and natural resources—each under the direction of a knowledgeable and trusted lieutenant. Another reason the conglomerate was profitable was because losses in one division were more than offset by profits in other, nonrelated divisions.

In 1975 Bluhdorn ran afoul of the federal government when the Securities and Exchange Commission began investigating Gulf + Western for improper financial reporting and fraudulent business conduct. Although he never admitted any wrongdoing, in 1981 he signed a consent agreement in which he promised that Gulf + Western would obey scrupulously all federal securities laws and tighten up the conglomerate's bylaws pertaining to such matters. In 1982 Gulf + Western reported annual sales of $5.3 billion; its assets were valued at $5.8 billion and it employed more than 100,000 workers. On February 19, 1983, Bluhdorn was flying back to New York City after visiting one of the company's sugar plantations in the Dominican Republic when he suffered a heart attack and died. His personal fortune was estimated to be more than $300 million. After his death, his successor Martin S. Davis succumbed to pressure from investors and the federal government alike and began selling off many of Gulf + Western's subsidiaries. By 1989 about all that was left was the leisure-time division, and the company was renamed Paramount Communications. In the 1990s Paramount was itself acquired by the media conglomerate Viacom.

Further Reading

Biskind, Peter. *Easy Riders, Raging Bulls: How the Sex-Drugs-and-Rock-'n'-Roll Generation Saved Hollywood.* New York: Simon & Schuster, 1999.

Bluhdorn, Charles G. *The Gulf + Western Story.* New York: Newcomen Society in North America, 1973.

Bogardus, James

(1800–1874) *inventor of cast-iron architecture*

The techniques for mass producing cast iron were invented in the mid-18th century. Almost 100 years later, James Bogardus, an inventor with no training as an architect or engineer, devised the idea of using cast iron as an architectural element. The result was an architectural craze that swept the United States for almost 80 years.

Bogardus was born on March 14, 1800, near Catskill, New York. His parents, John and Sara, were farmers. From 1814 to 1820 he worked as an apprentice watchmaker. He spent the next three years in Savannah, Georgia, learning the engraving trade, and in 1823 he returned to Catskill where he opened his own clockmaking and engraving shop.

In 1828 Bogardus invented the first of his many innovative machines, an eight-day clock that won first prize at the 1828 American Institute Fair in New York City. He then moved to New York, where he maintained a permanent residence until his death and where he made a comfortable living as an inventor. His most original invention, the sales from which provided him with a steady income until his death, was an eccentric mill that could grind everything from sugar to coal. Other notable inventions included a ring flyer for textile spinning, a mechanical pencil, a device for separating gold from ore, a dry gas meter for measuring illuminating gas, a diaphragm meter for measuring fluids, a device for cutting and corrugating India rubber, a glass presser, a pyrometer, a dynamometer, and an apparatus for sounding the depths of the ocean floor. In 1831 he married Margaret Maclay with whom he had no children.

In 1836 Bogardus went to London, England, to get a British patent for his dry gas meter. While there he became acquainted with the use of cast iron as a building material. Four years later, while touring Italy, it occurred to him that cast iron would make an excellent material for reproducing ornamental designs for buildings. By the time he got back to New York, he had conceived of constructing entire buildings, including walls, roofs, and floors, out of cast iron.

Bogardus's idea was not entirely original. Cast-iron storefronts were first advertised in New York City in the 1820s. However, Bogardus was the first to recognize that cast iron was strong, stable, durable, light, and fireproof, qualities that were perfectly suited for urban construction. Also, he realized that a building's various parts, no matter how intricate or ornate, could be cast in virtually any size or shape, machined and test-fitted at the foundry, and quickly assembled on the jobsite, thus making possible the prefabrication and mass production of attractive buildings and homes.

In 1849 Bogardus erected in New York City a factory made of cast iron for manufacturing his eccentric mills. While the building was under construction, he was ridiculed for building something that would either fall down under its own weight or be blown apart by lightning. However, the finished building was so eye-catching that the public's ridicule quickly changed to acceptance, and orders for cast-iron buildings began to pour in. In

California, where people were too busy prospecting for gold to build, Bogardus's cast-iron houses became extremely popular. Although his cast-iron commercial buildings were most popular in New York City, he also received orders to build them in Boston, Philadelphia, Baltimore, Washington, and Chicago.

Bogardus also employed cast iron in the erection of a number of New York City fire watchtowers and shot towers, where bullets were made by dripping molten lead from a height of more than 100 feet into a pool of cold water. As the tallest of these buildings was more than 200 feet tall, they are regarded by many architectural historians as the forerunners of the modern skyscraper.

Cast-iron architecture became popular all across the United States and did not fall into disfavor until the 1920s. However, in the late 20th century the fight to restore many beautiful old cast-iron buildings led to an increased public awareness of and appreciation for the uniqueness of Bogardus's invention. He died on April 13, 1874, in New York City.

Further Reading

Bogardus, James, et al. *The Origins of Cast Iron Architecture in America.* New York: Da Capo Press, 1970, reprint.

Gayle, Margot, and Carol Gayle. *Cast Iron Architecture in America: The Significance of James Bogardus.* New York: W. W. Norton, 1998.

Bok, Edward William
(1863–1930) *entrepreneur in magazine publishing*

Between the late 1800s and the mid-1900s, the most influential and widely read women's magazine in the United States was *Ladies' Home Journal.* Although Edward Bok did not found the *Journal* or serve as its first editor, he did convert it from a schmaltzy, sentimental magazine into a hard-hitting yet entertaining publication. By encouraging through the *Journal* the development of modern women who were capable, intelligent, and self-assured, Bok did much to instill women with the Progressive spirit of the day and lead them into the 20th century. In the process, he also transformed the style and content of women's magazines.

Bok was born on October 9, 1863, in Den Helder, Holland. His father, William, was a merchant, and his mother, Sieke, was a homemaker. At age seven he moved with his family to Brooklyn, New York. Over the next 12 years he briefly attended public school, then worked successively as a newspaper delivery boy, a baker's helper, an office boy for the Western Union Telegraph Company, and a reporter for the *Brooklyn Eagle.*

In 1882 Bok entered the world of book publishing by going to work for Henry Holt; two years later the hard-working Bok was hired away from Holt by Charles Scribner's Sons. In 1884 he founded the *Brooklyn Magazine*, a modest publication that featured the sermons of prominent ministers like Henry Ward Beecher as well as articles on various topics by famous people like William Tecumseh Sherman, the Civil War general. Two years later he sold *Brooklyn Magazine* to John Brisben Walker, who changed its name to *Cosmopolitan Magazine.* Bok then formed Bok Syndicate Press, which provided a variety of columns and features to more than 100 newspapers around the country. Its most popular feature was a full page of material with special appeal for women that was centered around a column written by the noted journalist Ella Wheeler Wilcox. The success of Bok Syndicate Press led Charles Scribner in 1887 to make Bok the head of the advertising department of a new project, *Scribner's Magazine.* It also brought Bok to the attention of Cyrus Curtis, publisher of *Ladies' Home Journal*, who in 1889 offered Bok the editorship of the Philadelphia-based magazine.

Under Bok's predecessor, Curtis's wife Louisa, *Ladies' Home Journal* had offered its readers a rather bland diet of religious exhortations and tales designed to bring a tear to the eye. Bok reinvented the *Journal* by recruiting some of the best fiction writers in the United States and Europe to submit work that was entertaining as well as intellectually stimulating, and by including nonfiction articles that informed women about their changing world while exhorting them to help change it for the better. Bok was not a muckraker, but he was very much in tune with the Progressive sentiments of his day, and he made sure the *Journal* called women's attention to a number of reform issues. For example, the *Journal* notified its readers of the danger of patent medicines, most of which were heavily laced with alcohol and few of which worked, and refused to accept advertising for such concoctions. The *Journal's* efforts in this regard are credited with helping to secure passage of the U.S. Food and Drug Act in 1906. The *Journal* also published photographs of run-down sections of various American cities and towns, in the process shaming many of its readers into petitioning their elected officials to do something about slum conditions in their communities. In addition to agitating for Progressive reform, Bok offered his readers a variety of interesting and stimulating information on virtually every topic from venereal disease to floor plans for their homes. Much of this information came in the form of regular features such as "Heart to Heart Talks" and "How America Lives."

In 1892 Bok married Mary Louise Curtis, daughter of Cyrus Curtis, with whom he had two children. In 1919 he retired as editor of the *Journal*, and spent his remaining years working for world peace and the resettlement of refugees displaced by World War I. He died on January 9, 1930, at his estate in Lake Wales, Florida.

Further Reading

Bok, Edward. *The Americanization of Edward Bok: The Autobiography of a Dutch Boy Fifty Years After.* Chicago: Lakeside Press, 2000.

Krabbendam, Johannes L. *The Model Man: A Life of Edward William Bok, 1863–1930.* Amsterdam: Rodopi, 2001.

Borden, Gail, Jr.

(1801–1874) *inventor of condensed milk*

Keeping milk fresh for any length of time in hot climates was virtually impossible until Gail Borden discovered a way to condense it. This process made it possible for Union troops to drink fresh milk during the Civil War—and for southerners and westerners to drink fresh milk after the war. Borden's Eagle Brand of condensed milk, an essential ingredient in a number of recipes, can still be found on store shelves today.

Borden was born on November 9, 1801, in Norwich, New York. His parents, Gail and Philadelphia, were farmers. As a young boy he moved with his family to Kennedy's Ferry, Kentucky, where at age 14 he helped survey the future town of Covington. At age 15 he moved with his family again, this time to New London, Indiana. In 1822 he left home and settled in Amite County, Mississippi, where he became the county surveyor as well as a schoolteacher. In 1828 he relocated to San Felipe, Texas, at the time still a part of Mexico. Over the next 20 years he farmed and raised cattle in San Felipe, helped write a constitution for Texas, compiled the first topographical map of Texas, founded a newspaper, the *Telegraph and Texas Land Register*, served as customs collector at Galveston Island, surveyed the town of Galveston, and designed the prototype of an amphibious vehicle he called the terraqueous machine, which was never actually built. In 1828 he married Penelope Mercer with whom he had five children. She died in 1843, and the following year he married the widow of Augustine F. Stearns. By 1860 she had also died, and that same year he married Emeline Eno Church.

In 1849 Borden conducted the first of many experiments involving food. His first invention was the meat biscuit, a combination of condensed beef broth and flour baked into cakes like pemmican, an old Indian trail food. The U.S. Army thought it was a great idea, as did the 1851 Great Council Exhibition in London, England, which awarded it a gold medal. However, for some reason, possibly because influential contractors used bribery to keep the army from procuring it, the meat biscuit never caught on, and in 1855 he gave up trying to make it a commercial success. Meanwhile, he had been experimenting with condensing other liquid foods such as coffee, tea, and apple cider, and in 1855 he moved to New Lebanon, New York, where he used the laboratories of the Shaker colony to develop a way to condense milk. Within a year he had received a patent for condensing milk by evaporating 75 percent of its water content in a vacuum over low heat, then sweetening the condensed milk with granulated sugar to make it taste good for long periods of time. Although Borden had no scientific training and therefore no idea why his process worked, his method anticipated the work of Louis Pasteur, the French scientist who developed pasteurization. By heating the milk in a vacuum, out of contact with the atmosphere, Borden killed a number of microorganisms that otherwise would have caused the milk to spoil.

By 1857 Borden had become partners with James Bridge, Thomas Green, and Reuel Williams and was operating two factories for condensing and canning milk in Connecticut. Although the partners did not lose money, neither did they make any, so in 1858 Borden's three partners sold out to Jeremiah Milbank, a New York City financier. Borden and Milbank formed the New York Condensed Milk Company, and under Milbank's skillful direction Borden's Eagle Brand of condensed milk became a fast-selling item. In 1861 the company replaced one of its factories with a newer one in Wassaic, New York. The Civil War occasioned a tremendous demand for condensed milk for troops in the field, and by the end of the war the company was operating six plants in New York and one in Illinois. After 1870, when the company became known as the Borden Condensed Milk Company, he spent his summers in White Plains, New York, and his winters in Borden, Texas, a small town which had been named in his honor. He died on January 11, 1874, in Borden.

Further Reading

Frantz, Joe B. *Gail Borden: Dairyman to a Nation.* Norman: University of Oklahoma Press, 1951.

"Gail Borden, Jr. (1801–1874)," Lone Star Junction. Available online. URL: http://www.lsjunction.com/people/borden.htm. Downloaded on June 30, 2009.

Wade, Mary D. *Milk, Meat Biscuits, and the Terraqueous Machine: The Story of Gail Borden.* Austin, Tex.: Eakin Press, 1987.

Brin, Sergey (1973–), and Larry Page (1973–)
founders of Google

In 2007, *Forbes* magazine published its annual ranking of the wealthiest Americans and tied for fifth on that list were two young business partners, Sergey Brin and Larry Page, who had revolutionized

Google cofounders Sergey Brin (left) and Larry Page talking about the new Google browser, Chrome. *(Photo by Paul Sakuma/AP)*

the Internet with the development of what would later become the world's top search engine, Google. Their enormously ambitious goal—as stated in Google's mission statement—"to organize the world's information and make it universally accessible and useful," and the rapid and enduring success they have enjoyed in pursuit of this goal have not only brought Brin and Page great riches but also made them among the most influential business leaders of the 21st century.

Sergey Brin was born in Moscow, Russia—then part of the Soviet Union—on August 21, 1973. Brin's father, Michael, was thwarted in his desire to pursue a professional career in astronomy because the ruling Communist Party barred Jews from physics positions at universities. Frustrated by the stifling anti-Semitism of Soviet culture and soon after attending a conference at which he met with American, British, and French colleagues and discovered that they were "not monsters," Michael applied for and was eventually granted an exit visa, and the family moved to the United States. Brin attended school in Maryland and graduated from a prestigious public high school in 1990. He enrolled at the University of Maryland, where he majored in computer science and mathematics, graduating with honors in 1993.

Lawrence Edward Page was born on March 26, 1973, in Lansing, Michigan. Page's father, Carl, was a computer science and artificial intelligence professor who, along with Larry's computer programming mother Gloria, encouraged their son's inclination and aptitude for science and math by encouraging him to tinker with computer components around the house. Page graduated from the University of Michigan—the school where his parents met—with a bachelor of science degree in computer engineering. In 2009, Page was presented with a honorary doctorate from the University of Michigan and delivered the commencement address, during which he described his alma mater as an "amazing institution that is responsible for my very existence."

Brin and Page met for the first time in 1995 at an orientation for doctoral candidates in computer science at Stanford University. Brin had already been in the program for two years and was serving as a guide for the new students, including Page. They soon began to collaborate on a project begun by Page that he later described as initially not seeking to create a search engine. Explained Page in a 2000 interview, "In late 1995, I started collecting the links on the Web, because my advisor and I decided that would be a good thing to do. We didn't know exactly what I was going to do with it, but it seemed like no one was really looking at the links on the Web—which pages link to which pages. In computer science, there's a lot of big graphs . . . I figured I could get a dissertation and do something fun and perhaps practical at the same time, which is really what motivates me."

In the same interview, Brin added, "I was really interested in data mining, which means analyzing large amounts of data, discovering patterns and trends . . . Our joint effort, just looking at the data out of curiosity, we found that we had technology to do a better job of search, and from that initial technology, we got really interested in the problem, and we realized how impactful having great search can be. So we built technology upon technology after that, to bring Google to where it is today, and we continue to develop lots of technology for tomorrow." Filling their apartments with inexpensive computers, Brin and Page continued to make great progress with their project and soon gained renown for it within the Stanford and broader northern California Silicon Valley com-

munities. The two men attracted just over $1 million from investors to begin Google, Inc., using the common misspelling of googol, which is the number one followed by 100 zeroes, which was the project's name when developed at Stanford.

Brin and Page ran Google out of a Menlo Park, California, garage in 1998. Within a year, Google moved to Palo Alto, California, and after continued growth moved to Mountain View, California, in 2003. In 2004, Google had a much-anticipated initial public offering (IPO) that raised over $1.7 billion. In subsequent years, Google has grown through new developments, acquisitions, and partnerships that have made Brin and Page billionaires. Especially profitable for Google have been simple advertisements that accompany the billions of web page clicks of their Web site. In 2006, over $10 billion of Google's revenue came from such advertisements. Another sign of Google's astounding success and impact on everyday life came in 2006, as the Oxford English Dictionary first included the word *google* as a verb, meaning "to use the Google search engine to obtain information on the Internet."

Despite their great wealth, both men have sought to focus on making Google an uniquely progressive company. *Fortune* magazine has repeatedly named Google its "#1 Place to Work" as the company has become well-known and respected for the perks it provides it employees, including first-class dining facilities, gyms, massage rooms, commuting buses, and dry cleaning services. In addition, Brin and Page have become very active philanthropists, providing millions for a variety of causes, particularly in the areas of energy, transportation, and health research. Among the health initiatives heavily invested by Brin and Page is research into Parkinson's disease, which afflicts Brin's mother and for which Brin explained he has a heightened chance of developing at some point in his life.

Brin has been married to biotechnology analyst Anne Wojcicki, the sister of the man from whom the Google founders rented their first garage as entrepreneurs, since 2007 and together they are the parents to a son. Also in 2007, Page married Lucy Southworth, a doctoral student in biomedical informatics.

Further Reading

"Enlightenment Man," *Economist*. Available online. URL: http://www.economist.com/sciencetechnology/tq/displayStory.cfm?story_id=12673407. Downloaded on June 30, 2009.

"Sergey Brin and Larry Page," Academy of Achievement. Available online. URL: http://www.achievement.org/autodoc/page/pag0bio-1. Downloaded on June 30, 2009.

Stross, Randall. *Planet Google: One Company's Audacious Plan to Organize Everything We Know.* New York: Free Press, 2008

Vise, David A., and Mark Malseed. *The Google Story.* New York: Delacorte Press, 2005.

Brown, John

(1736–1803) *entrepreneur in mercantile activity*

During the colonial period, virtually all economic activity was carried on by individuals rather than corporations. The mercantile firms that did exist were usually partnerships involving family members, whether related by blood or by marriage. John Brown typifies this sort of mercantile connection. Although he was one of the less cautious of the colonial New England traders, as evidenced by his involvement in privateering, slave trading, and the China trade, he usually conducted his business in partnership with his uncle, his brothers, or his son-in-law.

Brown was born on January 27, 1736, in Providence, Rhode Island. His father, James, was a merchant, and his mother, Hope, was a homemaker. At age three his father died, after which the major male presence in his life was his uncle, Obadiah Brown. As soon as John and his brothers Nicholas, Joseph, and Moses were old enough, Obadiah Brown made them his partners and put them to work in his extensive mercantile enterprises, known collectively as Obadiah Brown & Company. During the French and Indian War, which began when Brown was 18, he assisted his uncle in privateering against French merchantmen as well as trading with French merchants. In 1760 he married Sarah Smith with whom he had six children. When Obadiah Brown died in 1762, Brown and his brothers inherited their uncle's enterprises, which included a mercantile firm that traded extensively between Rhode Island and England and its possessions in the West Indies, a candle works, a rum distillery, and more than 80 ships. The brothers reorganized these activities as Nicholas Brown & Company, named after the eldest brother, while also embarking on new ventures, including an iron foundry, whaling, and a whale oil processing and distributing business.

Although Brown retained a lifelong interest in Nicholas Brown & Company, in 1771 he formed his own mercantile firm. Judging from the nature of the businesses Brown became involved in, the break was necessitated by his desire to engage in trade that the other brothers found either too risky or too distasteful. Brown's willingness to take risks is best exemplified by his involvement in the Gaspée Affair of 1772, when a British revenue cutter that had run aground was looted and burned to the waterline. Although the culprits were never brought to justice, by all accounts Brown had led the raiding party. In 1775 he received a contract from the Continental Congress to build two vessels for the nascent American navy. He also outfitted his own privateers for service against the British, supplied cannons, muskets, and gunpowder to the Continental Army, and invested rather heavily in securities issued by the Congress.

Brown maintained an interest in the transatlantic slave trade long after his brothers had lost theirs. In 1764 Nicholas Brown & Company had sent a slave ship to the coast of Guinea, where 17,000 gallons of the company's rum were exchanged for 200 slaves. Only 92 survived the trip to the West Indies, and the company lost money on the enterprise. This experience was enough to sour his three brothers on slave trading, but in 1769 Brown became involved without his brothers in another slave ship, with basically the same results. He tried again in 1797, despite a Rhode Island law prohibiting its citizens from participating in the slave trade, and he may have sent out one last slave ship in 1800.

The economic recession that followed the American Revolution, as well as the trade dislocations caused by the war, led Brown to look for new ways to make money. In the mid-1780s, he opened one of the first American gin distilleries, dabbled in cod fishing, and got involved more extensively in trading with Guinea, Suriname, and the countries touching the Baltic Sea. In 1787 Brown became partners with his son-in-law, John Francis, in a new mercantile firm, Brown & Francis. That same year their company sent out one of the first American merchant ships to travel to China and the East Indies via Africa and India. The ship exchanged a cargo of naval stores, iron goods, and alcoholic beverages for a cargo of tea, silk, china, spices, and lacquerware that sold in America for almost four times as much as the original cargo. By 1794 the firm was regularly operating four of the largest vessels ever to sail from Providence in the China trade. Two years later, however, the firm dissolved following Francis's untimely death.

In 1791 Brown helped found the Providence Bank, of which he served as president. In addition to his mercantile holdings, he owned several farms in Rhode Island as well as more than 200,000 acres of land in the Adirondack Mountains in New York. Along with his brothers Nicholas and Moses, he was a major supporter of the College of Rhode Island, which was moved from Warren to Providence and renamed Brown University. He died on September 20, 1803, in Providence.

Further Reading

"Brown, John, 1736–1803," Biographical Dictionary of the United States Congress. Available online. URL: http://bioguide.congress.gov/scripts/biodisplay.pl?index=B000927. Downloaded on June 30, 2009.

Hedges, James B. *The Browns of Providence Plantations.* 2 vols. Providence: Brown University Press, 1968.

Brown, Marie Dutton

(1940–   ) *entrepreneur in literary services*

For many years, the American publishing industry was fairly inhospitable to blacks. Few black authors could get their work published, and most blacks had trouble finding jobs as editors or agents. But this attitude began to change in the 1960s, and one of the first people to take advantage of the change was Marie Brown. In the process, she became one of the foremost literary agents for a rising tide of talented black novelists.

Brown was born Marie Dutton on October 4, 1940, in Philadelphia, Pennsylvania. Her father, Benson, was a professor of civil engineering, and her mother, Josephine, was a high school English teacher. As a young girl she moved with her family to Hampton, Virginia, and then to Nashville, Tennessee, both times because her father had obtained a new teaching position. At age 18 she enrolled in Pennsylvania State University and received her B.A. in psychology in 1962. After graduation she returned to Philadelphia and taught social studies in a public high school for three years.

By 1965 the civil rights movement was in full swing, and a number of businesses were waking up to the fact that black consumers constituted a significant portion of the American marketplace. In particular, Doubleday & Company, a major book publisher, was looking to expand its sales among black readers by publishing books that would be of special interest to them, and so the company began recruiting talented black professionals to learn the publishing business. In 1965 Brown was invited to work for Doubleday in New York City as a trainee and editorial assistant, and she was soon on a fast track to a top management position. However, two years later she left Doubleday to accompany her husband, Kenneth Brown—whom she had married in 1966 and with whom she had one child—to Los Angeles, California, where he had been accepted into art school. Unfortunately for Brown, the Los Angeles publishing community did not share the same interest in publishing diversity as did Doubleday, so she did freelance editorial work and managed Bronze Books, a bookstore that specialized in minority American literature and literature from developing nations.

In 1972 Brown returned to Doubleday's New York City office as an associate editor, and over the next eight years she worked her way up to senior editor. During this period she played a significant role in bringing top-quality black writers, such as Vertamae Smart Grosvenor, Mari Evans, and Carolyn Rodgers, into the Doubleday galaxy of stars. But by the late 1970s, the company's commitment to black literature was fading, in large part because sales of black-authored books were slumping. This slump was caused in part by the fact that many black authors had focused on shocking their readers with grim portrayals of life in the ghetto or in the racist South, and the novelty of this genre was wearing off among white readers, who had initially responded to such works with great enthusiasm. In 1980 she left Doubleday to become cofounder and managing editor of *Elan,* a women's magazine that covered the lifestyles of the black international upper middle class. However, one year and three issues later, the magazine folded; unable to find a suitable position in publishing, she took a job as a salesclerk with Endicott Booksellers, a Manhattan bookstore. Shortly thereafter she was promoted to assistant buyer, and within three years she was the store's assistant manager.

In 1984 Brown was convinced by a close friend to go into business for herself, doing what she had done so well at Doubleday, helping talented black

Marie Brown is one of America's leading literary agents. *(Photograph by Mel Wright)*

writers become black authors. That same year she formed Marie Brown Associates, a one-woman literary services agency operating out of her apartment in Harlem. She solicited manuscripts, reviewed them, and placed them for publication, then marketed her clients' books and handled their public relations. Like most fledgling businesses, Brown's struggled for a few years. But when publishers like Doubleday regained their interest in publishing black literature in the late 1980s, in part because many black writers were now focusing more on the human condition in general so that their work had tremendous appeal to both black and white audiences, her contacts and knowledge of the publishing industry enabled her agency to thrive. By 2001 she represented more than 100 talented black novelists such as Randall Robinson, Susan Taylor, Johnnetta Cole, Faith Ringgold, Donald Bogle, Colin Channer, Herb Boyd, and Queen Afua, and she employed several other literary agents in an upscale office in Greenwich Village.

Brown remains active as the president of Marie Brown Associates and continues to receive praise for her work as a pioneer in publishing. Such recognition is reflected in the words of noted journalist and former *60 Minutes* correspondent Ed Bradley, who said of Brown, ". . . she is determined and hardworking, someone who every day is pushing a boulder uphill and never stops."

Further Reading

Brennan, Carol. "Marie Dutton Brown." *Contemporary Black Biography* 12, Detroit: Gale Group, 1996, pp. 17–19.
"Marie Dutton Brown," Biography Resource Center. Available online. URL: http://www.africanpubs.com/Apps/bios/0383BrownMarie.asp?pic=none. Downloaded on November 19, 2001.

Brown, Rachel Fuller (1898–1980), and Elizabeth Lee Hazen (1885–1975)
inventors of antibiotic drugs

Rachel Brown and Elizabeth Hazen are the codiscoverers of the antibiotic drugs known as nystatin. This drug is used to treat all sorts of fungal infections from vaginal yeast infections to athletes' foot. It has also been used to counter the effect of fungus on everything from livestock feed to ancient murals and manuscripts. Most important, it made possible the use of penicillin for the widespread treatment of human diseases.

Brown was born on November 23, 1898, in Springfield, Massachusetts. Her father, George, was a real estate and insurance agent, and her mother, Annie, was a housewife. As a young girl she moved with her family to Webster Groves, Missouri. In 1912 her parents' marriage failed, and she and her mother and brother returned to Springfield. She graduated from Mount Holyoke College in 1920 with an A.B. in history and chemistry. She then moved to Chicago, Illinois, where she taught high school chemistry while doing graduate work at the University of Chicago. She received her M.S. in chemistry in 1921 and completed the work for her Ph.D. in chemistry in 1926, but for some reason her dissertation was not approved until 1933, when she received the degree. In 1926 she went to work as a biochemist with the division of laboratories and research of the New York State Department of Health in Albany, at the time one of the few places in the United States that hired women for research positions. Over the next 14 years she worked primarily to identify the bacteria that cause pneumonia; she also developed an antipneumonial vaccine that was used as late as the 1980s.

Hazen was born on August 24, 1885, in Rich, Mississippi. Her parents, William and Maggie, were cotton farmers. She was orphaned at age four and raised by an aunt and uncle who lived nearby. She graduated from the Mississippi Industrial Institute and College (today Mississippi University for Women) in 1910 with a B.S. in science. For the next six years she taught high-school science in Jackson, then enrolled in Columbia University where she earned an M.S. in bacteriology in 1917 and a Ph.D. in microbiology in 1927. For the next four years she taught at Columbia's College of Physicians and Surgeons. In 1931 she went to work as a microbiologist with the division of laboratories and research of the New York State Department of Health. For the next 10 years she primarily studied the spread of infectious diseases.

In 1940 penicillin was developed into an injectable antibiotic drug. However, one of its harmful side effects was that it stimulated the growth of fungus in the mouth and stomach, which sometimes developed into fatal infections. Unless this side effect could be neutralized, penicillin could only be used on a limited basis to combat bacterial diseases. In the early 1940s Hazen set out to solve this problem by developing an antibiotic that could kill fungus. Following Selman A. Waksman's discovery in 1944 that antibiotics are produced by actinomycetes (bacteria that live in soil), she began searching for an actinomycete that produced an antifungal antibiotic.

At this point Hazen and Brown became collaborators, having been introduced to one another by Gilbert Dalldorf, director of the division in which they both worked. It was agreed that Hazen would concentrate on finding suitable soil samples and that Brown would analyze the samples in the laboratory. In 1948, after four years of collecting and analyzing hundreds of samples from all across the country, Hazen found a sample on a friend's farm in Virginia that contained *Streptomyces noursei,* an actinomycete that produced two antifungal substances. One was too toxic to use on humans, but the other proved to be perfect: strong enough to kill fungal infections of the central nervous system, mouth, lungs, and vagina but mild enough to leave humans unharmed.

In 1950 Brown and Hazen announced their discovery and patented their antifungal antibiotic as nystatin, in honor of the New York State Department of Health. They licensed the patent to E. R. Squibb and Sons, a pharmaceutical firm that in 1954 began marketing nystatin in tablet form under the name Mycostatin. Over the years Brown and Hazen earned more than $13 million in royalties, but they kept little of it for themselves. They donated the bulk of the money to the Research Corporation, a nonprofit organization that specialized in general medical research, and the Brown-Hazen Fund, which promoted research in the field of biology and related sciences. For their discovery and development of nystatin, Brown and Hazen were awarded the Squibb Award in chemotherapy in 1955, and in 1975 they became the first women to win the American Institute of Chemists' prestigious Chemical Pioneer Award.

Brown and Hazen continued their search for actinomycetes until 1960, when Hazen retired. In 1953 they discovered phalamycin and in 1959 they discovered capacidin. Unfortunately, both proved to be too toxic for use in humans. After her retirement, Hazen worked as a guest investigator at the Columbia University Mycology Laboratory until she retired in 1973. That same year she moved into a retirement home in Seattle, Washington, to be near her sister; Hazen died in Seattle on June 24, 1975. Brown retired in 1968; she remained in Albany where she was active in local affairs until her death on January 14, 1980.

Further Reading

Baldwin, Richard S. *The Fungus Fighters: Two Women Scientists and Their Discovery.* Ithaca, N.Y.: Cornell University Press, 1981.

"Elizabeth Lee Hazen," The National Inventors Hall of Fame. Available online. URL: http://www.invent. org/Hall_Of_Fame/75.html. Downloaded on June 30, 2009.

"Rachel Fuller Brown," The National Inventors Hall of Fame. Available online. URL: http://www.invent. org/hall_of_fame/20.html. Downloaded on June 30, 2009.

Yount, Lisa. *A to Z of Women in Science and Math.* New York: Facts On File, 1999.

Brush, Charles Francis

(1849–1929) *inventor of electric arc lamp street lighting*

The first lightbulb was not THOMAS ALVA EDISON'S incandescent lamp, but the arc lamp. Invented by the English inventor Humphry Davy in 1807, the arc lamp maintains an electric arc between two conductors or rods, and the heated ends of the rods as well as the arc itself give off a bright light. The use of the arc lamp for commercial lighting, however, was not made practical until 1880, when Charles Brush installed the first commercially successful arc lamp lighting system.

Brush was born on March 17, 1849, in Euclid, Ohio. His father, Isaac, was a woolens manufacturer, and his mother, Delia, was a homemaker. As a young boy he became interested in electricity,

and while in high school he built a homemade battery with which he powered a small lighting system that used arc lamps. At age 18 Brush enrolled in the University of Michigan, earning a B.S. in mining engineering in 1869. After graduation he moved to Cleveland, Ohio, where he became a self-employed analytical and consulting chemist. In 1873 he expanded his activities to include the marketing of iron ore, and within two years he had made enough money to be able to devote most of his time to a resumption of his experiments with electric arc lighting. In 1875 he married Mary Morris with whom he had three children.

Since arc lighting is much too bright for indoor use, in 1875 Brush began looking toward using it as a means of providing outdoor illumination. His first problem was to develop a suitable power source for the lamps, since the electrical current they required was really more than could be supplied reliably by batteries alone. He began by taking a Gramme dynamo, in essence a direct-current generator invented by the French engineer Zenobe-Theophile Gramme, and making it compact and efficient enough to provide continuous power for four arc lamps. Next, Brush tackled the problem of the lights themselves. The conductors in the first arc lamps burned out after only a few hours, so he fashioned conductors out of carbon rods, which provided a bright light for at least 16 hours. To ensure that the arc gave off a uniform glow, he developed an electromagnetically actuated feedback device that maintained the gap between the carbon rods at a uniform distance, even as the rods were being consumed gradually by the current. The original arc lamps also flickered, a problem he solved by sheathing the carbon rods with copper plating. To prevent the system from redirecting a burned-out lamp's current to the remaining lamps, thus causing them to burn out prematurely, he invented an automatic regulator that maintained a constant current throughout the system.

In 1877 Brush's dynamo was awarded a prize by the Franklin Institute in Philadelphia, Pennsylvania, and the following year he installed an arc light system at the Philadelphia department store of JOHN WANAMAKER. In 1879 he designed and constructed a 12-lamp arc light system for illuminating a public square in downtown Cleveland, the first electric street lighting system to become operational in the United States. And in 1880, the year by which he had completed all of the above-mentioned technological improvements, he installed a street lighting system in San Francisco, California, that delighted the city's residents and greatly profited Brush.

That same year Brush and George Stockly formed the Brush Electric Company in Cleveland for purposes of manufacturing and installing electric arc street lighting systems. Within five years the company had illuminated streets in New York City, Philadelphia, and Boston, Massachusetts, among other cities. By 1885 it was producing more than 1,500 lamps per month and grossing more than $1 million annually. In 1889 Brush and Stockly sold Brush Electric to the Thomson-Houston Company of Lynn, Massachusetts; both men made enough money from the sale to live the rest of their lives in comfort.

Although perfecting the system of electric arc lighting was Brush's major contribution to the field of electricity, it was not his only one. In 1880 he invented a storage battery that operated by means of lead plates and sulfuric acid (a similar battery was invented at the same time by the French inventor Camille Faure). Brush had hoped that such a storage battery would permit him to use a smaller, and therefore less expensive, dynamo for street lighting. Although the lead-acid battery proved to be impractical for this application, it later found widespread acceptance as a starter battery for automobiles.

Over the last 30 years of his life, Brush dabbled with electrical experiments and other scientific investigations. He also formed Brush Laboratories, a small independent research facility, and in 1907 he cofounded and became the first president of the Linde Air Products Company, an early chemical manufacturing firm that eventually became a part of the Union Carbide Company. He died on June 15, 1929, in Cleveland.

Further Reading

Carlson, W. Bernard. *Innovation as a Social Process.* New York: Cambridge University Press, 1991.

Passer, Harold. *The Electrical Manufacturers, 1875–1900.* Salem, N.H.: Ayer Co., 1988.

Buffett, Warren
(1930–) *entrepreneur in financial investing*

Known as the Oracle of Omaha because of his legendary acumen in selecting investment opportunities, Warren Buffett was ranked by *Forbes* magazine in 2009 as the second wealthiest person in the world, with a net worth of $37 billion. Despite this staggering amount of riches, Buffett remains well known for his frugal and unassuming nature, as well as for his commitment to philanthropy.

Warren Edward Buffett was born in Omaha, Nebraska, on August 30, 1930. The second of three children born to his parents, Leila and Howard, Buffett spent his childhood years in Omaha and worked in his grandfather's grocery store when not in school. Buffett also delivered newspapers and filed his first tax return at the age of 13, famously taking a $35 deduction for his bicycle. When his stockbroker father won a seat to the U.S. House of Representatives, the family moved to Washington, D.C., where Buffett graduated from high school in 1947. Buffett enrolled in the University of Pennsylvania's Wharton School of Business, but transferred to the University of Nebraska, graduating from there in 1950 with a degree in economics.

Buffett then was accepted into Columbia Business School. During his studies at Columbia, he was greatly influenced by two prominent professors, Benjamin Graham and Phil Fisher, who were renowned for their analysis of securities. Of these

Warren Buffett during a press conference in New York, June 26, 2006 *(Photo by Seth Wenig/AP)*

mentors, Buffett later noted, "I'm 15 percent Fisher and 85 percent Benjamin Graham . . . The basic ideas of investing are to look at stocks as business, use the market's fluctuations to your advantage, and seek a margin of safety. That's what Ben Graham taught us. A hundred years from now they will still be the cornerstones of investing." Buffett graduated from Columbia with a masters in economics in 1951.

The professional career that would eventually make Buffett into the world's richest person began with a investment salesman job in Omaha, which was followed by a three-year stint working as a securities analyst with his former professor in New York at Graham-Newman Corporation. Buffett returned to Omaha in 1956 to work as the general partner in Buffett Partnership, Limited. He was very successful in this endeavor—becoming a millionaire in his early 30s—by using his value investing philosophy that emphasizes buying stocks that are trading below their intrinsic value to accumulate returns that were approximately 10 times the rate of growth in the Dow Jones Industrial Average during that same period.

In 1965 Buffett took control of the textile company Berkshire Hathaway and within a few years wound up the company's work in textiles. He kept the name Berkshire Hathaway for his portfolio of companies and investments. Through his careful and detailed research and adherence to his philosophy, Buffett invested in several companies, including American Express, the Washington Post, Coca-Cola, and Gillette to become very rich. During this time and later in his career, Buffett took a relatively meager salary for his work, relying on his investment income for his wealth. In 1979, Buffett made his first appearance on the *Forbes* magazine list of the 400 richest people in the United States, with an estimated net worth of $620 million.

Buffett's wealth and his now-sturdy legend as one of the most successful investors in history grew throughout the next few decades, culminating in his placement by *Forbes* as the world's richest person, with a estimated net worth of $62 billion (the significant drop in the stock market during 2008 dropped this figure to $37 billion in 2009). In addition to attracting countless admirers to his investment strategies, Buffett has also gained the respect of many for his personal style. He writes annual letters to shareholders and is an accessible and engaging speaker at Berkshire Hathaway conferences and in other public forums. Through these writings and speeches, Buffett has become well known for maxims that reflect his personality and business style, including, "Most people get interested in stocks when everyone else is. The time to get interested is when no one else is. You can't buy what is popular and do well," "You only have to do a very few things right in your life so long as you don't do too many things wrong," "If a business does well, the stock eventually follows," and "Price is what you pay. Value is what you get."

Buffett married Susan Thompson in 1952 and together they had two sons and a daughter. He separated from Thompson in 1977, but they remained close and never divorced. Soon after Susan's death in 2004, Buffett married his longtime companion, Astrid Menks. He remains intimately involved in all aspects of his firm and recently became more involved in public life with his active support in 2008 for presidential candidate Barack Obama and his informal role as an economic adviser to President Obama during economically tumultuous periods of 2009.

Further Reading

Lewis, Michael. "The Master of Money," *New Republic*. Available online. URL: http://www.tnr.com/story_print.html?id=12ef5554-1023-4be9-ad93-681003b280ef. Downloaded on June 30, 2009.

Lowenstein, Roger. *Buffett: The Making of an American Capitalist*. New York: Random House Trade Paperbacks, 2008.

Schroeder, Alice. *The Snowball: Warren Buffett and the Business of Life*. New York: Bantam, 2008.

"The World's Billionaires," *Forbes*. Available online. URL: http://www.forbes.com/lists/2009/10/billionaires-2009-richest-people_Warren-Buffett_C0R3.html. Downloaded on June 30, 2009.

Buick, David Dunbar

(1854–1929) *inventor of the Buick automobile*

One of the most popular makes of automobile in the United States is the Buick. Originally manufactured in 1904, Buicks were still selling well at the beginning of the 21st century. The car takes its name from its inventor, David Buick, who was a contemporary of HENRY FORD and whose Model B went on sale four years before Ford's famous Model T. Unlike Ford, however, Buick proved to be a poor entrepreneur, and as a result he was forced out of the automobile business just as his cars were becoming popular.

Buick was born on September 17, 1854, in Arbroath, Scotland. The occupations of his parents, Alexander and Jane, are unknown, although it is probable that they were both mill or factory workers. At age two he moved with his family to Detroit, Michigan, where his father died three years later. At age 11 he went to work to help support his family, and over the next four years he worked successively as a newspaper delivery boy, a farm laborer, and a machinist's apprentice. He completed his apprenticeship at the shop of James Flower and Flower's brothers, where Henry Ford would later work as an apprentice.

In 1869 the 15-year-old Buick was hired as a machinist by the Alexander Manufacturing Company, which made plumbing supplies; by 1878, the year he married Catherine Schwinck with whom he had four children, he had become a production foreman. In 1882 Alexander Manufacturing went out of business, so Buick and William S. Sherwood bought the company's assets and formed the Buick & Sherwood Plumbing and Supply Company. Buick concentrated on production and new product development, and by 1889 he had received 13 patents. His most important invention in this regard was a process for bonding porcelain to metal, which for many years was used to manufacture sinks and commodes. Partly as a result of Buick's inventions, the company thrived, and in 1899 the partners sold it for $100,000, at the time a substantial sum.

Although Buick stayed on for two years as the company's salaried president, he spent most of his time experimenting with his newest interest, the gasoline engine. In the late 1890s he had begun tinkering with motors for boats and tractors, but he quickly redirected his focus toward designing a powerful engine for the nascent American automobile industry. By 1901 he, Walter L. Marr,

and Eugene C. Richard had developed a motor that they called the "L-head engine." Shaped somewhat like a "V," this asymmetrical engine places all of the intake and exhaust valves in the extended half of the cylinder block, or the long part of the "L," while all of the spark plugs are placed in the shortened half. In 1902 he began building an entire car that featured another new motor design, the "valve-in-head" engine. This symmetrical design places the intake and exhaust valves directly above the cylinders, rather than to one side as in the L-head configuration, and mounts them entirely within the cylinder head, the result being a more powerful and efficient operation. By 1903 he successfully road tested his first car, and the following year he built an improved version, the Model B, which featured a two-cylinder, valve-in-head engine. Between 1904 and 1908, the Model B's annual sales rose from 37 to more than 8,800, more than the total number of Fords and Cadillacs combined.

Although Buick was a brilliant automotive inventor, he was inept as an automotive entrepreneur. The company he formed in 1901 to manufacture and sell L-head engines, the Buick Auto-Vim and Power Company, nearly went bankrupt within a year because the L-head engine's lopsided design was almost completely rejected by car manufacturers. He reorganized his company in 1902 as the Buick Manufacturing Company and began designing the Model B, but only as a result of two loans totaling $4,150 from Benjamin and Frank Briscoe, two Detroit auto parts manufacturers. In return for the loans, the Briscoes assumed 99.7 percent ownership of Buick's company. In 1904, when the Model B entered production, the Briscoes sold the company to several investors headed by James H. Whiting, president of the Flint Wagon Works in Flint, Michigan. Buick stayed on as secretary and general manager of the renamed Buick Motor Company, which was relocated to Flint. In 1905 he was removed from these positions after borrowing heavily from several Flint banks without developing a comprehensive business plan. Reassigned as head of the product development team, he was forced out of the company altogether in 1908.

At the time of his discharge from the company that bore his name, Buick was given $100,000 as severance pay. By the mid-1920s the money was entirely gone. Two great chunks of it were lost due to unfortunate investments in California petroleum and Florida real estate. The rest of it was used to start a carburetor manufacturing company and another automobile manufacturing firm, both of which failed. For the last several years of his life, Buick eked out a living teaching automotive mechanics in Detroit, where he died on March 6, 1929.

Further Reading

General Motors Corporation. *Buick's First Half-Century.* Flint, Mich.: The Corporation, 1952.

Gustin, Terry B., and Lawrence R. *The Buick: A Complete History.* Kutztown, Penn.: Automobile Quarterly Publications, 1997.

Burnett, Leo

(1891–1971) *entrepreneur in advertising*

Few, if any, people who have worked in advertising have done as much to elevate the power of the visual image as Leo Burnett. In a groundbreaking career that spanned five decades, Burnett created and left an indelible imprint on advertising that continues to be felt around the world.

Leo Burnett was born on October 21, 1891, in St. John's, Michigan. He grew up in that small town located about 30 miles north of the state capitol in Lansing and as a child he assisted his father in his dry goods store. As a teenager, Burnett pursued his love of writing by working as a reporter for local newspapers. After graduating from high school, Burnett attended the University of Michigan and received his bachelor's degree in 1914. He soon moved to Peoria, Illinois, where he briefly worked as a reporter before taking a job as an editor of a publication for Cadillac dealers. This led to a position as the advertising director with the company of the publication.

In 1918, Burnett married Naomi Geddes, and they eventually became parents to two sons and a daughter. After a short stint in the navy, Burnett moved to Indianapolis, where he worked as an advertising director for a new car company founded by former colleagues at Cadillac. He worked there for 10 years before moving to Chicago to work as the vice president and head of the creative department with the Erwin, Wassey advertising agency. Burnett stayed with Erwin, Wassey for five years but found it increasingly difficult to keep top talent, who were often lured by offers from New York–based agencies. Faced with this problem, Burnett decided in 1935 to open his own firm. He made the highly unusual choice to have the new Leo Burnett Company be based outside of New York City, which was the capital of the advertising world, because as he would later explain, "My associates and I saw the opportunity to offer a creative service badly needed in the Middle West. I sold my house, hocked all my insurance, and took a dive off the end of a springboard."

Burnett started with just three employees, three clients, and about $200,000 in billings. By 1945, those numbers grew to over 100 employees, 16 clients, and $7.4 million in billings, and by 1950 the company had almost 300 employees, 24 clients, and more than $20 million in billings. But this impressive growth was eclipsed by the stunning expansion during the 1950s, which was mainly powered by the increasingly popular advertising medium of television. Through the development of such enduring advertising icons as Tony the Tiger (Kellogg's cereals), Charlie the Tuna (StarKist Tuna), the Jolly Green Giant (Green Giant vegetables), and the Marlboro Man (Phillip Morris cigarettes), the Leo Burnett Company created visually appealing characters that became well known and loved by millions watching them on the commercials that filled television programming. Burnett's more visually oriented and less market research–oriented ads took hold exactly as television ownership boomed. At the beginning of the 1950s, about one in 10 U.S. households owned a television, but by the end of the decade about nine in 10 owned at least one television. Burnett's fortunes mirrored this increase. By the end of the 1950s, Burnett had 38 clients and $117 million in billings, an increase of more than 500 percent from the beginning of the decade.

The 1960s witnessed further growth for Burnett's company, leading it to become one of the top advertising agencies in the world. By the end of the 1960s, Burnett had almost 40 offices located in 25 countries. Powering this expanded reach and influence was Burnett himself, who had all his workers use the big black pencils he favored as a symbol of creative production. A 1962 *Time* magazine cover story that profiled Burnett and other leading advertising executives noted,

> "Legend has it that 70-year-old Leo Burnett works from before dawn till after dark 364 days a year—and takes Christmas morning off. Through his ability to confect folksy attention-getting ads, Chairman Burnett has lifted the billings of Chicago's Leo Burnett Co. to $136 million, largest for any agency west of the Hudson. Out of Burnett's oven came the Pillsbury cake-mix campaign, which set a much imitated standard for food ads by running a mouth-watering photo of a cake under copy that appealed to Mrs. America's subliminal desires and fears ("You triumph, you please, you make everybody very, very happy"). . . . Today, his personal trademark is the bowl of red apples that sits in each of his agency's reception rooms—a permanent rejoinder to a scoffing gossip columnist who warned years ago that Burnett, by going into business for himself, would 'wind up selling apples.'"

Burnett retired in December 1967 and addressed his Chicago employees with a renowned speech entitled, "When to Take My Name off the Door." In it, Burnett described several scenarios (e.g., "When you forget the sheer fun of ad making and the lift you get out of it . . . When you lose your itch to do the job well for it's sake—regardless of the client, or money, or the effort it takes . . . When you stop reaching the manner, the overtones, the marriage of words and pictures that produce the fresh, the memorable and the believable effect") with which he would not want his name associated in the future. The advertising agency that Burnett started against such long odds remains among the strongest in the world, beginning the 21st century with $8.3 billion in billings and 94 offices in 82 countries.

Burnett died of a heart attack in his home in Lake Zurich, Illinois, on June 7, 1971, but his unique legacy on advertising, and more specifically

on his iconic company, remains strong. In 1990, the *Forbes* magazine writer Rita Koselka reflected on this legacy by noting, "The Burnett agency has accomplished something that has eluded so many other businesses: It has managed to keep the spirit and drive of its founder alive and well almost two decades after the founder himself passed on." Other indications of Burnett's enduring impact are also seen on a visit to the Leo Burnett offices, which feature many symbols of its founder, including signs in the form of his autograph, black pencils, and his beloved apples.

Further Reading

Ewen, Stewart. "Leo Burnett," Time 100. Available online. URL: http://www.time.com/time/time100/builder/profile/burnett.html. Downloaded on June 30, 2009.

"Heritage" Leo Burnett. Available online. URL: http://www.leoburnett.com/. Downloaded on June 30, 2009.

"The Men on the Cover," *Time*. Available online. URL: http://www.time.com/time/magazine/article/0,9171,829288-3,00.html. Downloaded on June 20, 2009.

Burroughs, William Seward
(1857–1898) *inventor of the recording adding machine*

William Burroughs did not invent the adding machine. That honor goes either to Blaise Pascal, the French philosopher who invented a crude mechanical calculator in 1642, or to the anonymous Babylonian who invented the abacus thousands of years ago. By the time, however, that Burroughs had his idea, both Pascal's machine and the abacus were nothing more than curiosities to Americans. Burroughs, at the time a bank clerk, determined the need for a machine that would allow him to do his job faster and more accurately, and the machine he developed did exactly that.

Burroughs was born on January 28, 1857, in Auburn, New York. His father, Edmund, was a mechanic, and his mother, Ellen, was a homemaker. As a young boy he lived briefly with his family in Michigan, then returned with them to

Auburn. At age 15 he went to work as a clerk in a local bank. In 1878 he married Ida Selover with whom he had four children.

As a bank clerk, Burroughs' primary job was to account for monies paid out and taken in. He soon discovered that he spent most of his time checking his arithmetic, which at the time was done with a pencil on a piece of paper, and trying to correct mistakes. By 1882, when he had been working in the bank for 10 years, he had had the idea to invent a machine for adding and subtracting numbers. That same year he was diagnosed with tuberculosis; searching for a healthier climate, he moved to St. Louis, Missouri, where his father got him a job at the Hall and Brown Machine Company.

Constructing models for castings by day, Burroughs designed the adding machine by night. In 1884 his efforts came to the attention of Richard Scruggs and Thomas Metcalfe, senior partner and attorney, respectively, for a retail dry-goods store. The two men were fascinated by Burroughs's project and gave him $700 with which to build a prototype. Burroughs left Hall and Brown and spent the next year perfecting his machine. In this he was helped greatly by Joseph Boyer, a machine shop owner, who gave him space in his shop rent free. Boyer also loaned him the services of an apprentice, Alfred Doughty, who later became the president of the company Burroughs and his partners would found. Burroughs filed for a patent for a "calculating machine" in 1885, which he received three years later, but it was not until 1886 that he had developed a device (actually his third model) that added and subtracted accurately, while simultaneously recording the calculations and their totals by printing them on a piece of paper. The machine included a fail-safe device, a hand-operated calculating lever; after keying in the proper figures, the operator could double-check the entry before pulling the lever, which set in motion the adding mechanisms and the printer.

In 1886 Burroughs, Scruggs, Metcalfe, and William Pye formed the American Arithmometer Company, with Burroughs as vice president. The company was undercapitalized, however, and Burroughs spent most of his time raising money. In 1889, while he was in England looking for additional investors, his partners employed Boyer's machine shop to build 50 calculating machines. Not one of the machines worked correctly, mostly because of the calculating lever. Burroughs quickly discovered that different operators pulled the lever at different speeds, which caused the adding mechanisms to miscalculate. He solved the problem by attaching a hydraulic governor, actually a small oil-filled dashpot, to the lever so that, regardless of how hard it was pulled, it traveled at only one speed. In 1890 the company hired three salesmen, who also served as the company's repairmen, to begin calling on potential customers in the St. Louis area; the adding and listing machine sold for $475. Eventually the company branched out into other cities, and in 1895 it sold almost 300 machines. Five years later American Arithmometer was selling almost 1,000 machines per year.

Meanwhile, Burroughs's health had continued to worsen. In 1896 he resigned from the company and moved to Citronelle, Alabama, hoping that the change in climate would help him get over his tuberculosis. It did not, and on September 14, 1898, he died in Citronelle. In 1905 American Arithmometer was reorganized as the Burroughs Adding Machine Company, and it went on to become the world's largest manufacturer of adding and accounting machines.

Further Reading

Coleman, John Strider. *The Business Machine, with Mention of William Seward Burroughs, Joseph Boyer, and Others, Since 1880.* New York: Newcomen Society in North America, 1949.

"William Seward Burroughs," National Inventors Hall of Fame. Available online. URL: http://www.invent.org/hall_of_fame/23.html. Downloaded on June 30, 2009.

Busch, Adolphus
(1839–1913) *founder of Anheuser-Busch*

Most Americans think that the first light beer made in the United States was Lite, a product of the Miller Brewing Company. They are wrong; the first light beer made in America was Budweiser. The brainchild of Adolphus Busch, cofounder of what would become Anheuser-Busch, Inc.,

Budweiser eventually became the best-selling beer in the world.

Busch was born on July 10, 1839, in Mainz, Hesse, today part of Germany. His father, Ulrich, was a wealthy merchant and landowner, and his mother, Barbara, was a homemaker. After completing his schooling, he worked briefly for his father and then for a mercantile firm in nearby Cologne. At age 18 he emigrated to the United States, settling in St. Louis, Missouri, where several of his brothers lived, and for the next two years he worked as a clerk on a riverboat.

In 1859 Busch inherited a sum of money from his father's estate. He used it to form two partnerships—one with his brother Ulrich in a brewery supply house and the other with Ernst Wattenberg in a malt house—and began doing business with St. Louis's 40 breweries. One of his customers was Eberhard Anheuser, owner of one of the smaller breweries, and in 1861 Busch married Anheuser's daughter, Lilly, with whom he had 14 children. In 1864 he became a partner in Anheuser's brewery, and within five years annual sales had increased from 8,000 to 18,000 barrels of beer.

Despite this increase, Busch knew that the immediate future of the brewery did not lie in St. Louis, where there were a number of competing breweries, but in the vast, thirsty expanses of the Southwest. Unfortunately, beer did not travel well in those days, because it had to be kept cold to avoid spoilage. Undaunted, Busch solved this problem in 1872, when he began shipping barrels of beer to Texas; he kept the beer fresh by icing it down in St. Louis and then reicing it at icehouses he had built along the railroad. The following year Anheuser's technicians discovered that beer could be pasteurized by bottling it and then dunking the bottles in tubs of hot water for an extended period of time. Once the bottles were chilled, the beer regained its original flavor and stayed fresh indefinitely. In 1876 Busch helped develop a special refrigerated railcar for shipping unpasteurized beer in barrels, and two years later he organized the St. Louis Refrigerator Car Company to manufacture and operate these cars. Pasteurization and refrigeration enabled Busch to sell beer all over the western half of the United States, with draft beer

outselling bottled beer until 1939. By 1879, when the company was incorporated as the Anheuser-Busch Brewing Association, the brewery was selling more than 50,000 barrels of beer per year.

In 1883, Anheuser-Busch began selling nationally what would become the number-one beer in the world and what would make it the number-one brewery in the country. Prior to 1876, Anheuser-Busch brewed mostly a dark, heavy lager beer like the types enjoyed throughout central Europe. Although German-Americans loved this beer, Busch realized that many Americans of other ethnic origins did not care for it, so he decided to brew a pale, light lager beer similar to the pilsners preferred by eastern Europeans. With the help of his

This 1904 picture depicts Adolphus Busch as an early modern Dutch burgomeister. *(Library of Congress)*

friend Carl Conrad, Busch developed a light beer which he named in honor of the Bohemian town of Budweis (today known as Ceske Budejovice in the Czech Republic). For seven years, Budweiser was brewed by Anheuser-Busch but bottled and distributed by Conrad. When Conrad went out of business in 1883, Anheuser-Busch began shipping Budweiser all over the country. Budweiser proved to be exceptionally popular; by 1885 Anheuser-Busch's annual sales topped 300,000 barrels, and five years later that figure had increased by another 400,000 barrels. In order to keep up with the demand, Busch had the brewery outfitted with artificial refrigeration to take the place of the ice-cooled cellars he had used previously.

Meanwhile, Busch had been expanding his operations by acquiring breweries outside of St. Louis and by implementing an aggressive advertising campaign. In 1883 he acquired the Lone Star Brewery in San Antonio, Texas, and later bought other breweries in Texas and Louisiana. In 1896 he began giving away untold lithographed copies of a painting entitled *Custer's Last Fight,* with the Anheuser-Busch logo prominently displayed along one of the edges. It was said that, by 1900, one could hardly find a bar in America that did not have the lithograph on display. By 1900 Anheuser-Busch had passed Pabst as the number-one brewery in the United States, and the following year annual sales hit the 1-million-barrel mark for the first time.

In 1906 Busch's health began to fail; three years later he appointed his son August vice president and general manager with the authority to make the day-to-day operating decisions, although Busch retained the nominal title of president. Busch died on October 10, 1913, while hunting at his estate near Langenschwalbach, Germany. At the time of his death, his estate was valued at between $50 million and $60 million. In 2008 Anheuser-Busch was acquired by the Brazilian-Belgian brewing conglomerate InBev, ending 150 years of control by the Busch family.

Further Reading

Busch, August A. *Budweiser, a Century of Character.* New York: Newcomen Society in North America, 1955.

Hernon, Peter, and Terry Ganey. *Under the Influence: The Unauthorized Story of the Anheuser-Busch Dynasty.* New York: Avon Books, 1991.

Land, Stephen, et al. *Brewed in America.* New York: A&E Home Video, 1997, videorecording.

C

Candler, Asa Griggs
(1851–1929) *founder of Coca-Cola*

The most popular soft drink in the world is Coca-Cola. In fact, Coca-Cola has become an icon of American culture, both in this country and abroad, of the magnitude of baseball and apple pie. The person most responsible for Coca-Cola's success was Asa Griggs Candler, whose insistence on heavy advertising and quality control in the beverage's earliest days resulted in millions of loyal customers.

Candler was born on December 30, 1851, in Villa Rica, Georgia. His parents, Samuel and Martha, were farmers. As a boy he had dreamed of becoming a doctor, but his family's financial condition prevented him from being able to pay the tuition to medical school. At age 19 he settled for the next best thing by apprenticing himself to two physicians in Cartersville, who taught him how to be a pharmacist. Three years later he moved to Atlanta where he went to work as a clerk in the drugstore of George J. Howard. In 1877, the year before he married Howard's daughter Lucy with whom he had five children, Candler became partners with Marcellus B. Hallman in a wholesale drug company. After four years, Candler bought out his partner, then a year later sold a half interest to his father-in-law. In 1886 Howard retired and sold his interest back to Candler, who renamed the business Asa G. Candler & Company.

In 1888 Candler bought a one-third interest in a health elixir called Coca-Cola. The elixir's inventor, the Atlanta pharmacist John S. Pemberton, had been inventing exotic beverages for years, including Ginger and Coca Tonic and French Wine Coca. In 1885 he formed the Pemberton Chemical Company to distribute his products, and that same year he invented Coca-Cola. This beverage was a combination of sugar, soda water, and a patent medicine, the active ingredients of which were caffeine (derived from kola nuts) and cocaine (derived from coca leaves). Within a year Coca-Cola had become a very popular drink at a local pharmacy, in large part because of the addictive properties of caffeine and cocaine. In fairness to Pemberton, it must be noted that neither drug was properly understood in his day; cocaine was used extensively as a local anesthetic during surgery involving the eye, nose, or throat, and Pemberton honestly believed cocaine use was a safe means of providing relief from most common ailments.

By 1892 Coca-Cola was selling so well that Candler had bought the remaining two-thirds interest in the drink, closed his thriving drug business, and incorporated as the Coca-Cola Company in order to concentrate full time on promoting the sweet, fizzy beverage. He hired Frank Robinson, Pemberton's former bookkeeper and the person who had given Coca-Cola its name, to be in charge of advertising. Robinson designed the flowing white-on-red script version of "Coca-Cola" that became the drink's logo and flooded the media markets of the Southeast with advertising. Before long, Coca-Cola was being promoted via billboards, store posters, calendars, and novelty items like serving trays and drinking glass holders all over the South. For several years, Candler spent practically every penny of profit on advertising, and by 1909 the Associated Advertising Clubs of America called Coca-Cola "the best advertised article in America."

While Robinson was promoting Coca-Cola, Candler was making it a better product. Several people had earlier owned the rights to Coca-Cola, so they knew what its secret ingredients were. To keep the drink a proprietary item, Candler changed the way the drink tasted in addition to making some changes to prolong its shelf life. Most important, by 1905 he had become convinced of the addictive properties of cocaine, so he removed it from the formula, although he continued to flavor the beverage with decocanized coca leaves.

Perhaps the most important move Candler made to ensure the success of Coca-Cola was to license bottlers. At first, he tried to produce, package, and distribute all of the product via his own organization, but by 1899 this had proven to be a restraint on the growth of sales. That same year, he licensed Benjamin F. Thomas and Joseph B. Whitehead to bottle and distribute Coca-Cola. He gave them the right to establish bottling plants anywhere in the United States outside New England, the territorial rights to which he had previously sold. In addition, the Coca-Cola Company would pay for all advertising, and in return Thomas and Whitehead had to purchase their syrup only from the company. As a result of this arrangement, annual sales of Coca-Cola syrup increased from less than 400,000 gallons in 1899 to more than 12 million gallons in 1911. By 1919 there were almost 1,000 individual bottlers in the United States, Canada, Cuba, and Panama, and the company was selling almost 19 million gallons of syrup per year.

Despite the Coca-Cola Company's profitability, by 1919 Candler had decided, for several reasons, to terminate his association with it. The previous year he had concluded a nine-year-long legal battle with the federal government. The government had alleged that Coca-Cola violated the provisions of the 1907 Pure Food and Drug Act, either because it contained cocaine, which made it addictive, or because it did not contain cocaine, which made the company guilty of false advertising. The suit was finally settled when the company

agreed to reduce the amount of caffeine in Coca-Cola, but Candler feared further government interference in the years to come. In 1916 Candler had resigned as president to run for, and then serve as, mayor of Atlanta, and he was becoming more interested in politics and civic affairs than business. Most important, his first wife was dying, and he hoped she would be comforted by knowing that their children had been provided for financially. That same year he gave the company to his children, with his son Howard becoming president. But the children had no interest in running the company, so later that year they sold it to a group of Atlanta investors headed by Ernest Woodruff and Samuel C. Dobbs, Candler's nephew, for $25 million. According to legend, Candler found out about the sale by reading about it in the newspaper, and the news made him cry.

Candler spent his remaining years involved in church and civic affairs. He served as vice president of the American Bible Society, and he contributed the land and money necessary to relocate Emory College to Atlanta, where it became famous as Emory University. In 1923 he married Mary Reagan. He died on March 12, 1929, in Atlanta.

Further Reading

Candler, Charles Howard. *Asa Griggs Candler: Founder of Coca-Cola.* Alexander, N.C.: Alexander Books, 1997.

Graham, Elizabeth Candler, and Ralph Roberts. *The Real Ones: Four Generations of the First Family of Coca-Cola.* Fort Lee, N.J.: Barricade Books, 1992.

Pendergrast, Mark. *For God, Country, and Coca-Cola: The Definitive History of the Great American Soft Drink and the Company that Makes It.* New York: Basic Books, 2000.

Capone, Al
(Alphonse Capone)
(1899–1947) *entrepreneur in organized crime*

Prohibition in America was a dismal failure. Invoked by the Eighteenth Amendment in 1919 and revoked by the Twenty-First Amendment in 1933, this misbegotten adventure in federally enforced sobriety led instead to a general flouting of the law, which contributed to a lessening of respect for authority. It also gave rise to a new type of organized criminal, the bootlegger. By profiting obscenely from the importation and sale of illegal liquor and beer, bootleggers did much to entrench organized crime in American society; in fact, many of the leaders of organized crime during the mid- to late-20th century got their start by selling illegal alcohol during Prohibition. Although many of them were engaged in criminal activity for a longer time, none of the bootleggers gained as much notoriety as Al Capone, who became a legend in his own time.

Capone was born Alphonse Capone on January 17, 1899, in Brooklyn, New York. His father, Gabriel, was a barber, and his mother, Teresa, was a homemaker. At age 14 he dropped out of school and joined a gang of young hoodlums known as the James Street Boys. Four years later he had "graduated" to the James Street Boys' adult affiliate, the Five Points Gang, and was working as a bartender and bouncer in a brothel on Coney Island. One night, while trying to evict an unruly customer, Capone received a nasty slash across his left cheek. The resultant scar earned him the public nickname "Scarface," although his acquaintances usually called him "Snorky." In 1918 he married Mary Coughlin, with whom he had one child.

In 1919, the year that Prohibition went into effect, Capone moved to Chicago, Illinois, to manage a brothel for Johnny Torrio, a former New Yorker who had founded the James Street Boys. Torrio was partners with James "Big Jim" Colosimo, who had been Chicago's crime boss since 1902, in a number of brothel, saloons, and gambling joints on Chicago's working-class South Side and in its southern and western suburbs. The year after Capone's arrival, Colosimo was murdered by an unknown assailant; according to many accounts, that assailant was Capone. Shortly after Colosimo's death in 1920, Torrio took over his entire operation, and Capone became his chief lieutenant.

Prohibition presented a unique opportunity for organized crime, especially in those areas of the United States, like Chicago, that had been settled largely within the last half-century by immigrants from eastern and southern Europe, where people generally saw nothing harmful about consuming beer and wine. Beginning in 1920, Capone played a major role in Torrio's quest to become a serious bootlegger. With the assistance of his brothers Ralph and Salvatore, as well as Paul "The Waiter" Ricca, a former bodyguard turned chief aide, Capone established and oversaw the wholesale distribution of illegal liquor to speakeasies in the same general area where Torrio already operated, as well as to bootleggers in other parts of Illinois and neighboring states.

In 1924 Capone spearheaded Torrio's moves to expand his gambling interests into Cicero, a factory community west of Chicago; the move succeeded, but not until after a shootout with Cicero police left Capone's brother Salvatore dead. That same year he also undertook to expand Torrio's bootlegging activities into north Chicago. This move also ultimately succeeded, but again not without violence. Capone started what became known as the "beer wars" by ordering three of his men to kill Dion O'Bannion, an uptown Chicago bootlegger and leader of the North Side Gang. Others who died during the protracted struggle included Assistant State Attorney William H. McSwiggin in 1926 and six members of the archrival North Side Gang on St. Valentine's Day, 1929.

Another casualty of the beer wars was Torrio himself. Severely wounded in 1925 by an unidentified gunman after pleading guilty to one count of bootlegging, he eventually returned to New York City. His operations were taken over by a gangster junta consisting of Capone, his brother Ralph, his cousin Frank "The Enforcer" Nitti, and Jack Guzik, which forged an alliance of convenience with the mayor of Chicago, William Hale "Big Bill" Thompson. As senior partner, Capone became the crime boss of Chicago, and in 1927 his net worth was estimated to be almost $100 million.

Unlike most gangsters, Capone reveled in publicity. He gave interviews to reporters, frequented sporting events and fancy restaurants where he left enormous tips, and rode around rather conspicuously in an armored car. His love for the spotlight proved to be his undoing, as Thompson was forced by public pressure to move against him, despite their alliance. Although he was able to shift his base of operations to Cicero, in 1928 Capone bought a mansion on Palm Island in Miami Beach,

Florida, after which he spent little time in the Chicago area. In 1929, while returning from a bootleggers' convention in Atlantic City, New Jersey, he was arrested for carrying a concealed weapon as he boarded a train in Philadelphia, Pennsylvania, and was sentenced to one year in jail. Meanwhile, the Internal Revenue Service was investigating him for income tax evasion, and in 1931 he was convicted on 23 counts. He spent the next eight years in the Cook County, Illinois, jail and the federal penitentiaries in Atlanta, Georgia, and Alcatraz near San Francisco, California. In 1939 he was released on good behavior, whereupon he sought treatment for the advanced stages of syphilis at a hospital in Baltimore, Maryland. Upon leaving the hospital, he returned to his home in Florida, where he died on January 25, 1947.

Further Reading

Bergreen, Lawrence. *Capone: The Man and the Era.* New York: Simon and Schuster, 1994.

Haller, Mark H. "Illegal Enterprise: A Theoretical and Historical Interpretation," *Criminology* 28 (May 1990): 215–23.

Carlson, Chester Floyd

(1906–1968) *inventor of Xerox copier*

The proliferation of paperwork at almost every level of American government and business would not have been possible, nor remain bearable, without a mechanical means of reproducing documents. Although several wet-copying methods have been introduced over the years, they usually caused some degree of harm to the original document, thus making them impractical. Not until Chester Carlson invented xerography, or "dry writing" as the Greeks might have called it, did a practical means of copying documents exist. In the process of revolutionizing the workings of the typical office, Carlson made millions of dollars for himself. Ironically, Carlson never considered himself an inventor, but rather just an overworked patent attorney with too much paperwork to do.

Carlson was born on February 8, 1906, in Seattle, Washington. His father, Olof, was a barber, and his mother, Ellen, was a homemaker. While he was still a young boy, both of his parents developed tuberculosis, and the family moved to Mexico in the hope that the warm weather would help cure them. In 1910 the family moved to San Bernadino, California, where his parents became tenant farmers. By the time Carlson reached high school, his parents were too ill to work, so he supported his family by doing odd jobs after school in a local printing shop and in the testing laboratory of the Riverside Cement Company. At age 19 he enrolled in a work-study program at Riverside Junior College that permitted him to continue working at Riverside Cement; three years later he entered a similar program at the California Institute of Technology (Cal Tech), and in 1930 he received a B.S. in physics.

By 1930 both of his parents had died, so Carlson moved to New York City where he worked for Bell Telephone Laboratories as a patent attorney's assistant. Laid off in 1933 as a result of the Great Depression, he found similar positions with Austin & Bix and, in 1934, P.R. Mallory & Co., an electronics manufacturing firm. That same year he married Linda (maiden name unknown) with whom he had no children, and he decided to become a patent attorney. He took night courses at New York Law School for five years, received his law degree in 1939, and was put in charge of Mallory's patent department in 1940.

A major part of Carlson's work with patents, mostly as an assistant but also as an attorney, was to prepare many copies of each patent application, which included reams of text as well as a number of drawings that were not easily reproduced by hand. In the early 1930s he began thinking about how this material could be reproduced mechanically. Shortly thereafter he read a paper by Paul Selenyi, a Hungarian inventor, in which the author described how static electricity could be used to create an image on a chemically coated metal drum. Inspired by Selenyi's paper and undaunted by the burdens already imposed on him by a full-time job, night school, and a new marriage, in 1934 Carlson began developing an electrostatic copying process. He started out by turning his kitchen into a laboratory, but within a year he had moved his experiments into a small building in Astoria in the New York City borough of Queens.

Chester Carlson demonstrates the world's first copier. *(Courtesy of Xerox Corporation)*

By 1937 Carlson had learned enough about imposing an electrostatic image on a photoconductive plate that had been exposed to light to apply for a patent on the process, which he called "electro-photography." He made the photoconductive plate by rubbing a zinc plate with a cloth to give it an electrostatic charge, coating the plate with a thin layer of sulfur, then exposing the plate to several seconds of bright light. In 1938 he hired Otto Kornei, an expatriate German physicist, to help with the experiments. Kornei suggested dusting the sulfur-coated plate with lycopodium, an alkaloid powder made from club moss, to help transfer the image to paper. That same year they reproduced an image from the photoconductive plate onto a sheet of paper coated with wax. Shortly thereafter, Kornei went to work for International Business Machines (IBM), but Carlson continued to experiment on his own with various coatings and light sources. In 1940 he obtained several patents for what became known in 1947 as "xerography," essentially a Greek word for "dry writing."

For the next four years, Carlson demonstrated his electrostatic copier to more than 20 companies in the hope of either selling the patent rights or attracting enough capital to form his own manufacturing firm. In 1944 he came to the attention of the Battelle Memorial Institute, a nonprofit industrial research organization in Columbus, Ohio, that provided financial backing for promising inventions or industrial processes in order to bring them to the marketplace. In exchange for patent rights, Battelle gave Carlson a generous yearly payment and financed further research on Carlson's process that resulted in a number of improvements. For example, it was discovered that selenium made a better coating for the zinc plate than sulfur and that dim light facilitated the photocopying process better than bright light. In 1946 Battelle reached an agreement with the Haloid Company of Rochester, New York, a manufacturer of photographic paper, that permitted Haloid to make and market Carlson's copier. Subsequent agreements between Battelle and Haloid provided Carlson with a fixed yearly payment and 3.2 percent of Haloid's revenue from xerography.

In 1946 Carlson moved to Rochester to become a Haloid consultant. Two years later he demonstrated the first Xerox copier at a meeting of the Optical Society of America. This machine was basically an offset photocopier, still the most popular form of electrostatic photocopier in use today. Light that reflected off the markings on the document being copied created a mirror image on the photoconductive plate by energizing the selenium electrons, causing them to attract negatively charged particles of ink from a spray. When a sheet of paper was passed close to the plate, it attracted the ink particles from the plate, thus "printing" an exact copy of the original document. It was not until 1959, however, that Haloid-Xerox (the name had changed the previous year) had perfected this whole process. That same year the company introduced the first commercial copier, the Xerox 914 office copier. Within two years, the 914 had become immensely popular, and in 1961 the company changed its name to Xerox Corporation and began trading its stock on the New York Stock Exchange.

The Xerox copier made Carlson a multimillionaire. It also cost him his first marriage, which ended in 1945; several years later he married Dorris Hudgins with whom he had no children. Having no heirs, he gave away much of his money; his favorite charities were Cal Tech, the Center for the Study of Democratic Institutions, and various health agencies of the United Nations. Later in life he became interested in paranormal and mystical phenomena, which led him to fund a number of research programs involving physical research, extrasensory perception, and Zen Buddhism. He died on September 19, 1968, while visiting New York City.

Further Reading

American Society for Psychical Research. *Lecture Forum Honoring the Memory of Chester F. Carlson.* New York: The Society, 1969.

"Chester F. Carlson," National Inventors Hall of Fame. Available online. URL: http://www.invent.org/hall_of_fame/27.html. Downloaded on July, 1, 2009.

Pell, Erik M. *From Dreams to Riches: The Story of Xerography.* Rochester, N.Y.: Erik M. Pell, 1998.

Carnegie, Andrew
(1835–1919) *entrepreneur in steel*

"Watch the costs and the profits will take care of themselves." This was the motto of Andrew Carnegie, the Scottish immigrant who built the largest steel company in 19th-century America. In the process, Carnegie perfected such things as cost accounting and vertical integration. He also made lots of money, and by the time of his death he had probably given away more than $330 million to various charitable organizations in the United States, Great Britain, and Canada.

Carnegie was born on November 25, 1835, in Dumfermline, Scotland. His father, William, was a handloom weaver, and his mother, Margaret, was a homemaker. At age 12 he moved with his family to the United States and settled in Allegheny, Pennsylvania, which eventually became a part of Pittsburgh. In 1848 he got a job changing spindles in a cotton textile mill. Over the next five years he worked successively as a steam-engine tender, a telegram delivery boy, and a telegraph operator. He became so skilled at this last job that in 1853 he was hired by Thomas A. Scott, superintendent of the Pennsylvania Railroad's western division, to be his personal telegrapher and secretary. In this position, Carnegie learned every detail about how to run a railroad, and in 1859, at age 23, he took Scott's place when Scott became the

Pennsylvania's general superintendent. As division superintendent, Carnegie bought and began operating the Pennsylvania's first passenger cars; the cars were manufactured by Theodore Woodruff's company, in which Carnegie held a one-eighth stake. He also invested heavily in other manufacturing ventures related to the railroad industry, such as the Keystone Bridge Company, makers of the first iron railroad bridges in the United States, and the Pacific & Atlantic Telegraph Company, which later became part of Western Union.

In 1864 Carnegie entered the business that would bring him fame and fortune. He and Thomas Miller, a boyhood friend, formed the Cyclops Iron Company for purposes of manufacturing iron beams for Keystone and rail for the Pennsylvania. In 1865 the partners merged with another mill to form Union Mills, with Carnegie holding a controlling interest. By the end of the Civil War, Carnegie's holdings in Union and other commercial ventures were providing him with a yearly income of about $50,000, enough to allow him to leave the railroad in order to concentrate on other moneymaking activities.

By the early 1870s British steel rails were gaining favor with American railroads because they lasted far longer than American-made iron rails. In 1872 Carnegie met this challenge by building a large steel mill south of Pittsburgh. The mill used the so-called Bessemer process for making steel, which had been developed and patented in the United States by WILLIAM KELLY. The mill was named after J. Edgar Thomson, the president of the Pennsylvania, to whom Carnegie hoped to sell tons of steel rails. Instead of raising money by selling stock to the general public and hiring high-priced executives to run everything, Carnegie attracted talented people to be his top managers by giving them a small share, never more than 6 percent, of the business, thus making them his partners. In this way he avoided paying them high salaries while also giving them a vested interest to keep costs low, thus increasing the profits, which could then be reinvested in the business instead of being paid out as dividends.

As his motto suggests, practically everything Carnegie did with his business revolved around lowering the cost of production. Drawing

Andrew Carnegie contributed more than $300 million to charity during his lifetime. *(Library of Congress)*

on his experience with the Pennsylvania Railroad, he instituted a system of cost- and production-accounting procedures and a layer of trained middle managers to ensure smooth operations that minimized waste. He invested heavily in any new technology that lowered production costs, the most important of which was the Siemens open-hearth furnace for making steel. He was one of the first entrepreneurs to create a vertical organization, whereby the same corporation controlled everything from the raw materials used to make the product to the sales organization that sold it. In this regard, Carnegie acquired iron ore and coal mines, bought railroads and freighters to bring coal and iron to his mills and carry away the finished products, and developed his own sales force. At each step of the manufacturing process, he bought from himself, thus cutting out the middleman and further reducing the cost of the finished product. In 1883 he bought out Homestead Steel and Hartman Steel, and in 1889 he acquired the Duquesne steelworks. That same year he incorporated all of his ventures related to the making of iron and steel into the Carnegie Steel Company, which in 1890 posted an annual profit of $4.5 million, an astronomical sum for the day.

Although Carnegie's business interests were centered in Pittsburgh, he had continued to live in New York City since 1867. In 1887 he married Louise Whitfield with whom he had one child. Having made Henry C. Frick chairman of the board of Carnegie Steel and Charles M. Schwab its president, Carnegie was free to travel back and forth to Europe while overseeing the general expansion of the company. He also devoted much of his time to writing treatises on capitalism, something he had begun doing in the early 1880s. His most important work in this regard was an article called "The Gospel of Wealth," in which he declared that the accumulation of wealth in the hands of a few is a good thing if those few use their wealth for the betterment of society as a whole.

By 1901 Carnegie had grown weary of being one of America's most successful capitalists. A major labor strike at the Homestead plant in 1892 had generated a tremendous amount of negative publicity for Carnegie, and he remained stung by it for years to come. Partially as a result, his relationship with Frick deteriorated, as Frick increasingly showed signs of being his own man. Most important, for years Carnegie had feared that devoting all of his time to making money would condemn his soul to hell, and he had decided to do something with his wealth other than leave it to his heirs. In 1901 he sold Carnegie Steel to a group of investors headed by J. P. MORGAN for $480 million; Carnegie's share of the sale amounted to more than $225 million in interest-bearing bonds. Carnegie Steel was incorporated with Morgan's other steel mills into the newly formed United States Steel Corporation, the first billion-dollar company in the United States, with Schwab as president.

Over the course of his remaining years, Carnegie gave away nine-tenths of the money he had received from the sale of his company. He contributed millions to Carnegie-Mellon University, Carnegie Institute of Technology, and the Carnegie Institution of Washington, and provided for a national trust fund in Scotland which provided free tuition to all four Scottish universities. He donated money to build more than 2,700 public libraries in Great Britain, the United States, and Canada, and donated more than 7,000 pipe organs to churches of all denominations. Despite all this giving, the interest on his bonds accumulated faster than he could spend it, so in 1911 he founded the Carnegie Corporation of New York to dispense the rest of his money after his death. He died on August 11, 1919, at his summer home in Lenox, Massachusetts.

Further Reading

Crompton, Samuel W. *100 Americans Who Shaped American History*. San Mateo, Calif.: Bluewood Books, 1999.

Livesay, Harold C., and Oscar Handlin. *Andrew Carnegie and the Rise of Big Business*, 2nd ed. New York: Longman, 2000.

Smith, George D., and Frederick Dalzell. *Wisdom from the Robber Barons: Enduring Business Lessons from Rockefeller, Morgan, and the First Industrialists*. Cambridge, Mass.: Perseus Pub., 2000.

Wall, Joseph Frazier. *Andrew Carnegie*. Pittsburgh: University of Pittsburgh Press, 1989.

Wren, Daniel A., and Ronald G. Greenwood. *Management Innovators: The People and Ideas that Have Shaped Modern Business*. New York: Oxford University Press, 1998.

Carnegie, Dale
(Dale Breckenridge Carnegey)
(1888–1955) *entrepreneur in self-improvement courses and books*

Of all the authors who have written books designed to help people achieve their full potential, perhaps none is better known than Dale Carnegie. Although Carnegie's writings have focused on helping businesspeople become more successful, their basic principles have been applied in a number of ways by many others to improve their personal lives as well. Carnegie got his start as a teacher of public speaking; his course, and others derived from its basic principles, continue to be taught today by the Dale Carnegie Institute for Effective Speaking and Human Relations, which estimates that graduates of Carnegie courses number more than 4 million worldwide.

Carnegie was born Dale Breckenridge Carnegey on November 22, 1888, in Maryville, Missouri. His parents, James and Amanda, were farmers. His mother wanted him to become a minister, and to this end she strongly encouraged him to practice public speaking at their church and in high school. Despite having grown up in near poverty, he managed to get a good education, and in 1908 he graduated from State Teacher's College in Warrensburg (present-day Central Missouri State College), where he achieved some fame as a debater. After graduation, however, he became neither a minister nor a teacher; instead, over the next four years he peddled correspondence courses, bacon, and lard to farmers in Nebraska, South Dakota, and Wyoming; studied acting at the American Academy of Dramatic Arts in New York City; toured the East as a bit player with a theatrical company; sold trucks in New York City; and briefly attended Columbia and New York universities.

In 1912 Carnegie embarked on the career path that would make him rich and famous. He convinced the director of New York City's 125th Street Young Men's Christian Association (YMCA) to hire him to present a series of public speaking classes of Carnegie's design. Carnegie knew that the biggest obstacle preventing most people from becoming good public speakers was the fear of making fools of themselves, so during every class he helped his students overcome this fear by making them stand up and say something. To encourage them, he always praised them for having done something good; to help them improve, he drew on his training as an actor to point out what they could have done a little bit better. He also wrote up his own course materials in the form of pamphlets; many of the essays contained in the pamphlets were later published in various magazines and books. Although many of his students never actually improved their ability to speak before a group, almost all of them felt better about themselves by the time "graduation day" rolled around. The YMCA director was so impressed with the course, which became known as the Carnegie Course in Effective Speaking, that he told other YMCA directors about it. Within two years Carnegie was presenting the course at YMCAs in Philadelphia, Pennsylvania, and Washington, D.C., and earning more than $400 per week, at the time a substantial sum of money.

After 1914 Carnegie modified his public speaking course by including much useful information on how to influence people. His precepts were short but simple: smile and be friendly, take a genuine interest in other people, cooperate rather than compete with others whenever possible, and always treat others the way you would like to be treated. These rules differed markedly from the ones that had guided many late-19th-century entrepreneurs, whom later generations have come to know both as "self-made men" and "robber barons." However, Carnegie's guidelines were in perfect harmony with the changing attitudes of the Progressive Era, which made its most impressive gains in the 1910s. His expanded course became popular with business and civic organizations, and he was hired as

Dale Carnegie beams at the thought of helping another class of students achieve their full potential. *(Library of Congress)*

a sales and management trainer by several of New York City's manufacturing and utility companies. In the 1920s he began presenting lecture-length versions of his course throughout Canada and Great Britain, and in 1926 he published his first self-improvement book, *Public Speaking: A Practical Course for Business Men*. Originally a two-volume compendium of the pamphlets he had written for use in his course, in 1932 it was condensed into one volume and renamed *Public Speaking and Influencing Men in Business*. In 1934 he wrote *Little Known Facts about Well-Known People*, a collection of interesting stories that he often used to illustrate a point while teaching. This book led to a syndicated radio programs of the same name, and to the publication a year later of *Five-Minute Biographies*.

In 1936, in the middle of the Great Depression, Carnegie published the most popular and influential of all his books, *How to Win Friends and Influence People*. The book had a special appeal for success-hungry Americans, many of whom blamed themselves for their financial failures. It became an immediate bestseller, and over the next 50 years it sold more than 15 million copies and was translated into 30 languages. The book's basic message was nothing new; a similar message had lain at Americans' fingertips for years, in the Holy Bible. Carnegie's genius was to repackage that message—that enthusiasm and positive thinking could indeed work miracles in the here and now—in such a way that average people could comprehend and implement this basic precept to their great advantage, if they would try. Specifically, Carnegie argues that about 15 percent of success is having a good idea and about 85 percent is expressing that good idea in a persuasive and enthusiastic way so that others can get enthusiastic about it, too. He drove his point home by using examples from everyday life and from the experiences of historical persons and successful businesspeople, many of which were drawn from his earlier books. In this regard, his favorite person was Andrew Carnegie, the immigrant Scot whose talent and tenacity enabled him to rise up from modest means and become one of the most successful American businessmen of all time. Carnegie idolized Andrew

Carnegie to the point that in 1919, the year Andrew Carnegie died, he decided to pay homage to his departed hero by changing the spelling of his last name.

In 1921 Carnegie married Lolita Baucaire; they divorced 10 years later. In 1944 he married Dorothy Vanderpool, one of his former students, with whom he had one child. Although the Carnegie Course in Effective Speaking and his books made him a millionaire, he continued to write and teach until his death on November 1, 1955, in Forest Hills, New York.

Further Reading

Crainer, Stuart. *The Ultimate Book of Business Gurus: 110 Thinkers Who Really Made a Difference.* New York: AMACOM, 1998.

Friedman, S. M. "The Dale Carnegie Page." Available online. URL: http://www.westegg.com/unmaintained/carnegie/. Downloaded on July 1, 2009.

Kemp, Giles, and Edward Claflin. *Dale Carnegie: The Man Who Influenced Millions.* New York: St. Martin's Press, 1989.

Carothers, Wallace Hume
(1896–1937) *inventor of neoprene and nylon*

Two of the most useful synthetic materials ever developed are neoprene and nylon. Neoprene proved to be a superior substitute for natural rubber, and nylon was developed into a highly versatile textile fiber. The person most responsible for the invention of both materials was Wallace Carothers, whose achievements eventually drove him to commit suicide.

Carothers was born on April 27, 1896, in Burlington, Iowa. His father, Ira, was a teacher, and his mother, Mary, was a homemaker. At age five he moved with his family to Des Moines where his father had accepted a teaching position. After studying accounting for a year at a local business school, in 1915 he enrolled in Tarkio College in Missouri where he studied chemistry and physics while also teaching accounting. He received his B.S. in 1920, then went to the University of Illinois, receiving his M.S. in 1921 and his Ph.D. in organic chemistry in 1924. Over the next four years he taught chemistry for two years each at Illinois and Harvard University.

Although Carothers was a good teacher, he preferred to do research, and he longed to open an industrial laboratory similar to THOMAS ALVA EDISON's. In his spare time, he investigated the nature of the double covalent bond, whereby certain molecules share two electrons instead of one, and he published his findings in a scholarly journal in 1924. Three years later the article came to the attention of Charles M. A. Stine, director of the chemical department of E. I. Du Pont de Nemours & Company in Wilmington, Delaware. Du Pont was embarking on an ambitious research program, and Stine offered Carothers the position as director of research in organic chemistry. Specifically, Du Pont hoped to develop a wide range of synthetic materials via polymerization, the construction of complex molecules by stringing together long chains of simple molecules. Although the position sounded ideal, Carothers hesitated to accept it. Despite Edison's example, industrial research was still in its infancy, and most college-trained scientists believed that conducting research for commercial purposes rather than as a pure intellectual pursuit was beneath their dignity. Understandably, Carothers did not want to cut himself off from his colleagues by sullying his hands with money. In the end, though, Stine prevailed by assuring Carothers that Du Pont would give him the freedom and the funding to experiment with whatever he wanted to, provided it had something to do with polymerization.

Carothers joined Du Pont in 1928 and put together an eight-person research team. Taking the work of LEO HENDRIK BAEKELAND, the inventor of modern plastic, as a starting point, the team began combining alcohols and acids into long polymeric chains, making sure that the last molecule in the chain was capable of further bonding. In 1930, while experimenting with divinylacetylene, a short-chain polymer, Arnold M. Collins, a team member, isolated a liquid by-product that turned into a white, rubbery substance a few days later. Carothers called it chloroprene, and upon investigating it he discovered that it was chemically analogous to natural rubber. Further research transformed chloroprene into neoprene, the world's first synthetic

rubber, which Du Pont used to make a variety of products such as shoe soles, industrial hoses, and adhesives.

Next, Carothers decided to build the world's longest polymeric chain. In the process, he discovered that one of the by-products of combining alcohols and acids was water, which built up to the point that it impeded the ability of the alcohols and acids to continue bonding. After getting rid of the water via a molecular still, the team was able to produce an incredibly long polymeric chain. Further research showed that this chain, while in a molten state, could be drawn into workable filaments, and when the filaments cooled they could be stretched to form tough, elastic fibers. Unfortunately, the fibers melted at relatively low temperatures and so could not be used for commercial purposes. In their first several attempts to raise the melting points, the team produced fibers with melting points so high they could not be spun into yarn. Not until 1934 were Carothers and Donald D. Coffman, another team member, able to produce fibers with melting points within a range that made them spinnable. These fibers became known as nylon, which Du Pont developed into hundreds of products, the most notable being women's stockings. Nylon led to the development of other synthetic fibers such as Orlon and Dacron, and over the next 20 years (1935–54) the production of synthetic fibers increased Du Pont's annual sales by 600 percent.

Meanwhile, Stine had been replaced as director of Du Pont's research program by Elmer K. Bolton. Although Bolton supported Carothers's research to the same extent as did Stine—indeed, it was Bolton who oversaw the development of nylon—in 1934 he refused to allow Carothers to publish his findings in scientific journals, justly fearing that this would allow the competition to steal Du Pont's trade secrets. Bolton also tried to restrict Carothers's freedom to experiment, preferring instead to assign specific research problems for Carothers to solve. At this point, Carothers seems to have feared that he had sold his academic soul, and he began suffering bouts of depression and seeing a psychiatrist. In 1936, the same year he married Helen Sweetman, he suffered a nervous breakdown. His wife's pregnancy and his sister's death the following year seem to have further depressed him to the point that, on April 29, 1937, in a hotel room in Philadelphia, Pennsylvania, he committed suicide.

Further Reading

Furukawa, Yasu. *Inventing Polymer Science: Standinger, Carothers, and the Emergence of Macromolecular Chemistry.* Philadelphia: University of Pennsylvania Press, 1998.

Hermes, Matthew E. *Enough for One Lifetime: Wallace Carothers, Inventor of Nylon.* Washington, D.C.: American Chemical Society and the Chemical Heritage Foundation, 1996.

Hounshell, David A., and John Kenly Smith, Jr. *Science and Corporate Strategy: Du Pont R&D, 1902–1980.* New York: Cambridge University Press, 1988.

Carrier, Willis Haviland

(1876–1950) *innovator of air-conditioning systems*

Willis Carrier did not invent air-conditioning; that honor goes to JOHN GORRIE, the Florida physician who invented the first room air conditioner before Carrier was born. Nor did he invent the term "air-conditioning"; that honor belongs to Stuart Cramer, an engineer in a cotton mill where Carrier installed one of his air-conditioning systems. Carrier did, however, develop the science of designing and installing industrial and commercial air-conditioning systems, and his work contributed directly to just about every advance made in air-conditioning during the 20th century.

Carrier was born on November 26, 1876, in Angola, New York. His father, Duane, was a dairy farmer, and his mother, Elizabeth, was a schoolteacher. After completing high school in 1893, he taught school for four years, then enrolled in Cornell University where he received a B.S. in mechanical engineering in 1901. After graduation he went to work for Buffalo Forge in Buffalo as a designer of industrial heating and drying equipment. He soon realized that variables such as air pressure, relative humidity, absolute humidity, dew point, and temperature all affect the efficiency of a heating or drying system, yet no one in his department seemed to be bothered that their designs failed to take these factors into account. Over the next six months he devoted much of his spare time to finding ways to quantify these variables in an effort to design equipment that worked more efficiently with less horsepower. When he presented his findings to top management in early 1902, he was immediately put in charge of developing the company's first industrial research laboratory. That same year he married Edith Seymour with whom he had no children. She died in 1912, and the following year he married Jennie Martin with whom he adopted two children. She died in 1939, and two years later he married Elizabeth Wise.

In 1902 Carrier was approached by J. Irvine Lyle, Buffalo Forge's sales manager, with an urgent request. A New York City printer had experienced great difficulty over the previous two summers because high humidity had prevented ink from adhering properly to paper, and Lyle wanted to know if Buffalo Forge could do anything to rectify the situation. Carrier responded by undertaking a scientific analysis of the optimum atmospheric conditions under which to print. He determined that a printshop operates best when the air temperature is 80° Fahrenheit with a relative humidity of 55 percent. He then consulted U.S. Weather Bureau data to determine New York City's average temperature and humidity during the summer, and he concluded that a dehumidification system for a printshop in that city would have to remove about 60 gallons of water from the air each hour. He then designed the first mechanical industrial air-conditioning system. The system consisted of two sections of finned, coiled pipe in the printshop; one circulated cold water while the other circulated chilled liquid ammonia. A large fan blew room air across the coils. As the water and ammonia circulated, they absorbed the heat from the air, causing the moisture in the air to condense on the fins, from where it was drained. Meanwhile, another large fan recirculated the cooled air throughout the room. The system worked so well that soon Buffalo Forge was being approached by other manufacturers with humidity problems, particularly those companies that made textiles, pharmaceuticals, or tobacco products.

In 1906 Carrier came up with a way to dehumidify air in large spaces, such as in textile or tobacco warehouses, by spraying it with cold water. As the air was cooled by the water spray, it lost its ability to hold water and actually became drier, or less humid. Five years later he developed the Psychrometric Chart, a device that greatly assists design engineers in determining accurately the optimum air-conditioning system for any industrial activity. The chart permits the extrapolation of values for relative humidity, absolute humidity, and dew point by taking readings with a psychrometer, a device that consists of a wet-bulb thermometer and a dry-bulb thermometer. Although a few modifications have been made over the years, the chart was still being used almost a century later.

In 1907 Buffalo Forge formed the Carrier Air Conditioning Company of America as a wholly owned subsidiary, with Carrier as vice president. Eight years later the company had become one of the foremost design and installation firms in the country. In 1915, however, Buffalo Forge decided to focus on manufacturing, and it sold the company to Carrier, Lyle, and five others, who renamed it the Carrier Engineering Corporation. In the 1920s the company became involved in nonindustrial air-conditioning. One of its first big projects in this area came in 1922 when it designed and installed an air-conditioning system for Graumann's Metropolitan Theater in Los Angeles, California. Carrier designed an innovative system whereby air was drawn from floor level, cooled and dehumidified, and then fed back into the theater from the ceiling, so that it cooled the patrons as it slowly settled to the floor. By 1930 the company had designed and installed air-conditioning systems in a number of movie theaters across the country. Meanwhile, Carrier had begun air-conditioning other types of commercial buildings. In 1928 the company made the 21-story Milam Building in San Antonio, Texas, the first air-conditioned office building in the world. The system featured a central refrigeration unit in the basement that pumped cold water to small air-handling units on each floor. These units dumped the cold air from the ceiling, from where it was recirculated through louvers in the doors into the corridors and then back to the air-handling units. This system is still used today in many office buildings.

In 1930 Carrier Engineering merged with two competitors, Brunswick-Kroeschall and York Heating & Ventilating, to form the Carrier Corporation. For the next 20 years the company was the preeminent manufacturer of air-conditioning equipment in the United States. In 1948 Carrier retired from the active management of the company but continued to do design work. In 1949 he invented the "Weathermaster" system for the modern skyscraper's all-glass curtain walls. First installed in the United Nations building in New York City, this system features pipe coil convector units just inside the glass walls, and it can pump either warm or cold water to either heat or cool the building, as needed. Carrier died on October 7, 1950, in New York City.

Further Reading

Ingels, Margaret. *Willis Haviland Carrier, Father of Air Conditioning.* Louisville, Ky.: Fetter Printing Co., 1991.

Ivins, Molly. "King of Cool: Willis Carrier." Time 100. Available online. URL:http//www.time.com/time/time100/builder/profile/carrier.html. Downloaded on July 1, 2009.

Cartwright, Alexander Joy, Jr.
(1820–1892) *popularizer of modern baseball*

Everyone knows that baseball is "America's National Pastime," but no one knows who invented modern baseball. For years, the sport was accredited to General Abner Doubleday. Modern scholars, however, generally agree that the game's popularizer was Alexander Cartwright, a man who lived most of his adult life in Hawaii.

Cartwright was born on April 17, 1820, in New York City. His father, Alexander, was a merchant ship captain, and his mother, Ester, was a homemaker. Cartwright finished his formal schooling at age 16, then went to work, first as a clerk for a Wall Street stock broker and then as a bank teller. In 1842 he married Eliza Ann Gerrits with whom he had five children. In 1845 he and his brother Alfred opened a bookstore on Wall Street. In 1849 Cartwright caught "gold fever" and went to California in the hopes of striking it rich. But he came down with dysentery almost as soon as he got to San Francisco, so as soon as he could he took a ship to the Sandwich Islands, better known today as Hawaii. He made one trip to California as bookkeeper for a Honolulu ship's outfitter, then returned forever to Honolulu where he was joined by his wife and children.

In 1850 Cartwright founded Honolulu's first fire company and served as its first chief. He eventually founded Cartwright and Company, which offered a wide range of financial services including banking, insurance, and real estate. He also served as agent for American whaling ships and financial adviser to the Hawaiian royal family. In addition, he played a major role in the founding of Queen's Hospital, a public library, the American Seaman's Institute, and a Masonic lodge.

Despite these accomplishments, Cartwright would not be remembered were it not for his growing dissatisfaction with his favorite outdoor amusement, "base ball." Bat-and-ball games had been played in the United States since the colonial period, when a game similar to cricket was popular. "Playing at base" had been a pastime of George Washington's troops at Valley Forge in 1778 and of college students at Princeton in 1787. By 1823 the game, known also as rounders, one-old cat, and goal ball, had acquired the name "base ball." The primary difference between "base ball" and baseball is that "base ball" runners were not put out by being tagged with the ball but by being hit with it, similar to the way in which runners in kickball are put out. Not only did this rob runners of their dignity (whenever one was hit by a thrown ball, he would be subjected to a chorus of catcalls), but it also necessitated the use of a soft ball. Being soft, the ball could not be hit for any great distance, so the bases could be placed no more than 60 feet apart (the same distance as on a Little League field). To Cartwright, who played "base ball" as a young adult, the game was a rather comical farce involving large men careening and cackling around a tiny field.

In 1845 Cartwright organized his fellow Wall Street players into the Knickerbocker Base Ball Club. At the club's first meeting he proposed a simple but dramatic innovation in the rules: Stop hitting runners with the ball, and tag them out instead. This would permit the use of a hard ball which could be hit for much greater distances, thus necessitating moving the bases farther apart. This simple rule change transformed "base ball" from a slow, silly game for children into a faster-paced, graceful game for adults.

The first baseball game played under Knickerbocker rules was in 1846, between the Knickerbockers and the Hoboken (New Jersey) Nine. By the end of the Civil War, Knickerbocker rules had been adopted by "base ball" players all up and down the Atlantic seaboard. The first professional baseball team, the Cincinnati Red Stockings, was organized in 1869, and the first professional baseball league was formed in 1871.

Although Cartwright had little to do with the rise of professional baseball, he did introduce baseball to Midwesterners as he passed through their communities on his way to California. And in 1852 he laid out a baseball field in Honolulu's Makiki Park and taught the game to Hawaiians. In 1908 an investigating commission led by A. G. Spaulding, the sporting goods manufacturer, concluded that Doubleday had invented baseball at Cooperstown, New York, in 1839. This error was rectified in 1939 when Cartwright's role as the father of modern baseball was acknowledged with his induction into the Baseball Hall of Fame. He died on July 12, 1892, in Honolulu.

Further Reading

Haven, Jeffrey L. *Baseball: the Origins and Development of the Game Until 1903.* Ann Arbor, Mich.: University Microfilms International, 1982.

Peterson, Harold. *The Man Who Invented Baseball.* New York: Scribner, 1973.

Will, George F. *Bunts: Curt Flood, Camden Yards, Pete Rose, and Other Reflections on Baseball.* New York: Scribner, 1998.

Carver, George Washington
(ca. 1860–1943) *inventor of peanut butter*

George Washington Carver was not the first person to realize that peanuts could be made into dozens of things. That honor belongs to several anonymous experts at the U.S. Department of

Agriculture. Nor was he the first to actually make anything out of peanuts. That honor belongs to an anonymous Englishman who invented peanut milk two years before Carver began experimenting with peanuts. Carver did, however, develop more than 100 different uses for peanuts, including what may be the typical American child's favorite lunch, the peanut butter sandwich. He also transformed the face of southern agriculture by helping farmers improve their diets and their crop yields.

Carver was named George when he was born in the early 1860s on a farm owned by Moses and Susan Carver in Diamond, Missouri. His mother, Mary, was a slave, and his father, whose name is unknown, was probably a slave on a nearby farm who had died before Carver was born. As an infant he and his mother were kidnapped by raiders from Arkansas; Moses Carver, their master, succeeded in getting back George but not Mary. Freed from slavery by the Thirteenth Amendment in 1865, he was raised by the Carvers, whose last name he adopted.

In 1877 Carver moved to Neosho, Missouri, to attend a public school for blacks, supporting himself by exchanging household chores for room and board. From 1879 to 1884 he lived in several Kansas towns, working in commercial laundries and cooking while attending school. In one town he ran into another young black man with the same name, so he adopted the middle name Washington to avoid confusion. In 1884 he graduated from the public high school in Minneapolis, Kansas, and was accepted at Highland College. He was turned away, however, when it was discovered he was black, and for the next six years he drifted across the Kansas prairie, working variously as a wheat farmer and laundryman.

In 1890 Carver enrolled in Simpson College in Indianola, Iowa. Two years later he transferred to Iowa State College where he studied horticulture and botany, receiving a B.S. in 1894 and an M.S. in 1896. While in graduate school, he also taught freshman horticulture, managed the school's greenhouse, and demonstrated great skill at producing hybrid plants. In 1896 he moved to Tuskegee, Alabama, to become head of the agriculture department at Tuskegee Institute. Unfortunately, the school suffered from a severe lack

of funds—his first laboratory was an empty room which he was expected to stock with equipment he either made or purchased himself—and faculty members were required to play a significant role in the school's administration. His failure to perform this role satisfactorily kept him in constant trouble with Booker T. Washington, the school's founder. Carver was, however, a brilliant teacher and researcher, and it is in this latter role that he gained everlasting fame.

Although he had never lived in the South before coming to Tuskegee, Carver knew that southern farmers were in dire need of help. Most of them planted as much cotton as they could, year after year, and used the money from selling their crop to buy food and supplies for the following year. Whether boll weevils attacked the crop or not, the cotton plants leached the soil of valuable nutrients, thus reducing the size of the subsequent year's crop. Spreading fertilizer solved this problem, but most

Although he appears very dapper in this formal photograph, George Washington Carver was usually seen wearing old gardening clothes. *(Library of Congress)*

southern farmers were too poor to afford all they needed. And since cultivating cotton meant not growing food, southern farmers and their families usually did not eat well the year following a poor cotton crop.

Carver set out to combat this problem in several ways. First, he began looking for ways for farmers to supplement their diets with foods that were easy to grow and full of nutrition. In 1897 he began experimenting with sweet potatoes, and he soon figured out how to grow a large crop of the sugary tubers on a small plot. He then developed recipes—by 1918 they numbered 115—for making staples like flour, sugar, and bread out of sweet potatoes, as well as recipes for preparing sweet potatoes in tasty ways. He also encouraged farmers to increase the amount of pork in their diets by feeding their hogs acorns, which grow all over the South and which provide hogs with just as much nutrition as expensive cornmeal. In addition to teaching these methods to his students, he published bulletins that were distributed free of charge, and he even turned a wagon into a mobile school that he sent across the South like a bookmobile.

Carver also addressed the problem by looking for ways to replenish the nutrients in the soil without using commercial fertilizer. In 1902 he began experimenting with black-eyed peas, a legume that grew plentifully in the South. Black-eyed peas restored to the soil the very nutrients that cotton leached out, so he urged farmers to rotate their fields between cotton one year and black-eyed peas the next. He also developed recipes for black-eyed peas, and by 1908 he had come up with 40 delicious ways to fix them, including pancakes, pudding, and croquettes.

In 1903 Carver began experimenting with peanuts, another abundant southern legume. Until he took an interest in them, southerners mostly fed peanuts to their livestock. By the time he was done, he had transformed the humble peanut into one of the most versatile agricultural products in the world. At first, he promoted peanuts as a natural fertilizer much like black-eyed peas, but soon southerners were growing far more peanuts than their animals could eat, so he had to find other things to do with them. Carver quickly discovered that peanuts contain plenty of vegetable oil, which can easily be extracted by crushing them. By 1916 he had figured out how to convert peanut oil into 105 different products, including cheese, facial creams, printer's ink, medicine, shampoo, soap, vinegar, and wood stain. By far the most popular of his peanut products was peanut butter, which he made by grinding roasted peanuts into a smooth, creamy butter. Peanut butter contains more protein than butter made from corn oil, and it lasts longer than butter made from milk because it does not have to be refrigerated. By the 1920s people all over the United States were spreading peanut butter on bread to make a delicious, nutritious, and inexpensive snack.

Having taught farmers how to improve their diets and replenish the nutrients in their soil, there remained one last task for Carver to try: vanquishing the boll weevil. He had been a master of developing hybrid plants ever since his days at Iowa State, and he set out once again to develop a cotton plant that could somehow foil the boll weevil. In 1915 he succeeded in breeding such a plant. Called Carver's Hybrid, it matures so quickly that its cotton bolls can often be picked before the boll weevils emerge from their winter dormancy.

Although Carver was a gifted inventor, he took no interest in the business end of inventing. He never filed a patent application, and he showed little interest in making money from his discoveries. His one attempt at profit-making came in 1923 with the formation of the Carver Products Company, but even this venture was an initiative of a group of businessmen from Atlanta, Georgia, and not Carver. Moreover, he showed little interest in the company, and it soon failed. Indeed, Carver believed that the fruits of the land belonged to all people, and that he would be remiss in his duty to God if he charged anyone for his knowledge.

Carver died on January 5, 1943, in Tuskegee. Having never married, he left his small savings to the institute to establish a museum and research facility for agricultural chemistry.

Further Reading

Gates, Henry L., and Cornel West. *The African-American Century: How Black Americans Have Shaped Our Country.* New York: Free Press, 2000.

McMurry, Linda O. *George Washington Carver: Scientist and Symbol*. Norwalk, Conn.: Easton Press, 1994.

Perry, John. *Unshakable Faith: Booker T. Washington & George Washington Carver: A Biography*. Sisters, Oreg.: Multnomah Pub., 1999.

Tiner, John H. *100 Scientists Who Shaped World History*. San Mateo, Calif.: Bluewood Books, 2000.

Wellman, Sam. *George Washington Carver: Inventor and Naturalist*. Urichsville, Ohio: Barbour Pub., 1998.

Case, J. I.
(Jerome Increase Case)
(1818–1891) *inventor of the thresher-separator*

Anyone familiar with the construction industry knows that the Case Corporation is a major manufacturer of top-quality earth-moving equipment. The person most responsible for building Case into a major corporation was J. I. Case, the company's founder. But instead of building bulldozers and backhoes, Case got the company started by manufacturing farm implements, especially the thresher-separator, which he invented.

Case was born Jerome Increase Case on December 11, 1818, in Williamstown, New York. His parents, Caleb and Deborah, were farmers. When Case was 16, his father bought a horse-powered threshing machine that was known as a "ground hog." His father then taught him how to operate it, and for the next six years Jerome hired out his services to neighboring farmers. In 1841 he took an engineering course at the Rensselaer Academy in New York, the only formal education he ever received. The following year he bought six ground hogs and set out for Wisconsin Territory, where he had heard that wheat grew in abundance. By the time he got to Wisconsin he had only one ground hog left, having sold the others en route.

Case settled in Rochester, Wisconsin, where he hired out his services as a thresher. Meanwhile, he made improvements to the ground hog, turning it into a combination thresher-separator; in addition to beating the wheat kernels from the chaff, it also separated the wheat and chaff into different compartments. Believing that the machine held great commercial promise, in 1844 Case moved to Racine where he rented a shop to manufacture it.

He advertised his thresher-separator by demonstrating it all across Wisconsin, but for a while he sold just enough machines to feed himself. By 1847, however, he had raised enough money from the sale of thresher-separators to finance the construction of a real factory. In 1849 he married Lydia Bull with whom he had four children, and by 1857 his factory was the largest thresher production facility in the Midwest.

In 1863 Case took steps to take his operation nationwide by taking on three partners and forming the J. I. Case Company. In 1869 he built the first steam-powered thresher, and in 1876 he formed the J. I. Case Plow Works. In 1880 he bought out his partners and incorporated his various enterprises as the J. I. Case Threshing Machine Company. During the 1870s and 1880s, the company established a national network of branch sales offices while expanding its line of machines to include harvesters and reapers. By 1891 the company had grown into the largest manufacturing concern in Wisconsin, and it was shipping a wide range of farm implements all over the world.

Case was a stickler for quality, and he insisted that his equipment be the best available. According to legend, at age 65 he personally traveled to Faribault, Minnesota, where one of his threshers had broken down. Try as he might, he was unable to fix the machine, so he doused it with kerosene, set it on fire, and shipped the farmer who owned it a brand-new thresher to take its place. He also had a passion for horse racing, and his horse breeding operations in Wisconsin and Kentucky bred several champion trotters and pacers. Hickory Grove Farm, his 200-acre spread in Racine, featured steam-heated stables and a one-eighth-mile indoor track so the horses could work out during inclement weather. On Sundays he opened the farm to the public, and hundreds of people would come to watch his champions go through their paces. His favorite horse, Jay Eye See, was a small, ugly, black colt when he bought him for $500, but he turned the horse into the world's fastest trotter. He had a railroad baggage car remade into a traveling stable for Jay Eye See; the car featured every amenity a horse could want, including a set of lace curtains that Case's wife had bought to hang in their home.

Case died on December 22, 1891, in Racine. His company eventually became known as the Case Corporation. By 1912 it had branched out into the manufacture of farm tractors and construction equipment, especially steamrollers and road graders for building highways and roads. By 1940 it was also manufacturing combines and a host of other items of farm and construction equipment. By the end of the century Case's annual sales exceeded $5 billion.

Further Reading

"Case in History," Available online. URL: http://www.caseih.com/about/about.aspx?contentid=291&RL=ENEU&navid. Downloaded on July 1, 2009.

Holmes, Michael S. *J. I. Case: The First 150 Years.* Racine, Wisc.: Case Corp., 1992.

J. I. Case Company. *Jerome Increase Case: The Man and His Works.* Racine, Wisc.: The Company, 1949.

Case, Steve
(Stephen McConnell Case)
(1958–　) *founder of America Online*

In the late 1990s, two of America's favorite pastimes involved the use of computers. "Going online" allowed many people to chat with friends and strangers via E-mail and chat rooms, while "surfing the Net" permitted many others to access Web sites filled with strange and wonderful information. Before all this could happen, however, the country had to get "wired" for the computer age, and no single individual has played a greater role in making this happen than Steve Case.

Case was born Stephen McConnell Case on August 21, 1958, in Honolulu, Hawaii. His father, Daniel, was a lawyer, and his mother, Carol, was a schoolteacher. As a boy, he delivered newspapers, sold seeds and greeting cards door to door, and distributed discount coupons for local businesses. After receiving his B.A. in political science from Williams College in Massachusetts in 1980, he moved to Cincinnati, Ohio, to work for Procter & Gamble as a marketing specialist. His assignment was to drum up consumer enthusiasm

for a home-permanent kit and a hair conditioner that was applied by means of a towelette. In 1982 he took a corporate position with Pizza Hut in Wichita, Kansas, and spent the next year traveling the country in search of new and exotic toppings for pizza. He spent most of his evenings in his hotel room, using a personal computer (PC) and a modem to surf an early online subscription service called The Source.

In 1983 Case attended a consumer electronics show in Las Vegas, Nevada. At the show he saw a device that could run an Atari video game on a personal computer. He was so impressed with the product that he acquired a job as a marketing specialist with its manufacturer, Control Video Corporation. The device, however, never caught on, and two years later the company had almost folded. In 1985, the year he married Joanne Barker with whom he had three children, Control Video went through a major management reshuffling; the name was changed to Quantum Computer Services, Jim Kimsey was appointed chief executive officer, and Case was given the job of finding enough venture capital to keep the company alive. Partly because of Case's urging, the company also refocused its efforts to provide online services—E-mail, chat rooms, bulletin boards, and the like—for users of personal computers.

At the time, no universal Internet language like Java existed, and each brand of PC utilized its own proprietary operating system. This meant that a separate online service had to be developed for each brand of personal computer. Quantum chose to design its initial service to be compatible with Commodore PCs, which at the time were popular. This service was successful enough that in 1987 Case was able to convince Apple Computers to give Quantum access to its operating system so that it could develop an online service for Apple users. That same year, he arranged similar deals with the Tandy Corporation, makers of Radio Shack PCs, and with IBM, whose PCs ran on a system written by Microsoft. Although these three deals promised to bring Quantum a tremendous amount of business in the future, they greatly compromised the company by overloading its capabilities to finance and develop three new online services simultaneously. For five years nearly every nickel in subscription fees went to pay for the development of further enhancements to the three services. In 1991 the company changed its name to America Online (AOL), and the next year it went public, its initial stock offering raising more than $60 million, enough to bail out AOL financially.

In 1992 Kimsey became AOL's chairman of the board, and he named Case to replace him as CEO. Case immediately embarked on an aggressive campaign to improve the services, add new subscribers, and acquire or ally itself with various software companies and telephone networks so that it could compete more effectively against its two main rivals, CompuServe and Prodigy. In this way, AOL was able to offer its subscribers direct access to the Internet in late 1994, a browser that allowed them to surf the World Wide Web by late 1995, and dedicated transmission lines by late 1996. Meanwhile, subscriptions skyrocketed from 600,000 in 1994 to 6.3 million two years later; at a flat rate of $19.95 per month for unlimited access, this meant that the company was grossing more than $1.5 billion per year, far more than CompuServe and Prodigy combined. Six million subscribers also caused major problems for the company's system, particularly when large numbers of them tried to access the Internet at the same time. Beginning in 1994, subscribers began experiencing difficulty getting connected to the Internet and accessing and transmitting data, and many disgruntled subscribers took to calling AOL "America On Hold." In 1996 the entire system crashed for 19 hours when a maintenance installation procedure at the company's headquarters in Sterling, Virginia, a suburb of Washington, D.C., went awry. Despite these problems, Case managed to placate users in various ways, such as giving each subscriber a free hour (when the company charged by the hour) and then switching in 1996 to a flat rate per month. Best of all, he also made sure that the features and content provided as part of an AOL subscription were second to none. In 2000, AOL subscribers generated one-third of all the traffic on the Wide World Web, and the company grossed almost $7 billion.

In 1995 Case succeeded Kimsey as AOL's chairman. In this capacity, he oversaw the company's merger in 2000 with Time Warner, the entertainment giant, thus forming AOL Time Warner, the largest Internet and media company in the world, with Case as the new conglomerate's chairman. His annual compensation in this position was estimated to be almost $40 million. In 1996 he divorced his first wife, and in 1999 he married Jean Villanueva, a former AOL top executive.

As the economy—especially Internet companies—weakened in 2001–2002, Steve Case was bumped from the *Forbes* magazine annual list of billionaires. His net worth in 2002 was estimated at $760 million, down from $1.4 billion in 2001.

Case announced his resignation as chairman of AOL Time Warner in January 2003, though he stayed on the corporation's board of directors for three more years. The AOL Time Warner merger continued to endure financial struggles and heavy criticism, eventually becoming widely considered as one of the greatest business failures in American history. In 2007, even Case noted of the merger, "I'm sorry I did it." In December 2009, AOL and Time Warner officially severed their partnership.

Despite this setback, Case remained very active in the business and philanthropy realms. In 2005, he founded Revolution, LLC, which has acquired several companies in order to increase choice, convenience, and control in the health, financial, resort, and digital sectors. In November 2009, American Express bought Revolution for $300 million. In February 2010, Case was named chairman of Exclusive Resorts LLC, a luxury vacation membership club. In addition to these business interests, Case has established the Case Foundation, which provides funding to address world poverty and safe drinking water in poor regions of the world, and the Accelerated Brain Cancer Cure (ABC2) to help people who suffer from brain cancer and their families. Case was motivated to this cause after his older brother, Dan, died of brain cancer in 2002 at the age of 44.

Case lives in Virginia with his wife and their daughters from previous marriages in the mansion where Jackie Kennedy lived as a child.

Further Reading

Ashby, Ruth. *Steve Case: America Online Pioneer.* Brook-
field, Conn.: Twenty-First Century Books, 2002.

French, Laura. *Internet Pioneers: The Cyber-Elite.* Berkeley Heights, N.J.: Enslow Publishers, 2001.

Leibovich, Mark. *The New Imperialists.* Upper Saddle
River, N.J.: Prentice Hall, 2001.

"Stephen, M. Case," Academy of Achievement. Available online. URL: http://www.achievement.org/
autodoc/page/cas1bio-1. Downloaded on March 12,
2010.

Swisher, Kara. *AOL.COM: How Steve Case Beat Bill
Gates, Nailed the Netheads, and Made Millions in the
War for the Web.* New York: Times Books, 1998.

Chouteau, René Auguste
(1749–1829) *entrepreneur in the fur trade*

During the colonial period, one of the best ways to
make a fortune was to enter the fur trade. One of
the most successful American fur traders was René
Auguste Chouteau, who achieved this position in
part because as a baby he was abandoned by his
father.

Chouteau was born on September 7, 1749, in
New Orleans, Louisiana, which at the time was
owned by France. His father, Rene, was a tavern-
keeper, and his mother, Marie, was a homemaker.
By late 1750 Chouteau's father had returned to
France, leaving his wife and newborn son behind.
In 1757 Marie Chouteau began living with Pierre
Laclède Liguest, the senior partner of Maxent,
Laclède & Company, a fur trading company.
Although she and Liguest never married, they lived
together as husband and wife, and Liguest treated
René Auguste like a son.

In 1762 the French government gave Liguest's
company a monopoly on the fur trade west of the
Mississippi River, and when he went to explore
the area he took along Chouteau. In 1763 Liguest
decided to center his business near the conflu-
ence of the Missouri and Mississippi rivers, and he
began building forts on the Mississippi's west bank.
In 1764 he put Chouteau, who was 15 at the time,
in charge of building the village that grew into the
city of St. Louis, Missouri. For the next 14 years,
Liguest and Chouteau operated out of St. Louis,

and together they built a major fur trading empire
in the Missouri Valley.

Fur traders were not fur trappers. Liguest,
Chouteau, and their agents did not spend a lot of
time out in the wild looking for fur-bearing animals. Instead, they erected trading posts close to
Indian settlements where they exchanged manufactured goods such as boots, cloth, kettles, and metal
hatchets for buffalo hides, deerskins, and animal
pelts. Success in the fur trade did not require wilderness skills. Instead, it required the ability to
communicate with and gain the trust of a number
of different Indians tribes, each with its own language and culture. Chouteau was especially successful among the Osage Indians, who were the
dominant tribe along the fur-rich lower reaches of
the Missouri River, and this area became the center of his entrepreneurial activity.

When Liguest died in 1778, Chouteau took
over the firm. In 1786 he married Marie Thérèse
Carre, with whom he had seven children. By
1803, when the United States took possession of
Louisiana, Chouteau was the territory's most successful fur trader and St. Louis's wealthiest citizen. He served as a justice on the first territorial
court under U.S. jurisdiction, colonel in the St.
Louis militia, and U.S. Indian commissioner to the
Sioux, Iowa, Sauk, and Fox tribes with whom he
also did business.

After Liguest's death, Chouteau was ably
assisted by his half brother, Jean Pierre Chouteau.
René Auguste continued to concentrate on the
Osage Indians while Jean Pierre was notably successful among the Indians of present-day Oklahoma. In 1809 the two formed a separate company,
the St. Louis Missouri Fur Trade Company, with
Jean Pierre as its head. Among the firm's investors
were the legendary explorers Meriwether Lewis and
William Clark. The company's goal was to expand
the Chouteaus' business into the Pacific Northwest, but a combination of undercapitalization and
intense competition from the British North West
Company forced the new company out of business
in 1814. However, the original company continued
to prosper, and at the time of his death on February 24, 1829, in St. Louis, René Auguste Chouteau
was one of the wealthiest men west of the Mississippi River.

Further Reading

Burt, Olive W. *Young Wayfarers of the Early West.* New York: Hawthorn Books, 1968.

Fly, Shelby M. *The Saga of the Chouteaus of Oklahoma.* Norman, Okla.: Levite of Apache, 1988.

Foley, William E., and C. David Rice. *The First Chouteaus: River Barons of Early St. Louis.* Urbana: University of Illinois Press, 2000.

Claiborne, Liz
(Elisabeth Claiborne)

(1929–2007) *entrepreneur in women's sportswear*

Before 1975, women who worked in offices had to wear fancy clothes to work. This all changed when Liz Claiborne introduced a line of stylish sportswear that doubled as suitable business attire for women in most professions. Claiborne's designs contributed to making women's (and men's) business wear in the late 20th-century more casual and more comfortable.

Claiborne was born Elisabeth Claiborne on March 31, 1929, in Brussels, Belgium. Her parents were Americans; her father, Omer, was a banker, and her mother, Louise, was a homemaker. At age 10 she moved with her parents to New Orleans, Louisiana, their hometown, when the Nazis threatened to overrun Belgium. Instead of finishing high school, she studied fine arts in Belgium and France after the end of World War II because her father wanted her to be a painter. She preferred, however, to draw and to sew, and eventually she convinced him to let her become a fashion designer.

In 1950 Claiborne went to live with an aunt in New York City. Before long, she landed a job as a design assistant and model with Tina Lesser, perhaps the best out of a handful of designers who worked with women's sportswear, casual but stylish clothing that was originally intended for wear while playing golf or tennis. That same year Claiborne married Ben Schultz with whom she had one child. Over the next two years she also worked as an assistant to Ben Rieg, a tailored-clothing designer, and Omar Kiam, a high-fashion designer. She spent the next three years designing junior dresses for the Junior Rite Company and the Rhea Manufacturing Company in Milwaukee, Wisconsin, then in 1955 she returned to New York City to work as a dress designer for Dan Keller. In 1957 she divorced her first husband and married Arthur Ortenberg, a fashion executive. In 1960 she became chief designer for Youth Guild, and for the next 15 years she designed dresses for juniors.

While at Youth Guild, Claiborne became convinced that a growing market existed for mix-and-match women's sportswear if it were stylish enough to wear to work. Her own experience as a working mother told her that a number of women preferred to wear an attractive but comfortable pair of pants or slacks and a blouse with a sweater or jacket to the office instead of a fancy dress or a women's business suit with its skirt, tailored shirt and jacket, and floppy bow tie. She also knew that the growing number of women who worked outside the home held jobs which did not require getting dressed up every day. However, her repeated attempts to convince Youth Guild's management to design a line of stylish women's sportswear were unsuccessful.

By 1975 Claiborne's child and her two stepchildren had graduated from college and moved out on their own, and her husband had closed his old company and was looking for a new challenge. She convinced him and two friends to join her as partners in Liz Claiborne Inc. As president and head designer, she designed the clothes while the others took care of more mundane tasks such as business administration, production, and marketing. The company's first line in 1976 consisted primarily of pants, knickers, pleated skirts, sweaters, ponchos, and shirt jackets, all of them colorful and stylish and designed so that they could be mixed and matched in a number of combinations. Moderately priced so that the typical working-woman could afford them, Claiborne's designs were an instant hit, and the company's first-year sales topped $2 million.

In addition to shaking up the fashion industry with its designs, Liz Claiborne Inc. also introduced some new management and marketing techniques. Claiborne planned her lines several seasons in advance so that pieces from different year's lines would still mix and match with each other. She added two lines to the traditional four—fall, winter, spring, and summer—so that customers were constantly seeing new merchandise. She solicited requests and complaints from customers and store buyers, and she made efforts to address such comments in her next line. The company also introduced a computer tracking system, known as System Updated Retail Feedback (SURF) to keep up with how the different styles, colors, and sizes were moving from one week to the next.

Liz Claiborne's original line of active sportswear was augmented with a slightly dressier collection in the late 1970s, a dress division in 1982, a shoe division in 1983, and a girls' line in 1984. In 1985 the company bought the Kaiser-Roth Corporation, which manufactured women's accessories, and introduced Lizwear, a line of jeans, and Claiborne, a collection of men's sportswear. In 1986 the company developed a line of fragrances called Liz Claiborne. That same year the company's annual sales reached $1.2 billion. In 1988 the company began retailing its own merchandise through its own chain of stores called First Issue, while continuing to sell its various lines through approximately 3,500 department stores and women's shops across the United States.

In 1989 Claiborne and her husband retired from the active management of Liz Claiborne Inc. At the time they owned stock in the company that was estimated to be worth almost $100 million. She then lectured on fashion design at the Fashion Institute of Technology and the Parsons School of Design, while dividing her time between her apartment in Manhattan and her getaway homes in Fire Island, New York, the Caribbean island of St. Bart's, and Montana. In 1997, Claiborne was diagnosed with a rare form of abdominal cancer and she died of complications from it in 2007.

At the time of her death, the widely shared view of Claiborne's impact on the fashion industry was reflected in her own 1989 quote: "I wanted to dress busy and active women like myself, women who dress in a rush and who weren't perfect. But loving clothes, I knew clothes could do a certain thing for you from a flattering point of view. And I tried to bring good taste to a mass level." When she died, the fashion icon Calvin Klein noted of Claiborne, "She was really the first American designer to concentrate on clothes that a large segment of working women could afford. She had great taste and great style and she built one of the largest, most successful apparel companies."

Further Reading

Brands, H. W. *Masters of Enterprise: Giants of American Business from John Jacob Astor and J. P. Morgan to Bill Gates and Oprah Winfrey.* New York: Free Press, 1999.

Daria, Irene. *The Fashion Cycle: A Behind-the-Scenes Look at a Year with Bill Blass, Liz Claiborne, Donna Karan, Arnold Scaasi, and Adrienne Vittadini.* New York: Simon and Schuster, 1990.

Wilson, Eric. "Liz Claiborne, Designer, Dies at 78." *New York Times.* Available online. URL: http://www.nytimes.com/2007/06/27/fashion/27cnd-claiborne.html?_r=1&ei=5070&en=63233eb9f332b5c6&ex=1188014400&pagewanted=all. Downloaded on July 1, 2009.

Clark, James H.
(1944–   ) *founder of Netscape*

As the only person to ever start three different multibillion-dollar companies, Jim Clark holds a singular place in the history of American business. This astounding achievement is even more impressive when considering Clark's unusual path to great wealth and entrepreneurial success began as "a self-described child of hardscrabble Texas" and followed a wandering path that found him nearly 40 years old and seemingly lacking a prosperous future.

James H. Clark was born in 1944 in Plainview, Texas. Clark grew up in poverty in this dusty town in the heart of west Texas, and his parents divorced in 1958. He severed his relationship with his abusive father and remained in Plainview with his mother, brother, and sister. In high school, Clark's various episodes of misconduct resulted in his expulsion from school. At the age of 17, Clark received his mother's consent to enlist in the navy. In the navy, Clark again struggled with authority, though his demonstrated proficiency in mathematics led to his placement as an instructor for incoming recruits. Encouraged by supervisors to pursue his rare talent in math, Clark excelled in this role and after his discharge from the navy he enrolled at Tulane University. Within eight years, Clark had earned a bachelors degree in physics from Tulane, a masters in physics from the University of New Orleans, and a doctorate in computer science from the University of Utah.

Throughout most of the 1970s, Clark worked mainly as a professor, but restlessness and occasional insubordination led to short times in these positions. In 1979, Clark became an associate professor in electrical engineering at Stanford University. At Stanford, Clark soon became well known and admired for his groundbreaking research in the field of computer imagery by designing a computer chip that was able to process three-dimensional images in real time. This process allowed engineers to model their designs on a computer screen, which saved vast and precious amounts of time and money. Clark called his invention the "Geometry Engine," hired a handful of his students, and, in 1982, created Silicon Graphics Inc., one of the first and most important companies of the emerging technologically based economy. One of Clark's students later recalled, "Jim's logic was that the world was three-dimensional, and so the computer would have to be, too. He thought the right way to interact with machines is the way you interact with the world."

Silicon Graphics was enormously successful, garnering billions in annual revenues and attracting a wide variety of users, including the National Aeronautics and Space Administration, Hollywood directors such as Steven Spielberg, and legions of anonymous computer users around the world. Clark remained with Silicon Graphics until 1994, when fatigue over battles with colleagues and eagerness to explore new avenues of creative growth led him to leave the company. Initially, Clark was interested in interactive television but soon decided to pursue opportunities in the burgeoning field of the Internet. He partnered with Marc Andreesen, a 22-year-old recent graduate of the University of Illinois, and developed the Mosaic Web browser.

Learning from his experience at Silicon Graphics, Clark kept a 25 percent equity stake in the new Internet browsing company, Netscape Communications Corporation. Within a year, Clark took the highly unusual step of taking his company public, even though the venture had not posted any profits. This move proved to be filled with shrewd foresight, as investors were eager to pounce on this intriguing company. On the day of its initial public offering, the stock price of Netscape jumped from six dollars to $24, and within a month it was selling at $70 a share. As the largest stockholder in Netscape, Clark was Silicon Valley's newest billionaire, and his strategy helped set off countless Internet-related imitators in the next few years.

Always seeking what the author Michael Lewis called, "The New New Thing" in his book of the same name about Clark and the rise of Silicon Valley's influence, Clark soon focused his energy on a the health care industry. Seeking to improve efficiency and access for all stakeholders in the complex and often inefficient field of health services, Clark began the Healtheon Corporation, which did not enjoy the explosive growth of Silicon Graphics or Netscape but did become very profitable as it merged with the simultaneously developing WebMD.

In 2009, Clark—the father of two grown children—was married for the fourth time, to Australian model Kristy Heinze. He has become a leading American philanthropist, donating $150 million to Stanford for the creation of an interdisciplinary biological sciences program called Bio-X and $30 million to Tulane for academic scholarships. An avid sailor who has devoted much of his recent years to the sea, Clark has remained active on corporate boards and has not ruled out attempting to create another company in the future.

Further Reading

Greenfeld, Karl Taro. "Jim Clark." *Time.* Available online. URL: http://www.time.com/time/magazine/article/0,9171,49994,00.html. Downloaded on July 1, 2009.

Kenter, Larry. "Brilliant Careers: Jim Clark." *Salon.* Available online. URL: http://www.salon.com/people/bc/1999/11/24/clark/. Downloaded on July 1, 2009.

Lewis, Michael. *The New New Thing: A Silicon Valley Story.* New York: Penguin, 2001.

Cohen, Ben (Bennett Cohen) (1951–   ), and Jerry Greenfield (1951–   )
founders of Ben and Jerry's Ice Cream

Not too many successful corporations get started by people who really do not want to make a lot of money in the first place. But this is exactly what happened to Ben & Jerry's Homemade Inc., the brainchild of America's two most unusual businessmen, Ben Cohen and Jerry Greenfield. They started hanging around with each other in middle school, and they ended up creating some of the best-testing ice cream ever.

Cohen was born Bennett Cohen on March 18, 1951, in Brooklyn, New York. His father, Irving, was an accountant and his mother, Frances, was a homemaker. As a high-school senior, he got a job selling ice cream from a truck in various neighborhoods in Merrick on Long Island where he grew up. In 1969 he enrolled in Colgate University but dropped out after three semesters. Over the next five years, he worked a number of part-time jobs in and around New York City, including ice-cream vendor, McDonald's cashier, security guard, night janitor, assistant superintendent of an apartment complex, taxi driver, deliveryman, and hospital emergency-room clerk. He also took some college courses at various campuses, studied pottery and jewelry making, and interned as a craft therapist at Bellevue Hospital in New York City. In 1974 he moved to Paradox in New York's Adirondack Mountains, where he spent three years teaching crafts to troubled teenagers at the Highland Community School.

Greenfield was born on March 14, 1951, in Brooklyn. His father, Malcolm, was a stockbroker, and his mother, Mildred, was a homemaker. In 1969 he enrolled in Oberlin College as a premed student. After receiving his B.S. in 1973, he took a job in New York City as a lab technician, sharing a room with Cohen. A year later he moved to Chapel Hill, North Carolina, with his girlfriend; after bumming around for nine months, he went to work as a lab technician. In 1976 he moved in with Cohen once again.

In 1977 Cohen and Greenfield decided it would be fun to open some sort of a food business in a small college town. At first they wanted to

sell bagels, but gave up that idea when they realized they couldn't afford the equipment for making them. Eventually they decided to sell ice cream, so they took a correspondence course from Pennsylvania State University in ice-cream making. After successfully completing the course, in 1978 they moved to Burlington, Vermont, home of the University of Vermont. A few months later they were selling Ben & Jerry's homemade ice cream from a converted gas station in downtown Burlington. Their specialty was exotic, high-fat flavors with zany names like Dastardly Mash, chocolate ice cream liberally spiked with pecans, walnuts, chocolate chunks, and raisins. As business grew, Greenfield concentrated on making the ice cream while Cohen concentrated on selling it. By 1980 business had increased to the point that the partners felt a need to bring in someone who knew something about running a business, so they recruited Fred "Chico" Lager, a Burlington nightclub owner, to be their chief operating officer. Under Lager's direction, the company became highly profitable, and in 1980 it began packing pints in a converted textile mill and selling them to restaurants and grocery stores around the state. In 1981 the company opened a larger packing facility in South Burlington as well as its first franchise store in nearby Shelburne. Shortly thereafter, *Time* magazine featured Ben & Jerry's in an article about ice cream, and after that people from out of town began trekking to Burlington just to buy some Ben & Jerry's. Franchise stores began opening all over northern New England, and an independent distributor began selling Ben & Jerry's in Boston, Massachusetts. By 1984 the company was selling about $4 million worth of ice cream per year.

That same year Cohen and Greenfield realized that they were successful businessmen, something they had never intended to become. This thought bothered them so much that they decided to do something about it. They incorporated their business as Ben & Jerry's Homemade Inc., with Cohen as chairperson of the board and Greenfield as vice chairperson, and then set out to create the most unusual corporation in the United States. Believing that corporations by their very nature perpetuated the class inequalities in American society, the partners vowed that no employee, themselves included, would ever make more than five times the salary of the lowest paid worker in the company. They created the Ben & Jerry's Foundation, to which they contributed 7.5 percent of the corporation's pretax profits, to fund projects that benefitted the communities in which the corporation operated, as well as to national environmental and social justice organizations.

They introduced several new flavors that heightened awareness of certain social concerns while at the same time addressing those concerns. For example, the brownies used in Chocolate Fudge Brownie were made by homeless and otherwise unemployed people in Yonkers, New York; Wild Maine Blueberry was made from blueberries grown by impoverished Passamaquoddy Indians in Maine; and Rainforest Crunch was made from Brazil nuts harvested by Indians in the Amazon rain forest. Among the many corporate benefits were three free pints of ice cream per employee per day and the services of the Joy Gang, a rotating committee of regular employees who took turns improving employee morale via such things as giving massages.

But despite their best efforts to avoid being a for-profit corporation, Ben & Jerry's continued to make money. In 1985 they opened a new facility in Waterbury, Vermont, and began distributing ice cream in half a dozen states outside New England. By 1990 the company had 90 franchise stores in 38 states and did $58 million in sales. By 2000 annual sales had grown to $237 million. And in 2000 Ben & Jerry's came dangerously close to becoming just another part of the corporate world when it agreed to be bought by Unilever PLC, an international conglomerate headquartered in Holland, for $326 million. Although Cohen and Greenfield remained on Ben & Jerry's board of directors, their primary responsibility was to represent the company in their speaking engagements around the country. Cohen indicated that he would try to introduce social responsibility to the businesses under the Unilever umbrella, and the corporation was active in charitable activities, particularly environmental causes. Their annual Free Cone Day began in 1979, and it is often held on Earth Day (April 22) and tied to local and national causes. The pair most recently enjoyed a resurgence of their high profile by creating a popular ice cream flavor in 2007 in honor of satirical talk show host Stephen Colbert (Stephen Colbert's AmeriCone Dream) and another in 2008 in support of presidential candidate Barack Obama (Yes Pecan).

Further Reading

Cohen, Ben, and Jerry Greenfield. *Ben & Jerry's Double-Dip: How to Run a Values-Led Business and Make Money, Too.* New York: Simon & Schuster, 1998.

"History." Ben and Jerry. Available online. URL: http://www.benjerry.com/company/history/. Downloaded on July 1, 2009.

Lager, Fred "Chico." *Ben & Jerry's: The Inside Scoop: How Two Real Guys Built a Business with a Social Conscience and a Sense of Humor.* New York: Crown Publishers, 1994.

Colgate, William

(1783–1857) *entrepreneur in soap*

William Colgate was the first American to realize the business potential of manufactured soap. Although his business began as a one-man operation, it eventually grew and evolved into the Colgate-Palmolive Company, one of the world's largest manufacturers of household and personal products. An astute entrepreneur, he seems never to have suffered a serious business setback. More than any other individual, he is responsible for transforming the soap-making business from a marginal enterprise to a thriving industry.

Colgate was born on January 25, 1783, in Hollingbourne Parish, Kent, England. His parents, Robert and Sarah, were farmers. After emigrating to the United States in 1783, the Colgates tried and failed at farming in Maryland and Virginia before finally settling in Baltimore, Maryland, in 1800. That same year William and his father entered the soap- and candle-making business.

Most soap in early 19th-century America was homemade. Housewives put kitchen grease and animal fat in a big tub in the backyard, mixed in potash, and then stirred and boiled the mixture over a wood fire. The result was soap that cleaned fairly well but that irritated the skin and the nose. Soap manufactured in the United Sates was not as offensive in either category because it was made from low-grade oils and slaked lime, and it was easier to use because it could be bought in bar form, but it cost more and did not clean any better than homemade soap. And those who were inclined to purchase their soap were more likely to buy French imports, which were soft, scented, and highly effective. Consequently, the soap business in Baltimore, which was home to fewer than 10,000 people, was not good, and after two years Robert Colgate moved to New York to try farming once again.

William Colgate now found himself the sole proprietor of a struggling soap business. He quickly realized that profits would be much higher in a crowded city where most people could not make their own soap, so in 1803 he moved to New York City. After working for a competitor for three years, in 1806 he founded his second soap business, William Colgate & Company, in Manhattan.

As a means of attracting and keeping the business of homebound housewives, Colgate offered free home delivery on purchase as small as one bar. For his first year in business in New York he ran himself ragged by doing all of the company's buying, manufacturing, selling, delivery, and bookkeeping, so in 1807 he took on a partner, Francis Smith. Almost immediately business began to boom. War had broken out between France and Great Britain, and both sides worked to keep American ships out of each other's ports. The result was the U.S. Embargo Act of 1807 and the U.S. Non-Intercourse Act of 1809, which kept American ships from trading with either side, thus virtually eliminating the importation of French soap. By 1813 Colgate had made so much money selling soap to New Yorkers that he was able to buy his parents a farm, marry Mary Gilbert with whom he later had nine children, and buy Smith's share of the company. By the time French imports resumed after 1815 when the Napoleonic wars ended, Colgate was making soap that was good enough and inexpensive enough to hold its own in the marketplace.

Over the next few years Colgate learned to use starch as an inexpensive filler without unduly affecting the quality of his soap, and in 1820 he opened his own starch factory. In 1829 he learned how to produce scented soap by mixing the oil and lime with just the right amount of perfume. In 1838 he brought his oldest son, Samuel, into the business and changed its name to Colgate & Company. By 1845 business had grown to the point that he undertook the construction of the world's largest soap-boiling pan, with a capacity of more than 20 tons. His critics called it "Colgate's Folly" and swore it would bankrupt the company. Instead, two years later Colgate found it necessary to expand operations even further, so he opened a state-of-the-art facility across the Hudson River in Jersey City, New Jersey.

Colgate died on March 25, 1857, in New York City. At that time, Colgate & Company was a thriving enterprise under the capable management of his sons. In 1908 the company produced Colgate Ribbon Dental Cream, the world's first toothpaste in a tube. In 1928 the company merged with a major competitor, Palmolive-Peet Company, and eventually became known as Colgate-Palmolive Company. By the late 20th century the company had become one of two major producers of bar soap and laundry detergent in the United States and was manufacturing a variety of household and personal care products, food items, health care and industrial supplies, and sports and leisure time equipment.

Further Reading

Carver, Saxon Rowe. *William Colgate: Yeoman of Kent.* Nashville, Tenn.: Broadman Press, 1957.

Foster, David R. *The Story of Colgate-Palmolive: One Hundred and Sixty-Nine Years of Progress.* New York: Newcomen Society in North America, 1975.

Colt, Samuel
(1814–1862) *inventor of the repeating revolver*

Although the world's first revolver was invented sometime in the 17th century, it did not become available commercially until it was reinvented by Samuel Colt some 200 years later. By permitting a gunman to get off six shots before having to reload, Colt's revolver made the sidearm a truly formidable weapon and contributed significantly to the taming of the American West. It also helped to make American society more dangerous, as it put lethal firepower within the grasp of virtually everyone. As the old post–Civil War saying went, "Abe Lincoln may have freed all men, but Sam Colt made them equal."

Colt was born on July 19, 1814, in Hartford, Connecticut. His father, Christopher, was a merchant and cloth manufacturer, and his mother, Sarah, was a homemaker. By 1821 his father had gone out of business, and at age 10 Colt was apprenticed to a farmer. The following year he went to work in a dyeing and bleaching factory in Ware, Massachusetts. At some point he was sent to a private boarding school, but at age 16 he set off a fireworks display that nearly burned a school building to the ground. Before he could be caught and punished, he signed aboard a merchant vessel bound for India.

Colt had been interested in firearms for some time, having acquired his first pistol at age seven, and while at sea he began making wooden models of multibarrel pistols. He also carved a model of a revolver, having been inspired by the workings of the ship's capstan. This device, which was used to hoist the anchor, featured a rotating drum around which the anchor chain was wound, with a notched track on the base plate and large pins on the drum to keep the drum from rotating the wrong way. He returned to the factory in Ware in 1831, and at age 17 he developed a single-barrel revolver. This weapon featured a revolving cylinder in which the gunpowder and bullets were stored in chambers; cocking the hammer caused a capstan-like mechanism to rotate the cylinder so that the next full chamber was in line with the barrel and the hammer. The revolver's advantage over single-shot pistols was that it could fire several shots without having to be reloaded.

At age 18 Colt assumed the name Dr. Coult and went on a lecture tour demonstrating the effects of nitrous oxide, or laughing gas. He made enough money from the tour to perfect the revolver's design and to receive a patent in 1836. That same year his uncle put him in touch with a group of New Jersey investors, with whom he formed the Patent Arms Manufacturing Company in Paterson, New Jersey, and began turning out the world's first commercially produced revolvers. The revolver quickly proved its usefulness to U.S. Army officers

fighting against the Seminole Indians in Florida and to Texas insurgents fighting for independence from Mexico. However, the Army Ordnance Department decided that Colt's revolver was too fragile for military use, and it refused to buy more than a few of them. Outside of a few sales to civilian customers, Patent Arms did little business, and closed its doors in 1842.

Over the next four years, Colt devised a method to make electrical wire waterproof, and he started a company to manufacture telegraph line for underwater use. In 1846 the army, having become involved in a war with the Mexicans, came to realize the usefulness of Colt's revolver and tried to order 1,000 as sidearms for its officers. Upon finding out that Patent Arms was no longer in business, Captain Samuel H. Walker was dispatched to track down Colt and get him to make more revolvers. In the process of filling the government's order, Colt and Walker designed a larger-caliber pistol, known as the Colt-Walker revolver, which in 1847 was put into production in partnership with Eli Whitney, Jr., at his armory in Whitneyville, Connecticut. As Colt's revolvers (he eventually made three different models, as well as a line of rifles) became popular with western settlers as well as with the army, in 1848 Colt formed a new partnership and opened a factory of his own in Hartford. In 1849 he went on an extended sales tour of Europe, calling on military procurement officials in virtually every major country, and came home with several sizable orders, including one from the Ottoman Empire for 5,000 revolvers.

In addition to being a clever inventor and skillful salesman, Colt was also an innovative manufacturer. He had learned much about making interchangeable parts from his partnership with Whitney, Jr., who in turn had learned many techniques from his father ELI WHITNEY, who had introduced the concept at the federal armory in Springfield, Massachusetts. The Ottoman sale enabled Colt to build two new factories, one in London, England, and one in Hartford, that incorporated everything he had learned, as well as his own ideas about machining interchangeable parts. The new Hartford factory, built between 1852 and 1856, was the largest privately owned munitions plant in the world, and the London plant, which opened in 1851, was the first factory to be built in Europe by an American company. In addition to being heated and lit via gas lamps, these factories featured machines for producing about 80 percent of the metal parts of a firearm and for reducing significantly the handwork required for fitting the parts together. Most of this equipment had been invented or designed by E. K. Root, Colt's superintendent of manufacturing, although Colt was the one who encouraged its development and then popularized its use throughout the United States and Europe. By 1856 Colt's Patent Fire Arms Manufacturing Company was turning out about 150 firearms per day.

From 1852 to 1858 Colt spent much time in Europe, overseeing operations at his factory in London and making sales calls. In 1856 he married Elizabeth Jarvis, with whom he had four children. In 1858 he became too ill to travel, and he spent his remaining years at his palatial mansion, Armsmear, located next to his Hartford factory. Although he never served in the military, he was made an honorary colonel by the governor of Connecticut for services rendered to the state. At the time of his death on January 10, 1862, in Hartford, his estate was estimated to be worth $15 million.

Further Reading

Edwards, William B. *The Story of Colt's Revolver: The Biography of Colonel Samuel Colt*. Harrisburg, Penn.: Stackpole Co., 1957.

Grant, Ellsworth S. *The Colt Armory: A History of Colt's Manufacturing Company, Inc.* Lincoln, R.I.: Mowbray Pub., 1995.

Hosley, William N. *Colt: The Making of an American Legend*. Amherst: University of Massachusetts Press, 1996.

Kirkland, K.D. *America's Premier Gunmakers*. New York: Mallard Press, 1990.

Cone, Moses Herman (1857–1908), and Ceasar Cone (1859–1917)
founders of Cone Mills

Two of the most successful of all southern textile mill owners were Moses and Ceasar Cone. Having started in the textile business as commissioned sales agents, they eventually owned one of the largest mills in North Carolina. Ironically, this probably would not have happened had the customers of their original business been able to pay them in cash.

The Cones were born in Jonesboro, Tennessee—Moses on June 29, 1857, and Ceasar on April 22, 1859. Their father, Herman, owned a grocery store, and their mother, Helen, was a homemaker. In 1870 they moved with their family to Baltimore, Maryland, where their father went into the wholesale grocery business. Eight years later Moses, Ceasar, and two other brothers became their father's partners in the grocery business, which was renamed H. Cone & Sons.

After the Civil War, textile mills had begun popping up on the outskirts of virtually every community of any size in the cotton growing region of the South. By 1880, most mills had become separate communities of their own, with their own housing and shopping facilities. It became the responsibility of Moses and Ceasar to call on these mills and sell groceries, leather goods, and tobacco to their company stores. In 1888 Moses married

Moses Cone and his brother Ceasar founded one of the largest textile mills in the South. *(Courtesy of Cone Mills Corporation)*

Bertha Lindau with whom he had no children, and in 1894 Ceasar married Jeanette Siegel with whom he had three children.

Many of the Cones' customers fell on hard times during the 1880s, as the price of cotton goods rose and fell throughout the decade, and the Cones were often asked to accept cases of yarn and bales of textiles in lieu of cash. Not having much other choice but to accept, they did so reluctantly, finding themselves and their company in the wholesale textile business. Fortunately, they soon found out that the bartered goods could often be sold for more than the original debt, and they eventually expanded their services to the mills by also acting as commissioned sales agents for many of them. In 1887 they became mill owners themselves when they acquired part ownership of the C. E. Graham Manufacturing Company in Asheville, North Carolina. In 1888 they also became partners in the establishment of cotton mills in Salisbury and Gibsonville.

While selling the wares of the various mills the Cones represented to buyers in New York City and abroad, Moses realized that there was little diversity to the textiles being turned out by southern mills. Of the 50 or so mills in the region, almost all of them produced either inexpensive cotton plaids or heavy sheeting. None of them did any finishing or bleaching to their products, which reduced both their desirability and their price. He also knew that there was no good reason for this situation, other than the lack of organization and innovative thinking on the parts of the mill owners. In 1890 he and his brother began organizing southern mills into a loose-knit trade organization in order to help its members get better prices for their products, as well as to expand the repertoire and quality of what southern mills produced. They quickly convinced 38 mill owners of the wisdom of their plan, and in 1891 they established the Cone Export & Commission Company, with headquarters in New York City and with Moses as president, as the exclusive agent and banker of each member. Two years later, the company relocated its offices to Greensboro, North Carolina, where both Cones also settled, and eventually just about every cotton mill in the South joined Cone Export.

Ceasar and Moses Cone brought improved profitability and new markets to the southern textile industry. *(Courtesy of Cone Mills Corporation)*

By 1895 the Cones realized that the worldwide demand for denim greatly exceeded the supply, and that the mills Cone Export represented were turning out very little denim at all. That same year they formed the Proximity Manufacturing Company in Greensboro, with Ceasar as president, to address this situation. The company was located on the site of a defunct steel mill, where the Cones were able to obtain 25 acres of land for free. Within a short period of time, Proximity was producing about one-third of the world's supply of denim; its profits were used to open other mills near Proximity for the manufacture of corduroy and flannel. By 1908 the Cones' Greensboro mills sprawled over more than 2,000 acres, and the Cones were among the most prosperous mill owners in the South. In 1912 Ceasar established the Proximity Print Works in Greensboro, which was the first mill in the South to print colored fabrics.

The Cones made a fortune in the textile business, much of which they gave back to the community in the form of philanthropic and charitable contributions. They were paternalistic mill owners in the best sense, providing excellent schooling, housing, and recreational facilities for their employees and their children and even hiring social workers to teach their employees about nutritious cooking and proper sanitation. Having bought a 3,750-acre estate near Blowing Rock in North Carolina's Great Smoky Mountains in 1901, Moses donated generously to the schools in Blowing Rock and to what became Appalachian State University in nearby Boone. In his will he made provisions for the establishment of Moses H. Cone Hospital in Greensboro, where he died on December 8, 1908. Meanwhile, Ceasar donated much of his time and money to the Jackson Training School in Concord, North Carolina. He died in Greensboro on March 1, 1917.

Further Reading

Noblitt, Philip T. *A Mansion in the Mountains: The Story of Moses and Bertha Cone and their Blowing Rock Manor.* Boone, N.C.: Parkway Pub., 1996.

Zweigenhaft, Richard L., and G. William Domhoff. *A Century of Excellence: The History of Cone Mills, 1891–1991.* Greensboro, N.C.: Cone Mills Corp., 1991.

Coolidge, William David

(1873–1975) *inventor of the Coolidge X-ray tube*

William Coolidge did not invent either the lightbulb or the X-ray tube; these honors go to THOMAS ALVA EDISON and Wilhelm Roentgen, respectively. However, had it not been for Coolidge's improvements to both inventions, they might still be primitive devices unsuited for modern applications.

Coolidge was born on October 23, 1873, in Hudson, Massachusetts. His parents, Albert and Martha, were farmers. After receiving his B.S. in electrical engineering from the Massachusetts Institute of Technology (MIT) in 1896, he attended the University of Leipzig, Germany, where he received his Ph.D. in physics in 1898. He spent the next eight years as a researcher at MIT's Research Laboratory of Physical Chemistry, then in 1905 he joined the staff of the General Electric (GE) Research Laboratory in Schenectady, New York.

At the time, GE researchers were trying to develop an improved filament for the incandescent lightbulb that would last longer as well as generate more light than heat. In 1904 Willis R. Whitney, the laboratory's director, had developed a metalized carbon filament that lasted longer than any previous filament, but the following year two Hungarian researchers, Alexander Just and Franz Hanaman, made a longer-lasting filament from tungsten, a rare metallic element with a high melting point. Although tungsten converts electricity into light more efficiently than anything else (a century later it was still being used in lightbulb filaments), it is brittle, and researchers were having great difficulty fashioning it into the thin wires required for use in the lightbulb. The earliest method of making tungsten filaments involved molding the brittle metal into the required shape, an expensive and time-consuming process. In 1906 Coolidge devised a method for shaping tungsten into wire by heating a mixture of tungsten, cadmium, and mercury until the tungsten became soft, turning the mixture into wire by swaging (forcing it through a small hole in a die) and drawing it, then heating the wire until the cadmium and mercury melted away, leaving a wire made of pure tungsten. By 1909, the year after he married Ethel Woodward with whom he had two children, he had devised an even better method for making tungsten wire. His new method involved heating small blocks of densely packed tungsten until the metal got soft and malleable, hammering the blocks until the tungsten was thin enough to be swaged and drawn, and coating the wire with thorium to make it more flexible. Coolidge's method worked so well that tungsten wire could be produced by the mile, and filaments could be made simply by snipping off the required length of wire and shaping it by hand or machine. This method remained the standard way to make tungsten filaments into the 21st century.

Having improved the lightbulb, Coolidge then set out to improve the X-ray tube. In 1895 Wilhelm Conrad Roentgen had discovered X-rays and their ability to penetrate solid matter, and had constructed a simple device known as a Roentgen tube for producing X-rays. However, the Roentgen tube was a weak source of X-rays, partly because its filament could not withstand the high temperatures required for generating electrons (which in turn were used to create X-rays) and partly because it

William Coolidge was one of many distinguished researchers who worked for General Electric. *(Library of Congress)*

generated electrons by ionizing gas in a low vacuum, an inefficient method for doing so. In 1913 Coolidge and another GE researcher, Irving Langmuir, improved on the Roentgen tube by using a tungsten filament, completely evacuating the tube, and utilizing a method of pure electron discharge to generate X-rays. The result was the so-called Coolidge tube, modified versions of which continued to be used into the 21st century. Coolidge continued to work on X-ray equipment for the rest of his career. Having discovered that higher voltages produce X-rays that penetrate matter much more effectively than at low voltages, he eventually developed a powerful X-ray tube that could be operated at more than 1 million volts.

Coolidge remained at GE for his entire career. In 1932 he took Whitney's place as director of the research laboratory. He retired to his home in Schenectady 12 years later with his second wife, Dorothy MacHaffie, whom he had married in 1916,

the year after his first wife died. He spent his last years doing consulting work for GE, traveling, and dabbling with photography. He died on February 3, 1975, in Schenectady.

Further Reading

Suits, C. Guy. *William David Coolidge: October 23, 1873– February 3, 1975.* Washington, D.C.: National Academy Press, 1982.
"William D. Coolidge," National Inventors Hall of Fame. Available online. URL: http://www.invent. org/hall_of_fame/33.html. Downloaded on July 1, 2009.

Cooper, Kent

(1880–1965) *innovator for the Associated Press*

Associated Press (AP) is the nation's oldest and largest cooperative news agency. Prior to 1925, it functioned as a rather complacent clearinghouse for stories of national and international importance. After 1925, it became an innovative purveyor of local news, feature articles, sports and entertainment stories, and photographs, as well as the nation's foremost source of traditional news. The person most responsible for changing AP was Kent Cooper, its general manager and executive director from 1925 to 1951.

Cooper was born on March 22, 1880, in Columbus, Indiana. His father, George, was a lawyer, and his mother, Sina, was a homemaker. Between the ages of 11 and 18 he delivered newspapers part time, thus gaining some experience in the news business. At age 18 he enrolled in the University of Indiana but was forced to withdraw the following year when his father died. He then went to work as a journalist for the *Indianapolis Press*, but after a year he transferred to its rival, the *Sun*. In 1903 he became the Indianapolis correspondent of the Scripps-McRae Press Association, a cooperative news agency that shared stories among its member newspapers via telegram, or wire. In 1906, the year after he married Daisy McBride with whom he had one child, he began making telephone conference calls twice a day to Scripps-McRae subscribers to give them the national and foreign news. This method, known as a pony service, was more thorough yet less expensive than the traditional wire service method of sending each news article via short telegram. The pony service allowed him to sign up a number of small newspapers in Indiana which could not otherwise afford to subscribe to a wire service.

In 1907 Scripps-McRae became part of the United Press (UP) news agency, and Cooper was recruited to set up pony services for UP across the United States. Three years later he left the UP to join its larger rival, the Associated Press (AP). Hired by AP as a traveling inspector, he suggested so many improvements, the sum of which saved the company a substantial amount of money, that in 1912, when AP was restructured, Cooper was made head of the new Traffic Department. By 1916 he had installed the first teletype machines used by a news agency and developed a pony-service-like system for transmitting the World Series on a play-by-play basis to newspapers across the country. In 1918 Cooper developed AP into an international wire service by signing up 25 newspapers in South America. In 1920 his first wife died, and he married Marian Rothwell; they were divorced in 1940, and in 1942 he married Sarah Gibbs.

In 1925 Cooper was promoted to general manager, having served the previous five years as assistant general manager. To this point the AP had generally restricted itself to reporting only "hard news" of a national or international nature; local news, human interest stories, and features of an informational or entertaining nature had generally been ignored. Cooper changed all this. He set up state services that concentrated on local and state news, hired a science editor, created a features department, and provided members with illustrations, political cartoons, and comic strips. In 1935 he established a wire-photo service that reduced the time required to transmit photographs across the country from four days to four minutes.

One of Cooper's biggest contributions to AP was to convert it into a truly international news agency. Prior to the 1930s, four agencies—Reuters of Great Britain, Wolff of Germany, Havas of France, and AP—controlled the reporting of news from their respective corners of the world; in fact, Cooper had had to get special permission from Havas to sign up his South American correspon-

dents. By 1934, he had become frustrated with what he considered to be undue censorship and biased reporting of the news, especially by Wolff, in the wake of the Nazis' rise to power. That same year, he severed AP's ties with the international news cartel and began establishing independent AP bureaus around the world.

Cooper retired as general manager in 1948, but he continued to serve as AP's executive director until 1951. He spent the last years of his retirement in West Palm Beach, Florida, where he dabbled in songwriting and wrote two books; *The Right to Know* (1956) chronicled the history of press censorship, and *Kent Cooper and the Associated Press* (1959) was his autobiography. He died on January 31, 1965, in West Palm Beach.

Further Reading

Cooper, Kent. *Kent Cooper and the Associated Press: An Autobiography.* New York: Random House, 1959.
Schwarzlose, Richard. *The Nation's Newsbrokers.* Vol. 2. Evanston, Ill.: Northwestern University Press, 1990.

Cooper, Peter
(1791–1883) *inventor of the Tom Thumb steam locomotive*

The 19th century was a time of great opportunity, and many people who had nothing more than energy and intelligence became successful despite their lack of formal education or family fortune. One of these people was Peter Cooper, inventor of the *Tom Thumb*, the first steam locomotive designed and built in the United States.

Cooper was born on February 12, 1791, in New York City. His father, John, was a merchant of various trades, and his mother, Margaret, was a homemaker. As a young boy he moved with his family from town to town in New York, while helping his father do everything from keeping shop to making bricks. At age 17, he returned to New York City to become an apprentice coach maker. When he completed his apprenticeship four years later in 1812, he moved to Hempstead, New Jersey, where he worked in a factory that made a machine for shearing cloth. He soon patented several improvements to the machine, then set up shop in New York City where he manufactured his machine until around 1816, when the end of the War of 1812 depressed the demand for domestic cloth. He then opened a grocery business with the brother of Sarah Bedell, whom he had married in 1813 and with whom he had six children. In 1821 he sold his interest to his brother-in-law and bought a glue factory in New York. Within seven years he had become the foremost American manufacturer of glue and isinglass, a gelatinous substance used as a clarifying agent in glue and jelly, and was successfully competing with European imports in terms of quality and price.

Cooper's success in the glue business made him a wealthy man, and in 1828 he was approached by two shady characters who tried to swindle him out of some of his money. They convinced him to become their partner in the purchase of 3,000 acres of waterfront property in Baltimore, Maryland; in fact, the two men contributed nothing toward its purchase. When he realized the following year that he had been tricked, he ended the partnership by buying the interests of the two men. Serendipitously, he then discovered that the property was rich in iron ore. Leaving his glue factory in the hands of his son and son-in-law, he moved to Baltimore, opened the Canton Iron Works, and began making rails for the newly established Baltimore and Ohio Railroad (B&O).

The B&O was formed to give Baltimore merchants the same access to the nation's interior that the Erie Canal had given to New York merchants. Unfortunately, it soon became apparent that the rolling hills of western Maryland's piedmont region were too steep to be traversed by the steam locomotives of the day, which had been designed to haul freight and passengers on the flat grades in England. As the railroad was on the verge of declaring defeat, Cooper approached the B&O's board of directors with an offer to design a more suitable locomotive. He soon came up with the *Tom Thumb*, so called because it was considerably smaller than English locomotives. Basically a small steam boiler mounted on a rolling platform about 16 feet long, the *Tom Thumb* had smaller wheels and a shorter wheelbase (the distance between the front and rear axles) than English locomotives.

Although it was slow—top speed with a full load was about 10 miles per hour—it was powerful enough to pull a train of cars over Maryland's hills, as it demonstrated on its trial run from Baltimore to Ellicott's Mills (modern Ellicott City) in 1830. The *Tom Thumb* was the first steam locomotive designed and built in the United States, and it saved the fortunes of the B&O. It also inspired other efforts to penetrate the interior by rail, most notably those of the Pennsylvania Railroad.

In 1836 Cooper exchanged his interest in the Canton Iron Works for B&O stock, and he returned to New York City. He and his partner Abram Hewitt formed one of the first vertical combinations in U.S. business history by buying an iron mine in Andover, New Jersey; opening a blast furnace in Phillipsburg, New Jersey, to smelt the ore into pig iron; and constructing a rolling mill in Trenton, New Jersey, to convert the pig iron into wire, wrought iron, and rails. The Trenton mill was the first mill in the United States to produce structural iron (1854) and steel (1868) via the open-hearth method.

Peter Cooper invented the *Tom Thumb,* one of the first steam locomotives built in America. *(Library of Congress)*

In 1854 Cooper became a partner of CYRUS WEST FIELD in the laying of the first transatlantic cable. While Field provided the engineering know-how, Cooper took care of the business end of things. He served as president of the New York, Newfoundland & London Electric Telegraph Company from 1854 to 1866, when the project was finally completed. He was also president of the North American Telegraph Company, which in 1857 began stringing telegraph lines across the continental United States. Meanwhile, he continued to invent a wide variety of things, including a washing machine, a compressed-air engine for powering ferryboats, a chain mechanism for towing canal boats, and a musical cradle.

Cooper devoted much of his free time to civic affairs. He served as a New York city alderman for a number of years, and in 1876, at the age of 85, he was the Greenback Party's candidate for president of the United States. But his favorite hobby was the Cooper Union, a tuition-free school of science, engineering, and art in New York City. Despite his many accomplishments, Cooper himself had only one year of formal schooling, and he regretted that he had not been able to obtain an education because he lacked the funds. Founded in 1859 by Cooper, who endowed it generously so that it could continue to operate and expand, the Cooper Union continues to offer day and night classes free of charge to any student who passes the entrance exam. Cooper died in New York City on April 4, 1883.

Further Reading

Mack, Edward C. *Peter Cooper: Citizen of New York.* New York: Duell, Sloan and Pearce, 1949.

"Peter Cooper and His Legacy," About Inventors. Available online. URL: http://www.cooper.edu/engineering/chemechem/general/cooper.html. Downloaded on July 1, 2009.

Cornell, Ezra

(1807–1874) *founder of the Western Union Telegraph Company*

During the 19th century, it was sometimes possible for a would-be entrepreneur to become successful without much capital or education. Ezra Cornell was perhaps typical of this type of entrepreneur. He received little formal schooling as a youth, and he came from a middling economic background. However, he possessed vision and determination, as well as a knack for being in the right place at the right time.

Cornell was born on January 11, 1807, in Westchester Landing, New York. His father, Elijah, was a potter and schoolteacher, and his mother, Eunice, was a homemaker. At age 11 he moved with his family to De Ruyter where his parents had bought a farm. At age 17 he became a journeyman carpenter, and for the next four years he traveled throughout upstate and western New York before finally settling in Ithaca in 1828. That same year he became the foreman of a flour mill owned by Jeremiah S. Beebe, and in 1831 he married Mary Ann Wood with whom he had 11 children. He worked for Beebe until 1839, when the mill closed as a result of the panic of 1837.

Unemployed at the age of 30 and with a growing family to feed, Cornell bought a small farm near Ithaca and became partners in a grocery business. Although the grocery business did not thrive, the farm did, and Cornell became increasingly interested in better ways to grow crops. This interest led him to buy the patent rights for Maine and Georgia to a new plow with a double moldboard, which removed more dirt from the furrow than a single moldboard plow. In 1842, while in Maine to promote his plow, he met F. O. J. Smith, a farm journal publisher and chairman of the House Committee of Commerce. Smith had just signed a contract with SAMUEL F. B. MORSE, inventor of the telegraph, to lay a test telegraph line in an underground pipeline between Washington, D.C., and Baltimore, Maryland, and he was looking for a suitable ditch- digging machine. In no time, Cornell modified his double moldboard plow so that it could quickly cut a trench in which the pipeline could be installed. But as the project neared completion, Morse discovered to his horror that the wire was improperly insulated for underground use; unless he could buy enough time to solve the problem, the test would almost surely fail. At this point Cornell rose to the occasion; he "accidentally" destroyed his ditchdigger, thus delaying the project, then helped Morse develop a better method for insulating the wires. Ironically, during the delay it was decided to string the test line from poles, so the ditchdigger was no longer needed. However, a new problem arose: how to insulate the wire from the pole. Again Cornell came up with a solution: mount the wires on glass doorknobs. The entire project was completed in 1844, and Morse's first telegraph message was successfully transmitted that same year, thanks in no small part to Cornell.

Cornell clearly saw the potential of the telegraph to transform the country, and he became heavily involved in the construction of telegraph lines. He was one of the original investors in the Magnetic Telegraph Company, and in 1845 he supervised that company's efforts to string a line from New York City to Philadelphia. The following year he supervised construction of a line linking New York City and Albany, New York, and then served briefly as the line's superintendent. In 1847 he and John J. Speed, Jr., founded the Erie & Michigan Telegraph Company, which completed a line from Buffalo, New York, to Milwaukee, Wisconsin, as well as a branch line into Vermont and Quebec. In 1848 he founded the New York & Erie Telegraph Company for purposes of building a line between Buffalo and Albany, thus connecting New York City and Philadelphia with the Midwest. Throughout all this construction, Cornell battled bad weather, poor materials, and competition from rival companies, and by 1851 he owned a controlling interest in several lines but was deeply in debt. He managed somehow to struggle on until 1856, when the Western Union Telegraph Company was formed from a number of smaller lines, including all of Cornell's. He emerged from the merger as Western Union's largest stockholder and a wealthy man.

His fortune seemingly assured, Cornell retired after the merger and became involved in state politics. He played a central role in acquiring a federal land grant for a state college under the terms of the Morrill Act of 1862, then offered to endow the college if it were built in Ithaca. The result was Cornell University, which opened its doors in 1868. It was one of the first institutions of higher learning in the United States to admit women, and one of the few not affiliated with a religious

denomination. Toward the end of his life, Cornell made some bad investments in railroad stock and nearly lost his fortune. However, he continued to support the university generously, contributing more than $3 million before his death on December 9, 1874, in Ithaca.

Further Reading

Dorf, Philip. *The Builder: A Biography of Ezra Cornell.* Ithaca, N.Y.: Pine Grove Press, 1965.

Wren, Daniel A., and Ronald G. Greenwood. *Management Innovators; The People and Ideas that Have Shaped Modern Business.* New York: Oxford University Press, 1998.

Coston, Martha Hunt

(1826–unknown) *inventor of Coston Night Signals*

Martha Coston invented a signal flare system that revolutionized the way ships at sea communicate with one another. For about 60 years her signaling system was the primary means of ship-to-ship and ship-to-land communication at night.

Coston was born Martha Hunt in Baltimore, Maryland. Her father, who was evidently a man of means, died while she was young. Her mother moved the family to Philadelphia, Pennsylvania, where they were accepted into polite society. In 1842, at age 16, she married Benjamin Franklin Coston, a promising 21-year-old inventor. The couple moved to Washington, D.C., where he worked as head of the U.S. Navy's pyrotechnic laboratory. Over the next four years Coston gave birth to four sons.

In 1847 Coston's husband, mother, and youngest son died, probably from pneumonia. Heartbroken and penniless, Coston decided that the only way to support herself and her remaining children was to market one of her dead husband's unfinished inventions. Among his papers she found detailed plans for night signals, and she remembered her husband saying how interested the navy was in their development. At the time, ships used flags to communicate with one another and with the shore. The navy had developed a sophisticated flag system whereby approximately 1,300 sentences used in ordinary service could be signaled by using no more than four flags, one flag per numeral of the sentence's code. For example, "7-8-3" might be the signal for "return to port." However, the system did not work at night because the flags could not be seen without artificial light and the navy had never developed a satisfactory way to illuminate the flags. A night signal such as the one Benjamin Coston had been working on, whereby lights were substituted for flags, would be of great value to both the navy and to its inventor.

Martha Coston retrieved the prototype night signals from the laboratory and arranged to have the navy test them at sea. Unfortunately, the signals failed the test. Undaunted, Coston contracted with a procession of chemists in an attempt to develop a pyrotechnic device that could produce a very bright light in three different colors for an extended period of time. Within a few years the chemists developed white and red flares, but they were unable to produce a satisfactory blue flare. After several more years of unsuccessful experimentation, Coston found a pyrotechnical expert who could make a green flare of equal quality to the white and red ones. After 10 years of research, Coston finally had chemical recipes for red, white, and green night signals that could be seen at sea up to 15 miles away. She also developed a system whereby all 10 numerals could be indicated by various combinations of the three colors.

In 1857 Coston patented her pyrotechnic night signals in her husband's name. For the next two years she worked to get the navy to approve them. Finally, in 1859, she sold the right to use her system to the navy, signed a contract to supply enough Coston Night Signals to equip all of its ships, and found a manufacturer to fill the order. The first signals arrived just in time for the Civil War. By using Coston Night Signals, ships of the Union navy on blockade duty were able to coordinate their activities at night. This helped them capture a great number of southern blockade runners, most of whom made their run for port under cover of dark.

In 1859 Coston also obtained patents in England, France, Holland, Austria, Denmark, Italy, and Sweden, and in 1861 she left for Europe to sell the right to use her night signals to those governments. For 12 years she toured Europe with her sons, all the while promoting her invention. During this period her high-society lifestyle was financed with the money she made from selling signals to the various navies. While in Italy she became engaged to a Count Piccolomini, but he died before they could be married. In 1873 she returned to the United States and bought a home in Washington, D.C. The circumstances of her death are not known, but she probably died not long after her memoirs were published in 1886.

Further Reading

Coston, Martha. *A Signal Success: The Work and Travels of Mrs. Martha J. Coston, An Autobiography.* Philadelphia: J. B. Lippincott, 1886.

Macdonald, Anne L. *Feminine Ingenuity: Women and Invention in America.* New York: Ballantine Books, 1994.

Cottrell, Frederick Gardner

(1877–1948) *inventor of the electrostatic precipitator*

Most inventors are primarily interested in inventing something that will make them rich. However, a few inventors are more interested in developing devices that benefit the human race without regard to their own financial well-being. One of these latter inventors was Frederick Cottrell. Not only did he invent the electrostatic precipitator for cleaning the exhaust air emitted by factory smokestacks, but he also donated most of the money he made from the sale of the device to further scientific research.

Cottrell was born on January 10, 1877, in Oakland, California. His father, Henry, worked for a ship brokerage firm, and his mother, Cynthia, was a homemaker. He received his B.S. from the University of California, Berkeley, in 1896, then taught high school chemistry in Oakland for several years. He then enrolled in the University of Leipzig, Germany, where he received his Ph.D. in physical chemistry in 1902. After graduation he returned to UC-Berkeley where he taught chemistry for the next four years. In 1904 he married Jessie Fulton with whom he had no children. When an earthquake destroyed his laboratory in 1906, he left the university and went to work for the Du Pont Company as a researcher.

At the time, air pollution was just beginning to become a problem in the United States. The major cities of the Northeast and Midwest were filled with coal-burning factories, and most of them pumped billowing plumes of thick black smoke, heavily laced with sulfuric acid, into the atmosphere. Although no one knew exactly what effect air pollution had on humans, animals, and plants, many scientists were beginning to suspect that air pollution was not a good thing. Not long after joining Du Pont, it occurred to Cottrell that a simple and inexpensive way to reduce air pollution would be via electrostatic precipitation. This process removes solid and liquid particles from a gas stream by ionizing them, or giving them a negative electric charge. When ionized particles pass by electrodes with a positive charge, they are attracted to the electrodes, and can then be collected and discarded. The process was discovered in 1824 by M. Hohlfeld, a professor of mathematics at Leipzig, but it had never been developed commercially because of the high voltages required to charge a steady stream of particles. But by 1906 powerful transformers capable of producing up to 30,000 volts were readily available, and Cottrell set out to invent an electrostatic precipitator for commercial applications.

Within a year Cottrell had developed a device capable of removing dust from smokestacks. He mounted his precipitator in the stack, forcing the dust particles to pass through a high-potential electrostatic field that ionized them. Moments later the ionized particles were pulled aside by a powerful electrode that deposited them as dust in the bottom of the precipitator. In 1907 he applied for a patent and, with several partners, formed the International Precipitation Company and the Western Precipitation Company to manufacture and sell his electrostatic precipitator. Within two years electrostatic precipitators had been installed at a Du Pont sulfuric acid plant, two copper smelting facilities, and a cement plant.

In 1911 Cottrell left Du Pont to open a branch office of the U.S. Bureau of Mines in San Francisco, California. To avoid a conflict of interest—one of the bureau's responsibilities was to monitor

and reduce industrial air pollution—he assigned his patent rights to the electrostatic precipitator to the Smithsonian Institution, with the proviso that the proceeds from the patent be used to fund scientific research of a practical nature. In 1912 the institution created the Research Corporation, the first independent nonprofit foundation to support research and development projects that promise to aid humankind.

In 1921 Cottrell left the bureau to become director of the Department of Agriculture's Fixed Nitrogen Research Laboratory. Among other projects, he experimented with nitrogen-based fertilizers and explosives, and he developed a furnace for converting nitrogen and oxygen in the air into nitric acid. In 1930 he retired from government service and joined the Research Corporation, working as a consultant and director until his death on November 16, 1948, in Berkeley.

Further Reading
Bush, Vannevar. *Biographical Memoir of Frederick Gardner Cottrell, 1877–1948.* Washington, D.C.: National Academy of Sciences, 1950.
Cameron, Frank. *Cottrell, Samaritan of Science.* Tucson, Ariz.: Research Corp., 1993.

Curtiss, Glenn Hammond
(1878–1930) *inventor of the seaplane*

Next to WILBUR AND ORVILLE WRIGHT, the most important figure in the early history of American aviation is Glenn Curtiss. His skill at building lightweight engines with plenty of power enabled aircraft designers to build planes that could actually fly for some distance. He also designed and built the first practical seaplane.

Curtiss was born on May 21, 1878, in Hammondsport, New York. His father, Frank, owned a harness shop, and his mother, Lua, was a homemaker. At age 14 he finished his formal schooling and went to work as a stenciler for the Eastman Dry Plant and Film Company (present-day Eastman Kodak Company) in Rochester. The following year he bought a bicycle and got a job delivering telegrams for Western Union; he also took up the exhilarating but dangerous sport of bicycle racing.

In 1898 he married Lena Neff with whom he had two children, and he returned to Hammondsport where he went to work as a photographer.

Curtiss quickly found that taking pictures for a living was far too tame for his blood, and in 1900 he opened a bicycle repair shop, partly so he could devote more time to racing. His interest in speed naturally led him to develop an interest in motorcycles. By 1902 he and several partners had formed the G. H. Curtiss Manufacturing Company, whose main product was the Hercules motorcycle, featuring a lightweight, high-speed, two-cylinder, gasoline engine designed by Curtiss. Curtiss himself rode the Hercules to several world motorcycle speed records, including a subminute mile in 1903 and a 10-miles-in-nine-minutes ride in 1904. In 1907 he designed and built a monster bike with an eight-cylinder engine, then rode it to a world speed record of more than 136 miles per hour. At the time, this bike was the fastest machine in the world.

Curtiss's light but powerful motorcycle engines were exactly what aviators were looking for to power their aircraft. In 1907 ALEXANDER GRAHAM BELL, inventor of the telephone and a founder of the Aerial Experiment Association (AEA), recruited Curtiss to build and fly airplanes. The AEA built experimental planes by mounting Curtiss's engines and Bell's ailerons for improved steering on a basic "pusher" biplane (with the propeller mounted in the rear) of the kind designed and patented by Wilbur and Orville Wright. In 1908 Curtiss made the first public flight of more than a kilometer in an AEA plane called *June Bug*. In 1909 he left the AEA and became partners with Augustus M. Herring in the Herring-Curtiss Company. That same year the company's entry, *Golden Flyer*, equipped with an eight-cylinder, 50-horsepower engine capable of a top speed of 47 miles per hour, was piloted by Curtiss to a first-place finish at the world's first international air meet in Rheims, France.

Unfortunately, Curtiss proved to be a better pilot and engine designer that he was an entrepreneur, and his company went bankrupt in 1910. Part of the problem stemmed from bitter litigation with the Wright brothers over the use of ailerons, which the Wrights claimed was an infringement on their warped-wing design; the matter was finally settled in court in favor of the Wrights in 1913. Undaunted by his company's failure, Curtiss managed to scrape together enough money to form another firm, the Curtiss Aeroplane Company, which he devoted to the development of an amphibious airplane. Having relocated to San Diego, California, in 1911 he designed and built the Triad, a biplane with pontoons instead of landing gear, and began teaching military pilots how to fly it. The Triad quickly came to the attention of top U.S. Navy brass, who ordered one and redesignated it the A-1. Although the A-1 flew perfectly fine, it encountered some difficulties when taking off and landing, so Curtiss set out to build a true seaplane, a craft that featured wings mounted on a hull that could accommodate the pilot, passengers, and cargo. His biggest challenge was to figure out how to overcome the suction created by the water acting on the hull, which prevented the plane from taking off. He finally solved this problem by mounting wooden "steps" to the underside of the hull. As the plane picked up speed, it gradually rose out of the water onto the steps, thus creating a hydroplaning effect that greatly reduced suction and allowed the seaplane, dubbed the *Flying Fish*, to take off without difficulty.

By 1916 Curtiss's "aeroboat" had become so popular with military and civilian customers alike that he and a group of investors formed the Curtiss Aeroplane & Motor Company. Curtiss received almost $7 million in cash and stock and became the company's president. Within two years the company's New York factories were turning out more than 10,000 planes per year, many of which were bought by the British and Russian governments for use during World War I. Its most popular models were the JN-4 *Jenny* trainer plane, which became popular among barnstormers after the war ended, and the HS-1L coastal patrol seaplane for defending against German U-boats. Toward the end of the war, Curtiss designed and built the NC-4, a long-range seaplane powered with four 400-horsepower engines. Originally intended for antisubmarine warfare in the North Atlantic Ocean during World War I, the navy used the NC-4 to attempt the first transatlantic crossing by air. In 1919 the seaplane left Newfoundland and, after making several mid-ocean stops, arrived safely in Portugal.

Although Curtiss's company had thrived during the war, under his leadership it was unable to find its niche in the American economy once the war ended. In 1920 he was forced to step down as president, and although he was retained as a consultant, he had little more to do with the company. He moved to Florida where he used his fortune to buy and sell real estate. He died on July 23, 1930, in Buffalo, New York.

Further Reading

Carpenter, Jack. *Pendulum: The Story of America's Three Aviation Pioneers—Wilbur Wright, Orville Wright, and Glenn Curtiss, the Henry Ford of Aviation*. Carlise, Mass.: Ausdalen, Bosch & Co., 1992.

Casey, Louis S. *Curtiss, the Hammondsport Era, 1907–1915*. New York: Crown Pub., 1981.

Roseberry, C. R. *Glenn Curtiss: Pioneer of Flight*. Syracuse, N.Y.: Syracuse University Press, 1991.

D

Daché, Lilly
(1892–1989) *entrepreneur in ladies' hats*

Prior to the 1960s, adults of the upper and middle classes rarely appeared in public without a hat on their head. For the well-dressed woman, a stylish hat was not just an accessory; it was a fashion necessity. One of the best-known designers of ladies' fashion hats was Lilly Daché, a creative genius and skillful entrepreneur who made a fortune when hats were in vogue, then used her fortune to diversify into other areas of fashion before dress hats became an anachronism.

Daché was born in Begles, France. Her actual birth date, and the names and occupations of her parents, are unknown. About all that is known about her childhood is that, even then, she enjoyed making hats out of bits of fabric and decorating them with odds and ends. At some point she moved to Bordeaux to go to work for her aunt as a hatmaker for fashionable ladies. Her talent was such that her aunt sent her to Paris to learn the art of hatmaking from Caroline Reboux, Suzanne Talbot, and Georgette, France's best-known milliners. In 1924 she came to the United States, landing in New York City with no friends, family, or contacts and with less than $20 in her pocket. She soon found work in a small hat store called the Bonnet Shop; later, when the owner decided to sell, she and a coworker bought the store. Before long Daché bought out the coworker as well, and soon she was running the Bonnet Shop by herself.

Daché found herself without sufficient funds to stock her shop properly, but she hit upon a marketing technique that allowed her millinery business to thrive nonetheless: She insisted that each customer receive a hat that was custom-made just for her. The technique worked exceptionally well; the Roaring Twenties were in full swing, and New York City was full of well-to-do, fashionable women who wanted a unique look and who were not afraid to spend money to obtain it. After carefully measuring a customer's head, talking with the customer about where and with what outfit she intended to wear the hat, and arriving in her own mind as to what might look flattering and stylish, Daché would collect a $2 deposit. Then, after closing the shop in mid-afternoon, she would take the $2 to a fabric store and buy whatever material and notions were needed to make the hat. She would then return to the shop and stay up until the wee hours of the morning, folding and sewing so that her creation was almost perfectly fashioned to fit the customer's head. The next morning the customer would come back to pick up the hat, which Daché sold to her for an additional $10.50. As the business prospered, she hired more employees and relocated the Bonnet Shop to more fashionable locations, which in turn brought her into contact with a new clientele. By the end of the decade, she had become the milliner of choice for New York City's most fashion-conscious women.

Daché's millinery business continued to thrive even after the stock market crash of 1929 brought an end to the Roaring Twenties. In fact, the Great

Lilly Daché was the foremost women's hat designer of her day. *(Library of Congress)*

Depression, which brought about the ruin of many an American business, had little effect on Daché's, in large part because a woman who could not afford to buy a new outfit would buy a new hat instead. In 1935 she and Jean Despres, a French perfume salesman she had married four years earlier and with whom she had one child, bought an estate in Pound Ridge, New York; they relaxed and entertained there on the weekend, while continuing to work and live in the city during the week. Two years later, Daché moved her millinery enterprise into a nine-story building in downtown Manhattan that she had designed to be a reflection of her business. The outside was decorated in chromium and pink, and the interior was decked out in leopard skins, gold, and mirrors. The bottom seven floors housed the fitting salons, storerooms, and workshops, which eventually employed 150 milliners, and the upper two floors contained well-appointed living quarters for her and her husband.

By 1950 Daché had expanded her business across the United States. In addition to her opera-

tions in New York City, she had opened salons in Chicago, Illinois, and Miami, Florida, and sold ready-made hats to more than 40 stores across the country. Virtually every American woman of fortune or renown owned at least one Daché creation, some of which sold for as much as $500. Despite her success, Daché could sense that American fashion was changing and that the wearing of fashionable hats by women was about to come to an end. Having come to this realization in the late 1930s, she sought a solution in two ways. One was to design new hats that would appeal to younger women who preferred to appear in public bareheaded. In 1940 she won an American Design Award for the so-called half-hat, essentially a fancy headband that appealed to teenagers, and she later designed the "Mlle. Lilly" and "Dachette" lines, both of which targeted young adult women. The other was to diversify her operations. In 1954 she founded the General Beauty Products Corporation, which sold perfume, cosmetics, and hair products. She also expanded the range of her salons to include the design and sale of accessories, dresses, furs, jewelry, and lingerie, as well as men's shirts and ties.

In 1969 Daché closed her New York salon, sold her estate, and retired. She and her husband spent their winters in Delray Beach, Florida, and their summers in Meudon, a suburb of Paris. She died on December 31, 1989, in Louvecienne, France.

Further Reading

Daché, Lilly, and Dorothy Roe Lewis. *Talking Through My Hats*. London: John Gifford Ltd., 1946.
McDowell, Colin. *Hats: Status, Style, and Glamour*. New York: Thames and Hudson, 1997.
Morris, Bernadine. *The Fashion Makers*. New York: Random House, 1978.

Daly, Marcus
(1841–1900) *entrepreneur in copper*

When one thinks of miners striking it rich in the West, one usually thinks about the forty-niners in California or the cheechakos in the Yukon and Alaska, all of whom went looking for gold. An exception to this rule was Marcus Daly, who did not make his millions from mining precious metals but from finding copper. By striking one of the world's richest veins of this ordinary but useful metal, he became one of the wealthiest Irishmen who ever came to the United States.

Daly was born on December 5, 1841, in Ballyjamesduff, Ireland. His parents, Luke and Mary, were farmers. At age 15 he emigrated to the United States, settling in New York City. After working a number of odd jobs for five years, in 1861 he sailed to California where he became a silver miner. During the 1860s he worked as a miner and foreman in silver mines in California and Nevada, then around 1870 he went to Utah to manage several silver mines for the Walker brothers of Salt Lake City. In 1872 he married Margaret Evans with whom he had four children.

In 1876 Daly moved to Butte, Montana, to inspect a mine that he and the Walkers eventually bought. He managed the mine for four years, then in 1880 he sold his interest and bought the Anaconda mine for $30,000. At first it was thought that the Anaconda contained only silver, but Daly soon discovered that it also held a rich vein of copper, an important bit of news that he shrewdly kept to himself. As luck would have it, at that same time THOMAS ALVA EDISON and others were developing electrical power for residential and commercial use, and the demand for copper, which was used for making electrical wiring, was increasing dramatically. Needing money to buy as much of the land around the Anaconda as possible—thereby minimizing the number of competing claims to the Anaconda's copper vein, as well as to extract and process the Anaconda's copper—in 1881 he became partners with George Hearst, Lloyd Tevis, and Ben Ali Haggin and formed the Anaconda Copper Mining Company, with himself as general manager.

The Anaconda proved to contain the richest vein of copper ever discovered to that date, and Daly set out to exploit it for everything it was worth. Although he had taught himself much about silver mining, he knew that he did not know a lot about mining or processing copper, so he hired the best metallurgists he could find to advise and assist him. In 1893 he built the world's largest copper smelting facility. It was located on Warm Springs Creek, about 25 miles west of Butte, and around it Daly built the town of Copperopolis, later renamed Anaconda. The town boasted of such amenities as the Hotel Marcus Daly, one of the most ornate hotels in the country, and the *Anaconda Standard,* a newspaper with one of the most modern printing plants in the country. To fuel the smelter, he bought hundreds of acres of timberland and several coal mines, as well as the necessary sawmills and coke facilities. To get the copper ore to and from the smelter, he built a railroad connecting Anaconda and Butte. To get the copper out of the ground, he hired the best miners and supervisors he could find, paid them top wages, and took a personal interest in their physical well-being. By 1891 the Anaconda was producing so much copper that the four partners took it public as the Anaconda Mining Company. Over the next several years it became a favorite of European investors, who ended up owning about half of its stock.

In 1899 Daly became president of Anaconda Mining. That same year he oversaw the sale of the company to JOHN DAVISON ROCKEFELLER's Standard Oil company of New Jersey, his personal interest in Anaconda going for about $39 million. He stayed on as president of the mine until his death.

Other than copper, Daly's passions were horse racing and politics. On a 22,000-acre horse farm in the upper Bitter Root Valley near Anaconda, he bred champion racehorses that wore his colors of copper and green when they raced. Although he never ran for public office, he was dedicated to keeping fellow copper magnate William A. Clark from getting elected to the U.S. Senate, which he did by lavishly financing the campaigns of Clark's opponents. Daly died on November 12, 1900, in New York City, while on a business trip. At the time of his death, his estate was valued at $25 million.

Further Reading

Malone, Michael P. *The Battle for Butte: Mining and Politics on the Northern Frontier, 1864–1906.* Helena: Montana Historical Society Press, 1995.

Shoebotham, H. Minar. *Anaconda: Life of Marcus Daly, the Copper King.* Harrisburg, Penn.: Stackpole Co., 1956.

Davenport, Thomas

(1802–1851) *inventor of the electromagnetic motor*

The electromagnetic motor has been used to power everything from electric streetcars to small, precision pneumatic cylinders. Although the motor was anticipated by such scientific luminaries as Michael Faraday and Joseph Henry, it took a blacksmith, Thomas Davenport, to actually invent it.

Davenport was born on July 9, 1802, in Williamstown, Vermont. His parents, Daniel and Hannah, were farmers. At age 14 he became a blacksmith's apprentice, and seven years later he opened his own shop in nearby Brandon. In 1827 he married Emily Goss with whom he had two children. Around 1830 he relocated his business to nearby Forest Dale.

In 1833 Davenport paid a visit to the Penfield and Hammond Iron Works in Crown Point, New York. There he saw an electromagnet being used to separate iron ore from the various nonmetallic impurities with which it is usually found. Fascinated by this spectacle, he resolved to obtain an electromagnet of his own. He convinced his brother Oliver, an itinerant peddler, to get one for him. In order to do so, Oliver had to sell all the goods on his wagon and trade his good horse for a less-reliable horse. With the electromagnet in his hands, Davenport and his wife set out to find out what made it work. First, while she made notes, he reduced it to its constituent parts: battery, horseshoe-shaped iron core, wire coils wrapped around the ends of the core, and armature—the iron bar attached to the ends of the core that becomes magnetized by the electric current and that attaches to the load. Then he fashioned a new core, larger than the one he had bought, out of soft iron. Then, instead of rewrapping the wire coil around the core as on the one he had bought, they insulated the various turns of wire between strips of silk, which Emily had torn from her wedding gown. After reassembling the modified electromagnet, they discovered that it was even more powerful than the one his brother had obtained.

In 1834 Davenport built the world's first electromagnetic motor. He took a spoked wheel, attached electromagnets to two of the spokes, and then placed the wheel itself between two more electromagnets. All four electromagnets were connected through a commutator, which regulated the flow and direction of the electrical current, to a battery. When the motor was activated, the wheel spun at about 30 revolutions per minute. That same year he showed his motor to two professors at Middlebury College, who assured him that he had invented something revolutionary and urged him to apply for a patent immediately. After raising enough money from his friends to make a model, travel to the U.S. Patent Office in Washington, D.C., and file the paperwork, he departed on the trip. Unfortunately, he stopped off at several colleges along the way to demonstrate his machine to more professors, and by the time he reached Washington he no longer had enough money to file for a patent. Returning home, he spent the next two years demonstrating his motor as a means of raising more funds for applying for a patent. One of his demonstrations involved the operation of the world's first electric toy train. His second trip to Washington was more successful; this time he actually completed the application process. But no sooner had he done so than the model and the paperwork were destroyed in a huge fire at the Patent Office. In 1837 he again applied for a patent, and this time he received one.

In order to create a market for the electromagnetic motor, Davenport moved to New York City where he set up a workshop and laboratory. He also built an electromagnetic motor for powering a printing press, which he used to print and publish two journals, *Electro-Magnet and Mechanics Intelligencer* and *The Electro-Magnet*. Unfortunately, the publications failed, as did his other efforts to promote the electromagnetic motor. In fact, Davenport was ahead of his time. No one could imagine using an electromagnetic motor for any operation of any considerable size because, other than a small battery, no dependable source of electric power existed. This deficiency would not be addressed for another 40 years, when THOMAS ALVA EDISON and his associates began building electrical generation plants in the large cities. In 1843 Davenport gave up and returned home. He settled on a small farm in Salisbury, Vermont, where he died on July 6, 1851.

Further Reading

Davenport, Walter Rice. *Biography of Thomas Davenport: The "Brandon Blacksmith," Inventor of the Electric Motor.* Montpelier: The Vermont Historical Society, 1929.

Visser, Thomas D. "Smalley-Davenport Shop, Forestdale, Vermont," UVM Historic Preservation Program. Available online. URL: http://www.uvm.edu/~histpres/SD/hist.html. Downloaded on July 2, 2009.

Davis, Benjamin Jefferson

(1870–1945) *entrepreneur in newspaper publishing*

The Jim Crow South was a fairly hostile place for a black businessperson to seek his or her fortune. And yet, opportunity did exist for those who were fearless enough to seize it. Such a person was Benjamin Davis, who made a fortune in the early 20th century by selling newspapers in rural Georgia.

Davis was born on May 27, 1870, in Dawson, Georgia. His parents, Mike and Katherine, were farmers and ex-slaves. After completing the sixth grade, he worked successively as a bricklayer and an elementary schoolteacher before going to work for Tom W. Loyless, a Dawson printer and newspaper publisher. During the 1890s he started his own printing business and amassed a moderate amount of wealth. In 1898 he married Jimmie Porter with whom he had two children.

In 1903 Davis founded the *Independent*, a weekly newspaper geared toward blacks that was distributed throughout the state of Georgia. Within a year he reported a circulation of 100,000. The *Independent* gave rural black Georgians a voice they otherwise lacked. The paper devoted much of its space to society-page stories about club, social, and church activities, and it boosted black-owned businesses by serving as a forum for the products and services they offered. But it also featured hard-hitting editorials, written by Davis, that attacked such aspects of racial discrimination as convict labor, disfranchisement, and lynching, and it provided important news about the activities, speeches, and strategies of the principal black leaders of the day, especially Booker T. Washington, Marcus Garvey, and W. E. B. DuBois.

Since most of his advertising dollars came from businesses in Atlanta, in 1909 Davis moved his paper and his residence to that city. Meanwhile, he continued to distribute his paper to the small towns. In this regard he was fearless, despite the real possibility of racial violence. Many white-controlled towns had banned the *Independent*, and in 1912 a bundle of papers that he had sent to Carrollton came back with a death threat. Undaunted, the next day he drove to Carrollton and in broad daylight distributed that very bundle of papers from the busiest corner in town. While he did so, a large group of armed white men gathered on one side of the street, only to be dissuaded from taking action by an even larger group of armed black men that gathered on the other side.

By 1912 Davis had amassed a fortune. He threw lavish parties at his mansion in Atlanta and once hired a white orchestra to entertain his mostly black guests. At a time when most whites did not own an automobile, he owned three. He bypassed the Jim Crow laws that prohibited blacks from shopping in Atlanta's fancy, white-only stores by hiring white people the same size as him and his family and sending them to the stores to try on and buy clothing.

As the wealthiest black person in Atlanta, he played a major role in the black business community. By 1912 he had been a high-ranking member of the Grand United Order of Odd Fellows, the largest black fraternity in the South, for some time, and that same year he oversaw the development of the Odd Fellows Block in downtown Atlanta. The block became the center of the city's black commercial and professional community, and its centerpiece was the Odd Fellows Building, which housed the offices of the *Independent*.

Davis published the *Independent* until 1932, when he retired; by that time the paper's circulation had dropped to about 27,000. He devoted his remaining years to a variety of charitable and community activities. Next to publishing, his passion was politics, and for years he had been the central figure in the Georgia Republican Party. He died on October 28, 1945, while visiting his children in New York City.

Further Reading

Horne, Gerald. *Black Liberation/Red Scare: Ben Davis and the Communist Party.* Newark: University of Delaware Press, 1994. (This book is about Benjamin Davis's son but contains some information on him.)

Walton, Hanes, Jr. *Black Republicans: The Politics of the Black and Tans.* Metuchen, N.J.: Scarecrow Press, 1975.

Day, Benjamin Henry

(1810–1889) *inventor of the "penny press"*

The first newspaper to sell for one penny and not fold, the first newspaper to employ paperboys, and the first newspaper to use steam presses in the printing room—all these accolades belong to the *New York Sun,* brainchild of Benjamin Day. But as Day himself once averred, his success as a newspaper publisher happened "more by accident than design." In fact, had Day's printing business been more successful, he probably never would have entered the rough-and-tumble world of newspaper publishing.

Day was born on April 10, 1810, in West Springfield, Massachusetts. His father, Henry, was a hatmaker, and his mother, Mary, was a homemaker. At age 14 he went to work as an apprentice for the *Springfield Republican,* a local newspaper. Six years later he moved to New York City, and over the next two years he worked as a typesetter for three different newspapers. In 1832, the year after he married Eveline Shepard with whom he had four children, he started his own printing business.

For a little more than a year, Day struggled to make ends meet as a printer. Finally in 1833, he formed his own newspaper, mostly because he needed something to keep busy. At the time, New York City's leading newspapers, the *Morning Courier* and the *Enquirer,* sold for six cents an issue, a price that virtually precluded the middle and working classes from becoming regular readers of newspapers, and their editorial content appealed primarily to the upper class. One of Day's old workmates, Dave Ramsey, had often declared that a paper that sold for a penny would attract such a large and loyal readership that it could not

help but succeed. In fact, Ramsey's idea had been tried three times before, in New York City, Philadelphia, and Boston, and each time it had failed. Nevertheless, Day was desperate for work, so he began printing the *Sun*—its motto was "It Shines for ALL"—and selling it for one penny.

At first, the *Sun* was a one-man show. Day got his "news" by paraphrasing stories that had appeared in the previous day's papers, and to make it look like the *Sun* was a going concern, he also reprinted—for free—a number of the ads that his competitors were running. To hold down costs, he kept the paper small; the entire first issue was contained on four 8"x 11" sheets. Newsstands refused to sell the *Sun* because news dealers were afraid it

Benjamin Day was the first publisher to sell a newspaper for one cent. *(Library of Congress)*

would eat into their profits from the more expensive papers, so Day recruited enterprising young boys to sell his papers on the city's street corners. Within a few weeks he hired a reporter to cover the police courts, a beat that the six-penny papers turned up their noses at, but which Day's clientele found to be exceptionally interesting. Day made the *Sun* a popular paper by placing little editorial emphasis on politics, economics, and foreign affairs, which he left to the six-penny papers, and instead emphasized the human side of the news. Consequently, the *Sun* was filled with stories about the humorous side of life, as well as plenty of sex, crime, and violence, especially when the rich and powerful were involved. Within a year the *Sun*'s daily circulation was up to 8,000, and the upstart paper was seriously rivaling the six-penny papers. In the process, Day had revolutionized the newspaper business by covering a wide range of subjects in a popular writing style and selling it all at a price the general public could afford.

In 1835 Day began using steam-powered cylinder presses to print his newspaper, a first in American publishing. That same year he surpassed his competitors in terms of circulation by publishing what became known as the Moon Hoax. His reporter wrote a story about a scientist who had viewed the moon through a powerful telescope and discovered that humanlike creatures and Earthlike plants were living and thriving there, and their descriptions were published in great detail over several issues of the *Sun*. Naturally, Day's outraged competitors howled with self-righteous indignation that he was making a mockery of journalism's highest ideals; meanwhile, the *Sun*'s circulation climbed to more than 19,000, making it the most widely read newspaper in the world.

By 1838 the Sun's circulation rose to 50,000, more than that of all the six-penny papers combined. That same year Day sold the *Sun* to his brother-in-law and chief mechanic, Moses Beach, for $40,000, a tidy sum at the time, although Day later regretted letting it go so cheaply. After a brief retirement, in 1840 he began publishing another penny paper, the *True Sun*, which he sold a few months later. In 1842 he became partners with James Wilson and began publishing a monthly literary journal called *Brother Jonathan*, which

reprinted the most popular of England's novels. This publication eventually became the first American illustrated weekly journal, and Day continued his involvement with it for 20 years.

In 1862 Day retired from publishing, leaving his enterprises in the hands of his son Benjamin, Jr. He had made enough money as a publisher that he never had to work another day in his life. He died on December 21, 1889, in New York City.

Further Reading

Douglas, George H. *The Golden Age of the Newspaper.* Westport, Conn.: Greenwood Press, 1999.
O'Brien, Frank M. *The Story of the Sun: New York, 1833–1918.* New York: George H. Doran Co., 1918.

Deere, John
(1804–1886) *inventor of the steel plow*

When farmers tackled the Great Plains, they discovered that the soil there was not like anything they had ever seen before. Having been undisturbed for thousands of years, native grasses had put down a thick, extensive network of roots that was difficult to penetrate. Moreover, the yearly baking and freezing of the region's rich, black soil made it hard as a brick in some places, thus permitting many midwestern farmers to build their homes from prairie sod. This unique soil was not really mastered until John Deere invented the all-steel, one-piece plow, one of the tools that helped American farmers turn the Great Plains into the world's breadbasket.

Deere was born on February 7, 1804, in Rutland, Vermont. His father, William, was a tailor, and his mother, Sarah, was a seamstress. At age 17 he became an apprentice blacksmith, and in the mid-1820s he opened a shop of his own. In 1827 he married Demarius Lamb with whom he had nine children. By 1836 his business had failed, in large part because agriculture was on the decline in New England, so that year he decided to seek his fortune in the West. Settling in Grand Detour, Illinois, he discovered a booming agricultural economy, and he opened what quickly became a thriving blacksmith business.

Within a year Deere discovered that the soil of the Midwest was much more difficult and time-consuming to plow than the soil of the Northeast. Whereas New England soil was thin and loose, and therefore easily turned by the standard iron plow, Midwest soil was so thick and densely packed that it stuck to an iron plow's moldboard, the curved part of the plow that turns the soil (consider the difference between digging in sand versus digging in clay). Deere saw an opportunity to make money by solving this problem, and by 1837 he had designed a plow which featured a moldboard and share, the sharp blade that cuts through the soil, made from one piece of polished steel. Rather than get stuck like the iron plow, the polished steel plow slid through the rich, black soil without clogging. That same year he became partners with Leonard Andrus, and by 1838 the partners had built and sold 10 of Deere's plows. Over the next nine years, as sales gradually increased, Deere gradually abandoned his regular blacksmith work to concentrate on making plows.

By 1847 Deere had decided to build his own plow factory. That same year he sold his interest in the Grand Detour shop to Andrus and moved to Moline, Illinois, where the Mississippi River served as an excellent source of water power and transportation. Ten years later, his factory was making 13,000 plows per year, and his sales force was selling them in every state of the Union and in Canada. He offered a wide variety of plows, including breaking plows for cutting through the tough, thick sod of virgin prairie land, double-moldboard plows for making wide furrows, and shovel plows for making deep furrows, as well as a line of cultivators and harrows. Prior to the late 1850s, he imported most of his steel by ship and riverboat from England. After the steel mills in Pittsburgh, Pennsylvania, began making steel according to the Bessemer method (patented in this country by WILLIAM KELLY), he began buying domestic steel shipped by rail.

As his operation grew, Deere left factory activities in the hands of capable subordinates. Meanwhile, he worked on expanding and improving sales by advertising in regional and national farming magazines, demonstrating his wares at state fairs, and competing in plowing contests. In 1857 he turned over the day-to-day operation of the company to his son Charles, although

Deere retained the title of president. Over the next 29 years, he continued to devise small improvements to the various items in his product line, and in 1868 he incorporated the business as Deere & Company. In 1865 his first wife had died, and the following year he had married her sister Lusena. He died on May 17, 1886, in Moline. His company was owned and managed by Deeres for five generations. By 1984 it had become a major manufacturer of tractors, balers, and seeding and harvesting equipment, and it was the biggest builder of farm equipment in the United States.

Further Reading

Broehl, Wayne G., Jr. *John Deere's Company: A History of Deere & Company and its Times.* New York: Doubleday, 1984.

Genuine Value: The John Deere Journey. Moline, Ill.: Deere & Co., 2000.

De Forest, Lee

(1873–1961) *inventor of the audion vacuum tube*

One of the more interesting American inventors is Lee De Forest. He invented the audion, or vacuum tube, which served as an essential component in radio receivers and transmitters until the invention of the transistor, and for this reason he is sometimes called the "father of radio." Although he was a gifted inventor, he was also a poor businessman, and his many inventions enriched others but not him.

De Forest was born on August 26, 1873, in Council Bluffs, Iowa. His father, Henry, was a minister, and his mother, Anna, was a homemaker. At age 16 he moved with his family to Talladega, Alabama, where his father served as a college president. After finishing high school, he attended Yale University's Sheffield Scientific School, receiving a B.S. in 1896 and a Ph.D. in physics in 1899. While at Yale he became interested in electromagnetic wave propagation as a medium of wireless communications. After graduation he moved to Chicago, Illinois, to take a job with the Western Electric Company, which manufactured equipment for the American Telephone & Telegraph Company.

Starting out in the dynamo department, De Forest gradually worked his way to the experimental laboratory. On his own time, he continued to experiment with wireless communications, particularly after 1901 when Guglielmo Marconi successfully transmitted Morse code via radio waves across the Atlantic Ocean. Despite Marconi's feat, at the time the reception of radio waves was poorly understood, and De Forest set out to develop a receiver that would permit further developments in radio. By 1902 he had invented an electrolytic detector of radio waves; that same year he left Western Electric, took on several partners, and formed the De Forest Wireless Telegraph Company. To promote his device, he gave numerous public and private demonstrations, including one at the St. Louis World's Fair in 1904 that was given from atop a huge tower displaying his name in lights. Unfortunately, De Forest's backers were unscrupulous men who defrauded him twice and left the company bankrupt by 1906.

Undaunted, in 1907 De Forest unveiled his greatest invention, the audion vacuum tube. The audion was a modification of the two-electrode radio rectifier patented three years earlier by the English engineer John A. Fleming. Fleming's device converted radio signals from alternating current into direct current, which is much easier to convert into audible sound. However, the direct current produced by Fleming's rectifier was so weak it could be heard only by means of headphones or a telephone receiver. The audion inserted an amplifier grid between the cathode, which emits electrons, and the anode, which collects them, in Fleming's device. Increasing the electrical potential imposed on the grid amplified the flow of electrons caused by the weak direct current signal of Fleming's rectifier, so that the radio signal could be heard by the naked ear from across a room.

In 1907 De Forest took on another set of partners and formed the De Forest Radio Telephone Company to exploit the possibilities of the audion. But, once again, his partners swindled him; they also oversold the company's stock, among other misdeeds, and in 1912 De Forest had to stand trial for using the federal mails to defraud the public. In the ensuing legal brouhaha, the American Marconi Company acquired De Forest's company, and

then sued De Forest over the patent rights to the audion. The case was finally settled by the U.S. Supreme Court in 1916, which granted rights to the audion to both parties.

Although the audion worked better than any other radio receiver on the market, it still did not reproduce speech or music well. In 1912 De Forest solved this problem when he came up with the idea of "cascading," or arranging several audions in series. In this configuration, the first audion amplified the original signal, the second audion amplified the signal from the first audion, and so forth, until live speech or music was coming in loud and clear. That same year, both De Forest and EDWIN HOWARD ARMSTRONG discovered a way to replace cascading by creating a regenerative circuit. This process involved feeding back part of the audion's output signal to its amplifying grid, thus making the output signal progressively louder by using only one audion. Working independently, they also discovered how to use the regenerative circuit as a way to make a more powerful radio transmitter. From 1915 to 1934 the two inventors were locked in an intense legal battle over patent rights to the regenerative circuit, with the Supreme Court ultimately finding in De Forest's favor. Meanwhile, American Telephone & Telegraph (AT&T) had concluded that the audion could be used to amplify long-distance telephone signals. Between 1913 and 1917 the company bought De Forest's rights to the audion, and the device became an essential component in long-distance repeater circuits.

In 1920 De Forest developed a method for adding sound to motion pictures, but the tonal quality was poor and the major studios would have nothing to do with it. Ironically, when "talkies" came out a few years later, they used a method that was quite similar to the one De Forest had developed. During the 1930s he used the audion as a central component in various pieces of medical equipment designed to produce heat in body tissue for therapeutic purposes. During World War II he conducted military research with Bell Telephone Laboratories. None of these lines of inquiry, however, turned up much of anything useful.

De Forest was associated with dozens of firms during the course of his professional life—as a partner, consultant, or employee. He was at his best, however, when he worked alone. A capable inventor, he had absolutely no mind for business, and had he found reliable partners he might have become a wealthy man. As it was, he had to declare bankruptcy in 1936, and when he died his estate was estimated at only $1,200. His personal life was every bit as confused as his professional one. He was married four times, to Lucille Sheardown (1906), Nora Blatch (1908–1911, one child), Mary Mayo (1912–1930, three children), and Marie Mosquini (1930–1961). In 1930 he settled in Hollywood, California, where he died on June 30, 1961.

Further Reading

Hijiya, James A. *Lee de Forest and the Fatherhood of Radio.* Bethlehem, Pa.: Lehigh University Press, 1992.

Lewis, Tom. *Empire of the Air: The Men Who Made Radio.* New York: HarperPerennial, 1993.

CEO of Dell Inc., Michael Dell *(Photo by Manish Swarup/AP)*

Dell, Michael

(1965–) *founder Dell Computers*

As an undergraduate student at the University of Texas in 1984, a teenaged Michael Dell began a computer company with $1,000 and a business strategy centered on building relationships directly with consumers. Eight years later, Dell—powered by his vision, energy, and ingenuity, as well as the galvanizing force of the Internet—became the youngest chief executive officer to ever earn a ranking on the Fortune 500 list of wealthiest Americans.

Michael Saul Dell was born in Houston on February 23, 1964. Dell was the middle son of three born to his orthodontist father, Alexander, and stockbroker/financial consultant mother, Lorraine. He grew up in Houston and demonstrated a high interest and aptitude for math and science while still in elementary school. Although he came from an upper-middle-class home, Dell pursued work opportunities before he was a teen. When he was 12, Dell began working as a dishwasher and maître d' in restaurants before getting a job in a stamp and coin hobby shop, where one of his duties was assessing the value of metal and negotiating a purchase price with customers. Dell spent some of the money he earned from these jobs to invest in

stocks himself and purchased an Apple IIe computer, which he took apart and reassembled to satisfy his curiosity and joy in discovering how things worked.

Dell's business experience as a teenager also included a job selling subscriptions to a Houston newspaper. In researching the best way to do this, Dell discovered that the people most likely to sign up for a new subscription were newlyweds and people moving to a new home. Dell then collected the contact information from public records on these groups of people by hiring friends to visit each of the 16 counties in and around Houston. Armed with this information, Dell sent direct mail appeals and his efforts paid off. In one year he earned $18,000.

After graduating from Memorial High School in Hedwig Village, Texas, in 1983, Dell enrolled as a premed student at the University of Texas in Austin. However, instead of studying biology, Dell was spending much of his time starting a computer components business. Dell later explained, "Around Thanksgiving of 1983, my parents kind of made me commit that I wasn't going to do this computer business anymore. I was only going to focus on my studies. So that lasted about ten days. It was during that time that I decided that I was going to start a company. So actually, my parents telling me to stop doing it is probably what caused the company to get created. If they hadn't done that it might've just been a hobby. But what I kind of reflected on in those ten days is that I really love this, and it was enormously exciting, tremendously fun." It also quickly became tremendously successful and led the 19-year-old Dell to drop out of college to pursue his business endeavor, named PCs Limited, full time.

He started placing advertisements in computer magazines that appealed to businesspeople and selling computer upgrade kits and soon was able to expand most of his business beyond the Austin area. Dell's focus on making customized computers to order and getting them to the consumer typically quicker and at a lower cost than other companies led to fast success and growth. During its first year PCs Limited had more than $6 million in sales, and Dell became known throughout the computer world as a boy wonder. In 1987, he changed the company's name to Dell Computer Corporation and sales continued to rise, reaching nearly $160 million by the end of 1988. Also in 1988, Dell made an initial public offering which raised $30 million, with almost two-thirds of that money going to Michael Dell.

Dell and his computer company continued to enjoy prosperity into the 1990s, generating $800 million in sales in 1991 and $2 billion in 1992. However, intense competition and difficulty keeping up with its rate of growth led to problems. By mid-1993, the company's stock price was plummeting and several top executives were leaving. Dell decided to hire many high-priced and more experienced managers and—against much of the conventional wisdom of the time—to focus on business customers and direct marketing rather than retail sales. This strategy resuscitated the company. Selling fully customized PCs via the phone led to sales of approximately $5.5 billion by early 1996. In July 1996, Dell established the first direct-sale computer Web site, and within three years Internet sales accounted for $30 million a day in sales.

Throughout the first years of the 21st century, Dell amassed accolades as one of the world's top entrepreneurs and leading chief executive officers. The company—renamed Dell Inc. to reflect its expansion beyond computers—regularly ranked among the best places to work and enjoyed pop culture renown from the series of popular "Dude, you're getting a Dell" television ads. Critics pointed to the company's lack of innovation, but the company remained a leader among computer consumers. Dell stepped down as CEO in March of 2004 to focus more on his philanthropic activities, though he remained the chairman of the board. He returned as CEO in January 2007. In 2009, *Fortune* magazine ranked Dell as the 25th richest person in the world, with a total wealth of over $12 billion.

Michel Dell lives in Austin, near his company's Round Rock, Texas, headquarters. He has been married since 1989 to wife Susan and together they are the parents to three daughters and one son.

Further Reading

Dell, Michael. *Direct from Dell: Strategies That Revolutionized an Industry.* New York: Collins, 2000.
Fishman, Charles. "Face Time with Michael Dell." Fast Company. Available online. URL: http: //www.fastcompany.com/magazine/44/dell.html. Downloaded on July 28, 2009.
"Michael Dell Interview," Academy of Achievement. Available online. URL: http://www.achievement.org/autodoc/page/del0int-1. Downloaded on July 28, 2009.

Disney, Walt
(Walter Elias Disney)
(1901–1966) *pioneer in animation and cinematography, creator of Mickey Mouse*

Ask any red-blooded American child who is not old enough to drive where he or she wants to go, and the answer probably will be "Disneyland!" or "Disney World!" These citadels of fantasy, sentimentality, and nostalgia are permanent monuments to the artistic and business acumen of Walt Disney, the creator of Mickey Mouse. Disney was also one of the best animators, cinematographers, entertainers, and business promoters who ever lived.

Disney was born Walter Elias Disney on December 5, 1901, in Chicago, Illinois. His father, Elias, was a building contractor, and his mother, Flora, was a teacher. Shortly after his birth, his parents moved the family to Marceline, Missouri, where his father bought a farm. Having tired of farming within a few years, they moved to Kansas City, Missouri. With the help of Walt and his brother Roy, Elias supported the family by delivering the morning newspaper. While not flinging papers, Walt went to public school, took a correspondence course in cartooning, and briefly attended the Kansas City Art Institute and School of Design. At age 15 his family resettled in Chicago; Disney went to high school during the day and attended the Art Institute of Chicago at night in the hope of becoming a newspaper cartoonist. In 1918 he dropped out of school to serve as an ambulance driver for the American Red Cross during World War I. After the war he returned to Kansas City, finding work as an artist with the Pesman-Rubin Commercial Art Studio and then as an animator with the Kansas City Film Ad Company.

In 1922 Disney and Ub Iwerks, a fellow artist at Pesman-Rubin, formed Laugh-O-gram Films. They bought a used movie camera and began making short animated advertising films, which played before the main features in movie theaters. (In those days, a day at the movies included several ads, one or more cartoons and/or other short features, a newsreel, and a full-length feature movie.) They also made a series of animated cartoons called "Laugh-O-Grams" and a seven-minute feature called *Alice's Comedies.* But after a New York City film distributor swindled the two partners, they closed the company and Disney moved to Los Angeles, California.

In 1923 Disney and his brother Roy formed Disney Brothers Studio, with Roy as business manager and Disney as art director and producer. Shortly thereafter they signed a contract with Margaret Winkler, a national film distributor, to produce a series of short comedies featuring the Alice character. They were soon joined by Iwerks, who helped Disney design and draw a series of cartoons featuring a character called Oswald the Lucky Rabbit. By 1927 Oswald's adventures were being shown across the country in theaters affiliated with Universal Studios. Their popularity led to one of the first movie/merchandise tie-ins, Oswald the Lucky Rabbit candy bars. Unfortunately, Disney's success attracted the attention of Charles Mintz,

a movie producer who, as Winkler's husband, co-controlled the copyrights to Oswald. In an effort to force Disney to work for him, Mintz hired away all of Disney's illustrators except Iwerks; when Disney refused to join Mintz, he completed the Oswald series without Disney.

Undaunted, Disney and Iwerks created another character, the legendary Mickey Mouse. (The mouse's original name was Mortimer, but Disney's wife, the former Lillian Bounds whom he had married in 1925 and with whom he had two children, nixed that name in favor of Mickey.) Fortuitously, Mickey came along at about the same time as sound. After making two silent cartoons featuring Mickey, Disney contacted Pat Powers, a former Universal Studios executive turned film distributor and the proprietor of a sound process called Cinephone. Powers agreed to license Cinephone to Disney if he could distribute Disney's films. Disney's first production to include sound was "Steamboat Willie" (1928), starring Mickey Mouse, with Walt himself supplying Mickey's voice. "Steamboat Willie" received rave reviews from critics and the general public which clamored for more Mickey cartoons. Over the next two years, Disney Brothers produced a number of Mickey features, as well as a new series called "Silly Symphonies," featuring animated characters cavorting to classical music. But just as the studio seemed on the verge of becoming hugely profitable, in 1930 Powers hired away Iwerks and canceled the contract to distribute Disney's films, thus hoping to get Disney to work for him.

Unlike the distribution deal involving Oswald, Disney (ably advised by his brother Roy) had retained the copyrights to Mickey Mouse, so he simply hired more illustrators and found a new distributor. This was easy enough to do because his cartoon shorts were so unique that the public demanded more. Despite the vicissitudes of the Great Depression, or perhaps because of them, people flocked to see Disney productions in the movie houses. He created new characters such as Minnie Mouse, Donald Duck, and Goofy, and by 1935 his studio was putting out 20 short features per year. Unlike his competitors, whose cartoons were filled with slapstick and double entendres, Disney's short features focused on the wholesome activities of likeable little characters who were essentially human in spirit if not in form. Coupled with the profits from product tie-ins such as Mickey Mouse watches, dolls, shirts, and toys, the company showed a net annual profit of well more than $500,000 during the worst years of the depression.

In 1935 Disney Brothers made its first feature-length film, *Snow White and the Seven Dwarfs,* the first animated film with sound and color. The film received high praise for its production values, which Disney had honed by refining several animation techniques, closely monitoring story development, and establishing an in-house animator training school connected with Los Angeles's Chouinard School of Art. It also grossed $4.2 million from the initial release alone, enough to build a modern studio in nearby Burbank, and was the first animated movie ever to receive an Academy Award. Over the next 10 years, Disney produced a number of other highly successful full-length animated features. After World War II, MGM and Warner Bros., two major Hollywood studios, began competing with Disney by creating animation divisions of their own. This competition, coupled with the rising costs of animation, led Disney to eliminate animated shorts in favor of full-length animated features including *Pinocchio, Fantasia,* and *Bambi.* Soon the studio began making "true-life adventures" and live-action movies such as *Seal Island* (1949) and *Treasure Island* (1950).

In 1950 Disney Studio produced its first television show, *One Hour in Wonderland,* a feature promoting its latest animated film, *Alice in Wonderland.* Over the next 15 years, Disney would emerge as the unparalleled master of interweaving various media in a way that they promoted each other. In 1955 America's most unique theme park, Disneyland, opened in Anaheim, California. The park was owned jointly by Disney; American Broadcasting-Paramount Theaters, which distributed Disney movies and aired Disney television series such as *The Mickey Mouse Club, Zorro,* and *Davy Crockett;* and Western Printing and Lithographing Company, which published Disney juvenile books, coloring books, and comics. During the late 1950s, the park promoted the movies, television programs, and books, which in turn promoted the park. Meanwhile, Disney profited immensely from merchandise tie-ins with Mickey Mouse hats, Zorro swords and capes, Davy Crockett coonskin caps, and a plethora of items bearing the likenesses of his cartoon characters. By 1966 the Disney empire had become an awesome thing to behold. That same year, there were about 160 million people living in the United States, of whom 240 million saw a Disney movie, 100 million watched a Disney television program, 800 million read a Disney book or magazine, 50 million listened to a Disney record, 80 million bought a Disney toy or product, 150 million read a Disney comic strip, 80 million saw a Disney educational film, and 7 million visited Disneyland. Also that year, Disney plans for building an East Coast Disneyland, called Disney World, were well under way in Orlando, Florida.

Throughout his life, Disney cared little for critics who denigrated his work. It was his opinion that he sold entertainment, not art, and during his day fantasy, sentimentality, and nostalgia were in great demand. He died on December 15, 1966, in Burbank.

Further Reading

Brands, H. W. *Masters of Enterprise: Giants of American Business from John Jacob Astor and J. P. Morgan to Bill Gates and Oprah Winfrey.* New York: The Free Press, 1999.

Crompton, Samuel W. *100 Americans Who Shaped American History.* San Mateo, Calif.: Bluewood Books, 1999.

Thomas, Bob. *Walt Disney: An American Original.* New York: Hyperion, 1994.

Donovan, Marion O'Brien
(1917–1998) *inventor of the disposable diaper*

During her lifetime, Marion Donovan received a dozen patents. But her most important invention inspired the development of the modern disposable diaper. Although the diaper Donovan designed never went into production, it inspired other inventors to design more modern disposables. It has been said that Donovan, by inventing the disposable diaper, did more than any other female to liberate women from the drudgery of home life.

Donovan was born Marion O'Brien in Fort Wayne, Indiana. Her father and uncle were machinists who invented and manufactured machine tools for the automotive industry. As a young girl she spent much of her spare time helping out in their shop. After graduating from high school, she enrolled in Rosemont College in Philadelphia where she earned a B.A. in English literature in 1939. She then moved to New York City to work for *Vogue* magazine as assistant beauty editor. A few years later she married James Donovan, a leather importer, and moved to Westport, Connecticut, where she became a full-time housewife and mother.

In the 1940s babies wore cloth diapers held together with safety pins. When the baby urinated, the diapers got soggy and held the urine next to the skin which resulted in diaper rash. Once the diapers got wet, the baby's clothes and crib sheets got wet too. Rubber pants helped contain some of the moisture, but they often leaked, and during World War II they were virtually impossible to obtain. Consequently, babies stayed wet and cold, often had a skin rash, and often got pricked with safety pins. To make matters worse, mothers usually had a mountain of dirty diapers and laundry to wash.

At first Donovan simply wanted to make a better diaper cover. This she did by cutting a piece from an old rubber shower curtain and sewing it into a pair of baby pants. But then she got the idea to sew the piece of shower curtain into an envelope, then stuff the envelope with absorbent paper. The paper drew away much of the moisture from the diaper itself, thus helping to keep the baby's skin dry and rash free. She also added plastic snaps to eliminate the possibility of stabbing the baby with a safety pin. The result was the Boater, so called by Donovan because it helped baby "stay afloat."

In 1949 Donovan convinced Saks Fifth Avenue, a major New York department store, to buy a small quantity of Boaters. After consumers eagerly snapped them up, Donovan tried to sell her idea to various paper manufacturers. When none of them showed any interest in making baby pants, she stated her own company and began manufacturing Boaters herself. Boaters continued to sell well, and Donovan eventually sold her company for $1 million.

Meanwhile Donovan had also invented the first disposable diaper. By today's standards, it was crude; it was made entirely out of the same type of absorbent paper that lined Boaters. Once again Donovan tried to interest paper manufacturers in her invention, and once again these companies failed to see the profit in making a disposable baby product. Not until the 1950s, when Victor Mills, a design engineer with Procter & Gamble, created Pampers, did the first mass-produced disposable diaper come into existence.

Boaters was Donovan's most successful invention, but it was not her only one. She invented the Big Hangup, a compact closet hanger that held up to 30 garments; a soap dish that drained directly into the sink; and the Zippity-Do, an elastic cord that made it easier for a woman to zip up the back of her dress. In 1958 she earned a degree in architecture from Yale University and eventually designed her dream home, which she had built in Greenwich, Connecticut.

Disposables helped liberate babies from diaper rash and wet bottoms and helped liberate mothers from doing mounds of laundry. They also made traveling with babies much easier by eliminating the necessity of taking along powder, rash ointment, pins, and rubber pants, not to mention piles of bulky cloth diapers. Although Donovan received little credit for her role in the development of the disposable diaper, she played an instrumental part in making it a reality.

Further Reading

Macdonald, Anne L. *Feminine Ingenuity: Women and Invention in America.* New York: Ballantine Books, 1994.
"Marion Donovan (1917–1998)," The Lemuelson-MIT Program. Available online. URL: http://web.mit.edu/invent/iow/donovan.html. Downloaded on July 2, 2009.

Dorrance, John Thompson
(1873–1930) *inventor of condensed soup*

John Dorrance did not invent canned soup. He did, however, figure out how to condense it without losing any of the flavor and then how to sell it to grocers and homemakers. In the process, he made Campbell's Soup a household name.

Dorrance was born on November 11, 1873, in Bristol, Pennsylvania. His father, John, was a businessman, and his mother, Elizabeth, was a homemaker. After graduating from the Massachusetts Institute of Technology in 1895, he attended the University of Gottingen in Germany and received a Ph.D. in chemistry in 1897. His uncle, Arthur Dorrance, was president of the Joseph Campbell Preserve Company in Camden, New Jersey, and when Dorrance returned to the United States, he convinced his reluctant uncle to hire him as the company chemist. The company had been founded in 1869 by Joseph Campbell, a fruit merchant, and Abram Anderson, an icebox manufacturer, to can fruit preserves, tomatoes, and vegetables. In 1876 Anderson left the company and Arthur Dorrance took his place. In 1894 Campbell retired and Arthur Dorrance assumed control of the company. By the time Dorrance joined Campbell, it was canning almost 200 different products, including a handful of soups.

While in Germany, Dorrance had been impressed by how much soup Germans ate. He began to investigate the possibility of selling more soup to Americans, and he was surprised to find out that none of the three largest soup canners in the United States was making much money. Further investigation showed the reason why; none of them sold condensed soup but instead sold their soup in 32-ounce cans that were two-thirds full of water. Dorrance concluded that condensing the amount of water in the soup would reduce the price of a can by about two-thirds without affecting the quality of the soup in any way. Moreover, the soup could be marketed as a convenience product; all the customer had to do was add water, heat the soup which had already been cooked in the cannery, and eat it.

Dorrance's uncle was skeptical about his nephew's idea at first, but he eventually allowed Dorrance to produce a test batch to see how it would sell. Having attended college in Boston, Massachusetts, Dorrance chose it as his "test city." He was probably as shocked as his uncle was when he sold a carload of 10-ounce cans of condensed tomato soup to various grocers on just one sales trip in 1899. His uncle immediately embraced the idea and geared up Campbell for the production of condensed soup. He also promoted Dorrance to vice president.

Under Dorrance's direction, the Campbell soup division quickly gained almost total control over the American soup market. While competitors sold noncondensed soup for more than 30¢ per can, Campbell sold condensed soup for 10¢ per can. Heavy advertising on streetcars and in ladies' magazines convinced customers that "soup is good food" as well as being inexpensive and easy to fix. By holding down its per-can profit to less than a penny, Campbell discouraged other competitors from producing condensed soup.

While Campbell was taking over the soup market, Dorrance was taking over Campbell. He began buying stock in the company in the early 1900s, and by 1906, when he married Ethel Mallinckrodt with whom he had five children, he had become a major stockholder. In 1914 he became president, and by the following year he had acquired all but nine shares of Campbell stock. As president, he eliminated the production of all non-soup products except pork and beans, which were canned only on Mondays while the soup broth simmered. By focusing on soup, Campbell enjoyed an economy of scale not available to its more diverse competitors, further contributing to its dominance of the soup market. The company's near-total focus on soup was made clear in 1922, when the name was changed from Joseph Campbell Company (its name since 1905) to the Campbell Soup Company. Between 1915 and 1930, the years of Dorrance's presidency, Campbell produced almost 90 percent of all the canned soup sold in the United States.

Other than soup, Dorrance's tastes included a fondness for traveling throughout Europe and the United States. He died in Cinnaminson, New Jersey, where he had moved in 1911. At the time of his death, his estate was valued at $115 million.

Further Reading

Chapin, Earl. *The Canning Clan: A Pageant of Pioneering Americans.* New York: The Macmillan Co., 1937.

Collins, Douglas. *America's Favorite Food: The Story of Campbell Soup Company.* New York: Harry N. Abrams, 1994.

Drake, Samuel
(Samuel Drake Bryant)

(1768–1854) *entrepreneur in professional theater*

In the days before televisions and movie theaters, the only form of professional entertainment most Americans could enjoy was theatrical productions. Before 1815, the only stage performances Americans living west of Pittsburgh, Pennsylvania, could attend were those performed by local amateurs. Samuel Drake, a lifelong actor and director, changed this by establishing the first professional acting troupe on the frontier.

Little is known about the first 40 years of Drake's life. He was born in 1768 somewhere in England to parents whose names and occupations are unknown. However, it seems likely that their last name was Bryant, and that Drake dropped this name when he became an actor but kept his first and middle names. He seems to have worked briefly as a printer's apprentice, then ran away with a roving band of theatrical performers. He married Alexina Fisher, an actress, probably in the early 1790s; they had five children, all of whom eventually became stage performers. At some point Drake stopped touring to become the stage manager (who performed the same duties as a modern-day director in addition to acting) of a small theater in western England.

In 1809 Drake relocated to Boston, Massachusetts, where he became the stage manager for the Federal Street Theatre. In 1813 he took a similar position in Albany, New York. In 1814, following Alexina's death, Drake seems to have contemplated retiring from the stage when he was approached by Noble Luke Usher, an actor from Kentucky. Usher and his father had built several makeshift theaters in the principal settlements of Kentucky, and they needed a professional stage manager and troupe. Drake was captivated by the idea of taking professional theater to the frontier, and he organized a 12-person theatrical company, including himself and his five children, which left Albany for Kentucky the following year.

Transportation being primitive in the early 1800s, it took seven months for Drake's company to reach Kentucky. Between Albany and Olean, New York, a distance of almost 250 miles, they traveled on foot, carrying their costumes and scenery in an ox-drawn wagon. They earned their keep by performing in the towns along the way. At Olean, the troupe loaded itself into a flat-bottomed boat and continued its journey by way of the Allegheny River. Upon reaching Pittsburgh, the troupe was joined by five other actors and spent the summer season performing in a dilapidated building. Then they got back on the boat for the 400-mile voyage down the Ohio River to Kentucky, stopping and performing at river communities along the way.

Upon arriving in Kentucky, Drake discovered that Usher's "theaters" were actually converted barns and warehouses that were poorly suited to the needs of a professional company and its audience. Unperturbed, Drake arranged for the theater in Louisville to be renovated according to his own specifications, and for the next eight years he made this theater the troupe's home base. From Louisville he established a successful circuit for his troupe that included Lexington and Frankfort, where Drake had also had the theaters renovated. His goal, at which he succeeded admirably in Kentucky, was to provide quality plays performed by skilled actors and actresses on attractive sets. His troupe performed two plays per evening, mostly farces and sentimental comedies, which were highly entertaining without being scandalous. He also tried to establish a circuit that included the more distant river communities of Cincinnati, Vincennes, and St. Louis, but evidently the transportation obstacle was too great to overcome and the circuit was not successful. In 1823 Drake turned over the management of the troupe and the circuit to his eldest son Alexander and spent his remaining days on a substantial farm he had purchased in Oldham County. He died on his farm on October 16, 1854.

Further Reading

Casto, Marilyn D. *Actors, Audiences, and Historic Theaters of Kentucky.* Lexington: University Press of Kentucky, 2000.

Ford, George D. *These Were Actors: A Story of the Chapmans and the Drakes.* New York: Library Pub., 1955.

Drew, Richard Gurley
(1899–1980) *inventor of Scotch tape*

Before duct tape was invented, the all-purpose repair tool was Scotch tape. Scotch tape is still the perfect tool for repairing torn paper, posting notes, and hanging posters on a bedroom or office wall, but once upon a time it was also used to fix just about everything around the house. The inventor of this wonderful item was Richard Drew, who received most of his formal training as an engineer by taking correspondence courses.

Drew was born on June 22, 1899, in St. Paul, Minnesota. His father, Edward, was a clothing salesman, and his mother, Margaret, was a homemaker. By the time he finished high school he was a skilled banjo player, and he paid for his first year at the University of Minnesota by playing in a band at night. He dropped out and took a day job when his father died so he could help support his family, and he studied mechanical engineering via correspondence courses. In 1921 he went to work for the Minnesota Mining and Manufacturing Company (later known as 3M) as a laboratory technician with the coated abrasives division. One of his duties was to deliver and pick up sandpaper samples at local auto body shops, where they were tested.

In 1923 Drew became aware of a unique opportunity. Auto manufacturers had recently introduced the two-tone paint job, where the upper portion of the car is painted one color and the lower portion is painted another color. Although this new style was attractive and helped sell a lot of cars, it drove bodymen crazy when they had to repaint a car. At the time, there was no good way to mask one color while the other color was being applied; the various tapes and other masking alternatives either failed to properly mask the color that had already been applied, or they peeled off the paint they were masking when removed. One day Drew happened to be in a body shop when a commotion erupted because a particularly horrible masking failure ruined a beautiful paint job.

In the heat of the moment, Drew promised the workers at the body shop that he would solve the problem. Upon reporting back to the laboratory, his bemused boss allowed him to devote his spare time on the job to finding a solution. Drew quickly realized that the solution involved developing some sort of paper/glue tape, like a strip of sandpaper without the abrasive coating. Its paper backing had to be flexible enough to stretch flat around curved body parts without ripping, and it had to stand up to the corrosive properties of auto paint. Its adhesive had to be sticky enough so that finger pressure would make it adhere to body parts, but not so sticky that it peeled off the paint when it was removed or stuck to itself when rolled up. Also, the adhesive had to maintain the right degree of stickiness in hot or cold storage conditions.

For two years Drew experimented with various paper-and-glue concoctions, all to no avail. Then one day, while rummaging through the warehouse, he discovered a load of crimped paper, similar to the type used in paper towels found in modern public restrooms, that seemed perfect for the job. Shortly thereafter he applied a rubber-based adhesive to a long strip of the crimped paper. The result was Scotch Brand Masking Tape, and 3M began manufacturing it in 1925. Masking tape was a tremendous hit, with bodymen and a host of other workmen, and within a year 3M formed a new division, the 3M Tape Group, to keep up with the demand. In 1926 the new division formed a laboratory dedicated to adapting masking tape for other industrial applications, and Drew transferred into this unit.

In 1927 Du Pont developed cellophane as a transparent, moisture-proof packaging material, and it became popular as a way to wrap fresh foods so they could be displayed and preserved at the same time. Unfortunately, the only way to seal a cellophane package was by tying it with string or using a nontransparent tape, neither of which provided a moisture-proof seal and both of which ruined the appearance of the package. The following year Drew set out to develop a tape that could solve this problem. He figured that all he had to do was develop a transparent glue and then affix it to the back of a strip of cellophane. Doing all this by hand proved to be simple enough; however, when it came time to mass-produce cellophane tape, he ran into major problems. It turned out that cellophane was almost too brittle to be machined, plus it curled when it got too hot and split when coated with adhesive. Consequently, he had to design new machinery to cut it into long strips, coat it evenly with glue, and roll it up. He also had to devise a new adhesive that did not split cellophane. By 1930 he had created cellophane tape, popularly known as Scotch tape, and developed a way to manufacture it. Scotch tape turned out to be even more popular than masking tape. Serendipitously, it came out just before the Great Depression, when people were looking for ways to make their old stuff last longer. Scotch tape proved to be the perfect way to fix most household problems, from repairing torn lampshades to covering up mouse holes.

In 1935 Drew married Lorna Cassin with whom he had one child; after her death, in 1957 he married Margaret Page. In 1943 he became the technical director of 3M's products fabrication laboratory. He retired from this position in 1962, but stayed on as consultant for five more years. In 1967 he moved to Santa Barbara, California, where he died on December 14, 1980. Meanwhile, 3M continued to make tape, and by the end of the century it had developed more than 600 different industrial and household tape products, the annual sales of which exceeded $1 billion.

Further Reading

"3M History," 3M Worldwide. Available online. URL: http://www.3M.com/profile/looking/index.jhtml. Downloaded on July 2, 2009.

3M Technical Liaison Department. *Richard Drew, the Inventor.* St. Paul, Minn.: 3M Corp., 1996.

Duke, James Buchanan

(1856–1925) *founder of the American Tobacco Company*

James Duke did not invent the cigarette. That honor belongs to the beggars of 16th-century Seville, Spain, who shredded discarded cigar butts and rolled the shreds in scraps of paper. However, Duke is more responsible than any single individual for making cigarettes popular the world over. By becoming the first tobacconist to mass-produce cheap cigarettes and then promote them among the masses, Duke created an international demand for cigarettes.

Duke was born on December 23, 1856, near Durham, North Carolina. His parents, Washington and Artelia, were farmers. When Duke was nine years old, his father began growing nothing but bright-leaf tobacco for smoking and chewing, and in 1874 his father built a small factory in Durham for making pipe and chewing tobacco. Duke helped out with the business when not attending school, and upon graduating from the Eastman School of Business in Poughkeepsie, New York, in 1878, he, his brother Benjamin, and his father incorporated the business as W. Duke, Sons and Company.

At the time, most Americans who used tobacco either smoked it in a pipe or cigar or chewed it. Consequently, virtually every large American tobacco manufacturer made either pipe or chewing tobacco, usually both, while cigars were generally produced by hand in small shops. For various reasons, dark-leaf tobacco, particularly that which thrives in Virginia and Kentucky, was preferred by most chewers and pipe smokers, while Connecticut dark-leaf was preferred by cigar smokers. Bright-leaf tobacco, which thrives in North Carolina, was in little demand outside the state, and by 1881 W. Duke was forced either to find new uses for its tobacco or to go out of business.

At this point Duke convinced his father and brother to take a gamble on cigarettes. "Little cigars" had been introduced into the United States from Europe just before the Civil War, and in 1880 James Bonsack had invented a cigarette-rolling machine that fed shredded tobacco onto a continuous strip of paper, then formed, pasted, closed, and cut the cigarette into the desired length. Most American tobacco users, however, thought cigarettes were effeminate, and most of the ones who did smoke cigarettes preferred to roll their own out of pipe tobacco rather than buy machine-made ones. Nevertheless, Duke set out to create a market in the United States for manufactured cigarettes. He bought two of Bonsack's machines and then hired a mechanic to work out the design flaws; soon each machine was turning out 120,000 cigarettes per day. He also used lower-priced bright-leaf tobacco instead of the more expensive pipe tobacco. These two innovations allowed him to sell his cigarettes for a nickel a pack rather than a dime, the rate other cigarette manufacturers were charging. He also established a network of sales agents in major cities, spent heavily on advertising, offered customers premiums and prizes, and established contacts with jobbers in other countries. This marketing campaign was hugely successful, and in 1884 Duke opened a second cigarette factory in New York City, where he also moved the company's headquarters. By 1889 W. Duke was making more than 800 million cigarettes per year and doing annual sales of more than $4 million.

Meanwhile, four other companies had sprung up to compete with W. Duke for the cigarette market. Competition threatened to become so ruinous that in 1890 Duke successfully arranged a merger of the five leading cigarette manufacturers into the American Tobacco Company, with Duke as president. By 1898 American Tobacco was selling almost 4 billion cigarettes per year and controlled virtually the entire cigarette industry in the United States. This success led Duke to get involved in other aspects of the tobacco industry. In the mid-1890s he began buying pipe and chewing tobacco factories, modernizing their manufacturing operations, and initiating major advertising campaigns. His success permitted him to mastermind the formation of combinations of companies in other areas of tobacco production in much the same way as he had done with cigarettes. In 1898 he formed the Continental Tobacco Company, a conglomerate of chewing tobacco manufacturers with himself as president; in 1900 he helped organize the American Snuff Company; and in 1901 he helped consolidate a large part of the cigar industry by cofounding the American Cigar Company and the United Cigar Stores Company. In 1901 he oversaw the formation of the Consolidated Tobacco Company, a holding company that combined the assets of American Tobacco and Continental Tobacco; three years later the holding company was renamed American Tobacco. And in 1902 he helped arrange the agreement between Consolidated and the Imperial Tobacco Company, a British conglomerate, to stay out of each other's country and to cooperate rather than compete in the international market via the jointly owned British-American Tobacco Company, with Duke as chairman of the board. Duke's positions with these various firms made him the most important figure of his day in the U.S. tobacco industry, and his companies operated more than 150 factories around the world. In 1904 Duke married Lillian McCredy; they divorced two years later, and in 1907 he married Nanine Holt Inman with whom he had one child.

In 1904 Duke and his brother Benjamin founded the Southern Power Company, known today as Duke Power, for purposes of providing cheap hydroelectricity to industries in North Carolina. Although the U.S. Justice Department forced the breakup of American Tobacco in 1911, Duke continued to serve as chairman of British-American until 1923. In his later years he devoted most of his attention to his power company and to his charitable interests. In 1924 he created the Duke Endowment, a charitable foundation that provided the funding to move tiny Trinity College from Trinity, North Carolina, to Durham, where it was transformed into Duke University. He died on October 10, 1925, in New York City.

Further Reading

Chandler, Alfred D., Jr. *The Visible Hand: The Managerial Revolution in American Business.* Cambridge, Mass.: Belknap Press, 1977.

Durden, Robert F. *The Dukes of Durham, 1865–1929.* Durham, N.C.: Duke University Press, 1975.

"James Buchanan Duke." Duke University Archives. Available online. URL: http://library.duke.edu/uarchives/history/histnotes/james_b_duke.html. Downloaded on July 2, 2009.

du Pont de Nemours, Éleuthère Irénée

(1771–1834) *founder of the Du Pont Company*

Over the years, Du Pont has emerged as one of the most innovative developers of synthetic fibers in the world. Headquartered in Wilmington, Delaware, today the company has plants and offices all over the world. Ironically, the company was founded in the United States to make gunpowder by an expatriate Frenchman whose first name means "peace."

Du Pont was born on June 24, 1771, in Paris, France. His father, Pierre, the future comte de Nemours, was a political economist, and his mother, Nicole, was a socialite. As a student, he showed little enthusiasm for any subject other than gunpowder, which fascinated him. At age 14 he enrolled in the College Royal in Paris, and after two years of study he was offered a position in the Regie des Poudres et Salpítres, the French government's agency in charge of the manufacture of gunpowder. At the Regie, he studied under Antoine Lavoisier, the famous chemist, and then served an apprenticeship at Essonnes, the government's gunpowder plant. In 1791 he married Sophie Dalmas with whom he had eight children, and became the manager of the publishing house that his father had founded. Shortly thereafter, du Pont and his father became caught up in the French Revolution; both were arrested and narrowly escaped being killed by an angry mob. In 1799 his father sold the publishing house and the entire family emigrated to the United States. They settled in Bergen Point, New Jersey, and opened an office in New York City without knowing exactly what sort of business they were in.

In 1800 du Pont went hunting with Colonel Louis Toussard, a former French officer who had settled near Wilmington, Delaware, after taking part in the American Revolution. Du Pont was stunned that the domestic-made gunpowder they used cost so much and worked so poorly. After Toussard arranged for him to visit an American powder works, he discovered that Americans had no idea how to refine gunpowder. He convinced his father to allow him to go into the gunpowder business, and in 1801 he returned to France to obtain equipment and raise money for their venture from his father's old friends and acquaintances. The French government proved to be most supportive, and it even sold du Pont state-of-the-art equipment at cost. Du Pont located his company, which he named E. I. du Pont de Nemours & Company, on a tract of land south of Wilmington on Brandywine Creek close to Toussard's estate; in time, the area became known as Eleutherian Mills. Alexander Hamilton served as du Pont's legal counsel in arranging water rights and other matters. Du Pont also took on as a partner Peter Bauduy, who provided the funds needed to complete the powder works. In 1804 du Pont became an American citizen and his company opened for business; President Thomas Jefferson put in a good word for

the company with the War Department, largely because du Pont's father had used his influence in France to help bring about the Louisiana Purchase. Government orders for almost 45,000 pounds of powder allowed the company to show a profit of $10,000 its first year.

The company prospered further in the early 1800s, partly because the Embargo Act forbade the importation of gunpowder from either England or France, and partly because the War of 1812 generated a demand by the government for almost 1 million pounds of powder. In 1814 du Pont bought out Bauduy and took sole ownership of the company. Over the next 20 years du Pont built his company into the largest gunpowder manufacturer in the United States. He died on October 31, 1834, in Philadelphia, Pennsylvania. For more than 100 years Du Pont, as the company became popularly known, remained in the hands of his descendants, and in the 20th century it became one of the world's leading manufacturers of chemicals, plastics, and synthetic fibers. Two of the company's top researchers, WALLACE HUME CAROTHERS and STEPHANIE LOUISE KWOLEK, would develop two of the 20th century's most important fibers, nylon and Kevlar, respectively.

Further Reading

Colby, Gerard. *du Pont Dynasty*. Secaucus, N.J.: L. Stuart, 1984.

Vare, Ethlie Ann, and Greg Ptacek. *Women Inventors and Their Discoveries*. Minneapolis: Oliver Press, 1993.

Durant, William Crapo
(1861–1947) *founder of General Motors*

In terms of sales, General Motors Corporation is one of the largest corporations in the world. Its several divisions produce a car or truck for almost every budget and taste, and its many subsidiaries produce most of the parts that go into making those vehicles. The person most responsible for creating General Motors was William Durant, who was recruited into the auto industry because of his success as a manufacturer of horse-drawn carts.

Durant was born William Crapo Durant on December 8, 1861, in Boston, Massachusetts. His father, William, was a businessman, and his mother, Rebecca, was a homemaker. At age 10 his father deserted the family, and Durant moved with his mother to Flint, Michigan, where she had grown up. In 1879 he dropped out of high school, and went to work as a sawyer by day and a salesman of patent medicines by night. Over the next seven years he also sold cigars, worked as a bookkeeper for the local water company, and opened a fire insurance agency. In 1885 he married Clara Pitt with whom he had two children. They divorced in 1908, and that same year he married Catherine Lederer.

In 1886 Durant and J. Dallas Dort bought a company that made horse-drawn carts. They moved it to Flint, expanded its product line to include carriages, buggies, and wagons, and established small sales and service centers throughout the Great Lakes region. Six years later they renamed the company the Durant-Dort Carriage Company and began acquiring manufacturers of the various components that went into horse-drawn vehicles. They also moved these companies to Flint and made the company an integrated manufacturing concern that bought most of its parts from itself. By 1900 Durant-Dort was the largest maker of horse-drawn vehicles in the United States.

In 1901 Durant sold his interest in the company for a considerable amount of money and moved to New York City, without his family, to invest in the stock market. In 1904 he returned to Flint at the invitation of a group of investors headed by James H. Whiting, president of Durant's old company, who had purchased the ailing Buick Manufacturing Company. After test-driving one of the company's automobiles, Durant agreed to take over as president. He immediately began implementing the same strategy for making and selling cars that had worked so well with carriages. Buick was moved to Flint, its product line was expanded to include a vehicle for every budget, the old wagon works was retooled to manufacture auto parts, other parts manufacturers were acquired and moved to Flint, and a nationwide network of sales and service centers was established. Four years later, Buick was making more cars than anyone else in the industry, and it was selling cars as fast as it could make them.

In 1908 Durant moved to create a corporation that would consolidate the automobile industry in much the same way that United States Steel and Standard Oil had consolidated theirs. After trying and failing to arrange a merger among Buick, Ford, Oldsmobile, Cadillac, and other automakers, that same year he formed the General Motors Company. With Buick as a subsidiary, General Motors was able to borrow enough money to acquire several of the companies Durant had tried to merge with, including Oldsmobile, Cadillac, and Oakland (later known as Pontiac), as well as almost 20 smaller producers of autos, trucks, and auto parts. But except for Buick, which continued to operate smoothly and profitably, the other companies were never integrated in a coherent manner. Rather than cooperate, they continued to compete with each other, and the giant automaker seemed stuck in neutral. By 1910 General Motors was strapped for cash. Durant managed to borrow enough money to meet the company's obligations, but the price was loss of control of the company to a syndicate of investors.

Although Durant remained a major stockholder in General Motors, he also began building a new automaker. Louis Chevrolet, a former race-car driver for Buick, announced his intention to begin manufacturing a touring car, and in 1911 Durant became his principal financial backer. He also acquired two smaller automakers in Flint—Mason Motors and Little Motors—which he merged with Chevrolet's operation in 1913 to form the Chevrolet Motor Company. Over the next two years Chevrolet introduced several low-priced cars that sold extremely well, and by 1915 its sales were second only to Ford. He also began building an auto parts conglomerate, United Motors, which sold its products primarily to Chevrolet.

Meanwhile, General Motors was coming together as an integrated corporation, but its sales were still low and stockholders were grumbling about low dividends. In 1915 Durant began trading five shares of Chevrolet for one share of General Motors, and by 1916 he had acquired enough shares of his old company to take it over again. That same year he reincorporated the company as General Motors Corporation; Chevrolet and United Motors were made divisions in 1918, as was

Fisher Body, Detroit's leading chassis manufacturer, in 1919. By 1920, however, the corporation's sales, and its stock prices, had plunged, and Durant was again forced to resign as president.

Undaunted, in 1921 Durant formed yet another automaker, Durant Motors. Once again he followed the old formula that had worked so well for Durant-Dort and Buick, and by 1926 the company had climbed to number five in annual auto sales. However, once again Durant left Flint to play on Wall Street, and once again his company foundered in his absence. He built up a sizable fortune, but lost it all during the Great Depression and declared bankruptcy in 1936. He formed a few companies after that, but none of them attained the stature of Durant-Dort, Buick, or General Motors. He died on March 18, 1947, in New York City.

Further Reading

Madsen, Axel. *The Deal Maker: How William C. Durant Made General Motors.* New York: Chichester, Wiley, 2001.

Weisberger, Bernard A. *The Dream Maker: William C. Durant, Founder of General Motors.* Boston: Little, Brown, 1979.

Wren, Daniel A. and Ronald G. Greenwood. *Management Innovators: The People and Ideas that Have Shaped Modern Business.* New York: Oxford University Press, 1998.

Duryea, Charles Edgar (1861–1938), and James Frank Duryea (1869–1967)

inventors of the first American-made automobile

Most historians credit Charles and Frank Duryea with building the first practical American-made automobile. Although the brothers themselves got into a protracted disagreement about which of them contributed the most to its design, it now seems clear that the efforts of both were indispensable to its development.

Charles Edgar Duryea was born on December 15, 1861, in Canton, Illinois. James Frank Duryea was born on October 8, 1869, in Washburn, Illinois. Their parents, George and Louisa, were farmers who eventually settled their family in Wyoming, Illinois. In 1882 Charles left home, and for the next four years he built bicycles in St. Louis, Missouri, and Peoria, Illinois. In 1886, two years after he married Rachel Steer with whom he had three children, he moved to Washington, D.C. In 1888 Frank also moved to Washington, and the two brothers worked together in Herbert Owens's bicycle shop.

In 1888 Charles formed the Duryea Manufacturing Company and began making bicycles according to his own designs. One was a bicycle with a smaller wheel diameter that he designed just for women, which made it possible for large numbers of women to take up cycling for the first time. Another was the "Sylph," a graceful-looking machine that handled with greater ease than the high-wheel cycles that were popular at the time. The following year he moved his manufacturing operation to Rockaway, New Jersey, where he was joined once again by Frank. In 1890 the brothers moved to Chicopee Falls, Massachusetts, where Charles had contracted with the Ames Manufacturing Company to build his bicycles. Two years later Charles moved his operation again, this time to the Rouse-Hazard Company in Peoria, Illinois, while Frank continued to work for Ames. By the end of 1892, the brothers were living in Springfield, Massachusetts; the following year Frank married Clare Root with whom he had one child.

The Duryeas became seriously interested in building a horseless carriage after Charles attended the 1886 Ohio State Fair and saw a gasoline engine that seemed powerful enough to drive a small wagon. In 1892 the brothers began building an automobile; Charles, who was more of a visionary than Frank, designed the car, while Frank, who was a better mechanic than Charles, worked out the practical details necessary to make it run. By the following year they had converted a one-horse carriage into a one-cylinder car with electrical ignition that performed reasonably well during a test-drive of about 200 feet through Springfield. The vehicle, however, had not performed well enough to suit Charles's expectations, and so he abandoned the project shortly thereafter and returned to Peoria. Frank, on the other hand, was encouraged by the car's performance, and so he continued to make improvements without his brother's help. In 1894 he managed to get the vehicle to travel a full six miles. The following year he reworked Charles's design and came up with what became known as the "the Chicago car," because of its victory in the first American auto race in which more than two cars competed, a 50-mile course from Chicago to Evanston, Illinois, and back on Thanksgiving Day, 1895. Two months prior to the race, the brothers had formed the Duryea Motor Wagon Company, the first American automobile manufacturing firm. Charles held 48 percent of the stock while Frank held 33 percent, with the remainder going to David Allen Reed and George Henry Hewitt, the company's president and treasurer, respectively. Despite great promise, the company built only 13 cars in its first three years of existence, mostly because the Duryeas had focused their time and money on promoting the company's fortunes in Canada and England rather than just building and selling cars in the United States. In 1898 the brothers sold their stock to Reed and Hewitt and went their separate ways.

In 1898 Charles formed the Duryea Manufacturing Company in Peoria, which built a dozen three-wheeled vehicles and the first American-made armored car. Two years later he founded the Duryea Power Company in Reading, Pennsylvania, which built several hundred three- and four-wheeled autos. In 1911 he formed the Duryea Motor Company in Saginaw, Michigan, which made a few cars before Charles moved it to Philadelphia, Pennsylvania. Altogether Charles designed at least 10 different gasoline-powered vehicles before retiring as an active manufacturer in 1920. Having made little more than a decent living from his various ventures, he spent his remaining years as a consulting engineer and as a writer for two automotive journals. He died on September 28, 1938, in Philadelphia.

In 1900 Frank and several investors formed the Hampden Automobile and Launch Company. The following year he designed the Stevens-Duryea car, so called because it was manufactured under contract by the J. Stevens Arms and Tool Company in Chicopee Falls. In 1904 he organized the Stevens-Duryea Company, which built the first six-cylinder automobiles made in the United States. These vehicles, known as the Big Six and the Model Y, enjoyed great popularity well into the 1920s as limousines for the wealthy. Unlike his brother, Frank made a fortune in the automotive industry, and he retired from active manufacturing in 1915. Although he continued to design and engineer automobiles until his death, he spent his last 54 years in comfortable semiretirement in Greenwich, Connecticut, and, after 1938, in nearby Madison, Connecticut. He died on February 15, 1967, in Saybrook, Connecticut.

Further Reading

May, George W., et al. *Charles E. Duryea, Automaker.* Peoria, Ill.: Peoria Regional Museum Society, 1996.

Scharchburg, Richard P. *Carriage without Horses— J. Frank Duryea and the Birth of the American Automobile Industry.* Warrendale, Penn.: Society of Automotive Engineers, 1993.

E

Eastman, George

(1854–1932) *founder of the Eastman Kodak Company*

Most American families today think nothing of taking pictures at each and every family gathering or special event. Before George Eastman developed the Kodak camera, however, amateur photography was virtually nonexistent. Oddly enough, this invention probably would not have taken place were it not for a trip to the Caribbean that Eastman never took.

Eastman was born on July 12, 1854, in Waterville, New York. His father, George, was an educator, and his mother, Maria, was a homemaker. At age five he moved with his family to Rochester, where his father had founded the Eastman Mercantile College. Two years later his father died, and at age 13 Eastman went to work as an office boy in a real-estate firm. A year later he took a similar position with an insurance company, and at age 20 he became a bookkeeper for the Rochester Savings Bank.

In 1877, while making plans for a trip to the Caribbean island of Hispaniola (present-day Haiti and the Dominican Republic), Eastman decided that he would take some photographs while there. At the time amateur photography was virtually unheard of, mostly because photographs were developed from plates: flat pieces of glass that had been coated with fresh, wet chemicals. To take a picture, instead of using film, the photographer mounted a plate to the back of the camera.

This process meant that taking pictures in the field required the transportation of a batch of dry chemicals, plenty of water, various pieces of mixing equipment, and a dark tent, because wet-plate negatives had to be developed immediately. For various reasons, Eastman never made the trip. Nevertheless, Eastman was determined to learn how to take pictures, so he studied photography with several professional photographers. The following year he read in a photography journal about the new dry-plate method, whereby a plate could be coated with gelatin containing silver salts, thus making it more sensitive than wet plates. Perhaps even better, this method permitted the making up of plates in advance, so that instead of carrying a lot of equipment into the field, a photographer had only to carry as many pretreated plates as he planned to take pictures.

In 1880 Eastman patented a machine for coating dry plates and founded the Eastman Dry Plate Company. Before long he realized that using plates, whether wet or dry, was simply beyond the ability of most amateur photographers, and if he wanted to stay in business he would have to simplify photography for the amateur even further. He began experimenting with film made from collodion, a yellowish, viscous material, as a replacement for plates, and in 1884 he developed a roll of film with a layer of paper backing to hold the gelatin in place. The roll contained enough film to take about one hundred round photographs, each about 2 inches in diameter. That same year he and William H. Walker, a camera designer, became partners in the Eastman Dry Plate & Film Company; also that year they patented a roll holder by which the roll could be attached to the camera where the plate normally went. In 1886 the partners opened a photofinishing division in Rochester where customers could get their rolls of film developed.

In 1888 Eastman revolutionized amateur photography when it introduced the Kodak camera. A simple hand-held box camera, it came loaded with a roll of film; when the film was used up, the customer returned the camera to Eastman, where the film was developed and the camera reloaded. To emphasize how simple the whole process was for the amateur photographer, the company adopted as its motto, "You press the button, we do the rest." In fact, it was not quite that simple; the camera had no viewfinder and no exposure counter, so taking pictures still involved a bit of guesswork. Nevertheless, the Kodak camera greatly simplified picture taking, and as a result vast numbers of amateur photographers began buying the cameras, which sold for $25 apiece. In 1889 the company introduced a new type of film made out of nitrocellulose, and in 1900 Eastman introduced the Brownie camera, a smaller version of the Kodak which sold for $1 and came loaded with a short roll of film.

While he was advancing the art of photography, Eastman was also creating an international company. By 1892, when he reincorporated his organization as the Eastman Kodak Company, he had highly profitable branch operations in England, France, Germany, Italy, Belgium, and Sweden. Over the next 30 years he bought out a number of competing domestic manufacturers of photographic paper, plates, and cameras, and eventually became the country's only manufacturer of film for X-ray photography and cinematography. By 1915, when the U.S. Justice Department sued Eastman Kodak for antitrust violations, the company controlled virtually the entire photographic industry in the United States. In 1925 Eastman retired from actively managing his company and spent much of the next several years hunting and fishing in Alaska and Africa.

Eastman made more than $100 million for his contributions to the photography industry. He spent much of it on a 50-room mansion in

George Eastman loved to travel to Europe; here he is seen on the deck of the S.S. *Aquitania. (Library of Congress)*

Rochester, which included five gardens and a pipe organ in its central court. He also donated large sums of money to worthy causes such as the Mechanics Institute and the Rochester Orphan Asylum, known today as the Rochester Institute of Technology and the Hillside Children's Center, respectively. He established the School of Medicine and Dentistry and the Eastman Theater and School of Music at the University of Rochester, as well as the Rochester Dental Dispensary and a dental clinic at Meharry College in Nashville, Tennessee. He also gave generously to the Massachusetts Institute of Technology, Tuskegee Institute, and Hampton Institute. Having never married, Eastman had no heirs, and by the time of his death he had given away his entire fortune to charity. Late in life he contracted a painful and untreatable condition of the lower spine, and on March 14, 1932, he took his own life at his mansion in Rochester.

Further Reading

Brayer, Elizabeth. *George Eastman: A Biography.* Baltimore, Md.: Johns Hopkins University Press, 1996.

Brooke-Ball, Peter. *George Eastman and Kodak.* Watford, U.K.: Exley, 1994.

Eastman Kodak Co. *From Glass Plates to Photo CDs: The Kodak Story.* Rochester, N.Y.: Eastman Kodak, 1992.

Edgerton, Harold Eugene

(1903–1990) *inventor of the stroboscopic flash*

One of the most important inventions in the field of photography is the stroboscopic flash. This device enables photographers to film rapidly moving objects that would otherwise be impossible to photograph. The inventor of this device, as well as a number of ancillary devices to make it work in a variety of applications, was Harold Edgerton.

Edgerton was born in Fremont, Nebraska. His father, Frank, was a lawyer and his mother, Mary, was a homemaker. After receiving his B.S. degree in electrical engineering from the University of Nebraska in 1925, he went to work for the Nebraska Power and Light Company.

Edgerton was assigned to a team of engineers who were troubleshooting generators that were not running 100 percent smoothly. The problem was that the generators' moving parts moved so fast that no one could see what they were, or were not, doing. In 1926 Edgerton realized that if he could develop a light source that flashed at the same rate as the parts moved, then the effect would be to "freeze" the motion so that the engineers could see the parts as if they were standing still. By 1928 he had invented a high-speed electronic flash and the necessary electronic circuitry to make it work; he received a patent for this device, the stroboscopic flash, in 1933.

In 1928 Edgerton married Esther May Garrett with whom he had three children. He also enrolled at the Massachusetts Institute of Technology (MIT) where he received his doctorate in science in 1931. He remained at MIT as a professor of electrical engineering until his death.

Edgerton's lifetime research focused on developing further the components necessary to improve the operation of the stroboscopic flash, such as more sophisticated circuitry, brighter lamps, and faster camera shutters. By 1966 he had been awarded a total of 46 patents for his inventions. Many of these devices were manufactured and sold by Edgerton, Germeshausen, and Grier (later known as EG&G), a company Edgerton formed in 1934 with two of his MIT students. Next to the flash itself, his most important invention was a xenon-vapor lamp that could flash brilliantly for one microsecond, thus permitting the photographing of instantaneous actions that had never before been captured on film. Perhaps the most famous photograph made with the xenon-vapor lamp is one Edgerton himself took in 1938 of a drop of milk splattering into a saucer and creating a crownlike effect. Another famous set of pictures appeared in *National Geographic*'s August 1947 issue, showing the rapid movement of a hummingbird's wings in flight. Edgerton also developed ways to photograph a vast array of physical phenomena,

Harold Edgerton displays some of the equipment in his technology studio. *(Library of Congress)*

such as the tracks made by subatomic particles in bubble chambers and the explosion of a nuclear bomb. During World War II he adapted the stroboscopic flash to photograph enemy troop movements at night, and he developed a stroboscopic beacon capable of flashing light to distances of up to 50 miles.

After the war Edgerton became increasingly interested in underwater photography. Having designed the first underwater camera in 1937, he turned his attention to making flash equipment that could photograph sea creatures and objects at levels of the ocean where sunlight cannot penetrate. He developed a system of cameras and lights for bathyscaphes, the miniature submarines that explore the ocean's depths, and accompanied the noted oceanographer Jacques-Yves Cousteau on 10 voyages during which they obtained the first photographs of sea life near the bottom of the ocean. He also wrote more than 100 scientific articles regarding his inventions and their potential applications. In 1968 he retired to his home in Cambridge, Massachusetts, where he died in 1990.

Further Reading

Bedi, Joyce, et al. *Seeing the Unseen: Dr. Harold Edgerton and the Wonders of Strobe Alley.* Rochester, N.Y.: Trust of George Eastman House, 1994.

Edgerton, Harold, and James Rhyne Killian, Jr. *Moments of Vision: The Stroboscopic Revolution in Photography.* Cambridge, Mass.: MIT Press, 1985.

Edgerton, Harold E., et al. *Stopping Time: The Photographs of Harold Edgerton.* New York: Harry N. Abrams, 2000.

Mark, Lorraine. *Photographs that Changed the World: The Camera as Witness, the Photograph as Evidence.* New York: Doubleday, 1989.

Edison, Thomas Alva

(1847–1931) *inventor of electrical devices*

Thomas Edison was the most prolific inventor in the history of the world. His patented inventions, which totaled 1,093, contributed to major advances in telegraphy and created or made possible such modern conveniences as sound recording, mechanical dictation, motion pictures, electric lighting, and electric power generation and transmission. As the father of team-based industrial research, he also invented a new way to invent. In the process of achieving fame and fortune as an inventor and businessman, the "Wizard of Menlo Park" became one of America's best-loved heroes.

Edison was born on February 11, 1847, in Milan, Ohio. His father, Samuel, was a shopkeeper, and his mother, Nancy, was a schoolteacher. At age seven he moved with his family to Port Huron, Michigan. Much is made of Edison's lack of success in school; in fact, he was bored by his school's slow pace, and he learned prodigiously as a home-schooled child and from independent reading. At age 12 he began selling newspapers, sandwiches, and candy at the local train station, and before long had recruited several other boys to work for him. At age 15 he rescued a young boy from being run over by a runaway railcar; in gratitude, the boy's father, a telegrapher, taught Edison how to operate the telegraph. Over the next six years Edison developed into a first-class telegrapher while working as an operator all over the Midwest. Meanwhile, he had become interested in the electromechanical principles by which telegraphy works. In his spare time he experimented with ways to make telegraphy work faster and easier, and he devoured the works of Michael Faraday, the British scientist who wrote brilliantly about electricity, magnetism, and other physical and chemical phenomena. In 1869, the year after he had moved to Boston, Massachusetts, to work as a telegrapher, Edison devoted himself full time to invention.

Edison's first patent was for a voting machine. Other early inventions included a municipal fire alarm system, a prototype of the modern fax machine, and improvements in the method and equipment for printing out ticker tape. Before 1875, however, his primary interest was making improvements to telegraphy. He developed and installed dedicated telegraph systems for companies with offices in downtown Boston and factories on the outskirts of town. In 1869 he moved to New York City to become superintendent of the Gold and Stock Reporting Telegraph Company, and the following year to Newark, New Jersey, where he and William Unger established the Newark Telegraph

Thomas Alva Edison was the most prolific American inventor of all time. *(Library of Congress)*

Works. Eventually Unger supervised the manufacture of the company's main product, the Edison Universal Stock Printer, while Edison focused on improving existing equipment and raising capital to finance further research, much of which came from the Western Union Telegraph Company. In 1871 he married Mary Stilwell with whom he had three children.

While in Newark, Edison began developing the strategies that he would later make famous at his industrial research laboratory in nearby Menlo Park. He began hiring talented individuals, particularly immigrants, to whom he assigned specific research responsibilities. He also began keeping meticulous logbooks concerning what he and each of his assistants did and discussed on a daily basis, thus generating records that could later be used to Edison's great benefit during patent lawsuits. In 1875 he built a laboratory on the fourth floor of his factory where he and his team of researchers could work undisturbed by production problems on the floors below. In this laboratory, Edison and his team invented the electric pen, in essence a prototype of the mimeograph machine, and an acoustic telegraph, which used tuning forks to send several telegraphic messages at different sound frequencies simultaneously.

In 1876 Edison moved his laboratory to Menlo Park. Over the next six years he and his researchers, the chief ones being Charles Batchelor and John Kruesi, made major discoveries involving the telephone, the phonograph, the electric lightbulb, and the electric generator. The acoustic telegraph evolved into the speaking telegraph, which evolved into the telephone. For a while Edison, ELISHA GRAY, and ALEXANDER GRAHAM BELL were all in the running to receive the first telephone patent. Bell won because he demonstrated publicly a working model in 1876, before Edison and Gray, but two years later Bell's telephone was using a carbon-button transmitting device of Edison's design. Further experiments with strengthening telephone signals so they could be transmitted over long distances led to the discovery of recorded sound in 1877 and the invention that same year of the cylinder phonograph. It was this invention that earned Edison the nickname "Wizard of Menlo Park." Over the years Edison devoted further attention to developing the phonograph into a commercial success and a closer approximation of the modern record player.

Perhaps the greatest invention by Edison and his team was incandescent lighting, or light produced by heat. Arc lighting had already been invented and installed in auditoriums and street lamps, but it had proven impractical for use in homes, offices, and shops. Edison set out to develop an entire electrical system—lightbulb, generator, and distribution system—as if he were solving a problem in telegraphy. The main step was to design the receiving unit, or lightbulb, and in 1879 his researchers developed a high-resistance, carbon filament that gave off light while it "burned" inside an evacuated glass globe when an electrical current was passed through it. Meanwhile, that same year Edison and Francis Upton had developed a generator capable of producing direct current, which

Edison deemed best suited for incandescent lighting. The development of a rudimentary distribution system came about in 1880, the same year Edison, J. P. MORGAN, and other investors formed the Edison Electric Illuminating Company of New York. In 1881 this company began building the first electrical generating station and laying underground cables throughout New York City for the distribution of electricity.

In 1882 Edison closed his Menlo Park operation and moved it to New York City. Assisted by SAMUEL INSULL, he began establishing companies to build central power stations across America as well as to manufacture lightbulbs, generators, and other apparatus needed to provide business and residential customers with electric light. By 1886 the majority of Edison's manufacturing operations had been moved to Schenectady, New York. In 1891 they were combined with the holdings of the Thomson-Houston Electric Company to form the General Electric Company, under the control of J. P. Morgan. Shortly thereafter, Edison began selling his stock in the company and concentrated on other interests.

In 1887 Edison had completed construction on a new five-story laboratory in West Orange, New Jersey. He also built a new home nearby for his new wife; Mary Edison had died in 1882, and four years later he married Mina Miller with whom he also had three children. Most of the activity in the new laboratory centered around three very different ideas—motion pictures, mining, and storage batteries. Edison got interested in motion pictures following an 1888 visit to his laboratory by Eadweard Muybridge, the British photographer who specialized in photographing animals in motion. Shortly thereafter Edison began approaching the problem of recording movement as if it were sound. By 1894 he and his researchers had invented the kinetograph, in essence the first motion-picture camera, and the kinetoscope, by which one viewer could watch images on a roll of film as they passed beneath a peephole. Throughout the 1890s, Edison developed a method for extracting iron from low-grade magnetite ore mined in New Jersey's Musconetcong Mountains by using gigantic electromagnets. He put this equipment to work at a processing plant he had constructed near

Ogdensburg; unfortunately, the price of iron ore dropped shortly thereafter as a result of the discovery of high-grade iron ore in Minnesota's Mesabi Range, and he was eventually forced to shut down his mining operation. Much of the equipment from the ore processing plant was transferred to New Village where he built a huge facility for producing cement, having also developed a method for building homes and factories out of poured concrete. In the late 1890s he began working on a powerful alkaline storage battery that could be used for everything from powering phonographs in homes that lacked electricity to powering telegraph signals along remote stretches of railroad track. This battery was later modified for use in submarines during World War I and in automobiles as a means of starting the motor and running the lights.

Edison continued to put in a full day's work in his laboratory until the year he died. While his sons managed his phonograph, motion-picture equipment, and battery manufacturing operations, he devoted his last years to developing new chemical compounds and a synthetic substitute for rubber. He died on October 18, 1931, at his home in West Orange, New Jersey.

Further Reading

Crompton, Samuel W. *100 Americans Who Shaped American History*. San Mateo, Calif.: Bluewood Books, 1999.

Josephson, Matthew. *Edison, A Biography*. New York: J. Wiley, 1992.

Millard, Andre. *Edison and the Business of Innovation*. Baltimore: Johns Hopkins University Press, 1993.

Wren, Daniel A. and Ronald G. Greenwood. *Management Innovators: The People and Ideas that Have Shaped Modern Business*. New York: Oxford University Press, 1998.

Elion, Gertrude Belle
(1918–1999) *inventor of 6-MP and acyclovir (pharmaceutical drugs)*

As an inventor, Gertrude Elion is unique for two reasons. First, she was one of the first recipients of the Nobel Prize for medicine who conducted her research under the auspices of a pharmaceutical firm instead of a university, medical center, or other nonprofit organization. Second, she was the first woman, and one of the first developers of pharmaceutical drugs, to be inducted into the National Inventors Hall of Fame.

Elion was born on January 23, 1918, in New York City. Her father, Robert, was a dentist, and her mother, Bertha, was a homemaker. As a young girl, she became interested in science, particularly the exploits of Marie Curie, winner of two Nobel Prizes for her work with radium. As a teenager, Gertrude was profoundly moved by her grandfather's suffering as he slowly died from stomach cancer, and she resolved to devote her life to trying to find a cure for this disease. She graduated from Hunter College in 1937 where she majored in chemistry. She spent most of the next two years working as an assistant to Alexander Galat, a research chemist for a small pharmaceutical company. During this time she became engaged, but her fiancé died before they could be wed, and she never considered marrying anyone else. In 1939 she enrolled in New York University where she received her master's in chemistry in 1941.

For the next three years Elion worked successively as a quality control chemist for the Quaker Maid Company and as a research assistant in Johnson & Johnson's fledgling pharmaceutical division. But these rather routine jobs frustrated her and certainly did not allow her to search for a cure for cancer as she desired to do. So in 1944 she interviewed with George H. Hitchings, a research chemist with the Burroughs Wellcome Company in Tuckahoe, New York, in the hope of becoming his chief research assistant.

Hitchings was trying to develop a variety of new drugs to cure previously incurable diseases such as leukemia, malaria, and herpes, and his approach to developing pharmaceuticals differed considerably from the approach taken by most drug researchers. Instead of developing a drug, then testing it to see what it would do, Hitchings studied the biochemical differences between healthy cells and diseased cells. He believed that once he understood these differences, he could develop drugs that would attack the diseased cells while leaving the healthy cells alone.

Specifically, Hitchings was an advocate of the antimetabolite theory, first proposed around 1940 by two pharmacologists, Donald Woods and Paul Fildes. This approach focused on understanding how diseased cells produce deoxyribonucleic acid, or DNA, which is essential to cell growth, then using that knowledge to create drugs that would interrupt their production of DNA. The trick was to develop a "camouflaged" chemical substance that closely resembled one of DNA's building blocks but that also contained a substance that could inhibit cellular growth; getting the cancerous cell to bond with the camouflaged substance would then retard or stop altogether its growth. Figuratively speaking, effective antimetabolite drugs would have to be "appetizing" enough to diseased cells that they would "eat" the drug, but instead of gaining "nutrition" the diseased cell would get "sick." As Hitchings's assistant, Elion became convinced that this approach to pharmaceutical research was the correct one, and she was guided by this philosophy throughout her research career.

One of Elion's first projects with Hitchings was to look for a cure for leukemia, a type of blood cancer that ultimately leads to death. After discovering how leukemia cells produce DNA, the next step was to develop a drug that would interfere with DNA production by leukemia cells without also interfering with DNA production in normal cells. By 1948 she had developed a drug known as 2,6-diaminopurine that she thought would do this, but the drug induced such intense nausea and vomiting that only one patient was ever able to take it, and after two years this patient had died from leukemia anyway. Undaunted, Elion continued to look for a better drug, and in the early 1950s she developed 6-mercaptopurine, or 6-MP. This drug caused remission in child leukemia patients for up to one year without the deleterious side effects of 2,6-diaminopurine. Although better antileukemic drugs were later discovered, 6-MP continues to be prescribed for patients in remission; after taking 6-MP for several years, most former leukemia patients experience a complete cure.

6-MP proved to be of use for the treatment of other conditions as well. The American surgeon Joseph E. Murray developed a derivative of 6-MP, known as azathioprine, to suppress the body's immune system so that it would not reject transplanted organs. In 1962 he used azathioprine to achieve the first successful kidney transplant in which the donor and the recipient were not related. In the mid-1960s Elion discovered that allopurinol, which breaks down 6-MP, successfully treats gout, leishmaniasis, and Chagas' disease.

Elion's early career had been marred by several incidents of gender discrimination. After graduating from Hunter, the attractive redhead struggled to find a job as a research chemist; one interviewer, no doubt echoing the sentiments of others, told her she could not be hired because she would distract the male chemists from their research. When she finally did get a job with Galat's company, it was only because she agreed to work for free for six months. Quaker Maid and Johnson & Johnson gave her mostly trivial tasks, such as measuring the tensile strength of sutures. But Hitchings always treated her as a valuable colleague, allowing her to conduct her own line of research without micromanaging her. In 1967 she ended 23 years as Hitchings's assistant to become head of Burroughs Wellcome's department of experimental therapy. Three years later, when the company relocated to North Carolina's Research Triangle Park near Chapel Hill, she made the move also.

In 1968 Elion returned to her earlier experiments with 2,6-diaminopurine after reading a medical journal article that suggested to her that the drug could be enhanced in such a way that it could inhibit DNA viruses. Further experimentation with a compound known as 2,6-diaminopurine arabinoside showed that it was mildly effective against those forms of the herpes virus that cause genital herpes, herpes encephalitis, and shingles. Curious as to why 2,6-diaminopurine arabinoside worked on a virus, she soon discovered that, just as with diseased cells, it tricked viruses into thinking it was a DNA building block. She then directed a massive research effort to develop a stronger strain of the drug. The result was acyclovir, which was 100 times more effective than 2,6-diaminopurine arabinoside. Introduced in 1982 as Zovirax, the drug was the first effective drug for the treatment of herpes. It also proved to be an effective treatment for chicken pox, and it helps prevent viral infections in people whose immune systems have been suppressed by chemotherapy or AIDS.

In 1983 Elion retired to her home in Chapel Hill but continued to consult for Burroughs Wellcome. As a consultant, she participated in the discovery of AZT, the first drug approved by the federal government for the treatment of AIDS. In 1988 she and Hitchings shared the Nobel Prize for medicine with England's Sir James Black, who had developed drugs for treating heart disease and ulcers. She died on February 21, 1999, in Chapel Hill, North Carolina.

Further Reading

Avery, Mary Ellen. *Gertrude B. Elion: January 23, 1918– February 21, 1999.* Washington, D.C.: National Academy Press, 2000.

Wasserman, Elga. *The Door in the Dream: Conversations with Eminent Women in Science.* Washington, D.C.: Joseph Henry Press, 2000.

Yount, Lisa. *A to Z of Women in Science and Math.* New York: Facts On File, 1999.

Ellison, Larry
(1944–   ) *founder of Oracle Corporation*

Admirers and detractors alike tell the following joke about Larry Ellison: What is the difference between Larry Ellison and God? God does not think he is Larry Ellison. The joke reflects Ellison's place among the business world's most powerful figures and his identity as an enormously ambitious, aggressive, visionary, and ultimately successful leader of business software development.

Lawrence Joseph Ellison was born on August 17, 1944, in New York City to a 19-year-old single mother named Florence Spellman. Feeling that she could not properly care for her newborn son, Spellman asked her sister and her husband, Lillian and Louis Ellison of Chicago, to raise him. The Ellisons consented and became the adoptive parents of Larry when he was nine months old. Ellison grew up in a two-bedroom apartment in a mainly Jewish, lower-middle-class neighborhood on Chicago's South Side. He was a bright but often inattentive student who preferred playing baseball and basketball with his friends to academic pursuits. Ellison

Cofounder and CEO of Oracle Corporation, Larry Ellison *(Oracle Corporate Communications/Used under a Creative Commons license)*

enjoyed a close relationship to his adoptive mother, but not with his adoptive father, who had emigrated from Russia years earlier and changed his long Jewish last name to honor the place—Ellis Island—where he arrived in the United States. Ellison recalls his father frequently telling him that he would never amount to anything, adding, "That was his form of greeting, as opposed to, 'Hi' or, 'Good morning.'"

In 1962 Ellison graduated from Chicago's South Shore High School and enrolled at the University of Illinois. He stayed there until the end of his sophomore year when he returned to Chicago following the death of his adoptive mother from kidney cancer. He spent one semester at the University of Chicago but dropped out and decided to travel west to northern California. His aptitude in physics helped him gain employment in a variety of technical jobs, including several in the burgeoning field of computer programming.

Ellison continued to gain work and programming expertise well into the 1970s. He took a position with Ampex, a computing company in Sunnyvale, California, that did a great deal of contract work for the federal government. With Ampex, Ellison contributed to a database for the Central Intelligence Agency that was code-named Oracle. In 1977 Ellison seized on the emerging breakthroughs in database technology to start a software development business with two former Ampex colleagues that focused on the computing needs of businesses. Ellison pursued advancements in relational databases—many of which were described in a published IBM study—that would allow businesses to organize connections among bits of data to improve clarity, efficiency, and profit. Together, Ellison and his partners built their business with little outside resources while constantly developing the relational database project that they named Oracle. In 1979 they put out the first version of their database, and within five years the company that would become known as Oracle Corporation was generating nearly $13 million a year in sales.

Oracle continued to prosper into the 1980s as a forerunner of Silicon Valley technology firms. Oracle held an initial public offering in 1986 with shares beginning at $15 and closing at $20.75, making Ellison's net worth nearly $100 million. The business made huge strides financially by following the aggressive style of Ellison who demanded much from his growing number of employees and compensated them very well for their work. A former Oracle salesperson from the mid to late 1980s described it, "The management theory was simple. Go out and don't come back until you have a signed contract."

Despite Oracle's high-flying success, the company ran into severe problems in the early 1990s, much of which Ellison blamed on himself. Years of sales discounts and negligent accounting led Oracle to state higher revenues than they actually had. This led several top executives to flee and to a plummeting stock price. Ellison vowed to run the company in an "adult" manner and within a few years it was again highly profitable. During this period Ellison—who had been married and divorced three times—decided to find and contact his biological mother, who was living in Connecticut. They established a relationship and remained in contact until her death in 1999.

Ellison and Oracle enjoyed unprecedented success and influence as the Internet boom continued into the 21st century. Oracle was the chief provider of business database software for many of the world's leading banks, airlines, auto companies, and retail stores. Ellison also foresaw opportunities in Internet commerce as well, leading Oracle to become a top company in the business application field for e-commerce. Even as many companies failed or suffered during the dotcom bust period, Oracle thrived as did its stock value. This stability and growth made Ellison one of the world's richest people, ranking fourth on the *Forbes* magazine list of the 400 wealthiest people in 2009, with a net worth of $22.5 billion.

Much of Ellison and Oracle's success came from his renowned—and to some notorious—reputation for aggressive acquisitions of other companies. From 2004 to 2008, Ellison increased Oracle's market share through the acquisition of nearly 50 companies for more than $25 billion. Included in this strategic maneuvering was the takeover of small and large companies that managed data, retail inventory, and logistics, such as PeopleSoft, Siebel Systems, Hyperion Solutions, and Sun Microsystems. Oracle is now the world's largest business software company, supplying all 100 of *Fortune* magazine's Global 100 companies.

Ellison has been married to his fourth wife, novelist Melanie Craft, since 2003. He is a certified pilot and an active yachtsman, whose BMW Oracle racing team sailed to a 2010 victory for the United States in sailing's prestigious America's Cup. Ellison lives in Woodside, California, and remains the only chief executive officer that Oracle Corporation has ever had.

Further Reading

"Lawrence J. Ellison," Academy of Achievement. Available online. URL: http://www.achievement.org/autodoc/page/ell0bio-1. Downloaded on July 1, 2009.

Leibovich, Mark. *The New Imperialists.* Upper Saddle River, N.J.: Prentice Hall, 2001.

Ellison, William
(April Ellison)
(1790–1861) *entrepreneur in planting and manufacturing*

In 1860, wealthy white slave owners were hardly exceptional in the South. Wealthy black slave owners, on the other hand, were exceptionally rare outside of Louisiana and uncommon even there.

Perhaps the wealthiest black slave owner outside Louisiana, and one of the most unusual success stories of any black American, was William Ellison, who was born into slavery and died rich before the Civil War abolished slavery.

Ellison was born in Fairfield District, South Carolina, and given the name April. His father was probably either Robert Ellison, the owner of the plantation on which April was born, or Robert's son William. April's mother was an unidentified slave woman. Although the Ellisons never acknowledged a blood relationship between themselves and April, they treated him with as much affection as the law allowed. At age 10 he was transferred to the ownership of William Ellison, who apprenticed him two years later to a cotton-gin maker in nearby Winnsboro. For the next 14 years April built cotton gins, learned reading, writing, and arithmetic, earned the respect of all the important planters in the district, and worked overtime in order to purchase his freedom. In 1816 April became a free black, and opened a cotton-gin repair shop in Stateburg, South Carolina, where he spent the rest of his life. In 1817 he purchased a slave woman named Matilda whom he freed and married; they had three children. In 1820 he changed his legal name to William Ellison.

Ellison's cotton gins were top-quality machines, and he received orders for them from as far away as Mississippi. By 1822 he had made enough money to buy one acre of land in the center of Stateburg and two slaves. On this land he erected shops for building cotton gins and doing general blacksmith and carpentry work. By 1840 his business had prospered so much that he owned 330 acres of fertile farmland and 30 slaves, most of whom either worked in his cotton fields or were leased to other planters. By 1860 Ellison owned 900 acres and 63 slaves. He was wealthier than nine-tenths of the white people in central South Carolina, and one of the wealthiest black men in the South. Perhaps even more impressive is that he was acknowledged as an upstanding member of the community by his fellow planters, all of whom were members of the white elite and who held strong prejudices against black equality. One measure of the esteem in which Ellison was held is the fact that he was permitted to purchase and occupy the home of a former governor.

Ellison's rise to fortune was probably unique in the annals of Southern history. Certainly other free blacks had become wealthy by hard work and good fortune. In 1860 Virginia's Eastern Shore was heavily populated with free blacks whose ancestors had gained their freedom in the early 1600s, and Louisiana was home to a number of wealthy slaveholding free blacks whose ancestors had gained their freedom under French rule. But Ellison achieved his fortune and maintained his independence in the heartland of the state that would be the first to secede from the Union over the issue of slavery. Clearly, Ellison possessed exceptional interpersonal skills and intelligence to have pulled off such a remarkable feat. He died on December 5, 1861.

Further Reading

Johnson, Michael P., and James L. Roark. *Black Masters: A Free Family of Color in the Old South*. New York: W. W. Norton, 1984.

Koger, Larry. *Black Slaveholders: Free Black Slave Masters in South Carolina, 1790–1860*. Columbia: University of South Carolina Press, 1994.

Ertegun, Ahmet
(1923–2006) *entrepreneur in music industry*

A strong case can be made that there is no one—outside of the musical performers themselves—who has made a more significant impact on the music recording industry as Ahmet Ertegun. In his nearly 60-year career as an executive that reflects the history of popular music, Ertegun played a critical role in discovering, signing, or producing acts as diverse, influential, and successful as Ray Charles, Aretha Franklin, the Rolling Stones, Led Zeppelin, the Bee Gees, and Kid Rock.

Ahmet Ertegun was born in Istanbul, Turkey, on July 31, 1923. His father, Munir, served as a legal counselor to Kemal Ataturk, the founder of modern Turkey. Ertegun moved with his family as his father received various ambassadorships in Switzerland, France, Great Britain, and eventually the United States. A lifelong love of music was

Tribute to Ahmet Ertegun at a Led Zeppelin concert in London, December 10, 2007 *(Photo by P. A. H./Used under a Creative Commons license)*

sparked in Ertegun when he was only nine years old and went with his older brother Nesuhi to see the Duke Ellington and Cab Calloway orchestras perform in London. Ertegun graduated from St. John's College in Annapolis, Maryland, in 1944 and was taking graduate courses in philosophy at Georgetown University when his father died. Though most of Ertegun's family returned to Turkey, he remained in Washington, D.C., and pursued work in the music industry, later recalling that time to an audience of music students by saying, "I had to decide whether I would go into a scholastic life or go back to Turkey in the diplomatic service, or do something else. What I really loved was music, jazz, blues, and hanging out."

With the help of a $10,000 loan from his family dentist, Ertegun formed Atlantic Records in 1947 with partner Herb Abramson. For several years Atlantic Records operated out of a one-room office in New York City with a staff of fewer than 10 people. In the daytime, Ertegun worked on promotions and sales, and in the evening he scouted new artists at clubs around the city or made recordings with artists Atlantic had already signed to contracts. The company was able to survive until finally prospering in the early to mid-1950s thanks to the addition of partner Jerry Wexler and Ertegun's brother Nehusi and the popularity of such artists as The Drifters, John Coltrane, and Ray Charles.

By the mid to late 1950s, Atlantic under Ertegun's leadership had established itself as among the leading recording studios. Following Ertegun's love for a variety of musical styles—but especially rhythm and blues—Atlantic helped pioneer an American sound that often featured and sometimes integrated the best of jazz, blues, and swing. Ertegun established and enjoyed strong relationships with many of the artists he produced and occasionally contributed as a songwriter (including "Mess Around" by Ray Charles) and backup performer (including "Shake, Rattle, and Roll" by Big Joe Turner). Like the music that came from the Atlantic studios, the management and performers of Atlantic were an eclectic bunch, including the Muslim Ertegun, his Jewish partners, and several black musicians.

Ertegun continued to be among the music industry's most prominent business figures throughout the 1960s and 1970s. He established partnerships with many other smaller record companies, including the renowned Chess Records in Chicago and Stax Records in Memphis, to help develop artists such as Otis Redding, Wilson Pickett, and Percy Sledge. These partnerships—and the signing and producing of new bands such as Led Zeppelin and becoming the label of the already-established Rolling Stones—resulted in huge sales for the artists and companies and played a key role in redefining mainstream American musical tastes, with rhythm and blues and rock and roll increasingly occupying the center.

Ertegun and his partners sold the Atlantic label to Warner Brothers-Seven Arts in 1967 for $17 million in stock, but when that company was acquired by the Kinney National Service conglomerate of nonmusical brands (later becoming Time Warner), Atlantic was revived with Ertegun in charge. Although Ertegun's direct management dwindled in the 1980s and 1990s, he remained a beloved and symbolic figure of Atlantic, and he continued to pursue his love of music by scouting bands in nightclubs. Ertegun also delved into other areas of business by forming the New York Cosmos soccer club in the fledgling North American Soccer League in 1971. The Cosmos eventually signed high-profile global stars, including the Brazilian

icon Pelé and the German Franz Beckenbauer, on their way to five championships before the league folded after the 1984 season.

For his pioneering role in the music industry, Ertegun was the recipient of many honors. In 1987 Ertegun was inducted into the Rock and Roll Hall of Fame, and in 1995 the Hall's main exhibit hall was named in his honor. In 2000 the U.S. Library of Congress named Ertegun a Living Legend, and in 2003 he was inducted into the National Soccer Hall of Fame. In 2005, the National Academy of Recording Arts Sciences named Ertegun the first recipient of its President's Merit Award to Industry Icons.

Ertegun died on December 14, 2006, in New York City from complications related to a brain injury he suffered in a fall six weeks earlier. The injury occurred backstage at the Beacon Theater in Manhattan while he was waiting for the Rolling Stones to play at the 60th birthday party of former president Bill Clinton. He was survived by his wife of 45 years, Mica. He is buried in Istanbul, Turkey, next to his brother and father.

The rock and roll legend Neil Young wrote of Ertegun soon after his death, "The last time I saw Ahmet, we just sat and talked. He was a regular guy. He happened to also be one of the most powerful guys in the music business. But he had no use for wielding the power. The only time he ever used his power was with other executives. He didn't use it on the musicians. And it's suitable that his last conscious moments were at a concert. Because that's the way he lived. He went to a show. And the encore was heaven."

Further Reading

Bardach, A.L. "Interrogating Ahmet Ertegun: The Atlantic Records founder on Ray Charles, Islamic fundamentalism, and his own hipness." Slate. Available online. URL: http://www.slate.com/id/2114074/. Downloaded on July 1, 2009.

Wade, Dorothy, and Justine Picardie. *Music Man: Ahmet Ertegun, Atlantic Records, and the Triumph of Rock'N'Roll.* New York: W. W. Norton & Co., 1990.

Weiner, Tim, "Ahmet Ertegun, Music Executive, Dies at 83." New York Times. Available online. URL: http://www.nytimes.com/2006/12/15/arts/music/15ertegun.html. Downloaded on July 1, 2009.

Evans, Oliver
(1755–1819) *inventor of the automated flour mill*

The two most important inventors of the late 18th and early 19th centuries were probably ELI WHITNEY and Oliver Evans. While Whitney is well known for his work with the cotton gin and firearms, Evans's contributions to factory automation, the steam engine, and steam-powered transportation are all but forgotten. In fact, Evans designed the first continuous production line, built the first high-pressure steam engine, and invented the first self-propelled land vehicle in the United States.

Evans was born on September 13, 1755, in Newport, Delaware. His father, Charles, was a shoemaker, and his mother, Ann, was a homemaker. At age 15 he was apprenticed to a wheelwright, and he worked at that profession for the next six years. In his spare time, he tinkered with various mechanical innovations. His most successful invention during this period was a machine for making cards, comblike devices used to prepare the fibers of raw wool or cotton for spinning into yarn. He also began thinking about how to use steam for various commercial purposes. In 1783 he asked the Pennsylvania legislature to grant him a patent for a steam-powered wagon, but he had no working model and so his request was refused.

By 1783 Evans had moved to Tuckahoe, Maryland, where he and a brother ran a small store. That same year he married Sarah Tomlinson with whom he had seven children. He also began tinkering with ways to automate the grinding of grain into flour. Although grindstones had been powered by water, wind, and animals for centuries, the rest of the flour-making operations, such as carrying grain and raking flour, were done by hand. By 1785 he had perfected a mechanical system for performing all these tasks at a water-powered mill. The machinery was powered by the waterwheel that turned the grindstones via a system of shafts, gears, and leather belts. The operator merely dumped the grain into a hopper and engaged the clutch, thus setting the system in motion. An "elevator," a leather belt with leather cups, carried the grain up to a "conveyor," a screwlike rod, which positioned the grain between the grindstones. The ground flour was carried by a chute to a hopper in the drying room, where a "hopper-boy," a mechanized rake that swept around in a circular motion, sifted the flour so it could dry more evenly. Once it was dried, the flour was bagged by hand.

In 1785 Evans and two brothers opened an automated flour mill on Red Clay Creek in Delaware, not far from Philadelphia. The operation was a financial success because it cut the cost of making flour by almost half. Over the next three years he obtained patents from four states and sold his interest in the store because he expected to make a fortune licensing his system to other millers. They, however, showed little enthusiasm for adopting his system, partly because of the initial expense involved and partly because it meant throwing people, in many cases family members, out of work. Most of those who did adopt his methods refrained from paying him a licensing fee, even though by 1790 he held a federal patent. Evans's experience with the automated flour mill was similar to Whitney's experience with the cotton gin, in that he spent most of the money he made from licensing fees on legal fees suing patent infringers.

In 1792 Evans sold his interest in the Red Clay Creek mill and opened a store in Philadelphia. He also built a machine shop and returned to tinkering with his earlier idea about steam-powered transportation. By 1801 he had built a stationary steam engine, which he used to power a rotary crusher for making lime. He started by designing a direct, high-pressure steam engine with a cylindrical boiler (the first built in the United States) rather than a condenser-equipped model of the type invented by James Watt. Then he connected the steam cylinder to the crankshaft by means of an innovative straight-line linkage, thus permitting the entire mechanism to work more efficiently. Soon he had connected steam engines to machinery for doing everything from sowing seed to sawing wood. By 1804 he had devised a way to use his steam engine to power a wagon for hauling freight over long distances, but the authorities refused to grant him permission to operate it on the Pennsylvania Turnpike because they were afraid it would frighten horses. In 1805 he invented the Orukter Amphibolos, a Greek term that means Amphibious Digger. Orukter Amphibolos was a 30-foot steam-powered barge he built under contract to the city of Philadelphia for dredging the city's waterfront. The dredging mechanism was an elevator-type device similar to the one he had designed for his flour mill. He also outfitted Orukter Amphibolos with wheels so that it could operate on land as well as in the water, thus making it the first self-propelled vehicle to operate on land in the United States.

In 1806 Evans constructed a factory in Philadelphia for manufacturing steam engines. Called the Mars Works, it included an iron foundry and a machine shop. Over the next 13 years it turned out more than 100 steam engines and boilers, as well as a host of mill machinery and other mechanical devices. Many of his steam engines provided the motive power for steamboats plying the nation's great rivers. In 1819 the Mars Works burned to the ground, the fire destroying virtually all of Evans's patterns and molds. Four days later, on April 15, 1819, Oliver Evans died in New York City while on a business trip.

Further Reading

Bathe, Greville, and Dorothy Bathe. *Oliver Evans; A Chronicle of Early American Engineering.* New York: Arno Press, 1972.

Ferguson, Eugene S. *Oliver Evans, Inventive Genius of the American Industrial Revolution.* Greenville, Del.: Hagley Museum, 1980.

"Oliver Evans, 1755–1819," District Energy Biographies. Available online. URL: http://www.history.rochester. edu/steam/evans/. Downloaded on July 2, 2009.

Everleigh, Ada (Ada Lester) (1876–1960), and Minna Everleigh (Minna Lester) (1878–1948)
entrepreneurs in prostitution

Prior to 1920, when women's suffrage was passed into law, business opportunities for women in the United States were severely circumscribed. In fact, the best way for a woman of the late 18th/early 19th century to make a lot of money on her own was to become the madam of a house of prostitution. Few, if any, madams did better than the Everleigh sisters, Ada and Minna, who made more than $8 million in 11 years and then lived the rest of their lives in aristocratic luxury.

The Everleigh sisters were born Ada and Minna Lester on February 15, 1876, and July 13, 1878, respectively, in the backwoods of Kentucky. Their father was a lawyer and their mother was a homemaker. In 1897 they married a pair of brothers (names unknown), who turned out to be wife beaters. Leaving the brothers behind, in 1898 the sisters moved to Omaha, Nebraska. Having no skills and little education, and with the Trans-Mississippi Exposition in town, the sisters earned their keep as prostitutes in a part of the exposition known as the "Streets of Cairo." By the end of the exposition the following year, they had made enough money to open a brothel of their own. In 1900 Ada and Minna Everleigh, as they called themselves, sold the brothel, moved to Chicago, Illinois, and opened the Everleigh Club, a pleasure palace for high-rollers in the center of the Windy City's red-light district.

The Everleighs set out to make their establishment the finest one in Chicago. At the opposite end of the spectrum from the 25-cent whorehouses that catered to the dregs of male society, the Everleigh Club charged $50 for admission and required a recommendation from a regular patron. In return, a gentleman could spend one hour with any one of 30 gorgeous "butterflies," as the Everleighs called their girls. The club itself was a three-story mansion with 50 rooms, many of them decorated in themes such as the Copper Room and the Hall of Mirrors. The rooms in which the butterflies entertained patrons were soundproof; they were also lavishly appointed with marble inlaid brass beds, pianos, rare books, Persian rugs, gilded bathtubs, and gold-plated spittoons. In the ballroom, where the butterflies put on many an exotic and erotic show for the patrons, three orchestras played around the clock.

The Everleighs had no trouble finding women to work as butterflies. At the time, young women from the country like the Everleighs and female immigrants from all over Europe were flocking to Chicago and other cities, all of them desperate to find employment. "Honest" work for a woman usually meant a job as a domestic, where she was required to work long hard hours, six days a week, for about $1 a day. Moreover, many domestics were expected to provide, as part of their jobs, sexual gratification for either the man of the house or one of his sons. On the other hand, prostitution, at least within the confines of a high-class brothel like the Everleigh Club, provided an attractive young woman with a safe, comfortable place to live, a bevy of "sisters" with whom to socialize and draw on for support, an opportunity to meet marriage-able men of means, and a daily wage of about $4. Nor did the Everleighs have trouble finding men to be their customers. The Victorian morals of the day frowned upon married women having frequent sexual relations with their husbands, while the pseudoscience of the day taught that male mastur-bation caused insanity. Meanwhile, the rapid pace of industrialization was concentrating enormous amounts of money into the hands of a small num-ber of men, who thought nothing of trading a little of it for a night of pleasure.

As a result, the Everleigh sisters became mil-lionaires, taking in an average of $15,000 each week. In fact, the sisters faced only one major business problem: Prostitution was illegal. They countered this problem in several ways. First, they helped keep antivice bills from being passed by the state legislature by admitting state legislators free of charge. Second, they greased the palms of corrupt judges, aldermen, and police officials with healthy bribes, thus protecting themselves from being raided excessively (the nature of their clientele helped cut down on raids, too). Third, they con-tributed generously to the campaign funds of nearly every public official in Chicago, going so far as to allow their butterflies to appear gratis at the First Ward Democratic Club's annual ball.

Despite all these precautions, in 1911 the Ever-leighs were forced out of business. The one element they could not control was the growing reform movement in America, better known as Progres-sivism. Moral reformers across the country hated prostitution and vowed to shut it down. In 1905, just days before a mayoral election, hundreds of reformers, led by an evangelist on a month-long antivice campaign, invaded the Everleigh Club and held a prayer meeting in the ballroom. The club remained shut down until after the election, when an anti-antivice candidate was elected. In 1907 a Republican reformer was elected mayor, and he personally led raids on the major bawdy houses, including the Everleigh Club. In 1911 the club was closed down for good.

Undaunted, the Everleighs left Chicago, never to return. They had invested the millions of dol-lars they had earned from the brothel wisely, and they spent the rest of their lives traveling about Europe and living as aristocrats on New York City's West Side. After Minna died on September 16, 1948, Ada moved to a secluded country estate in Virginia, where she died on January 3, 1960.

Further Reading

"Chicago: City of the Century," PBS. Available online. URL: http://www.pbs.org/wgbh/amex/chicago/peopleevents/p_everleigh.html. Downloaded on July 2, 2009.

Washburn, Charles. *Come into My Parlor: A Biography of the Aristocratic Everleigh Sisters of Chicago.* New York: Arno Press, 1974.

F

Fairchild, Sherman

(1896–1971) *entrepreneur in airline and semiconductor industries*

Many entrepreneurs and business leaders enjoy success because of their laserlike concentration on one aspect of commerce. Others gain renown by starting in one area and branching out into a related field. Then there are the few, such as Sherman Fairchild, who become pioneers in several disparate fields. Fairchild—whose diverse interests and abilities led him to design an indoor tennis court and become a gourmet cook—would eventually own 30 patents and make an indelible impression on the burgeoning field of aeronautics and the creation of Silicon Valley.

Sherman Mills Fairchild was born in Oneonta, New York, on April 7, 1896. He was the only child of Josephine and George. Fairchild's father was successful in a wide range of endeavors, including newspaper publishing, election to the U.S. House of Representatives, and ownership of a company that manufactured clocks and adding machines that eventually merged with two others to form International Business Machines (IBM). Fairchild was an intelligent and inquisitive child who was fascinated with the relatively new field of photography. He enrolled at Harvard in 1915, where he developed a flash camera that he used to take pictures in his role as managing editor of the *Harvard Illustrated.*

Fairchild left Harvard after only a year because he contracted tuberculosis and, seeking a dry and hot climate for his health, transferred to the University of Arizona where he studied aerial photography and worked to assist the military during World War I through the development of new shutter technology for aerial cameras. With his health restored, Fairchild transferred to Columbia University in New York City. He soon left Columbia and—with his father's support and financial backing—established the Fairchild Aerial Camera Corporation, eventually became Fairchild Camera and Instrument.

The photography produced by Fairchild's company was enormously useful in mapmaking and surveying and led the curious and ambitious Fairchild to explore airplane manufacturing. In 1927, Fairchild completed his first aircraft, which was the first with an enclosed cabin and folding wings. Development of related airplanes later played a crucial role in a variety of capacities, such as training and surveying, during World War II and the Korean War. Fairchild also explored other interests, and in 1931 he established the Fairchild Recording Equipment Corporation to test his theories of sound recording. He continued to advance camera technology by developing a front projection background system.

Fairchild continued to run his companies while also garnering extensive wealth as the largest stockholder in IBM, which he inherited from his father upon his death in 1925. He also was a key shareholder in PanAmerican Airlines, which he helped build. Fairchild's role in the evolution of the semiconductor business evolved from his formation of Fairchild Semiconductor in 1957, a company that began with his financial backing of engineers—dubbed the "Traitorous Eight" because they left Shockley Semiconductor as a group— who blazed trails in the development of solid-state transistors. Fairchild Semiconductor quickly became an incubator of leading talent and breakthroughs that would ultimately lead to Silicon Valley becoming the center of the high technology business.

Though he would be credited for his impact on the rise of the telecommunications industry later in the century, Fairchild was also recognized for his accomplishments during his time. A July 25, 1960, *Time* magazine cover story that focused on business leaders noted of Fairchild, "A big part of Fairchild Camera's magic lies in the man who lent it—and several other companies—his name: Sherman Mills Fairchild, 64. Fairchild talks about his present and future products with all the excitement of a 20-year-old with his first sports car. He is the epitome of the new scientist-businessman-inventor who is the driving force behind the success of the growth and glamour stocks. Cut from the same Yankee tinkerer mold as Ben Franklin, Thomas Edison and Henry Ford, he never got an engineering degree–yet has more than two dozen patents in his name. He flatly says, 'I have no urge to make money'—yet has piled up a fortune of more than $80 million."

Fairchild died in New York City after a long illness on March 28, 1971. He left most of his $200 million estate to two charitable foundations formed in his name. Fairchild's name graces the Library of Engineering and Applied Science at the California Institute of Technology in Pasadena. He is buried near his boyhood home in Oneonta, New York.

Further Reading
"Sherman Fairchild," Cal Tech. Available online. URL: http://library.caltech.edu/sherman/fairchild.htm. Downloaded on May 28, 2009.
"The Yankee Tinkerers," *Time.* Available online. URL: http://www.time.com/time/magazine/article/0,9171,826520,00.html. Downloaded on July 1, 2009.

Farnsworth, Philo Taylor
(1906–1971) *inventor of the image dissector*

Although VLADIMIR KOSMA ZWORYKIN is considered to be the father of television, Philo Farnsworth deserves a share of the title; the modern television transmission tube is a composite of the ideas of both men. Zworykin came up with his idea at the age of 34, but Farnsworth got his when he was just 15 years old.

Farnsworth was born on August 19, 1906, in Indian Creek (present-day Manderfield), Utah. His parents, Lewis and Serena, were farmers. At age 12 he moved with his family to a ranch in Rigby, Idaho. By this time he had already developed a keen interest in science. He loved to tinker with electrical devices and make models of automobile engines. He also loved to read about science and chemistry, and he became fascinated with the photoelectric cell and the cathode-ray tube.

Farnsworth knew so much about chemistry when he entered high school that he was put into the senior chemistry class. One day he and his chemistry teacher, Justin Tolman, got into a discussion about television, which was a hot topic in the science magazines Farnsworth read. He confided to Tolman that he believed mechanical scanners, which all existing television systems used at the time, would never work fast enough to transmit a clear picture. Instead, he was convinced that, in order to get sharp pictures, images would have to be converted into electronic waves, the same way sound is converted into radio waves. The 15-year-old Farnsworth then showed a sketch of his idea to the astonished Tolman and explained how it could be done: A camera lens would focus an image on a photoelectric cell, thus changing the image into electronic signals, which would then be transmitted as radio waves to a receiver, which would project the waves onto a cathode-ray tube, which would convert the waves back into the original image.

At age 16 Farnsworth moved with his family to Provo, Utah. After finishing high school he served a brief stint in the U.S. Navy, then enrolled at Brigham Young University. He dropped out after two years when his father died, and in 1926 he and Clifford Gardner opened a radio repair shop in Salt

Lake City. That same year he married Gardner's sister, Elma, with whom he had four children.

Still dreaming of developing his idea about television, in 1926 Farnsworth saw a newspaper advertisement, calling for fundraiser assistants, that had been placed by George Everson, a professional fundraiser from San Francisco. After getting hired by Everson, Farnsworth explained his idea to Everson, who was impressed enough to introduce Farnsworth to Mott Smith, a scientist of some renown. Smith assured Everson and his partner, Leslie Gorrell, that Farnsworth's idea was scientifically sound, and the two partners agreed to fund Farnsworth's efforts to make his idea a reality. That same year Everson and Gorrell acquired backing from additional investors and set up Farnsworth in a laboratory in San Francisco.

In the process of perfecting a photoelectric cell for use as a transmission tube, Farnsworth invented the image dissector. This electronic tube transmits pictures with a high degree of resolution, resulting in a sharp picture at the receiver. However, because it is highly insensitive to light, only very bright images can be transmitted accurately. Nevertheless, by 1927 Farnsworth had progressed enough to file for a patent for an all-electronic television, which was granted in 1930. While waiting for the patent, Farnsworth gave public demonstrations in his laboratory, and in 1929 Everson, Gorrell, and their partners formed Television Inc. as a subsidiary of the Philco Radio Company, a radio manufacturer. Two years later Farnsworth moved to Philadelphia, Pennsylvania, where he gave more demonstrations on Philco's experimental television station.

Meanwhile, in 1924 Vladimir Zworykin, an engineer with the Radio Corporation of America (RCA), had also invented an all-electronic television. Instead of using an image dissector like Farnsworth, Zworykin's system used an iconoscope, a storage pickup tube that does not produce as sharp an image as the image dissector but that is much more sensitive to light, thus allowing it to transmit not-so-bright images much better than the image dissector. Also, Zworykin's picture tube, which he called the kinescope, was markedly better than Farnsworth's cathode-ray tube, which he called the oscillite.

By 1934 RCA was using as a transmission tube a combination image dissector and iconoscope, so Farnsworth sued the company for patent infringement. That same year the U.S. Patent Office conducted a hearing into the matter, during which Zworykin claimed to have invented a device similar to the image dissector in 1923, four years before Farnsworth filed for his patent. But the examiners found in Farnsworth's favor after his old chemistry teacher, Justin Tolman, testified about what Farnsworth had said and shown him in 1922. RCA appealed the ruling but lost the appeal in 1936. After three years of trying unsuccessfully to invent another form of the image dissector, RCA agreed to enter into a licensing arrangement with Farnsworth for the rights to use the image dissector in their televisions.

In 1939 Farnsworth and his backers bought a company that manufactured phonographs and radios in Fort Wayne, Indiana, renamed it the Farnsworth Television and Radio Corporation, and began making televisions. However, the partners lacked the necessary expertise to make it successful; in order to avoid bankruptcy, in 1949 they sold the company to International Telephone and Telegraph (ITT).

Farnsworth became a research engineer with ITT, and eventually he began experimenting with nuclear fusion as part of an ITT contract with the federal government. When the contract was canceled in 1966, he spent a year relaxing in Maine, then moved to Salt Lake City where he started another company to continue his experiments with fusion. Using a laboratory at Brigham Young University for his experiments, he got a government contract of his own, but it, too, was canceled, and in 1970 Farnsworth went out of business. He retired to Holladay, Utah, where he died on March 11, 1971.

Further Reading

Everson, George. *The Story of Television: The Life of Philo T. Farnsworth.* North Stratford, N.H.: Ayer Publishing, 1998.

Godfrey, Donald G. *Philo T. Farnsworth: The Father of Television.* Salt Lake City: University of Utah Press, 2001.

Schwartz, Evan I. *The Last Lone Inventor: Tale of Genius, Deceit, and the Birth of Television.* New York: Harper-Collins, 2002.

Field, Cyrus West

(1819–1892) *entrepreneur in transatlantic cable*

Cyrus Field did not invent telegraphy, or the telegraph line, or even come up with the idea of laying telegraph lines underwater. He did, however, conceive of the idea of connecting Europe and North America via a transatlantic cable. When the project finally succeeded after 12 frustrating years, Field was hailed as the "new Columbus" for once again bringing together the Old World and the New.

Field was born Cyrus West Field on November 30, 1819, in Stockbridge, Massachusetts. His father, David, was a minister, and his mother, Submit, was a homemaker. At age 15 he moved to New York City and went to work as an errand boy in Alexander T. Stewart's dry-goods store. After several years he had worked his way up to senior clerk, at which point he returned to Massachusetts and took a job as a salesman for a paper mill. In 1840 he married Mary Stone with whom he had seven children, and returned to New York City to become a partner in E. Root & Company, a paper wholesaler. Six months later the company failed, so he became partners with his brother-in-law and formed Cyrus W. Field & Company, another paper wholesaler. By 1851 he had made enough money to pay off E. Root & Company's debts in full, with $250,000 left over.

In 1854 Field was introduced to Frederick N. Gisborne, a Canadian engineer. Gisborne sought financial aid for a project of his that would improve communications between Great Britain and North America: the laying of a submarine telegraph cable between the United States and Nova Scotia, which would be linked more closely to Ireland by a line of fast steamships. Field knew Gisborne's plan was feasible, because underwater cables had already been laid between England and Holland and between Scotland and Ireland. Being a bit of an adventurer, Field suggested that Gisborne modify his plan by dropping the steamship line and extending the underwater cable all the way to Ireland. That same year Field formed the New York, Newfoundland, & London Electric Telegraph Company, with PETER COOPER as president, which raised about $1.6 million from private investors

Despite numerous setbacks, Cyrus Field succeeded in laying the first transatlantic cable. This photo is a daguerreotype made between 1844 and 1860 by the famous photographer Mathew Brady. *(Library of Congress)*

and the governments of the United States and Great Britain. To make sure his cable had customers in place as soon as it was reliably operable, in 1854 he formed the American Telegraph Company, with lines stretching from Newfoundland to New Orleans, Louisiana, and in 1856 he formed the Atlantic Telegraph Company, with lines throughout Great Britain.

Unfortunately, it took 12 years to make the transatlantic cable reliably operable. The first telegraph line snapped in 1857 before it could be completed, and it had to be abandoned. The second line was finished in 1858 and worked fine for about a month before its insulation failed and the line went dead. At this point, many of his investors pulled out and threw their support to the establishment of an intercontinental telegraph line connecting Asia and North America via a submarine cable in the Bering Strait. Before he could mount a third attempt, the Civil War broke out and all work stopped on the project for four years. In 1865 the line snapped in the middle of the Atlantic once again. Undaunted, Field tried again, and in 1866 his company managed to lay another transatlantic cable. That same year his crews recovered the snapped line from the year before and successfully completed it, too, thus making the cable doubly reliable.

Field profited greatly from the transatlantic cable. He also profited from investments in Western Union, which eventually acquired his Newfoundland-to-New Orleans lines, the New York Elevated Railroad Company, the Wabash Railroad, and the New York Mail and Express. By 1887 his fortune was worth about $6 million. That same year, however, he became overextended financially as a result of a failed investment deal and lost almost all of his fortune in one day. He died on July 12, 1892, in New York City.

Further Reading

Carter, Samuel III. *Cyrus Field: Man of Two Worlds.* New York: Putnam, 1968.
"Cyrus W. Field," Atlantic Cable and Undersea Communications. Available online. URL: http://www.atlantic-cable.com/Field/papermerchant.htm. Downloaded on July 2, 2009.
Judson, Isabella F. *Cyrus W. Field, His Life and His Work.* New York: Garrett Press, 1969.

Field, Marshall

(1834–1906) *founder of Marshall Field & Company*

Along with Alexander T. Stewart in New York City and JOHN WANAMAKER in Philadelphia, Chicago's Marshall Field was one of America's department-store pioneers. Although each went about it in his own way, these three men popularized such modern retail policies as the one-price system and "satisfaction guaranteed." They also established clean, attractive stores that offered a plethora of goods and customer services. Although Field was the last of the three pioneers, he eventually surpassed the other two when his Chicago store became the largest department store in the United States.

Field was born on August 18, 1834, in Conway, Massachusetts. His parents, John and Fidelia, were farmers. At age 16 he moved to Pittsfield and went to work as a clerk in Deacon Davis's dry-goods store, a category that includes just about anything one might find in a modern department store. In 1856 Davis offered him a partnership in the store, but Field decided instead to move to Chicago, Illinois, where a brother lived. Upon his arrival he took a job as a clerk with Cooley, Wadsworth and Company, the city's largest wholesaler of dry goods. Over the next four years, Field worked as a clerk and a traveling salesman, demonstrating a talent for moving a variety of goods while creating customer goodwill. In 1860 he was made a junior partner in the firm, as well as its sales manager and credit manager. By 1863 he was a full partner in the firm, which changed its name that same year to Farwell, Field & Company. In 1863 he married Nannie Scott with whom he had two children. She died in 1896, and in 1905 he married Delia Caton.

By 1865 Field had become interested in expanding his wholesale operation to include retail sales, but his partner, Joseph Farwell, balked at the idea. That same year they ended their partnership amicably, and Field became partners with Potter Palmer, a prosperous Chicago retailer, and Levi Z. Leiter, a junior partner in Farwell, Field, in the wholesale/retail firm of Field, Palmer, and Leiter. Over the next 16 years the company's retail trade thrived, and Field became more and more interested in getting out of the wholesale trade altogether. Once again his partners demurred, and by 1881 Field had bought out both of them and reorganized the firm as a retail-only business called Marshall Field & Company.

Although Stewart and Wanamaker had been exerting much positive influence on retailers in the East, midwestern storekeepers had learned few of their lessons. It remained to Field to teach them about modern retailing. Like Stewart and Wanamaker, Field refused to make his customers haggle over prices as if they were buying a horse. He established a one-price policy, whereby the price of each item was clearly posted for all to see. He cheerfully refunded the entire purchase price of an item if that item failed to give complete satisfaction. He offered goods that appealed to the well-to-do and the price conscious alike. He established liberal credit policies, practiced truth in advertising, imported high-quality consumer goods from Europe and Asia, offered an in-store restaurant, and, except for groceries and hardware, displayed practically everything anyone could possibly want to buy in 73 acres of floor space. By 1900 Marshall Field & Company was doing business in the largest department store in the country, and its book, china, shoe, and toy departments were believed to be the largest departments of their kind in the world.

Field had few interests outside of retailing. He did contribute generously to several charities, including the University of Chicago, the Art Institute of Chicago, and Chicago's Columbian Museum, later renamed the Field Museum of Natural History. He died on January 16, 1906, while on a business trip in New York City. After his death his estate was valued at $125 million.

Further Reading

Koehn, Nancy F. *Brand New: How Entrepreneurs Earned Consumers' Trust from Wedgwood to Dell.* Boston: Harvard Business School Press, 2001.

———. *Marshall Field, 1834–1906: The Retail Brand as a Customer Experience.* Boston: Division of Research, Harvard Business School, 1999.

Wendt, Lloyd, and Herman Kogan. *Give the Lady What She Wants! The Story of Marshall Field & Company.* South Bend, Ind.: And Books, 1979.

Filo, David (1966–), and Jerry Yang (1968–)
founders of Yahoo!

In future centuries, when historians document the first days of the technological breakthrough of the Internet, there will almost certainly be a great deal of attention given to the people who were among the first to tame the seemingly endless and exponentially increasing amount of data available to its users. When that historical examination occurs, David Filo and Jerry Yang—who began working together as scruffy graduate students in a small, dark office—will emerge prominently for their role in changing the role of high technology in business.

David Filo was born on April 20, 1966. He moved with his family from Wisconsin to Lake Bluff, Louisiana—a suburb of the southwestern

Louisiana town of St. Charles—when he was six years old. Filo was an excellent student and graduated from Sam Houston High School in Lake Charles before enrolling at Tulane University in New Orleans, where he graduated with a bachelor's degree in computer engineering. He then earned master's in science from Stanford and remained there to pursue a doctorate degree.

Jerry Yang was born Yang Chih-Yuan on November 6, 1968, in Taipei, Taiwan. His father died when he was only two years old, and he moved with his mother and brother six years later to San Jose, California. Yang adopted the first name Jerry, and, although he knew very little English when he arrived, he quickly learned the language while excelling at science and mathematics. Yang graduated from Piedmont Hills High School—where he played on the tennis team and was elected senior class president—before receiving bachelor's and master's degrees in electrical engineering in only four years at Stanford.

Filo and Yang met in 1989 when both were studying at Stanford. They became close friends in 1992 while in Japan on a six-month academic exchange program. Soon after they returned to the United States, Filo and Yang began finding time away from their doctoral studies to pursue the development of software that could organize sites from the burgeoning World Wide Web into categories. They named their newly created site Jerry's Guide to the World Wide Web though they soon changed the name to Yahoo! (an acronym for yet another hierarchical officious oracle).

Quickly, Filo and Yang were working 20-hour days on their project, which they ran out of a makeshift trailer on the Stanford campus. As word spread about their project, they began to attract the attention of venture capitalists. They decided to partner with the venture capitalist Mike Moritz of Sequoia Capital. Yang later explained, "We weren't so much looking for money as for another partner who could help us with the aspects of the business that we didn't understand and give us skills that we didn't have . . . [Moritz] . . . shared our values. Like us he's cheap, and he's not a big believer that technology solves everything. But he does believe in the human element and in the art of what we were doing as well as the science."

Yahoo!'s popularity spread largely through word of mouth, as millions of Internet users found its services useful and exciting. Yahoo! made most of its revenues from advertising, mainly banner and button ads that decorated the margins of many Web pages. In addition, Yahoo! closely targeted those ads to users' specific interests simply by observing the Web-surfing patterns of individual users. Yahoo also advanced methods of measuring the effectiveness of a particular ad, primarily by determining whether a Web user clicked on it, which was a service for which advertisers were willing to pay more money. By 1996, Yahoo!'s advertising revenue was about $19 million. Through strategic plans for growth and the Internet's popularity explosion, Yahoo!'s advertising revenue rose to approximately $2.5 billion by 2004.

Though Yahoo! has remained among the Internet's greatest successes, Filo and Yang have recently been the target of criticism. Yahoo!'s reported role in providing the Chinese security agencies with information on the Internet surfing activity of a reporter and a political dissident led the advocacy group Reporters Without Borders to call Yahoo! "a Chinese police informant" whose actions led to the conviction of a journalist and writer. They were also criticized for what was viewed by many as the bungled opportunity to be acquired by Microsoft in 2008.

Yahoo! has its headquarters in Sunnyvale, California, and remains a leading global Internet communications, commerce, and media company that—according to its Web site—serves more than 345 million individuals each month worldwide. As the first online navigational guide to the Web, www.yahoo.com is the leading guide in terms of traffic, advertising, and household and business user reach. Yahoo! is the No. 1 Internet brand globally and reaches the largest audience worldwide. Filo, who is married to photographer and former teacher Angela Buenning, still holds the title of "Chief Yahoo" and is the company's director of technological operations. The success of the company has made both Filo and Yang billionaires. Yang, who is married to Akiko Yamazaki—a student he met on his academic exchange trip to Japan—stepped down from his 18-month tenure as CEO and returned to his role as "Chief Yahoo" in 2009.

Further Reading

Patsuris, Penelope, "Old Souls." *Forbes.* Available online. URL: http://www.forbes.com/1998/10/02/feat.html. Downloaded on July 1, 2009.

Schlender, Brent, "How A Virtuoso Plays the Web Eclectic: Inquisitive and Academic, Yahoo's Jerry Yang Reinvents the Role of the Entrepreneur." *Fortune.* Available online. URL: http://money.cnn.com/magazines/fortune/fortune_archive/2000/03/06/275253/index.htm. Downloaded on July 1, 2009.

Fitch, John
(1743–1798) *inventor of the steamboat*

Robert Fulton made the steamboat an economically viable means of transportation following the successful trial run of his vessel, the *Clermont,* in 1807. John Fitch, on the other hand, never made a nickel from his steamboat, but it made its successful trial in 1787, 20 years before Fulton's. Despite his success as an inventor, Fitch was a failure at just about everything else, and that may be why Fulton's name and not Fitch's is most closely associated with the invention of the steamboat.

Fitch was born on January 21, 1743, in Windsor, Connecticut. His parents, Joseph and Sarah, were farmers. As a teenager he ran away to sea, but he came back home after spending a few weeks on a ship that was engaged in the coastal trade. He then apprenticed himself to two clock makers, neither of whom taught him much about making clocks. In 1765 he went to work in a brass foundry, and two years later he married Lucy Roberts with whom he had two children. By the time the second child was born in 1769, he had abandoned his family. He did not see any of them again until 25 years later, by which time his children no longer acknowledged him as their father. He made his way to Trenton, New Jersey, where he spent the next six years making brass buttons, repairing clocks, and eventually working as a silversmith and gunsmith. After serving for five years in the New Jersey militia during the American Revolution, he went to Kentucky where he lost what little money he had in a failed land deal. In 1782 he was surveying along the Ohio River when he was captured by Indians allied with the British, and he spent nine months in a British prisoner-of-war camp in Montreal, Canada. After the war he settled in Bucks County, Pennsylvania, and he got involved in another land deal that failed when the U.S. Congress invalidated his claims.

For some unknown reason, in 1785 Fitch was inspired to invent the steamboat. He insisted throughout the rest of his life that he had never heard of a steam engine, which had been perfected by the British inventor James Watt some 20 years earlier, before he built one himself. Regardless, that same year he built a steam engine much like the one invented by the British inventor Thomas Newcomen around 1700, and he designed a boat with side paddles on which to mount it. With the help of Henry Voight, a watchmaker, and the financial backing of a group of investors from Philadelphia, Pennsylvania, he built a side-paddle steamboat that was powered by a steam engine of Fitch's design that more closely resembled Watt's version. In 1787 the boat was demonstrated successfully on the Delaware River near Philadelphia before a group of observers that included several of the signers of the U.S. Constitution. Later that same year Fitch and Voight built a 45-foot-long steamboat on which the paddles were mounted on the rear. This boat, named the *Perseverance*, could reach speeds of up to eight miles per hour, and spent the entire summer of 1790 traveling back and forth between Philadelphia and Trenton for a total of about 2,000 miles.

Although the boat was a mechanical success, it never became a commercial success. The public showed little interest in traveling or shipping goods by steamboat, so the summer excursions lost money. Meanwhile, in 1785 James Rumsey, a Maryland inventor, had also built a steamboat which he claimed to have originally invented in 1784, a year before Fitch got the idea. For six years the two men battled each other for preeminence. The U.S. Patent Office had yet to come into existence, so the two rivals appealed to the various state legislatures for state patents. Although Fitch gained patents from Delaware, New Jersey, New York, Pennsylvania, and Virginia, Rumsey received the support of such influential Americans as George Washington, Thomas Jefferson, and Benjamin Franklin. The battle between Fitch and Rumsey left both men

drained of energy and money—it did, however, contribute significantly to the passage of the Patent Act in 1790—and the fact that both received a patent for the steamboat issued on the same day in 1791 settled nothing. Rumsey died the following year, and Fitch's backers pulled out when his newest steamboat sank in a storm in 1791. The departures of Fitch and Rumsey from the field brought a temporary halt to the development of steam travel in the United States.

Fitch returned to Kentucky where he became involved in yet another failed land deal. Broken financially and in spirit, he lived out his remaining days in bitter solitude and committed suicide in Bardstown, Kentucky, in June or July 1798. In 1807 Robert Fulton, apparently acting in complete ignorance of the accomplishments of Fitch and Rumsey, successfully demonstrated his steamboat, the *Clermont*, on the Hudson River between New York City and Albany, New York, and went on to develop the first commercially successful steamboat operation in the United States.

Further Reading

Fitch, John. *The Autobiography of John Fitch*. Philadelphia: American Philosophical Society, 1976.

Flexner, James Thomas. *Steamboats Come True*. New York: Fordham University Press, 1992.

Harris, C. M. "The Improbable Success of John Fitch." *American Heritage of Invention & Technology* 4, no. 3 (Winter 1989): 23–31.

Flagler, Henry Morrison

(1830–1913) *entrepreneur in the development of Florida*

Contrary to what many young people may believe, Florida was not built by WALT DISNEY. The person most responsible for developing Florida into a vacation center was Henry Flagler, a partner of JOHN DAVISON ROCKEFELLER in the Standard Oil Company and Trust. Flagler built hotels and a railroad along the state's sleepy Atlantic coast, thus transforming Florida's economy and providing the springboard from which it would become one of the most vibrant and bustling states in the country.

Flagler was born in January 2, 1830, in Hopewell, New York. His father, Isaac, was a Presbyterian minister, and his mother, Elizabeth, was a homemaker. At age 14 he left home; working his way west as a deckhand on the Erie Canal and Lake Erie, he settled in Republic, Ohio, where he found a job as a clerk in a general store. He later moved to nearby Fostoria where he also clerked. By 1850 he had saved enough money to become a grain commission merchant in Bellevue, and he began shipping grain to customers in Cleveland, among them John D. Rockefeller. In 1853 he married Mary Harkness with whom he had three children. Around 1860 he moved to Saginaw, Michigan, where he entered the lumber and grain businesses. He also got into the business of mining and selling salt, which did exceptionally well until the end of the Civil War, when demand dropped off and he found himself overextended financially. In 1865, after selling his businesses, he borrowed enough money from his wife's uncle, Stephen Harkness, to open a general store in Cleveland. Within two years he had made a considerable amount of money, and in 1867 he became partners with Rockefeller in Rockefeller & Andrews, a Cleveland oil refinery.

Over the next 15 years Flagler was an active partner with Rockefeller in the creation and management of the Standard Oil conglomerate. When the Standard Oil Company was founded in 1870, Flagler was named secretary and treasurer, in effect making him the number-two man in the company. In 1873, the year Standard Oil became the largest oil refiner in the United States, he arranged lower shipping rates with the major oil-hauling railroads in exchange for guaranteed minimum daily shipments from Standard Oil's refineries. Since these rates were made available to any refinery that would merge itself into Standard Oil, they played a major role in permitting the company to acquire controlling interest in 90 percent of the nation's oil refineries. In 1877 he moved to New York City to take control of the company's affairs in the East. In 1882, when the partners created the Standard Oil Trust as a means of coordinating the operations of their holdings, he was elected president of the trust; however, effective day-to-day control of the company continued to be exercised by Rockefeller.

Although Flagler played a nominal management role in Standard Oil Trust until its dismantling in 1911, his active involvement in the trust's affairs ended in 1882.

That same year Flagler's personal holdings were worth about $15 million, and his interests soon turned to spending some of that money in Florida. In 1883 he married Ida Shourds, his first wife having died two years earlier, and the newlyweds went to Jacksonville and St. Augustine, Florida, on their honeymoon. While there, Flagler was impressed mightily by two things: northern Florida's incredible beauty and mild weather, and the backward condition of the state's transportation and tourist accommodations. It occurred to him that if railroads and first-class hotels were built in Florida, then the state could be transformed into a winter resort for wealthy Americans. In 1885 he decided to build a magnificent hotel in St. Augustine, the Ponce de Leon, and by the time it was completed three years later he had already begun building another hotel, the Alcazar, nearby.

At the time, Jacksonville was the southern terminus of the standard-gauge rail system in the East, so Flagler purchased a run-down, narrow-gauge line connecting St. Augustine to Jacksonville and widened and improved its right-of-way. By 1894 the railroad had been extended south through Ormond Beach, where he bought the run-down Hotel Ormond and where Rockefeller eventually built a large winter estate, to Palm Beach, where Flagler built two more hotels, the Royal Ponciana and the Breakers. Palm Beach attracted a number of wealthy visitors and residents and became known as "the American Riviera" because of its similarity to the strip of high-class Mediterranean beach resorts in France and Italy known as the Riviera. In addition to hauling passengers to his hotels, the railroad hauled citrus fruit from the Indian River region around Cocoa, where some of the tastiest oranges and grapefruit in the world are grown. He also acquired several land development companies with the intention of building up industries and communities along his railroad, which in 1895 was renamed the Florida East Coast Railway.

By 1896 the railroad had been expanded south as far as Miami. Flagler set out to transform the sleepy little tropical town by building the Royal

Palm Hotel, a water and sewage system, and an electrical power plant. He also dredged part of Biscayne Bay, on which Miami is located, and formed the Florida East Coast Steamship Company, which offered regular service between Miami and Nassau in the Bahama Islands. These improvements led to the incorporation of Miami as a city in 1896. In 1901 he divorced his second wife, married Mary Lily Kenan, and moved into a fine mansion he had built in Palm Beach. By 1912 he had completed the railroad all the way to Key West. At the time of his death on May 20, 1913, he had invested more than $50 million in various development projects in Florida. These projects repaid him handsomely, however, for he left behind an estate estimated at nearly twice that amount.

Further Reading

Martin, Sidney W. *Florida's Flagler.* Athens: University of Georgia Press, 1977.

———. *Henry Flagler: Visionary of the Gilded Age.* Lake Buena Vista, Fla.: Tailored Tours Pub., 1998.

Standiford, Les. *Last Train to Paradise: Henry Flagler and the Building of the Railroad that Crossed the Ocean.* New York: Crown, 2002.

Flanigen, Edith Marie

(1929–) *inventor of the synthetic emerald and molecular sieve*

Emeralds are well known as some of the world's most precious gemstones. Few people know that a molecular sieve is a crystalline compound that is used to do everything from converting crude oil into gasoline to removing water from refrigerant lines in refrigerators and automobile air conditioners. Edith Flanigen played a leading role in devising ways to produce emeralds and molecular sieves synthetically.

Flanigen was born on January 28, 1929, in Buffalo, New York. Her father worked in the lumber business and her mother was a homemaker. In high school she became interested in chemistry, in which she majored at D'Youville College where she earned her B.A. in 1950. After receiving her M.S. in chemistry from Syracuse University in 1952, she went to work as a research chemist for Union Carbide Corporation's Linde Division in Tonawanda, New York. In 1988 she left Union Carbide to work for UOP in Tarrytown, New York, a joint venture of Union Carbide and Allied Signal. She stayed with UOP until her retirement in 1994, although she continued to do consulting work for UOP for several years.

In 1960 Flanigen became part of a special research team assigned to develop a synthetic emerald. The maser (microwave amplification by stimulated emission of radiation) was invented in 1953 as a means of amplifying radio waves without adding any noise to the original signal. The first masers used a crystal rod as the amplifying device, and at the time it was thought that the most "noiseless" crystal for this application was the emerald. Unfortunately, emeralds are rare, so the U.S. government officials who were most interested in maser research began looking for someone who could make emeralds synthetically. Linde Division was already making artificial sapphires for other applications, so it accepted a government contract to "grow" emeralds in the laboratory. Flanigen and Norbert Mumbach, a Union Carbide colleague, figured out how to make a gelatinous mixture of silicon, oxygen, aluminum, beryllium, and chromium, the five elements that make up emeralds. After much experimentation, they determined the exact amount of heat and pressure that must be applied to the gel so that emeralds could be created in the laboratory. This process became known as the hydrothermal emerald synthesis process. Rubies later proved to work better than emeralds as maser amplifiers, and masers themselves were generally discarded in favor of lasers, so the industrial demand for synthetic emeralds never materialized as expected. However, for more than five years the synthetic emeralds developed by Flanigen and Mumbach were sold in a line of jewelry known as the Quintessa Collection.

In 1967 Flanigen assumed leadership of Union Carbide's molecular sieve research team. A molecular sieve is a porous, crystalline compound that does the opposite of a filter. While filters remove larger molecules and let the smaller ones pass through, a molecular sieve removes smaller molecules and lets the larger ones pass through. This is because the molecular sieve contains a number of small, ionized (electrically charged) cavities and channels that trap and remove the smaller molecules.

Flanigen's first task as team leader was to develop a new family of molecular sieves. At the time, molecular sieves existing in nature were composed of aluminum and silicon, and their cavities were too large to remove very small molecules. Flanigen directed the team in synthesizing a molecular sieve out of aluminum and phosphorus, which she hoped could be used to produce molecular sieves with smaller cavities. After experimenting with a number of different aqueous gels, pH levels, and temperatures, the team produced the first aluminophosphate molecular sieve. By 1985 Flanigen's team had produced more than 200 different sizes of molecular sieves. In addition to using aluminum, silicon, and phosphorus as the basic elements for synthesizing molecular sieves, the team also discovered how to make molecular sieves out of 10 other metals including cobalt, iron, and zinc. The team's efforts revolutionized the field of inorganic chemistry by demonstrating the feasibility of synthesizing a virtually unlimited number of new compounds.

Flanigen's work made a huge impression on the chemical industry. In 1991, she received the American Institute of Chemists' Chemical Pioneer Award. In 1992, she became the first woman to receive the Society of Chemical Industry's Perkin Medal. In 1993, she was also awarded the American Chemical Society's Garvan-Olin Medal.

The accolades for Flanigen's contributions to technological progress and invention continued into the 21st century, as she was presented with the Lifetime Achievement Award by the Massachusetts Institute of Technology. Also in 2004, Flanigen—who is the inventor or coinventor of over 100 patents—was inducted into the national Inventors Hall of Fame for her work in molecular filters and petroleum processing.

Further Reading

Camp, Carole Ann. *American Women Inventors.* Berkeley Heights, N.J.: Enslow Pub., 2002.
"Edith M. Flanigen," Lemuelson-MIT Program. Available online. URL: http://web.mit.edu/invent/a-winners/a-flanigen.html. Downloaded on June 30, 2009.
Stinson, Stephen. "Edith M. Flanigen Wins Perkin Medal." *Chemical and Engineering News* 70 (9 March 1992):25.

Fleischmann, Charles Louis
(1834–1897) *inventor of packaged baker's yeast*

From the time of the ancient Egyptians to the Industrial Revolution, the commercial production of bread changed little. After the mid-19th century, however, major improvements in baking equipment and processes permitted bakers to bake bread in greater quantity and with more uniform results than ever before. A major contributor to this evolution was Charles Fleischmann, whose solid baker's yeast gave commercially produced bread a superior taste and texture.

Fleischmann was born on November 3, 1834, in Budapest, Hungary, which was at the time part of the Austrian Empire. His father, Alois, was a distiller and yeast maker, and his mother, Babette, was a homemaker. Charles finished school at age 19 and went to work as a clerk in a general store in Tasgendorf, Austria. In 1866 he emigrated to New York City, where his older sister lived. That same year, while attending the reception following her wedding, he realized that American bread tasted flat because American bakers used a liquid yeast that did not leaven the dough sufficiently to give the bread a full body and flavor. Shortly thereafter, he paid a quick visit to Budapest to obtain some solid yeast his father had developed. Upon returning to New York City, he was unable to interest local bakers in the superiority of his yeast, perhaps because solid yeast is a bit more difficult to use than the liquid version. By 1868 he had married Henrietta Robertson with whom he had three children.

After working in a local distillery for two years, in 1868 Fleischmann moved to Cincinnati, Ohio, where he, his brother Maximilian, and James W. Gaff opened their own distillery under the name Gaff, Fleischmann and Company. Over the next 20 years Fleischmann received five patents for processes related to the distillation or aging of beer and liquor. His most important patent, however, concerned baker's yeast. In 1870 he and his brother Henry patented a high-quality, solid yeast that was similar to their father's, made from the froth formed during the fermentation of beer. For the next six years, he tried to sell the yeast to local bakers, but his lack of sales skills, probably the result of his eastern European accent, and the novelty of the product—a number of bakers apparently feared that bread made with Fleischmann's yeast would taste like beer—prevented the product from catching on. Finally, in 1876, he put together what he called the Model Vienna Bakery, a stunning exhibit at the Philadelphia Centennial Exposition. The exhibit permitted visitors to watch as the yeast was made, the dough was set, and the bread was baked, and then to sample the bread in a small café. Because Fleischmann's yeast fermented the sugars in wheat flour more completely than liquid yeast, the results were much more consistent. Bread from the Model Vienna Bakery was so uniformly light, thick, and tasty that visitors went away craving more.

Before long, bakers in Pennsylvania, New Jersey, and New York were inquiring about the yeast. To assuage their fears about the relative difficulty of using solid yeast, Fleischmann offered the services of a trained baker to help them get started. Because yeast must be used while it is fresh, Gaff, Fleischmann and Company opened distilleries on the outskirts of Philadelphia and New York City, as well as one outside Cincinnati, and established a daily delivery-wagon service to local bakers. By 1879 the company was also selling yeast to grocers where homemakers could buy it, and it had expanded its product line to include malt, syrup, vinegar, and feed by-products. Following the deaths of Gaff in 1879 and Maximilian Fleischmann in 1890, Charles Fleischmann became the sole proprietor of the company. By 1897 the company had branch operations in every major city in the United States and was operating the world's largest yeast plant in Peekskill, New York.

Fleischmann's inventive and entrepreneurial interests were not limited to the business interests of Gaff, Fleischmann and Company. By 1888 he had patented improvements to the cotton gin, sewing machine, and plow, as well as a method for extracting oil from cottonseed. His business involvement in Cincinnati included partnerships

in the Market National Bank; the *Cincinnati Commercial Tribune* newspaper; and the Cincinnati Cooperage Company, which made barrels and casks. He used his wealth to support a number of charitable organizations, especially orphanages, and to have fun. He developed a taste for French oil paintings and bronze statuary, and he became a major figure in East Coast yachting. Told by his doctor to spend more time outdoors, in 1890 he and his son Julius established Fleischmann & Son, which bred horses in Ohio and New Jersey and raced them with considerable success. At the time of his death on December 10, 1897, his fortune was estimated to be about $2 million.

Further Reading

Butterick Publishing Co. *The Story of a Pantry Shelf: An Outline History of Grocery Specialties.* New York: Butterick Publishing, 1925.

"History of Fleischmann's Yeast," Bread World. Available online. URL: http://www.breadworld.com/history.aspx. Downloaded on July 2, 2009.

Flora, William

(ca. 1750s–1820) *entrepreneur in cartage and real estate*

Not all blacks who lived in Virginia before 1865 were slaves. Between 1620 and 1660, blacks who had been purchased from slave ships calling on the colony were treated as if they were indentured servants, meaning they were given their freedom after a certain period, usually four to seven years. From them were descended a number of free blacks who, although they lived in a slave state, never experienced slavery personally. By 1820, perhaps two or three thousand free blacks lived in Virginia, mostly on the Eastern Shore or in the communities bordering Hampton Roads. The majority eked out a livelihood as farmers and were treated as second-class citizens, but a few became successful businessmen and entrepreneurs with the full support and backing of the white community. William Flora is the best-known of these free black entrepreneurs.

Nothing is known about the circumstances of Flora's birth. He was probably born around 1750 in the vicinity of Portsmouth; the names and occupations of his parents are unknown. In fact, nothing is known about his life before 1775, when he distinguished himself at the Battle of Great Bridge near Portsmouth. He was probably already well thought of at this time, however, because he was allowed to furnish his own musket, while colonial statutes prohibited free blacks from owning firearms.

By 1784 Flora owned a thriving cartage business. He hauled imported goods and supplies from the wharves and stores of Portsmouth to the plantations and farms of Norfolk and Suffolk counties, and he returned to town with loads of tobacco and other farm products. He also operated a livery stable and rented out riding carriages. By 1810 he owned three large wagons, three two-wheeled carriages, and six horses, a considerable amount of property at that time. Beginning in 1784, when he bought two unimproved lots in Portsmouth, he used the profits from his several businesses to buy and sell real estate. When he died, he owned two houses and a lot. He left them to his wife, a slave woman he married and set free sometime after 1782, and their two children. He may also have left them 100 acres of land in the Virginia Military District in southwestern Ohio, which he had received in 1818 for serving during the American Revolution.

Flora's success as an entrepreneur depended not only on his business acumen, but also on his skill at exploiting the opportunities made available to him as a war hero without exceeding the limitations imposed upon him by prevailing racial mores. At a time and place when most blacks were slaves, Flora was a self-employed businessman, a remarkable achievement of its own. He died around 1820 (the exact date is unknown) in Portsmouth.

Further Reading

Jackson, Luther Porter. *Virginia Negro Soldiers and Seamen in the Revolutionary War.* Norfolk, Vir.: Guide Quality Press, 1944.

Kaplan, Sidney. *The Black Presence in the Era of the American Revolution.* Amherst: University of Massachusetts Press, 1989.

Quarles, Benjamin. *The Negro in the American Revolution.* Chapel Hill: University of North Carolina Press, 1996, reprint.

Forbes, Malcolm Stevenson
(1919–1990) *entrepreneur in magazine publishing*

The period between 1945 and 1970 was corporate America's Golden Age. Having skated through World War II without incurring any damage to their industrial capability, American businesspeople were uniquely poised to rebuild two continents ravaged by war. They were also in a position to provide people across the country and around the world with the consumer goods many of them had done without since the beginning of the Great Depression in the 1930s. It was a boom time like no other, and no one covered it better than Malcolm Forbes, publisher and later owner of *Forbes* magazine. In addition to reporting on the Golden Age's top executives and free-spending successes, Forbes himself became a symbol of the people and culture he covered and an apostle of unapologetic wealth.

Forbes was born on August 19, 1919, in New York City. His father, Bertie, was a newspaper columnist and the publisher of *Forbes* magazine, and his mother, Adelaide, was a homemaker. In 1941 he received his B.A. in political science from Princeton University. That same year, with his father's financial backing, he became publisher of the *Fairfield* (New York) *Times* and the *Lancaster* (Ohio) *Tribune,* but both newspapers folded when he enlisted in the U.S. Army the following year to fight in World War II. In 1946, the same year he married Roberta Laidlaw with whom he had five children and whom he divorced in 1985, he joined the editorial staff of *Forbes* magazine, which had been founded by his father. The following year he was made associate publisher, and in 1954, the year his father died, he assumed total responsibility for the magazine's nonadvertising content.

In 1954, *Forbes* magazine was a rather stuffy journal focused largely on the doings of Wall Street. Founded in 1917 as the first business magazine in the United States, it had been eclipsed by its rivals, *Business Week* and *Fortune,* both of which had been founded in the late 1920s. By 1964, Forbes had transformed it into a vibrant magazine that covered the broad spectrum of American business, thus making it more competitive with magazines like *Fortune* and *Business Week*. Much of the coverage that had originally appeared in *Forbes* magazine was relegated to a new publication, *Forbes Investor,* which was published by the Investors Advisory Institute, founded in 1948 by Bertie Forbes as a means of providing better financial analysis for his readers. Meanwhile, *Forbes* magazine concentrated on reporting about companies engaged in virtually every type of economic endeavor, with an eye toward giving its readers a good sense of the relative prosperity of the various companies within the various industries.

In 1964, when his older brother Bruce died, Forbes took his place as president of *Forbes* magazine. Shortly thereafter, he acquired his stock, thus giving him control of the business and advertising side of the publication as well as its editorial content. Having no one to report to or satisfy other than readers and advertisers, Forbes set out to cover the business world in such a way that would appeal to the average person as well as to the corporate executive and investor. For the former, he provided breezy descriptions of corporate activity and cutting-edge trends as well as colorful stories about how top executives and entrepreneurs spent their money. For the latter, he provided rather detailed information about how successful companies got things done and, on occasion, how the failures had managed to fail. He also provided a creditable ranking of the top 500 companies in the United States as well as a ranking of the 400 wealthiest people in the world. It was a mix that worked well; by 1975 *Forbes* magazine had more than 600,000 subscribers and was attracting more advertising dollars than either *Fortune* or *Business Week.*

Part of Forbes's success formula was his hiring and relatively loose management of James W. Michaels as editor, but a significant part was the public image he created of himself. By 1970 he had made enough money from his publishing activities that he could afford to spend it just as lavishly as the big spenders covered in his magazine. He gave fancy parties on the lawn of his mansion in Far Hills, New Jersey, on his company yacht, and at the company townhouse in New York City; many of the parties were high-society soirees that were covered in the society pages and sometimes on television, thus generating excellent publicity among the people he wanted to reach as readers. The fanciest party of all was the birthday he threw for himself in 1989 that reportedly cost $2 million. He engaged in two rather exotic recreational activities, motorcycle racing and hot-air ballooning, collected a variety of expensive treasures such as Renaissance-era paintings and original historical documents, and acquired real estate holdings in exotic places such as Tangier, Fiji, and Tahiti. His other business interests included a development company that converted a 260-square-mile ranch in Colorado into vacation homes and retirement communities, an antiques dealer, and a motorcycle dealership. At the time of his death on February 24, 1990, at his home in Far Hills, his estate was estimated to be worth $600 million.

Further Reading

Jones, Arthur. *Malcolm Forbes: Peripatetic Millionaire.* New York: Harper and Row, 1977.
Winans, Christopher. *Malcolm Forbes: The Man Who Had Everything.* New York: St. Martin's Press, 1990.

Ford, Henry
(1863–1947) *inventor of the Model T automobile*

Perhaps no single individual did more to bring America out of the 19th century and into the 20th than Henry Ford. By inventing the Model T, the world's first automobile for people of limited means, Ford made it possible for the average farmer and worker to buy a car, which in turn gave them a sense of freedom they had never experienced before. Ford put America on wheels, and in the process he contributed indirectly to the growth of cities, the rise of suburbs, and the advent of motoring vacations. The mass-production methods he used to make Model Ts changed American industry forever.

Ford was born on July 30, 1863, in Springwells (present-day Greenfield) Township, Michigan. His parents, William and Mary, were farmers. At age 16 he moved to Detroit where he went to work as an apprentice machinist. Three years later he got a job with the Westinghouse Engine Company servicing and repairing steam-powered tractors throughout southern Michigan. In 1891, three years after he married Clara Bryant with whom he had one child, he returned to Detroit to take a job as a night engineer with the Edison Illuminating Company, the local electric utility.

Like many other young machinists of the day, Ford hoped to build an automobile from which he could make a fortune. In 1896, in a shed behind his apartment, he built his first car, the Quadricycle, essentially a gasoline-powered buggy frame mounted on four bicycle wheels. Three years later he built a sturdier, heavier car that attracted the attention of several investors. In 1899 he and a group led by William H. Murphy, a Detroit lumber merchant, formed the Detroit Automobile Company (later known as the Henry Ford Company), with Ford serving as superintendent of production. Ford soon became more interested in racing cars than building them, and in 1902 he was fired, the company having made less than two dozen vehicles in three years. Undaunted, he continued to build racers, and after two of his cars, the 999 and the Arrow, beat vehicles designed by Alexander Winton, the country's top auto designer, Ford attracted interest from a new set of investors. In 1903 he and a group led by Alexander Y. Malcomson, a Detroit coal dealer, formed the Ford Motor Company, with Ford serving as vice president and general manager.

At the time, automobiles were considered to be the playthings of the wealthy, and many manufacturers vied with one another to make a vehicle that was larger, more powerful, and more luxurious than the competition. Ford, however, decided to focus on making cars that were inexpensive and therefore attainable by the average working-class person. One of his first production cars for Ford Motor, the Model N, weighed only 800 pounds, was powered by a 15-horsepower, four-cylinder engine, and sold for $600. Malcomson and the other investors were unhappy with this and similar models, believing that more money could be made by selling more luxurious vehicles in the neighborhood of $2,000, and they pressured Ford to abandon his cheap runabouts. Ford's response was to change the way Ford Motor built autos.

Like most early automakers, Ford Motor did not actually manufacture anything; it simply

Henry Ford's Model T is one of the best-known automobiles of all time. *(Library of Congress)*

assembled a vehicle out of the various parts, such as the engine, chassis, and body, which were made by subcontractors. In 1905 Ford founded his own company, Ford Manufacturing Company, to manufacture engines and various chassis components for the Model N. Ford Manufacturing charged Ford Motor so much for the various subassemblies that Malcomson and the others gained little profit; meanwhile, Ford himself was pocketing huge sums of cash. In 1906 Malcomson and many of the other investors agreed to sell their shares to Ford. This gave him control of 58 percent of the company's stock, and the following year he took over as president and merged Ford Manufacturing into Ford Motor. The company continued to manufacture an increasing number of parts in its own shops, and by 1913 virtually all of the components that went into a Ford were made by Ford. In addition to getting rid of most of the stockholders who tried to interfere with the way he ran the company, Ford also found a much more profitable way to manufacture automobiles that would allow him to dominate the auto market into the mid-1920s.

In 1908 Ford unveiled to the general public the most famous American automobile of all time, the Model T. Designed by a team headed by Ford, the Model T was intended to be a people's car, plain but rugged, and especially suited for farmers who had to drive many miles on poor roads. The Model T was powered by a 22-horsepower, four-cylinder engine, and included practical features available on cars that sold for more than twice its sticker price of $825. As Ford's operations became more and more streamlined over the years, the cost of the Model T dropped; the 1927 model, which was virtually unchanged from the original, was priced at only $290 brand new. Over time, Ford sold more than 15 million Model Ts, making it one of the most popular cars of all time.

Ford held down the price of the Model T in several ways. One was by eliminating frills; to the end, the Model T came in only one color—black. He also controlled production costs by becoming the first automaker to use mass production, or Fordism, as it was originally called. Beginning in 1910 at the company's new Highland Park plant, Ford built cars on a moving assembly line. Rather than complete a subassembly and then transport it to a final assembly area, like other manufacturers did, the company built subassemblies like motors and transmissions on conveyor belts which intersected the main assembly line at strategic intervals. Materials were placed next to workers at waist height so that no time was lost to stooping or lifting, and the necessary machines were located next to the appropriate stations rather than in a central machine shop. All movement of both lines and workers was scrutinized by time-and-motion experts, who then developed the most time-efficient way to do every task. Although eventually this system made it possible to turn out a new Model T every 24 seconds, it also resulted in workers doing the same thing over and over, all day every day. Ford made up for the monotony by paying his people well, at least in the early days. In 1914 he started paying most of his workers $5 for eight hours of work, which was twice as much pay for one less hour than other autoworkers were

getting. In addition to improving employee morale and productivity, cutting each shift back to eight hours allowed him to add a third shift at night. Last but not least, he kept down costs by buying materials from himself. By 1920, the year after Ford assumed total ownership of the company, Ford Motor owned coal and iron ore mines, stamping mills and foundries, forests and lumber mills, rubber plantations, glass factories, a fleet of ships, and a railroad, all of them dedicated to providing Ford's auto plants with the materials they needed. By 1928 Ford's corporate headquarters in Dearborn, Michigan, oversaw the production of cars in 21 countries on every continent but Antarctica.

Although the Model T continued to sell well into the 1920s, by 1927 it had clearly become obsolete. By then roads had generally improved, a more sophisticated buying public wanted something more stylish than just basic transportation, and most new cars were being sold to people who were replacing their first car and wanted something more upscale. Unlike Ford, other car makers had seen this trend coming much earlier and were making different models (and changing their basic styling every year or so) to appeal to various segments of the market. In 1927 General Motors's annual sales surpassed Ford's for the first time ever. This new reality forced Ford to overcome his stubborn resistance to change, and in 1927 he finally halted production of the Model T, retooled his new, state-of-the-art facility at River Rouge southeast of Detroit, and introduced the Model A later that same year. However, little distinguished the Model A from the competition, so in 1932 Ford introduced the Model 18, which featured a 65-horsepower, V-8 motor with an engine block that was cast as a single piece to cut down costs. Unfortunately, the Model 18 did little to reverse the trend of declining auto sales of Ford, although truck and tractor sales continued to be areas of strength for the company. By 1936 Ford was the number-three automaker in the United States in terms of annual sales, having been passed by both General Motors and Chrysler.

Although Ford was a genius in several respects, he was also a man of limited education, great stubbornness, and deeply held prejudices. These latter two characteristics were exacerbated by a stroke in 1938 from which Ford never fully recovered. Although he remained in control of Ford Motor Company, he seemed to lose touch with reality as the years passed. At one point he had become convinced that World War II was just an elaborate plot by the federal government to take control of his company. In 1945 he retired as president of Ford Motor Company and was replaced by his grandson, Henry Ford II. Perhaps Ford's last great move was the creation of the Ford Foundation. Established in 1936 when Ford put all his shares of Ford stock into it to avoid paying an excessive amount of income tax, the foundation became one of the richest and most benevolent private foundations in the world. He died on April 7, 1947, at his estate in Dearborn.

Further Reading

Crainer, Stuart. *The Ultimate Book of Business Gurus: 110 Thinkers Who Really Made a Difference.* New York: AMACOM, 1998.

Crompton, Samuel W. *100 Americans Who Shaped American History.* San Mateo, Calif.: Bluewood Books, 1999.

Lewis, David L. *The Public Image of Henry Ford.* Detroit, Mich.: Wayne State University, 1987.

Nevins, Allan, and Frank E. Hill. *Ford: The Times, the Man, the Company.* New York: Scribner, 1976.

Smith, George D., and Frederick Dalzell. *Wisdom from the Robber Barons: Enduring Business Lessons from Rockefeller, Morgan, and the First Industrialists.* Cambridge, Mass.: Perseus Pub., 2000.

Forten, James

(1766–1842) *inventor of sail-hanging device*

Before the American Revolution, Philadelphia was the largest city in the 13 colonies. In addition to being home to a great many white residents, the City of Brotherly Love included a thriving community of hundreds of free blacks. One of the most prominent members of this community was James Forten, owner of a prosperous sail-making firm and the inventor of a device that made sail-hanging much easier. Forten's success is a testimony to his own hard work and vision but also to the ability of whites and blacks in the United States to work together, at least in some places, in the early days of the American republic.

Forten was born on September 2, 1766, in Philadelphia, Pennsylvania. His father, Thomas, was a sailmaker, and his mother, Margaret, was a homemaker. At age nine, two years after his father died, he went to work in the grocery store of Anthony Benezet, the famous teacher and abolitionist. At age 15 Forten signed up to serve as a powder boy aboard the *Royal Louis,* an American privateer, during the American Revolution; the ship was captured and he spent seven months on a prison ship in New York harbor until he was released as part of a general prisoner exchange. After the war he sailed for a year on a merchant ship, then in 1784, at the age of 18, he apprenticed himself to Robert Bridges, the Philadelphia sailmaker who had earlier employed Forten's father.

Bridges took a liking to Forten, who was a hardworking, industrious, intelligent youth. Within two years he had promoted his young protégé to foreman of the loft, the upper portion of a sail-making shop, and over the years Bridges taught Forten everything he knew about the sail-making trade. When Forten needed money to buy a house, Bridges loaned it to him. By 1798, when Bridges decided to retire, Forten had become a master craftsman, so Bridges sold him the business. Forten borrowed money for the purchase from Thomas Willing, a Philadelphia merchant. Because of his skill, Forten was able to retain most of Bridges's employees and customers, and over the years the business thrived. He gained a reputation for being able to fit sails precisely to any given ship, and by 1807 his enterprise employed 30 workers.

At some point—no one knows exactly when because he never applied for a patent, although it probably occurred between 1784 and 1796 while he was foreman of the loft—Forten invented a device that made it much easier to handle the large, bulky sails used by merchantmen. Unfortunately, none of the details about how the device worked are known, either, except that it speeded up the rigging process, whereby a ship is outfitted with the necessary sails and other paraphernalia, to the point that it gave his business a competitive edge over other sailmakers.

Over the years, Forten became a wealthy man; he lived in a fashionable house and employed several servants. He augmented his income from the sail yard by shrewdly investing the profits, first in Philadelphia real estate and by lending money at interest, then later by buying stock in various banks, canals, and railroads. A staunch opponent of slavery, he refused to rig any ship that he suspected of being employed in the slave trade, and he loaned enough money to William Lloyd Garrison to publish the first issues of the abolitionist newspaper, the *Liberator.* In 1803 Forten married Martha Beatte, who died the following year, and in 1805 he married Charlotte Vandine with whom he had eight children. He played an active role in the management of his business until 1841, when declining health forced him to turn over the business to his children. He gave away more than $250,000, partly to further the cause of abolition and partly as loans or gifts to his fellow blacks. At the time of his death on March 4, 1842, in Philadelphia, his estate was estimated to be worth more than $67,000, a substantial amount of money for that day.

Further Reading

Douty, Esther M. *Forten the Sailmaker: Pioneer Champion of Negro Rights.* Chicago: Rand McNally, 1968.

James, Portia P. *The Real McCoy: African-American Invention and Innovation, 1619–1930.* Washington, D.C.: Smithsonian Institution Press, 1989.

Winch, Julie. *A Gentleman of Color: The Life of James Forten.* New York: Oxford University Press, 2002.

Franklin, Benjamin
(1706–1790) *publisher and inventor extraordinaire*

Benjamin Franklin is perhaps the most interesting American of all time. Known to all because his portrait is on the 100-dollar bill, Franklin was one of the world's leading scientists, politicians, and diplomats. What few people realize about Franklin, however, is that he was also a multifaceted inventor as well as a brilliant entrepreneur whose skill as a publisher paid for the lifestyle he enjoyed over the last 40 years of his life.

Franklin was born on January 6, 1706, in Boston, Massachusetts. His father, Josiah, was a soap maker and candle maker, and his mother, Abiah, was a homemaker. At age 12 he became an apprentice printer in the shop of his brother, James. Within four years he had become a skilled typesetter, and he also contributed anonymous articles to his brother's newspaper, the *New-England Courant.* In 1722 James was jailed for printing libelous material in his paper, and to keep the *Courant* running he made Franklin, at the time 16 years old, the publisher of record and released him from his indenture. But shortly after James's release from prison in 1723, he and Franklin quarreled so bitterly that Franklin left James's shop and moved to Philadelphia, Pennsylvania. After working for a year in the printing shop of Samuel Keimer, he went to London, England, where he hoped to raise enough money to open his own shop. Instead, he ended up working for Samuel Palmer, an English printer, until 1726, when he returned to Philadelphia. He worked for a year as a clerk and accountant in the store of Thomas Denham, then in 1727 returned to Keimer's establishment. In 1728 Franklin and Hugh Meredith opened their own printing shop, of which Franklin became the sole proprietor two years later. In 1730 Franklin took Deborah Read as his common-law wife; in addition to having two children of their own, they raised Franklin's illegitimate son, whose mother is unknown.

Franklin's printing business thrived. In addition to being the public printer of the colonies of Pennsylvania, New Jersey, Delaware, and Maryland, in which capacity he printed their paper money among other things, he was the publisher of the *Pennsylvania Gazette,* the most influential newspaper published in the 13 colonies. His most famous publication, however, was *Poor Richard's Almanack,* a collection of astrological data, proverbs, predictions, and other useful and entertaining material, much of which was written by Franklin himself. *Poor Richard's Almanack* first appeared in 1732 and was soon selling almost 10,000 copies per year. He also published the first American German-language newspaper and one of the first American magazines, neither of which succeeded. His other projects, however, brought him considerable wealth, and by 1748 he had made so much money that he ended his active participation in the printing trade to devote his life to science. But first, being a practical man above all else, that same year he and David Hall formed Franklin & Hall, which, under Hall's direction, continued to publish the *Gazette* and *Poor Richard's Almanack* while also fulfilling Franklin's many printing contracts. Between 1748 and 1766, when the business became Hall's, Franklin received an average of 500 pounds per year from Franklin & Hall, a considerable sum of money for the day.

In addition to being a capable entrepreneur, Franklin was also an accomplished inventor. During the winter of 1741–42, he invented what he called the Pennsylvania fireplace but is better known today as the Franklin stove. This wood-burning heating stove had an iron grate on which the fire was fed air from a draft, and a tall, hollow iron flue with iron baffles that extracted every bit of heat from the gases escaping from the fire on the grate. It could be installed either in a tall fireplace or as a free-standing stove by connecting it via a flue to a chimney. The Franklin stove remained a popular way to heat cabins, farmhouses, and even city dwellings until the mid-20th century, mostly because it gives off twice the heat produced by a regular fireplace while using half the wood.

Franklin's experiments with electricity led him to the conclusion that lightning is nothing more than a huge bolt of electricity. This conclusion led him in turn to invent the lightning rod, whereby lightning bolts can be prevented from setting fire to tall buildings. He proved the efficacy of this invention in the mid-1750s by erecting a lightning rod atop the new steeple of Philadelphia's Christ Church. In 1784, no doubt prompted by his own need for a pair of reading glasses that could also be used for distance viewing, he invented bifocals. The first pair was simply a top lens for seeing afar and a bottom lens for seeing close-up; the two lenses were held together by a special frame of his design.

Franklin also invented a number of other items. His armonica, also called the glass harmonica, was a hand-played musical instrument that produced such expressive sounds that Beethoven and Mozart composed music to be played on it. He invented a device for removing books from the upper shelves of a library, a chair that folded out

into a ladder, a chair with a writing arm on one side that became a model for the modern school desk, and a rocking chair with an automatic fan. Unlike his printing business, which brought him considerable wealth, Franklin profited little from his inventions. He refused to apply for patents, believing that brilliant ideas should be made available to the public free of charge.

Of course, Franklin also played a major role in the formation of the American republic. He was the only person to sign the Declaration of Independence, the Treaty of Paris ending the American Revolution, and the U.S. Constitution. He died on April 17, 1790, in Philadelphia.

Further Reading

Brands, H. W. *The First American: The Life and Times of Benjamin Franklin.* New York: Doubleday, 2000.

Campbell, James. *Recovering Benjamin Franklin: An Exploration of a Life of Science and Service.* Chicago: Open Court, 1999.

Crompton, Samuel W. *100 Americans Who Shaped American History.* San Mateo, Calif.: Bluewood Books, 1999.

Franklin, Benjamin, and L. Jesse Lemisch, ed. *The Autobiography and Other Writings.* New York: Signet Classics, 2001.

McCormick, Blaine. *Ben Franklin's 12 Rules of Management.* Irvine, Calif.: Entrepreneur Press, 2000.

Frasch, Herman

(1851–1914) *inventor of sulfur extraction processes*

The Frasch process refers to two different chemical processes, both of which involve the extraction of sulfur. One is a way to remove it from crude oil, while the other is a way to remove it from the ground. Both processes were developed by Herman Frasch, who used them to make himself rich.

Frasch was born on Christmas Day, 1851, in Gaildorf, Wurttemberg, now part of Germany. His father, Johannes, was a pharmacist, and his mother was a homemaker. After working briefly as an apprentice pharmacist, at age 16 he emigrated to the United States and settled in Philadelphia, Pennsylvania. Over the next five years he worked as a laboratory assistant at the Philadelphia College of Pharmacy, and in 1873 he opened a chemical research laboratory. That same year he married Romalda Berks with whom he had two children. She died in 1889, and three years later he married Elizabeth Blee.

When not conducting research for Philadelphia manufacturers, Frasch performed experiments of his own. By 1876 he had developed a process for refining paraffin wax, a petroleum by-product, which he sold to the Standard Oil Company. That same year Standard Oil engaged him as a consultant and established a laboratory for him in Cleveland, Ohio. Over the next nine years he developed several improvements in the refining of crude oil and discovered a way to use paraffin to make waxed paper. In his spare time, he invented an oil lamp that gave off brighter light, developed a process for manufacturing carbon for electric arc light filaments, designed several parts for electric generators, and developed processes for synthesizing soda ash and extracting white lead pigment from lead sulfide.

By 1885 Frasch had made enough money to buy an oilfield in Canada. He acquired it for next to nothing because the oil it produced had a high sulfur content. Known as sour crude oil and skunk oil, this oil smelled so bad and emitted gases that were so corrosive that it could be sold only as a low-grade fuel oil, and then only with great difficulty. Within a year, Frasch had developed a chemical process for removing the sulfur from skunk oil. Basically, he just added copper oxide to a batch of the oil, and then heated the mixture. This caused the sulfur to combine with the copper oxide which, when removed, left high-grade petroleum. Meanwhile, he had formed the Empire Oil Company, which extracted, refined, and marketed desulfurized skunk oil. By 1886 Standard Oil had acquired the Lima oil field in Ohio and Indiana, which had almost as high a sulfur content as Frasch's skunk oil, and retained him to desulfurize oil from this field. In 1888 he exchanged the American rights to his desulfurization process for enough shares of Standard Oil to make him rich.

Frasch next turned his attention to extracting sulfur from the ground. Then as now, sulfuric acid was used in a number of industrial processes, and large sedimentary deposits of sulfur, its basic ingredient, had been discovered in Louisiana and east Texas. Unfortunately, these deposits lay under successive descending layers of swamp, gravel, clay, shale, and limestone. Normally, sulfur was extracted in much the same way as coal, but digging a mine shaft in the middle of the swamp clearly would not work. By 1891 Frasch had developed a process for extracting sulfur from the ground that took advantage of the fact that sulfur, although a quartzlike substance, melts at about 250° Fahrenheit. Basically, he drilled through the overlying layers, as one would when drilling for oil, until he reached the tip of the sulfur deposit. Then he inserted a system of three concentric pipes. Through the outer pipe he pumped superheated water at about 350° Fahrenheit into the deposit. As the heat melted the sulfur, compressed air at about 100 pounds per square inch was pumped into the deposit via the inner pipe, which forced the liquid sulfur to the surface via the middle pipe. As the water cooled, the sulfur solidified. In 1892 he formed the Union Sulphur Company with himself as president, and by 1903 the company had become the leading producer of sulfur in the world.

Around 1900 Frasch also became president of the International Sulphur Refineries, which was headquartered in Marseilles, France. He moved to France shortly thereafter, and for the rest of his life he divided his time among his office in Marseilles, his home on the French Riviera, and Paris. He died on May 1, 1914, in Paris.

Further Reading

Byrnes, Donia. "A History of the Louisiana Sulphur Industry," Loyola University Student Historical Journal. Available online. URL: http://www.loyno.edu/history/journal/1985-6/byrnes.htm. Downloaded on July 2, 2009.

Hayne, Williams. Brimstone: The Stone That Burns; The Story of the Frasch Sulphur Industry. New York: D. Van Nostrand, 1959.

Fuller, Alfred Carl

(1885–1973) *founder of the Fuller Brush Company*

For much of the 20th century, the "Fuller Brush Man" was a common sight in residential neighborhoods across America. This door-to-door salesman—and, as time passed, saleswoman—sold a variety of brushes, which were carried in a large leather satchel, to customers who were encouraged to try the products before purchasing them. The person most responsible for creating the Fuller Brush Man, Alfred Fuller, did not invent door-to-door selling, but he did contribute to making it a respectable business.

Fuller was born on January 13, 1885, in Welsford, Nova Scotia, Canada. His parents, Leander and Phebe, were farmers. At age 18 he moved to Boston, Massachusetts, where his five older siblings lived, and rented a room from his sister. After spending the next two years working successively as a streetcar operator, a horse's groom, and a wagon driver, in 1905 he joined the Somerville Brush and Mop Company as a door-to-door salesman. The company's product line consisted primarily of mops and bristle brushes in various sizes for scrubbing the floor, cleaning clothes, and scouring pots and pans. Fuller proved to be an exceptional brush salesman, mostly because he was able to empathize with the typical homemaker's cleaning needs. He quickly discovered that several of the company's brushes did not work well because they were designed to be used by someone who had larger hands and more muscles than the typical homemaker. Although he tried on several occasions to get his boss to correct these design deficiencies, the boss repeatedly refused.

In 1906 Fuller took matters into his own hands by forming the Fuller Brush Company. His sister allowed him to convert her basement into a workshop; during the day he sold the brushes that he had made in his workshop the night before. His specialty quickly became the custom-designed brush, which he was delighted to provide for the customer with a special cleaning need. Many of these customized brushes became part of his regular product line, and within a few years he offered a brush for just about every conceivable cleaning problem that could be found in the typical home.

After less than a year in business, Fuller's business had outgrown his sister's basement, so in late 1906 he moved his operation to Hartford, Connecticut. As his custom brush business increased, he began taking orders during the week

and delivering brushes on the weekend, since most family breadwinners got paid on Fridays. He also began to hire and train New England college students to sell brushes on a part-time basis. By 1908 he had begun to recruit salespeople in New York and Pennsylvania. That same year he married Evelyn Ells with whom he had two children; Evelyn later became one of his best salespeople. The most effective means of recruitment was ads placed in national magazines, and by 1910 Fuller had more than 250 distributors in the field, each of whom had paid a $17-deposit for a leather case filled with sample brushes. Because turnover was high, after 1915 Fuller provided training at the local level by promoting successful salesmen into management positions and by teaching his workforce how to develop a positive mental attitude. He also insisted that his goods be made to the highest quality standards, and he offered a no-questions-asked, money-back guarantee to any dissatisfied customer.

As these techniques were successfully implemented, annual sales increased, from $30,000 in 1910 to $1 million in 1919. In 1921 Fuller built a large brush factory in Hartford to keep up with demand, and in 1923 sales rose to an annual high of $15 million. Sales slipped somewhat over the rest of the decade, and the company took a heavy hit during the Great Depression. It was not until the United States entered World War II that sales returned to the $15 million mark. Meanwhile, the Fuller Brush Man had become an icon of American society. Fuller's salespeople became familiar sights in virtually every community, and by 1930 caricatures of the Fuller Brush Man had appeared in comic strips and cartoons. In 1948 Red Skelton, one of America's funniest comedians, starred in *The Fuller Brush Man,* a motion-picture comedy about a door-to-door brush salesman who gets involved in a murder. In 1950 Lucille Ball, one of America's funniest comediennes, starred in *The Fuller Brush Girl,* a sequel to the earlier movie. Both movies were box office hits.

Fuller had become an American citizen in 1918, divorced his first wife in 1930, and married Mary Pelton in 1932. In 1942 he became chairman of the board while his son Howard became president and took over the day-to-day management of the company. Howard was replaced by his brother

Avand in 1959, with Fuller continuing as chairman until the company was purchased in 1968 by the Sara Lee Corporation. He spent his remaining years doing volunteer work in Hartford, where he died on December 4, 1973.

Further Reading

"Alfred C. Fuller," Horatio Alger Association of Distinguished Americans. Available online. URL: http://www.horatioalger.com/member_info.CFM? Downloaded on July 2, 2009.

Fuller, Alfred Carl, with Hartzell Spence. *A Foot in the Door: The Life Appraisal of the Original Fuller Brush Man.* New York: McGraw-Hill, 1960.

Fuller, R. Buckminster
(Richard Buckminster Fuller)
(1895–1983) *inventor of the geodesic dome*

Perhaps the most influential architectural design of the 20th century is the geodesic dome. This structure has been used to house any number of sports arenas as well as a variety of other buildings of various sizes and functions. The man who invented the geodesic dome was R. Buckminster Fuller, who also achieved fame for coining the phrase "Spaceship Earth" and lecturing around the world on the uses of technology to make life on this planet better.

Fuller was born Richard Buckminster Fuller on July 12, 1895, in Milton, Massachusetts. His father, Richard, was a merchant, and his mother, Caroline, was a homemaker. In 1913 he enrolled in Harvard University, but he was expelled twice for being excessively indifferent to his studies and never received a college degree. In 1915 he moved to New York City where he obtained a management position at Armour and Company's meat-packing distribution facility. In 1917 he married Anne Hewlett with whom he had two children.

Fuller's career as an inventor began during World War I. While patrolling the Maine coast for German U-boats, he also became involved in rescuing airmen whose planes had crashed into the sea. To this end he developed a combination winch, mast, and boom that quickly flipped cap-

sized aircraft, thus saving the lives of the pilots. After the war he and his father-in-law, James Hewlett, formed the Stockade Corporation. Under Fuller's direction, the company manufactured modular homes from blocks of compressed fibers invented by Hewlett according to a system developed by Hewlett. Although the Stockade Building System worked fine—it was later bought by Celotex and marketed under the name Soundtex—at the time it failed to catch on, and in 1927 the two partners were forced out of the company by a group of investors.

Later that same year, Fuller found himself in Chicago, Illinois, on a Lake Michigan beach, unemployed, broke, drunk, and suicidal. But just as he was about to drown himself, he heard a voice that denied him the right to take his own life and instructed him instead to devote his life to developing ideas that served humanity. Thus redeemed, he immediately set out in search of ideas worth developing. Although he eventually developed a number of innovative ideas, including an omnidirectional automobile, most of his inventions would be related to architecture.

In 1927 Fuller designed the 4D or Dymaxion House, a factory-built modular home that included its own utilities. The two-bedroom house's six aluminum-and-glass walls were suspended by cables from a central mast that also incorporated a spiral stairwell and most of the house's wiring and plumbing. In 1930 he developed a die-stamped modular bathroom unit that could be plugged into a conventional home like a ready-to-use appliance. Neither concept captured the public imagination. However, in 1940 he developed the Dymaxion Deployment Unit for the federal government, which used the modular structure as barracks and radar stations in hard-to-reach places. And in 1945 he invented the Wichita House, in essence an updated version of the Dymaxion House. Made from steel, aluminum, and Plexiglas, this circular building featured a ventilating system that completely replaced the air in the house. Since the house was popular with those consumers who were able to examine the prototype and cost less than $3,500 to build, it promised to alleviate the housing shortage that occurred after World War II. Unfortunately, Fuller and his financial backers had a falling-out over the final design of the house—they wanted to begin production before he believed the design was satisfactory—and the project was abandoned before any Wichita Houses could be sold.

In 1947 Fuller began experimenting with the architectural design that would make him famous, the geodesic dome. Using his knowledge of the tetrahedron, or pyramid-shaped, lattice structure of most crystalline metals, he combined triangular and polygonal shapes to create a strong, space-efficient structure that requires no inner support from columns or trusses because the triangles and polygons along the dome's geodesic lines, or great circles, provide the structural support of an arch while also distributing stresses within the structure itself. The geodesic dome is the only large domed structure that can be placed directly on the ground as a completed building. Unlike most other architectural structures, it gets stronger as it increases in size, and therefore has no upper limit to its size. Best of all, it is safe to build because the top can be hoisted on a mast and lower sections added on from the ground level. Fuller's first geodesic dome, built in 1948 at Black Mountain College in North Carolina, collapsed, mostly because it was made out of venetian blind strips, but a second dome, constructed the following year from aluminum tubing, remained standing.

By 1955 the geodesic dome had captured the imagination of builders and the general public everywhere. That same year Fuller formed Synergetics Inc. and Geodesics Inc. to build geodesic domes all over the world. He quickly discovered that his companies could not keep up with the demand, so he began licensing other companies to build domes according to his patent. By 1966 almost 200 companies were licensed, and they had constructed more than 3,000 domes, in addition to the thousands that Fuller had built. It is estimated that during Fuller's lifetime, more than 300,000 geodesic domes were constructed around the world. Meanwhile, in 1959 Fuller had become a professor at Southern Illinois University at Carbondale, where he taught until his retirement in 1975. From 1959 until his death, he gave lectures at college campuses around the world concerning his ideas about humankind's role in the universe and on what he called Spaceship Earth. He was particularly interested in the rational use of technology as a means of solving societal ills such as starvation, disease, homelessness, poverty, and waste. He died on July 1, 1983, in Los Angeles, California.

Further Reading

Pawley, Martin. *Buckminster Fuller*. London: Grafton, 1992.

Sajkovic, Miriam T. *Visionaries of Our Times: An Introduction to Their Creative Legacy*. Pittsburgh: Dorrance Pub., 1994.

Sieden, Lloyd Steve. *Buckminster Fuller's Universe*. Cambridge, Mass.: Perseus Publishing, 2000.

Zung, Thomas T. K. *Buckminster Fuller: Anthology for the New Millennium*. New York: St. Martin's Press, 2001.

G

Gabe, Frances
(Frances Grace Arnholtz)
(1915–) *inventor of the self-cleaning house*

Frances Gabe hated to do housework so much that she set out to invent a house that cleans itself. Although her house is a bit impractical for most people, it may someday prove to be the perfect residence, especially for those too handicapped to do housework.

Gabe was born Frances Grace Arnholtz in 1915 on a ranch near Boise, Idaho. Her father, Frederick, was a building contractor. Her mother, whose name is unknown, died mysteriously when Gabe was young. Gabe's father's business took him all across the Pacific Northwest, and she traveled with him from one construction site to another. Her "family" were the men on her father's crews, who taught her everything they knew about building houses. After attending 18 different grade schools and being privately tutored off and on, at age 12 she was enrolled in the Girl's Polytechnic School in Portland, Oregon. She graduated in 1929, having completed six years of middle and high school education in two years. In 1932 she married Herbert Bateson, by training an electrical engineer, with whom she had three children.

Gabe's husband seems never to have worked at anything other than odd jobs, so she was forced to support herself, him, and their children. She did this for a while by working for her father. After her first child was born, she settled down in Portland where she started her own home-repair service. Her husband was so embarrassed by her business success that he eventually told her to stop using his name. She decided to call herself "Gabe," which is derived from the initials of her middle, maiden, and married names (she added the "e" to avoid being called "Gab"). In 1978, shortly after adopting her new name, she and her husband separated.

Gabe's business kept her busy most of the time, and when she did have free time she wanted to spend it with her family, not doing household chores. So in 1955 she decided to use her skill as a house builder to design and build a home in nearby Newburg, Oregon, that would keep itself clean. After 40 years and 68 patents, Gabe now lives in a 1,350-square-foot house that cleans itself.

Almost everything in the house is made of materials that can be cleaned easily with water and then dried. The furniture is made of plastic and wood, and the walls, ceilings, and floors are heavily coated with marine varnish. The beds are covered with plastic before being cleaned, reading material and bric-a-brac are protected behind clear plastic sleeves or stored in plastic boxes with special watertight lids, and curtains and carpeting have been completely eliminated. Perhaps the most impressive device in her home is a 10-inch-square cleaning, drying, cooling, and heating device that is mounted in the ceiling of each room. At the push of a button, the apparatus dispenses a fine mist of soapy water throughout the room. Then it dispenses a mist of rinse water, after which it blow-dries everything in the room. Runoff water is removed via drains in the corners of the slightly sloped floor. The device can also dispense germicide or insect spray, as needed.

Other specialized devices are found throughout the house. The dish-washing cabinet washes and dries dirty dishes and stores them for future use. The clothes-washing closet does the same thing with wash-and-wear garments, and also doubles as a personal shower. The chair-shaped bathtub rinses itself out as soon as the bather is done, and the sinks and toilets clean themselves the same way. The fireplace automatically dumps ashes and the bookshelves automatically dust themselves.

Gabe persevered with building her dream house despite a number of setbacks. She struggled with partial blindness for 18 years following the birth of her first child, her husband divorced her, and she suffered the ridicule and harassment of her neighbors for 40 years. And to date only one model of the self-cleaning house exists, despite Gabe's efforts to have houses like hers made available to the general public. But the house is perfect for elderly or handicapped people who cannot do housework, so one day it may become the rule rather than the exception.

Further Reading

Blashfield, Jean F. *Women Inventors 4: Sybilla Masters, Mary Beatrice Davidson Kenner and Mildred Davidson Austin Smith, Stephanie Kwolek, Frances Gabe.* Minneapolis, Minn.: Capstone Press, 1996.

Macdonald, Anne L. *Feminine Ingenuity: Women and Invention in America.* New York: Ballantine Books, 1994.

Gates, Bill
(William Henry Gates III)
(1955–) *founder of Microsoft*

The youngest person to become a billionaire in the history of the United States was Bill Gates, who did so just before his 31st birthday. In the process of achieving fame and fortune, Gates revolutionized the computer industry more than once and will probably continue to do so for years to come.

Gates was born William Henry Gates III on October 28, 1955, in Seattle, Washington. His father, William, is a surgeon, and his mother, Mary,

was an educator. His parents sent him to Lakeside School, a private school in Seattle, where at age 12 he had his first encounter with a computer. At the time, personal computers (PCs) did not exist; instead, operators used terminals that were connected to a large mainframe computer. In 1967, Lakeside's Mothers Club purchased a computer training terminal and had it hooked up by telephone to the mainframe computer at Seattle's Computer Center Company (CCC) so that the school's students could gain some hands-on experience with what was surely to be a technological phenomenon of the future. Gates and three friends became so fascinated with this arrangement that they devoted virtually every moment of their free time to exploring its possibilities. They quickly formed the Lakeside Programming Club, and soon they were writing and running programs for the school, including one that arranged class schedules, for pay. To learn more about programming and how to write code, they snooped around CCC after hours, digging through its daily trash in search of trial programs and notes that had been written by the company's programmers. Before long, the club members had become so proficient that they were able to identify errors that CCC's programmers had made. After writing a long report about the errors and sending it to CCC, the company put the club members to work as part-time programmers.

Shortly thereafter, Gates wrote a program that deliberately caused a major operating system to crash. Reprimanded by CCC and rebuked by his fellow club members, he gave up computers temporarily. Meanwhile, the programming club had begun to take on commercial work to pay for computer time but found that it needed Gates's abilities to succeed at this endeavor. One of their projects was a method for tabulating traffic data by computer, and at age 14 Gates became president of Traf-O-Data, the company formed by the club to sell their method to municipalities. The company made about $20,000 before city managers realized that Traf-O-Data was run by high schoolers.

After graduating from Lakeside in 1973, Gates enrolled in Harvard University. During his sophomore year, MITS, a company headquartered in Albuquerque, New Mexico, released the Altair 8080, the first commercially available microcomputer, a forerunner to the personal computer. Although the device generated much interest, it was actually of little use because it had limited programmable memory and no software, the internal programming that directs its operation. Almost immediately, Gates and Paul Allen, a fellow Harvard student and a former member of the Lakeside Programming Club, decided to write an operating program for the Altair 8080. Despite not having one of the microcomputers or any knowledge of the machine other than a book that described it, they abandoned their college studies and began writing a program in BASIC (Beginner's All-purpose Symbolic Instruction Code), an interactive computer language that was designed specifically for people with little programming ability. They also developed what they hoped was an Altair 8080 simulator, which they ran through a terminal connected to Harvard's mainframe computer. Amazingly, given their seat-of-the-pants approach as well as the major limitation posed by the Altair 8080's limited memory, their program worked so well when it was tested at MITS headquarters in mid-1975 that the company contracted with them to produce software for the Altair 8080 and other MITS products.

That same year Gates and Allen dropped out of Harvard, moved to Albuquerque, and formed Microsoft, with Gates as president, to write BASIC programs for MITS. Within two years, the company was writing programs for major computer retailers such as Apple, Commodore, and Radio Shack. In 1980, two years after the partners relocated Microsoft to Bellevue, Washington, the company was earning $4 million annually.

In 1980 Microsoft got its big break when Gates arranged a deal with IBM, at the time the world's largest manufacturer of business machines, to develop the software for a PC it was building. Once the contract was signed, Gates paid $50,000 to Tim Patterson, a Seattle programmer, for a program Patterson had written called Q-DOS, short for Quick and Dirty Operating System. Using Q-DOS as his basic program, Gates then modified it so that it would run the IBM PC. He also added a number of new features to the program, which he called MS-DOS, short for Microsoft Disk Operating System. Then, in a particularly brilliant

maneuver, he convinced IBM to "declassify" the design specifications of their personal computer so that other programmers could make software that was compatible with the IBM PC. When IBM agreed, it opened the door for dozens of software companies to design application software specifically for the IBM PC, thus enhancing its usefulness and value. It also boosted Microsoft's business, since any new program written by any software company for the IBM PC would have to be based on MS-DOS. Soon other hardware manufacturers in the United States and Japan had contracted with Microsoft for the rights to use MS-DOS to develop operating systems for their projects, and within a year the company's sales quadrupled. Licensing fees and royalties from programs utilizing MS-DOS (and, after 1990, the various versions of Windows) would be a major source of Microsoft's income into the 21st century.

Having established MS-DOS as the industry's standard operations system, Gates led Microsoft to begin developing applications software, which allows computers to run all sorts of programs. By 1983, nearly 40 percent of all personal computers, not just IBMs, were using operating and applications software developed by Microsoft. As the company grew in size—from 125 employees in 1981 to 1,200 in 1986—Gates proved to be an adept manager as well as a skilled software designer. Unlike many executives of highly successful start-up companies, he did not sell his company to a large competitor once the company started to prosper, nor did he retain all the decision-making authority. Instead, he hired top-quality managers from other computer companies to manage Microsoft's new divisions. To provide these managers with the proper incentive to remain with Microsoft, he sold them shares in the company and gave them stock options. Then, to increase the value of these shares and options, in 1986 he took the company public, with himself as chairman of the board. Within a year the company's stock had risen from $21 per share to almost $91 per share; Gates, who had retained 45 percent of the stock for himself, became a billionaire at age 30.

Meanwhile, Gates continued to serve as Microsoft's chief software architect. He built on his earlier success by forging ahead with new operating systems to replace MS-DOS. The first replacement was OS/2, which came out in 1987. But by far the most influential, and the one that set the standard for the industry for years to come, was Windows 3.0. This system was the first to replace typed commands with a hand-held mouse and click-on icons. Within a year of going on the market in 1990, Windows 3.0 sold more than 6 million copies. Over the next 10 years, Windows was updated several times, and by 1998 it included a variety of office applications such as Word (word processing), Outlook (electronic mail, better known as E-mail), Excel (spreadsheets), Access (database management), Explorer (Internet access), and PowerPoint ("slide" presentations). These applications proved to be very popular, and by 2000 Microsoft was doing annual sales of almost $23 billion, with 39,000 employees in 60 countries around the world.

Gates himself emerged from all this as the world's wealthiest man. He was married in 1994 to Melinda French with whom he has three children. In 2002 Gates's net worth was estimated to exceed $52 billion. A large part of that money has been used to endow the Bill and Melinda Gates Foundation, which contributes millions each year to global health care and education.

In recent years, Gates has become increasingly active in the work of the foundation, and as of 2007 he and his wife ranked second among the most generous philanthropists, behind only investor WARREN BUFFETT, with more than $28 billion in total funding. The work of the foundation, which focuses its resources on global health and development and education, earned Bill and Melinda Gates the shared distinction with rock and roll star and philanthropist Bono as *Time* magazine's 2005 Persons of the Year.

By 2009, Gates remained among the world's wealthiest people as well as a cultural symbol of a business icon. Gates had some fun with this image by appearing in a series of offbeat television advertisements for Microsoft alongside comedian Jerry Seinfeld. Only in his mid-fifties, Gates has long been among the brightest lights in the world of business and indeed in the history of business. Still the chairman and chief software architect of Microsoft, Gates recently noted, "We've really achieved the ideal of what I wanted Microsoft to become." Though that suggests a level of contentment, Gates continues to lead his company and push previously known boundaries of wealth and business accomplishment.

Further Reading

Andrews, Paul, and Stephen Manes. *Gates: How Microsoft's Mogul Reinvented an Industry and Made Himself the Richest Man in America.* New York: Simon and Schuster, 1994.

Brands, H. W. *Masters of Enterprise: Giants of American Business from John Jacob Astor and J. P. Morgan to Bill Gates and Oprah Winfrey.* New York: Free Press, 1999.

Crossen, Cynthia. *The Rich and How They Got That Way: How the Wealthiest People of All Time from Genghis Khan to Bill Gates Made Their Fortunes.* London: N. Brealey, 2001.

Leibovich, Mark. *The New Imperialists.* Upper Saddle River, N.J.: Prentice Hall, 2001.

Lowe, Janet. *Bill Gates Speaks: Insight from the World's Greatest Entrepreneur.* New York: Chichester, Wiley, 2001.

Gates, John Warne
(1855–1911) *entrepreneur in steel wire*

Between 1898 and 1903, hundreds of mergers involving thousands of companies changed the face of American business. One of the leading promoters of industrial mergers during this period was John "Bet-A-Million" Gates, a former hardware store owner who earned a fortune selling barbed wire as well as a reputation as the quintessential robber baron.

Gates was born on May 8, 1855, in Turner Junction, Illinois. The occupations of his parents, Asel and Mary, are unknown. After graduating from high school, he briefly attended college and business school, and at age 19 he became a partner in a hardware store in St. Charles. In 1876 he married Dellora Baker with whom he had one child.

One of the most popular items that Gates sold in his hardware store was barbed wire. Invented in 1873, barbed wire consisted of long strands of steel wire studded with hook-shaped wire barbs. The new wire was the perfect fencing material for the western prairie, where rocks and trees were virtually nonexistent. The barbs were sharp enough to keep animals from trampling the fence to get at crops; the wire could easily be strung over the flat plain; it was much cheaper and easier to obtain than lumber or stone; and it could not be destroyed by wind or fire.

By 1878 Gates had realized that there was far more money to be made in selling barbed wire than in owning a small-town hardware store. That same year he tried to become a partner in the Barb Fence Company, manufacturers of the barbed wire he sold in his store. When his offer was rejected, he went to work for the company as a salaried salesman operating out of San Antonio, Texas. Gates believed passionately in his product, and on one occasion he overcame objections that the wire was too flimsy to contain cattle by erecting a small corral of barbed wire and betting ranchers that their meanest steers could not escape from it. He sold wire faster than Barb Fence could ship it, so in 1879 he and a partner put up $8,000 each and opened a barbed-wire factory in St. Louis, Missouri. Barb Fence tried to sue Gates for infringing on its barbed-wire patent, but he frustrated the attempts of several sheriffs to serve him with an injunction by moving from town to town. The dispute ended in 1879 when Barb Fence reluctantly sold Gates permission to manufacture barbed wire according to their patent.

Over the next 17 years Gates established himself as the leading figure in the barbed-wire industry. In 1880 he bought out his partner and established the Southern Wire Company. Two years later he merged this company with his leading competitor to form the Braddock Wire Company, which slowly began to acquire its rivals. By this time Gates had realized the benefits to be had from vertical integration, so he began looking for ways to control every aspect of the barbed-wire business from the extraction of the raw materials for making steel wire to the shipping of the finished product by rail. In 1894 he became president of the Illinois Steel Company, and he later acquired a substantial interest in several iron mines, coal mines, and railroads. By 1898 Gates was able to use his vast enterprises as the nucleus around which to form the American Steel & Wire Company, a conglomeration of every major barbed-wire manufacturer in the United States, with a stock value of $90 million. By controlling American Steel & Wire, Gates enjoyed a virtual monopoly in the barbed-wire business.

Gates made a fortune as a barbed-wire entrepreneur, and he used this fortune to gain control of other industries as well. He moved to New York City and purchased a seat on the New York Stock Exchange. After he and several partners were unsuccessful in buying Carnegie Steel in 1899, Gates led the syndicate that created the Republic Iron & Steel Company. In 1902 he organized the group of investors that gained control of the Louisville & Nashville Railroad and helped combine American Steel & Wire into the United States Steel Corporation, the nation's first billion-dollar corporation. In 1906 he helped form the group that put together the Tennessee Iron & Coal Company. He also played a major role in the formation of the American Sheet Steel Company, the American Steel Hoop Company, the American Tin Plate Company, and the National Steel Company.

Gates's high-rolling lifestyle earned him the sobriquet "Bet-A-Million." An inveterate gambler, he bet on horses, cards, and roulette, and he reputedly earned his nickname by losing $1 million on a single hand of poker. He also wagered on the stock market, and in 1900 his activities set off a minor panic on the New York Stock Exchange. He had sold short a large block of shares in American Steel & Wire, which at the time was doing very well. To make the stock's price drop, he closed one of its mills in Chicago, thus throwing hundreds of his employees out of work and setting off rumors of the company's imminent demise. Then, as soon as the price had plummeted sufficiently to enable him to make a nice profit on the stock deal, he reopened the mill and American Steel & Wire went back to business as usual.

After 1906 Gates retired to Port Arthur, Texas, to concentrate on his oil and real-estate investments in that state. He played a major role in developing Port Arthur into a center for the refining and shipping of oil. He died on August 9, 1911, in Paris, France, while visiting a medieval castle he had purchased.

Further Reading

Paskoff, Paul F. *Encyclopedia of American Business History and Biography: Iron and Steel in the 19th Century.* New York: Facts On File, 1989.

Wendt, Lloyd, and Herman Kogan. *Bet a Million! The Story of John W. Gates.* New York: Arno Press, 1981.

Gayley, James

(1855–1920) *inventor of the dry-air furnace*

Before 1890, one of the major problems faced by manufacturers of iron and steel was high humidity. Moist air results in lower furnace temperatures, which impede the conversion of iron ore into pig iron, the basic ingredient for making cast iron, wrought iron, and steel. James Gayley solved this problem by inventing the dry-air furnace.

Gayley was born on October 11, 1855, in Lock Haven, Pennsylvania. His father, Samuel, was a Presbyterian minister, and his mother, Agnes, was a homemaker. As a baby he moved with his family to West Nottingham, Maryland. At age 21 he graduated from Lafayette College with a B.S. in mining engineering. In 1884 he married Julia Gardiner with whom he had three children; they were divorced in 1910.

Gayley spent his entire professional life in the iron and steel industry. He specialized in the operation of blast furnaces, the huge ovens in which the impurities are removed from iron ore to make pig iron. He entered the industry in 1876 as a chemist for the Crane Iron Company in Catasauqua, Pennsylvania. Four years later he became the superintendent of the Missouri Furnace Company in St. Louis. In 1882 he returned to Pennsylvania to manage the blast furnaces of the E. & G. Brooks Iron Company in Birdsboro. Three years later he took a similar position with the Carnegie Steel Company's Edgar Thomson Steel Works in Pittsburgh, and in 1897 he was made managing director of Carnegie Steel. When Carnegie Steel was merged with a number of other iron and steel companies in 1901 to form the United States Steel Corporation, he was made first vice president of the new corporation and assumed responsibility for obtaining and transporting iron ore and coal from the mines to the furnaces. He retired from U.S.

Steel in 1909 and moved to New York City where he served as president of the American Ore Reclamation Company and the Sheffield Iron Corporation until his death.

In addition to overseeing the operation of blast furnaces, Gayley invented a number of devices to make them run more efficiently. He was greatly encouraged in this endeavor by his 12-year association with ANDREW CARNEGIE whose obsession with driving down operating costs made his mills the most efficient and profitable ones in the world. Gayley's primary interest was to get the furnaces to operate at higher temperatures, thus removing a greater percentage of the impurities from iron ore, while using less fuel. To this end he designed charging bins that mixed rather than heaped the iron ore, coke, and limestone while loading them into the furnaces, thus permitting the ingredients to burn more evenly. He also designed an improved blast engine for forcing air into the furnaces, thus enhancing combustion.

Gayley's greatest contribution to improved blast furnace efficiency was the dry-air furnace. One factor that contributed to the inefficiency of blast furnaces was water vapor in the air that was forced under pressure into the furnace. This vapor absorbed heat that could otherwise be used to heat the iron ore to higher temperatures, and in iron-making centers in regions with high humidity such as Richmond, Virginia, and Birmingham, Alabama, the excess moisture in the air actually reduced the quality of the pig iron, which led to the production of inferior iron and steel. In 1894 Gayley mounted a condenser to his blast engine, thus removing the moisture from the air before blasting it into the furnace. Over the next 17 years he fine-tuned the operation of the condenser and added certain features to the furnace to further enhance the removal of water vapor. In 1908 he received the Franklin Institute's Elliott Cresson Medal for designing the dry-air furnace.

Gayley's other inventions include a bronze cooling plate, mounted between layers of brick and through which cool water circulates, thus keeping the furnace's firebrick walls from burning out and having to be replaced; a machine to unload iron ore more efficiently from a ship; and an ore ship that could be easily unloaded by means of his ore-unloading machine. In 1913 he received the American Society of Mechanical Engineers' Perkins Gold Medal for his contributions to the American iron and steel industry. He served as president of the American Institute of Mining Engineers (AIME) from 1904 to 1905 and published a number of papers regarding the making of iron and steel in the AIME journal. He died on February 25, 1920, in New York City.

Further Reading

"James Gayley." *Transactions of the American Institute of Mining Engineers* 67 (1922): 639–40.

Swank, James M. *History of the Manufacture of Iron in all ages and Particularly in the United States for Three Hundred Years, from 1585 to 1885.* Philadelphia: NCR Educational Products, 1979, microfiche.

Genovese, Vito

(1897–1969) *entrepreneur in organized crime*

One of the most powerful figures in the history of organized crime in the United States was Vito Genovese. A ruthless thug who completed only five grades in school, he rose through the ranks to become the most influential leader in the American Mafia. In the process, he made a fortune from his involvement in gambling, extortion, prostitution, and drug dealing.

Genovese was born on November 21, 1897, in Ricigliano, Italy. His father, Philip, was a construction worker, and his mother, Nancy, was a homemaker. At age 17 he emigrated to New York City, taking up residence in that part of Lower Manhattan known as Little Italy. Either unable or unwilling to find honest work, he soon joined a local Italian gang and embarked on a life of crime. At first he was content to commit acts of petty thievery and do battle with rival Irish and Jewish gangs, but gradually he became involved in the protection racket, whereby he extorted cash payments from small businesses in exchange for not vandalizing the establishments and not harming the proprietors or their family members. He gained a reputation for being both clever and cruel, and he was arrested several times on suspicion of battery or murder. In the late 1920s he came to the attention of Charles

"Lucky" Luciano, the boss of one of the five families of New York City's Mafia, a nationwide organized crime syndicate whose members tended to be Italian. Having found favor with Luciano, Genovese was able to become a collector for the Italian lottery, which was illegal in the United States. In the late 1920s Genovese became a legitimate businessman by starting a company that hauled wastepaper and rags. However, this enterprise existed merely to protect him from being prosecuted for income tax evasion, the downfall of another legendary criminal, AL CAPONE. By 1931 Genovese had become Luciano's chief lieutenant, and as such was now also heavily involved in prostitution and illegal drug dealing, especially heroin.

In the early 1930s, Genovese was implicated in three murders. In 1931 his wife of seven years, whose name is unknown, died suspiciously. In 1932 Gerard Vernotico was murdered; two weeks later Genovese married Vernotico's widow, Anna, with whom he would have two children. In 1934 he murdered Ferdinand Boccia, who had been his partner in an extortion scheme. After Luciano was jailed in 1936 on charges related to prostitution, the federal government stepped up its investigation of these three murders and of Genovese's position in the Mafia, and in 1937, the year after he became a naturalized citizen of the United States, he returned to Italy.

Despite his self-imposed exile, Genovese continued to play a major role in the American Mafia. He oversaw the production of heroin in southern Italy, and then had it smuggled into the United States. The profits from this operation were returned to him by his wife, who made several trips to Italy each year. He protected his operation by becoming friendly with Benito Mussolini, the Italian fascist dictator, who awarded Genovese the Order of the Crown of Italy in return for financing several major construction projects. Had World War II not occurred, Genovese might have stayed in Italy forever. But not long after U.S. troops liberated Italy in 1944, he was arrested for masterminding Italy's postwar black market, whereby supplies intended for the relief of the hungry and homeless were stolen and sold to the highest bidder. He returned to the United States to stand trial for Boccia's murder, but when Peter La Tempa, the

After making millions of dollars during his criminal career, Vito Genovese died in prison. *(Library of Congress)*

by state police in Appalachin, New York, while attending a high-level Mafia meeting. Two years later he was convicted for smuggling and distributing narcotics and received a 15-year sentence in the federal penitentiary in Atlanta, Georgia. Despite being in jail, he continued to run his criminal organization from behind bars until the mid-1960s. In 1963, Joseph Valachi, a former Mafia associate and cellmate of Genovese's, testified before a congressional committee about Genovese's continued involvement in organized crime. This led to Genovese's transfer to the federal penitentiary in Leavenworth, Kansas, where his contact with the outside world was almost completely cut off. He died of a heart attack on February 14, 1969, at the Medical Center for Federal Prisoners in Springfield, Missouri.

Further Reading

Hanna, David. *Vito Genovese.* New York: Belmont Tower Books, 1974.

Maas, Peter. *The Valachi Papers.* New York: Pocket Books, 1986.

Sifakis, Carl. *The Encyclopedia of American Crime,* Second Edition. New York: Facts On File, 2001.

"Vito Genovese," Spartacus Educational. Available online. URL: http://www.spartacus.schoolnet.co.uk/ USAC genovese.htm. Downloaded on November 19, 2001.

Gernsback, Hugo
(Hugo Gernsbacher)
(1884–1967) *inventor of science fiction*

By the end of the 20th century, science fiction had become a multibillion-dollar industry. Most of the credit for founding this industry belongs to Hugo Gernsback, the writer and publisher of the first science-fiction magazine in the United States, a man who got his intense interest in science from his mother.

Gernsback was born Hugo Gernsbacher on August 16, 1884, in Luxembourg City, Luxembourg. His father, Moritz, was a wine maker and his mother, Berta, was a housewife. He was educated in various boarding and technical schools in Luxembourg, Germany, and Belgium. Gernsback's

chief witness against Genovese, was poisoned while in protective custody, the case against Genovese collapsed and in 1946 he was set free.

Over the next 12 years, Genovese continued his involvement with gambling, extortion, prostitution, and narcotics, while becoming criminally involved in the dealings of several trade unions. All the while he became more powerful within the Mafia, and in 1957 he made a bid to become the head of the five families in New York City by having rival bosses assassinated. Having already arranged the murder of Willie Moretti in 1951, he ordered the executions of Frank Costello, who survived, and Albert Anastasia, who did not. As a result of these attacks, Genovese became generally recognized as "boss of all the bosses" in New York City. His personal fortune was estimated to be $30 million.

Not long after Genovese assumed control of the Mafia in New York City, he fell from power. In late 1957 he and 60 other mobsters were arrested mother was fascinated with electricity, and her enthusiasm for electricity influenced him. While still in school he invented the world's most powerful dry-cell battery; unfortunately, it was too expensive to manufacture to be sold in sufficient quantity to be profitable.

At age 20 Gernsback emigrated to the United States, settling in New York City. In 1905 he founded the Electro Importing Company, a mail-order house that sold a variety of parts for building amateur radios as well as the Telimco Wireless Radio, which Gernsback had designed. Amateur radio was just becoming popular, and the company's products sold so well that within five years Electro employed 60 people.

One reason for the firm's success was *Modern Electrics*, which Gernsback began publishing in 1908. Originally a catalog of parts and equipment available from Electro, it quickly blossomed into a monthly magazine featuring editorials and how-to articles of interest to amateur radio operators. In 1911 the magazine included the first installment of a futuristic piece of fiction called "Ralph 124C 41+." Written by Gernsback, the story was his attempt to prove that popular fiction could be used to teach science to the masses; in it he prophesied such far-out contraptions as microfilm, radar, tape recorders, and television. Although the story itself was mediocre, its focus on the scientific possibilities of the future captured the imaginations of a number of readers, and *Modern Electrics* continued to publish such pieces as a regular feature.

In 1926 Gernsback founded the Experimenter Publishing Company and began publishing *Amazing Stories*, the first English-language magazine devoted entirely to science fiction. Despite this magazine's popularity, Experimenter was forced into bankruptcy after just three years. Undaunted, in 1929 Gernsback launched the Stellar Publishing Corporation and began publishing four new science-fiction magazines: *Air Wonder Stories, Science Wonder Stories, Science Wonder Quarterly,* and *Scientific Detective Monthly.* Within a year the first two magazines were merged into *Wonder Stories,* which Gernsback sold in 1936 to Standard Publications, while the other two quietly disappeared after a few months. Gernsback made two more attempts at publishing commercially successful science-fiction

magazines, *Superworld Comics* in 1940 and *Science-Fiction Plus* in 1953, but neither lasted more than seven issues.

Gernsback's science-fiction magazines were commercial flops, mostly because he published pieces that were strong along scientific and technical lines but weak in terms of plot and general readability. However, he did much better with other magazines that were devoted to popular science. *Modern Electrics* had its scope expanded and its name changed to *Science and Invention* before it was merged in 1931 with *Popular Mechanics,* perhaps the most popular and long-running popular science magazine in U.S. history. Gernsback also achieved success with *Radio-Electronics, Radio Craft,* and *Popular Electronics,* all of which were modeled after *Modern Electrics.*

In addition to Electro Importing and his publishing activities, Gernsback operated a radio station and a television station in New York City. He invented more than 100 electrical and electronic devices, and he received at least 37 patents. He was married three times: in 1906 to Rose Harvey with whom he had two children; in 1921 to Dorothy Kantrowitz with whom he had three children; and in 1951 to Mary Hancher with whom he had no children. The first two marriages ended in divorce. He died on August 19, 1967, in New York City, and in his will he left his body to the Cornell University Medical School.

Gernsback was evidently the type of person whom one either loved or hated. On the one hand, he received the Veteran Wireless Operators' Marconi Memorial Wireless Pioneer Medal in 1950, Luxembourg's Gold Medal of Luxembourg in 1953, and the Helios Society of Belgium's Silver Jubilee Trophy in 1953. In 1953 science-fiction fans named their annual achievement award the "Hugo" in his honor and awarded him a Hugo in 1960. On the other hand, he alienated most of the top-rank science-fiction writers of his day, mostly by not paying them on time or at all. Many science-fiction critics vilify him for giving the nascent genre a bad name by publishing weak stories and then folding his magazines before they had a chance to mature, and they suggest that science fiction would have grown faster had it not been for his shortsightedness. Modern critics are divided over whether

Gernsback was the best thing or the worst thing that ever happened to science fiction.

Further Reading

Moskowitz, Sam. *Explorers of the Infinite: Shapers of Science Fiction.* New York: World Pub., 1963.

Siegel, Mark. *Hugo Gernsback, Father of Modern Science Fiction.* San Bernardino, Calif.: Borgo Press, 1988.

Westfahl, Gary. *The Mechanics of Wonder: The Creation of the Idea of Science Fiction.* Liverpool, U.K.: Liverpool University Press, 1998.

Getty, J. Paul
(Jean Paul Getty)
(1892–1976) *entrepreneur in petroleum*

At the time of his death, the wealthiest man in the United States, and probably in the world, was J. Paul Getty, oil tycoon. Getty was worth billions of dollars, yet for much of his life he never carried cash and spent little on anything other than his art collection. His wealth seems to have soured his personal relationships and made him more miserable than if he had been broke.

Getty was born Jean Paul Getty on December 15, 1892, in Minneapolis, Minnesota. His father, George, was an attorney and oil investor, and his mother, Sarah, was a socialite. At age 11 Getty caught "oil fever" when he accompanied his father to Indian Territory, now Oklahoma, where George Getty owned several oil wells under the name Minnehoma Oil Company. At age 13 Getty moved with his family to Los Angeles, California; he attended military school there and worked in the Oklahoma oil fields during summer vacations. After graduating from military school in 1909, he studied briefly at the University of Southern California and the University of California at Berkeley, then attended Oxford University where he received a diploma in economics and political science in 1913.

Getty traveled through Europe for a year before becoming an oil field scout for Minnehoma. He also began investing in oil leases of his own. He seemed to have a knack for knowing where the next big strike would come, and by 1916 he was worth $1 million. That same year he and his father combined their holdings to form Getty Oil Company. Two years later Getty became convinced that the best oil investments were to be made in California, not Oklahoma. His intuition proved to be correct, and Getty Oil prospered as a result.

In 1923 Getty's father separated his holdings from Getty Oil to form his own company, George F. Getty, Inc. After his father died in 1930, Getty became president and, in 1933, majority stockholder of his father's company. By this time he had also acquired controlling interest in Pacific Western Oil Company, into which he merged Getty Oil. After acquiring Skelly Oil Corporation in 1937 and Tidewater Associated Oil Company in 1951, which he consolidated with the rest of his holdings under the name Minnehoma Financial Corporation, Getty was one of the richest oil investors in the United States.

Getty's fortune got even bigger when he struck oil in the Middle East. In 1949 he purchased a 60-year oil lease in Saudi Arabia near its border with Iraq, and for four years Pacific Western drilled for oil without success. Finally, in 1953 the company struck oil in a field estimated to hold more than 13 billion barrels. This strike put Getty's estimated net worth at more than $1 billion, thus making him one of the wealthiest people in the world. Over the years his oil companies prospered while his oil leases increased in value, and at the time of his death he was estimated to be worth between $2 and $4 billion dollars, making him possibly the richest person on Earth.

Unfortunately for Getty, his billions did not seem to have bought him happiness. Most of his fortune was tied up in stocks, bonds, and oil leases that were not easily converted into cash. In fact, he carried little if any cash and lived a surprisingly frugal lifestyle, which may have prompted his famous remark that "a billion dollars isn't what it used to be." Between 1949, when he became involved in Saudi Arabia, and 1960, he lived mostly in hotel rooms around the world. In 1960 he rented space at Sutton Place, a large estate in Surrey, England, and he made this his home until his death.

Getty's only extravagance seems to have been collecting art. He was particularly fond of Greek and Roman antiquities, 18th-century French decorative art, and medieval and modern European paintings. In 1974 he moved his collection from Sutton Place to the newly constructed J. Paul Getty Museum in Malibu, California; the building itself was a re-creation of a Roman villa of the Augustan period that cost $12 million to build. He endowed the museum with $40 million and gave it an annual operating budget of $2 million. When he died, he left more than $1 billion to the museum in his will.

Getty's wealth seems to have made his relationships with his parents, spouses, and children difficult. He and his father split following a disagreement as to who should supervise their oil fields; the dispute became bitter and the two never reconciled. Getty managed to gain control of his father's corporation by buying thousands of shares for millions of dollars from his mother, but he refused to pay her until she agreed to put the money into a trust fund to benefit her heirs, thus alienating her as well. He was married and divorced five times, to Jeannette Demont (1923–1925), Allene Ashby (1926–1928), Adolphine Helmle (1928–1932), Ann Rork (1932–1935), and Louise Lynch (1939–1958). He and his eldest son, George F. Getty II, had a falling-out over how Getty Oil should be run, and before they could be reconciled George died. Another son, Gordon Peter Getty, sued him for $7.4 million, the amount Gordon claimed was due him from his grandmother's trust fund but which he had not received because Getty had never paid it into the fund as promised. In 1973 one of his grandsons, J. Paul Getty III, was kidnapped and held ransom for $17 million, but Getty bargained the kidnappers down to $1 million, which he then loaned, with interest, to the boy's father, Eugene Paul Getty, in the hope of deterring future kidnappers from snatching his other grandchildren.

Although Getty could be quite parsimonious with family members, rumors of his miserliness were largely unfounded. The pay phone he supposedly installed at Sutton Place for guests to use was actually put there by the company that owned and ran the estate for the use of its employees. It was reported in the press that Getty had invited 16 guests to dine at a fancy restaurant in Paris, France, and then refused to pay the bill, but Getty was himself a guest at this dinner party, not the host. In fact, he contributed quite generously throughout his lifetime to the World Wildlife Fund and the American Hospital in Paris.

J. Paul Getty died on June 6, 1976. For the last three years of his life he cut himself off from the outside world, seeing few people other than his personal staff, one son, and one ex-wife.

Further Reading

De Chair, Somerset S. *Getty on Getty: A Man in a Billion.* London: Cassell, 1989.

Glassman, Bruce. *J. Paul Getty: Billionaire Oilman.* Woodbridge, Conn.: Blackbirch Press, 2001.

Lenzner, Robert. *Getty: The Richest Man in the World.* London: Grafton, 1987.

Miller, Russell. *The House of Getty.* New York: H. Holt, 1986.

Pearson, John. *Painfully Rich: J. Paul Getty and His Heirs.* London: Macmillan, 1995.

Giannini, Amadeo Peter
(1870–1949) *entrepreneur in consumer banking*

As the son of Italian immigrants and fatherless at the age of seven, Amadeo Giannini seems an unlikely entry into the status of the great business leaders in U.S. history. But the innovations and personal approach he forged helped create significant changes in the field of banking, to the extent that Giannini is considered by many America's banker, the person who did more to serve the banking needs of ordinary Americans than any individual before or since.

Amadeo Pietro Giannini was born on May 6, 1870, in San Jose, California. His father, Luigi, had come to California from Genoa, Italy, in an unsuccessful search for gold and settled in California with his new wife, Virginia. Less than a year later the couple welcomed their son, who was often referred to as A. P. When Giannini was seven, his farmer father was killed in a dispute over a dollar. Giannini's mother remarried a produce salesman named Lorenzo Scatena and Amadeo left school at the age of 14 to assist him in the business. Within five years, Giannini was a partner in the successful enterprise and had developed a reputation as a trusted person of high integrity.

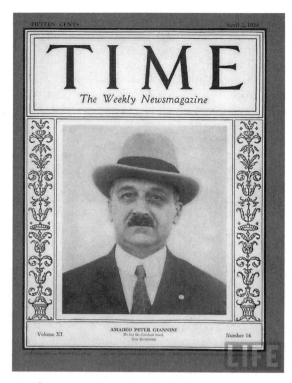

FIFTEEN CENTS   April 2, 1928

TIME
The Weekly Newsmagazine

Volume XI   AMADEO PETER GIANNINI   Number 14
                     He has the Corsican touch.
                            (See Business)

Amadeo Peter Giannini, head of the Bank of America National Association on the cover of *Time,* April 2, 1928 *(TIME magazine)*

Giannini married Clorinda Cueno in 1892, and they would eventually have six children. When he was 32, Giannini joined the board of Columbus Savings & Loan Society, a small bank located in the largely Italian North Beach section of San Francisco, when he assumed the seat of his recently deceased father-in-law. Giannini soon left this position, largely because his fellow directors consistently opposed his ideas to make banking services more accessible to the working-class, largely immigrant population of the area who Giannini knew from personal experience would be dependable clients. In 1904, he raised $150,000 from his stepfather and 10 friends to open the Bank of Italy in a converted saloon across the street from the Columbus Savings & Loan. Giannini quickly took the then very unconventional step of soliciting business by stopping people on the street and ringing doorbells. Though traditional bankers viewed this

as extremely distasteful, Giannini soon proved that extending banking services to common people was good for them and profitable for bankers.

Giannini solidified his reputation as a man of the people in the immediate aftermath of the 1906 San Francisco earthquake. A 1998 *Time* magazine profile listing Giannini as one of the 100 most important people of the 20th century explained, "Giannini quickly set up shop on the docks near San Francisco's North Beach. With a wooden plank straddling two barrels for a desk, he began to extend credit 'on a face and a signature' to small businesses and individuals in need of money to rebuild their lives. His actions spurred the city's redevelopment."

Over the next few decades, Giannini continued to be a pioneer in banking by helping usher in home mortgage and auto loans as well as formulating what would later be widely adopted as a national and international system of branch banking, explaining, "Branch banking is the only way a small town can get the resources, brain power and equipment of a $4 billion bank. And when they have got it, the town starts growing." He also played an important role in the booming expansion of California in the first half of the 20th century, helping provide much-needed investment in the wine and motion picture industries, including extending a $2 million loan to Walt Disney to complete his film, *Snow White.*

An April 2, 1928, *Time* magazine cover story on Giannini reflected the sterling reputation he had earned and which served him so well in his business dealings. Noted the article, "Amadeo Peter Giannini, a Sicilian peasant by ancestry, acts the Roman patrician by nature. He believes himself the guardian as well as the leader of his clients. Because he knows that the ever-expanding activities of his bank and investment corporation tend to stir up speculation in their securities, he warns the unwary." Also in 1928, Giannini started the financial services corporation, TransAmerica, and in 1930 he founded the Bank of America, which grew to be the largest bank in the United States. Giannini provided critically needed financial support during the Great Depression, including funding the Golden Gate Bridge construction and during World War II funding defense industries.

After a brief retirement in 1930, Giannini returned to serve as chairman of Bank of America until 1945, when he retired again and left the leadership of the bank to two of his six children. Giannini died on June 3, 1949, of heart failure at his home in San Mateo, California. Although his Bank of America was the largest bank in America with over 500 branches (mostly in California) and about $6 billion in assets, Giannini was not extraordinarily wealthy, leaving behind an estate worth about half a million dollars. This was by choice, as Giannini believed that accumulating too much wealth would keep him from being connected to the "little fellow" that he sought to serve, so he regularly took a modest salary and gave much of his wealth to various philanthropies.

Giannini's legacy remains strongly felt in the banking world and more particularly in San Francisco, where his name graces the plaza at the Bank of America building, a middle school, and the building that houses the Department of Agricultural and Resource Economics at the University of California at Berkeley. He is buried at Holy Cross Cemetery in Colma, California.

Further Reading

"Amadeo Ginannini," Time 100. Available online. URL: http://www.time.com/time/time100/builder/profile/giannini3.html. Downloaded on July 1, 2009.

"Business and Finance: Bankitaly, Bancitaly." Time. Available online. URL: http://www.time.com/time/magazine/article/0,9171,731707,00.html. Downloaded on July 1, 2009.

"Who Made America? A.P. Giannini," PBS. Available online. URL: http://www.pbs.org/wgbh/theymadeamerica/whomade/giannini_hi.html. Downloaded on July 1, 2009.

Gillette, King Camp

(1855–1932) *inventor of the disposable razor blade*

Before 1900, men had to shave with bulky straight razors. These devices took time to sharpen and were unwieldy to the point of being dangerous, so much so that many men went to a barber to get a shave. But in 1903 the advent of the safety razor made it possible for men to shave quickly and safely. Oddly, King Gillette, the man who invented and profited handsomely from its sale, was an opponent of capitalism, the same economic system that allowed him to become wealthy.

Gillette was born on January 5, 1855, in Fond du Lac, Wisconsin. His father, George, was a hardware wholesaler, and his mother, Fanny, was an author. As a young boy he moved with his family to Chicago, Illinois. His family lost everything they owned in the Great Chicago Fire of 1871, and at age 16 he went to work as a clerk in a hardware store. A few years later he followed in his father's footsteps by becoming a traveling salesman of hardware items. He loved to tinker with mechanical things and in 1879 he received a patent for a water faucet component. In 1890 he married Atlanta Gaines with whom he had one child.

In 1891 Gillette moved to New York City to take a job as a salesman for the Baltimore Seal Company. Its president, William Painter, had invented a throwaway tin bottle cap, and he advised Gillette that if he ever wanted to become wealthy he should invent something disposable. For four years Gillette wracked his brain for such an idea. One day while stropping one of the large straight razors of the day, it occurred to him that a disposable razor blade might be just the thing he had been looking for; not only would a disposable blade eliminate the need to sharpen the razor by hand before shaving, but also it might make shaving a lot safer. He reasoned that a thin blade could be held rigid if it were clamped securely into a T-handle, which could be designed in such a way that only a small portion of the blade would come in contact with the skin. But when he told others about his idea, they scoffed at the notion that a thin piece of metal could be made sharp enough to give a satisfactorily close shave.

Although he knew nothing about metallurgy, Gillette persisted in finding a way to make his idea work. When William Nickerson invented a machine in 1901 that could sharpen ribbon-thin steel, Gillette was able to move forward with his project. In 1903 he formed the Gillette Safety Razor Company. Although the first year's sales were disappointing—less than 200 blades and about 50 T-handles—he embarked on an

Before King Gillette invented the disposable razor blade, many men sported full-length beards. *(Library of Congress)*

aggressive advertising campaign that emphasized both the speed and the safety of his invention. The results of the campaign were instant and dramatic; in 1904 the company sold almost 90,000 T-handles and more than 12 million blades. By 1913 he had made so much money from his invention that he retired from the active management of the company and moved to a large estate in Calabasas, California.

Despite his success as a capitalist, at heart Gillette was a socialist. Instead of letting businesspeople do whatever they liked regardless of its effect on the general public, socialists wanted the government to take control of the factories and businesses, and distribute the profits among the workers. As early as 1894 he began looking for alternatives to the dog-eat-dog lifestyle espoused by unfettered liberal capitalism. His book *The Human Drift* (1894) blamed all of mankind's misery on the unbridled competition celebrated by robber baron capitalism. He proposed instead that all means of production be consolidated in the hands of one super-corporation that would manage the world's resources for the good of all its residents. Once his fortune was assured, he continued to press for social change. He hired Melvin L. Severy to write two books outlining his utopian views, *Gillette's Social Redemption* (1907) and *Gillette's Industrial Solution* (1908). Gillette himself wrote *World Corporation* (1910) and *The People's Corporation* (1924), the latter with the assistance of the radical novelist Upton Sinclair. In 1910 Gillette established the World Corporation in Arizona Territory and tried unsuccessfully to interest former president Theodore Roosevelt, whose New Nationalism called for a kinder, gentler version of capitalism, to manage it. Gillette later maintained that such arch-capitalistic industrial monopolies as United States Steel and Standard Oil were the forerunners of the socialist world corporation of which he dreamed.

While espousing worldwide socialism, Gillette continued to invest heavily in California real estate and the New York Stock Exchange. He explained this apparent hypocrisy to critics by declaring that only a fool would not take advantage of whatever opportunities presented themselves. The collapse of the stock market in 1929 and of the California real estate boom shortly thereafter ruined him financially. He died on July 9, 1932, in Calabasas.

Further Reading

Adams, Russell B., Jr. *King C. Gillette: The Man and His Wonderful Shaving Device.* Boston: Little, Brown, 1978.

Dowling, Tim. *Inventor of the Disposable Culture: King Camp Gillette, 1855–1932.* London: Short Books, 2001.

Mariott, Steve, et al. *The Very, Very Rich: How They Got That Way and How You Can, Too!* Franklin Lakes, N.J.: Career Press, 2000.

Glidden, Joseph Farwell

(1813–1906) *inventor of barbed wire*

The taming of the American West depended in large part on the development of a suitable method for fencing in land without using wood or stone, both of which were in short supply on the

Great Plains. Although several alternative forms of fencing were invented during the 19th century, the most successful was the style of barbed wire invented by Joseph Glidden, a 60-year-old farmer who got his idea while attending a county fair.

Glidden was born on January 18, 1813, in Charlestown, New Hampshire. His parents, David and Polly, were farmers. While still a baby he moved with his family to Orleans County, New York. After completing his secondary education, he taught school until 1834, then spent the next six years working on his parents' farm. In 1837 he married Clarissa Foster with whom he had three children. In 1843 his wife died, and in 1851 he married Lucinda Warne with whom he had one child.

Glidden loved to farm, but the price of farmland in western New York was so high that he could not afford to buy enough acreage to support his family. In 1840 he decided to move west where good farmland was considerably cheaper. Taking two threshing machines with him, he paid for the trip by hiring himself out to farmers along the way. By 1842 he had reached De Kalb, Illinois, where he was able to buy 600 acres of prairie land and happily settle down to spend the rest of his life farming.

In 1873 Glidden attended the De Kalb County Fair where he saw an exhibit by Henry Rose of "armored wire fencing," which consisted of wire points imbedded in wooden strips. Rose's invention was intended to provide farmers with a cheap means of keeping farm animals and cattle out of their crops, but his use of wood was impractical on the prairie where timber was scarce. However, Rose's fence inspired Glidden, who substituted metal rods for the wooden posts and smooth wire strands for the wooden strips, then strung barbed points along the strands. At first the barbs kept coming loose and sliding toward the posts, thus making the fence ineffective, so he twisted a second strand around the first strand and the barbs to keep them from sliding. It was this second strand that made Glidden's fence unique from a host of other designs for wire fences, several of which had been invented in the 1860s, and he received a patent for "armored wire" in 1874.

Glidden sold a half interest in his patent to Joseph Ellwood, a hardware store owner in De Kalb who had also been inspired by Rose's fence to tinker with an improved version. In 1874 Glidden and Ellwood founded the Barb Fence Company and began manufacturing barbed wire. Despite the fact that the company employed no salesmen and sold the wire mostly out of Ellwood's store, the demand for barbed wire almost exceeded the company's ability to manufacture it. By the 1870s the Illinois prairie was dotted with farms, and wandering cattle and farm animals posed a major threat to crops—which made fencing a necessity. Glidden's barbed wire provided a cheap, easy-to-use form of fencing that resisted wind and fire while providing an effective barrier to the movement of animals.

Despite the commercial success of his invention, Glidden had no interest in being a manufacturer. In 1876 he sold his half interest in the barbed wire patent to the Washburn and Moen Manufacturing Company of Worcester, Massachusetts, which manufactured the smooth wire strands from which Barb Fence made its wire; he received $60,000 in cash and substantial royalties for fifteen years. He used the money to buy several farms and a number of investment properties in De Kalb, including a hotel, a newspaper, and a mill. He also invested heavily in a Texas ranch with 15,000 head of cattle. Except for the fact that the ranch was fenced in with 150 miles of barbed wire of his design, for the rest of his life Glidden had little to do with the barbed wire industry he had created. He died on October 9, 1906, in De Kalb.

Further Reading

"Joseph Farwell Glidden," New Perspectives on the West. Available online. URL: http://www.pbs.org/weta/thewest/people/d_h/glidden.htm. Downloaded on July 2, 2009.

McCallum, Henry D., and Frances T. McCallum. *The Wire That Fenced the West*. Norman: University of Oklahoma Press, 1965.

Godfrey, Thomas
(1704–1749) *inventor of the octant*

Before 1730, sailors had a difficult time determining their position at sea. In 1731 a device known as the octant was invented, making it much easier to determine one's latitude, or distance north or south of the equator. This device was invented independently by two men; one of them was Thomas Godfrey, a self-educated artisan and comrade of BENJAMIN FRANKLIN, who enjoyed drinking with sailors.

Godfrey was born on January 10, 1704, in Bristol Township, Pennsylvania. His parents, Joseph and Catherine, were farmers. At age 12 he became a glazier's apprentice and learned how to install window glass. At age 21 he inherited his father's farm, but instead of settling down on the family homestead he moved to Philadelphia where he went into business as a glazier and plumber. From time to time he served the city government as an excavation supervisor for a number of public works projects. In 1727 he became a founding member, with Benjamin Franklin, of the Leather Apron Club or Junto, a group of artisans and mechanics with little formal education who aspired to improve themselves intellectually and socially. As a member of the Junto, Godfrey helped establish a public library, a hospital, a fire insurance company, and the American Philosophical Society. By 1736, Godfrey had married an unknown woman with whom he had two children. He lived his entire adult life in Philadelphia.

Despite his lack of formal education, Godfrey developed an intense interest in mathematics and astronomy. Having borrowed some books, he was able to teach himself enough about both subjects to develop ephemerides, tables showing the positions of the planets and stars on a sequence of future dates, for almanacs published by Benjamin Franklin and William Bradford. By 1740 Godfrey had become so adept at astronomy that he started teaching classes in navigation and astronomy in his home.

Godfrey's interest in astronomy and mathematics led him to invent the octant, a forerunner of the modern-day sextant. Although he never went to sea, he was a regular patron of the taverns along Philadelphia's waterfront where he enjoyed discussing various topics of navigation with sailors. At the time, one of the biggest navigational problems was determining latitude. The standard method was to use a backstaff, essentially a staff about three feet long that was marked off in degrees and fitted with a sliding crosspiece. The navigator held the bottom end of the staff up to one eye, then adjusted the crosspiece until one end lined up with the horizon and the other with the North Star. The degree mark indicated by the position of the crosspiece gave the North Star's altitude, from which could be determined the ship's latitude. There were three major problems with using the backstaff; first, the North Star is not aligned perfectly with the earth's axis, so a daily adjustment had to be made when calculating latitude; second, on a bright day the North Star can be difficult to see with the naked eye; and third, as one approaches the equator, the North Star falls below the horizon so that it cannot be seen at all.

Godfrey was glazing windows one day in 1730 when he noticed the double reflection from a pane of glass that had fallen on the ground. This observation led him to the realization that, by using two mirrors, one stationary and one movable, he could reflect the sun so that it appeared to be on the horizon, thus making it possible to determine latitude by measuring the altitude of the sun at high noon, when it was aligned perfectly with the earth's axis from the navigator's point of view. He borrowed a backstaff from George Steward, a ship's mate who was a friend of his, and converted it into what Godfrey called a reflecting quadrant. Steward tested it on his next voyage and reported that it worked better than the backstaff. Then Godfrey had an improved model made by Edmund Woolley, a carpenter, which he gave to Steward to test on voyages to Jamaica and Newfoundland. When the device passed the test with flying colors, in 1731 Godfrey contracted with Anthony Lamb, an instrument maker in New York City, to produce and sell the reflecting quadrant, better known today as the octant.

Before Godfrey could apply to the king of England for a patent, John Hadley, vice president of the Royal Society of London, announced his invention of a similar device. He demonstrated it before the society in 1732 and was awarded a patent, thus the device became known as Hadley's quadrant. However, most historians acknowledge that the two men arrived at the same idea independently of each other. In any case, the octant was made obsolete in the mid-18th century by the sextant, which uses mirrors to determine both latitude and longitude. Thomas Godfrey died in Philadelphia in December 1749.

Further Reading

Bedini, Silvio A. "At the Sign of the Compass and Quadrant: The Life and Times of Anthony Lamb." *Transactions of the American Philosophical Society* 74, pt. 1 (1984): 37–47.

Coulson, Thomas. "Godfrey's Invention of the Reflecting Quadrant." *Journal of the Franklin Institute* 266, No. 5 (November 1958): 336–37.

Goldman, Sylvan Nathan

(1898–1984) *inventor of the folding shopping cart*

Imagine going shopping for groceries in a supermarket that had no shopping carts. Even if you used a handbasket, you could only carry a few items, and so you would probably not purchase any impulse or nonessential items. You might also have to come back another day to finish your shopping. Fortunately, modern shoppers can buy as many items as they want, thanks to Sylvan Goldman's folding shopping cart.

Goldman was born on November 15, 1898, in Ardmore, Indian Territory, in what is today Oklahoma. His parents, Michael and Hortense, owned a general store. At age 15 he moved with his family to Tulsa, and shortly thereafter he went to work for his mother's brothers, who owned a wholesale grocery and produce business in nearby Sapulpa. In 1917 he enlisted in the U.S. Army and saw action in France during World War I. In 1919 he became partners with his brother and an uncle and opened a wholesale grocery business in Cisco, Texas. After the business failed two years later, he went to California where he worked as a clerk in several stores. In 1926 he returned to Oklahoma and cofounded with his brother the Sun Stores chain of grocery stores. The chain grew phenomenally, and three years later the brothers sold out to Skaggs-Safeway Stores. However, the profits they made from the sale were wiped out in the stock market crash of 1929, so in 1930 they opened another chain, Standard Stores, which in 1934 they renamed Humpty

Dumpty. In 1931 Goldman married Margaret Katz with whom he had two children.

Goldman's grocery stores were too big to operate like general stores, where the store clerk rounded up the items that the customer wanted to purchase. Instead, Goldman's customers roamed the store, found what they wanted, and then carried their selections back to the cash register. His customers could buy only what they could carry in their arms or in a handbasket, thus they rarely bought more than a dozen items at a time, which was never as many items as they wanted to buy. One day it occurred to him that if his customers could carry more they would buy more, in which case they would probably buy more high-profit impulse and luxury items as well as the essentials.

In 1936 Goldman had the idea of mounting two handbaskets on a wheeled frame, thus making a cart that could hold twice as much and could be pushed instead of carried. With the help of his employee Fred Young, Goldman built such a cart on a folding frame, so that the baskets could be removed and the cart could be collapsed for easier storage. Several years later he designed the nesting cart familiar to modern-day shoppers, with the swinging rear gate that allows carts to be stored one inside the other. The original model worked so well in his own stores that in 1937 he formed the Folding Basket Carrier Company to manufacture and sell his folding shopping cart to other grocery stores. When store owners proved to be skeptical about the potential of the cart to boost sales, Goldman had his salesman show them a film of professional actors pushing his carts around the store and filling them up with groceries. Goldman's carts were a big hit with store owners and customers alike, and during the 1930s and 1940s Goldman made millions of dollars selling them. However, even though he had patented the cart and its various improvements, he found it virtually impossible to stop others from imitating his design and gradually encroaching on his sales.

In the 1940s Goldman began buying farms on the outskirts of Oklahoma City. As the city grew outward, he converted the farms into shopping centers anchored by one of his grocery stores. In 1955 he merged Humpty Dumpty with several other chains into a new corporation called

ACF-Wrigley, with himself as president. He sold his interest in this company in 1959, and in 1960 he founded Goldman Enterprises, a conglomeration of his holdings in real estate, financial institutions, and hotels across the Southwest. He spent the last 20 years of his life giving away money to charitable organizations via the Goldman Foundation. He died on November 25, 1984, in Oklahoma City.

Further Reading

Lienhard, John H. "No. 995: Shopping Carts," Engines of Our Ingenuity. Available online. URL: http://www.uh.edu/engines/epi995.htm. Downloaded on July 2, 2009.

Wilson, Terry P. The Cart That Changed the World: The Career of Sylvan N. Goldman. Norman: University of Oklahoma Press, 1978.

Goldmark, Peter Carl

(1906–1977) *inventor of color television*

Long-playing records have been replaced by CDs, and videocassettes are being replaced by DVDs, but color television, which is older than both, just might live forever. The inventor of color television, Peter Goldmark, also invented the long-playing record and helped develop the forerunner to videocassettes, thus marking him as one of the foremost inventors of 20th-century entertainment technology.

Goldmark was born on December 2, 1906, in Budapest, Hungary. His father, Alexander, was a hatmaker, and his mother, Emmy, was a homemaker. At age 12 he moved with his family to Vienna, Austria. As a schoolboy, he built a miniature television set from a mail-order kit, then received an Austrian patent for devising an enlarged viewing screen. After completing his basic education, he enrolled in the Physical Institute of Vienna and received his B.Sc. in 1930 and his Ph.D. in 1931. He then emigrated to London, England, where he worked as a television design engineer. Two years later he left for the United States, finding work in New York City as a consultant to various radio and television networks. In 1936 he became the chief television engineer for the Columbia Broadcasting System (CBS). He

became an American citizen in 1937, and in 1939 he married Frances Trainer with whom he had four children; they divorced in 1954, and that same year he married Diane Davis with whom he had two children.

In 1940 Goldmark went to see the epic movie *Gone With the Wind*. He was so impressed with the film's vivid color that he decided to invent color television. That same year he developed the field-sequential system, an electromechanical system that uses a whirling disk with thousands of red, blue, and green phosphor dots on it to record color images, then transmits the images to the television set, which depicts them in color by means of another whirling red, blue, and green disk. In 1940 he used this system to make the first color television broadcast to a small audience in New York City. The field-sequential system became and remains the system of choice for closed-circuit applications. However, it never caught on for use in individual home television sets because of the high cost of retrofitting black-and-white televisions with the disks. After years of struggling to gain wider acceptance for the field-sequential system, Goldmark gave up and came up with another system instead. By 1954 he had figured out how to superimpose the colored phosphor dots onto the inside of the television screen itself. Although the arrangement has been modified a number of times since then, in essence it remains the method for projecting color television images into modern homes.

In addition to color television, Goldmark was interested in classical music. He loved to play the cello and piano, at which he was quite good, and listen to classical music records. He was particularly distressed that the recordings of his day, which were basically disks of pressed shellac, had a scratchy, tinny sound to them and could hold only a few minutes of music per side. By 1948 he had invented the long-playing (LP) record. He substituted vinyl for shellac, which eliminated a lot of the scratchiness. He increased the number of grooves and slowed down the record speed from 78 revolutions per minute (rpm) to 33 1/3 rpm, thus increasing the playing time to about 20 minutes per side, which was usually sufficient to hold an entire symphonic movement. LPs made recorded music more appealing, thus greatly increasing the number of record customers. As the first company to release LPs, CBS quickly became a giant in the recording industry as well as in radio and television.

Goldmark was promoted from chief television engineer to director of engineering research and development in 1944, to vice president of CBS Laboratories in 1951, and to president of the laboratory in 1954. During his presidency, the laboratory invented more than 160 devices or processes related to acoustics, film reproduction, phonograph recording, and television. In the 1960s it developed electronic video recording (EVR), a system for recording moving images on videotape that could then be viewed on a home television. This system was later used as the springboard to the development of videocassette recordings. It also developed a lighter, smaller version of the field-sequential system so that the Lunar Orbiter and the first moon walkers could transmit high-resolution pictures of the Moon back to Earth.

In 1971 Goldmark retired from CBS and formed Goldmark Communications, later a subsidiary of Warner Communications. He hoped to use EVR to bring cultural, educational, and sports programs to rural viewers so they would not be isolated from the technological sophistication of the cities. Before he could make much progress in this direction, he was killed in an automobile accident on December 7, 1977, near Rye, New York.

Further Reading

Goldmark, Peter, with Lee Edson. *Maverick Inventor: My Turbulent Years at CBS*. New York: Saturday Review Press, 1973.

"Peter Carl Goldmark," The National Inventors Hall of Fame. Available online. URL http://www.invent.org/hall_of_fame/1_3_07_induction_Goldmark.asp. Downloaded on June 30, 2009.

Goodyear, Charles

(1800–1860) *inventor of vulcanized rubber*

Before the discovery of vulcanization, natural rubber was good for little else than erasing pencil marks. Afterward, natural rubber found ready uses in the manufacture of hundreds of flat items made from rubber sheeting, and it eventually was used to make a variety of industrial items from automobile tires to hoses to shoes. Ironically, Charles Goodyear, the man most responsible for the rise of the multimillion-dollar rubber industry, made little money from his invention and died in debt.

Goodyear was born on December 29, 1800, in New Haven, Connecticut. His father, Amasa, made hardware and farm implements, and his mother, Cynthia, was a housewife. At age 17 Goodyear moved to Philadelphia, Pennsylvania, where he went to work for a hardware manufacturer; four years later he returned to New Haven to enter his father's business. In 1824 he married Clarissa Beecher with whom he had nine children. In 1826 he returned to Philadelphia and, with his father, opened the first retail hardware store in the United States. The concept was too new to be received enthusiastically and the partners went bankrupt after four years.

In 1830 Goodyear opened a small shop and attempted to make a living as an inventor. By 1834 he had received six patents for various mechanical devices. That same year he became obsessed with rubber, which had just come into commercial production in 1820, after visiting the New York City showroom of the India Rubber Company, a Massachusetts firm that manufactured a variety of items from rubber. He quickly grasped that natural gum rubber, also known as India rubber, is moldable, strong, durable, and water resistant, qualities that had great appeal to him as an inventor. He immediately began looking for ways to incorporate rubber into his inventions, and in 1835 he invented the first rubber sheeting by treating the rubber with nitric acid. Two years later, he won a government contract to make mailbags out of sheet rubber, but the sheeting was too sticky and too susceptible to heat and cold; letters stuck to the inside of the mailbags, which were too brittle in the winter and too soft in the summer.

In 1838 Goodyear purchased from Nathaniel Hayward the Eagle India Rubber Company in Woburn, Massachusetts. He also purchased Hayward's patent for solarization, a process whereby rubber sheeting is dusted with sulfur and placed in the sunlight to cure, thus solving the problem of stickiness. For a year Goodyear devoted himself untiringly to perfecting Hayward's process via trial and error. At one point it occurred to him that adding lead oxide to the sulfur-rubber compound might work. He prepared such a sample, which he unintentionally placed on top of a hot stove. At first, he expected the high heat to melt the rubber, but instead it caused the rubber to harden without losing its strength or stretch.

Goodyear's discovery was later named vulcanization by an English rubber manufacturer in honor of the Roman god of fire. It was one of those serendipitous discoveries that could only have been made by accident; at the time, everyone who knew anything about rubber knew that heat ruined it. As for the chemical reaction itself, more than 150 years later scientists are still hard-pressed to explain exactly how it works. For some reason and in some way, the sulfur is not dissolved or dispersed throughout the rubber, but it combines with the long-chain molecules to form cross-links, making the rubber stronger and stretchier. The lead oxide simply accelerates the reaction between sulfur and rubber. Thus Goodyear's lack of formal training in chemistry did not hold him back at all; indeed, had he possessed such training he might never have made the discovery.

Unfortunately for Goodyear, his obsession with finding a way to make rubber commercially useful led to his complete impoverishment. Throughout the 1830s, he was often forced to make ends meet by selling his furniture and other household items. On several occasions he was sent to debtor's prison by his creditors, where he continued to experiment with rubber. His discovery of vulcanization permitted him to begin manufacturing various items out of rubber sheeting, but his business did not have sufficient capital and by 1843 he was forced once again into bankruptcy and debtor's prison. The sale of licenses to use his patent, which he received in 1844, supplied him with much-needed cash, but most of that was used to finance lawsuits against American manufacturers who infringed on his patent and by travels to England and France, where he tried unsuccessfully to establish his patent rights. In 1844 the British government awarded its patent for vulcanized rubber to Thomas Hancock, who had founded the world's first rubber factory

Charles Goodyear is probably the most famous inventor who never made any money from his invention. *(Library of Congress)*

in 1820. That same year the French government awarded Goodyear a patent but later revoked it because he had brought a pair of American-made rubber shoes into the country without authorization. From 1852, when the American courts established once and for all Goodyear's patent rights to vulcanization, to 1858, he spent most of his time in England and France attempting to establish his patent rights in those countries, but his efforts only drained him of cash and resulted in him being thrown into debtor's prisons in both countries.

Goodyear's first wife died in 1853, and the following year he married Fanny Wardell with whom he had three children. In 1859 he moved to Washington, D.C. He died on July 1, 1860, in New York City, while traveling to the funeral of one of his daughters. Instead of leaving his heirs a hefty fortune, he left them debts totaling more than $200,000.

Further Reading

Fanning, Leonard M. *Charles Goodyear: Father of the Rubber Industry.* New York: Mercer Pub., 1955.

Korman, Richard. *The Goodyear Story: An Inventor's Obsession and the Struggle for a Rubber Monopoly.* San Francisco, Calif.: Encounter Books, 2002.

Norman, Jon. *Nineteenth-Century Inventors.* New York: Facts On File, 1992.

Quackenbush, Robert M. *Oh, What an Awful Mess!: A Story of Charles Goodyear.* Englewood Cliffs, N.J.: Prentice Hall, 1980.

Smith, Tom. *Goodyear: The India Rubber Man in Woburn.* Woburn, Mass.: Black Flag Press, 1986.

Gordy, Berry, Jr.

(1929–   ) founder of Motown Records

One of the best-known African-American executives in the 1960s and 1970s was Berry Gordy, Jr. As founder and chairman of Motown Records, Gordy transformed the music industry by popularizing soul music for young black and white audiences. In the process, he launched the musical careers of such luminaries as Smokey Robinson, Diana Ross, and Michael Jackson.

Gordy was born on November 28, 1929, in Detroit, Michigan. His father, Berry, Sr., owned a plastering and carpentry business, and his mother, Bertha, was a homemaker. After dropping out of high school, he worked on an auto assembly line while pursuing a career as a professional boxer. In 1951 he was drafted into the U.S. Army where he received his high school equivalency diploma. He was discharged in 1953, the same year he married Thelma Coleman with whom he had three children, and went back to work on the assembly line. Two years later he borrowed enough money from his parents and siblings to open the 3-D Record Mart, a short-lived record store that specialized in jazz recordings (before CDs and cassette tapes, recorded music was played on vinyl disks called records; singles contained one song on each side and were played on a turntable at a speed of 45 revolutions per minute [rpm], while albums or LPs usually contained six songs per side and were played at 33 1/3 rpm). He had also taken up songwriting, and in 1957 he and two partners penned a hit tune for Jackie Wilson, who was just embarking on an illustrious career as a soul singer. Over the next two years Gordy wrote or cowrote four more songs that Wilson would turn into hits. In 1958 Gordy formed Jobete Music Company to publish the songs written by him and his partners. He also began producing records independently, although in this capacity he basically acted as an agent for national record labels such as Chess and United Artists. It was around this time that he met and befriended Smokey Robinson, whom Gordy would help become one of the greatest recording artists of his day. In 1959 Gordy divorced his first wife. Shortly thereafter he married Raynoma Liles with whom he had two children; they were divorced in 1962.

By 1959 Gordy had grown tired of the way the national labels were taking his songs and the talent he had recruited and giving him little in return. That same year, at Robinson's urging, he borrowed $800 from his family and friends and formed his own record company, Motown Record Corporation. Operating at first out of an apartment in downtown Detroit, in 1959 the company released its first single. Three years later, it released its first number-one hit, "Please Mr. Postman" by the Marvelettes. This tune became so popular that even the Beatles, perhaps the greatest rock 'n' roll band of all time, recorded a version of it on one of their early albums.

Motown's early efforts were aimed at a mostly black audience who preferred what they called rhythm and blues (R & B) and what white people called soul. But around 1962, when the civil rights movement was making whites think seriously about their commitment to segregation, Gordy realized that, properly packaged, R & B could be made to appeal to white audiences as well, especially young ones who were not as ingrained with racial prejudice as their parents had been. Taking as Motown's motto "The Sound of Young America," he set out to produce crossover hits, tunes that placed high on both the R & B and pop charts. By 1964 Motown had several acts, among them Stevie Wonder, Martha and the Vandellas, and the Supremes, who were beginning to cross over on a regular basis. A large part of their success was Motown's songwriters; in addition to Gordy and his changing cast of partners, the trio of Eddie Holland, Lamont Dozier, and Brian Holland penned a number of hits for the Supremes and other Motown acts. And Gordy's ability to manage Motown like one big, mostly happy family allowed the company to churn out hits with assembly-line-like precision and speed.

In 1966 Gordy began moving Motown in new directions. He established an office on Sunset Boulevard in Los Angeles, California, with the intention of getting Motown's stars into the movies and on television. Two years later he moved his residence to Los Angeles, and in 1972 Motown's corporate offices were relocated to Los Angeles from Detroit. Motown's first movie hit was *Lady Sings the Blues* (1972), in which Diana Ross, the multitalented lead singer of the Supremes, played Billie Holiday, the legendary blues singer. In 1983 the company produced a two-hour NBC-TV special called *Motown 25—Yesterday, Today and Forever,* featuring appearances by such popular Motown acts as Ross, Michael Jackson, Marvin Gaye, the Jackson 5, Smokey Robinson and the Miracles, and the Supremes. The show drew one of the biggest audiences ever for a television variety show.

In 1973 *Black Enterprise* magazine recognized Motown Records as the largest business enterprise owned or managed by a black person. That same year Gordy resigned as president of Motown Records to assume the chairmanship of Motown Industries, which included Motown Records, Jobete, and movie and television production divisions. In 1988 he sold Motown Records to MCA for $61 million and reorganized Motown Industries' other three divisions into the Gordy Company, with himself as chairman.

Also in 1988, Gordy was inducted into the Rock and Roll Hall of Fame in recognition of his enormous contribution to the recording industry. After selling most of his stake in Jobete to EMI Publishing, Gordy has been largely out of the public eye, though he did receive honorary degrees from Michigan State University and Occidental College in Los Angeles after giving commencement addresses at those schools in 2006 and 2007.

Further Reading

Clark, Dick et al. *Motown 25: Yesterday, Today, Forever.* New York: MGM/UA Home Video, 1985, videorecording.

Early, Gerald. *One Nation Under a Groove: Motown and American Culture.* Hopewell, N.J.: The Ecco Press, 1995.

Robinson, Louie. *The Black Millionaire.* New York: Pyramid Books, 1972.

Gorrie, John

(1802–1855) *inventor of the ice-making machine*

John Gorrie was not the first American to design an ice-making machine, nor was he the first American to produce ice commercially. Those honors go to OLIVER EVANS, who in 1805 designed but never built an icemaker in Philadelphia, Pennsylvania, and to Alexander C. Twinning, who in 1856 went into the ice-making business in Cleveland, Ohio. Nevertheless, Gorrie developed the first practical icemaker by using a method that is still widely used today.

Several versions exist as to the circumstances of Gorrie's life before 1834. The most likely account says he was born on October 3, 1802, in Charlestown on the Caribbean island of Nevis. His father was a Captain Gorrie, a Scottish captain in the Spanish navy, and his mother was an unidentified Spanish woman who met Captain Gorrie on Nevis. In 1803 Gorrie accompanied his parents to Charleston, South Carolina, and shortly thereafter his father returned to sea, never again to see Gorrie or his mother. By 1824 he was living with his mother in Columbia and working as an apprentice apothecary, and in 1825 he enrolled in the College of Physicians and Surgeons of the Western District of the State of New York in Fairfield, New York. After graduating in 1827, he opened a medical practice in Abbeville, South Carolina, and in 1831 he moved with his mother to Sneads, Florida. By 1833 she had died, and he moved to Appalachicola where by 1834 he had opened another medical practice.

Over the next four years Gorrie became one of Appalachicola's leading citizens. He was elected to several town offices, including mayor. He was also a part owner of the Mansion House Hotel, a cofounder of the Marine Insurance Bank, president of the Branch Bank of Appalachicola, and director of the Appalachicola Mutual Insurance Company. He also helped establish an Episcopal church and a Masonic lodge. In 1838 he married Caroline Myrick Beman with whom he had two children.

After 1838 Gorrie concentrated his efforts on finding a cure for malaria. Although he did not suspect that mosquitoes were the carriers of the disease, he did suspect that swamps had something to do with the disease's spread, so he encouraged his fellow citizens to fill in or drain marshy areas. He also believed that malaria could be treated more effectively if the patient's body temperature could be controlled by confining the patient in a cool room with low humidity. Since such a room was unheard of in Florida for most of the year, he set out to invent an air-cooling machine, and in 1844 he succeeded. First, Gorrie's machine heated air by compressing it in a chamber by means of a pump, then released the hot air through a series of coils that contained circulating water. As the cooled air re-expanded into another chamber, its temperature dropped enough to turn water into ice. At this point the expanded air could either be released into the room to cool it or circulated over trays of water to make ice.

In 1845 Gorrie contracted with the Cincinnati (Ohio) Iron Works to make a working model of his icemaker. Six years later he received a patent, and then set out to mass-produce it. Although he traveled across the South in search of investors, he was never able to raise enough money to build an ice-machine factory before his death on June 29, 1855, in Appalachicola. In 1859 Ferdinand Carre, a Frenchman, learned of Gorrie's machine and devised a similar one that used ammonia instead of air. Carre's machine became popular, and the process for chilling air and making ice—which it employed and which Gorrie had first put to use— was utilized well into the 21st century.

Further Reading

Chapel, George L. "Dr. John Gorrie, Refrigerator Pioneer," University of Florida Dept. of Physics. Available online. URL: http://www.phys.ufl.edu/~ihas/fridge.html. Downloaded on July 2, 2009.

Sherlock, Vivian M. *The Fever Man: A Biography of Dr. John Gorrie.* Tallahassee, Fla.: Medallion Press, 1982.

Gould, Jay
(Jason Gould)
(1836–1892) *entrepreneur in railroads*

One of the most influential men in the history of American railroading was Jay Gould. In the 1870s and 1880s, this financial genius put together the largest railroad empire in the United States, while encouraging other railroad executives to expand and consolidate their own systems. Because he was unscrupulous in his tactics early in his career, Gould became known during his day and for many years thereafter as the quintessential robber baron, an unprincipled schemer who acquired companies and cornered markets without a second thought as to the consequences for the American public. However, later in his career Gould developed into the model entrepreneur who resurrected several failing railroads by implementing sound management practices.

Gould was born Jason Gould on May 27, 1836, in Roxbury, New York. His parents, John and Mary, were farmers and storekeepers. At age 16 he opened his own surveying business, having taught himself surveying at night while working in his parents' store during the day. At age 20 he moved to the eastern Pennsylvania countryside where he and a partner opened a tannery. Three years later he sold his interest in the business and moved to New York City.

Gould gravitated to Wall Street, where he became a successful stockbroker in a short time. In 1863 he married Helen Miller with whom he had six children. By 1867 he had accumulated enough speculative know-how to become a partner in the brokerage firm of Smith, Gould & Martin. That same year he joined forces with James Fisk and Daniel Drew to do battle with Cornelius Vanderbilt for control of the relatively unimportant Erie Railroad. Vanderbilt had just acquired the New York Central Railroad a year earlier, and he wanted to acquire the Erie as well because it competed directly with the New York Central, even though it was small and poorly managed. Gould and his partners believed the Erie had great promise to become a major east-west competitor of the New York Central. To thwart Vanderbilt's takeover, the three partners illegally printed 50,000 shares of Erie stock and sold them on the market. When a New York court ordered their arrest, they fled to New Jersey, from where Gould worked to introduce a bill before the New York state assembly to legalize what he had done. Both sides bribed as many New York legislators as they could in an effort to swing the vote on the bill in their favor. The three partners won, and Gould emerged from the so-called Erie War as president and chief stockholder of the Erie.

As president, Gould embarked on a program of westward expansion by trying to gain control of the smaller railroads that connected the New York Central and other major eastern railroads to Chicago and St. Louis. But after five years of trying, he had failed to build up the Erie, and in 1872 he was forced to resign as president.

Gould might have succeeded had he not become involved in the events leading to Black Friday, the near-collapse of the gold market in 1869. Gould and Fisk had schemed to corner the gold market by buying up privately held gold while bribing government officials to keep government-held gold off the market. The two partners had bid the price of gold up from $100 to $163.50 per ounce when President Ulysses Grant realized what was happening and ordered the sale of government gold. The price fell back to $133, causing a major dislocation on all financial markets and throwing stock prices into disarray. Had Gould's plan worked, he might have obtained enough money to buy several western railroads; instead, he lost a considerable sum while Vanderbilt used his fortune to acquire at a discount the very lines Gould sought.

Following his resignation, Gould returned to Wall Street where he continued to speculate in railroad stocks. In 1874 he acquired controlling interest in the Union Pacific Railroad, at the time a poorly managed line whose reputation had been severely tarnished by its involvement in the Credit Mobilier scandal a few years earlier. By 1879 he, as president of the line, had built the Union Pacific into a profitable railroad; however, he was unable to strengthen its connections with the east, so he

Toward the end of his lifetime, Jay Gould was probably the most hated man in America. *(Library of Congress)*

sold his interest and set out to build an intercontinental rail system of his own.

At first Gould tried to build his system through the central United States, but this plan of action brought him into direct competition with the Union Pacific, which he himself had just finished strengthening. So he abandoned this plan and concentrated on acquiring and building lines through the Southwest, which was still virgin territory for a major railroad. He made the Missouri Pacific, a road connecting St. Louis and Kansas City, the central road in his system, then acquired the Texas & Pacific to connect with the West, the Missouri, Kansas & Texas to connect with the South, the International & Great Northern to connect with the North, and the Wabash to connect with the East. He also acquired controlling interest in several smaller railroads in the East so that his lines connected virtually every major city in the United States. So successfully and so swiftly did

Gould move that in 1880, after one year of frantic scrambling, he controlled more than 8,000 miles of railroad, more than any other person in the world.

Unfortunately for Gould, his system was so large that he could not manage it as if it were one railroad. One reason was that, as in 1869, he distracted himself from building and operating a railroad empire. In 1881 he succeeded in gaining control of the Western Union Telegraph Company, which operated most of the nation's telegraph lines. Another reason was that he made little effort to consolidate operations, preferring instead to let each line operate individually. This failure to consolidate, coupled with a major recession that drove down stock prices, forced him to sell his interest in most of his eastern roads in 1884. From that point on, he concentrated on expanding the Missouri Pacific into a first-class regional railroad in the heartland of America.

Known as the "Mephistopheles of Wall Street" for his exploits during the Erie War and Black Friday, Gould seems to have mellowed later in life, especially after 1888 when he discovered he had tuberculosis. Although he was perhaps the most hated man in America—the press vilified him after he gained control of Western Union, largely because many people believed he would use his power to read other people's wires and use the knowledge gained from them to take over the country—he was a devoted husband and father who loved orchids and books. He died on December 2, 1892, in New York City.

Further Reading

Ackerman, Kenneth D. *The Gold Ring: Jim Fish, Jay Gould, and Black Friday, 1869.* New York: Harper Business, 1990.

Floyd, E. Randall. *The Good, the Bad & the Mad: Weird People in American History.* Augusta, Ga.: Harbor House, 1999.

Klein, Maury. *The Life and Legend of Jay Gould.* Baltimore, Md.: Johns Hopkins Press, 1997.

Ogilvie, J. S. *Life and Death of Jay Gould, and How He Made His Millions.* New York: Arno Press, 1982.

Wren, Daniel A. and Ronald G. Greenwood. *Management Innovators: The People and Ideas that Have Shaped Modern Business.* New York: Oxford University Press, 1998.

Graham, Bette Nesmith
(Bette Claire McMurray)
(1924–1980) *inventor of Liquid Paper*

As all typists know, one of the handiest inventions of all time is correction fluid. However, few of them also know that its inventor was Bette Graham, a 27-year-old single mother.

Graham was born Bette Claire McMurray on March 23, 1924, in Dallas, Texas. Her father, Jesse, was an auto wholesaler, and her mother, Christine, was a homemaker. At age 17 she dropped out of high school and went to work as a secretary. In 1942 she married Warren Nesmith with whom she had one child, Michael; they were divorced in 1946.

Following the divorce, Graham completed her high school education at night school. She also went to work for Texas Bank and Trust, and in 1951 she became the executive secretary of the bank's chairman. In this position, Graham did a lot of typing on the newly invented electric typewriter. The electric typewriter made characters that were much sharper than those made by a manual typewriter. Unfortunately, these characters were also nearly indelible. Erasing them, something one could do to characters made by a manual typewriter, either smudged the character or put a hole in the paper, neither of which were acceptable in a business letter.

Graham began looking for ways to correct typos neatly so that entire letters would not have to be retyped. She finally hit on the idea of covering up her mistakes with tempera, a thin, water-based paint used by artists. While no one was looking, she would daub tempera over the typo with a watercolor brush, wait for it to dry, then type over it. Although the tempera was too thin to cover the typo with just one application and it took a while for it to dry, the end result was a perfect correction that no one noticed.

For five years Graham secretly corrected typos in this way. Eventually, her fellow secretaries found out what she was doing and insisted that she share her secret with them. In 1956 she began selling them little bottles of "Mistake Out," as she called it. Soon every secretary at the bank was using Mistake Out, and Graham realized she had a moneymaking idea on her hands. After several trips to the local library and several conversations with Michael's chemistry teacher, she came up with a combination of pigments, wetting agents, and resins that made a thicker, faster-drying correction fluid. Changing its name to "Liquid Paper," she began making it in the kitchen and bottling it in the garage, all with the help of Michael and his friends.

In 1956, Graham tried to sell the rights to Liquid Paper to International Business Machines (IBM), a major manufacturer of electric typewriters, but the company politely declined. Meanwhile, word traveled among the secretaries of Dallas, and Graham soon had enough business to distract her from her duties at the bank but not enough to support her and Michael. In 1958, she got fired for accidentally signing her company's name to a letter to one of the bank's most important customers. She decided at this point to sink or swim financially with Liquid Paper. This was a bold move, because at the time Graham was selling less than 2,000 0.6-ounce bottles of Liquid Paper per year.

Fortunately, that same year Liquid Paper began attracting national attention. Graham had sent samples to the national secretarial and office supply trade journals and had received favorable reviews, which resulted in hundreds of orders. And when Michael got his driver's license in 1959, he began calling on office supply distributors throughout central Texas and receiving sizable orders. By 1962, the same year she married Robert Graham with whom she had no children, Graham's business had grown enough to justify erecting a 2,600-square-foot shop and office in her backyard and hiring two full-time employees. A successful display at the 1963 National Office Products Association convention in Memphis, Tennessee, generated a huge volume of orders from major office supply distributors across the United States. In 1968, Liquid Paper Corporation sold 1 million bottles and moved into a major production and office facility. Sales increased to 5 million bottles in 1970 and to 25 million in 1975.

In 1976 Graham stepped down as chairperson of Liquid Paper Corporation, which by now was selling its product internationally. In 1979, when the Gillette Company bought Liquid Paper Corporation for $47.5 million, she became a multimillionaire. A devout Christian Scientist all her life, she spent her retirement in Dallas doing church work and contributing money to charities. She died on May 12, 1980, in Dallas.

Further Reading

Altman, Linda Jacobs. *Women Inventors.* New York: Facts On File, 1997.

Vare, Ethlie Ann, and Greg Ptacek. *Mothers of Invention.* New York: William Morrow and Co., 1988.

Graham, Katherine
(1917–2001) *entrepreneur in newspaper publishing*

Throughout the first half of Katherine Graham's life, there was little or no expectation that she would become a towering figure in American business. She had lived a life of privilege and had demonstrated intelligence and ambition, but by virtue of her gender was not groomed for a leading role in her family's publishing empire. But Katherine Graham was not to be defined by her early life, but rather by a remarkable second act, in which she took over her family's newspaper empire to become one of the most successful and influential newspaper publishers in the history of the United States and a pioneering woman in the annals of American business.

Katherine Graham was born Katherine Meyer on June 16, 1917, in New York City. She was the fourth of five children born to her father, Eugene Meyer, a prominent financier who eventually served as the chairman of the Federal Reserve and as the first president of the World Bank, and her mother, Agnes, who was a writer, philanthropist, and social activist. Graham spent much of her childhood away from her parents at boarding schools, graduating from the Madeira School in Virginia in 1935 before enrolling at Vassar. After only one year at Vassar, Graham transferred to the University of Chicago. She returned to Washington during the summers to work with the *Washington Post*, a struggling newspaper purchased by her father in 1933 for less than $1 million. In 1938, Graham graduated from the University of Chicago before leaving for San Francisco where she worked as a newspaper reporter. In 1939, she returned to Washington to work in the editorial department for the *Post* and a year later married Phillip Graham, who had worked as a clerk for Supreme Court justice Felix Frankfurter.

During World War II, Graham briefly gave up reporting to move with her husband who had enlisted in the army. When he was transferred to the Pacific, she returned to Washington, but after the war she left reporting again to focus on raising her growing family, which eventually included a daughter and three sons. During this time, Phillip Graham had been given control of the *Post* by Meyer and helped elevate it to great success, including the acquisition of *Newsweek* magazine as well as several other communication ventures. However, despite the positive business fortunes and the improved editorial reputation of the *Post*, Phillip Graham suffered from severe bipolar depression, and he committed suicide in 1963. To fill the void he left, Katherine Graham stepped in as the de facto publisher of the newspaper, though she would not formally possess that title for another 10 years.

Among Graham's first major decisions after assuming leadership of the *Post* was hiring Ben Bradlee as assistant managing editor. She would eventually elevate him to executive editor in 1968. With Bradlee, Graham took what she later described as a "big gulp" and made the historic decision to publish articles based on the Pentagon Papers—secret documents smuggled by former analyst Daniel Ellsberg that detailed the depth of America's long-standing involvement in Vietnam and Southeast Asia—despite a temporary judicial order prohibiting their publication. Within a week, a case brought by the Nixon administration against the *New York Times* and the *Washington Post* was heard by the U.S. Supreme Court. The court ruled 6-3 in favor of the newspapers, and articles based on and including excerpts from the Pentagon Papers continued to be published.

Though this was a significant victory for the First Amendment right to freedom of the press, it would not be Graham's last constitutional and consequential battle with President Nixon. That would occur with the *Post's* publication of investigative articles by reporters Bob Woodward and Carl Bernstein that exposed and described the Watergate scandal, which eventually led to the resignation of President Nixon. Again, Graham led the *Post* in the face of strong governmental opposition, this time in pursuit of private recordings made by Nixon that proved his role in the cover-up of various forms of illegal activity. Graham later directly described her goals for the *Post* during the heated days of Watergate as "The best we could do was to keep investigating, to look everywhere for hard evidence, to get the details right, and to report accurately what we found."

Graham's tenure as chief executive of the *Post* has been highly celebrated both for its historical significance and as an example of a woman's success at the head of a major business enterprise, a situation that was extremely rare at that time. Graham's reputation for setting a clear course, hiring talented people, and allowing those people to work without meddling has been used as a model by many in publishing and other fields.

In 1991, she handed over her chief executive duties to her son Donald. Her 1997 memoir, *Personal History*, was lauded by critics and reading audiences and received a Pulitzer Prize. Graham—who never remarried—died in Sun Valley, Idaho, on July 14, 2001, three days after suffering a serious fall. Years earlier, Graham reflected on her time as head of the *Post* and her central role in history, noting, "I became absorbed by the challenge . . . I was trying to learn all the time. And I loved what I was doing."

Further Reading

Graham, Katherine. *Personal History*. New York: Alfred Knopf, 1997.

"Katherine Graham: First Lady of the Post," BBC. Available online. URL: http://news.bbc.co.uk/2/hi/americas/1443672.stm. Downloaded on July 1, 2009.

"Katherine Graham Remembered," *Washington Post*. Available online. URL: http://www.washingtonpost.com/wp-dyn/metro/specials/graham/. Downloaded on July 1, 2009.

Grandin, Temple

(1947–   ) inventor of low-stress livestock handling equipment

Autism is a neurobiological disorder that is still imperfectly understood and treated. Most people who suffer from autism remain withdrawn from reality all their lives, preferring instead to live in their own worlds. All the more surprising, then, that Temple Grandin, who is autistic, would become one of the foremost designers of livestock handling systems in the world.

Grandin was born on August 29, 1947, in Boston, Massachusetts. Her father, Richard, was a real-estate agent, and her mother, Eustacia, was a writer, singer, and actress. At age two, she was diagnosed with autism (probably a very mild case); among autism's many symptoms is an intense physical reluctance to being held or hugged. Never told about her condition, she was educated in a normal school environment and received tremendous emotional support from her mother. She did not even discover that she was autistic until she entered graduate school. During the summer between her junior and senior years in high school, she spent some time on a cattle ranch that one of her aunts owned. Here she became acquainted with the squeeze chute, a mechanical device that immobilizes livestock so they can be inoculated or stunned. After seeing how calm the device made cattle when they were in it, she got in it herself while her aunt worked the controls. Grandin was pleasantly surprised to feel waves of both stimulation and relaxation pass through her body as the sides of the squeeze chute gently pressed against her. Upon returning to high school, a science teacher helped her to build her own squeeze chute. Using the chute on herself almost daily, she was able to overcome much of her reluctance to being touched physically, which enabled her to open up more to other people. Ten years later, after several psychologists and occupational therapists reported similar results with other patients with autism and related conditions, she sold the rights to her machine to the Therafin Corporation.

After graduating from high school, Grandin enrolled in Franklin Pierce College where she received a B.A. in psychology in 1970. That same year she enrolled in Arizona State University's graduate psychology program. Shortly thereafter she took two part-time jobs, one as a cattle chute operator at a feedlot and the other selling cattle chutes and feed wagons. These experiences awakened in her a growing empathy for livestock and their feelings of fear and anxiety while being led to slaughter, and in 1973 she transferred to the animal science program. In 1974 she took a job with a corral construction company as an equipment designer, which led her to write her master's thesis on the design of cattle chutes in feedlots. After receiving her M.S. in 1975, she founded Grandin Livestock Handling Systems Inc., and she began designing livestock handling facilities full time. Over the next 11 years, Grandin designed corrals, feedlots, chutes, ramps, veterinary clinics, slaughterhouses, and other livestock handling systems for cattle, sheep, and pigs in 30 states and 10 foreign countries.

In 1986 Grandin invented the double-rail restrainer system for use in stunning and shackling cattle and sheep. This system is a vast improvement over the standard "V" restrainer because it allows the operator to stand up straight while stunning the restrained animal rather than doing it bent over. It also maneuvers the animal into a more comfortable position without a lot of prodding and restricts the animal's field of vision, both of which tend to keep the animal calm, thus increasing the stunner's accuracy, minimizing the suffering by the livestock, and reducing the potential of injury to the operator. Over the last 15 years, the double-rail restrainer has been adopted for use by almost one-half of all the meat plants in North America.

In 1989 Grandin received a Ph.D. in animal science from the University of Illinois. She also teaches courses on livestock behavior and facility design at Colorado State and works as a consultant in the livestock industry. Grandin continues to add to the more than 300 articles she has authored on animal handling, welfare, and facility design. In 2010, HBO produced and aired a full-length film on her life, *Temple Grandin*, starring Claire Danes.

Further Reading

Ambrose, Susan A. *Journeys of Women in Science and Engineering: No Universal Constants.* Philadelphia: Temple University Press, 1997.

Chang, Laura. *Scientists at Work: Profiles of Today's Groundbreaking Scientists from Science Times.* McGraw-Hill, 2000.

Grandin, Temple. *The Way I See It: A Personal Look at Autism and Asperger's.* Arlington, Tex.: Future Horizions, 2008.

———. *Thinking in Pictures: My Life With Autism.* New York: Vintage, 2010.

Gray, Elisha

(1835–1901) *inventor of telegraphic devices*

Elisha Gray was a gifted inventor of telegraphic equipment. During his lifetime he received patents on more than 70 such devices, including one that contributed to the invention of the modern fax machine. He was also one of the founders of Western Electric, a major manufacturer of telegraphic and telephonic equipment. However, Gray is best remembered as the man who almost invented the telephone.

Gray was born on August 2, 1835, in Barnesville, Ohio. His parents, David and Christiana, were farmers. As a young boy he became fascinated with the telegraph, and by age 10 he had built his own transmitters and receivers. When he was 12 his father died, and for the next 10 years Gray helped to support his family by working as a carpenter and boatbuilder. Meanwhile, he continued to study and experiment with electricity until one day he came to the attention of a professor at nearby Oberlin College. In 1857 the professor convinced Gray to enroll in the college's preparatory school; five years later Gray graduated from Oberlin. After graduation he continued to build furniture and boats and experiment with telegraphy. In 1865 he married Delia Shepard with whom he had one child.

In 1867 Gray received a patent for a telegraphic relay, which he sold to the Western Union Telegraph Company. The company then loaned him the money to become partners with Enos Barton in the making of telegraphic equipment.

Two years later the partners moved their shop from Cleveland to Chicago, Illinois, and in 1869, with more financial backing from Western Union, incorporated their shop as the Western Electric Manufacturing Company. Three years later Gray sold his interest in Western Electric, receiving enough money from the sale to establish himself as a full-time inventor of telegraphic devices. His best-known invention was the TelAutograph, a short-line telegraph that transmitted handwriting and sketches made with a special mechanical stylus. Invented in 1895, Gray's TelAutograph was a forerunner of the modern fax machine.

In 1874 one of Gray's nephews managed to produce a whiny sound by attaching himself to a weak battery and rubbing his hand on a zinc bathtub. Intrigued, Gray discovered that variations in the frequency of the current resulted in variations in the pitch of the whiny noise. This led him to develop a metal diaphragm receiver so that the noise could be amplified and then to experiment with ways to use this phenomenon to transmit multiple telegraphs on the same wire. Although he claimed to have conceived of the basic concept of transmitting externally generated sounds, such as the human voice, in 1875, it seems more likely that the idea of inventing a telephone did not occur to him until after he had spent several weeks at the U.S. Patent Office in Washington, D.C., reviewing patent applications as part of his own application for a patent for the multiple telegraph. On the same day that ALEXANDER GRAHAM BELL filed his formal application for a patent for the telephone, Gray filed a caveat for the telephone, an official notice of intention to file for a patent within 90 days accompanied by a rough drawing but no apparatus.

Although Bell's and Gray's telephones were remarkably similar, the minor variations in each design suggest that the two men arrived at their ideas independently. What seems to have tipped the scales in Bell's favor in the slew of patent lawsuits that followed was their respective attitudes toward the commercial profitability of the telephone. While Gray returned to his shop to continue working with the telegraph, Bell returned to his to perfect the telephone. Bell demonstrated an improved model of the telephone at the 1876

Centennial in Philadelphia, and the following year he organized the Bell Company to begin commercial production of the telephone. By the time it became clear to Gray that the telephone possessed tremendous commercial potential, Bell had already established himself in the public mind as the inventor of the telephone. Gray's claim to having invented the telephone was advanced in hundreds of lawsuits, and every time it was rejected by the court.

Although Bell got the greater glory, Gray made more money from his many inventions than Bell made from the telephone. Nevertheless, Gray went to his grave convinced that he had been cheated of fame and fortune. He died on January 21, 1901, in Newton, Massachusetts, while visiting a friend.

Further Reading

Baker, Burton H. *The Gray Matter: The Forgotten Story of the Telephone.* St. Joseph, Mich.: Telepress, 2000.

Evenson, A. Edward. *The Telephone Patent Conspiracy of 1876: The Elisha Gray-Alexander Bell Controversy and Its Many Players.* Jefferson, N.C.: McFarland, 2001.

Green, Hetty
(Harriet Howland Robinson)
(1834–1916) *entrepreneur in high finance*

One of the shrewdest investors of all time, particularly in a bear market, was Hetty Green. She started out in 1865 with about $2 million, and by 1916 she had built it into a fortune of about $200 million, thriving through two major financial panics. The richest woman in America, Green was also a parsimonious person who seemed to love money more than her husband, her children, or even herself, and she was known as the "Witch of Wall Street."

Green was born Harriet Howland Robinson on November 21, 1834, in New Bedford, Massachusetts. Her father, Edward, owned a whaling company, and her mother, Abby, was a homemaker. As a young girl she was sent to live with her grandfather and her mother's sister Sylvia; one of her chores was to read the financial pages of the newspaper to him, which may be where she developed her

keen talents as an investor. She attended boarding school from ages 10 to 13 and returned to her parents' home in 1847. She lived with her parents until 1860, when her mother died and her father moved to New York City. She lived with her Aunt Sylvia for several years and then followed her father to New York City. The death of her father and aunt in 1865 left her richer by $2 million, which she inherited from their estates. In 1867 she married Edward Green, with whom she had two children, and moved with him to London, England.

While in London, Green greatly increased her wealth by investing shrewdly in the gold market and railroad stocks. Although the financial affairs of her husband, who was in the import-export business, suffered during the panic of 1873, hers thrived. She always made sure that her financial situation was fairly liquid so that she could "buy low, sell high," and the panic gave her plenty of opportunities to buy low. In 1874 the Greens settled in Bellows Falls, Vermont, his hometown. While his affairs continued to spiral, hers continued to prosper, and by 1885 she was worth about $25 million while he was $700,000 in debt. They were separated that same year, and from then on she went by the name Mrs. Hetty Green.

Green's fortune increased again during the panic of 1893. While most other investors had overextended themselves, she had remained fairly liquid, and she began loaning millions of dollars to individuals who put up their real estate as collateral. In this way she acquired more than $17 million worth of income property scattered across seven states. She received $40,000 per month in rent alone just from her holdings in Chicago, Illinois. She seems to have seen the panic of 1907 coming, and before it hit she converted all of her holdings to either cash or first mortgages. Consequently, she had plenty of money on hand to "help" people out of trouble when they found themselves overextended. At the time of her death, her estate was valued at around $200 million.

Green was undeniably a shrewd investor, perhaps the best of her day when times were bad and the stock market was slumping. But a darker and more disturbing reason for her success was that she exhibited a love of money that bordered on the pathological. Her father left home in 1860 because she nagged him about his disbursement of her mother's trust fund, Green having received (in her opinion) only a pittance. Her aunt Sylvia threw her out because Green had nagged her to change her will to make Green the sole beneficiary, and when Sylvia died, Green produced a forged will to that effect. She insisted on a prenuptial agreement with Edward Green that stated he pay all household expenses, keep his financial affairs separate from hers, and absolve her from paying his debts. When her children got sick, she disguised herself and them so they could get free medical treatment at charity clinics; on one occasion, her son lost a leg because she refused to pay a doctor to treat an infection that turned gangrenous. When her husband lost his fortune, she threw him out. She wore the same black dress and bonnet and carried the same black briefcase and umbrella for years, thus contributing to the nickname "Witch of Wall Street." When her one-legged son went to work for her as a rent collector, she paid him a measly $3 per day. She moved about from one cheap place to another, so as to avoid paying taxes of any kind. She died on July 3, 1916, in New York City, as a result of a stroke brought on by an argument over the price of a meal.

Further Reading

Clarke, William K. *The Robber Baroness*. New York: St. Martin's Press, 1979.

Crossen, Cynthia. *The Rich and How They Got That Way: How the Wealthiest People of All Time from Genghis Khan to Bill Gates Made Their Fortunes*. New York: Crown Business, 2000.

Floyd, E. Randall. *The Good, the Bad & the Mad: Weird People in American History*. Augusta, Ga.: Harbor House, 1999.

Moore, Samuel Taylor. *The Witch of Wall Street, Hetty Green*. Garden City, N.Y.: Doubleday, 1948.

Gregg, John Robert

(1867–1948) *inventor of Gregg shorthand*

In the days before the invention of the Dictaphone, secretaries and clerks took down conversations, dictation, speeches, legal testimony, and the like by using shorthand, a form of speed writing that substitutes simple strokes, abbreviations, and symbols for letters, words, and phrases. Although many forms of shorthand exist, the most popular form in the United States is Gregg shorthand, which was invented by John Gregg when he was just 19.

Gregg was born on June 17, 1867, in Shantonagh, County Monaghan, Ireland. His father, George, was a railroad stationmaster, and his mother, Margaret, was a homemaker. At age 11 he moved with his family to Glasgow, Scotland, where he went to work as an office boy in a law office. Gregg was introduced to shorthand, also known as stenography and phonography, in the law firm, and by age 15 he had learned six different shorthand systems, including Pitman and Sloan-Duployan, the two most popular. However, he found them all to be deficient in some way and set out to develop a better system.

At age 18 Gregg won a Sloan-Duployan shorthand contest. Part of the prize was a certificate of proficiency from J. M. Sloan, the system's coinventor, which enabled Gregg to begin teaching Sloan-Duployan shorthand for a living shortly thereafter. Meanwhile, he continued to perfect his own system by borrowing the best features from the existing ones and joining them with his own ideas. By age 19 he had developed what is known today as Gregg shorthand. Gregg's system was a marked improvement over the others because it used the curvilinear motion of longhand writing while employing phonetic rather than alphabetic spelling; it also placed all components on the same line rather than above or below the line, thus maintaining the natural flow of the writing. In 1888 Gregg published *Light-Line Phonography*, his first of many manuals on shorthand, and opened the Light-Line Phonography Institute in Liverpool, England.

Gregg was somewhat of a missionary when it came to his shorthand system, so in 1893 he emigrated to the United States to teach Gregg shorthand to Americans. Settling in Boston, Massachusetts, he found that teachers of the Graham, Beale, Pitman, and other styles were too well entrenched for him to make any headway, and when he tried to get the Charles Scribner Publishing Company to print his shorthand manual, he was rebuffed. Undaunted, in 1895 he moved to

Chicago, Illinois, where fewer shorthand teachers existed. He established the Gregg School that same year and the Gregg Publishing Company in 1896.

Because Gregg shorthand was easier to learn and to use than other systems, it quickly caught on in Chicago, and then it gradually spread throughout the rest of the United States. Part of the reason for its spread was the many innovative manuals Gregg wrote. *Gregg Speed Practice* (1907) juxtaposed actual text with the shorthand version, and *Gregg Speed Studies* (1917) presented all practice material in shorthand form. Altogether Gregg published at least nine manuals and seven magazines related to shorthand. Many of these texts were translated into other languages, including French, German, Italian, Spanish, Portuguese, Polish, and Esperanto. By 1911, his publishing company was also publishing books on other topics related to business education.

Gregg became an American citizen in 1896. In 1899 he married Maida Wasson with whom he had no children; she died in 1928, and in 1930 he married Janet Kinley with whom he had two children. Around 1908 he moved to New York City where he died on February 23, 1948. He received several awards, including the Ulster-Irish Society of New York's Gold Medal for Notable Service to the Nation (1936), the New York Academy for Public Education's Distinguished Service to Education Award (1938), and Great Britain's King's Medal for Service in the Cause of Freedom.

Further Reading

Cowan, Leslie. *John Robert Gregg: A Biography of the Shorthand Inventor, Educator, Publisher and Humanitarian, Whose Achievements Enriched the Lives of Millions.* Oxford, England: Pre-Raphaelite Press at Oxford, 1984.

Gregg, John Robert. *Key to Supplementary Exercises in Gregg Shorthand.* Googlebooks. Available online. URL: http://books.google.com/books?id=cHUPAA AAYAAJ&dq=john+robert+gregg&source=gbs_ navlinks_s. Downloaded on July 2, 2009.

"Shorthand." The Columbia Encyclopedia Sixth Edition. Available online. URL: http://www.bartleby. com/65/sh/shorthan.html. Downloaded on November 20, 2001.

Griffin, Merv
(Mervyn Edward Griffin, Jr.)
(1925–2007) *inventor of game shows*

One of the most successful game show producers in television history is Merv Griffin. Two of his concepts were developed into *Jeopardy!* and *Wheel of Fortune*, the two longest-running game shows on television. Surprisingly, Griffin did not get his start in show business as an executive, but as a singer.

Griffin was born Mervyn Edward Griffin, Jr., on July 6, 1925, in San Mateo, California. His father, Mervyn, Sr., was a stockbroker, and his mother, Rita, was a homemaker. After graduating from high school in 1942, he spent a year at San Mateo Junior College, followed by a year at the University of San Francisco. In 1944 he dropped out of school to go into show business. He spent the next nine years as the male vocalist with Freddy Martin's Orchestra and as a solo artist; one record, "I've Got a Lovely Bunch of Coconuts," sold more than 3 million copies. In 1953 he signed an acting contract with Warner Bros., but after getting only a few small roles he returned to singing the following year. For the next four years his career was a hodgepodge of nightclub performances and brief stints as host/emcee of various radio and television shows. In 1958 he married Julann Wright, with whom he had one child; they divorced in 1976.

In 1958 Griffin was hired to host *Play Your Hunch*, a daytime game show. The program ran for three years, largely because Griffin managed to inject his own personality, which one critic called "affable but adventurous," into the otherwise lame proceedings. After the show's cancellation in 1961, he appeared a number of times as the guest host replacement for Jack Paar on *Tonight*, NBC's hugely popular late-night talk show. He did such a good job that it was rumored he would become the regular host when Paar retired. Instead, NBC hired Johnny Carson to host the program, and Griffin was offered the opportunity to host an afternoon version of *Tonight*. *The Merv Griffin Show* was a witty and controversial alternative to soap operas; although it attracted a small but intensely loyal following, it was canceled after two years. In 1963 Griffin formed Merv Griffin

Productions to revamp his show and sell it to another network. In 1965 he succeeded, and *The Merv Griffin Show* ran uninterrupted on various networks for another 21 years.

Although Griffin was one of television's better talk-show hosts, he also demonstrated considerable talent as a producer of game shows. His first effort was *Word for Word,* a morning show hosted by Griffin that survived for only one year. In 1964 he struck gold when he came up with the idea for *Jeopardy!* the second-most popular television game show of all time. *Jeopardy!* employs a new twist on the old game-show format; instead of asking contestants questions, the host gives them the answers, and they have to figure out what the questions are. To do well on the show, a contestant has to possess a broad range of general information and remember to phrase the answer in the form of a question. The show became immensely popular almost overnight, and it remains one of television's highest-rated shows, drawing 30 million viewers each week. Part of its success is the fact that luck plays virtually no role in winning—generally speaking, winning contestants possess above-average intelligence—and that its format is so unique that it cannot easily be copied.

In 1975 Griffin struck gold a second time when he developed the most popular game show in the history of television, *Wheel of Fortune.* In essence, *Wheel of Fortune* is a glitzy version of the old paper-and-pencil word game called "Hangman," in which the players try to guess a secret word by guessing which letters are in it. *Wheel* makes the game more difficult by turning the word into a phrase and by giving a clue that often does more to confuse than to help. It also adds an element of chance to the whole affair by making contestants spin a large glittery wheel before guessing a letter; the wheel's sections contain mostly money prizes but also a few booby prizes, such as "bankrupt." By 2000 *Wheel of Fortune* was drawing more than 50 million viewers each week, and its hosts, Pat Sajak and Vanna White, had become well-known celebrities.

In 1986 *The Merv Griffin Show* aired for the last time. That same year, Griffin sold Merv Griffin Productions to Columbia Pictures for $250 million and a share of the production company's future profits. He then bought and operated hotels and resorts in California, Arizona, Florida, and Ireland; in one of them, the Beverly Hilton, he opened a replica of the old Cocoanut Grove, at one time one of Los Angeles's most popular nightclubs. He also owned Merv Griffin Events, which stages corporate promotions and other extravaganzas, and a winery in California's Carmel Valley. In 2000 he gave one of his resorts, the Wickenburg Inn and Dude Ranch in Arizona, to Childhelp USA for use as a rehabilitation center for severely abused children.

In 2007, Griffin died of prostate cancer in Los Angeles. His funeral was attended by hundreds of friends, including former first lady Nancy Reagan, California governor Arnold Schwarzenegger, as well as stars of his beloved game shows. He is buried at Westwood Village Memorial Park Cemetery in Los Angeles where his headstone reads, "I will not be right back after this message."

Further Reading

Griffin, Merv, with Peter Barsocchini. *Merv, An Autobiography.* New York: Simon & Schuster, 1980.

"Merv Griffin, Television Innovator, Dies at 82." *New York Times.* Available online. URL: http://www.nytimes.com/2007/08/13/arts/television/13griffin.html?_r=1. Downloaded on October 15, 2009.

Grove, Andrew

(1936–) *cofounder of Intel Corporation*

Andrew Grove has survived scarlet fever, World War II, and political oppression in his native Hungary to become a leading physicist, an expert in corporate management, and a man considered by many to be among the most influential business leaders of the late 20th century. When he was named 1997's Person of the Year by *Time* magazine, the writer Walter Isaacson noted of Grove's remarkable path and profound impact, "His character traits are emblematic of this amazing century: a paranoia bred from his having been a refugee from the Nazis and then the Communists; an entrepreneurial optimism instilled as an immigrant to a land brimming with freedom and opportunity; and a sharpness tinged with arrogance that comes from being a brilliant mind on the front line of a revolution."

Andrew Steven Grove was born Andras Istvan Grof on September 2, 1936, in Budapest, Hungary. He grew up in a secular and comfortably middle-class Jewish family, the only child of George, who owned a dairy business, and Maria, a bookkeeper. Grove experienced a difficult childhood, surviving a serious case of scarlet fever as a four-year-old that claimed much of his hearing and enduring the absence of his father, who served with Hungarian forces fighting the invading Germans early in World War II. Grove and his mother eventually moved into the home of friendly Christian neighbors who protected them with the aid of false identities. Grove and his mother survived the war, as did his father, who returned to the family weakened to near death from typhoid and pneumonia after being captured and forced into hard labor in a Nazi work camp.

After the war, Grove remained in Hungary, which was soon a satellite state of the Soviet Union under communist rule. A bright, curious, and successful student, Grove enjoyed opera and journalism, but instead decided to pursue the study of science. Fulfilling his and his parents' dream that he attend college, Grove was a university student in Budapest when the Soviet Union invaded Hungary to crush a budding rebellion. As word spread that the Soviets were rounding up perceived agitators—including many students—Grove and a friend decided to attempt to flee the country. They successfully evaded checkpoints and made it across to Austria, before he traveled on a ship to live with relatives in the Brooklyn section of New York City.

Grove, who had been taunted in Hungary for being Jewish before and during World War II and for being the son of what was considered a capitalist after the war, immediately felt both at ease and invigorated in America. He Americanized his name and later recalled of his introduction to his new nation, "I grew up to be 20 years old, and I was always told I was undesirable for one reason or another. I got to the United States, and I expected there would be some of the same because I was an immigrant. And there wasn't." While working a summer job as a waiter in 1957, Grove met another

Hungarian refugee Eva Kastan. They fell in love and were married within a year. He excelled at the City College of New York, graduating magna cum laude in 1960. Grove then enrolled in a Ph.D. program in chemical engineering at the University of California at Berkeley, completing the demanding requirements in just three years. He was in high demand among the leading scientific research labs and chose to work for Fairchild Camera and Instrument, which would later change its name to Fairchild Semiconductor.

Among the earliest projects Grove pursued at Fairchild was an attempt to improve the speed of computer function by creating technology that would reduce the amount of heat caused by processing. Grove and two other scientists soon made a breakthrough in the usability of silicon for this purpose, and they received recognition and awards for their research. However, management at Fairchild was embroiled in infighting and failed to see the effective applications of the technology, which led Grove and many other top employees to leave the company. With the help of the investor Arthur Rock, Grove and a few other former Fairchild workers in 1968 founded a new company, initially named Integrated Electronics, but almost immediately known as Intel.

Intel's main focus was on the production of memory chips for large mainframe computers. Grove served as the company's head of engineering as well as its chief operations officer. He developed a reputation as a demanding and tough-minded boss, even once going so far as to require employees to work on Christmas Eve. However, Grove was widely respected within Intel for his collegiality (he preferred that coworkers call him Andy), intelligence, problem-solving skills, and encouragement. Compact and physically fit, Grove underwent several surgeries to restore much of the hearing he lost as a child due to scarlet fever. Grove became the president of Intel in 1979 and ascended to chief executive officer in 1987. Under Grove's leadership, which shared many qualities of informality and rigorous efficiency with the Hewlett Packard Company, Intel enjoyed enormous success, creating within its own company thousands of millionaires. As a result of his influence on the development of and reliance on blazingly fast and ubiquitous Intel semiconductors, Grove was named 1997's Person of the Year by *Time* magazine.

Despite Grove's ultimate success with Intel, his tenure with the company featured many significant challenges. In the late 1970s, there was weak demand for microchips and various manufacturing difficulties. In the early 1980s, competition from Japanese companies, many of which were "dumping" products in American markets at prices far below market value, also put stress on Intel. The greatest crisis for Intel under Grove's watch occurred in 1994, when the company released millions of slightly flawed Pentium chips that potentially could have malfunctioned. The glitch led to intense media coverage as consumers—most of whom had computers that had the "Intel Inside" sticker on them indicating the presence of the company's processors—became concerned with the reliability of the product. Grove decided to spend nearly half a billion dollars to recall the processors and offered in-home service for those affected.

Grove, who overcame a diagnosis of prostate cancer in 1996, stepped down as CEO of Intel in 1998 and retired as chair in 2005. He remains with Intel as a senior adviser and is active as a lecturer at the Stanford Graduate School of Business, teaching a course entitled, "Strategy and Action in the Information Processing Industry." Grove has been a very active philanthropist, including a gift of $26 million to his alma mater, City College of New York. He and Eva have been married for more than 50 years and are the parents of two adult daughters.

Further Reading

Grove, Andrew. *Only the Paranoid Survive: How to Identify and Exploit the Crisis Points That Challenge Every Business.* New York: Doubleday Business, 1996.

———. *Swimming Across: A Memoir.* New York: Warner Books, 2001.

Heilemann, John. "Andy Grove's Rational Exuberance," *Wired.* Available online. URL: http://www.wired.com/wired/archive/9.06/intel_pr.html. Downloaded on October 19, 2009.

Isaacson, Walter. "The Digital Age . . . Driven by the Passion of Intel's Andrew Grove," *Time.* Available online. URL: http://www.time.com/time/magazine/1997/int/971229/cover1.html. Downloaded on October 19, 2009.

H

Hall, Charles Martin
(1863–1914) *inventor of the aluminum extraction process*

Before Charles Hall discovered how to extract aluminum from bauxite via electrolysis, aluminum was a semiprecious metal. For the most part, it was used only to make jewelry and dinnerware, but it was also used for special items—like a nonconductive capstone for the Washington Monument to protect it from lightning strikes. After Hall's discovery, aluminum became as common as iron or steel, and it found uses in just about as many applications as those two workhorse metals.

Hall was born on December 6, 1863, in Thompson, Ohio. His father, Herman, was a minister, and his mother, Sophronia, was a homemaker. At age 10 he moved with his family to Oberlin. As a teenager he became interested in chemistry, and he soon developed a fascination with aluminum because it was so hard to extract from bauxite, the ore in which it is found. In 1880 he entered Oberlin College where he became friends with Frank Jewett, a chemistry professor who also was interested in aluminum. For four years he and Jewett studied the various properties of aluminum and experimented with ways to extract it.

After receiving his B.A. in 1885, Hall returned home to continue experimenting with aluminum. In 1886, in a woodshed he had converted into a laboratory, he succeeded in producing a few precious beads of aluminum metal via electrolysis. He designed a crucible out of graphite, filled it with bauxite dissolved in molten cryolite, and then applied a charge of direct current from a homemade battery to the mixture. In the ensuing reactions, the oxygen in the bauxite was released to the atmosphere, and the aluminum adhered loosely to the crucible's graphite lining. When Hall applied for a patent in July 1886, he was informed that a Frenchman, Paul Heroult, had filed an application for the same process two months earlier. Under U.S. law, however, precedence went to Hall because he had made his actual discovery in February, several months before Heroult's application was filed, and he was issued a U.S. patent in 1889. As a result, the process, which is still used today to extract aluminum from bauxite, became known as the Hall-Heroult process.

In 1889 Hall and a group of investors headed by Alfred E. Hunt formed the Pittsburgh Reduction Company to extract aluminum from bauxite on a massive scale. That first year, the company produced about five tons of aluminum. Over the next 25 years Hall refined the techniques and equipment necessary to extract aluminum via electrolysis. In the 1890s, a major extraction facility was built near Niagara Falls to take advantage of the abundance of cheap electricity being produced there. As a result of such developments, the per-pound price of aluminum fell from $12 to 50¢. As the cost went down and the supply went up, aluminum was used in an increasing number of industrial and commercial applications requiring a light, nonconductive metal. By 1914 the Aluminum Company of America (Alcoa), as Pittsburgh

Reduction had been known since 1907, produced almost 50,000 tons of aluminum.

Hall never married. His other passion besides his work was playing the piano. He made a fortune from the Hall-Heroult process, much of which he donated during his lifetime to Oberlin College. He worked as the chief technical person for Alcoa until he died on December 27, 1914, in Daytona Beach, Florida. At the time of his death, his estate was estimated at $15 million, most of which he donated to furthering higher education.

Further Reading

"Charles Martin Hall," National Inventors Hall of Fame. Available online. URL: http://www.invent.org/hall_of_fame/72.html. Downloaded on July 2, 2009.

Edwards, Junius. *The Immortal Woodshed: The Story of the Inventor Who Brought Aluminum to America.* New York: Dodd, Mead, 1955.

Hammer, Armand

(1898–1990) *entrepreneur in petroleum*

Most people are not surprised to learn that doctors make a lot of money. They are surprised, however, when doctors make a lot of money by selling pharmaceutical drugs while still in school, making pencils for the Russians, or discovering oil in Africa. One doctor who did all three was Armand Hammer, who graduated from medical school, never practiced medicine, and made three different fortunes without losing any of them.

Hammer was born on May 21, 1898, in New York City. His father, Julius, owned Good Laboratories, a pharmaceutical company, and his mother, Rose, was a homemaker. As a teenager he went to work for his father, and at age 19 he took over active management of the company when his father became ill. By 1921 he had made a million dollars in the pharmaceutical business. At the same time, he studied medicine, and in 1921 he received his M.D. from the Columbia College of Physicians and Surgeons.

In 1921 Hammer went to the Soviet Union to donate medical aid and pharmaceutical supplies to the victims of a typhus epidemic. While there he met Vladimir I. Lenin, the Soviet leader, with whom he discussed various business arrangements of interest to them both. He received a government concession to mine asbestos and to form the Alamerico Corporation for purposes of exchanging Russian furs and caviar for American wheat. By 1925 he had built a factory for making lead pencils, which were in short supply in the thousands of public elementary schools that had sprung up across the Soviet Union following the Russian Revolution, and arranged for the sale of American-built tractors to the Soviets. In 1927 he married Olga von Root with whom he had one child. They divorced in 1934, and in 1943 he married Angela Zevely. They divorced in 1956, and that same year he married Frances Barrett.

Hammer made a second fortune from doing business in the Soviet Union. However, his business interests in Russia were threatened in 1928 when Joseph Stalin, Lenin's successor, began collectivizing virtually every aspect of the Soviet economy. That same year, Hammer sold his businesses to the Soviet government and returned to the United States, settling in New York City. He brought with him a huge collection of Russian art and artifacts, most of which he sold through Lord & Taylor's department store as well as his own Hammer Galleries in New York City. He also became involved in the liquor business, acquiring a rum distillery in New England and a bourbon distillery in Kentucky, and the cattle business, acquiring several Black Angus breeding operations across the United States. In 1955 he moved to Los Angeles, California, presumably to enjoy the "good life" of retirement in a sunny climate.

In 1956 Hammer, in need of a tax write-off, went shopping for a company that was losing money. He found the Occidental Petroleum Company. Founded in 1920, this small, unprofitable operation had a gloomy history of drilling oil wells in California that produced very little oil. Ironically, after Hammer invested in the company, two of its wells started producing an abundance of oil. In 1957 he bought controlling interest in the company and became its chief executive officer and chairman of the board. Then he mounted a high-risk search for natural gas in the Sacramento Valley, and he made a major strike. At that point he decided that Occidental might be worth more to him as a profit maker than as a tax write-off, so he began building the company by expansion, acquisition, and diversification. In 1961 Occidental took another major risk by drilling in Libya, only to discover two huge oil fields, one with reserves of about 2 billion barrels. By 1966 Occidental had purchased Island Creek Coal and Hooker Chemical, two of the biggest companies in their industries, as well as a number of fertilizer companies. Having acquired the latter, Hammer received permission from the U.S. State Department to sell fertilizer to the Soviets at the height of the cold war. By 1986 Occidental's annual gross income exceeded $15 billion, and the company had become one of the largest in the United States. That same year he bought the Church & Dwight Company, makers of Arm & Hammer baking soda, just so he could tell inquisitive reporters that, yes, he did own it.

In addition to business, Hammer had a passion for art. He collected a number of valuable paintings, estimated to be worth $400 million, which he frequently loaned to museums and art galleries around the world. He was also an active worker for peace between the United States and the Soviet Union during the cold war, and he used his business contacts in both countries to arrange high-level meetings between their leaders. He remained active in Occidental's affairs until his death on December 10, 1990, in Los Angeles.

Further Reading

Epstein, Edward J. *Dossier: The Secret History of Armand Hammer.* New York: Carroll & Graf, 1996.

Lamb, Brian. Booknotes: *Life Stories: Notable Biographies on the People Who Shaped America.* New York: Times Books, 1999.

Weinberg, Steve. *Armand Hammer: The Untold Story.* London: Abacus, 1992.

Handler, Ruth
(Ruth Mosko)
(1916–2002) *inventor of the Barbie doll*

One of the most popular toys of all time is the Barbie doll. Inspired by a voluptuous Swiss doll for adults, Barbie's inventor, Ruth Handler, named her doll after her daughter.

Handler was born Ruth Mosko on November 4, 1916, in Denver, Colorado. Her father, Jacob, made custom truck bodies, and her mother, Ida, was a homemaker. When Handler was six months old her mother developed serious health problems, so her father sent her to live with her oldest sister, Sarah, and Sarah's husband, Louis Greenwald. The Greenwalds owned a drugstore in downtown Denver, where Handler worked after school. After graduating from high school, she attended the University of Denver for a year, then transferred to the University of California at Los Angeles where she studied business education for a year. In fact, she had moved to Los Angeles to be near her high school sweetheart, Elliot Handler, whom she married in 1938 and with whom she had two children.

In 1939 the Handlers and Zachary Zemby formed the Elzac Company. Elliot designed and made knickknacks out of acrylic plastic, and Ruth sold them to trendy shops. In 1941 she left the company to have her first child, Barbara, but after three years of being a stay-at-home mom she was ready to return to work. In 1944, the same year she had her second child, Kenneth, the Handlers and Harold "Matt" Matson formed the Mattel Company. Since most materials were rationed during World War II, the company collected scrap wood from local munitions factories and turned it into picture frames and dollhouse furniture. As at Elzac, Elliot designed and made the pieces, and Ruth sold them. Shortly after the company was founded, Matson sold his interest to Ruth's foster parents, the Greenwalds. In 1947 Mattel started selling a line of musical toys such as the Uke-A-Doodle, a plastic ukelele with a hand crank that operated a music box.

In 1951 Handler noticed that, when Barbara and her young friends played with paper dolls, they usually pretended to be grown-ups doing grown-up things. This gave Handler the idea to create a doll that looked like an attractive young woman. But her partners said "no," so she put the idea aside. Then, in 1956 while on vacation in Switzerland, she saw a doll very much like the one she had thought of. This 11-inch doll named "Lilli" had a gorgeous figure and wore beautiful clothes, but she was a novelty item for adults rather than a plaything for little girls. For three years Handler worked to design a more wholesome-looking doll that would appeal to girls her daughter's age without offending their parents. In 1959 Mattel introduced Handler's new doll, a 20-something blue-eyed blonde wearing a striped, one-piece swimsuit and named "Barbie" in honor of her daughter, at a national toy show in New York City.

Although Barbie received a cool reception at the show, Mattel did manage to receive a few small orders. But once the little girls of America found out about Barbie, it seemed like every one of them wanted a Barbie of her own. From 1959 to 1962 Mattel received more orders for Barbie than it could fill. In 1961 Barbie was joined by Ken (named after Handler's son) when thousands of girls wrote to Mattel begging for a boyfriend for Barbie. One of the fun things to do with Barbie and Ken (and all the cousins and friends who would eventually join them) was to dress them up in stylish clothes. Then, of course, they had to have their own cars, apartments, beach houses, swimming pools, offices, clubs, and other venues where they could wear their new clothes and be grown-up. This insatiable desire for Barbie merchandise resulted in Mattel becoming, not only the largest toy manufacturer in the United States during the 1970s, but also the country's largest manufacturer of women's fashion garments.

In 1970 Handler's world began to change dramatically. That same year she was diagnosed with breast cancer and her left breast was removed. Meanwhile, Mattel was growing so fast that she, as company president, was having difficulty keeping up with the changes. An aggressive corporate acquisition campaign, by which Mattel bought up a number of rivals, suppliers, and related companies, resulted in Handler losing effective control of the company she and her husband had started 30 years before. In 1975 she retired from Mattel; she returned briefly in 1994 to help the company celebrate Barbie's 35th birthday.

Following her surgery in 1970, Handler had tremendous difficulty finding an artificial breast to wear under her clothing. She had finally solved the problem by commissioning Peyton Massey, a local craftsperson of artificial limbs, to make a breast to her specifications. In 1975 she formed a new company to design, manufacture, and sell natural-looking artificial breasts that fit snugly and come in a number of standard bra sizes. Two years later Handler's company began selling "Nearly Me" nationwide. Although not as big a seller as Barbie, Nearly Me enjoyed considerable success among women who had had mastectomies. When Handler's health failed in 1991, she sold the company and retired. She died on April 27, 2002.

Further Reading

Altman, Linda J. *Women Inventors.* New York: Facts On File, 1997.

Handler, Ruth, with Jacqueline Shannon. *Dream Doll: The Ruth Handler Story.* Stamford, Conn.: Longmeadow Press, 1994.

Lord, M. G. *Forever Barbie: The Unauthorized Biography of a Real Doll.* New York: William Morrow and Co., 1994.

"Ruth Handler." The Lemelson-MIT Program's Invention Dimension. Available online. URL: http://web.mit.edu/invent/iow/handler.html. Downloaded on July 2, 2009.

Vare, Ethlie Ann, and Greg Ptacek. *Women Inventors & Their Discoveries.* Minneapolis: Oliver Press, 1993.

Harriman, E. H.
(Edward Henry Harriman)
(1848–1909) *entrepreneur in railroads*

From the 1860s to the 1890s, the Union Pacific Railroad was touted as a major vehicle for settling and civilizing the American West according to the standards of the American East. Unfortunately, in 1893 the line was forced to declare bankruptcy as a result of the Credit Mobilier scandal. The individual who played the single most important role in turning the Union Pacific around so that it could contribute to the Americanization of the West was E. H. Harriman. As a result of his efforts, the Union Pacific survived and thrived, and more than one hundred years later the railroad is still a major link in the transcontinental rail network.

Harriman was born Edward Henry Harriman on February 20, 1848, in Hempstead, New York. His father, Orlando, was a minister, and his mother, Cornelia, was a homemaker. At age 13 he went to work as an office boy for a Wall Street investment firm, and by age 21 he had become the managing clerk for the D. C. Hayes Company. In 1870 he borrowed enough money from an uncle to buy his own seat on the New York Stock Exchange and form his own brokerage firm, E. H. Harriman & Company. In 1879 he married Mary Averell with whom he had six children.

Harriman became involved in the railroad industry in 1880, when his father-in-law, the president of the Ogdensburg & Lake Champlain Railroad, made him a director. The following year Harriman and several partners bought controlling interest in the Lake Ontario Southern Railroad, and by 1883 he had become that line's sole owner. The following year he succeeded in creating a bidding war for his railroad between the New York Central and the Pennsylvania, the two largest railroads in the East. Later that year he became a director of the Illinois Central, and in 1885 he was made a vice president. He resigned from his Wall Street firm that same year in order to assist the Illinois Central's president, Stuyvesant Fish, create and direct a highly centralized management structure for the railroad.

In 1897 Harriman became a member of the executive committee and a director on the reorganized board of the Union Pacific Railroad, which had declared bankruptcy four years earlier. The following year he became the line's chairman of the board, and he immediately began to implement his own plan to upgrade the Union Pacific and make it into one of the nation's strongest railroads. He reduced the line's overhead and settled its debt to the federal government, which had partially funded the Union Pacific's construction. Finding the line in poor physical shape, he began spending millions of dollars to improve track and buy new freight cars and locomotives. Under Harriman's management, the Union Pacific became a well-run railroad, and it gradually became a highly profitable one as well. Over the years it played a major role in shipping the agricultural and mineral wealth of the West to the East, thus greatly stimulating the growth of the western economy.

In 1899 Harriman got involved with three separate acquisition ventures. First, he and several partners bought the Chicago & Alton Railroad, which they fixed up and made profitable. Second, he became part of the investment group that bought the Kansas City, Pittsburg & Gulf Railroad, and helped turn that line around. Third, he got involved in a battle with the Northern Pacific Railroad for control of the Chicago, Burlington & Quincy Railroad. At the time, the Union Pacific's eastern terminus was Omaha, Nebraska, while the Northern Pacific's was Minneapolis/St. Paul, Minnesota. Whichever line gained control of the Burlington, which connected Omaha and the Twin Cities to Chicago, Illinois, would gain a major connection to the East and probably become the dominant railroad in the West. After the Northern Pacific's JAMES JEROME HILL outbid him for the Burlington, in 1901 Harriman started buying stock in the Northern Pacific to gain control of the Burlington that way. As a way of making peace, Hill proposed to "share" the Burlington with Harriman and placed him and several of his associates on the boards of the Northern Pacific, the Burlington, and the Northern Securities Company, the holding company that held the stock of both lines.

While expanding the Union Pacific's lines eastward, Harriman also took steps to expand them westward. By 1901 he had gained control of the Central Pacific and the Southern Pacific, which greatly expanded his connections in California and the Southwest. As with the Union Pacific, Harriman cut overhead, improved track and equipment, and increased the profitability of the freight and passenger services of both lines.

At the time of his death, Harriman's railroads controlled more than 60,000 miles of track, making him the most influential railroad magnate in the country. Despite his success at rebuilding bankrupt or nonprofitable lines, he was attacked relentlessly in the press for being a robber baron of the same ilk as JAY GOULD. The charge was not true, not even always in Gould's case, but on occasion circumstantial evidence made it appear to be true. In 1907 President Theodore Roosevelt got into the act by accusing Harriman of being an "undesirable citizen." The charges stemmed partly from Harriman's involvement in the bidding war with the Northern Pacific, which almost brought chaos to Wall Street, and the controversy over Northern Securities, which in 1904 the U.S. Supreme Court declared an illegal monopoly.

However, it also stemmed partly from various disputes within the Republican Party, to which both Roosevelt and Harriman belonged. Harriman died on September 9, 1909, at his country estate in Turner, New York.

Further Reading

Eckenrode, H. J. *E. H. Harriman: The Little Giant of Wall Street.* New York: Arno Press, 1981.

Klein, Maury. *The Life and Legend of E. H. Harriman.* Chapel Hill: University of North Carolina Press, 2001.

Mercer, Lloyd J. *E. H. Harriman, Master Railroader.* Boston: Twayne Pub., 1985.

Wren, Daniel A., and Ronald G. Greenwood. *Management Innovators: The People and Ideas that Have Shaped Modern Business.* New York: Oxford University Press, 1998.

Hearst, William Randolph

(1863–1951) entrepreneur in newspaper publishing

William Hearst was one of the most flamboyant and influential newspaper publishers of all time. Unlike Adolph S. Ochs, whose commitment to serious news reporting gave the *New York Times* the motto "all the news that's fit to print," Hearst often instructed his editors to print whatever would boost circulation, regardless of whether or not it was true. His commitment to "yellow journalism" transformed the way American newspapers reported the news, and it ultimately resulted in Hearst's building the largest newspaper chain of his day.

Hearst was born on April 29, 1863, in San Francisco, California. His father, George, was the part owner of hundreds of western mines, and his mother, Phoebe, was a socialite. In 1882 he enrolled in Harvard University but was expelled after three years for excessive misbehavior. After working briefly as a reporter for the *New York World,* which had just been purchased by JOSEPH PULITZER, he returned to California and took over as publisher of the *San Francisco Examiner,* which his father had bought in 1880. Using the *World* as a model, Hearst remade the *Examiner* from a money-losing, pro-Democrat organ into a newspaper that attempted to reform San Francisco via hard-nosed investigative reporting. He also set out to entertain his readers with a hearty dose of lurid sensationalism. The transformation was funded by millions of his father's dollars, and within two years the paper was a money-making proposition that established his reputation as a successful newspaper publisher.

In 1895 Hearst returned to New York City, this time to buy the *New York Journal.* As with the *Examiner,* Hearst poured millions of dollars of his father's money into the paper, and he quickly turned it into the *World's* leading rival. He lured away the entire staff of the *World's* Sunday edition by doubling their salaries, and he paid outrageous amounts of money to such talents as writer Stephen Crane, editor Arthur Brisbane, and color cartoonist Richard Outcault. He boosted circulation by replicating the editorial policies of investigative reporting and lurid sensationalism that had made the *Examiner* popular, while using many illustrations and big headlines and lowering the per copy price to one penny. He also garnered much favor in the community by giving away coal, sweaters, and food to poor residents who could barely afford to buy his paper and by putting on a number of celebrations that were free to the public.

Within a short time the *World* was forced to respond with sensationalistic coverage of its own. The result was "yellow journalism"; the name derives from one of Outcault's cartoon characters, The Yellow Kid, who appeared at various times in both the *Journal* and the *World.* Yellow journalism reached its peak in 1898 during the Spanish-American War, when Hearst ordered his editors to report as news various fabrications and exaggerations of the truth regarding alleged atrocities of Spanish troops fighting against Cuban rebels. The *Journal* called repeatedly for war against Spain, and it is credited in part with actually bringing about the U.S. declaration of war. Hearst certainly thought he knew where the credit belonged, for he once asked in his newspaper, "How do you like the *Journal's* war?" During the actual conflict, both papers hysterically reported battlefield events, but by the end of the war Pulitzer had ordered his editors to restrain themselves, while Hearst continued to urge the *Journal's* editors to outdo themselves.

In addition to building up the *Journal*, Hearst also acquired other newspapers and magazines by using the profits from his own newspapers as well as a $10,000 per month allowance provided to him by his mother until her death in 1919. By that same year, the Hearst publishing empire included seven daily newspapers, five magazines, two news services, and a film company. Hearst, however, was not welcomed in every community in which he did business. His stridently anti-British attitude coupled with his strong support of the German kaiser during the early days of World War I caused several of his papers to be banned in their communities. Similar events occurred following his support for the Bolshevik revolution in 1917 and his admiration for the policies of Adolf Hitler and Benito Mussolini during the 1930s. But in most communities, the Hearst editorial policy worked as it had in New York and San Francisco, thus providing him with the profits to continue expanding his publishing empire. By 1933 he owned 28 newspapers, 18 magazines, and several radio stations, as well as the news services and the film company. His papers accounted for 14 percent of all daily newspaper sales and almost 25 percent of all Sunday sales.

During the Great Depression, Hearst began to lose control of his empire. His lavish spending on salaries and promotional events finally began to exceed his revenues, and he found himself unable to cut back on his spending until it was too late. By 1937 he was more than $125 million in debt, and he was forced to sell off about half of his assets. By this time Hearst's social commitments had changed. Whereas before he had been an unabashed promoter of what he considered to be the best interests of the working class, he later took more of a pro-business, antilabor stance that cost him millions of readers. Still, at the time of his death his papers accounted for almost 10 percent of daily newspaper sales, more than any other single newspaper chain in the country.

In his personal life, Hearst was every bit as flamboyant as his newspapers. As publisher of the *Examiner* in the 1880s, he lived openly with his mistress, Tessie Powers, with whom he had lived while attending Harvard. In 1903 he married Millicent Willson, a chorus girl, with whom he had five children. After 1920, however, he spent little time

with his wife, who lived in New York City; instead, he lived more or less openly with a second mistress, Marion Davies, a Hollywood actress. His California home was La Casa Grande, a grandiose castle in San Simeon, and his passion was art, on which he spent untold millions. Charles Foster Kane, the main character in Orson Welles's epic 1941 movie *Citizen Kane*, was modeled after Hearst. Hearst spent the last years of his life in virtual seclusion at San Simeon, and he died on August 14, 1951, in Beverly Hills, California.

Further Reading

Crompton, Samuel W. *100 Americans Who Shaped American History.* San Mateo, Calif.: Bluewood Books, 1999.

Kastner, Victoria, and Victoria Garagliano. *Hearst Castle: The Biography of a Country House.* New York: H. N. Abrams, 2000.

Nasaw, David. *The Chief: The Life of William Randolph Hearst.* Boston: Houghton Mifflin, 2001.

Robinson, Judith. *The Hearsts: An American Dynasty.* New York: Avon Books, 1992.

Hefner, Hugh Marston (1926–   ), and Christie Ann Hefner (1952–   )
entrepreneurs in Playboy Enterprises

One significant event in the history of 20th-century American publishing was the creation of *Playboy* magazine in the 1950s. Although *Playboy* was not the first magazine to feature photographs of beautiful naked women, it was the first to do so with class. In addition to challenging the nation's strait-laced sexual mores, *Playboy* also challenged prevailing American attitudes about obscenity, censorship, domesticity and single life, and male and female identity. The brainchild of Hugh Hefner, who guided the magazine to the heights of respectability and profitability by the mid-1970s, *Playboy*'s longevity since that time can be attributed in large part to Hefner's daughter, Christie, who guided the magazine and the empire that was built around it into new and profitable ventures in the late 20th century.

Hugh Hefner was born Hugh Marston Hefner on April 9, 1926, in Chicago, Illinois. His father,

Glenn, was an accountant, and his mother, Grace, was a homemaker. As a high-school student, he developed an interest and ability in drawing and writing comic strips, which he often provided for the school paper. He graduated from high school in 1944 and was immediately drafted into the U.S. Army. Discharged two years later, he enrolled in the University of Illinois where he majored in psychology and wrote cartoons and articles for the school paper. His most memorable articles were a series called "Coed of the Week" and a review of Alfred C. Kinsey's *Sexual Behavior in the Human Male,* also known as the Kinsey Report, in which Hefner endorsed an uninhibited attitude toward human sexual behavior. In 1949 he received his B.A. and married Mildred Williams with whom he had two children; his first child was Christie Ann Hefner, who was born on November 8, 1952, in Chicago.

Returning to Chicago after graduation, Hugh Hefner worked as a personnel director of a manufacturing company and wrote advertising copy for a department store before joining the staff of *Esquire* magazine as a writer of subscription promotion copy. At the time, *Esquire* was the nation's leading magazine for men. Its articles, features, and advertising were geared toward the educated, upwardly mobile male; most issues included photographs of women who were scantily clad but never totally nude or even bare breasted. In 1952 *Esquire* closed its Chicago office and offered Hefner a position in New York City, which he turned down.

Hugh Hefner spent the next two years as a promotion, then circulation, manager for two different publishers. Meanwhile, he had decided the time was ripe for a new men's magazine, like *Esquire* in many respects but with a more open attitude toward nudity and sex. He borrowed $10,000 from his friends to put together the first issue of *Playboy;* its highlight was a nude photograph of Marilyn Monroe, the famous actress. The issue hit the newsstands in December 1953, and within a short period it had sold out its press run of more than 50,000 copies.

Over the years Hugh Hefner built *Playboy* into a how-to guide for young, white urban males. In addition to featuring a number of nude photos of buxom young women, including a centerfold of the Playmate of the Month, the magazine offered original short stories, ribald humor and cartoons, and plenty of educational articles about music, clothing, wine, cigars and pipes, automobiles, stereo equipment, movies, plays, sports, and other topics that would appeal to young men. The magazine promoted its founder's own increasingly hedonistic beliefs, which seemed to be in step with an America that was getting used to enjoying the prosperity of the 1950s after the depression and war that had dominated American life in the 1930s and 1940s. And the nude photos were unlike those in the so-called girlie magazines, which depicted low-class women in provocative poses. By contrast, Playboy's nudes were freshly scrubbed and smiling, and they kept their genitalia covered. The accompanying copy made it clear that these women were just wholesome but fun-loving, All-American girls of whom any young man's parents might approve.

By 1971, the year Hefner took the company public, he had turned *Playboy* magazine into a business empire called Playboy Enterprises. In addition to the magazine, which sold about 7 million copies per month, the company also operated two resort hotels; a string of theaters; 23 Playboy Clubs, members-only nightclubs in which the waitresses were attractive young women of the type featured in the magazine; a line of clothing, jewelry, and other accessories emblazoned with the trademark rabbit's head logo; and several casinos and betting shops in Great Britain and the West Indies. The capstone of the empire was the Playboy Mansion, Hefner's personal pleasure palace in Chicago where he lived, worked, and hosted lavish parties promoting the magazine and its hedonistic lifestyle.

In 1972 *Playboy* magazine's monthly circulation peaked at 7.2 million. From there on, the magazine gradually declined in popularity as its many imitators began showing women with exposed genitalia, something Hugh Hefner would never permit. Fortunately for Playboy Enterprises, in 1975 Christie Hefner joined the company, and after getting her feet wet for 10 years, she would lead the company in a new and prosperous direction.

Hugh Hefner had divorced his first wife in 1959, after which Christie Hefner lived with her mother and stepfather in Wilmette, a suburb of

Chicago. She graduated from Brandeis University in 1974 with a B.A. in English and American literature and went to work for an alternative newspaper in Boston, Massachusetts. In 1975 she joined Playboy Enterprises as a special assistant to her father. Her first assignment was to make a profit with Playtique, a women's clothing and record shop in the lobby of the Playboy office building. Then she planned the company's gala 25th-anniversary celebrations, followed by an assignment to inaugurate the Playboy Guides To, special issues devoted to one topic such as men's fashion or stereo equipment. Following the cancellation of the company's gambling license in Great Britain in 1982 for numerous violations of British gaming laws, and her disclosure to her father that the profits from the gambling operations had been keeping the rest of the company afloat, she was made "president" of Playboy Enterprises. In fact, for six years she shared the duties of the office with other executives such as Marvin Huston, the executive vice president until 1984, and Richard Rosenzweig, Hugh Hefner's chief aide; then as now, all major decisions had to be cleared through Hugh Hefner, the corporation's major stockholder. She set out to restore the Playboy empire to profitability by cutting costs. The resort hotels having already been sold, the next step was to close the Playboy Clubs, sell the theaters, and shut down the Playboy Mansion. By 1986 *Playboy* magazine's circulation had fallen to 3.4 million, so she directed the expansion of its videocassettes by adapting the magazine's pictorials, spreads of several pages of photos devoted to one model, into hour-long videos.

Upon being elected chairperson and chief executive officer of Playboy Enterprises in 1988, Christie Hefner was able to implement more of her own ideas about how the business should be run, most of which had to do with the globalization of the company. She began publishing *Playboy* magazine in 17 foreign language editions, which eventually boosted *Playboy*'s total monthly circulation to 15 million, and licensed manufacturers of Playboy-logo apparel and merchandise in more than 70 countries. She also guided the company's movement into electronic formats—in 1994 *Playboy* became the first national magazine on the World

Wide Web—and its return to gambling with the opening of a casino on the Mediterranean island of Rhodes. These moves made the company profitable through the end of the decade. In 2001, however, renewed competition from cable TV providers and magazines forced Playboy Enterprises back into the red.

While Christie Hefner was transforming the way Playboy Enterprises did business, Hugh Hefner remained in charge of *Playboy* magazine itself. He moved into a new Playboy Mansion, this one in Beverly Hills, California, and in 1989 he married Kimberly Conrad, a former Playmate of the Month, with whom he had two sons. They separated in 1998 and eventually divorced. In 1995, Christie Hefner married former Illinois state senator and real estate developer and lawyer William Marovitz.

In recent years, the Hefners have pursued different paths in a joint effort to boost *Playboy*, which has struggled to compete with the growing availability of inexpensive, online, adult-related content. Christie remained an energetic and innovative force as *Playboy*'s chief executive officer, but stepped down from that role in 2008, explaining, "I've always known that I wanted to move on at some point in my career. I've given a great deal of my life to the company." Since 2005, Hugh has enjoyed renewed fame as a star in *The Girls Next Door*, a popular reality show on the E! cable television network. Soon after entering his 80s, he noted of his legacy, "I would like to be remembered as somebody who has changed the world in some positive way, in a social, sexual sense and I'd be very happy with that . . . I'm a kid who dreamed the dreams and made them come true."

Further Reading

Burns, Kevin. *Hugh Hefner, American Playboy*. New York: A&E Home Video, 1999, videorecording.

Coyote, Peter, et al. *Sex in the 20th Century*. New York: A&E Television Networks, 2001, videorecording.

Edgren, Gretchen. *Inside the Playboy Mansion: If You Don't Swing, Don't Ring*. London: Aurum, 1998.

Greer, Tammy Lee. *Playboy and the Culture of Sexuality, Patriarchy, Capitalism and Ideological Representations of the Erotic*. Ottawa, Canada: National Library of Canada, 1996.

Helmsley, Harry
(Henry Brakmann Helmsley) (1909–1997), and
Leona Helmsley
(Leona Mindy Rosenthal, Leona Panzirer, Leona Lubin, Leona Roberts) (1920–2007)
entrepreneurs in real estate

One of the most remarkable entrepreneurial relationships in the history of American real estate was the one between Harry and Leona Helmsley. By most accounts, he was a kind, low-key, big-deal-making genius, while she was a cruel, flamboyant, little-deal-making genius. And yet, at heart, they seemed to be one of a kind; except for a deep and abiding love they had for each other, neither was interested in much else besides making a lot of money, and they were not always scrupulous about how they made it. Although Leona caught most of the flak from the press, which dubbed her the "Queen of Mean," it seemed clear that Harry was a willing partner in most of her cruel and illegal shenanigans.

Harry Helmsley was born Henry Brakmann Helmsley on March 4, 1909, in New York City. His father, Henry, was wholesale dry-goods buyer, and his mother, Minnie, was a homemaker. After graduating from high school in 1925, he went to work as an office boy for Dwight, Voorhis & Perry, a real-estate brokerage and property management firm in New York City. Shortly thereafter he was promoted to broker, and in 1938 he became a partner. That same year he married Eve Green with whom he had no children. In 1949 Helmsley and Lawrence A. Wien formed an informal partnership; Helmsley found undervalued commercial and residential buildings and Wien raised the money to purchase them via public syndication, a process of his own design by which the investors legally paid no federal income tax on their profits. By 1955 Harry had become the principal owner of Dwight, Voorhis & Perry, which he merged with another brokerage firm to form Helmsley-Spear Inc., while continuing to do business with Wien. In 1961, after years of negotiating, the partners bought one of the most famous pieces of real estate in America, the Empire State Building. By 1969 Harry owned a controlling interest in hundreds of buildings in New York City and other cities that were worth close to $3 billion.

Leona Helmsley was born Leona Mindy Rosenthal on July 4, 1920, in Marbletown, New York. Her father, Morris, was a hatmaker, and her mother, Ida, was a homemaker. Shortly after her birth, she moved with her family to Brooklyn. After leaving high school, she worked for several years as a store clerk and receptionist. In 1940 she married Leo Panzirer with whom she had one child; they divorced in 1952. The following year she married Joseph Lubin; they divorced in 1960, although he continued to support her and the child for another two years. In 1962 she adopted the last name Roberts and went to work as a receptionist for Pease & Elliman, a real-estate brokerage firm. Shortly thereafter she was promoted to broker, and eventually was put in charge of renting the apartments in a specific brand-new building for which the company was the rental agent. Charmingly aggressive, she quickly earned a reputation as a saleswoman par excellence. In 1967 she became an executive vice president and partner in Sutton & Towne Residential Inc., a new company that specialized in converting residential buildings, where tenants rented their apartments, to cooperatives and condominiums. In cooperatives, the residents shared in the ownership of the building, and in condominiums, they owned outright their individual apartments.

In 1969 Harry met Leona at a realtors' social function. That same year, he hired her to be the senior vice president and director of cooperative sales of Brown, Harris, Stevens, a Helmsley-Spear subsidiary that specialized in renting and selling some of the most expensive apartments in New York City. Their business relationship turned into a romantic one, and in 1972 Harry divorced his first wife and married Leona.

Shortly after their marriage, Harry appointed Leona his troubleshooter. In fact, the title was largely honorific and carried few duties with it, so for about eight years she dropped in unannounced on Harry's various holdings in New York City and caused trouble. By 1980 he owned or managed about 40 hotels in the eastern United States, and he appointed Leona president of the hotel division. Given her total lack of experience in the hotel industry, the move was questionable at best. Quite simply, she had no idea how to manage the far-flung empire, and she was totally unable to establish a rapport with any of the staff members at any of the hotels, so she made her employees fear her rather than respect her. As a result, the division lost money steadily until outside managerial expertise was brought in to turn things around. However, she did demonstrate a real interest in hearing from guests about their stays, and she worked assiduously to correct whatever problems they revealed to her via comment cards. This very real caring attitude on her part was translated into two highly successful advertising campaigns for the division's flagship hotels, the New York Harley and the Helmsley Palace. For the Harley, she developed the "Why should you?" campaign, each ad featured a picture of Leona and a heading; for example, "I couldn't get along without a phone in the bath. Why should you?" Almost overnight, the campaign helped boost the Harley's occupancy rate from 25 percent to 70 percent, and it took the hotel out of the red and into the black. And for the Helmsley Palace, Leona's advertising agency turned her into a veritable queen. Ads depicted Leona inspecting every aspect of the hotel and demonstrating its many features and amenities, all under a heading that said, "The Only Palace in the World Where the Queen Stands Guard."

As Harry got older, Leona took over more and more of the responsibilities of managing his real-estate empire. A cold and cunning woman, she trusted no one other than Harry, and she relied on fear generated by the prospect of imminent dismissal to keep her employees in line. She also fired a number of Harry's longtime associates, people who had helped make him wealthy, all with his tacit approval.

Despite their billions, the Helmsleys insisted on getting kickbacks and freebies from suppliers that amounted to millions of dollars over the years. Worse, the couple evaded paying almost $2 million in federal income tax by fraudulently charging millions of dollars' worth of renovations to their mansion in Greenwich, Connecticut, to their expense accounts of their various properties in New York City. Following a 1989 trial in which a former housekeeper testified that Helmsley told her that, "We don't pay taxes. Only the little people pay taxes," Leona was found guilty of

33 counts of tax fraud; Harry had been deemed mentally unfit to stand trial. She was sentenced to four years in prison (she actually served 18 months, plus 10 months' house arrest), fined more than $7 million, and ordered to pay nearly $2 million in back taxes. While under house arrest, she took over Harry's role at Helmsley-Spear after he died on January 4, 1997, in Scottsdale, Arizona. She transferred his holdings in the company, valued at approximately $5 billion, to a new entity, Helmsley Enterprises, Inc., of which she was the sole owner. By 2001 she had sold many of those holdings for an undisclosed amount of money.

Leona Helmsley died of heart failure on August 20, 2007, at her summer home in Greenwich, Connecticut. Earlier that year, she was ranked by *Forbes* magazine as the 369th richest person in the world, with a net worth of $2.5 billion.

Further Reading

Hammer, Richard. *The Helmsleys: The Rise and Fall of Harry and Leona.* New York: Signet, 1991.
Kohn, George Childs, ed. *The New Encyclopedia of American Scandal.* New York: Facts On File, Inc., 2001.
Moss, Michael. *Palace Coup: The Inside Story of Harry and Leona Helmsley.* New York: Doubleday, 1989.
Pierson, Ransdell. *The Queen of Mean: The Unauthorized Biography of Leona Helmsley.* New York: Bantam Books, 1989.

Henry, Vickie Lea
(Vickie Lea Hixon, Vickie Rosenburg)
(1945–) *entrepreneur in mystery shopping*

Mystery shoppers are business consultants disguised as customers. They actually go shopping in their client's business, then they evaluate and make recommendations for improving the ways in which their clients' employees deal with customers. As owner and chief executive officer of Feedback Plus, Vickie Henry earned the reputation as "America's Mystery Shopper" and played a significant role in making mystery shopping an important part of the customer service evaluation industry.

Henry was born Vickie Lea Hixon on August 13, 1945, in Iola, Kansas. Her father, Clarence, was superintendent of a local meatpacking company, and her mother, Pearl, was a homemaker. At age seven Henry discovered she had both a talent and a passion for selling when she won the first of five local titles as top Girl Scout cookie salesperson. In 1963 she graduated from high school, married Bill J. Rosenburg, and moved to New Mexico. For the next five years she worked as a bank teller in the small towns of Roy and Portales, and in 1968 she became an assistant vice president of a local bank in Clovis. In 1970 she and her husband moved to Dallas, Texas, and had the first of their two children. Wanting to spend time with her new baby, she left the banking industry to sell Tupperware, a top-quality line of plastic homeware products that are sold primarily at in-home parties during the evening. Despite her success with Tupperware— she eventually became a district manager—in 1974, when her second child was born, she took a job with First City Bank and quickly worked her way up to vice president of marketing. In 1977 she divorced Rosenburg, and in 1979 she married E. W. "Reb" Henry with whom she had no children.

As vice president of marketing, one of Henry's duties was to ensure that First City's tellers gave the best possible service to the customers in the nine branches under her supervision. In 1982 she had her tellers evaluated independently by Feedback Plus, a small Dallas consulting firm founded in 1971 by Ted Dreier. The company studied the behavioral patterns of local businesses' salespeople and customers in order to improve customer service, satisfaction, retention, and sales. At the time such evaluations were conducted mostly by private investigators as a sideline to such activities as loss prevention, so Dreier was attempting to break new ground with his approach to customer evaluation. Henry was so impressed with the results of the Feedback Plus evaluation that she implemented a number of changes that materially boosted customer service in the nine branches.

Another of Henry's marketing duties involved keeping a close eye on developments in the banking industry, particularly the wave of bank mergers that in the late 1970s was just beginning to sweep the United States. About the same time that the Feedback Plus survey was completed, she realized that these mergers, by reducing the number of competitors in the financial services industry, were

also reducing her prospects of moving into a top management position with First City or any other financial institution. In 1983 she decided to seek greater opportunity by developing more fully her own natural abilities as a salesperson and entrepreneur, so she quit her job with First City to become one of Dreier's partners in Feedback Plus.

Henry's background in sales, marketing, and customer service gave her some unique insights for expanding the company's business that the other partners did not fully appreciate, partly because she lacked a college degree. These insights included the development of a sophisticated customer satisfaction index survey, the use of direct mail and telemarketing to collect and record customer-salesperson interactions, and the utilization of sophisticated econometric statistical techniques for evaluating customer service data. In 1988, after five years of a somewhat strained relationship, she bought her partners' shares and became sole owner of Feedback Plus. She also enrolled in Northwood University where she received her B.A. in business administration in 1993.

Going solo and finishing her education paid off handsomely for Henry; by 1995 she had boosted Feedback Plus's revenues by 4,000 percent, broadened its customer base to more than 200 clients across the United States, and was utilizing the services of almost 100,000 field representatives or secret shoppers. She also developed the highly successful "Would You Do Business With You?" seminar training program and authored two books, *Feedback on Sales* and *Feedback on Calls*. In 1997 she helped organize the Mystery Shopping Providers Association and later served as its third president.

Henry did not invent mystery shopping, nor did she start the first successful mystery shopping consulting firm. However, she did introduce a number of new techniques to the industry and in the process helped it to gain acceptance among U.S. retailers and financial service providers. In recent years, Henry has been active serving as the CEO of Feedback, Plus, authoring two books, and presenting talks to business groups.

Further Reading

Bacher, Renee. "The Shopper Who's a Spy," *Good Housekeeping*, May 1995, p. 28.

Moore, Dorothy P., and E. Holly Buttner. *Women Entrepreneurs: Moving Beyond the Glass Ceiling*. Thousand Oaks, Calif.: Sage Publications, 1997.

Henson, Jim
(James Maury Henson)
(1936–1990) *inventor of the Muppets*

One of the most phenomenally popular international television programs of all time was *The Muppet Show*. This program revived global interest in an old art form, puppeteering, while adapting its techniques to the modern medium of television. The person most responsible for the show's success was the creator of the Muppets, Jim Henson.

Henson was born James Maury Henson on September 24, 1936, in Greenville, Mississippi. His father, Paul, was an agronomist with the U.S. Department of Agriculture, and his mother, Elizabeth, was a homemaker. As a young boy he moved with his family to Hyattsville, Maryland, when his father was transferred. Upon graduating from high school, he was offered admission to the University of Maryland as well as a job as a puppeteer on a Washington, D.C., children's television program. He decided to accept both opportunities on a part-time basis, and for the next six years he entertained television audiences of wee folk with puppet shows of his own creation while studying art and stage design. Two of his early influences were Bill and Cora Baird, master puppeteers who are credited with reviving an interest in American puppet theater in the 1940s. The Bairds' singing frogs served as an inspiration for Henson's most famous creation, Kermit the Talking Frog, who made his first appearance on a regular five-minute segment called "Sam and Friends." In 1959 Henson married Jane Nebel with whom he had five children, and in 1960 he received his A.B. from the University of Maryland.

After graduation Henson expanded his puppeteering to include puppet shows for television commercials and network variety programs such as *The Ed Sullivan Show*. In 1969 he got his big break when he was invited to join the staff of the Children's Television Workshop in New York City and create puppet characters for *Sesame Street*. This daily educational program was designed to teach preschoolers their numbers and ABCs, as well as a few simple lessons in how to get along in life. Henson invented the Muppets, a cross between the words "marionettes" and "puppets." Joining Kermit were such *Sesame Street* regulars as Miss Piggy, Bert, Ernie, Cookie Monster, Oscar the Grouch, the Count, and Big Bird, as well as a host of supporting characters such as Snuffleupagus. Unlike most marionettes and puppets, the Muppets were made from nontraditional materials such as sculptured foam rubber, plastic, and various bits of fabric and feathers. Nor were they operated the same way. Whereas traditional puppeteers stand above and behind their creations to manipulate them, Henson and his associates held the Muppets directly over their heads and watched their actions by looking at a TV monitor placed below the stage in front of them. Regardless, the Muppets became enormously popular among children, and *Sesame Street* was eventually adapted for viewers in practically every country in the world.

In 1976 Henson got his own television program, *The Muppet Show*. This weekly one-hour program featured the Muppets and a famous real-life guest star who changed from one show to the next. Produced in England by Lord Lew Grade, an independent producer, the show became a worldwide hit. In the late 1970s it aired in more than 100 countries with an estimated global audience of more than 200 million viewers. The show's phenomenal success led Henson to put the Muppets on the big screen. In 1979 he came out with *The Muppet Movie*, followed by *The Great Muppet Caper* (1981) and *The Muppets Take Manhattan* (1984); all three were big box office hits. In 1983 he created Muppetlike characters for *Fraggle Rock*, another children's program, and in 1984 he created "Jim Henson's Muppet Babies," pint-sized animated versions of the "grown up" Muppets.

Henson's artistic abilities were matched by his entrepreneurial skills. Making the most of the Muppets' popularity, his company, Henson Associates Inc., licensed a number of product spinoffs such as toys, clothing, books, a magazine, and a comic strip, and was negotiating to be acquired by Walt Disney Enterprises, the entertainment conglomerate, at the time of Henson's death. How much money he made from the various Muppet enterprises is not known; however, it is estimated that he grossed $40 million from *The Muppet Show* alone. Not all of Henson's creative endeavors were commercial successes, however, particularly the ones that were aimed at a more adult audience. He made two movies with non-Muppet characters, *The Dark Crystal* (1982) and *Labyrinth* (1986) that drew poorly, and in 1989 he produced *The Jim Henson Hour*, a family entertainment program that flopped after five shows. But the endeavors that were geared primarily toward a younger audience were highly successful, partly because they used modern technology and portrayed modern situations, thus appealing to children, while affirming traditional values and attitudes, thus appealing to their parents.

In 1982 Henson endowed the Henson Foundation as an institution for promoting the art of puppetry. He died in New York City in 1990.

Further Reading

Gourse, Leslie. *Jim Henson, Young Puppeteer.* New York: Aladdin Paperbacks, 2000.

Inches, Alison. *Jim Henson's Designs and Doodles: A Muppet Sketchbook.* New York: H. N. Abrams, 2001.

Hershey, Milton Snavely

(1857–1945) *entrepreneur in chocolate candy*

Over the years Americans have enjoyed hundreds of different candy bars, but the most enduring one of all is the plain milk-chocolate Hershey Bar. The man who invented it, Milton Hershey, revolutionized the candy business in the United States by being the first to make chocolate with fresh milk. However, Hershey's repeated failures at selling caramels instead almost prevented him from ever inventing the Hershey Bar.

Hershey was born on September 13, 1857, in Derry Church, Pennsylvania. His father, Henry, was at various times a farmer, a cough-drop manufacturer, and a salesman; his mother, Fannie, was a homemaker. The family moved quite often to wherever his father sought opportunity, and Hershey's formal education ended after the fourth grade. At age 14 he was apprenticed to a printer

in Lancaster, Pennsylvania, but he did such a poor job that he was fired and sent home. The following year he returned to Lancaster, this time as an apprentice to Joseph H. Royer, a confectioner and ice-cream parlor operator, and for the next four years he learned how to make candy.

In 1876 Hershey borrowed enough money from his mother's brother to open a candy store in Philadelphia. The city was hosting the Great Centennial Exposition, a grand celebration of American independence that featured exhibits and drew visitors from all over the United States and Europe. He exploited this unique business opportunity by making caramels and taffy at night, then wheeling them downtown on a pushcart to sell them to exhibition goers while his mother and her sister ran the shop. While the exposition was in session, business boomed, but once it closed down, he was barely able to pay his bills. Finally, after six years in Philadelphia, he sold his business and moved back to Lancaster. He bounced around for a little over a year, working briefly as a candy maker in Denver, Colorado, then exploring the possibility of opening candy stores in Chicago, Illinois, and New Orleans, Louisiana. In 1883 he settled in New York City where he opened another candy store. Unfortunately, this one did worse than the one in Philadelphia, and within two years he was back in Lancaster again.

In 1885 Hershey opened his third candy business, but this time he did two things that ensured his success. First, he took on a partner, William H. Lebkicher, who had worked for him in Philadelphia, and together they opened the Lancaster Caramel Company. Second, he began making "Hershey's Crystal A Caramels" with fresh milk, a technique he had learned while in Denver and which makes caramels taste better and stay fresh longer. Crystal A Caramels soon came to the attention of an English importer who placed an order so large that it virtually guaranteed the success of the company. By 1893 Hershey and Lebkicher had opened another plant in nearby Mount Joy and two more in the Chicago vicinity, all of them making Crystal A Caramels.

In 1894 Hershey began making chocolate, having learned that the Swiss dipped their caramels in chocolate, which they also made with fresh milk. At first the Hershey Chocolate Company only made chocolate-coated caramels, but shortly thereafter it began turning out solid chocolate novelties in the shapes of bicycles and cigars as well. In 1900, two years after Hershey married Catherine Sweeney with whom he had no children, the company produced its first Hershey Bar, a solid block of milk chocolate that sold for a nickel. The Hershey Bar did so well that Hershey sold his interest in the Lancaster Caramel Company to concentrate on the manufacture of milk chocolate. In 1903 he began building what would become the world's largest chocolate factory on a 1,500-acre site surrounding his parents' old farm in Derry Church. Since the site was in the middle of Pennsylvania Dutch dairy country, Hershey also built a model company town, christened Hershey in 1905, that included housing with electricity and indoor plumbing, a shopping and entertainment district, churches, schools, a trolley line, a hospital, a park, and a zoo. Later additions, paid for by Hershey, included a hotel, high school, community center, and sports arena.

In addition to the Hershey Bar, the new plant also began producing the Hershey Kiss, a teardrop-shaped morsel of milk chocolate wrapped in silver foil, in 1907. The two products sold so well that by 1921 the company was grossing about $20 million in annual sales. That figure went up considerably over the years, especially after the company introduced Mr. Goodbar, a Hershey Bar with peanuts, in 1925; the Krackel Bar, a Hershey Bar with crispy rice, in 1938; and Hershey's Miniatures, smaller versions of the Hershey Bar, in 1939. During World War II, the company sold millions of specially designed chocolate bars to the U.S. military. Known as Field Ration D, the four-ounce bar contained 600 calories and did not melt, making it the perfect food item for troops in the field. It also became extremely popular among European children, to whom American GIs gave the bars as they liberated them, and helped to generate a tremendous demand for American-made chocolate in Europe after the war.

Hershey was a generous man who gave away almost all of his fortune. About $60 million of it endowed the M. S. Hershey Foundation, which he had established in 1918 to support what became known as the Milton Hershey School. Originally founded in 1909 as an orphanage and vocational school for boys, the school continued to grow until it housed, fed, and provided 13 years of vocational, business, and college preparatory education for more than 1,000 boys and girls. In 1944 Hershey stepped down as chairman of the board of Hershey Chocolate. He died on October 13, 1945, in Hershey.

Further Reading

Brenner, Joel G. *The Emperors of Chocolate: Inside the Secret Worlds of Hershey and Mars.* New York: Broadway Books, 2000.

Houts, Mary D., and Pamela C. Whitenack. *Hershey.* Cumberland, S.C.: Arcadia Pub., 2000.

Malone, Mary, and William M. Hutchinson. *Milton Hershey, Chocolate King.* Champaign, Ill.: Garrard Publishing, 1971.

McMahon, James D., Jr. *Built on Chocolate; The Story of the Hershey Chocolate Company.* Santa Monica, Calif.: General Pub. Group, 1998.

Hewitt, Peter Cooper

(1861–1921) *inventor of the mercury-vapor lamp*

Many inventors are driven to invent in large part by the profit motive, hoping to strike it rich by developing some new method or device. But some do it the other way around; having already acquired a fortune, they indulge themselves by giving free rein to their creative instincts while hoping to improve human society in some way. Peter Hewitt is typical of this latter group. His father and grandfather were wealthy men who left him enough money so that he never had to work, thus enabling him to devote his life to invention.

Hewitt was born on March 5, 1861, in New York City. His father, Abram, was an iron manufacturer, and his mother, Sarah, was a homemaker. He was named in honor of PETER COOPER, his mother's father and his father's business partner who invented the *Tom Thumb*, the first American-built steam locomotive. Hewitt attended the Stevens Institute of Technology and the Columbia University School of Mines during the 1880s, and in 1887 he married Alice Work with whom he had no children. Like many other scientific-minded young men, he was inspired by THOMAS ALVA EDISON's success as an independent inventor, and he created a laboratory of his own in a converted greenhouse in the tower of New York City's old Madison Square Garden. Also like Edison, he was interested in electricity, and his early experiments were devoted to building a better lightbulb.

Edison's original incandescent bulb, which was invented in 1879, was short-lived and inefficient. Its carbon filament could convert only about 5 percent of the electrical energy flowing into the bulb into light, the rest being turned into heat that quickly burned up the filament. For years a host of researchers attempted to solve this problem by inventing a more efficient filament, which was finally developed by a General Electric research team between 1904 and 1909. But after a few unpromising starts at inventing a better filament, Hewitt embarked on a different path.

In the late 1890s Hewitt realized that an electrical charge can be conducted by a gas, a principle that had been demonstrated in 1855 by Johann Geissler, a German glassblower. This realization led him to consider dispensing with a solid filament altogether and using a gaseous medium in its place. He focused his attention on making such a medium from mercury. Being a metal, mercury is an excellent conductor of electrical current; also, it can easily be converted to the gaseous state by roasting cinnabar, a mineral composed of mercury sulfide, and capturing the resulting vapor. By 1901 he had developed a lightbulb that featured a sealed quartz tube filled with mercury vapor. The bulb gave off an intense, cool light, which was exactly what Hewitt was hoping for.

Unfortunately, the light was a garish hue of blue, making it unsuitable for use in the home. Although Hewitt later developed a transformer that could add enough red light rays to balance the blue, the total package was too bulky and expensive to make it widely acceptable in homes. However, the mercury-vapor lamp was perfectly suitable for workshop conditions where the hue was unimportant. It also turned out to be an excellent source of ultraviolet light, and by the end of the 20th century the mercury-vapor lamp was used in such diverse industrial applications as curing polymers, detecting art forgeries and spoiled chicken eggs, producing glass, and treating water. It had also found ready acceptance as a lighting source for high-ceilinged industrial spaces, parking lots, and roadways. In 1902 Hewitt and GEORGE WESTINGHOUSE, the noted electrical manufacturer, formed the Cooper Hewitt Electric Company and began manufacturing mercury-vapor lamps. The company thrived, and in 1914 it was acquired by General Electric.

After inventing in 1904 a mercury-arc rectifier for converting alternating current into direct current, Hewitt refocused his attention from electricity to transportation. He designed a governor for controlling an automobile's speed, and he helped his brother Edward design and build the Hewitt automobile. In 1907 he developed a hydroplane motorboat, in 1915 he received a patent for a dirigible balloon and supporting framework, and in 1920 he invented a helicopter-like device capable of lifting 225 pounds. None of these inventions achieved commercial success, and they did little to inspire future inventors of similar devices. However, while experimenting with the flow of electricity through rarified gases, he discovered the fundamental principle of the vacuum-tube amplifier, which contributed tremendously to developments in electronics over the next few decades.

Hewitt was one of the founders of the Inventor's Guild, which was established in 1910. Membership in this 50-member club was by invitation only, and it was open only to successful inventors. The purpose was to protect the rights of inventors everywhere and to counsel the federal government on the relative value of potential inventions it was considering. The guild advised the U.S. Navy during World War I, but otherwise seems to have had little significance.

Hewitt spent much of his later life in Paris, France. Having divorced his first wife, in 1918 he married Maryon Andrews Bruguiere, an expatriate American whose first husband was a Frenchman. Hewitt died on August 25, 1921, in Paris.

Further Reading

"Lamp Inventors 1880–1940: Cooper Hewitt Lamp." Lighting a Revolution. Available online. URL: http://americanhistory.si.edu/lighting/bios/hewitt. htm. Downloaded on July 2, 2009.

Pupin, Michael I. *In Memoriam of Peter Cooper Hewitt*. Washington: Library of Congress Photoduplication Service, 1987.

Hewlett, William (1913–2001), and David Packard (1912–1996)
founders of Hewlett Packard

In Palo Alto, California, there is a garage that has been designated a historical landmark. Its importance stems from its role as the place where two friends from Stanford University—William Hewlett and David Packard—began a technology company and lifelong personal and business relationship that established Silicon Valley as the global capital of high technology and advanced management techniques admired and emulated around the world.

William Redington Hewlett was born on May 20, 1913, in Ann Arbor, Michigan. At the age of three he moved with his family to California after his father took a faculty position at Stanford Medical School. Hewlett reveled in the nature of northern California and enjoyed a wide variety of outdoor activities. Though he excelled in science, he struggled with reading and writing, which later was ascribed to an undiagnosed case of dyslexia. When Hewlett was 12 years old, his father died of a brain tumor, but the family remained in the San Francisco area and he enrolled as an undergrad at Stanford in 1930. He received a bachelor's degree in electrical engineering from Stanford in 1934 before heading east, where he earned a master's in electrical engineering in 1936 from the Massachusetts Institute of Technology.

David Packard was born on September 7, 1912, in Pueblo, Colorado. He grew up in Pueblo, then a small town located about 50 miles south of Colorado Springs, and was an outstanding student and athlete at Centennial High School. Following his graduation, Packard enrolled at Stanford, where he received both his bachelor's and master's degrees in electrical engineering.

The friendship between Hewlett and Packard that would eventually have such a significant impact on business began when the two young men met as freshmen at Stanford. After Hewlett returned from his studies at MIT and a job in New York with General Electric, they were encouraged by a Stanford radio engineering professor named Frederick Terman to start a company. Terman was hoping to help stem the flow of talented engineers from the west to places in the east such as New York. While on a mountain climbing trip in Colorado, Hewlett and Packard decided to go into business together. After winning a coin flip, Hewlett's name was placed first in the newly formed company, Hewlett Packard.

The men began working in a garage near Packard's Palo Alto home. Starting with just over $500 and a drill press from Sears, Hewlett and Packard created several new devices, including an automatic urinal flusher and a tuner for the harmonica. Soon, Hewlett invented the audio oscillator, which became the company's first major product. The oscillator solved problems with generating audio signals for newly released Federal Communications Commission guidelines. They called this new invention the HP200A, intentionally choosing a big number to create the impression that their company was well established. The oscillator helped the fledgling entrepreneurs partner with another California start-up, Walt Disney Studios, which ordered eight units for work on its new film *Fantasia*.

Hewlett Packard became one of the top companies in the world during the last half of the 20th century through the innovative creation of countless scientific devices, some of which have become ubiquitous in American homes. Hewlett—considered the idea man of the pair, while Packard was viewed as the sharper business mind—challenged engineers to create a computing device that could fit in his shirt pocket and the company created the first handheld, or "pocket," calculator. Hewlett Packard also created the first inkjet printer and remains among the top-selling printer-producing companies in the world.

Despite the impact of these inventions and the catalytic effect their company had on the evolution of Silicon Valley, Hewlett and Packard's greatest influence is perhaps felt in the area of business management. In what became known as the "HP Way," Hewlett and Packard consciously sought to create a business environment that emphasized, encouraged, and valued the intellectual and personal contributions of employees. The stated

"HP Way" noted such beliefs as, "We encourage flexibility and innovation. We create an inclusive work environment, which supports the diversity of our people and stimulates innovation. We strive for overall objectives which are clearly stated and agreed upon, and allow people flexibility in working toward goals in ways that they help determine are best for the organization. HP people should personally accept responsibility and be encouraged to upgrade their skills and capabilities through ongoing training and development. This is especially important in a technical business where the rate of progress is rapid and where people are expected to adapt to change."

In a 2004 article, the *Business Week* writer Peter Burrows described the HP Way as, "an egalitarian, decentralized system . . . The essence of the idea, radical at the time, was that employees' brainpower was the company's most important resource. . . . [resulting in] . . . one of the first all-company profit-sharing plans . . . [providing] shares to all employees . . . [offering] tuition assistance, flex time, and job sharing . . . Today, the behavior of the two founders remains a benchmark for business . . ." Many of these management innovations—as well as the famed Hewlett and Packard technique of "walking around management" that featured the company heads personally interacting on regular basis with workers and their projects—have been adopted by other companies and still serve as best practices models in much of the business world.

The global success of Hewlett Packard made both men billionaires. However, neither man lived a particularly lavish lifestyle and both made significant contributions of their time and resources. Hewlett established The Hewlett Foundation, which is among the 20 largest philanthropic foundations in the United States. It focuses on many issues including conflict resolution, education, environment, family and community development, the performing arts, population issues, and United States-Latin American relations. With his wife Lucile, to whom he was married for nearly 50 years until her death in 1987, Packard established the David and Lucile Packard Foundation. Upon his death, Packard gave all of the Hewlett Packard shares he owned—nearly 47 million—to

the foundation. Packard was also very involved as a business ambassador around the world, serving presidential or cabinet level invitations on trips including several to the Soviet bloc nations during the cold war.

David Packard died of pneumonia on March 26, 1996, in Palo Alto. He was survived by his son and three daughters. William Hewlett passed away at his home in Portola Valley, California, on January 12, 2001, and was survived by his second wife of 22 years, Rosemary (his first wife, Flora, died in 1977), five children, and five stepchildren. In his later years, Packard was the founder and a major contributor to the Monterey Bay Aquarium Research Institute. In 1987, he spoke of the work on this oceanographic endeavor and, in doing so, reflected the essence of his and his longtime partner Hewlett's work, saying, "Take risks. Ask big questions. Don't be afraid to make mistakes; if you don't make mistakes, you're not reaching far enough."

Further Reading
"David Packard (1912–1996)," Hewlett Packard. Available online. URL: http://www.hp.com/hpinfo/execteam/bios/packard.html. Downloaded on July 1, 2009.

Malone, Michael S. *Bill & Dave: How Hewlett and Packard Built the World's Greatest Company.* New York: Portfolio, 2001.

Packard, David. *The HP Way: How Bill Hewlett and I Built Our Company.* New York: Collins Business, 2006.

"William Hewlett (1913–2001), Hewlett Packard. Available online. URL: http://www.hp.com/hpinfo/execteam/bios/hewlett.html. Downloaded on July 1, 2009.

Hill, James Jerome
(1838–1916) *entrepreneur in railroads*

During the Great Age of American Railroads, two types of railroad tycoons emerged. One was the financier who built a line as rapidly as possible in an effort to beat the competition to a particular market, but from then on either neglected the line or engaged in price gouging so that the railroad's business declined. The other was the railroad man who built a line in order to serve a particular market, then carefully managed it to his and others' profit.

Perhaps no one typifies the second type better than James J. Hill. In the process of building the Great Northern Railway from St. Paul, Minnesota, to Seattle, Washington, Hill took care to ensure the economic viability of the customers served by his railroad, thus contributing perhaps more than any other single individual to the growth and prosperity of the American Northwest.

Hill was born James Jerome Hill on September 16, 1838, in Rockwood, Ontario, Canada. His parents, James and Anne, were farmers. At age 18 he moved to St. Paul, and for the next nine years he worked a variety of jobs for a succession of companies engaged in the dry-goods and grocery businesses. In 1865 he became a freight agent for the Northwestern Packet Company, which operated steamboats on the upper reaches of the Mississippi River, and the Milwaukee and Mississippi Railroad. A year later he opened the James J. Hill Company, which delivered freight in and around St. Paul. In 1867 he married Mary Theresa Mehegan with whom he had 10 children.

On Hill's 30th birthday, the American Northwest was still relatively unsettled. The northern reaches of Minnesota were still mostly wilderness, and North and South Dakota, Montana, Wyoming, Idaho, and Washington were still territories. It was a land full of opportunities for a person with energy and a vision, and Hill made the most of his opportunities. He invested the profits from his freight company in fur, land, and timber enterprises in northern Minnesota, and in 1870 he bought a steamboat and began providing service north along the Red River from its junction with the St. Paul and Pacific Railroad at Breckinridge, Minnesota. In 1875 he formed the Northwestern Fuel Company to supply coal to his steamboat company as well as to the St. Paul and Pacific. Three years later he and several associates acquired the bankrupt St. Paul and Pacific; Hill became the line's general manager in 1879 and its president in 1882.

Hill knew from his previous dealings with the railroad that it had not failed because of lack of business, but because it had been built hastily and then managed without any thought toward developing future business. He made the line an integral part of the communities through which it ran by improving local service. He also embarked

on a decade-long expansion program that by 1887 had extended the St. Paul's main line as far west as Great Falls, Montana Territory. However, unlike the owners of the rival Northern Pacific Railroad, he was in no hurry to complete the line all the way to the Pacific Ocean until it had become profitable in its eastern reaches, so he also constructed branch lines throughout the fertile farmland of southern Minnesota and Dakota Territory, in the process encouraging the growth of the local agricultural economy. Having provided these areas with good transportation, he then began encouraging Swedish and Norwegian immigrants to settle along his tracks and start farming.

In 1890 Hill and several associates created the Great Northern Railway, in essence the recapitalized St. Paul and Pacific under a different name, and he became its president three years later. By then, the main line had been completed to Seattle, Washington, and branch lines were under construction in Montana and Idaho. To encourage settlers in these new areas, he sponsored crop and livestock breeding programs and sent special classroom trains to teach farmers state-of-the-art agricultural techniques. In addition to developing a profitable trade by hauling local grain and livestock to market, the Great Northern also became a major bridge route for westbound cotton, flour, and metals and for eastbound lumber.

While the Great Northern prospered, the Northern Pacific floundered, mostly because it was controlled by financiers rather than conscientious railroad men like Hill. Nevertheless, the rival road created competition for Hill's line, and in 1896 he and J. P. MORGAN, the famous eastern financier, acquired control of the Northern Pacific. In 1901 Hill and Morgan also acquired the Chicago, Burlington, & Quincy Railroad, which connected St. Paul, the eastern terminus of the Great Northern and Northern Pacific, to Chicago, Illinois, the rail center of the nation. That same year these three railroads were consolidated under the Northern Securities Company, with Hill as president, thus effectively consolidating all railroading in the American Northwest in his hands.

Hill seems never to have used his monopolistic control to gouge farmers or other shippers, preferring instead to build up the strength of his railroads by building up the strength of the communities they served and the farmers and merchants who lived in them. Nevertheless, many shippers in the American Northwest feared that he would be mightily tempted to exercise his near-total control over their economic destinies to their detriment. Their fears were communicated to the federal government, which in 1902 sued Northern Securities for restraint of trade under the Sherman Antitrust Act of 1890. Two years later the U.S. Supreme Court ruled against Northern Securities and ordered its breakup. Although the order was complied with in the most technical sense, in reality the three roads continued to cooperate; in 1905, the year after the breakup, the Great Northern and the Northern Pacific jointly built the Spokane, Portland, and Seattle Railroad in Washington state.

In 1907 Hill stepped down as president of Great Northern in favor of his son Louis and then assumed the duties of chairman of the board, which he exercised for the next five years. He spent his remaining years in St. Paul as a bank president while also establishing the James J. Hill Reference Library and putting together an impressive art collection. He died on May 29, 1916, in St. Paul.

Further Reading

Malone, Michael P. *James J. Hill: Empire Builder of the Northwest.* Norman: University of Oklahoma Press, 1996.

Martin, Albro. *James J. Hill and the Opening of the Northwest.* St. Paul: Minnesota Historical Society Press, 1991.

Wren, Daniel A., and Ronald G. Greenwood. *Management Innovators: The People and Ideas that Have Shaped Modern Business.* New York: Oxford University Press, 1998.

Hilton, Conrad Nicholson

(1887–1979) *founder of Hilton Hotels*

In the late 20th century, Hilton Hotels was one of the most prestigious hotel chains in the world. Although never a large chain—in 1979 it consisted of fewer than 200 properties—it had a reputation among American travelers as one of the best places to stay anywhere in the world. The chain was the creation of Conrad Hilton, who got his start in the hospitality business by getting traveling salesmen to stay at his father's house for $2.50 per night.

Hilton was born Conrad Nicholson Hilton on Christmas Day, 1887, in San Antonio, New Mexico Territory. His father, Augustus, owned several businesses, including a general store and a coal mine, and his mother, Mary, was a homemaker. At age 17 he dropped out of school to work in his father's store, and the following year he moved with his family to Long Beach, California, after his father sold the coal mine for a sizable amount. But two years later the money was gone, most of it lost to risky investments, and he and his family returned to the store in San Antonio. That same year his father converted part of their large adobe house into a small hotel, and for the next two years Hilton attended the New Mexico School of Mines while helping out in the hotel. His main job was to recruit overnight guests, which he did by meeting the three daily trains that stopped in San Antonio and striking up conversations with whoever got off the train. Hilton dropped out of school for the last time in 1909, and for the next 10 years he helped organize a local bank, served a term in New Mexico's first state legislature, traveled throughout the state's wilderness trading groceries to trappers and miners for furs and gold dust, and served with the U.S. Army in France during World War I.

During the war Hilton had been convinced by one of his army comrades that postwar economic prosperity could best be found in the Lone Star State, so in 1919 Hilton moved to Cisco, Texas. Foiled in his efforts to buy the local bank, he bought the rundown, 40-room Mobley Hotel for $5,000 instead. After breathing life back into the Mobley, the next year he bought the equally decrepit Hotel Melba in Fort Worth. For several years he continued to purchase existing hotels that were past their prime, fix them up, put them in the hands of capable managers, and then leave them alone. In 1925, the same year he married Mary Barron with whom he had three children, he built a hotel in Dallas, and by 1929 he had built six more.

Like many other entrepreneurs in the hospitality business, Hilton took a heavy hit during the Great Depression. As business travelers became fewer and fewer, he found it increasingly difficult to come up with the money to repay his construction loans. At one point he was so destitute that he had to borrow money from one of his bellmen so he could buy groceries. But he managed to weather the storm, in large part due to the income from an oil lease he had invested in as a lark. By 1938 he was even able to expand his business outside of Texas, buying the Sir Francis Drake Hotel in San Francisco, California. By the end of World War II he had also bought hotels in Los Angeles, New York, and Chicago, and opened his first foreign property, the Palacio Hilton in Chihuahua, Mexico. Meanwhile, the ups and downs of the hotel business played havoc with his personal life; he divorced his first wife in 1934, then married the Hollywood actress Zsa Zsa Gabor in 1942, only to divorce her four years later.

In 1946 Hilton formed the Hilton Hotels Corporation, with sufficient capital to enable it to become the first hotel company to be traded on the New York Stock Exchange. Two years later he created the Hilton International Company to expand his operations overseas, and in 1953 he built his first European property, the Castellana Hilton in Madrid, Spain. In 1954 he merged the prestigious Statler hotel chain into Hilton Hotels. Up to this point, all of Hilton's hotels were owned by his corporations, but after 1960 he began selling Hilton franchises to hotel operators around the world. By 1966 his corporations owned, leased, or managed 61 properties in 19 countries. Most of his hotels catered to affluent American business travelers or vacationers, and many of them were among the world's most luxurious hotels.

In 1966 Hilton relinquished his position as president of the corporation to his son Barron, and he retired to his estate in Bel Air, California, with an estimated fortune of $150 million. An active man all his life, he enjoyed dancing and playing golf until his final days, and in 1977, at age 89, he married Mary Frances Kelly. He died on January 3, 1979, in Santa Monica, California.

Further Reading

"Conrad N. Hilton, 1950," Horatio Alger Association of Distinguished Americans: Members. Available online. URL: http://www.horatioalger.com/member_ info.cfm?memberid=hil50.htm. Downloaded on July 2, 2009.

Dabney, Thomas E. *The Man Who Bought the Waldorf: The Life of Conrad N. Hilton.* New York: Duell, Sloan and Pearce, 1950.

Hilton, Conrad. *Be My Guest.* New York: Simon and Schuster, 1994 reprint.

Hollerith, Herman
(1860–1929) *inventor of the tabulating machine*

The modern computer is a direct descendent of the electromechanical tabulating machine. Although mechanical calculators have been around since the French scientist and philosopher Blaise Pascal built one in 1642, the first practical tabulating machine was invented by Herman Hollerith. Although it was designed specifically to help tabulate census data, the tabulating machine revolutionized the way businesses keep track of numerical data, and it eventually led to the invention of the electronic computer. For his contributions to digital computing, Hollerith has become known as "the first statistical engineer" and "the father of data processing."

Hollerith was born on February 29, 1860, in Buffalo, New York. His father, Johann, was an absentee landlord, and his mother, Franciska, was a homemaker. As a boy he hated formal schooling so much that he once jumped out of a second-story schoolhouse window to get out of class, and so he had to be tutored at home. As he matured he outgrew his hatred of school, and at age 19 he graduated from the Columbia College School of Mines. In 1879 Hollerith went to work for the U.S. Census Bureau, and for the next two years he compiled statistics on manufacturers as well as tables regarding vital statistics. One of his supervisors, John S. Billings, casually mentioned one day that someone ought to invent a machine for tabulating statistics. This offhand remark got Hollerith thinking about the problem, and he decided to try his hand at solving it.

Hollerith left the Census Bureau in 1881, and for the next nine years he worked successively as an instructor of mechanical engineering at the Massachusetts Institute of Technology, a self-employed

Although Herman Hollerith did not invent the computer, his electromechanical tabulating machine inspired its invention. *(Library of Congress)*

inventor in St. Louis, Missouri, an examiner in the U.S. Patent Office in Washington, D.C., and a self-employed patent counselor. Meanwhile, in his spare time he worked to build an electromechanical calculator, which he completed in 1884 and received a patent for in 1889. His machine recorded data by "reading" the holes punched in rolls of nonconducting paper that were fed between electrically charged pins and a conducting metal surface. The holes were punched with the same tool a train conductor used to punch passengers' tickets, and were made in predesignated areas corresponding with certain numbers. As the nonconducting paper passed through the machine, electrical charges tried to pass from the pins to the metal surface, but they could only penetrate the paper through the punched holes. Every time a charge passed through a hole, it flipped a switch that advanced a counter, thus keeping track of the accumulated data. Because of the difficulty of punching holes on

a long roll of tape, he soon discarded the tape in favor of index cards about the size of a dollar bill.

Between 1887 and 1890, Hollerith's tabulating machine was used by the Census Bureau to compile mortality statistics for Baltimore, Maryland, New York City, and the state of New Jersey. In 1890, the same year he married Lucia Talcott with whom he had six children, the Census Bureau chose his machine over two others to compile all of the data generated by the Census of 1890. Previously, this job had not been completed until it was almost time to take the next census, but the tabulating machine got the job done in less than three years and at an estimated savings to the federal government of $5 million. Hollerith's tabulating machine quickly came to the attention of census officials outside the United States, and by 1915 it had been used to tabulate census data in Austria, Canada, Cuba, France, Great Britain, Norway, Puerto Rico, and Russia.

In 1896 Hollerith formed the Tabulating Machine Company to build and sell tabulating machines and punch cards. In a unique marketing strategy, he gave his machines to customers who agreed to buy all their punch cards from his company. Within a few years, many of the country's largest manufacturers and retailers had acquired a Hollerith tabulating machine for use in accounting and business analysis. To keep up with the demand for machines and cards, in 1901 he bought a manufacturing company in Woonsocket, Rhode Island, and formed manufacturing ventures in Great Britain and Germany. Meanwhile, he continued to improve the tabulating machine, and by 1905 he had replaced the conductor's tool with a desktop punch and the electrically charged pins with brushes, added a feature that allowed the machine to add as well as count, incorporated a device for sorting punch cards, installed a plugboard that permitted the machine to be programmed more easily, and incorporated a continuous feed mechanism that permitted the rapid reading of punch cards. The tabulating machine remained the standard calculator until the 1950s, when electronic computers became practical and affordable. However, modern computers still incorporate Hollerith's idea of using electrical sensing devices to read and record data, and for a number of years computers read data from punch cards virtually indistinguishable from the ones Hollerith designed. Although Hollerith's machines have been replaced by electronic computers in most business applications, they continued to be used as voting machines in electoral contests across the country and around the world through the end of the 20th century.

In 1911 Hollerith sold his companies to Charles R. Flint, a financier and speculator who immediately merged it with three other manufacturers of scales and industrial time clocks to form the Computing-Tabulating-Recording Company (C-T-R). Hollerith was retained as general manager of the Tabulating Machine Division and served on C-T-R's board of directors. In 1924 C-T-R was renamed International Business Machines Corporation and achieved fame in the late 20th century as IBM. In 1921 he retired from C-T-R to his home in Washington, D.C., to manage his stock and real-estate investments and to devote more time to inventing. He died on November 17, 1929, in Washington, D.C.

Further Reading

Austrian, Geoffrey D. *Herman Hollerith: Forgotten Giant of Information Processing.* New York: Columbia University Press, 1982.

Noonan, Jon. *Nineteenth-Century Inventors.* New York: Facts On File, 1992.

Spencer, Donald D. *Great Men and Women of Computing.* Ormond Beach, Fla.: Camelot Pub., 1999.

Zientara, Marguerite. *The History of Computing: A Biographical Portrait of the Visionaries Who Shaped the Destiny of the Computer Industry.* Framingham, Mass.: CW Communications, 1981.

Hopper, Edna Wallace

(unknown–1959) *entrepreneur in cosmetics*

During the 1930s many women dreamed of being either perpetually youthful looking or financially independent, but few could scarcely hope to achieve both in a lifetime. One woman who did was Edna Hopper, who starred as an actress, prospered as a stockbroker, and never seemed to get old.

Little is known about Hopper's childhood or even the circumstances of her birth. What is known is that she was born Edna Wallace in San Francisco, California, and that her father's name was Walter. His occupation and her mother's name are unknown, all records of her birth having been destroyed during the earthquake of 1906. And to perpetuate her image as "the woman who never grew old," she refused to disclose her real age or any details about her early life. Most observers guessed she was between 85 and 100 years old when she died, putting the year of her birth somewhere between 1859 and 1874.

By 1891 Hopper was living in Boston, Massachusetts, where she became an actress. Her specialty was playing the soubrette, a young, flirtatious lady's maid who loves to engage in intrigue. Although she was not a particularly skilled actress, she did an exceptionally fine job of portraying herself. Standing five feet tall, weighing 85 pounds, and being full of life, Hopper playing herself was a treat most audiences enjoyed, regardless of the

Although Edna Hopper earned her fortune by selling cosmetics, she earned her fame as an actress. *(Library of Congress)*

role she was supposed to be playing. But by 1913, despite her youthful looks, she had become too old to play the soubrette any longer, and by 1920 her acting career had come to an end. Meanwhile, she had had two marriages fail; the first, in 1893 to the musical comedy star DeWolf Hopper, ended in divorce after five years, while the second, in 1908 to Albert Brown, a stockbroker turned theatrical manager, ended in a separation in 1913. Neither marriage produced any children. To make matters worse, by 1920 she had frittered away every penny she had ever earned on the stage, so that when her acting career ended she was completely broke.

Undaunted, Hopper embarked on a new career as a businesswoman. Although by now she was probably in her mid-40s, her small stature and youthful face made her seem at least 20 years younger. She decided to capitalize on her looks by developing a new line of cosmetics and beauty aids, which she supposedly concocted from her mother's personal formulas. She then became partners with Otis Glidden, a food manufacturer in Waukesha, Wisconsin, and formed the Edna Wallace Hopper Cosmetic Corporation, with Glidden as president and herself as vice president. To promote her company's products, she became a fixture on the vaudeville tour and made appearances around the country. In 1927 she took advantage of the new medium of talking motion pictures to record on film her first face-lift, which she then showed to audiences in movie houses around the country while promoting her products. In addition to showing the film clip, she lectured her audiences about how to stay young looking and full of energy: live sensibly, eat healthy, do not drink or smoke, get plenty of sleep, and exercise. She enhanced her youthfulness by wearing youthful attire and doing a bit of acrobatic dancing, and in the process made a substantial sum of money from the sale of cosmetics.

Unfortunately for Hopper, she lost most of her money during the stock market decline of the 1930s. Once again, it was time for a new career. She gave up touring and devoted her energies to managing her company and her remaining money. Instead of listening to others give her advice about how to invest, she started making her own decisions and was soon doing better than the so-called experts. The managers of the brokerage firm where she did business, L. F. Rothschild & Company of New York City, were so impressed with her skill that in 1938 they offered her a desk in their office. She eagerly accepted, thus becoming the firm's first female stockbroker and one of the first in the United States. She loved her work, and continued to sell stocks and bonds until two days before her death on December 14, 1959, in New York City.

Further Reading

Obituary, *New York Times*, December 15, 1959, p. 39.

Strang, Lewis C. *Prima Donnas and Soubrettes of the Light Opera and Musical Comedy in America.* Boston: L. C. Page and Co., 1900.

Hopper, Grace
(Grace Brewster Murray)
(1906–1992) *inventor of the computer language compiler*

In many respects, the world of computer programming is a man's world. Television shows and movies rarely depict women as computer hackers or geeks, in large part because few women pursue careers as computer programmers. This makes it all the more surprising, then, that one of the first programmers, and the one who invented the computer language compiler so that average people can communicate with computers, was a woman, Grace Hopper. Hopper also became the oldest rear admiral in the history of the U.S. Navy.

Hopper was born Grace Brewster Murray on December 9, 1906, in New York City. Her father, Walter, was an insurance broker, and her mother, Mary, was a homemaker. As a child she received a private-school education, and in 1928 she graduated from Vassar College with a B.S. in mathematics and physics. She enrolled in graduate school at Yale University and received her M.A. in mathematics in 1930; that same year she married Vincent Hopper with whom she had no children. From 1931 to 1934 she worked on her doctorate at Yale while teaching mathematics at Vassar. After receiving her Ph.D. in mathematics and mathematical physics in 1934, she taught at Vassar for seven more years. In 1941 she went to New York

Grace Hopper's computer language compiler made it easier for people to communicate with computers. *(Library of Congress)*

University's Courant Institute to do postdoctoral studies for a year, then she taught for a year at Barnard College.

In 1943, at age 37, Hopper decided to get involved in World War II by joining the U.S. Naval Reserve. She chose the navy in large part because a great-grandfather whom she had greatly admired had been a rear admiral. In 1944 she was commissioned a lieutenant junior grade, assigned to the Bureau of Ordnance, and sent to Harvard University to compute mathematical tables on the newly completed Automatic Sequence Controlled Calculator, better known as the Mark I. Developed jointly by the navy and the International Business Machines Corporation (IBM), the Mark I processed data by means of electric relay switches, which were controlled by a sequence of instructions coded on punched paper tape. Compared to modern computers, it was terribly big and very slow; it took up more than 400 square feet of floor

space and could perform only three additions per second. The user's manual, which Hopper edited, was about 500 pages long. But the Mark I could compute tables and other mathematical problems faster and more accurately than humans could, and so it was regarded as a wonder.

In 1946 Hopper was promoted to lieutenant commander. When she applied for a regular commission, she was turned down because of her age, so she went on inactive reserve status. She remained at Harvard as a research fellow and part-time mathematics professor in order to help build two larger and faster computers, the Mark II and Mark III, which were also funded by the navy. One day in 1947, she and her colleagues, while trying to figure out why the Mark II was acting temperamentally, found a dead moth stuck in a relay switch. They removed the moth, thus "debugging" the computer and, in the process, adding a new word to the American English lexicon.

When the Mark III contract ran out in 1949, Hopper went to work for the Eckert-Mauchly Computer Corporation, developers of the Electronic Numerical Integrator and Calculator (ENIAC), the world's first all-purpose, all-electronic digital computer. When Remington Rand acquired the company a year later, she was promoted to senior computer programmer and began working with the Universal Automatic Computer (UNIVAC) I, the first computer that could easily handle both numerical and alphabetical information. Sperry-Rand took over the company in 1955, and she was made director of programming for Sperry's UNIVAC Division.

All of the computers that Hopper had worked with so far had been programmable, but just barely. Basically, these computers were just big binary calculators that processed 0s and 1s very rapidly. In order to program them, it was necessary to "speak" their language, that is, 0s and 1s. For example, "1" meant "turn yourself on" while "0" meant "turn yourself off." (These codes still appear by the on-off switch of many pieces of computer hardware.) Relatively simple commands had to be given to the computer in the form of a long string of 0s and 1s, also known as binary code, and the slightest goof invalidated the command and caused the programmer to begin again. This process was time consuming and frustrating, and it was capable of driving programmers to alcoholism, insanity, or suicide.

While working on UNIVAC, Hopper decided to do something about the situation. She put together and headed a team of programmers to build a compiler, a machine that could translate short strings of numbers that could easily be written by a programmer into long strings of 0s and 1s that could easily be read by a computer. For example, the programmer might enter "789," the code to run a particular program, rather than several hundred 0s and 1s. In 1952 the team succeeded in building what became known as the A-2 compiler. The next step was to design a compiler that could translate plain English into programmer language for translation into binary code. This effort led to the development in 1957 of the B-0 compiler and of Flow-Matic, the first computer language to be written in words rather than numbers. These developments led in turn to the development by 1960 of computer programming languages that could easily be learned by nonprogrammers, such as Formula Translation (FORTRAN), preferred by the scientific community, and Common Business-Oriented Language (COBOL), preferred by the business community. Although Hopper did not develop COBOL, which was the most popular computer language between 1960 and 1980, she did develop several COBOL compilers in the early 1960s.

In 1966 Hopper retired from Sperry-Rand; she also retired from the naval reserve, having been promoted to commander in 1952. Seven months later, the navy recalled her, this time to active duty; how it was that she was too old for such duty at age 40 but not at age 60 was never sufficiently explained. Appointed director of Programming Languages and assigned to the Office of the Chief of Naval Operations in the Pentagon, she went to work standardizing the navy's computer operations. In some cases this meant writing easier-to-use languages, in other cases it meant getting navy programmers to understand the basics of data management, and in many cases it simply meant convincing high-ranking officers that computers could actually help them get their jobs done faster and more accurately. These tasks kept her busy for 20 years. Her services were deemed

to be so indispensable that every year the navy got Congress to pass a bill exempting "Amazing Grace," as she became known, from the mandatory retirement age. She was promoted to captain in 1973, and in 1983 she was promoted to commodore at a special White House ceremony hosted by President Ronald Reagan. When she finally retired from the navy in 1986, three months before her 80th birthday, she did so as a rear admiral.

Hopper then went to work for the Digital Equipment Corporation as a senior consultant in the public relations department. In this capacity she traveled the country giving four or more talks a week about computers and what they could do. In 1990 she retired to her home in Arlington, Virginia, where she died in 1992.

Further Reading

Billings, Charlene W. *Grace Hopper: Navy Admiral and Computer Pioneer.* Hillside, N.J.: Enslow Publishers, 1989.

Spencer, Donald D. *Great Men and Women of Computing.* Ormond Beach, Fla.: Camelot Pub., 1999.

Tiner, John H. *100 Scientists Who Shaped World History.* San Mateo, Calif.: Bluewood Books, 2000.

Vare, Ethlie Ann, and Greg Ptacek. *Women Inventors & Their Discoveries.* Minneapolis, Minn.: Oliver Press, 1993.

Houdry, Eugene Jules
(1892–1962) *inventor of high-octane gasoline*

One of the drawbacks to building a more efficient engine in the early age of automobiles was the nature of the gasoline of the day. Without high-octane gasoline, an engine cannot develop enough compression to generate a lot of power. This problem was solved by Eugene Houdry, who developed a chemical catalyst for refining petroleum.

Houdry was born on April 18, 1892, in Domont, France. His father, Jules, owned a steel mill, and his mother, Emilie, was a homemaker. In 1911 he received a degree in mechanical engineering from the Ecole des Arts et Metiers in Paris, then went to work in his father's mill as an engineer. Over the next ten years he developed a keen interest in automobile racing, which was heightened by visits in 1922 to the Ford Motor Company plant in Detroit, Michigan, and the Indianapolis 500. That same year he married Genevieve Quilleret with whom he had two children.

Houdry's interest in racing cars led him to experiment with improving the quality of gasoline, which at the time had an octane rating of around 30 or 40 (octane rating is the ratio of isooctane, a component of gasoline that inhibits engine knock, to heptane, a component that causes engine knock; reducing engine knock makes cars go faster). This interest brought him to the attention of the French government, which in 1925 invited him to find a way to synthesize petroleum, which France lacked, from lignite coal, of which France possessed an abundance. He succeeded later that year, but the cost of the synthesizing process cost more than imported oil, so the project was abandoned. However, it led Houdry to a new way to develop gasoline from crude oil. At the time, petroleum was refined by heating it, which caused it to "crack" into heavier and lighter grades of oil, as well as hydrocarbon gases and gasoline. Houdry, on the other hand, had extracted oil from coal by using a catalyst, and he began experimenting with a method of catalytic cracking as a way to obtain gasoline with a higher octane rating.

By 1927 Houdry left his father's mill and set up a small independent research laboratory dedicated to developing a process for cracking petroleum catalytically. That same year he developed a catalyst composed of aluminum oxide and silicon dioxide that cracked low-grade crude oil more completely than using heat, in the process producing a gasoline with a higher octane rating than had ever been produced before. After trying in vain for three years to interest French petroleum refineries in catalytic cracking, in 1930 he began working on American refineries. Almost immediately, the Vacuum Oil Company became enthusiastic about catalytic cracking, and that same year it invited him to emigrate to the United States, which he did. In 1931 he formed the Houdry Process Corporation (HPC) in Philadelphia, Pennsylvania; three years later the company had become a joint venture between Vacuum and the Sun Oil Company, with Houdry retaining a one-third

interest and serving as president and director of research. By the end of 1936, HPC was cracking petroleum catalytically at a refinery in Paulsboro, New Jersey, which turned out 2,000 barrels of high-octane gasoline per day. By 1940 14 refineries in the United States had converted to the catalytic cracking process.

During the 1940s Houdry adapted the catalytic process for two other purposes besides making high-octane gasoline. In 1942 he developed a catalyst for changing butane, a hydrocarbon gas, into butadiene, from which synthetic rubber is produced. In 1948 he became convinced that automobile exhaust was polluting the atmosphere and causing an increase in lung cancer, so the following year he resigned from HPC and formed the Oxy-Catalyst Company, which later developed the first catalytic converter for automobiles.

Houdry became an American citizen in 1942. He died on July 18, 1962, in Upper Darby, Pennsylvania.

Further Reading
"Eugene Houdry," National Inventors Hall of Fame. Available online. URL: http://www.invent.org/hall_of_fame/82.html. Downloaded on July 2, 2009.

McMurray, Emily, ed. *Notable Twentieth-Century Scientists.* Detroit, Mich.: Gale Research, 1995.

House, Royal Earl
(1814–1895) *inventor of the printing telegraph*

Most Americans are familiar with the way Morse code represents letters and numerals by a series of dots and dashes. Most of them, however, have never heard of the House system, another form of electric telegraphy that came out just a few years after SAMUEL F. B. MORSE invented Morse code. Royal House invented a method of electric telegraphy that did not have to be translated from code into English because it printed out messages in regular letters and numerals. This system was eventually abandoned in favor of Morse code, mostly because the equipment it used kept breaking down; had this not happened, Morse code might never have become an important means of communicating.

House was born on September 9, 1814, in Rockingham, Vermont. His parents, James and Hepsibah, were farmers. As an infant he moved with his family to Susquehanna, Pennsylvania. Little else is known about his life before 1840, except that at some point he invented a waterwheel that worked like a turbine and in 1839 he received a patent for a machine that sawed barrel staves, neither invention making him any money. In 1840 he moved to Buffalo, New York, to study law with a relative who was a lawyer. Shortly thereafter he became interested in electric telegraphy, which had recently been developed in the United States by Morse. In 1844 House developed a prototype of a telegraph machine that printed a message in Roman letters and numerals rather than code. After demonstrating this machine at the American Institute Fair in New York City, he attracted enough financial backing to solve the problems with the original design. In 1846, the same year he married Theresa Thomas with whom he adopted one child, he received a patent for the printing telegraph.

House's invention introduced a third system of sending messages via electric telegraphy, and the only one that did not make use of some sort of code. The Cooke and Wheatstone method, named for its two British inventors, used five needles arranged on a diamond grid to point to the intended letter or numeral, and Morse code translated letters and numerals into short and long signals called dots and dashes. House's system was radically different from both of these systems. His transmitter had a piano-type keyboard with a separate key for each of 28 characters. Behind the keyboard was a cylinder with 28 pegs arranged in helical fashion. The cylinder, which was powered by compressed air, revolved until one of the pegs was blocked by a depressed key. This sent an impulse through a series of contacts and electromagnets to a ratchet on the printing telegraph on the receiving end. The ratchet positioned a printing wheel, which struck the appropriate character on an endless paper strip through a blackened silk ribbon. The system was a bit cumbersome; while one operator worked the keyboard, another operator pumped a foot peddle to provide the necessary compressed air. Nevertheless, House's system sent messages that were much easier to read than either the Cooke-Wheatstone or the Morse systems, and sent them at a rate of about fifty words per minute, about twice as fast as could be done with Morse code.

In 1847 House sold his patent rights to a group of investors, and two years later this group constructed a telegraph line between New York City and Philadelphia, Pennsylvania, that used the printing telegraph. House served as a consultant and troubleshooter during the line's construction. He also designed the first glass insulators for telegraph lines as well as a machine for making them. In 1851 several investors from this group formed the New York and Mississippi Valley Telegraph Company and began building lines using the printing telegraph all across the country. At first, House's system competed advantageously against Morse code (Cooke-Wheatstone was used primarily in Europe), and the profits its use generated allowed the New York and Mississippi Valley to acquire several lines that used Morse code. In 1856 the New York and Mississippi Valley merged with several telegraph lines owned by EZRA CORNELL, among others, to form the Western Union Telegraph Company. Ironically, by 1860 House's printing telegraph had been abandoned in favor of Morse code, partly because its transmission range was shorter than Morse code and partly because it used machinery that was difficult to synchronize on both ends of the line and too intricate to perform reliably.

By that time, however, the printing telegraph had made wealthy people of the parties involved in its use, including House. He retired to a life of leisure in Binghamton, New York, where he continued to dabble with electricity and telegraphy. In 1885 he moved to Bridgeport, Connecticut, where he died on February 25, 1895.

Further Reading

Blondheim, Menahem. *News over the Wires: The Telegraph and the Flow of Public Information in America, 1844–1897.* Cambridge, Mass.: Harvard University Press, 1994.

Thompson, Robert L. *Wiring a Continent: The History of the Telegraph Industry in the United States, 1832–1866.* New York: Arno Press, 1972.

Howe, Elias

(1819–1867) *inventor of the lock-stitch sewing machine*

Elias Howe did not invent the sewing machine. This honor belongs to Barthelemy Thimonnier, a French inventor who in 1830 designed and built 80 single-thread machines to stitch uniforms for the French army. Unfortunately for Thimonnier, every one of his machines was destroyed by angry tailors who feared the machines would put them out of work, and he never made any more. Nor did Howe invent the first American-made sewing machine. That honor belongs to Walter Hunt of New York, who in 1834 also designed and built a single-thread sewing machine. Unfortunately for Hunt, he did not attempt to patent his machine until 1853, by which time Howe's patent rights had already been firmly established by the courts. However, Howe did invent the first lock-stitch sewing machine, which uses two threads instead of one, and he was the first to patent a sewing machine in the United States. Howe's machine revolutionized the production of garments in factories and made it much easier to make and repair garments in the home.

Howe was born on July 9, 1819, in Spencer, Massachusetts. His parents, Elias and Polly, were farmers who also operated a gristmill and a sawmill. At age 12 he went to work on a neighboring farm, but after a year he returned to work in his family's mills. At age 16 he moved to Lowell where he became an apprentice in a factory that made machines for spinning cotton. When the factory closed two years later, he worked briefly as an operator of a hemp-carding machine for a Cambridge company, then apprenticed himself to Ari Davis, a Boston watchmaker who taught Howe the machinist trade. In 1841 he married Elizabeth Ames with whom he had three children.

In the early 1840s, Howe happened to overhear one of Davis's customers remark that whoever invented a machine that could sew would make himself rich. Immediately, Howe set out to invent such a machine. As his wife was a seamstress working out of their home, he started by studying her motions as she sewed by hand, then tried to design a machine that would replicate those motions. His original design used a double-pointed needle

with a hole in the middle of the shank, which the machine drove entirely through the material on each pass, but this design did not work well. In 1844 he had a dream in which he was surrounded by African warriors who were carrying spears with eye-shaped holes in the tips of the spears. This dream gave him the idea to use an eye-pointed needle, which led him to the realization that the machine did not have to sew the way humans do. He then decided to curve the needle and drive only its eye-pointed tip through the material, making its thread interlock with a second thread carried by a shuttle running back and forth on a track beneath the garment being stitched. In 1845 he used this design to sew together two suits of men's clothes, and the following year he received the first American patent for a sewing machine.

Meanwhile, Howe had left Davis's company in 1844 to develop and sell his sewing machine. Thinking that garment manufacturers would be delighted to buy his machine, he was disappointed with the reception he received when he called on various factories in Boston. One after the other turned him down, claiming that buying enough sewing machines for a whole factory would cost far more than could be recovered from their use, and that the machines might lead to labor unrest and even cause seamstresses to walk off the job. In 1846 Howe's brother Amasa persuaded Howe to let him take a sewing machine to England, where manufacturers might be more interested in it. In fact, the sewing machine was received in England in much the same way it had been in the United States. After many rebuffs, Amasa Howe was able to sell the machine and the right to patent it in England for $1,250 to William Thomas, owner of a corset factory in London, who agreed to pay Howe a royalty on each sewing machine sold in England. Thomas also hired Howe to modify the sewing machine so that it could sew corsets and advanced him the money to come to London. But once Howe had designed a corset-sewing machine Thomas fired him, and once sewing machines began to sell in England, Thomas refused to pay him royalties. In 1849 Howe was completely out of money, and he had to pawn some of his belongings to pay his way to New York City, where he found a job in a machine shop.

Shortly after his return to the United States, Howe was shocked to discover that several Boston garment manufacturers had reconsidered their objections to the sewing machine and were now using them in violation of his patent rights. By 1850 he had raised enough money to start manufacturing sewing machines on his own in New York City and to challenge in court the several infringements of his patent. That same year he sued ISAAC SINGER, the biggest seller of sewing machines, who had made several substantial improvements in Howe's original design. The biggest difference was that Howe's machine was powered by a hand crank, whereas Singer's machine was powered by a foot-operated treadle, thus freeing up both of the operator's hands to guide the material. In 1854 the court ruled in Howe's favor, and Singer was ordered to pay Howe $15,000 in royalties for machines he had sold prior to the decision. All other suits filed by Howe were also decided in his favor, and the result was that all American sewing machine manufacturers had to pay him a royalty of $25 for each machine they sold until 1867, when his patent expired. These royalties amounted to about $4,000 per week for the rest of his life, thus making him the wealthy man he had set out to become by inventing the sewing machine. In 1863 he added further to his fortune by founding the Howe Machine Company in Bridgeport, Connecticut, which built and sold sewing machines. He died on October 3, 1867, in Brooklyn, New York.

Further Reading

Hunkin, Tim, et al. *The Secret Life of the Sewing Machine.* Morris Plains, N.J.: Lucerne Media, 1988, videorecording.

Salamon, N. *The History of the Sewing Machine, From the Year 1750, With a Biography of Elias Howe.* Pietermaritzburg, South Africa: University of Natal, 1960.

Hughes, Howard Robard, Sr.
(1869–1924), and
Howard Robard Hughes, Jr. (1905–1976)
inventors of tools and airplanes

Two of the most fascinating entrepreneurs in American history are Howard Hughes, father and son. Hughes Senior made a modest fortune by inventing and selling a revolutionary drill bit, while Hughes Junior expanded that fortune into one of the world's largest. Despite their close blood relationship, the two men could hardly have been more different. The father was a gregarious, outgoing socialite, while the son became one of the world's most famous recluses. Senior was happiest when he was drilling deep in the ground, while Junior preferred to fly high in the sky. And yet, in some ways, the two were remarkably similar. Both were gamblers and risk takers, albeit in their own ways, and neither placed a high premium on family. The failure of either to produce a large family meant that their billions would ultimately be left in the hands of total strangers, something that most wealthy people go to great lengths to avoid.

Hughes Senior was born on September 9, 1869, in Lancaster, Missouri. His father, Felix, was a lawyer, and his mother, Jean, was a homemaker. At age 11 he moved with his family to Keokuk, Iowa. As a boy, he showed a remarkable ability for two things: taking things apart and putting them back together; and getting into trouble, a trait that two military schools could not break. In 1893, at age 24, he enrolled in Harvard University, but dropped out before completing his sophomore year. He studied law briefly at the University of Iowa, then passed the Iowa bar examination and went to work at his father's law firm. By 1897 he had grown tired of practicing law, and after working briefly as a telegraph operator, he went to Colorado to prospect for silver.

Hughes Senior failed to strike it rich in Colorado, or in Indian Territory (present-day Oklahoma) in search of zinc, or in Missouri in search of lead. So when oil was discovered near Beaumont, Texas, in 1901, he went there hoping to cash in on the petroleum bonanza. He had some success drilling in the Spindletop and Sour Lake fields, but when saltwater got into his wells in the Batson field, it almost ruined him. At one point he convinced Walter Sharp, a tool supplier and future partner, to let him have the equipment he needed by giving Sharp a diamond stud as collateral. Had it not been for substantial loans from his father, Hughes Senior most likely would have failed utterly. In 1904 he married Allene Gano, a Dallas debutante; their only child was Hughes Junior, who was born on December 24, 1905, in Houston, Texas.

Between 1905 and 1907, Hughes Senior drilled for oil in the vicinities of Oil City and Shreveport, Louisiana, without much success. In 1907 he acquired some petroleum leases in the Goose Creek field in Texas, but he was prevented from making a big strike when the standard drill bits he was using proved unable to penetrate a granite shelf that protected the oil. Undaunted, he designed a new type of bit that replaced the standard cutting edge with 166 rolling cutters. Rather than scrape off layers of rock at a tedious pace, the rollerbit, as he called it, ground the rock into dust at a rate of more than one foot per hour, at the time a phenomenally rapid pace. After receiving a patent in 1909, Hughes Senior and Walter Sharp formed the Sharp-Hughes Tool Company, opened a 20 x 40-foot shop in Houston, and began

A dapper Howard Hughes, Jr., poses in front of his airplane. *(Library of Congress)*

manufacturing rollerbits. The company grossed a half million dollars in sales its first year in business, and the partners decided that from then on they could make more money by leasing rollerbits rather than selling them. By 1918 Hughes Senior had acquired total ownership of the firm, which he renamed the Hughes Tool Company. The following year it was estimated that 75 percent of the world's oil wells were being drilled with rollerbits, partly because Hughes Senior continued to refine and improve them (he held 25 patents related to the rollerbit), and partly because he had given up searching for oil to become a tireless salesman of his revolutionary invention.

Unfortunately, Hughes Senior's success seems to have had a deleterious effect on Hughes Junior's upbringing. The young boy rarely saw his father, who was usually either away on sales trips or with his mother on visits to Los Angeles, California, where Hughes Senior's brother Rupert worked for a Hollywood movie studio. At age 14, Hughes Junior was sent to boarding school in Massachusetts for a year, after which he attended a boarding school in California. In 1922 his mother died from complications related to surgery, and in 1924 his father died of a heart attack, leaving him an orphan at age 18. No doubt as a result of these various experiences, he grew up to be an eccentric loner who feared death and was scared to death of germs. Fortunately, his father's death also left him a wealthy man, because Hughes Junior inherited 75 percent of Hughes Tool Company, at the time a multimillion-dollar operation.

Once his father's will was settled, Hughes Junior dropped out of Rice Institute and set out to obtain control of the rest of Hughes Tool. This resolution led to a bitterly personal squabble with his Uncle Rupert and his father's parents, who owned the other 25 percent. The squabble permanently soured Hughes Junior's relations with the only people to whom he might have become attached. He then hired capable managers to run Hughes Tool, and in 1925 he married Ella Rice, a Houston debutante, and moved to Hollywood to become a film producer.

Over the next eight years Hughes Junior produced 11 movies. The most remarkable was *Hell's Angels*, a 1930 film about aviation during World

War I. The film is noteworthy for four reasons: It cost $4 million to make, an astronomical sum for those days; in the process of shooting it, he acquired hundreds of hours of film, far more than could ever possibly be used in the final cut; the movie was so well received and played in theaters for so long that it actually recouped its production costs; and it provided the name for what would become the nation's most notorious motorcycle gang. Otherwise, Hughes Junior's films were unremarkable, although his total involvement in their production did lead to the breakup of his marriage in the 1930s. Afterward, he had a long string of brief romances with young actresses, including Billie Dove, Faith Domergue, and Jean Peters. He made three more movies between 1943 and 1948, and in 1948 he bought RKO Studios on a whim. However, by this point he no longer had any interest in making movies, so he sold RKO in 1953 for $25 million.

Although Hughes Junior rarely listened to advice from anyone, in 1933 he heeded the advice of the managers of Hughes Tool and got out of the movie business, at least temporarily. Instead, he turned his attention to aviation, something that had been a passion of his since his father had taken him on a ride in a seaplane. In 1932 he founded the Hughes Aircraft Company in Glendale, California. A division of Hughes Tool, the company was profitable almost from the beginning. Its sales skyrocketed during World War II when it produced armaments and radio equipment for the air forces of the United States and its allies. After the war, Hughes Aircraft focused on the production of advanced radar systems and radar-guided missiles. In the 1960s and 1970s, the company became a pioneer in the development of imaging, detection, and signal processing systems for satellites. Combined with the profits from the rest of Hughes Tool, the money Hughes Junior made from Hughes Aircraft made him one of the wealthiest men in the country.

Hughes Aircraft also built a number of experimental aircraft, which Hughes Junior himself would often fly as the test pilot. He was an accomplished aviator, having set a transcontinental speed record in 1936 and an around-the-world record in 1938. In 1946 he almost died when a jet plane

he was piloting, the XF-11, crashed and burned in Beverly Hills. Most observers thought he would never walk again, much less fly, but the following year he successfully flew a new and improved version of the XF-11. Perhaps his most famous flight was made in 1947, when he flew the *Spruce Goose,* a monstrous, eight-engine seaplane that could carry 750 people, on its only flight, a one-mile excursion over Long Beach Harbor with no one but himself and a copilot on board.

Hughes Junior's love of aviation led him in 1939 to buy stock in Transcontinental & Western Air Inc., a small air carrier that flew regularly between Newark, New Jersey, and Los Angeles. Renamed Trans World Airlines (TWA) in 1950, it offered one of the world's first intercontinental air services, connecting New York City with Paris, France, and from there with the rest of Europe, Africa, and Asia. Over time, Hughes Junior acquired 78 percent of TWA's stock, which he sold in 1966 for $566 million after refusing to appear in court to answer charges of antitrust activity.

Despite his millions, Hughes Junior seems to have led a tortured personal life. The crash of the XF-11 in 1946 left him in near-constant pain for the next 30 years and caused him to become addicted to codeine. His marriage to Jean Peters in 1957 was followed a year later by a nervous breakdown, after which they lived apart and were divorced in 1971. By 1967 his ill health and childhood fears had combined to make him a hypochondriac; that same year, he bought the Desert Inn resort hotel in Las Vegas, Nevada, where he lived in semi-isolation for three years. During an income tax dispute with the Internal Revenue Service, he left the country in 1970 and spent his remaining years living in almost total isolation in fancy hotels in the Bahamas, Nicaragua, Canada, England, and Mexico. He managed his business affairs through a handful of trusted aides, and he often worked for days without sleeping or eating, keeping himself going by taking an assortment of vitamins and prescription drugs. As a result, he became emaciated and deranged, refusing medical treatment until it was too late. He died in an airplane on April 5, 1976, somewhere between Acapulco, Mexico, and Houston, where his aides were taking him to be hospitalized. His estate was estimated to be worth about $2 billion; having no heirs or close relatives, he left most of it to the Howard Hughes Medical Institute.

Further Reading

Bartlett, Donald L., and James B. Steele. *Empire: The Life, Legend and Madness of Howard Hughes.* New York: Norton, 1979.

Brown, Peter Harry, and Pat H. Broeske. *Howard Hughes: The Untold Story.* New York: Signet, 1997.

Huizenga, Harry Wayne

(1939–   ) *entrepreneur in video rental*

One of the largest video rental companies in the world, and one of the most profitable entertainment companies in the United States, is Blockbuster Video. Although Wayne Huizenga did not found Blockbuster, he turned it into the multibillion-dollar business that it became. Along the way, he also made a fortune collecting garbage and spent a fortune on professional sports teams.

Huizenga was born Harry Wayne Huizenga on December 29, 1939, in Evergreen Park, Illinois. His father, Gerrit, was a cabinetmaker and builder, and his mother, Jean, was a homemaker. At age 13 he moved with his family to Fort Lauderdale, Florida, where his father tried but failed to make a fortune speculating in real estate. After graduating from high school, he went to work as a bulldozer operator. In 1957 he enrolled at Calvin College in Grand Rapids, Michigan, but dropped out after three semesters. Following a brief stint in the U.S. Army, he returned to Fort Lauderdale, and took a job driving a garbage truck in nearby Pompano Beach. In 1960 he married Joyce VanderWagon with whom he had two children. By 1962 he had scraped up enough money to buy his own truck and some household accounts in Broward County. At first, his business, Southern Sanitation Service, was a one-man operation; after picking up his customers' trash in the morning, he would solicit new business from their neighbors during the afternoon. Six years later, he owned 20 trucks, and his employees collected garbage throughout the extended suburbs of Miami.

In 1968, Huizenga became partners with his cousin Dean L. Buntrock, who operated a refuse hauling business in Chicago, Illinois, that had been started by Huizenga's grandfather. The partners called their new business Waste Management, Inc., and they set out to expand their company across the country. For the next 16 years, Huizenga operated out of the company's headquarters in Oak Brook, Illinois, while living in Fort Lauderdale, and built Waste Management into the largest company of its kind in the world. As vice chairman of the board, president, and chief executive officer, he grew the company in three ways. First, he won a number of contracts to dispose of toxic and hazardous waste that other companies shied away from. Second, in 1972, the same year he married Marti Goldsby (he had divorced his first wife in 1966), he and Buntrock took the company public. Within a year, they had raised enough money to buy out 90 small competitors, and they used the profits from these companies to buy more competitors. Third, he engaged in sharp business practices that bordered on being illegal. In 1976, following a lawsuit by the U.S. Securities and Exchange Commission alleging that Waste Management had bribed a number of local politicians in order to obtain trash-hauling contracts, Huizenga signed a consent decree in which he promised that his company would no longer engage in such improprieties. Meanwhile, Waste Management continued to pay millions of dollars in fines for such violations as harassing competitors, intimidating customers, and illegally dumping and storing hazardous materials. By 1984 the company was taking in more than $1 billion each year.

Despite his success, Huizenga had become bored with the trash business. In 1984 he resigned from his executive positions with Waste Management, although he retained full ownership of his shares, and began buying small businesses in Fort Lauderdale. Within two years he had acquired more than 100 service businesses as well as a number of commercial properties such as hotels, office buildings, shopping centers, and warehouses. Organized as Huizenga Holdings, by the end of 1986 the annual sales of the various units was about $100 million.

In 1987 John J. Melk, an executive with Waste Management who had worked for Huizenga, convinced his former boss to investigate a small company called Blockbuster Video. The brainchild of David P. Cook, Blockbuster operated a chain of 19 video rental stores in the Dallas, Texas, area. Unlike the majority of video rental outlets, each Blockbuster store stocked thousands of titles that were suitable for family viewing. In addition, the stores were clean and brightly lit, and they were staffed with people who enjoyed and could speak knowledgeably about the movies they stocked. Within weeks, Huizenga, Melk, and Donald F. Flynn, another Waste Management executive, exchanged $18 million for a one-third share of the company. By the end of 1987, Cook had stepped down as Blockbuster's chairman, and Huizenga took his place at the company's helm. As he had at Waste Management, he embarked on an aggressive expansion program with the intention of making the company the biggest one of its kind in the country. Huizenga was a great admirer of RAY KROC, the marketing genius who had made McDonald's a household word, and he used Kroc's model of expansion via franchising to build Blockbuster. By 1994 the company had almost 4,000 outlets, most operated by franchisees, and its annual sales exceeded $2 billion. Meanwhile, between 1990 and 1994 Huizenga had purchased Joe Robbie Stadium in Miami, the Miami Dolphins of the National Football League, the Florida Marlins of baseball's National League, and the Florida Panthers of the National Hockey League, thus making him the first person in the history of American professional sports to own franchises in three different sports.

In 1994 Huizenga sold Blockbuster to Viacom, a major entertainment corporation, for $8.4 billion, in the process becoming vice chairman of Viacom's board of directors while staying on as Blockbuster's chairman. Within a year, however, he had resigned both positions to become chief stockholder, chairman of the board, and chief executive officer of Republic Waste Industries, which operated nine landfills in six states. He also founded AutoNation USA, a nationwide chain of automobile dealers; Extended Stay America, a nationwide lodging chain that caters to long-term guests; and Boca Resorts, a vacation getaway in south Florida. By 1999 these ventures had been consolidated under Republic Industries, with Huizenga as chairman of

the board. In 2001, his net worth was estimated at more than $1 billion.

In recent years, Huizenga has been an active philanthropist and sports team owner, though he sold all of most of his stake in the Marlins, Panthers, and Dolphins by 2009. He has been a major contributor to Nova Southeastern University in Fort Lauderdale, Florida, and the business school there is named the H. Wayne Huizenga School of Business and Entrepreneurship. Huizenga—who has garnered several business awards including the accounting firm Ernst & Young's 2005 World Entrepreneur of the Year—has spent much of his increased leisure time aboard his luxury yacht, *The Floridian,* which he purchased from golf star Greg Norman for $77 million in 2004.

Further Reading

DeGeorge, Gail. *The Making of a Blockbuster: How Wayne Huizenga Built a Sports and Entertainment Empire from Trash, Grit, and Videotape.* New York: John Wiley & Sons, 1996.
"H. Wayne Huizenga, 1992," Horatio Alger Association of Distinguished Americans: Members. Available online. URL: http://www.horatioalger.com/member_info.cfm?memberid=hui92.htm. Downloaded on July 2, 2009.

Hunt, H. L.
(Haroldson Lafayette Hunt, Jr.)
(1889–1974) *entrepreneur in petroleum*

Oilmen seem to be naturally flamboyant and reckless, no doubt because of the risks they must take to find new reserves of petroleum. Even so, H. L. Hunt seems to have been one of the most colorful oilmen of all time. Reckoned at one point to be the richest person in the United States, Hunt's larger-than-life existence inspired a 1980s hit television series, the prime-time soap opera *Dynasty.*

Hunt was born Haroldson Lafayette Hunt, Jr., on February 17, 1889, in Ramsey, Illinois. His parents, H. L. and Ella Rose, were farmers. At age 16 he went west in search of his future, working as a laborer as he traveled about. He returned home around 1910 and briefly attended Valparaiso University before heading off to Arkansas in 1911 with

$50 of borrowed money to become a cotton farmer. Before long he discovered that growing cotton was not nearly as lucrative an endeavor as land speculation, and he began buying and selling farmland. He was particularly adept at buying a farm and then selling it immediately for more than he had paid for it, thus making money without actually having spent any.

In 1921 Hunt began buying and selling oil leases in Arkansas, and shortly thereafter he developed a business relationship with Columbus "Dad" Joiner, the legendary Texas wildcatter. In 1930 Joiner struck oil on 4,000 acres he had leased in East Texas. Acting on a hunch that Joiner had made a major find, Hunt bought him out for $30,000 down and up to $1 million in royalties from the sale of oil. By 1936, when he formed the Hunt Oil Company to manage his various petroleum holdings, Hunt had become the largest independent oil producer in the East Texas oil field, which was eventually determined to be one of the richest petroleum reservoirs in the world. In 1938 he moved to Dallas, Texas, and took up residence in an oversized replica of Mount Vernon, George Washington's home.

By the late 1930s, over-drilling and the Great Depression combined to depress domestic oil prices, so Hunt began diversifying his holdings. He invested some of his profits from oil in farms and ranches, and he eventually owned more than 1 million acres of prime agricultural land in Texas, Oklahoma, and Montana. In time he formed the HLH Products Company, a subsidiary of Hunt Oil, to market the produce raised on his land, which included just about everything from sugar to health foods. He also began exploring for petroleum overseas, in which he was ably assisted by three of his sons, Nelson Bunker, Herbert, and Lamar. Although Hunt Oil failed to gain concessions in Kuwait, or to find oil in Pakistan after gaining concessions there, the company acquired substantial oil and natural gas holdings in Canada, and in the 1960s it profited tremendously from a major oil strike in Libya. Meanwhile, Hunt's business acumen and luck had made him incredibly wealthy; in 1948 his fortune was estimated to be $600 million, and feature stories in two magazines identified him as the richest person in the United States. At the time of his death, his fortune was estimated at between $2 billion and $3 billion, a figure that reportedly grew by about $1 million each week.

Part of Hunt's success stemmed from his vision of himself as *sui generis*, a unique individual for whom the normal rules and regulations did not always apply. For example, he divided his time as husband and father among as many as three different families at the same time. In 1914 he married Lyda Bunker with whom he had seven children. During the 1920s he established a relationship which lasted at least into the late 1930s, and which some sources describe as bigamous, with Frania Tye, who bore him four more children. After Lyda Hunt died in 1953, two years later he married Ruth Ray; on the day of their wedding, they had already had four children together. In addition, Hunt was a staunch conservative who was vehemently opposed to any and all forms of government regulation of business. In 1951 he founded Facts Forum, which he replaced in 1958 with the Life Line Foundation, to produce a newsletter and radio and television programs in support of arch-conservative views such as those espoused by Senator Joseph McCarthy and the John Birch Society. In 1960 Hunt wrote a utopian novel, *Alpaca*, about a government that is run by the wealthy in the (supposedly) best interests of all citizens. In 1963 he emerged as a vocal opponent of the liberal policies of President John F. Kennedy. He published a derogatory and inflammatory advertisement against Kennedy in a Dallas newspaper on the morning that the president was assassinated. Although it was later suspected that Hunt had played a role in Kennedy's death, nothing was ever proven. H. L. Hunt died on November 29, 1974, in Dallas.

A certain portion of Hunt's sense that he was unique apparently rubbed off on his sons Nelson and Herbert. In mid-1979, a little less than five years after their father's death, the two brothers attempted to corner the world silver market. They managed to gain control of about half the world's supply, in the process bidding up the price of an ounce of silver from between $10 to $15 in mid-1979 to $53 in early 1980. Then the silver market collapsed, causing a minor panic on Wall Street in which one brokerage firm alone, Bache, Halsey, Stuart, Shields, Incorporated, may have lost as much as $50 million. The brothers themselves lost almost $400 million in the fiasco, including a $130 million fine imposed by a federal jury as a result of an investigation by the U.S. Commodity Futures Trading Commission.

Further Reading

Brands, H. W. *Masters of Enterprise: Giants of American Business from John Jacob Astor and J. P. Morgan to Bill Gates and Oprah Winfrey.* New York: Free Press, 1999.

Burst, Ardis. *The Three Families of H. L. Hunt.* New York: Weidenfeld & Nicolson, 1988.

Hill, Margaret H. et al. *H. L. and Lyda.* Little Rock, Ark.: August House Pub., 1994.

Hurt, Harry III. *Texas Rich: The Hunt Dynasty from the Early Oil Days through the Silver Crash.* New York: W. W. Norton, 1982.

Hunt, John Wesley

(1773–1849) *entrepreneur in mercantile activity*

Before the Civil War, Kentucky became known for its production of four commodities: corn liquor, loose-leaf tobacco, Thoroughbred racehorses, and hemp. Although he was not the first to distill, grow, breed, or market any of these things in Kentucky, John Hunt was one of the first to become involved in all four endeavors. In the process, he came to be regarded as the first American millionaire to live west of the Allegheny Mountains.

Hunt was born in August 1773 in Trenton, New Jersey. His parents, Abraham and Theodosia, owned a general store, and his father also bred racehorses and milled flour. By the time Hunt was 19 years old, he had been well trained in all three endeavors. In 1792 he moved to Richmond, Virginia, where he became partners with Harry Heth in a general store. He left after two years for Norfolk, where he hoped to take advantage of the war that had just broken out between England and France. Unfortunately, he lost most of his money instead, as the result of two unlucky investments. He put half of his money into a merchant ship that traded between Norfolk and the French West Indies, but the ship and its cargo were seized by the British on its first voyage. He put the other half of

his money into a French privateer that was being outfitted in Norfolk, but the U.S. government, not wanting to be accused by the British of violating its neutrality, seized the vessel before it could leave port.

In 1795 Hunt and his cousin Abijah Hunt became partners in a general store in Lexington, Kentucky. Three years earlier, Lexington had become the state capital of Kentucky. By 1800 it was the most populous and sophisticated city in the United States west of the Alleghenies, and in time it would become known as "the Athens of the West." Taking advantage of family contacts in Philadelphia, Pennsylvania, the partners acquired manufactured goods from back East and bartered them for whiskey, tobacco, pork, and salt, which they then sold to various U.S. Army outposts along the Ohio River as well as to merchants in Natchez and New Orleans, at the time Spanish possessions. Business was so good that by 1797, the year he married Catherine Grosh with whom he had 12 children, the partners had opened three more stores in Kentucky.

Horse racing had long been a popular pastime in Lexington, so popular that when the town fathers banned it from the town common in 1787, a racecourse was built almost immediately on the outskirts of town. By 1801 the breeding of racehorses was a growing industry in the Kentucky Bluegrass region, of which Lexington was the center. That same year Hunt sold his half of the mercantile business to become a full-time horse breeder. He is credited with improving local bloodlines by importing English Thoroughbreds, especially Royalist, a horse bred by King George IV while he was the prince of Wales. In large part because of Hunt's early efforts, the Kentucky Bluegrass region became the nation's top area for breeding and racing Thoroughbreds.

In 1803 Hunt got involved in another industry in which Kentucky became a national leader, hemp manufacturing. Hemp was the best source of natural fiber for making netting and rope with which to bag and bale cotton, and as the production of cotton rose throughout the South, the demand for hemp products rose with it. Hemp thrived in the Bluegrass region's sandy loam, and by 1800 Lexington was becoming the center for its growth and manufacture. Hunt opened his hemp factory in 1803, and by 1810 he had also established himself as a commissioned agent for other manufacturers' hemp products.

In 1816 Hunt entered the banking business when he was appointed by President James Madison as a commissioner of the Bank of the United State's Lexington branch. Two years later this involvement led him to cofound and serve as president of the Farmers and Merchants Bank of Lexington. At that time, private banks could issue their own bank notes, which circulated exactly like money because they were supposedly backed up by a certain amount of specie (gold and silver) on deposit with the bank; usually these notes were put into circulation in the form of loans given to farmers and speculators with which to buy land. As bank president, Hunt insisted that the dollar value of the notes that Farmers and Merchants had in circulation not exceed the amount of specie in its vaults, a policy that was highly unusual for banks of the day. Consequently, when the panic of 1819 led many private banks to declare bankruptcy because their mortgagees were unable to repay their loans and their creditors insisted on cashing in their bank notes, Farmers and Merchants continued to do business as usual, thus gaining a reputation as the soundest bank in Lexington. This reputation eventually led to Hunt's appointment as director of the Kentucky Insurance Company and the Lexington Fire, Life and Marine Insurance Company.

Hunt died on August 21, 1849, in Lexington. At the time of his death, his estate was appraised at almost $900,000. Given the practice of the day to appraise estates conservatively, it may well have been worth more than $1 million. Although he was probably not the first millionaire to live west of the Alleghenies (fur traders in St. Louis and sugar planters in Louisiana must surely have accomplished this feat before him), in his day he was the wealthiest resident of Kentucky.

Further Reading

"Hunt-Morgan House," National Park Service. Available online. URL: http://www.nps.gov/history/Nr/travel/lexington/hun.htm. Downloaded on July 2, 2009.

Ramage, James A. *John Wesley Hunt: Pioneer Merchant, Manufacturer and Financier.* Lexington: University Press of Kentucky, 1974.

Hyatt, John Wesley
(1837–1920) *inventor of celluloid*

John Hyatt did not invent the first modern plastic; that honor goes to LEO HENDRIK BAEKELAND, whose Bakelite was the first plastic that did not lose its shape when heated. However, Hyatt did invent the first synthetic plastic material, celluloid. This tough, moldable, but flammable material was used to make a number of items in the late 19th and early 20th centuries that today are made from the more heat-resistant modern plastics, and it also helped inspire Baekeland to invent Bakelite. Oddly enough, Hyatt made his breakthrough discovery while searching for a cheap material from which to make billiard balls.

Hyatt was born on November 28, 1837, in Starkey, New York. His father, John, was a blacksmith, and his mother, Anne, was a homemaker. At age 16 he moved to Illinois where he completed his printer's apprenticeship. Sometime during the mid-1860s he relocated to Albany, New York, to work as a printer. Shortly after settling in Albany, he learned that a billiard supply dealer in New York City was offering $10,000 to the first person to invent a suitable substitute for ivory, from which billiard balls were made. In an effort to win the reward, he created a compound from the dust of bone, wood, and ivory, which he held together by means of shellac. Although this compound did not compress into the hard, smooth material required to make a billiard ball, it did prove to be moldable, and he soon learned how to make a variety of other objects by forming and pressing the compound in machines. By 1869, the year he married Anna Taft with whom he had two children, he and his two brothers had formed the Embossing Company of Albany for purposes of manufacturing items from Hyatt's compound.

Meanwhile, Hyatt continued to look for a substitute for ivory. He began experimenting with collodion, a yellow, viscous solution of cellulose, or plant fiber, and nitric acid. At the time collodion was used to make photographic film and bandages for wounds by thinning and drying it into a transparent film, but he hoped to be able to pack it tightly into a hard ball. At first he succeeded only in producing a shapeless, brittle mass, but then he became acquainted with the experiments of Alexander Parkes, a British chemist and inventor. In 1855 Parkes had invented Parkesine, a plasticlike material made from chloroform and castor oil, and had attempted to make a similar material by dissolving collodion in camphor. In 1869 Hyatt built on this latter experiment by mixing equal amounts of collodion and camphor, adding some alcohol, heating and pressurizing the mixture, then allowing it to harden at room temperature and pressure. The result was what Hyatt called celluloid, a plasticlike substance that could be molded into solid shapes with smooth surfaces that could be colored.

Although celluloid proved to be a tough material with great tensile strength and good resistance to water, oil, and diluted acids, it made lousy billiard balls. It did, however, prove useful as a material for the manufacture of a number of other items. In 1871, the year after he received a patent for celluloid, Hyatt and his brother Isaiah formed the Celluloid Manufacturing Company in Albany. The following year the Hyatts brought in new partners, including Marshall Lefferts to serve as president, and moved the company into a new factory in Newark, New Jersey, where they began turning out combs, brushes, and knife handles, as well as collars and cuffs for shirts. Hyatt designed and built a number of different machines, especially presses, for shaping and molding various items, and by 1891 he had received 60 patents for such inventions.

Meanwhile, Hyatt was also devoting some attention to solving other problems. In the 1870s he designed a filter for purifying moving water, as well as several machines for refining sugar. In this latter endeavor he encountered a problem involving the heavy rollers that were used to crush sugarcane. The bearings that supported them were constantly heating up and then locking up due to friction. Hyatt solved the problem by replacing the solid-cylinder rollers in the bearings with helical-shaped rollers made from flat spring steel. These rollers proved to be more flexible and to last longer under heavy usage. After receiving two patents for the flexible roller bearing, in 1892 he formed the Hyatt Roller-Bearing Company in Harrison, New Jersey, with himself as general manager, and began manufacturing flexible roller bearings for use in heavy equipment. After seven years, however, the flexible roller bearing had yet to catch on, so Hyatt turned the management of the company over to Alfred P. Sloan. Sloan did such a good job of selling bearings to the nascent automotive industry that the General Motors Corporation later bought Hyatt Roller-Bearing; Sloan became a vice president, and in 1923 president and chief executive officer of General Motors.

After 1899 Hyatt continued to invent machinery, receiving patents for devices for sewing machine belting and straightening steel shafts. And in 1908 he finally got into the manufacture of billiard balls. At first, he tried to make them by mixing ground ivory with celluloid, but when Baekeland invented Bakelite in 1909, Hyatt enthusiastically switched to the newer material. He remained an active inventor and manufacturer almost until his death on May 10, 1920, at his home in Short Hills, New Jersey.

Further Reading

Friedel, Robert. *Pioneer Plastic: The Making and Selling of Celluloid.* Madison: University of Wisconsin Press, 1983.

"The History of Plastics," American Chemistry. Available online. URL: http://www.americanchemistry.com/s-plastics/doc.asp?CID=1102&DID=4665. Downloaded on July 2, 2009.

I

Icahn, Carl Celian

(1936–) *entrepreneur in corporate acquisitions*

Nothing infuriates Carl Icahn more than being called a corporate raider. His proficiency at risk arbitrage has made him the sworn enemy of many a board chairman, while making him the hero of many a stockholder who benefitted from Icahn's "raid" on a given company. He prefers to see himself as an activist who works to protect the financial interests of stockholders against the self-serving practices of corporate managers. Whichever he is, Icahn has used his skill at risk arbitrage to become a billionaire several times over.

Icahn was born Carl Celian Icahn on February 16, 1936, in New York City. His father, Michael, was a lawyer, and his mother, Bella, was a schoolteacher. In 1957 he received a B.A. in philosophy from Princeton University. He then enrolled in New York University's School of Medicine but dropped out after two years and joined the U.S. Army. While in the service he became a proficient poker player, and when he was discharged in 1961 he had a grubstake of $4,000 in his pocket. An uncle got him a job as an apprentice broker with Dreyfus and Company, where in one year he turned his own grubstake into $50,000. However, he lost it all the next year; the experience made him a more cautious trader and convinced him that he needed to specialize in something if he was going to be a successful broker. Consequently,

he decided to become a trader in stock options, the right to buy stock in a specific corporation at a specific price within a stated period. By 1963 he was good enough at options trading to become an options manager, first with Tessel, Patrick and Company, and the following year with Gruntal and Company where he helped start the options department. In 1968 he borrowed $400,000 from another uncle, used it to buy a seat on the New York Stock Exchange, and went into business as Icahn and Company. At first the company was just another Wall Street brokerage firm, but in the early 1970s it began focusing on Icahn's specialty, options trading.

In 1978 Icahn discovered that the stock of the Tappan Company, a manufacturer of kitchen appliances, was selling at $8 per share while its book value, the value of the company's assets, was $20 per share, thus making it a likely candidate for a takeover. When this happened, the price of Tappan's stock was sure to rise much closer to its book value. Within months, Icahn had purchased almost 300,000 shares of Tappan and was waiting for the takeover to occur. But after several months passed and no takeover was in sight, he instigated one. He won election to the company's board of directors by promising stockholders that he would find a buyer who would pay close to book value for their stock. Later that year AB Electrolux, a Swedish company, offered $18 per share for Tappan. At this point Icahn sold all of his shares at a profit of almost $3 million.

The Tappan affair convinced Icahn that he had found a lucrative way to make money. Today it is called risk arbitrage, whereby a group of investors buys millions of shares of a particular undervalued stock, waits for (or instigates) a takeover, then sells the stock at a considerable profit. Over the next six years, Icahn became the undisputed master of risk arbitrage. Between 1978 and 1984 he made approximately $125 million by putting "into play" such major corporations as Hammermill Paper, Marshall Field, American Can, and Phillips Petroleum. In the process, he discovered that he could make money even by losing a takeover bid. The target company's management would often borrow millions of dollars so it could buy Icahn's stock at a higher price than he had paid, thereby gaining voting control of his shares and avoiding a takeover. This practice became known as "greenmail," and Icahn and others who emulated him were roundly criticized in the press and the halls of Congress for disrupting the profitable activities of soundly managed companies. For his part, Icahn insisted that he was doing the stockholding public a favor by forcing up the value of their shares and therefore enriching them, even if the stockholder who was enriched the most was himself.

In 1984 Icahn broadened his horizons by acquiring a company, ACF Industries, after putting it into play. Under Icahn's management, the railcar manufacturer divested itself of several losing divisions, eliminated a number of top management positions, and consolidated its operations. The result was a dramatic increase in profits and share value. In late 1985 he acquired majority control of Trans World Airlines (TWA), which was saddled with a number of problems and had lost $140 million in 1985 alone. Icahn took over as chairman of the board in 1986, and by the end of the year TWA was making money again. But by 1993 TWA had run into trouble once again, and he was forced to resign the chairmanship. Two years later, when TWA declared bankruptcy, he arranged an unusual sort of options deal; he forgave a $190 million personal loan he had made to TWA in exchange for the option to purchase TWA tickets at about half price through 2003. Over the next several years, Icahn purchased hundreds of millions of dollars' worth of tickets, which he resold through Lowestfare.com Inc., a travel agency of which he was the majority owner.

Meanwhile, Icahn had continued to make millions by putting corporations into play. In 1989 he forced Texaco's stock up by 30 percent when he bought 24 million shares in a failed takeover attempt. In 1999 he forced RJR Nabisco to sell off its cookie and cracker divisions in order to avoid an Icahn-generated takeover. In 2000 he forced General Motors to sell its electronics subsidiary in order to buy back more than one billion shares, thus boosting the value of its stock. And in 2001 he became embroiled in a bitter takeover battle with American Airlines, which wanted to acquire TWA and cancel his option to buy tickets. In 2001 Icahn's holdings were estimated to be worth more than $4 billion.

Icahn has remained very active in corporate acquisitions in recent years, and he has also increasingly applied his vast wealth to various philanthropic endeavors, including funding for homeless shelters and hospitals, support for charter schools, and donations to his alma mater, Princeton University. With an estimated worth of $9 billion, Icahn was listed in 2009 by *Forbes* magazine as the 43rd richest person in the world.

Further Reading

Kadlec, Daniel J. *Masters of the Universe: Winning Strategies of America's Greatest Deal Makers.* New York: HarperCollins, 1999.

Stevens, Mark. *King Icahn: The Biography of a Renegade Capitalist.* New York: Dutton, 1993.

Insull, Samuel

(1859–1938) *entrepreneur in electric utilities*

Samuel Insull was one of the pioneers of the electric utility industry. At one time he was probably the king of the largest electric utility system in the country. He was the first to use electric meters as a way to charge customers for electricity as well as to gather important data regarding electrical usage. He also pioneered the creation of large, efficient power stations that generated electricity via state-of-the-art steam turbines. Unfortunately, Insull financed the spread of his empire in such a way that ultimately led to its downfall and his expatriation.

Insull was born on November 11, 1859, in London, England. His father, Samuel, was a clergyman, and his mother, Emma, was an innkeeper. After finishing his education, he worked for several years as an auctioneer's assistant and then became an assistant to one of THOMAS ALVA EDISON's representatives in London. In 1881 he emigrated to the United States and settled in Menlo Park, New Jersey, where he became Edison's private secretary. One of his first assignments was to help build in New York City the world's first electric generating station dedicated primarily to providing in-home lighting. In 1882 he began helping Edison establish companies to build central power stations across America as well as to manufacture lightbulbs, generators, and other apparatus needed to provide business and residential customers with electric light. In 1889 he was made a vice president of the Edison General Electric Company, one of Edison's manufacturing companies in Schenectady, New York. When this company was merged in 1892 with Edison's other companies to form the General Electric Company, Insull moved to Chicago, Illinois, where he became president of the Chicago Edison Company, an electric utility.

One of the earliest problems faced by electric utilities was figuring out how to predict the daily and hourly demand for electricity. In essence, electric power is like a fried egg in a restaurant; if it is not served the minute it is made, it just will not get consumed. Power companies have no way to store electricity, so they must operate only those generators that they need. In 1892, however, power companies had no way of guessing how much electricity their customers would require over the course of the day, nor did they have any idea how much power their customers actually used. Consequently, they charged their customers a flat rate per month and ran their expensive generators all day long, while selling only about 25 percent of the electricity they produced. Insull set out to solve this problem by installing meters at each customer's residence or business. He then charged for usage, and used the data he collected via the meters to predict customer demand and schedule the operation of his generators accordingly. In this way he was able to use more efficiently the equipment at his disposal, which in turn allowed him to gain new industrial customers by charging low rates for electricity during nonpeak hours. In the 1890s he married Margaret Bird with whom he had one child.

By 1900 Insull was easily outperforming his competitors in Chicago, and he began to acquire their operations and their customers. As he did so, he closed small, inefficient power stations and consolidated them into larger, more efficient stations that generated electricity via steam turbines. By 1907, when the company's name was changed to Commonwealth Edison, he had merged it with all of his 20-plus competitors in Chicago and its environs, and the company was providing electricity to Chicagoans at rates that were about the cheapest in the world. By that same year, he had also succeeded in getting the state of Illinois to regulate electric utilities, rather than leaving such matters in the hands of corrupt city councilmen and county commissioners, although he himself had resorted to bribery to help bring this about.

In 1908 Insull began acquiring streetcar lines, elevated trains, and electric railways in and around Chicago, which consumed about 65 percent of the electricity generated by Commonwealth Edison. Two years later he began expanding the company's operations into Indiana, Wisconsin, Ohio, and other midwestern states. To finance this expansion, he created seven holding companies that sold bonds to the general public. The money raised was used to purchase small competitors, while the interest on the bonds was paid from the profits generated by the expansion. Since the bonds did not confer voting rights upon their holders, Insull remained in complete control of his electric empire. By 1929 he was one of the most powerful people in Chicago. His companies served more than 5,000 communities in 32 states, and his personal fortune was estimated to be $150 million.

Insull's empire began to crumble in 1929, following the stock market crash. The onset of the Great Depression made matters worse, because the downturn in the economy led to a decrease in the demand for electricity. As his operating companies generated less profit, his holding companies found it harder and harder to pay the dividends on their bonds, which by this time were worth more than $2.6 billion. In 1932 three of the holding companies were forced into bankruptcy. By the time all the claims against the companies were settled, Insull's investors had lost $638 million. In the ensuing brouhaha, in which he was accused by a number of people of having greedily and fraudulently manipulated the financial affairs of his companies, Insull fled to Europe to avoid prosecution. In 1934 he was apprehended while on his way to Turkey and extradited to the United States to stand trial. Despite the best efforts of three different prosecutors—he was tried separately for mail fraud, embezzlement, and violations of the bankruptcy act—he was acquitted each time. After his last trial in 1935, Insull returned to Europe where he spent his remaining years. He died on July 16, 1938, in Paris, France.

Further Reading

Hatcher, Harold O. *Within the Law: The Insull Empire.* Boston: Pilgrim Press, 1935.

Kohn, George Childs. *The New Encyclopedia of American Scandal.* New York: Facts On File, 2001.

J

Jacuzzi, Candido
(1903–1986) *inventor of Jacuzzi hot tub*

One of the most relaxing things a person can do is sit in a hot tub and let the warm water and the pulsing action of the jet pumps soothe one's muscles. Although nowadays most hot tubs are used for recreational purposes, the Jacuzzi, as it is also known, was invented by Candido Jacuzzi as a way to treat his child's arthritis.

Jacuzzi was born on February 24, 1903, in Casarsa della Delizia, Italy. His parents, Giovanni and Teresa, were farmers. At age 17 he moved to Berkeley, California, where he went to work as an apprentice machinist for the Jacuzzi Brothers Company, a machine shop owned by five of his brothers that specialized in the production of pumps for agricultural wells. In 1925 he married Inez Ranieri with whom he had four children. In 1933 he became the company's sales manager, and seven years later he took over as general manager. By 1963 Jacuzzi Brothers was shipping swimming pool equipment and water pumps of all kinds all over the country. That same year the company relocated its headquarters to Little Rock, Arkansas, so that it could be more centrally located to its customers in the United States. Two years later Jacuzzi became president of the company, and he implemented an aggressive marketing campaign to sell Jacuzzi products abroad. By the early 1970s, the company had factories in Canada, Mexico, Brazil, Chile, and Italy.

Although Jacuzzi Brothers makes a wide range of products, the one for which it is most famous is the Jacuzzi, or hot tub. In 1943 Jacuzzi's 15-month-old son was diagnosed with rheumatoid arthritis. Five years later, his condition had gotten so bad that doctors recommended hydrotherapy of the kind that was available only at expensive spas. By this time Jacuzzi had received four patents for improvements to water pumps of various types, so he decided to build a home spa for his child. By 1948 he had developed a submersible aerating pump that could churn the water in a regular bathtub into a whirlpool. When used in conjunction with a tubful of hot water, the water jet created a spalike effect that effectively treated his child's symptoms. Over the years word of Jacuzzi's invention filtered out, but the company was so busy manufacturing its other products that it only made a few of the whirlpool pumps, and then only as special orders. Finally, in 1955, it became clear that a great demand for the water jet existed, so Jacuzzi modified the original design to make it safe for in-home use and easier for his company to manufacture. Originally, Jacuzzi Brothers sold the pump in drugstores and bath supply shops as a therapeutic aid. But later his whirlpool pump became popular among Hollywood stars and others who did not suffer from rheumatoid arthritis but who just wanted to unwind after a hard day. To meet the demand of this clientele, in 1968 Jacuzzi developed a large tub with built-in seats and a number of jets so that several people could enjoy one another's company while relaxing. The product became known as the hot tub and then later as the Jacuzzi, and Jacuzzi Brothers created a special division to manufacture and market it. By 1971 the company was selling about $250 million worth of hot tubs each year. Even so, the Jacuzzi accounts for only a fraction of the company's total sales.

In 1971 Jacuzzi stepped down as president and retired to Scottsdale, Arizona. He remained active on the company's board of directors for another four years until he was paralyzed by a stroke. He died on October 7, 1986, in Scottsdale.

Further Reading

Aaseng, Nathan. *The Problem Solvers*. Minneapolis, Minn.: Lerner Publications, 1989.

Gelbert, Doug. "Who Invented the Jacuzzi?" PageWise, Inc. Available online. URL: http://njnj.essortment. com/whoinventedthe_rgty.htm. Downloaded on July 3, 2009.

Jay-Z
(Shawn Carter)
(1969–   ) *entrepreneur in music industry*

A street hustler and drug dealer as a teenager, Jay-Z rose to become head of his own record label, a hugely successful and Grammy-winning musical performer, and the first African American to serve as the top executive of a major music company. Throughout his ascent, Jay-Z has expanded into other areas of business enterprise, while solidifying his reputation among many fans and observers as the most important person in the history of hip-hop.

Jay-Z was born Shawn Corey Carter in the Brooklyn section of New York City on December 4, 1969. He grew up in the Marcy Houses, a public housing project in a rough area of Brooklyn's Bedford-Stuyvesant neighborhood, where as a child his charismatic personality earned him the nickname "Jazzy." Soon this name was slightly altered to Jay-Z, which would remain his moniker throughout his youth and into his adulthood. Jay-Z experienced an often difficult childhood. His father left the family in his adolescence, and he spent much of his teenage years seeking money and status selling crack cocaine and other drugs. He dropped out

of high school and pursued his long-held dream of becoming a star rapper.

Jay-Z spent his late teens and early 20s trying to break through in the recording industry but failed to find much success. Frustrated with the record companies that did not offer him a deal, he created his own label, Roc-A-Fella Records. Jay-Z was then able to merge his reputation throughout the streets of New York City as a skilled hip-hop mc (microphone controller) with a deal with a distributor to release his first album, entitled "Reasonable Doubt," in 1996. The record sold well, was hailed by critics, and launched a prolific string of successful album releases every year until 2003, when Jay-Z announced his retirement as a music performer (he returned from retirement in 2006).

In 1997, the seminal hip-hop and rap label Def Jam, a groundbreaking company founded by Russell Simmons, who Jay-Z has often referred to as a "godfather" for budding hip-hop entrepreneurs, bought half of Roc-A-Fella Records and five years later paid $22 million to extend the partnership through 2005. From 2004 to 2007, Jay-Z served as president of Def Jam, solidifying and advancing the companies preeminent position in the lucrative and growing area of rap and hip-hop recording. In addition to his success in the music industry boardroom, Jay-Z branched out with a clothing brand, Rocawear, and diversified his business portfolio in deals with Budweiser, the development of upscale

Shawn "Jay-Z" Carter, founder of Roc Nation
(Photo by Elaine Thompson/AP)

sports bars, and acquiring part-ownership of the National Basketball Association's New Jersey Nets franchise that is constructing a new arena in Jay-Z's former home of Brooklyn.

In 2008, Jay-Z bought out the remaining portion of his contract with Def Jam and launched a new venture, Roc Nation, which describes itself as, "a fully-functioning 360° entertainment company . . . [that incorporates] all facets of the industry through vertical integration from a grassroots approach, we manage the development, production, administration, branding, marketing and distribution of our product." Jay-Z, estimated to have a net worth of about $300 million and an annual income in 2008 of $82 million by *Forbes* magazine, explained his own business management style to a reporter for *Rolling Stone* in 2005 by referencing a philosophy of karate film legend Bruce Lee. Said Jay-Z, "Be water. If you pour water in a cup, it takes the shape of a cup. If you pour it in a teapot, it takes the shape of a teapot. Be fluid. Treat each project differently. The best style is no style. Because styles can be figured out. And when you have no style, they can't figure you out." Of his power and success in commerce, Jay-Z has noted, "I'm not a businessman, I'm a business, man."

Jay-Z entered his 40s among the wealthiest and most influential figures in music. The fame that he earned as a performer and businessman was enhanced with his marriage to singing superstar Beyonce in 2008 as well as by his well-publicized philanthropic efforts, which have included large contributions to aid victims of Hurricane Katrina in New Orleans and efforts to alleviate the effects of drought in Africa.

Further Reading

Grigoriadis, Vanessa, "Smooth Operator." *New York* magazine. Available online. URL: http://nymag.com/nymetro/arts/music/pop/10869/. Downloaded on August 27, 2009.

"Jay-Z." All Music. Available online. URL: http://allmusic.com/cg/amg.dll?p=amg&sql=11:hjftxqrgldhe~T1. Downloaded on September 2, 2009.

Sanneh, Kelefa, "Uneasy Lies the Head." *New York Times.* Available online. URL: http://www.nytimes.com/2006/11/19/arts/music/19sann.html. Downloaded on August 27, 2009.

Toure, "The Book of Jay." *Rolling Stone.* Available online. URL: http://www.rollingstone.com/news/coverstory/book_of_jay-z. Downloaded on August 27, 2009.

Jobs, Steven Paul (1955–) and
Stephen Gary Wozniak (1950–)
founders of Apple Computer

The first personal computer was designed by Stephen Wozniak and popularized by Steven Jobs. Together the two formed Apple Computer Inc. as the vehicle for making their machine available to the masses. In the process, they both became multimillionaires. But for various reasons, Apple never became the personal computer of choice, even though it had a good head start on its competitors.

Wozniak was born Stephen Gary Wozniak on August 11, 1950, in San Jose, California. His father, Jerry, was an engineer, and his mother, Margaret, was a homemaker. As a young boy he moved with his family to Sunnyvale in California's Silicon Valley. Although he was fascinated by computers as a teenager, he could never afford to own one or even have access to one. However, he did manage to get his hands on several computer manuals, and using these books he would "redesign" his favorite computers by making them smaller. After graduating from high school in 1968, he enrolled in the University of California at Berkeley, but he soon dropped out when he realized that he knew as much about computers as his professors did. By this time computers had become affordable, so he bought one and spent the next two years playing with it. In 1971 he moved to Cupertino to work as an engineer for the Hewlett Packard Company, a manufacturer of electronic testing and measurement devices. In his spare time he worked on a design for an easy-to-use personal computer, and he hung around with a group of Bay Area "techies" called the Homebrew Computer Club.

Jobs was born on February 24, 1955, in California. Shortly after his birth, he was adopted by Paul and Clara Jobs, a machinist and accountant, respectively, who lived in Mountain View, and was given the name Steven Paul Jobs. At age 13 he moved with his family to nearby Los Altos, where he attended high school and developed an interest in computers and other electronics. In 1972 he enrolled at Reed College in Portland, Oregon, but dropped out after a semester. He hung around Portland for a year and dabbled with the hippie lifestyle, then moved to Sunnyvale, California, where he went to work as a game designer for Atari, an electronic arcade-game manufacturer. After a few months he had made enough money to go to India to study yoga and other philosophic practices; upon returning to California in 1974, he spent a summer picking apples on a commune. In 1975 he moved to Palo Alto where his parents then lived, went back to work for Atari as a video-game salesman, and joined the Homebrew Computer Club.

Wozniak and Jobs met at a club meeting in 1975. Jobs was immediately impressed with Wozniak's homemade computers, as well as his idea about building a personal computer. Having decided to form their own computer company, they sold Jobs's van and Wozniak's programmable calculator, used the money to buy parts, and set up shop in Jobs's parents' garage. With Wozniak doing the design work and Jobs taking care of business administration and sales, by 1976 they had a fully developed personal computer, the Apple I, and their first big sale. The machine itself, which Jobs named in fond memory of his summer on the commune, was simple; it was little more than a circuit board with online read-only memory (ROM) and a video interface. The sale was to a Bay Area computer store for 25 machines, which the partners sold for $50,000. After building 50 machines in the garage, they started selling the Apple I, through ads in electronics magazines, for $666.66.

In 1977 Jobs and Wozniak took on Mike Markkula, a venture capitalist, as a partner in exchange for $250,000, enough to move the company into its own building in Cupertino. Meanwhile, Wozniak had designed a new user-friendly computer, the Apple II. Like the Apple I, it connected directly to a video monitor or a television screen. Unlike the Apple I, it had color graphics, a keyboard, a power supply, and a carrying case, and it sold for about $1,300. By 1980 the company had sold about 100,000 Apple IIs and was ready to go public. In one of the most amazing episodes in

the history of American finance, Apple Computer's initial offering of 46 million shares sold at $22 per share in a matter of minutes. Almost instantly, Wozniak and Jobs, who each held about 8 million shares, became multimillionaires.

Ironically, Apple's financial success led indirectly to the departure of both of its founders. Wozniak left first; an engineer at heart, he had no interest in working for a big corporation like Apple had become. In 1981 he took a leave of absence and formed Unuson, a music production company that promoted music festivals in San Bernardino, all of which lost money. That same year he divorced his first wife, the former Alice Robertson, and married Candi Clark, with whom he had three children. He returned briefly to Apple in 1983, but left again in 1985, this time for 12 years. He went back to Cal-Berkeley and got a degree in computer science in 1986 under the alias "Rocky Clark," so as not to intimidate his professors and fellow students. Then he formed CL9, which made remote-control units for home electronics, but this venture was ultimately unsuccessful and he gave it up in 1990. That same year he divorced his second wife and married Suzanne Mulkern. Between 1990 and 1997 he donated Apple computers to public schools in Silicon Valley, and he spent most of his time teaching teachers and students how to use them.

Jobs continued as Apple's chief executive officer after Wozniak departed but soon found himself in trouble. The first 14,000 Apple IIIs had to be recalled, and the company's next computer, the Lisa was too sophisticated and too expensive for the average user.

In 1984 Jobs was ousted as CEO; he remained with the company but without title or duties, and in 1985 he sold his Apple stock and moved on. That same year he started NeXT, a software company that he hoped would produce a product that could replace MS-DOS, Microsoft's operating system. Although the company did eventually develop a system called NeXTStep, which made computers easier to program and easier to use, Microsoft's grip on the industry was too powerful to dislodge, and so NeXTStep never caught on. The NeXT computer, introduced in 1989, was a technological marvel, but its price tag of almost $10,000 precluded it from catching on with the general user. In 1991 he married Laurene Powell, with whom he has two children. Meanwhile, in 1986 Jobs had bought Pixar Animation Studios, which specialized in computer-generated animation for movies. In 1995 Pixar produced the smash hit *Toy Story*, the first feature-length movie made entirely with computer animation. This success led Jobs to take Pixar public later that year, after which his stake in the company was valued at more than $1 billion.

In 1996 Apple bought NeXT, thus facilitating Jobs's return to his former company. He was reunited with Wozniak two years later, when both men became members of Apple's executive board. Though not a full-time employee of Apple, Wozniak remains a major shareholder and a friend of Jobs. In recent years, Wozniak has been involved in various technology-related business endeavors and in 2006 he cowrote an autobiography, *iWoz: From Computer Geek to Cult Icon: How I Invented the Personal Computer, Co-founded Apple, and Had Fun Doing It.* In 2008, Wozniak—divorced since 2004 from Mulkern—married for the fourth time, to Janet Hill, and in 2009 he was a featured performer on the popular ABC television network show *Dancing with the Stars.*

Since returning to Apple, Jobs has left an indelible imprint on the company. He was named interim chief executive officer in 1997 and the success of the Apple increased dramatically following the popularity of the iMac computer. In 2000, Jobs was named as the permanent chief executive officer and Apple has continued to thrive. The iPod music player and iPhone have garnered high praise for design and innovation and earned the company unprecedented sales. Jobs has solidified his iconic status among technophiles with his business acumen as well as his yearly appearances at highly anticipated MacWorld Expos, where he introduces and describes new products while dressed in his trademark black mock turtleneck, blue jeans, and running shoes.

In 2009, Jobs—who has taken a salary of only one dollar from Apple for several years—issued a statement to help dispel rumors that he was dying after appearing ill and later failing to appear at the 2008 MacWorld Expo. Jobs explained that he was indeed suffering from a "hormone imbalance" and that he would take a six-month leave of absence while remaining closely involved in major strategic decisions. In June 2009, Jobs received a liver transplant, and in January 2010 he appeared healthy and vibrant when introducing Apple's new iPad—a tablet-style personal computer—at the annual MacWorld Expo in San Francisco.

Further Reading

Carlton, Jim. *Apple: The Inside Story of Intrigue, Egomania, and Business Blunders.* New York: Random House, 1997.

Crompton, Samuel W. *100 Americans Who Shaped American History.* San Mateo, Calif.: Bluewood Books, 1999.

Greenberg, Keith E., and Jim Spence. *Steven Jobs and Stephen Wozniak: Creating the Apple Computer.* Woodbridge, Conn.: Blackbirch Press, 1994.

Mariotti, Steve, et al. *The Very, Very Rich: How They Got That Way and How You Can, Too!* Franklin Lakes, N.J.: Career Press, 2000.

Spencer, Donald D. *Great Men and Women of Computing.* Ormond Beach, Fla.: Camelot Pub., 1999.

Jones, Amanda Theodosia

(1835–1914) *inventor of vacuum canning*

Inventors receive inspiration from a wide variety of sources. Amanda Jones, inventor of vacuum canning, claimed to receive her inspiration from the spirits of the dead. Wherever the inspiration for its invention came from, her method of vacuum canning was widely used well into the 20th century.

Jones was born on October 19, 1835, in East Bloomfield, New York. Her father, Henry, was a master weaver, and her mother, Mary, was a homemaker. At age 10 she moved with her family to Black Rock, a small town outside Buffalo. In 1850 she completed her elementary education, and for the next four years she taught in the local elementary school while attending high school in Buffalo during the summer, an arrangement that was fairly typical for its day. In 1854 she left teaching, partly because her health was failing (it would remain fragile throughout her life) and partly because she had just published some poems in a magazine. That same year she became interested in spiritualism, a belief that the living could communicate with the dead via mediums. For the next 15 years she supported herself by writing poems and editing magazines, meanwhile traveling about western New York holding séances.

In 1869 Jones became convinced that a spirit she identified as "Dr. Jonathan Andrews" told her to move to Chicago, Illinois, and open a home for prostitutes who wished to reform their ways. She moved immediately and attempted to raise the funds needed to purchase and operate the home by working as an editor for several small magazines. However, this work barely paid her own living expenses. In 1872 she received word from another spirit, whom she identified as "Mr. J. R. Evelyn," that she could best raise the money she needed by inventing vacuum canning.

Canning, the preservation of fruits and vegetables in sealed glass jars, had become popular in the United States early in the 19th century. The original method had been to cook the food and then seal it in a jar; unfortunately, food preserved in this manner loses practically all of its taste and nutrients. Instead of cooking the food, Jones's idea was to suck out the air from the jar and replace it with hot liquid, either a light syrup of sugar and water or the juice of the food being canned, thereby preserving the food longer and making it taste much better.

Up to this point, Jones had demonstrated no mechanical aptitude whatsoever. To help her work out the technical details, she contacted Leroy Cooley, her mechanically gifted brother-in-law's cousin who lived in Albany, New York. Between Jones describing the basic workings of her vision and Cooley figuring out how to make it work, in 1873 the two invented and patented the Jones Preserving Process and the various apparatus required for vacuum canning.

In 1879 Jones founded the U.S. Women's Pure Food Vacuum Preserving Company in Chicago. She envisioned the company to be part of her ministry to reform prostitutes; only women would be allowed to build the factory and equipment and work the processing lines. Initially, she even refused to allow men to own stock in the company, and since few women were willing or able to invest in the company, her venture was slow getting off the ground. Meanwhile, she attempted to raise the necessary capital by inventing the automatic safety burner. This time her inspiration was not a spirit but a Pennsylvania petroleum dealer, who hoped such an invention would enable him to sell crude oil to heat homes. But neither she nor the oilman could raise the capital to manufacture the burner, and so the project came to nothing. By 1890 she had succeeded in finding enough women investors to open the Woman's Canning and Preserving Company in Chicago. Except for Cooley, who operated the patented equipment, and the boiler man, all of the company's officers and employees were women who had been either hired or trained by Jones. The company did everything she had hoped it would do—turn a profit and provide a new start for desperate women—until its president persuaded Jones to allow a group of men to buy stock. These men had no sympathy for Jones's vision of an all-woman company, and in 1893 they forced Jones out of the company. She went to live with her sister in Junction City, Kansas, where she resumed her career as a poet. At some point she moved to Brooklyn, New York, where she died on March 31, 1914.

Further Reading

Altman, Linda Jacobs. *Women Inventors*. New York: Facts On File, 1997.
"Amanda Theodosia Jones," About Inventors. Available online. URL: http://inventors.about.com/library/inventors/bljones.htm. Downloaded on July 3, 2009.

Joyner, Marjorie Stewart
(1896–1994) *inventor of the permanent-wave machine*

Some inventors never make a nickel from their inventions. Sometimes this results from poor entrepreneurial skills, and other times it results because the inventor assigns the patent to a charitable or nonprofit group. And sometimes it occurs because the inventor's employer is entitled to the invention, either because it was designed and built at work or because of an employment contract that automatically assigns the patent to the employer. Marjorie

Joyner is a good example of this latter inventor. Having invented the permanent-wave machine at work, her employer, the Walker Manufacturing Company, claimed ownership of the patent. However, Joyner never seemed to care, because she continued to enjoy working at Walker for another 40-plus years.

Joyner was born Marjorie Stewart on October 24, 1896, in Monterey, Virginia. Her father, George, was a schoolteacher, and her mother, Annie, was a homemaker. At age eight she moved with her family to Dayton, Ohio, where her father had been offered a teaching position. Shortly thereafter, her parents divorced, and she was raised by a succession of family members scattered across the South. When she turned 16, she moved to Chicago, Illinois, to live with her mother. She went to work as a house cleaner and waitress, then enrolled in the A. B. Molar Beauty School. In 1916, the same year she married Robert Joyner with whom she had two children, she became the school's first black graduate and opened her own beauty salon.

Unfortunately for Joyner's black customers, she had not learned how to do black people's hair in beauty school. Not long after opening her salon, she did such a miserable job on her mother-in-law's hair that the elder woman insisted that Joyner learn something about black hairdressing. MADAME C. J. WALKER had recently opened a Walker School of Beauty Culture in Chicago, which taught beauticians how to use the Walker Hair Care System for treating black hair, and Joyner's mother-in-law paid for Joyner to take the course. She was an apt pupil, and Walker quickly realized that she had the potential to be a major asset to the business. Walker trained her in how to use and sell the products and methods she had perfected, and within three years Joyner had become the national supervisor in charge of Walker's chain of more than 200 beauty schools. After Walker's death in 1919, Joyner became a vice president of the Walker Manufacturing Company, of which the beauty school chain was a part, a position she held for almost 50 years.

In 1928 Joyner invented the permanent-wave machine, a device that automated part of the hair-straightening process that had previously been done by hand. In essence, Joyner's device was a curling iron that straightened hair. To use it, the beautician twisted a strand out of the hair from a one-square-inch section of the customer's head, wrapped the strand in flannel, then wrapped the strand around a metal electrode. She then put a special protective device on the customer's scalp, made sure the cords to the electrodes lifted the strands away from the head, and turned on the power. When done by a hairdresser who knew how to set the hair after disconnecting it from the permanent-wave machine, the result was a head of hair that stayed straight and neat looking. Joyner never received a penny from her invention; since she designed and built the machine at a Walker beauty school, the company declared the patent belonged to it. However, she never seemed to be bothered by this, choosing instead to focus on using the machine to improve the lives of herself, her customers, and her students.

Joyner also developed a preparation known as "Satin Tress," the prototype of the modern hair relaxer. In 1945 she founded the United Beauty School Owners and Teachers Association, a trade organization for black entrepreneurs who had been barred from joining whites-only trade associations. And in 1954 she organized a trip to Paris, France, for almost 200 black beauticians so they could see firsthand what the newest European hair fashions looked like.

Joyner was active in her community in several other ways. In 1929 she organized a parade in downtown Chicago honoring Bud Billiken, a character out of black folklore who is a special friend and protector of young people. The event proved to be so popular that for years it was held annually, and for decades Joyner chaired the parade committee. In the 1930s she cofounded the Cosmopolitan Community Church, and in 1935 she became a charter member of the National Council of Negro Women. She also directed the Chicago Defender Charities, a philanthropic venture of the city's preeminent black newspaper. For the last 30 years of her life she worked as a fundraiser for and contributed generously to Bethune-Cookman College.

Joyner retired from active participation in the hairdressing business in the 1960s, but she never really slowed down. At age 98, she was still going to work five days a week at her office in the

Chicago Defender building. She died on December 27, 1994, in Chicago.

Further Reading

Amram, Fred M. B. *African-American Inventors: Laurie Johnson, Frederick McKinley Jones, Marjorie Stewart Joyner, Elijah McCoy, Garrett Augustus Morgan.* Mankato, Minn.: Capstone Press, 1996.

Macdonald, Anne L. *Feminine Ingenuity: Women and Invention in America.* New York: Ballantine Books, 1992.

Julian, Percy Lavon

(1899–1975) *inventor of hormone production processes*

Trained as a chemist, Percy Julian became an inventor and an entrepreneur. As an inventor, he developed 94 patented processes for extracting derivatives from vegetative sources, primarily soybean oil, including a substance from which human hormones could be produced. As an entrepreneur, he found ways to convert these derivatives into highly useful and commercially viable products.

Julian was born on April 11, 1899, in Montgomery, Alabama. His father, James, was a railway mail clerk and his mother, Elizabeth, was a teacher. As a young black man, Julian experienced considerable difficulty getting a quality education in the segregated South. However, he managed to overcome this obstacle and was admitted to DePauw University, where he received his A.B. in 1920. After teaching chemistry for two years at Fisk University, he received a fellowship to Harvard University and received his M.A. in 1923. Over the next six years he conducted research in organic chemistry at Harvard and taught chemistry at West Virginia State College and Howard University. Like most black American scholars of his day, he went overseas to obtain his Ph.D., which he received in organic chemistry in 1931 from the University of Vienna in Austria. He then taught at Howard for a year before returning to DePauw in 1932 as a professor of chemistry. In 1935 he married Anna Johnson with whom he had two children.

As a student, Julian became interested in soybean oil as a source of stigmasterol, a chemical compound from which human hormones could be synthesized. (A hormone is a chemical compound secreted by the body to regulate the function of a specific tissue or organ.) It had just been discovered that hormones could be used to treat medical conditions such as glaucoma and myasthenia gravis. However, the problem of how to mass-produce hormones had yet to be solved. Julian was just beginning to work on this problem when in 1936 he decided to leave teaching and go into business with the Glidden Company in Chicago, Illinois.

Glidden, primarily a manufacturer of paint, was looking for ways to expand its product base. Its management was convinced that soybean oil had market potential similar to the peanut, from which GEORGE WASHINGTON CARVER had developed more than 100 different products. Julian's interest and experience in working with soybean oil made him the perfect candidate to attempt to exploit this potential. As director of research of the company's soy products division, Julian oversaw the planning and construction of a state-of-the-art soybean oil extraction facility. Once the facility was producing sufficient amounts of oil, he turned his attention to developing new products from the oil. His first discovery was that the vegetable protein in soybean oil made an excellent coating for paper. Other Julian discoveries included soybean-oil-based products for use in the manufacture of paint, animal feed, candy, cosmetics, food additives, ink, and textiles. One of his more interesting discoveries was "bean soup," formally known as Aero Foam, which proved to be highly effective at smothering petroleum-based fires.

In 1940 Julian turned his attention once again to the medical applications of soybean-oil derivatives. A large quantity of water had somehow gotten into a tank of soybean oil and turned the tank's contents into an oily paste. Rather than throw out the "ruined" oil, Julian began experimenting with the paste. He soon discovered that stigmasterol could be cheaply extracted from the paste, thus providing a cheap and abundant source of a chemical compound that could be converted into various hormones by adding or subtracting certain elements. Glidden quickly turned its attention to the manufacture of hormones such as progesterone, which prevents miscarriages and eases certain menstrual complications; testosterone, which is an effective treatment against some forms of breast cancer; and cortisone, which is highly effective in treating rheumatoid arthritis.

After 1940 Julian began to search for even better sources than soybean oil to make progesterone. He discovered that the root of a wild Mexican yam known as *Dioscorea* was the source he was looking for. In 1954, after 18 years with Glidden, Julian went into business for himself. He founded Julian Laboratories, with a research facility in the Chicago suburb of Oak Park and a factory and farm in Mexico where the company converted *Dioscorea* roots into hormones. In 1956 Gregory G. Pincus and Min Chueh Chang discovered that an oral contraceptive made from progesterone produced from *Dioscorea* root was safe and highly effective. When the U.S. Food and Drug Administration approved the sale of birth control pills in 1960, Julian's fortune was assured. He sold Julian Laboratories the following year to the pharmaceutical firm Smith, Kline and French, although he continued to serve as president for three years. In 1964 he founded Julian Research Institute and Julian Associates in Franklin Park, both of which specialized in the discovery and production of synthetic drugs. He died on April 19, 1975, in Waukegan, Illinois.

Further Reading

Beckner, Chrisanne. *100 African-Americans Who Shaped American History.* San Francisco: Bluewood Books, 1995.

Robinson, Louie. *The Black Millionaire.* New York: Pyramid Books, 1972.

Witkop, Bernhard. *Percy Lavon Julian: April 11, 1899–April 19, 1975.* Washington, D.C.: National Academy Press, 1980.

K

Kaiser, Henry John
(1882–1967) *entrepreneur in construction and heavy industry*

Cavalrymen and cowboys may have won the West, but it was tamed by building contractors. They helped transform the Pacific Coast from a sparsely populated agrarian region into an urban industrial region by building roads, dams, mills, and factories. Perhaps the best-known western construction entrepreneur was Henry J. Kaiser, who also gained prominence in the automobile and primary metals industries. None of this might have happened, however, had Kaiser not fallen in love.

Kaiser was born Henry John Kaiser on May 9, 1882, in Sprout Brook, New York. His father, Frank, was a shoemaker, and his mother, Mary, was a homemaker. After finishing the eighth grade, he dropped out of school and went to work as a clerk in a dry-goods store in nearby Utica. He also became interested in photography, which he learned on his own, and at age 16 he started his own photography business. The following year he became a photographic supplies salesman for Eastman-Kodak, and the year after that he bought a half-interest in a photographic studio in Lake Placid. At age 20 he began spending his winters in Florida, and within a year he had opened several small photography studios there.

In 1906 Bess Fosburgh, the daughter of a wealthy Virginia businessman, visited one of Kaiser's studios while on vacation. They quickly developed a romantic relationship and decided to marry. But when Kaiser asked her father for her hand, he refused, insisting that Kaiser first give up photography and become a "real" businessman. So Kaiser sold his studios and moved to Spokane, Washington, to take a job as a traveling salesman for McGowan Brothers, a major wholesale hardware supply house in the Pacific Northwest. Kaiser became the company's star salesman, and within a year he was respectable enough to satisfy Bess's father; the wedding took place in 1907, after which the newlyweds settled in Spokane and had two children.

In 1913 one of Kaiser's customers, a road construction company in Canada, went bankrupt in the middle of a major project; Kaiser took out a loan, bought the company, and finished the project on time and within budget. The experience made him realize just how woefully deficient the Pacific Northwest's transportation infrastructure was, and the following year he founded Kaiser Construction Company, a road-building outfit in Vancouver, Washington. By 1921 the company had built hundreds of miles of concrete roads in Washington, Oregon, and California, and moved its corporate headquarters to Oakland, California. Kaiser Construction gained a reputation for building good roads quickly, partly because it produced its own concrete using materials from its own sand and gravel plants. Over the next 10 years the company got involved in a variety of other construction projects, building dams in California, levees in Mississippi, and roads and bridges in Cuba.

In 1931 Kaiser organized the Six Companies, a consortium of the largest construction firms in the West, which was contracted by the federal government to build Hoover Dam on the Colorado River. After the successful completion of this project, at the time the largest dam in the world, the Six Companies won contracts to build the Bonneville and Grand Coulee dams in the Northwest. When the consortium lost the bid to build Shasta Dam in California in 1939, Kaiser won the contract to supply construction materials for the project. He built a huge cement plant in Permanente, just south of San Francisco, and transported more than 6 million barrels of concrete via a seven-mile-long conveyor to the dam site.

Shortly after World War II broke out, Kaiser won a contract to build 30 cargo ships for the British government. In early 1941 he and A. L. Todd, an experienced naval construction executive, organized the Seattle-Tacoma Shipbuilding Corporation and constructed a large shipyard in Richmond, California. After the Japanese attack on Pearl Harbor, the company was situated perfectly to build the ships needed to fight the Japanese and to provide the cement for building military bases and airfields in the Pacific Ocean. In 1942 he formed the Kaiser Steel Company, which built the West's first steel mill in Fontana, just east of Los Angeles, and in 1944 he opened several more shipyards in Portland, Oregon, and on Puget Sound. During the war his yards built almost 1,500 ships, including 50 small aircraft carriers. Many of these vessels were completed from start to finish in fewer than five days. Accomplishments such as these contributed to American victory in the Pacific, and the press dubbed Kaiser the "Miracle Man" and the "Number One Industrial Hero."

The war effort required the rationing of virtually every building material, especially steel, which resulted in a dearth of consumer items. Kaiser realized that after the war consumers and returning servicemen would demand things such as automobiles and appliances, and that the wages they had earned during the war would enable them to buy them. In 1945 he and Joseph W. Frazer, an automobile executive, formed the Kaiser-Frazer Corporation, bought a government-owned aircraft plant in Willow Run, Michigan, and started making cars.

Kaiser anticipated the day when small cars would be popular, so he encouraged the design of the "Henry J," a small vehicle made of aluminum that got good gasoline mileage. Having gotten the jump on Ford, General Motors, and Chrysler, which had yet to reconvert their factories from producing war matériel, Kaiser-Frazer sold about 15,000 cars per month. But by 1948 the Big Three had retooled their factories; when they began designing newer, larger models, which was what American motorists really wanted to drive, the upstart automaker found itself unable to compete and in 1955 it went out of business. Meanwhile, Kaiser's other industries did exceptionally well. Kaiser Steel became the leading supplier of steel west of the Rocky Mountains, while Kaiser Aluminum & Chemical Corporation, which had been established to supply aluminum to Kaiser-Frazer, captured a significant share of the aluminum and manganese markets from Alcoa and Reynolds Metals.

In addition to his industrial accomplishments, Kaiser was a medical pioneer as well. In 1942 he established the first health maintenance organization (HMO) in the United States for the workers at his Richmond shipyard. Eventually Kaiser expanded this organization and opened it to the general public, and at the time of his death the Kaiser Foundation Medical Care Plan operated 19 hospitals and provided managed care for more than 1 million Americans.

In 1951 Kaiser's wife died after a long illness. When he married Alyce Chester, her nurse and his junior by more than 20 years, it created a minor scandal in the press. Three years later he went into semiretirement in Honolulu, Hawaii, partly to avoid media attention. He formed a construction company to build Hawaiian Village, a resort center that he sold to Hilton Hotels in 1961 for $21 million, and he participated in the construction of Hawaii Kai, a planned city on Oahu. He died on August 24, 1967, in Honolulu.

Further Reading

Foster, Mark S. *Henry J. Kaiser: Builder in the Modern American West.* Austin: University of Texas Press, 1989.

"Henry J. Kaiser, 1882–1967," U.S. Dept. of Labor Hall of Fame. Available online. URL: http://www.dol.

gov/dol/oasam/programs/laborhall/hjk.htm. Downloaded on July 3, 2009.

The Kaiser Story. Oakland, Calif.: Kaiser Industries, 1968.

Keith, B. F. (Benjamin Franklin Keith)
(1846–1914), and
E. F. Albee (Edward Franklin Albee)
(1857–1930)
entrepreneurs in vaudeville

Between 1885 and 1925, the most popular form of public entertainment in the United States was vaudeville. No two people did more to promote such entertainment than B. F. Keith and E. F. Albee, who at one time owned and managed the nation's largest chain of vaudeville theaters. By insisting that their performers offer nothing but good clean fun, they made vaudeville the family entertainment of choice in the days before radio, movies, and television.

Keith was born Benjamin Franklin Keith on January 26, 1846, in Hillsboro Bridge, New Hampshire. The occupations of his parents, Samuel and Rhoda, are unknown. At age 17 he ran away with the circus, and for most of the next 13 years he toured the country with a number of circuses as a grifter, selling worthless "miracle gadgets" to gullible locals. In 1873 he married Mary Catherine Branley with whom he had one child. In 1880 he gave up circus life after a circus he had acquired finished an unsuccessful tour. He settled in Providence, Rhode Island, his wife's hometown, where he went into business making and selling brooms. Three years later he moved to Boston, Massachusetts, where he opened a combination store and circus-type sideshow featuring several freakish attractions. The following year he became a partner in Boston's Gaiety Theatre.

Albee was born Edward Franklin Albee on October 8, 1857, in Machias, Maine. His father, Nathan, was a shipbuilder, and his mother, Amanda, was a homemaker. At age 16 he, too, ran away with the circus, and for 10 years he worked as a tent boy, animal feeder, and shill, a fast-talking salesman of tickets to sideshows. In 1881 he married Laura Smith with whom he had one child; two years later he left the circus and returned to Boston where he became manager of the Gaiety Theatre.

In 1885 Keith acquired Boston's Bijou Theatre and hired Albee to be general manager. At the time, vaudeville was just becoming popular. The first vaudeville show had been put on in New York City four years earlier, and its incredible success prompted Keith and Albee to turn the Bijou into Boston's first vaudeville venue. But the Bijou went beyond regular vaudeville; whereas most vaudeville shows consisted of between 10 and 15 unrelated acts featuring actors, acrobats, comedians, dancers, jugglers, magicians, singers, and trained animals, Keith and Albee put on a continuous performance from 10 in the morning until 11 at night. For 10¢—15¢ if one wanted to sit—a patron could watch 13 uninterrupted hours of variety entertainment. They hired bouncers to throw out hecklers and other troublemakers and, as the result of strong encouragement from Keith's wife, they insisted that each act refrain completely from profanity, suggestive allusions, double entendres, and "off-color monkey business."

Having made vaudeville a forum for wholesome family entertainment, Keith and Albee won the support of Boston's churchmen and public officials for their enterprise. This support led to packed houses, which permitted them to borrow money to construct a theatrical empire. By 1893 the B. F. Keith Corporation, with Keith as president and Albee as general manager, owned theaters in Boston, Providence, New York, and Philadelphia. By the mid-1890s the Keith-Albee chain of vaudeville theaters had become known as the "Sunday School Circuit" for its moral probity; it was also one of the three largest in the Northeast. In 1906 it became the largest in the United States by acquiring the vaudeville chain of Frederick F. Proctor, thus giving the two partners control of hundreds of theaters in the East and Midwest.

As vaudeville became more popular, the booking agents who controlled the top acts acquired greater importance than theater operators. In 1900 Keith and Albee set out to change this by trying to organize theater owners into the Association of Vaudeville Managers. Although this attempt failed, they succeeded in 1906 with the United Booking Office of America (UBO), with Albee as president.

Performers hired by UBO were guaranteed a 30-week tour of UBO-member houses, but performers who irritated UBO management or refused to play by its rules were barred from performing at UBO-controlled venues. As organizers and managers of UBO, Keith and Albee pocketed 15 percent of each act's salary, with another 5 percent going to the act's agent. When a rival group attempted to break up UBO's monopoly by forming the United States Amusement Company (USAC), UBO blacklisted any act that performed in a USAC theater. After several years of this "vaudeville war," USAC's managers accepted $250,000 from Keith and Albee to abandon their operation for 10 years.

In 1909 Keith retired to Palm Beach, Florida, leaving the management of the company to Albee; when Keith died on March 26, 1914, he bequeathed a half-interest in the B. F. Keith Corporation to Albee. In 1916 Albee extended UBO's control over talent by forming National Vaudeville Artists, a union of vaudeville performers; any vaudeville artist who refused to join the union was blacklisted from UBO theaters, thus giving Albee control over virtually every top act in the country. By 1918, when Keith's son died and left Albee the other half-interest in B. F. Keith, Albee was the dominant figure in vaudeville. In 1927 he merged B. F. Keith with Orpheum Theaters, the largest chain of vaudeville theaters west of the Mississippi River, to form Keith-Albee-Orpheum, giving him ownership of 450 theaters and control over bookings in almost 300 more.

Meanwhile, vaudeville was beginning to face stiff competition from the motion picture industry. Partly because of the movies' growing popularity and partly because of Albee's heavy-handed tactics, many of vaudeville's top performers left the circuit and became Hollywood performers instead. In 1928, the year after sound was introduced into motion pictures, the Radio Corporation of America (RCA) tried to acquire Keith-Albee-Orpheum, mostly because it wanted to turn Albee's theaters into movie houses. Albee refused to sell, thus setting off a bitter takeover battle, which RCA won. The new chain, Radio-Keith-Orpheum (RKO)—Albee's name was left out of the title for reasons of revenge, not style—became the dominant chain of movie theaters for years to come, while the million-

aire Albee retired to Palm Beach, where he died on March 11, 1930.

Further Reading

Stein, Charles. *American Vaudeville as Seen by Its Contemporaries.* New York: Da Capo Press, 1985.
"A Vaudeville Timeline," Deluxe Vaudeville Orchestra. Available online. URL: http://home.earthlink.net/~deluxevaudeville/pages/timeline.html. Downloaded on July 3, 2009.

Keith, Minor Cooper
(1848–1929) *entrepreneur in railroads and bananas*

The independent nations of Central America are often referred to derisively as banana republics. Perhaps no individual is more responsible for making bananas the principal export crop of these countries, thus giving rise to their pejorative nickname, and building the railroads to get them to market, than Minor Keith.

Keith was born on January 19, 1848, in Brooklyn, New York. His father, Minor, was a lumber merchant, and his mother, Emily, was a socialite. He grew up in Stamford, Connecticut, a suburb of New York City. At age 14 he completed his education, then spent the next seven years working as a clerk in a New York City store, a helper in his father's lumberyard, and a hand on several ranches in Texas.

In 1871 Keith went to Costa Rica to join three brothers and an uncle who had just acquired a concession from the Costa Rican government to build a railroad. The line was to connect the deepwater port of Limon on the Atlantic coast to the coffee-rich central highlands around San Jose, a distance of about 75 miles. The project took almost 20 years to complete, mostly because the first part of the line ran through mosquito-infested swamp and the second part ran across mountains so treacherous that as late as 1990 the two cities remained unconnected by highway. It is believed that 4,000 laborers died between 1872 and 1884 while laying the first 25 miles of track, including Keith's three brothers. Keith himself thrived in the environment and society of his adopted land; in 1883 he married

Cristina Castro, daughter of the president of Costa Rica, with whom he had no children.

By 1884, however, it appeared that the project was doomed to fail. As an inducement to continue, Keith was given a 99-year lease on the railroad and 800,000 acres of virgin land along the railroad's right-of-way on which no taxes would be collected for 20 years; in return, Keith agreed to finish the railroad and fund the Costa Rican national debt. In order to start making a profit while the line was being built over the mountains, Keith organized the Tropical Trading and Transport Company to plant bananas on his land, haul them to port on his railroad, and ship them to Europe and the United States. By the time the railroad was completed in 1890, Keith had already made a fortune.

In the 1890s Tropical Trading acquired the banana plantations of the Colombian Land Company on Colombia's Caribbean coast and the Snyder Banana Company in what was then the Colombian province of Panama. Motivated by the financial recession of the mid-1890s, intense competition from other banana growers, and the spirit of merger that infected American businessmen during the late 1890s, in 1899 Keith merged Tropical Trading with its chief rival, Boston Fruit, and a host of lesser growers to create the United Fruit Company. Keith was made first vice president and received a 40 percent share in the new company, which produced about 80 percent of the world's bananas.

Nevertheless, United Fruit experienced considerable difficulty with its remaining rivals, and Keith spent much time trying to resolve disputes. In 1905 United Fruit got into a shooting war with the American Fruit Company over conflicting land claims in the Sixaola region between Costa Rica and Panama, which both countries claimed but neither controlled. And between 1905 and the mid-1920s, gunmen and diplomats in the company's employ waged war with the Cuyamel Fruit Company over conflicting land claims in Guatemala along the Motauga River, where Keith was building another railroad. But by the time of Keith's death all such disputes had been settled; United Fruit had acquired another 20 fruit growers and fruit shippers; the company was shipping fruit in its own private merchant navy of refrigerated steamships that was so large it became known

as the Great White Fleet; and United Fruit was the largest single employer in Central America.

The disputes did not keep Keith from refocusing his attention after 1904 on building railroads in Central America. That same year he acquired the Guatemala Railway Company and in 1908 completed its line from Puerto Barrios on the Caribbean coast along the Motauga River to Zacapa and from there to Guatemala City in the highlands. In 1909 he finalized a deal to build El Salvador's main railroad, which in 1929 he tied to the Guatemala Railway, thus giving El Salvador access to the Atlantic Ocean and the European market. In 1912 he organized his railroads in Costa Rica, Guatemala, and El Salvador into the International Railways of Central America. His ultimate goal was to complete a continuous rail connection from Mexico to Colombia, but he did not live to see this happen.

In addition to railroads and bananas, Keith had a passion for pre-Columbian artifacts. He collected some 15,000 items of gold ornaments and pottery, which he left to the Brooklyn Museum, the American Museum of Natural History in New York, and the National Museum in Washington, D.C. At the time of his death on June 14, 1929, in New York City, his fortune was estimated at more than $180 million.

Further Reading

"Minor Cooper Keith (1848–1929)," The United Fruit Historical Society. Available online. URL: http://www.unitedfruit.org/keith.html. Downloaded on July 3, 2009.

Stewart, Watt. *Keith and Costa Rica: A Biographical Study of Minor Cooper Keith.* Albuquerque: University of New Mexico Press, 1980.

Kellogg, John Harvey (1852–1943), and W. K. Kellogg (Willie Keith Kellogg) (1860–1951)
inventors of breakfast cereals

One of the most popular ways to start the day in the United States is to have a bowl of cold cereal with milk. For this, Americans can thank John Harvey and W. K. Kellogg, who invented the process of turning grains into cereal flakes. While

John Harvey originally intended that his cereals be nutritious, it was W. K. who insisted that his cereals taste great.

John Harvey Kellogg was born on February 26, 1852, in Tyrone, Michigan. His parents, John and Anne, were farmers. By age four he had moved with his family to Battle Creek, Michigan, where his father opened a store and broom-making shop. At age 12, he became an apprentice printer at the Seventh-Day Adventist publishing house in Battle Creek. At age 20 he enrolled in the teacher training program at Michigan State Normal College, but after a year he decided to study medicine so that he could better promote good health habits such as abstinence from meat, tobacco, and alcohol, plenty of fresh air and sunshine, regular exercise, good posture, the use of natural herbs as medicines, and 8 to 10 glasses of water per day. He studied briefly at the Hygieo-Therapeutic College in New Jersey and the University of Michigan Medical School before enrolling in the Bellevue Hospital Medical College in New York City where he received his M.D. in 1875. Meanwhile he served on the editorial staff of the Seventh-Day Adventist monthly publication, *Health Reformer,* later renamed *Good Health,* and became editor in 1874. In 1876 he returned to Battle Creek to become superintendent of the Adventists' Western Health Reform Institute, which he renamed the Battle Creek Sanitarium. In 1877 he married Ella Eaton with whom he had no children.

W. K. Kellogg was born Willie Keith Kellogg on April 7, 1860, in Battle Creek. As a teenager he became a traveling broom salesman, and at age 19 he was hired to manage a broom factory in Dallas, Texas. In 1880 he returned to Michigan, married Ella Davis with whom he had five children, and briefly attended Parson's Business College in Kalamazoo. In 1881 he went to work for his brother as the sanitarium's business manager.

By 1881 John Harvey had realized that the meals his patients were being served were monotonous and nonnutritious, so he and W. K. set out to remedy this. John Harvey was a great believer in the nutritive value of cereal grains, so they set out to develop several tasty products made from grains that could be served at breakfast. First they developed "Granola," a biscuit about one-half inch thick made from the meal of wheat, oats, and corn.

The dough was baked until it was fairly dry, then it was ground and packed into biscuits. In 1894 they decided to experiment with a batch of cooked wheat that had gone stale. Instead of turning into a long sheet of dough, as it normally did when it was rolled, the cooked wheat kernels flattened into small, thin flakes that were light and crispy after being baked. The sanitarium's patients greatly enjoyed the wheat flakes, especially when they were served with milk. In fact, some of them liked the wheat flakes so much that they insisted the Kelloggs ship them to their homes after they were discharged from the sanitarium.

The Kelloggs were a striking contrast. John Harvey was the inventor who was primarily interested in the nutritive value of his new food items, while W. K. was the entrepreneur who was primarily interested in the profit potential that the

With his brother W. K., John Harvey Kellogg made corn flakes a popular breakfast cereal. *(Courtesy of the Kellogg Company)*

new items offered. Given these differences, it seems odd that W. K. and not John Harvey invented the process for making flakes out of corn in 1898. W. K. was particularly galled by the fact that C. W. POST, a former patient at the sanitarium, had started selling a wheat-flakes cereal of his own in 1897, three years after the Kelloggs had patented their flaking process, and was making a fortune. In 1899 he convinced his brother to form the Sanitas Nut Food Company, with W. K. as general manager, and start selling breakfast flakes via mail order. In 1905 W. K. finally persuaded John Harvey, who had never taken much interest in Sanitas, to sell him his share of the patent for making corn flakes. The next year W. K. founded the Battle Creek Toasted Corn Flake Company, with John Harvey as a silent partner.

W. K. Kellogg bought out his brother and made the Kellogg Company a major corporation. *(Courtesy of the Kellogg Company)*

The company was successful, but it also served as a bone of contention between the two brothers. In 1910 W. K. sued John Harvey for the exclusive use of their last name on cereal products sold in the United States. The following year John Harvey sold his interest in the company to W. K. for $300,000, then in 1916 he sued W. K. to keep him from using the family name on products sold outside the United States. After five more years of squabbling, in 1921 W. K. finally won the right to use the Kellogg name on all his company's products wherever they were sold. The following year he changed the name of the company to the Kellogg Company. By this time the company had became a mass producer of breakfast cereals and one of the heaviest advertisers in the country. He insisted that advertising copy stress the fact that the company's products were not just nutritious, but also delicious. He also stressed the technological aspects of packaging and is credited with developing the concept for keeping cereal fresh by sealing it in a waxed-paper liner before putting it in the box. At the time of W. K.'s death on October 6, 1951, in Battle Creek, the Kellogg Company enjoyed more than 40 percent of the American market for ready-to-eat breakfast cereals and an even higher percentage of the market overseas. He donated most of his interest in the company to the W. K. Kellogg Foundation, which he had founded in 1930.

Meanwhile, John Harvey had developed some other food items, such as imitation meats made from wheat gluten and nuts, a coffee substitute made from cereals, and milk made from soybeans. Throughout his life he lectured and wrote about what he called "biologic living," in essence the good health habits he had always promoted. He continued to supervise the sanitarium and edit *Good Health* until his death on December 14, 1943, in Battle Creek.

Further Reading

Butler, Mary, et al. *The Battle Creek Idea: Dr. John Harvey Kellogg and the Battle Creek Sanitarium.* Battle Creek, Mich.: Heritage Publications, 1994.
Powell, Horace B. *The Original Has This Signature— W. K. Kellogg.* Battle Creek, Mich.: W. K. Kellogg Foundation, 1989.

Kelly, William

(1811–1888) *inventor of the Bessemer process for making iron and steel*

A surprisingly large number of inventions are not named after their inventors. The Bessemer process for making cast iron and steel is a case in point. The process was "invented" in England by Henry Bessemer several years after William Kelly invented it in the United States. However, for several reasons, one having to do with marketing, the process was named in this country as well as in England after Bessemer and not Kelly.

Kelly was born on August 21, 1811, in Pittsburgh, Pennsylvania. His father, John, was a landlord, and his mother, Elizabeth, was a homemaker. Little is known about the first 35 years of Kelly's life other than he received a public-school education. At some point he became a partner in McShane & Kelly, a wholesale dry-goods business in Pittsburgh and Philadelphia, with the responsibility of handling new and existing accounts in western Pennsylvania, Ohio, Indiana, Kentucky, and Tennessee. In 1846 he married Mildred Gracy of Eddyville, Kentucky, with whom he had several children.

While courting his bride-to-be in Eddyville, Kelly became fascinated with an old ironworks located nearby. The ironworks sat in the middle of a rich vein of iron ore, much of it on the surface, and a forest from which charcoal could be made to smelt the ore. In 1846 he and his brother John sold their interests in McShane & Kelly, bought the ironworks and 14,000 acres of surrounding timberland, formed the Eddyville Iron Works, and began manufacturing iron kettles.

After about a year of operation, Kelly became concerned that the company would soon run out of iron ore and timber, so he began looking for a more efficient way to operate. The brothers were making cast iron in the time-honored tradition, stacking up layers of charcoal and pig iron (smelted iron ore) in the furnace, lighting the charcoal, and then blasting air onto the burning mass, thus melting away the impurities from the pig iron and leaving behind molten iron from which the kettles could be cast. It occurred to Kelly that the furnace could be made to burn hotter, thus conserving timber and removing more impurities from the pig

iron, if a blast of cold air were introduced into the middle of the furnace rather than just around the edges. In 1847 he built what he called a converter, better known today as a blast furnace, to test his idea. By 1852 he had built a series of converters, each one better than the previous model, and had worked out most of the bugs of what he called the "pneumatic process," better known today as the Bessemer process.

In 1857 Kelly found out that an Englishman, Henry Bessemer, had received a U.S. patent the previous year for making steel in a furnace exactly like the one Kelly had invented to make cast iron. He immediately applied for a patent of his own, claiming rightly that he had invented the process years before Bessemer had applied for the patent, and received it that same year.

Unfortunately for Kelly, the panic of 1857 drove Eddyville Iron Works into bankruptcy. He moved to Johnstown, Pennsylvania, where he built an improved converter at the Cambria Iron Works, then in 1858 he moved to Wellsville, Ohio. In 1861 he sold his patent to Eben Ward and Z. S. Durfee, who then established the Kelly Pneumatic Process Company in Wyandotte, Michigan; Kelly was given a small interest in the enterprise. In 1862 Kelly moved to Louisville, Kentucky, where he opened an ax factory and speculated in real estate.

Both Bessemer and Kelly applied for renewal of their U.S. patents; Bessemer was turned down in 1870, although he continued to hold a British patent for the process, while Kelly's patent was renewed the following year. He assigned the renewed patent to Ward and Durfee, who by now were calling the process the Bessemer process, because this name was associated with imported English steel, which commanded a higher price. Between 1871 and his death on February 11, 1888, in Louisville, Kelly received more than $400,000 in royalties from Ward and Durfee.

Further Reading

Boucher, John Newton. *William Kelly: A True History of the So-Called Bessemer Process.* New York: Little and Ives, 1924.

Skinner, Bartley, and Thomas E. Prince. *Bessemer Steel Process Was Discovered in Kentucky.* Louisville, Ky.: Horsehead Pub., 1994.

Kennedy, Joseph Patrick
(1888–1969) entrepreneur in the stock market

Most Americans know that not every kid born in America can grow up to be the president. In addition to having an incredible amount of political savvy and good luck, the successful candidate requires millions of dollars to fuel the campaign machine. Although ROSS PEROT was the first multimillionaire to finance a personal run at the presidency, Joseph P. Kennedy was perhaps the first to use his millions to finance a presidential campaign for his son.

Kennedy was born Joseph Patrick Kennedy on September 6, 1888, in Boston, Massachusetts. His father, Patrick, ran a saloon, and his mother, Mary, was a homemaker. Despite (or perhaps because of) his occupation, his father became a prominent politician among Boston's Irish working-class constituency, and this prominence enabled Kennedy to obtain a private-school education and attend Harvard University. After graduating in 1912, he worked for a year as a state bank examiner. In 1914, at the age of 25, he was made president of Columbia Trust Company, a bank his father had helped found. That same year he married Rose Fitzgerald, the daughter of Boston's mayor, with whom he had nine children.

Over the next 20 years Kennedy used his enormous ambition and drive to become a multimillionaire. In 1917 he left the banking business to become assistant general manager of the Bethlehem Steel Company's Fore River Shipyard near Boston. Two years later he became a stockbroker with Hayden, Stone and Company, and by 1920 he had made himself a millionaire. Rumors persisted throughout his lifetime that during the early years of Prohibition, which began in 1919, he engaged in the illegal importation of liquor from Nova Scotia to New England. In 1927 he moved to New York City where he got profitably involved in the motion picture industry. Two years later he returned to Boston to become manager of Hayden, Stone's stock division. Sensing that the New York Stock Exchange was about to contract, he divested himself of most of his personal holdings just before the market crashed in 1929. Over the next five years he demonstrated a remarkable ability for selling short, whereby one sells at a high price stocks one does not own in the hope of being able to buy them at a lower price in the future. By 1934 his personal fortune was estimated to be $100 million.

At first, Kennedy used his fortune to further his own political ambitions. An ardent supporter of President Franklin D. Roosevelt, in 1934 he was made the first chairman of the Securities and Exchange Commission, and in 1937 he was appointed ambassador to Great Britain. However, his opposition to Roosevelt's running for a third term as president, coupled with his zeal for appeasing Adolf Hitler and keeping the United States neutral during World War II, ended his hopes for high elected office. In 1940 he resigned his ambassadorship, retired from public life, and returned to the world of high finance where he reportedly made another $100 million during World War II.

Denied a long-term political career of his own, Kennedy determined to use his fortune and political contacts to achieve one for one or more of his children. At first his efforts focused on his oldest son, Joseph Jr., but after the young man died in combat during World War II, he fixed his attention upon his second-born son, John Fitzgerald Kennedy. Largely because of Kennedy's sizable contributions to the Democratic Party and his courtship of his many contacts within the party, John F. Kennedy won election to the U.S. Senate and, in 1960, to the presidency. Meanwhile, Kennedy devoted considerable effort to the careers of his other sons, Robert ("Bobby") and Edward ("Teddy"). Bobby and Teddy both served in the U.S. Senate and, at various times, were strong candidates for the Democratic nomination for president. Bobby was assassinated during the presidential campaign of 1968, and Teddy's aspirations received a serious setback following his involvement in a fatal automobile accident the following year. (Ted Kennedy continued to serve in the U.S. Senate until dying in 2009.)

In 1961 Kennedy suffered a stroke that left him partially paralyzed and unable to speak. He died on November 18, 1969, at his palatial manor in Hyannis, Massachusetts.

Further Reading
Kessler, Ronald. *The Sins of the Father: Joseph P. Kennedy and the Dynasty He Founded.* New York: Warner Books, 1996.

Leamer, Lawrence. *The Kennedy Men: 1901–1963: The Laws of the Father.* New York: W. Morrow, 2001.

Smith, Amanda, ed. *Hostage to Fortune: The Letters of Joseph P. Kennedy.* New York: Viking, 2001.

Kettering, Charles Franklin
(1876–1958) *inventor of automotive equipment*

Charles Kettering was one of the most inventive automobile engineers of all time. He developed or played a major part in the development of the electric starter motor, battery, generator, voltage regulator, leaded gasoline, yearly model change, automotive paint, and V-8 engine. This list is all the more impressive when one considers that Kettering began his professional career by tinkering not with cars but with cash registers.

Kettering was born on August 29, 1876, in Loudonville, Ohio. His parents, Jacob and Martha, were farmers. After completing high school, he taught for two years, then enrolled at Ohio State University where he received his B.S. in engineering in 1904. After graduation, he went to work as a design engineer for the National Cash Register Company (NCR) in Dayton, Ohio. He invented an electric cash register with automated accounting features, and within five years he had become chief of the inventions department. In 1905 he married Olive Williams with whom he had one child.

In 1909 Kettering left NCR to open his own design engineering firm. Shortly thereafter Edward Deeds, NCR's chief executive, offered to back Kettering financially and helped him incorporate as Dayton Engineering Laboratories Company, better known as Delco. The two partners planned to invent and market a reliable electric start system for automobiles. At the time cars had to be started by manually cranking the engine. At the front of the car was a large hand crank that was attached to the flywheel, a heavy disk connected to the engine by a shaft. When the hand crank was turned, it spun the flywheel, the weight of which eventually "turned" the crankshaft that started the engine. Crank-starting an automobile was too strenuous for most women and the elderly, and many able-bodied men sprained their elbows or dislocated their shoulders when the crank jammed.

Clearly, if the horseless carriage were ever to gain widespread acceptance, an easier way to start it had to be found, and whoever found it stood to make a lot of money.

Having gained much experience with small electric motors while at NCR, Kettering was able to design one motor that was powerful enough to turn the flywheel. Then he designed a battery, voltage regulator, and generator to enable the starter motor to perform on demand. In 1912 Cadillac ordered 12,000 of Kettering's systems, and then the system's major flaw quickly came to light; the starter motor was not securely attached to the flywheel, so it did not always work. But when VINCENT HUGO BENDIX solved this problem shortly thereafter by inventing a reliable starter motor linkage, the door was opened for Kettering's electric start system to become standard equipment on virtually all American automobiles. By 1914 Delco employed more than 2,000 workers and was realizing annual profits of more than $1 million.

In 1916 Delco was acquired by WILLIAM CRAPO DURANT, president of General Motors (GM), who merged it with five other automotive companies to form United Motors. Kettering received more than $2 million in cash and a large number of shares in the new company. When United became part of GM in 1919, Kettering became a major stockholder in GM; the following year he was made a vice president and director of GM's corporate research laboratory.

Kettering's first major project was to make GM cars more fuel efficient, in case a projected post-World War I fuel shortage occurred. In the course of pursuing this goal, one of Kettering's engineers, Thomas Midgely, discovered that engine knock is caused by a deficiency in engine fuel, not in the engine itself. This discovery led to the invention in 1921 of leaded gasoline, originally known as ethyl, which completely eliminated engine knock. In order to refine and market ethyl to the motoring public, in 1923 GM joined with Standard Oil of New Jersey to form the Ethyl Corporation, with Kettering as president.

Kettering's next design project was an inexpensive air-cooled engine, which he hoped would allow GM to compete with HENRY FORD's immensely popular and low-priced Model T. But the project failed at the cost of millions of dollars, and in 1923 it was decided that in the future Kettering's laboratory would focus on designing new models every year. This meant adding new features to each model sold by GM's operating divisions. It was an enormous challenge, but Kettering proved to be up to the task.

Over the years Kettering's designers made GM cars more luxurious and comfortable without making them more expensive. In addition to making each year's Buicks, Cadillacs, Chevrolets, Oldsmobiles, and Pontiacs cosmetically different from the previous year's models, they made the cars ride better; for example, they figured out how to keep the crankshaft from vibrating the passenger seats and how to get the brakes to stop the car more smoothly. Kettering himself developed Duco, an automotive lacquer that dried within hours, stood up to extensive wear and tear, and, most important, came in a variety of colors. At a time when GM's main rival, Ford, offered cars in black only, this last feature greatly enhanced GM's position among consumers. All of these small improvements eventually paid off; by 1930 GM was selling more than half the cars bought in the United States.

Kettering's inventions were not confined to the automotive industry alone. During World War I, he helped formed the Dayton-Wright Airplane Company and designed what was in effect the world's first cruise missile, a bomb-laden biplane with an automatic guidance system. He could never get it to work the same way twice, however, so the project was eventually scrapped. He also invented a two-stroke diesel engine with fuel injection that enabled GM's Electromotive Division to compete with General Electric for dominance of the diesel-electric railroad locomotive market.

Kettering retired to his home in Dayton in 1947 as one of the wealthiest men in the United States. He continued to consult for GM, and in 1951 he helped develop the V-8 engine. Previously, automobile engines had a row of four cylinders mounted directly above the crankshaft; Kettering figured out how to add another row of cylinders by mounting both rows at an angle to the crankshaft in a V-shaped pattern, thus giving the engine twice as much power without materially increasing its size. Most of his retirement, however, was devoted

to funding medical research. He and Alfred Sloan, chief executive of GM, founded the Sloan-Kettering Institute for Cancer Research in New York City. He also established the C. F. Kettering Foundation for the Study of Chlorophyll and Photosynthesis. In addition, he funded a number of community hospitals and the Kettering College of Medical Arts in Kettering, Ohio; formerly known as Van Buren Township, the town renamed itself in his honor in 1952. He died on November 25, 1958, in Dayton.

Further Reading

"Charles Franklin Kettering," National Inventors Hall of Fame. Available online. URL: http://www.invent.org/hall_of_fame/86.html. Downloaded on July 3, 2009.

Leslie, Stuart W. *Charles F. Kettering, 1876–1958.* Newark, Del.: Leslie, 1980.

Zehnpfennig, Gladys. *Charles F. Kettering: Inventor and Idealist; a Biographical Sketch of a Man Who Refused to Recognize the Impossible.* Minneapolis: T. S. Dennison, 1962.

King, Don

(1931–   ) *entrepreneur in boxing promotion*

Next to Muhammad Ali, the three-time heavyweight champion of the world, the most flamboyant character in the history of boxing is Don King. King is one of the few promoters in the Boxing Hall of Fame, and he is the only boxing promoter named by *Sports Illustrated* as one of the 40 most influential sports figures in the last 40 years. Nattily attired in a black tuxedo and a haircut that defies gravity, King has done more to make professional boxing a big-money sport than any other individual. In the process, he has made millions of dollars while getting into and out of a never-ending series of scrapes with the law.

King was born on August 20, 1931, in Cleveland, Ohio. His father, Clarence, was a steelworker, and his mother, Hattie, was a homemaker. At age 10 his father was killed in an industrial accident; although the insurance settlement paid for a new house, it left little to live on. Hattie King supported her family by baking pies and roasting peanuts, which King and his brothers sold throughout their neighborhood. At the time, "playing the numbers" was a popular, if illegal, pastime in black communities across America. For a nominal fee, a player picked a three-digit number, and if that number won, the player received a handsome payoff (most state-run lottery games are simply legalized versions of the numbers game). To get people to buy his peanuts, King included a "lucky number" in every bag. Several of his customers played their lucky numbers and won, and in short order people began buying the peanuts more for the lucky number than the nuts.

As a teenager, King became involved in the numbers racket as a runner, picking up numbers slips and payments from players, delivering them to the racketeers who ran the game, and returning to the winning players with their payoffs. By 1951, at the age of 20, he had moved up in the numbers hierarchy and was making so much money that he decided to drop out of Case Western Reserve University. Meanwhile, he had also married Luvenia Mitchell with whom he had no children; they later divorced, and by 1960 he had married Henrietta King with whom he had three children.

Although King's numbers racket was lucrative, it was also dangerous, and it eventually got him thrown into jail. In 1954, he killed Hillary Brown whom King allegedly caught trying to rob one of his gambling houses. The shooting was ruled a justifiable homicide, sparing King a prison sentence. However, 13 years later King was found guilty of second-degree murder for stomping to death a gambling associate, Sam Garrett, who allegedly failed to repay a debt of $600 to King. The charge was later reduced to manslaughter, and King served less than four years in Marion Correctional Institution in Ohio before his release in September 1971.

While in jail, King decided to leave his life of crime behind him once he got out. While casting about for something legitimate to do for a living, in 1972, the year after his release from prison, he organized a charity boxing match for the benefit of Cleveland's Forest City Hospital. The benefit was a huge success, mostly because he persuaded Muhammad Ali, a friend of King's since 1960, to fight 10 rounds against four different opponents. This event convinced King that there was plenty

of money to be made as a boxing promoter, and he started putting together a series of minor fight cards. In 1974 he formed Don King Productions and engineered a deal with Video Techniques, a closed-circuit television company, and the government of Zaire to put on what he billed as the "The Rumble in the Jungle," a heavyweight title bout between Ali and George Foreman, the titleholder, in Kinshasa, Zaire. It was the first heavyweight title fight held outside the United States and Europe, the first to have its own name, and the first in which both fighters were guaranteed $5 million. The Rumble in the Jungle was broadcast around the world to millions of viewers and made millions of dollars for King. He followed up this huge success the following year with the "Thrilla in Manila," a heavyweight title bout between Ali, who won in Kinshasa, and Joe Frazier, Ali's boxing nemesis, in Manila, the Philippines. By 1975 King was the top promoter in boxing. He sponsored six more of Ali's championship fights, and he became the exclusive promoter for six other heavyweight champions including Larry Holmes and Mike Tyson.

One reason for King's tremendous success was his ability to arrange multimillion-dollar purses for both the winner and loser of his bouts. Prior to King, most boxers had made paltry amounts of money, but after King exploded upon the scene, many of them could now make millions of dollars. In large part, this was the result of King's flamboyant style (he adopted a hairstyle that looks as if every strand of hair on his head had been sucked straight up by a vacuum cleaner) and his considerable talents as a promoter. He used his skill as a salesman to arrange multimillion-dollar deals with closed circuit and cable television networks, then spent heavily on television advertising that often portrayed his bouts as being personal feuds between two fighters who had every intention of killing each other. Before King, title fights did not have snappy names or take place in exotic locations; after King, boxing matches became media events with closed-circuit screens set up in auditoriums and coliseums around the world.

Despite his success, King continued to be dogged by legal problems. In 1977 he set up a series of fights to be shown on the American Broadcasting Companies (ABC) television network, but the series was canceled after the Federal Bureau of Investigation (FBI), which was investigating alleged criminal activity in boxing, revealed that King had falsified the records of many of the scheduled fighters to make them look better than they really were. In the early 1980s, the FBI released more details about King's business dealings; although the report certainly made King out to be a shady character, it did not prove that anything he had done was illegal. In 1984, he and his secretary Constance Harper were indicted for tax evasion; she was convicted, but he was acquitted. In 1992 Joseph Maffia, King's former accountant, publicly accused him of being involved in a scam involving an insurance payment for a canceled bout; charges against King of wire fraud and falsification of documents related to the scam resulted in a mistrial in 1995. Meanwhile, a number of his former fighters have gone public with allegations that King defrauded them. Some fighters claim that King has kept as much as half their share of the purse as his management fee; one of them, Tim Witherspoon, sued King and settled out of court for a considerable amount.

King seemed undaunted by all these difficulties. He thumbed his nose at the legal authorities, who had tried and failed to convict him of anything related to his boxing activities. He recouped much of the money he lost due to the cancellation of the ABC series by forming the Don King Sports and Entertainment cable network in 1981 and by promoting the Jacksons' Victory Tour of musical concerts in 1984, at a time when Michael Jackson was at the peak of his popularity. King dismissed his fighters' allegations as bellyaching, and pointed out that he had given 93 of them at least one million-dollar payday apiece. In the mid-1990s he formed KingVision, a joint venture with Showtime, the cable television network, which grossed tens of millions of dollars from pay-per-view bouts. One of King's fights, the first title fight between Mike Tyson and Evander Holyfield, was seen by more than 2 billion people in more than 100 countries.

In 1984 King's fortune was estimated to be in excess of $50 million, and he had moved out of Cleveland to a 400-acre cattle ranch in Orwell, Ohio. The farm doubles as a training and health care center for his fighters, many of whom are managed by his son Carl. The business offices of Don King Productions are presently located in Oakland Park, Florida, on the outskirts of Miami. He has donated much of his money to charity, his favorite causes being the National Association for the Advancement of Colored People (NAACP), the United Negro College Fund, UNICEF, and the Don King Foundation, which contributes to a wide range of charities.

King remains among boxing's top promoters almost 40 years after he first became involved in the business. He recently has enjoyed success licensing his name for several boxing-related video games. Despite his long record of influence and prominence, King has many detractors. The noted sports biographer Jack Newfield noted, "Don King is a hip exploiter, an intelligent flesh peddler . . . He knows which fighters to steal, how to exploit anyone's vice, vanity or insecurity and make a profit for himself." King typically responds to such frequent criticism by pointing out his role in helping scores of fighters gain millions before adding with a smile his trademark phrase repeated in nearly every one of his many public appearances: "Only in America."

Further Reading

"Don King," International Boxing Hall of Fame. Available online. URL: http://www.ibhof.com/pages/about/inductees/nonparticipant/kingdon.html. Downloaded on July 3, 2009.

Newfield, Jack. *Only in America: The Life and Crimes of Don King.* New York: William Morrow, 1995.

King, Richard
(1825–1885) *founder of King Ranch*

Not surprisingly, the largest ranch in the United States, the King Ranch, is located in Texas. In fact, the most surprising thing about the King Ranch is that it was not originally started by a cowboy or a lifelong Texan, but by a second-generation Irishman from New York City who had earned his living on a riverboat for more than 20 years.

King was born on July 10, 1825, in New York City. His parents were Irish immigrants whose names and occupations are unknown. At age eight he was apprenticed to a jeweler, but after three years of mistreatment he ran away. He stowed away aboard a ship bound for Mobile, Alabama, and once he arrived he went to work as a cabin boy on a riverboat on the Alabama River. At age 15 he was befriended by the captain of the boat he was working on, who taught him to read and sent him to live with his sisters in Connecticut. He got eight months' formal education there before joining the U.S. Army to fight against the Seminole Indians in Florida. He stayed in Florida after the war to work on a riverboat that plied the Apalachicola River, and in 1843 he earned his pilot's license. Four years later he moved to Texas to became the pilot of a Rio Grande riverboat that hauled men and supplies for the U.S. Army during the Mexican War. In 1849 he bought the riverboat from the government and began providing ferry service between Brownsville on the Texas side and Matamoros on the Mexican side. In 1850 he became partners with Mifflin Kenedy and James Walworth in M. Kenedy & Company, which built and operated riverboats on the Rio Grande. The firm prospered during the Civil War by hauling Confederate cotton to Mexico, thus avoiding the Union blockade, but was disbanded in 1872 when it could no longer compete with railroads.

In 1852 King traveled by horse from Brownsville to Corpus Christi to attend the Lone Star Fair. About halfway through a desolate area known as the Wild Horse Desert, he came across the San Gertrudis Creek, an oasis of shade and cool, sweet water. Upon reaching the fair, he convinced a friend, Gideon K. Lewis, to form a partnership for raising livestock on the San Gertrudis. The following year, the partners bought part of the old Santa Gertrudis land grant, and started their operation. By 1854, the year King married Henrietta Chamberlain with whom he had five children, the partners had acquired the entire Santa Gertrudis land grant of almost 70,000 acres for about 3¢ an acre. For their first three years in business, Lewis ran the ranch while King was busy on the river, but when Lewis died in 1855, King assumed management of the spread. By 1860 he had sold partnerships in the ranch, now known as R. King & Company, to Kenedy and Walworth, increased its acreage to 80,000 acres, and begun raising horses,

mules, hogs, sheep, and goats. By 1867 the ranch included more than 200,000 acres. Labor was provided by Mexican vaqueros, or cowboys, who came to be called Los Kineños (King's Men). Meanwhile, Walworth's widow had sold her interest to King and Kenedy, who in 1867 decided for various reasons to split the ranch's land and livestock between them and amicably go their separate ways.

Before the Civil War, King's Longhorn cattle had grazed on the scrub and chaparral of the Texas coastal plain and never developed much size. As a result, their meat was in low demand locally, and they were valued mostly for their hides. After the Civil War, the demand for beef in the eastern United States increased dramatically. To get fatter cattle, he imported Durhams from England and crossbred them with his Longhorns; his heirs continued this practice after his death, and around 1910 they produced the Santa Gertrudis breed, known for its red color and resistance to hot weather. Around 1866 he began driving his cattle annually to the railhead in Abilene, Kansas, where they sold for 20 times their worth in Texas. He used the profits from these drives to buy more land and cattle, and by 1885 he owned 60,000 head of cattle and more than 600,000 acres of land. Known as the King Ranch, the spread was centered around the present-day community of Kingsville, which was named in his honor.

King died on April 14, 1885, in San Antonio, Texas. He left his entire estate, valued at more than $20 million, to his wife, who turned over the management of the King Ranch to her son-in-law, Robert J. Kleberg. Over the years, the Kleberg family expanded the ranch's activities by purchasing more land in Texas, growing sorghum, wheat, and cotton, leasing land to oil and natural gas companies, manufacturing leather goods, and buying millions of acres in Florida, Argentina, Australia, Brazil, Morocco, and Venezuela. By 1990 the King Ranch's holdings in Texas exceeded 800,000 acres, making it the largest ranch in the United States.

Further Reading

Frost, Dick. *The King Ranch Papers: An Unauthorized and Irreverent History of the World's Largest Landholders, the Kleberg Family.* Chicago: Aquarius Rising Press, 1985.

Sizer, Mona D. *The King Ranch Story: Truth and Myth: a History of the Oldest and Greatest Ranch in Texas.* Plano, Tex.: Republic of Texas Press, 1999.

Kluge, John Werner
(1914–) *founder of Metromedia Company*

John Kluge is one of the most unusual entrepreneurs in American history. An assembly-line worker at age 18, he had built up a billion-dollar corporation by the time he was 70. Then, instead of retiring, he almost completely dismantled it, in the process making several billion dollars. Then, instead of retiring, he built it back up into a multibillion-dollar corporation.

Kluge was born John Werner Kluge on September 21, 1914, in Chemnitz, Germany. His father, Fritz, was an engineer, and his mother, Gertrude, was a homemaker. At age eight his father died, and he moved with his mother to Detroit, Michigan. After graduating from high school in 1932, he worked on an automobile assembly line for a year, then enrolled in Wayne State University. In 1935 he received a scholarship to Columbia University where he received his B.A. in economics in 1937. He returned to Detroit where he went to work for Otten Brothers, gradually rising to vice president and sales manager. In 1947 he became president of New England Fritos, a position he held until 1955 when he and David Finkelstein formed Kluge, Finkelstein and Company, a food wholesaler in Baltimore, Maryland. Meanwhile, Kluge was doing double duty as an executive in the broadcasting industry. During World War II he had served as an army intelligence officer in Washington, D.C., and upon being discharged in 1946 he had bought a radio station in one of D.C.'s Maryland suburbs. By 1954 he was also president of broadcasting companies in Orlando, Florida; Pittsburgh, Pennsylvania; St. Louis, Missouri; and Nashville, Tennessee.

In 1959 Kluge bought the Metropolitan Broadcasting Company, which owned two television stations and four radio stations. He took over as president, changed the name to Metromedia Company, and set out to rejuvenate its properties. His most amazing feat came in Washington with WTTG, a run-down station that was a distant fourth to the three major network stations. He increased the station's audience by showing lots of old black-and-white movies and reruns from old sitcoms. (This is the same strategy that TED TURNER would use in 1970 to transform a station he bought in Atlanta, Georgia, into Superstation TBS.) By the mid-1960s, WTTG was outdrawing the networks in the late afternoon and early evening. Meanwhile, he began acquiring stations in other parts of the country. By 1984 Metromedia owned seven television stations and 11 radio stations, making it the largest independent broadcasting group in the United States. Kluge expanded Metromedia's holdings in other areas as well. In 1960 he bought three major outdoor advertising companies, giving Metromedia 35,000 billboards nationwide. He bought the Ice Capades in 1963; the Harlem Globetrotters in 1967; Wolper Productions, a movie and television production company, in 1968; and a cellular telephone and paging business in 1982.

In 1984, at age 70, Kluge shocked the business world when he borrowed $1.2 billion so that he could buy all of Metromedia's stock, thus making it a private company. The plan was to sell the company's assets for more than he had borrowed, thus repaying the loan and pocketing the difference. Although most industry analysts were skeptical about his ability to accomplish such a huge deal, within two years he had sold enough properties to repay the loan. By 1992 he had sold almost all of Metromedia's assets for almost $5 billion, leaving him with a tidy profit of more than $3 billion.

Having paid back the loan, Kluge shocked the business world again when he began rebuilding Metromedia into a conglomeration of telecommunications, steak houses, and computer printing operations. In 1983 he paid $30 million for LDS, a regional long distance telephone carrier in Texas that he renamed Metromedia Long Distance (MLD). Instead of selling MLD along with the rest of Metromedia's assets, he built it up by buying other carriers and merging it with still others. By 1993 he had expanded the company, now called LDDS Metromedia Communications, into a billion-dollar company. In 1988 he began buying steak house chains, and within a few years he owned Ponderosa, Bonanza, Steak & Ale, and Bennigan's, for a total of more than a thousand steak houses across the country. Although he had sold off his outdoor advertising companies, in 1987 he founded Metromedia Technologies, which prints billboard posters by computer. These machinations left Kluge with a net worth estimated at $5 billion in 1989, enough for *Forbes* magazine to declare him the richest man in the United States in 1989, 1990, and 1991 (he was knocked from the top spot in 1992 by BILL GATES). In 1995 Kluge and longtime partner Stuart Subotnick formed the Metromedia International Group, a publicly held corporation that has invested heavily in cable television, wireless and land-based telephone systems, radio stations, and long-distance carriers throughout the countries in the former Soviet communist bloc and China. Other endeavors include the Metromedia Fiber Network, which manages fiber-optic networks in several big cities, and Metromedia Energy, a coal and petroleum broker. By 2001 Kluge was likely worth more than $8 billion.

Kluge is married to Maria Tussi Kluge, his fourth wife. He has two children by his second wife, Yolanda Zucco. Kluge owns homes in New York City, Albermarle County, Virginia, Palm Beach, Florida, and France. His charitable contributions $60 million to the Library of Congress and over $100 million to his alma mater, Columbia University. In addition, Kluge has pledged a $400 million contribution to Columbia to be given upon his death solely in support of financial aid.

Though well into his 90s, Kluge remains an active investor and business mind. He still follows his basic philosophy that, ". . . it is very important to have imagination and very important to dream, but I also think it is important to keep ideas to yourself until your are implementing them."

Further Reading

Marcial, Gene G. "Kluge's Move at Metromedia," Business Week. Available online. URL: http://www.businessweek.com/1996/48/b3503136.htm. Downloaded on July 3, 2009.

"Metromedia International Group, Inc. (MMG)," Lens Inc. Available online. URL: http://www.lens-inc.com/companies/mmg/mmg.html. Updated on November 20, 2001.

Murray, James B. *Wireless Nation: The Frenzied Launch of the Cellular Revolution in America.* New York: Perseus Books, 2001.

Knight, Margaret
(1838–1914) *inventor of the bag-making machine*

Anyone who has ever carried a purchase home in a paper sack or a lunch to school in a paper bag is familiar with the handiwork of Margaret Knight. Her invention, the bag-making machine, greatly simplified the production of flat-bottomed paper bags, thus making these bags a common feature of 20th-century life.

Knight was born on February 14, 1838, in York, Maine. Her parents, James and Hannah, were cotton mill workers. When Knight was young she moved with her family to Manchester, New Hampshire. As a girl she was known as a tomboy, preferring to whittle things out of wood rather than play with dolls. Her formal education consisted of a few years of elementary school, and by age 10 she was working with the rest of her family in a mill. At age 12, after witnessing an accident on the work floor, she designed her first invention, a device to keep a shuttle from slipping out of its loom. She left the mill around 1857 and for the next 10 years she traveled about New England, supporting herself by upholstering chairs, repairing homes, and engraving silver.

In 1867 Knight went to work for the Columbia Bag Company in Springfield, Massachusetts. The company made flat-bottomed brown paper bags, similar to the paper grocery bags of the late 20th century. At the time the bags were cut, folded, and pasted together by hand. Knight became intrigued with the idea of inventing a machine that would perform all three steps mechanically, and for two years she experimented with different bag-making machines. When her supervisor complained that her experiments wasted valuable company time, she got him to leave her alone by suggesting that she might sell him the rights to whatever machine she invented. (In fact, she kept the rights to herself.) Finally, she came up with a workable wooden model, which she sent to a Boston machinist to copy in iron. But while the machinist had the machine, a fellow named Charles F. Annan saw it, copied it, and applied for a patent. Outraged, Knight hired a lawyer and sued Annan for stealing her idea. In 1870, after a lengthy, heated hearing, the U.S. Patent Office examiners found in Knight's favor.

After receiving her patent, Knight entered into an agreement with the Eastern Paper Bag Company in Hartford, Connecticut. Knight received $2,500 for the right to use her machine, $25,000 in royalties, and 200 shares of company stock, which paid quarterly dividends. She reportedly sold the patent rights at a later date for between $20,000 and $50,000.

Around 1890 Knight moved to Framingham, Massachusetts, where she worked in a shoe factory. Over the next four years she patented several machines for cutting shoe leather. She sold her four patents to a group of Boston investors while retaining a one-fourth interest in each patent; she later sold this interest to the Boston Rubber Company. Around 1900 she became interested in automobiles, and for the rest of her life she designed various automobile parts including valves, rotors, and at least two types of motors. By now Knight, who never married, enjoyed a lifestyle comfortable enough that she could afford to assign most of her automotive patents to her favorite nieces and nephews.

In addition to profiting handsomely from her inventions, Knight achieved a measure of fame in her own lifetime. In 1872 the *Women's Journal*, a feminist publication, published an interview with Knight and an accompanying article that praised her for her achievements. Her obituary in the *Framingham Evening News* called her a "woman Edison." Altogether she is credited with having been awarded 27 patents, and she invented a number of things that she never bothered to patent. She died on October 12, 1914, in Framingham.

Further Reading

Macdonald, Anne L. *Feminine Ingenuity: Women and Invention in America.* New York: Ballantine Books, 1994.

"Margaret Knight," National Inventors Hall of Fame. Available online. URL: http://www.invent.org/hall_of_fame/285.html. Downloaded on July 3, 2009.

Vare, Ethlie Ann, and Greg Ptacek. *Mothers of Invention: From the Bra to the Bomb, Forgotten Women and Their Unforgettable Ideas.* New York: William Morrow and Co., 1988.

Knight, Sarah Kemble

(1666–1727) *entrepreneur in innkeeping and land speculation*

Colonial American society assumed that a woman needed a male figure, usually either a father or husband, to manage her financial affairs. However, widows fell into a different situation. Having lost their husbands, and usually their fathers as well, these women had little choice but to become financially independent, and society had little choice but to allow them to do so. Not surprisingly, many of these women not only survived but prospered as independent businesswomen, usually as owners of taverns, inns, and boardinghouses but occasionally in other business ventures as well. An example of the colonial era's self-made woman is Sarah Knight, successful merchant, innkeeper, and land speculator.

Knight was born Sarah Kemble on April 19, 1666, in Boston, Massachusetts. Her father, Thomas, was a merchant, and her mother, Elizabeth, was a homemaker. Little is known about the first 38 years of her life other than she married Richard Knight, with whom she had a daughter, Elizabeth, and by 1704 both her father and husband had died.

In 1704 Knight went to New York to tie up several loose ends regarding a family estate, possibly in connection with the death of either Thomas Kemble or Richard Knight. She kept a diary of her trip, which depicts her as being an intrepid woman. At a time when women rarely ventured away from their hometowns except in the company of a father or husband, she traveled alone and on horseback through a country with poor roads, signage, and accommodations. She overcame all these problems and settled the legal affair to her satisfaction.

By 1707 (and probably much earlier than 1704) Knight was supporting herself and Elizabeth by running her father's old shop in Boston. She also took in boarders and served as a notary public, copying legal documents and witnessing deeds. When Elizabeth married John Livingston in 1713, Knight moved with the newlyweds to New London, Connecticut; whether she sold her shop in Boston is unclear. She opened a shop in town and purchased a tavern and inn on the outskirts of town on the road to Norwich, Connecticut. Using the profits from these businesses and drawing upon her experience as a notary public in Boston, she began to speculate in land, at which she evidently did quite well. She was able to re-acquire some land that her son-in-law had sold, then entered into a lucrative partnership with Joseph Bradford, a wealthy local landowner. Her holdings gradually increased to the point that she had to employ Joshua Hempstead, a local jack-of-all-trades, to survey her land and draw up leases for her tenants. In 1718 she ran afoul of the local authorities for selling alcohol to a small band of Mohegan Indians who lived near Norwich. At the time of her death on September 25, 1727, in New London, her estate was valued at more than 2,000 pounds, a considerable amount for the day.

Knight's diary of her adventures in 1704 was published in 1825 by Theodore Dwight. Known today as *The Journal of Madam Knight*, this diary gives many insights into the nature of colonial living in early 18th-century New England and New York. Knight's life also serves as a good example of what colonial women could do in business when given an opportunity.

Further Reading

Dubnick, Randa K. *Women and Literature: Four Studies.* Emporia: Emporia Kansas State College, 1976.
Gerba, Janet Burnett, ed. *The Journal of Madam Knight.* Rutland, Vt.: Colonial American Press, 1995.

Kraft, James Lewis

(1874–1953) *inventor of processed cheese*

Before 1900, store-bought cheese was an insignificant part of the American diet, mostly because it was difficult to preserve for any length of time. One hundred years later, cheese and products made with cheese were staples at mealtime throughout the United States, mostly because packaging, pasteurization, and advertising had stimulated the American appetite for cheese. The person most responsible for this transformation is James Kraft, who spent much of his professional life improving and promoting cheese.

Kraft was born on November 11, 1874, in Fort Erie, Ontario, Canada. His parents, George and Minerva, were farmers. After finishing high school, he spent 10 years as a clerk in a local general store. In 1903 he moved to Buffalo, New York, to attend business school; while there he worked as a janitor and delivered cheese, eggs, and ice. In 1904, at age 30, he moved to Chicago, Illinois.

As a clerk and deliveryman, Kraft had gained a good deal of knowledge about the selling and handling of cheese. At the time, grocers sold cheese by slicing it from large wheels that sat on display, uncovered and unrefrigerated. Periodically, the hardened "skin" of the wheel had to be scraped off and thrown away, something Kraft had done countless times. He reasoned that if he could find a way to eliminate this waste, he could probably make a decent living selling cheese.

Shortly after he arrived in Chicago, Kraft started his own cheese delivery business. He bought cheese wheels from wholesalers, cut them into small pieces, wrapped the pieces in tin foil or sealed them in glass jars, and delivered the small packages to grocers, who could sell them to customers without the added expense of handling or wasting the cheese. By 1909 Kraft's business was doing well enough to support himself and four brothers, and that same year he incorporated it as J. L. Kraft and Brothers. In 1910 he married Pauline Pratt with whom he had one child, and in 1911 he became an American citizen.

Kraft's Mennonite upbringing had given him a strong work ethic, and he combined this with a natural flair for business and a love for selling cheese to build an innovative and highly successful company. He promoted his services to grocers all over Chicago by mailing them flyers, and he promoted his products to consumers by advertising on billboards and in the city's elevated trains. By 1916 he had opened his own cheese factory and was selling 31 different varieties of cheese, including blends of two or more "flavors." That same year he received a patent for a process by which his blended cheeses could be pasteurized and canned, thus extending the shelf life of cheese indefinitely. This was tremendously effective in the South, where store-bought cheese spoiled so fast in the high heat and humidity of summer that it was a seasonal item, and with the U.S. military, which bought 24 million quarter-pound cans of cheese during World War I.

Kraft took his company public in 1917, after which he continued to find new ways to process, market, and sell cheese. In 1919 he began placing color advertisements in national magazines, and by 1920 he was doing business in Canada, England, and Germany. In 1924, the same year he changed the corporate name to Kraft Cheese Company, he set up a test kitchen and hired a home economist to develop recipes using cheese; within six years the kitchen had grown into the world's largest cheese research laboratory. In 1928 he merged with the Phenix Cheese Company, the makers of Philadelphia Cream Cheese and with whom he shared several cheese-processing patents. Kraft-Phenix Cheese, with Kraft as president, employed 10,000 people and did business in 30 states and four foreign countries. In 1931 Kraft-Phenix was acquired by the National Dairy Products Company, but the new owners did little to interfere with Kraft's management practices.

Although most American businessmen regarded the Great Depression as a nightmare, Kraft saw it as a golden opportunity. In 1933 he embarked on the biggest advertising campaign in his company's history to sell a new line of nutritious but inexpensive cheese and dairy products, which by 1937 included Velveeta, Miracle Whip, Kraft Macaroni and Cheese Dinner, and Parkay Margarine. Having survived the Great Depression virtually unscathed, Kraft was able, once again, to sell millions of pounds of packaged cheese to the U.S. military during World War II. The last innovation that came about under Kraft's leadership was the introduction in 1949 of processed cheese slices. In 1951 he retired to his home in Chicago.

Throughout his life, Kraft remained a deeply religious man. He was an active member of North Shore Baptist Church where he taught Sunday school for 40 years. He also provided many scholarships to the Northern Baptist Theological Seminary, of which he was a trustee. Aside from church and cheese, he enjoyed collecting and working with jade. He especially loved to make jade rings, which he would often give to employees who were doing a good job. He died on February 16, 1953, in Chicago.

Further Reading

"James L. Kraft, 1951." Horatio Alger Association of Distinguished Americans: Members. Available online. URL: http://www.horatioalger.com/member_info.cfm?memberid=KRASI. Downloaded on July 3, 2009.

National Dairy Products Corporation. *Kraft History.* Chicago: The Corporation, 1966.

Kroc, Ray
(Raymond Albert Kroc)
(1902–1984) *founder of McDonald's Corporation*

Before 1955, the phrase "fast food" meant nothing. The quickest meal one could find on the road was at a roadside diner, where the service was not always fast. Ray Kroc, founder of McDonald's Corporation, changed all that. His pioneering efforts created the multibillion-dollar fast-food industry, which by the 21st century had become a mainstay of modern American life. Ironically, Kroc's original intention was not to create an industry but to sell more milk-shake mixers.

Kroc was born Raymond Albert Kroc on October 5, 1902, in Oak Park, Illinois. His father, Louis, worked for Western Union, and his mother, Rose, was a homemaker. At age 15 he dropped out of high school with the intention of driving an ambulance in France during World War I, but the war ended while he was still in training. He returned briefly to school, then dropped out again to become a jazz pianist. At age 20 he married Ethyl Fleming with whom he had one child, and he became a traveling salesman with the Lily-Tulip Cup Company, selling paper cups and other supplies to restaurants. Except for a brief, disastrous stint selling land in Florida in 1926, he stayed with Lily-Tulip for 15 years and eventually became sales manager for the company's midwestern region.

In 1937 Kroc realized that he was never going to get rich working for someone else. Despite the fact that the country was still mired in the worst economic depression in its history, he and his boss at Lily-Tulip quit their jobs, formed the Prince Castle Company, and became the exclusive national distributors for the multimixer, a milk-shake maker that one of Kroc's customers had invented that could make five milk shakes at one time. Sales were so poor during the first two years that the partners could barely make ends meet. In 1939 Kroc's partner gave up and sold his half of the business to Kroc. Kroc struggled along for six more years, then watched as sales took off after World War II when soda fountains and corner malt shops became extremely popular. But when the soda-fountain industry began to slump in the mid-1950s, so did Prince Castle's sales.

Looking for a new way to market multimixers, in 1954 Kroc decided to pay a visit to McDonald's, an eatery in San Bernardino, California, that had bought eight of his mixers. Thinking it would be a huge restaurant, he was shocked to discover that McDonald's was a small, white-tiled drive-in with a walk-up window and a garish yellow arch on each side. The menu consisted entirely of hamburgers, French fries, and beverages. What amazed Kroc the most, however, was how clean everything was and how fast the food was prepared; instead of the usual short-order-cook approach, whereby one cook prepared one order from start to finish, McDonald's had one employee frying hamburger patties, another squirting condiments onto buns, another making French fries, and another fixing milk shakes and sodas and making coffee. The whole operation worked so efficiently that orders were filled almost as fast as they were placed.

Almost immediately, Kroc envisioned McDonald's from coast to coast, each one equipped with eight multimixers. The McDonald brothers, Maurice and Richard, were skeptical; they had already sold 14 franchises in California and Arizona, were unhappy with the way the franchisees were doing things, and did not know how to get them to change. With great enthusiasm, Kroc assured them that he could and would make franchisees serve good food quickly from clean establishments, that the brothers did not have to get involved with the chain's operations in any way, and that the three of them would soon be rich. Convinced that Kroc was a man of his word, the McDonald brothers signed a 99-year contract making him their exclusive agent. In return, they would receive one-half of 1 percent of each franchise's gross sales; Kroc, for taking on

all sales and management duties, would receive 1.4 percent.

Thinking that he had found the perfect way to sell more multimixers, Kroc founded the McDonald's Company with himself as president and began selling franchises. He opened the first one in 1955 in Des Plaines, Illinois, with himself as part owner, and by the end of the year there were seven more. At this point he realized that his fortune was to be made by selling franchises, not multimixers, and so he strove to make the McDonald's concept work by making sure that franchisees succeeded. To this end, he required all franchise owners to be their own managers, thus cutting down on slipshod management practices. He drew on his many years as a salesman in the food-service industry to develop a training program to teach owner-managers how to purchase quality ingredients, how to prepare menu items quickly and properly, how to keep the establishment clean, how to handle the public, how to advertise—in short, how to succeed as a McDonald's restaurant. By 1960 there were more than 200 McDonald's restaurants nationwide; with average yearly gross sales of more than $150,000 per franchise, Kroc's percentage worked out to be more than a half million dollars per year, so he sold Prince Castle and said good-bye to the multimixer business forever.

In 1961 Kroc paid the McDonald brothers $2.7 million for their rights to the McDonald's concept. Four years later he incorporated McDonald's and sold stock to raise funds for further expansion. By 1968, when he stepped aside as president to become chairman of the board, there were almost 1,500 sets of "golden arches" selling hamburgers across America. The primary reason for the phenomenal increase in the number of franchises was that owning a McDonald's was like owning a license to print money. By 1968 McDonald's was known across the country, by word of mouth as well as by a massive advertising campaign, for offering good food and service at an inexpensive price. The corporation recruited and trained its franchisees and enforced its strict standards of cleanliness, quality, and service so well that from 1955, when the company was started, to 1984, when Kroc died, only one McDonald's franchise, in Bedford, Virginia, went out of business.

Next to McDonald's, the two great loves of Kroc's life were Joan Smith and baseball. He met Smith in 1956, fell in love with her, and divorced his first wife in 1961 to court her. When she refused his proposal of marriage, he married Jane Green instead in 1962. However, he was still in love with Smith, and in 1968 he finally convinced her to marry him. He divorced his second wife that same year and married Smith in 1969. As for baseball, Kroc grew up a fan of the Chicago Cubs. Once he became a millionaire, he tried to buy the team but was turned down. In 1974 he bought the San Diego Padres, then moved to San Diego so he could watch them play. He retired as chairman of the board in 1977, but he remained senior chairman until his death on January 14, 1984, in San Diego.

Further Reading

Brands, H. W. *Masters of Enterprise: Giants of American Business from John Jacob Astor and J. P. Morgan to Bill Gates and Oprah Winfrey.* New York: Free Press, 1999.

Crompton, Samuel W. *100 Americans Who Shaped American History.* San Mateo, Calif.: Bluewood Books, 1999.

Kroc, Ray, with Robert Anderson. *Grinding It Out: The Making of McDonald's.* New York: St. Martin's Paperbacks, 1987.

Love, John F. *McDonald's: Behind the Arches.* New York: Bantam Books, 1995.

Mariotti, Steve, et al. *Entrepreneurs in Profile: How 20 of the World's Greatest Entrepreneurs Built Their Business Empires . . . and How You Can, Too!* Franklin Lakes, N.J.: Career Press, 2000.

Kwolek, Stephanie Louise

(1923–   ) *inventor of Kevlar*

By the time Stephanie Kwolek invented Kevlar, synthetic fibers had been around for a number of years. However, previous synthetics such as rayon and nylon had been used solely as replacements for textile fibers. Kevlar, on the other hand, proved to be a suitable substitute, in a number of applications, for a wide range of materials, including plastic and steel.

Kwolek was born in 1923 in New Kensington, Pennsylvania. Her father, John, was a mold maker in an iron foundry, and her mother, Nellie, was a homemaker. When Kwolek was 10 years old, her father died and her mother took a production job in an aluminum factory to support the family. Kwolek developed a great deal of independence at an earlier age than did most girls, so her childhood dream of becoming a doctor is hardly surprising, even though female physicians were rare at that time. In 1946 she graduated from the Carnegie Institute of Technology (today Carnegie-Mellon University) with a B.S. in chemistry. She then went to work for E. I. du Pont de Nemours and Company in Buffalo, New York, as a research chemist. She intended to stay only long enough to earn the tuition money for medical school. But she soon discovered that the world of industrial chemistry was more interesting and challenging that she had ever imagined, and she eventually transferred to Du Pont's main laboratory in Wilmington, Delaware, where she stayed for the rest of her career.

Kwolek was assigned to the textile fibers department where she became involved in making synthetic fibers from polymers, complex molecules consisting of long chains of simple molecules arranged in repetitive configurations. At the time, all of the known synthetic fibers had been produced by melting polymers into solutions that were forced through a tiny hole, thus "spinning" a long strand that hardens when it cools. Kwolek's team worked with a group of polymers known as polyamides, whose melting temperatures are so high they cannot be spun into yarn. In the 1950s Kwolek began developing solvents that could dissolve polyamides rather than melt them, a process that became known as low-temperature polymerization. This process fascinated her so much that she remained with Du Pont for years without receiving a promotion. Her long-awaited first promotion finally came in 1961, when she began receiving patents for her discoveries in low-temperature polymerization.

In 1964 Kwolek began experimenting with substances known as liquid crystals. When heated, these multimolecular compounds turn from a crystalline solid into a quasi-liquid state, at which point they possess characteristics of both solids and liquids. Given their unique properties in this liquid-crystal state, they seemed to be good candidates for making synthetic fibers with unique capabilities. About a year later she produced a milky white liquid-crystal solution; it was so unlike any other polymer solution that at first her lab assistant did not want to spin it. But once it was spun and tested, it proved to be lighter than asbestos and stronger than steel. It would neither rust nor burn; it was highly resistant to cutting and abrasion; and it could be spun into sheets and pellets as well as into yarn. Her discovery was so different from all the other polymeric fibers that it was originally called Fiber B, a name that was later changed to Kevlar. She received a patent for Kevlar in 1971, which she assigned to Du Pont in exchange for a generous bonus and another promotion.

At first Kevlar was used to make aramid fibers for use in automobile tires in place of steel cord. Tires reinforced with these fibers proved to be puncture proof and resistant to high speeds, thus making them perfect for race cars and police cars. When Kevlar came to the attention of officials at the National Institute of Justice, it occurred to them that Kevlar might make the perfect bullet-proof vest for police officers. Existing vests were made either of steel cord (too heavy) or many layers of nylon (too thick). Kevlar vests, however, proved to be light, flexible, and able to stop a bullet fired from a range of only three feet. Between 1975, when the Kevlar vest was first made available, and 2000, Du Pont estimated that it had saved the lives of more than 1,300 law enforcement officers, not to mention a host of employees who work in environments that are prone to robbery. Eventually Kevlar was used to make parachutes, linings for rocket engines, circuit boards, protective gloves and helmets, building materials, and in a host of other applications.

Kwolek holds 28 patents, most of them related to low-temperature polymerization. The development of Kevlar and her other work have earned Kwolek many prestigious awards, including induction in 1994 into the National Inventors Hall of Fame, becoming only the fourth woman among the 113 inductees at that time to gain that honor. Kwolek also has been recipient of the National Medal of Technology (1994), the American Section of the Society of Chemical Industry's Perkin Medal (1997), and the Lemelson-Massachusetts Institute of Technology Award (1999). Kwolek retired from Du Pont in 1986, but she has remained active as a consultant for the corporation and for the National Academy of Sciences.

Further Reading

Macdonald, Anne L. *Feminine Ingenuity: Women and Invention in America.* New York: Ballantine Books, 1994.

"Stephanie Kwolek," National Inventors Hall of Fame. Available online. URL: http://www.invent.org/hall_of_fame/90.html. Downloaded on July 3, 2009.

Vare, Ethlie Ann, and Greg Ptacek. *Women Inventors & Their Discoveries.* Minneapolis: Oliver Press, 1993.

L

Land, Edwin Herbert
(1909–1991) *inventor of instant photography*

Many people know that THOMAS ALVA EDISON received more U.S. patents that anyone else. Few people, however, know that the holder of the second-most number of U.S. patents is Edwin Land, the father of instant photography. Oddly enough, Land began his career as an inventor by looking for a way to reduce the glare of automobile headlights.

Land was born on May 7, 1909, in Bridgeport, Connecticut. His father, Harry, was a scrap dealer, and his mother, Martha, was a homemaker. In 1926 he enrolled at Harvard University to study physics. He became interested in the possibility of polarizing, or focusing, light for a number of useful applications, such as keeping himself from being blinded by the glare from oncoming headlights. Soon he was spending more time in his own primitive laboratory than on course work. In 1929 he married Helen Maislen, with whom he had two children, and dropped out of school. For the next three years he worked odd jobs while continuing to experiment with light polarization. By 1932 he discovered that treating a sheet of plastic with iodoquinine sulfate produced an excellent material for polarizing light, which he called Polaroid J sheet. That same year, he and George Wheelwright, a retired Harvard physics professor, formed Land-Wheelwright Laboratories in Cambridge, Massachusetts, and began working to mass-produce and market Land's filter material. By 1935

the partners were selling Polaroid J to the American Optical Company for use in sunglasses, and to the Eastman Kodak Company for use as camera lens filters.

In 1937 Land-Wheelwright became the Polaroid Corporation. Despite the contracts with American Optical and Eastman Kodak, the company struggled to show a profit until the outbreak of World War II. During the war Polaroid was swamped with government contracts to produce such things as infrared filters, range finders and gun sights, night-vision goggles, and three-dimensional aerial photography.

Land became interested in instant photography while on vacation in 1943. He had just taken some photographs when one of his children asked why she could not see them immediately. Intrigued by the question, he began thinking of the answer, and within an hour he had it all worked out in his head. After the war, he devoted himself to developing an instant camera, and in 1947 he demonstrated the Model 95. The camera featured a sealed pod containing the film processing chemicals in gel paste form to permit dry processing inside the camera. The Model 95 was bulky and expensive—$89.50 without film, batteries, or a case—and it still took a full minute to develop a picture, which then had to be coated to keep it from fading. Nevertheless, the public loved it, and within eight years more than a million Model 95s had been sold. Meanwhile, Land had continued to make improvements to the camera, film, and developing process, and by 1960 the company's

Polaroid Land camera could develop a finished black-and-white picture in 10 seconds. In 1965 the company introduced the Swinger, an inexpensive camera that was so small it came with a wrist strap and could be carried easily in the palm of one hand. In 1972 the SX-70 was introduced, which could fully develop a color picture in less than a minute. By 1985 Polaroid had introduced self-processing film for developing 35mm black-and-white and color slides.

Land was clearly a gifted inventor, as his 537 patents attest. His performance as Polaroid's leader, however, is harder to assess. He showed little interest in market research and none at all in advertising. In the 1950s the company became heavily involved in developing equipment for 3-D movies, which proved to be only a momentary fad. The SX-70 was put into production before all the kinks concerning its battery and film had been worked out, so it contributed both to record high sales in 1972, when it came out, and to record low sales two years later. Partly as a result, Land was forced out as president, although he continued as chairman of the board. In 1977 Land committed much of the company's resources to developing Polavision, 8mm color film for taking silent instant movies, at a time when competitors were clearly moving toward audio-video cameras using videotape. For two years he persisted in promoting Polavision, at a loss of $70 million. Coming on the heels of the SX-70, Polavision contributed to Land's resignation as chairman in 1982.

In 1979 Land had founded the Rowland Foundation, a nonprofit research organization, in Cambridge. After leaving Polaroid, he spent his remaining years at Rowland, conducting research on various topics related to optics and light. He died on March 1, 1991, in Cambridge.

Further Reading

Friends of Photography. *Innovation/Imagination: 50 Years of Polaroid Photography.* New York: H.N. Abrams, 1999.

McPartland, Scott. *Edwin Land, Photographic Pioneer.* Vero Beach, Fla.: Rourke Enterprises, 1993.

Wensberg, Peter C. *Land's Polaroid: A Company and the Man Who Invented It.* Englewood, Colo.: Newstrack, 1988.

Latimer, Lewis Howard

(1848–1928) *inventor of the lightbulb apparatus*

In 1918 the Edison Pioneers was formed of people who had been associated with the famous inventor THOMAS ALVA EDISON prior to 1885. In this distinguished group was one black man, Lewis Latimer. Latimer's main claim to fame is that he invented a superior carbon filament and other improvements for the incandescent lightbulb. Ironically, he had done this before joining Edison, while he was working for Edison's chief rival.

Latimer was born on September 4, 1848, in Chelsea, Massachusetts. His father, George, was a barber, and his mother, Rebecca, was a homemaker. As a young boy, he helped out around his father's barber shop and worked occasionally as a paperhanger's assistant. At age 10, following the mysterious disappearance of his father, a former slave who may have been kidnapped by his former master from Virginia, he and his brothers were apprenticed to the Farm School, a state-run work camp. The three brothers ran away after only a short stay and returned home, and Latimer spent the next six years doing odd jobs and working as an office boy for Isaac Wright, a Boston lawyer. At age 16 he enlisted in the Union navy and spent the last year of the Civil War at sea. Upon being discharged in 1865, he found work as an office boy for Crosby and Gould, Boston patent attorneys. He eventually taught himself the art of mechanical drawing, and over the next 10 years he gradually moved up in the company until he became chief draftsman. Surrounded as he was by invention, he invented a few things of his own, most notably an improved toilet for use in railway passenger cars, for which he received a patent in 1872. In 1873 he married Mary Lewis with whom he had two children.

By 1879 Latimer had tired of working for Crosby and Gould, so he moved to Bridgeport, Connecticut, where he found work as a paperhanger. He also took on a part-time job as a draftsman at the Follandsbee Machine Shop, where he chanced to meet Hiram S. Maxim, chief engineer of the U.S. Electric Lighting Company and Edison's principal rival in the race to invent the better lightbulb. Maxim was looking for a draftsman and personal secretary, and on their second meeting he hired Latimer to do both jobs. When U.S. Electric relocated to New York City in 1880, Latimer went, too, having been put in charge of developing a better filament for Maxim's lightbulb.

The major problem with lightbulbs in the 1870s was that their filaments, which were made out of carbon, burned out too quickly. Whoever could invent a long-lasting filament would be able to corner the lightbulb market, and this is the contest at which Maxim, Edison, and others competed. Latimer scored an important victory for Maxim when, in 1880, he invented an improved version of the carbon filament. He treated the standard filament with hydrocarbon vapor so that its resistance to the electricity flowing through it was equalized and standardized, thus making it last longer than competitors' filaments. Two years later he scored another victory when he invented an improved method for bonding carbon into filaments. At the same time he discovered that shaping the filaments into an elongated, loopy "M" made the filament easier to construct by hand and also contributed somewhat to its longevity. By 1882 he had also invented a sturdier base for the lightbulb's globe. All of these inventions helped give the Maxim lightbulb the edge over its competitors until 1904, when Willis R. Whitney invented a metalized carbon filament that lasted even longer.

Meanwhile, Latimer was also involved in other aspects of Maxim's operations. He helped install the country's first commercial incandescent lighting system in the Equitable Building, and in 1881 he supervised such installations in other buildings in the United States. Later that year he went to London, England, where he supervised the establishment of a lightbulb factory for Maxim's English affiliate. By 1882 he was in great demand as an electric-light technician, and he used this position to his advantage by going to work for the Olmstead Electric Lighting Company in Brooklyn. He soon moved to the Acme Electric Company of New York, and then in 1883 to the Excelsior Electric Company, which was controlled by Edison.

Latimer was involved in a wide range of Edison's activities after 1883. He took a position in the engineering department in 1885, then in 1889 he became one of Edison's patent-law advisors. To this end he traveled the country, gathering affidavits from various people who had been involved in the development of electric lighting and the invention of the associated apparatus, and providing legal testimony in the various court hearings involving patent rights. His knowledge about the early history of electric lighting is reflected in his book, *Incandescent Electric Lighting, a Practical Description of the Edison System* (1890). From 1896 to 1911 he served on the Board of Patent Control, a joint endeavor of the General Electric Company, which included Edison's companies, and the Westinghouse Electric Company, which had acquired Maxim's company. In this position he arranged cross-licensing of patents and assisted inventors of both companies. When the board was dissolved in 1911, he went to work as a patent consultant for the law firm of Hammer and Schwartz.

In 1924 Latimer retired to his home in Flushing, New York, to concentrate on his favorite hobbies, painting and writing poetry. He died on December 11, 1928, in Flushing.

Further Reading

Ayer, Eleanor H. *Lewis Latimer: Creating Bright Ideas.* Austin, Tex.: Raintree Steck-Vaughn, 1997.
Russell, Dick. *Black Genius and the American Experience.* New York: Carroll & Graf, 1999.
Sullivan, Charles F. *Lewis H. Latimer: Inventor and Scientist.* Queens, N.Y.: Sullivan, 1984.

Lauder, Estée

(1906–2004) *entrepreneur in women's cosmetics*

The reigning queen of the booming and lucrative field of women's cosmetics for most of the last half of the 20th century, Estée Lauder was one of the most successful businesswomen of her time. Her eponymous company, whose rise both spurred and mirrored that of beauty aids, still remains among the world's leading enterprises that create, market, and sell what she once called "jars of hope."

Estée Lauder was born Josephine Esther Mentzer in the Corona, Queens, section of New York

City on July 1, 1908. Her family had rather modest means and she grew up living above her father's hardware store. In her 1985 autobiography, Lauder described her father and her mother Rose, recalling that her mother was, "a Hungarian beauty whose mother was a French Catholic and whose father was a Hungarian Jew" and her father as, "an elegant, dapper monarchist in Europe, who, when transported to a new country, still carried a cane and gloves on Sundays." Estèe attended Newtown High School in Queens, where she was renowned for her attention to her appearance.

In the 1920s, Estée began to sell skin creams that were created by her mother's brother, John Schotz, who worked as a chemist in New York City. Estée developed the personal sales skill that would always remain a prominent trait by persuading beauty shops and beach clubs to stock the products developed by her uncle. During this

Estée Lauder, in a 1966 vivid print from Yves Saint Laurent, puts today's face on a customer by using a darker shade of lipstick. *(Photo by Bill Sauro for the World Journal Tribune/Library of Congress)*

time, in 1930, she married Joseph Lauter (they soon changed their last name to Lauder), whom she divorced in 1939, before remarrying him in 1942. Estée and Joseph remained together until his death in 1982.

In the early 1940s, Lauder met a Dutch industrialist named Arnold van Ameringen, who came to provide financial and technical support for the beauty products sold by Lauder. Armed with this critically important infusion of capital, the Estée Lauder company was established in 1946. Throughout the 1950s, Lauder encouraged the growth of her company by personally visiting stores where her products were sold and those higher-end department stores where she hoped they would be sold. Boosted by the success of the company's bath oil, "Youth Dew," as well as her own persistence, Estée Lauder products soon came to be very popular at stores such as Saks Fifth Avenue.

The widespread demand for Estée Lauder products grew with the rise of American prosperity in the 1950s and 1960s. Supporting this rise was the tireless effort of Lauder—who always served as the CEO of her company—to promote the products and herself as an extension of them. Lauder explained, "I love my product. I love to touch the creams, smell them, look at them, carry them with me. A person has to love her harvest if she's to expect others to love it." Lauder blazed the trail for new marketing methods, such as the now common beauty aid–related "free gift with purchase" and free samples of relatively expensive and highly desired products. She led the expansion of her company to include in-store spas, such as the first one that opened in a Manhattan Bloomingdale's in 1965. She later reflected on the successful and widely imitated spas by describing her attention to detail, saying, "I'd make sure the color I chose was the same wonderful 'in between a blue and a green' that whispered elegance, aristocracy, and also complemented bathroom wallpapers."

The aristocracy referenced in speaking about the spas was an attraction of Lauder's in personal relationships as well. Lauder enjoyed friendships with royalty, including the Duchess of Windsor, Princess Grace of Monaco, and other prominent women of their time, including First Lady Nancy

Reagan. She regularly invited these and other high-profile friends to social gatherings organized at one of her many homes. In January 1978, Lauder received induction into the government of France's Legion of Honor and was praised by a French official that she "represents what we French admire most about Americans—brains and heart."

The growth of the Estée Lauder company continued into the 1980s and 1990s, largely through the success of Lauder brands Clinique, Origins, and Aramis, a product line for men. Licensing and distribution pacts, such as the 1990s' agreements with the Tommy Hilfiger Corporation and MAC further strengthened Lauder's position in the marketplace.

Lauder died at the age of 97 on April 24, 2004, in her home on the Upper East Side of Manhattan. The company she built, now led by her grandson William, employs over 20,000 people, sells products in over 130 countries, and has a net worth of approximately $10 billion.

Further Reading

Mirabella, Grace. "Estée Lauder." Time 100. Available online. URL: http://www.time.com/time/time100/builder/profile/lauder.html. Downloaded on August 27, 2009.

Severo, Richard. "Estée Lauder, Pursuer of Beauty and Cosmetics Titan, Dies at 97." *New York Times.* Available online. URL: http://www.nytimes.com/2004/04/26/nyregion/estee-lauder-pursuer-of-beauty-and-cosmetics-titan-dies-at-97.html. Downloaded on August 27, 2009.

Lauder, Estée. *Estée: A Success Story.* New York: Ballantine Books, 1986.

Lear, William Powell

(1902–1978) *inventor of airplane autopilot and the Learjet*

One of the most important aviation devices ever built is the autopilot. This control system allows an airplane to stay on course while the pilot rests, thus greatly facilitating long-distance air travel. The autopilot's inventor, William Lear, also revolutionized business aviation by designing one of the world's most popular private airplanes, the Learjet.

Lear was born on June 26, 1902, in North Hannibal, Missouri. His father, Reuben, was a carpenter, and his mother, Gertrude, was a homemaker. His parents divorced when he was six years old, and he moved with his mother to Chicago, Illinois. His childhood was an unhappy one; his stepfather seems to have taken no interest in him, and his mother belittled his precociousness. As a boy he was somewhat of a loner, preferring to spend his spare time constructing electrical devices from scavenged parts. His ability to make something out of practically nothing led him at age 12 to dedicate his life to becoming an inventor.

Bored with school, he dropped out after completing the eighth grade and somehow talked his way into a job as an airplane mechanic. In 1918, at age 16, he ran away to Denver, Colorado, where he lied about his age to join the U.S. Navy. Instead of being sent to Europe to fight against the Germans in World War I, he was sent to radio repair school at the navy's training center in Chicago, where he stayed until the war ended.

For 13 years after the war, Lear worked a succession of jobs—telegraph operator, salesman, radio repairman, electrical engineer—quitting each as soon as he had mastered it. Meanwhile, he moonlighted as an inventor. One of his inventions was the Lazy Boy, a remote-control radio tuner. Another was a radio that was small enough to fit in an automobile; other car radios existed but they were too bulky to be practical. Lacking the funds at age 23 to go into the radio-manufacturing business, in 1924 he sold the car radio design to the Motorola Corporation.

Having finally grown weary of working for other people, in 1931 Lear went into business for himself as the Lear Development Company. Three years later he sold to the Radio Corporation of America (RCA) a coil he had designed that could amplify the sound produced by any radio, regardless of its design. In 1934 he used the proceeds from the sale to move to Dayton, Ohio, and establish the Lear Avia Corporation (renamed Lear Inc. in 1939), which specialized in developing and manufacturing navigational aids for private airplanes. At the time, most private pilots had to navigate by following rivers or railroad tracks, which limited their ability to fly wherever they wanted. Lear addressed this problem by inventing the Radioaire, the Lear-O-Scope, and the Learmatic Navigator, all of which used radio waves to help pilots determine their exact location. During World War II Lear sold more than $100 million worth of navigational equipment to the U.S. military for use in fighters, bombers, and cargo planes. He also seems to have straightened out his personal life during the war. Married and divorced three times by age 40, in 1942 he married Moya Olesen; they had four children and remained together until his death.

For years Lear had been concerned about pilot fatigue during long flights. Unlike an automobile driver, a tired pilot cannot simply pull over to the side of the road and rest, and at the time few airports existed across the country. During the war he began experimenting with an autopilot, an electromechanical control system that would automatically keep an airplane on a steady course. In 1946 he perfected a device that could keep an aircraft from pitching, rolling, and yawing. At first he sold autopilots exclusively to the U.S. military for use on jet fighters, but soon he was selling them to private pilots as well. Modified over the years by Lear and others so that it could practically fly a plane by itself, the autopilot revolutionized flying, and in 1949 the National Aeronautics Association presented Lear with its Collier Trophy, symbolic of great achievements in aviation.

After World War II Lear expanded his company's operations by buying used Lockheed Lodestar twin-engine jets. After refurbishing the interiors with more luxurious appointments and outfitting the cockpits with his newest navigational devices, he renamed them Learstars and sold them to private corporations. By 1962 Lear was ready to start building his own small jets for use as corporate planes. However, there were already two competitors in the field, and his board of directors feared that the customer base for corporate jets was too small to support a third. Undaunted by his directors' lack of support, Lear sold his interest in Lear Inc. for $14 million and formed Lear Jet International. He located his new company in Geneva, Switzerland, because the Swiss government had just canceled a contract on a fighter-bomber with the exact wing design he wanted to use, and tooling for building the wing was available there. However,

he encountered so many production difficulties in Switzerland that in 1963 he relocated the company to Wichita, Kansas. That same year Lear unveiled the first Learjet, a downsized, lower-priced version of his competitors' offerings that held six passengers and cruised at speeds of more than 500 miles per hour. Within a year the company had sold more than 100 planes, and the company seemed poised for success. Unfortunately, by 1966 several Learjets had crashed, mostly because their wings had iced prior to takeoff, and sales crashed with them. Beset by cash-flow problems and spurred once again by the desire to tackle a new challenge, in 1967 Lear sold the company for $28 million to Gates Rubber Company. Eventually Gates Learjet, as the company was renamed, solved its technical and financial problems, and the Learjet became one of the most popular private jets in the world.

Lear spent the remaining years of his life in Stead, Nevada, where in 1967 he had formed Lear Motors Corporation. He planned to solve the nation's air pollution problem by developing a steam-powered automobile, but the car burned too much fuel to be practical and the company went out of business after two years. He also developed the Learfan, a propeller that pushes rather than pulls an aircraft, but the basic concept never caught on. He died on May 14, 1978, in Reno, Nevada.

Further Reading

Rashke, Richard. *Stormy Genius: The Life of Aviation's Maverick, Bill Lear.* Boston: Houghton Mifflin, 1985.

"William P. Lear," National Inventors Hall of Fame. Available online. URL: http://www.invent.org/hall_of_fame/94.html. Downloaded on July 3, 2009.

Leslie, Miriam
(Miriam Florence Follin, Minnie Montez, and Frank Leslie)
(1836–1914) *entrepreneur in newspaper and magazine publishing*

Miriam Leslie was one of the most unusual women of the 19th century. By all accounts a beautiful woman well into her 60s, she was married four times and would have been married a fifth had the

Spanish count she was engaged to lived. She was the center of more than one scandal and, late in life, declared herself to be a French baroness. More important, she was also a good writer, a better editor, and the best businesswoman of her day.

Leslie was born Miriam Florence Follin on June 5, 1836, in New Orleans, Louisiana. Her father, Charles, was a merchant, and her mother, Susan, was a homemaker. At age 10 she moved with her family to Cincinnati, Ohio, and then four years later to New York City. At age 18 she married David Peacock, but they never lived together and the marriage was annulled two years later. In 1857 she toured the Northeast with the famous actress Lola Montez, adopting the stage name Minnie Montez and masquerading as the star's younger sister. That same year she married Ephraim Squier and settled in New York City.

Leslie got her start in publishing in 1858, when she translated a play by Alexandre Dumas *fils* into English. The following year she helped her husband publish a Spanish-language newspaper in New York City. In 1863, when Squier was hired by Frank Leslie, the proprietor of Frank Leslie Publishing House, to be the editor of *Frank Leslie's Lady's Magazine,* she joined the staff as well. Two years later, Frank Leslie hired her to plan and edit *Frank Leslie's Chimney Corner,* which contained stories that appealed to every age and emotion. In 1871 she translated a travel book about Central America from French to English and became editor of *Frank Leslie's Lady's Journal.* Meanwhile, she and Frank Leslie had become romantically involved; by 1873 they had divorced their spouses, and the following year they married. Over the next six years she served as editor of *Lady's Magazine, Lady's Journal,* and *Chimney Corner,* and she wrote a critically acclaimed book about her travels through the West.

Frank Leslie believed in publishing a lot of newspapers and magazines so just about everyone could find something to their taste in one of his publications. He also was one of the first publishers to provide high-quality illustrations in his publications, along with equal doses of sensationalism and folksy humor. For a while, this formula made him one of the most successful publishers in the United States. But by 1877 his company found itself in seri-

ous financial difficulty because he was spending more than he was earning. When he died in 1880, he left Miriam with a pile of debts and precious little income to pay them with.

Undaunted, Miriam Leslie took immediate steps to save her crumbling publishing empire. She pawned her jewels to raise enough money to pay the bills and to keep the doors open. She changed her legal name to Frank Leslie so that she could sign checks without changing the accounts and continue to use his name on the mastheads. When President James Garfield was assassinated in early 1881, she published several extra editions of *Frank Leslie's Illustrated Newspaper,* complete with engraved artist's renditions of the assassination, thus boosting circulation from 30,000 to 200,000. Most important, she folded or merged most of the company's publications, and by 1885 only two weeklies and four monthlies were left, including *Frank Leslie's Illustrated Newspaper* and *Frank Leslie's Popular Monthly.* Finally, in 1889 she incorporated Frank Leslie Publishing House with a capitalization of $1 million, then sold off both weekly publications. For her success at preserving her company, she earned from an adoring press the nickname "The Empress of Journalism."

In 1892 Leslie married William Wilde; they were divorced two years later. In 1895 she began winding down her publishing career by leasing her monthlies to a syndicate headed by Frederic L. Colver. Three years later, *Popular Monthly* was floundering, so she came back to serve as its editor until 1900, when she left the publishing business for good. For the next 14 years, she invested in Manhattan real estate and toured Europe. She died on September 18, 1914, in New York City. At the time of her death, her estate was valued at $2 million, most of which she left to Carrie Chapman Catt, a suffragist, to further the cause of gaining women the right to vote.

Further Reading

Jackson, Donald Dale. "Miriam Leslie: Belle of the Boardroom." *Smithsonian,* November 1997: 151–162.

"Miriam Florence Leslie Biography," PageWise, Inc. Available online. URL: http://ma.essortment.com/miriamflorence_rapg.htm. Downloaded on July 3, 2009.

Levitt, Abraham
(1880–1962) *inventor of tract housing*

Before Abraham Levitt founded Levitt and Sons in 1929, every new home in the United States was custom built, most new homes built in the country were huge, and the concept of suburban or tract housing had yet to be developed. Under Levitt's general management, Levitt and Sons changed all that. Responding to an enormous demand for inexpensive housing after World War II, the company revolutionized the way houses are built by introducing the concept of mass production to the residential construction industry. Although many people criticized Levitt's homes for looking alike, which they did, those homes provided millions of Americans with the opportunity to escape overcrowded cities and live in the suburbs.

Levitt was born on July 1, 1880, in Brooklyn, New York. His father, Louis, was a rabbi, and his mother, Nellie, was a homemaker. At age 10 he dropped out of school to deliver newspapers, and over the next 10 years he helped support his family by working as a dishwasher, waiter, and stevedore (longshoreman). Having read voraciously as a young man, in 1900 he passed the entrance exam and won a scholarship to New York University Law School. He specialized in real-estate law, and in 1902 he wrote a student manual on the subject; it was adopted by the school, and the proceeds from its sale paid the rest of his way through college. The following year he received his law degree and opened a private practice that thrived for 25 years. In 1906 he married Pauline Biederman with whom he had two children, William and Alfred.

In 1929 Levitt and his two sons formed Levitt and Sons, a residential construction company. In addition to providing general management and a broad vision of the future, Levitt focused on matters related to landscaping and law. Meanwhile, William took care of construction management, finance, and sales, while Alfred was in charge of building design. The company got off to a slow start because the stock market crashed that same year, but despite the onset of the Great Depression, the company managed to prosper. During the 1930s, as New York City became more and more overcrowded, it became imperative to develop resi-

dential communities on Long Island. Levitt and Sons contributed to this development by building more than 2,500 custom homes in the communities of Rockville Centre and Manhasset.

During World War II the company won a government contract to build 2,300 homes for military and civilian personnel in Norfolk, Virginia. Unlike the Long Island homes, the Norfolk housing was not custom built but was to be constructed according to the same basic design. About halfway through the project, the Levitts realized that they could mass-produce these houses, almost in assembly-line fashion. Beginning with the last 750 houses, they experimented with different ways to build homes quickly and cheaply without sacrificing quality. By the time they were done, they had perfected the basic system for building suburban tract housing.

After the war, there was a tremendous demand for new homes among veterans and civilians alike, and the Levitts set out to satisfy that demand as best they could. In 1946 they bought more than 4,600 acres in Nassau County on Long Island and began mass-producing homes, using the techniques they had developed in Norfolk. Levitt reckoned that the greatest demand would be for starter homes for young families, so he had Alfred design a two-bedroom, Cape Cod-style house of about 800 square feet on a quarter-acre lot that served as the basic model for the entire project. Next, they subcontracted the manufacture of items that could be mass-produced off-site, such as kitchen cabinets, shower stalls, and windows. Most important, they organized their workers into crews that specialized in one aspect of home building, such as concrete work, framing, or roofing; instead of building one complete home, these crews performed their specialty on a number of homes. Once they got things rolling, Levitt and Sons was building as many as 36 houses per day. As the first sections were finished, the company offered to rent each house for $65 per month or to sell it for $6,990. Demand was so great that within three years the purchase price for the homes had increased by $1,000. In response to consumer demand, the company also built a number of larger, ranch-style homes with three or more bedrooms, but even the largest house sold for less than

$10,000. By 1951 Levitt and Sons had built more than 17,000 houses, as well as parks, playgrounds, schools, and shopping centers, in what became known as Levittown.

Having grossed about $150 million from building Levittown, Levitt and Sons set out to do it again, this time on the outskirts of Philadelphia, Pennsylvania. In 1951 the company bought 5,500 acres in Bucks County; over the next four years, the company constructed 16,000 homes, most of them ranch style and selling for between $9,000 and $17,500. The next Levittown was built in the mid-1950s in New Jersey near Willingboro, which from 1959 to 1963 was renamed Levittown. Other Levittowns were constructed in Florida and Puerto Rico.

In 1962 Levitt retired from the company. Alfred had long since left Levitt and Sons, so its management fell to William, who sold it in 1968 to International Telephone and Telegraph for $492 million. Levitt died on August 20, 1962, in Great Neck, New York.

Further Reading

Boulton, Alexander. "The Buy of the Century." *American Heritage* 44, July 1993: 62–69.

"Levittown USA: A Brief History," Levittown Historical Society. Available online. URL: http://www. levittownhistoricalsociety.org/history.htm. Downloaded on July 3, 2009.

Little, Arthur Dehon
(1863–1935) *entrepreneur in industrial research*

The first independent industrial research firm in the United States was founded by Arthur D. Little. Eventually known as Arthur D. Little Inc., it provided chemical and engineering expertise to industry and government in a wide range of areas. By the time of his death, Little had helped to overcome the scientific community's reluctance to use its knowledge to make improvements and discoveries of commercial value, while helping to overcome the business community's reluctance to invest in scientific research.

Little was born Arthur Dehon Little on December 15, 1863, in Boston, Massachusetts. His father, Thomas, was an army captain, and his mother, Amelia, was a homemaker. At age two he moved with his family to Portland, Maine. As a youth he developed an intense interest in chemistry, and during one particularly memorable experiment he nearly blew up the house. He studied chemistry for three years at the Massachusetts Institute of Technology, then in 1884 he went to work as an apprentice chemist at the Richmond Paper Company's wood pulp mill in Rumford, Rhode Island. Six weeks later he became plant superintendent after his two bosses got into an argument with each other and quit. The mill was the first in the United States to use the sulfite process, whereby wood is turned into pulp by boiling it in a pressure cooker filled with acid bisulfite solution until the cellulose, the part of the wood from which paper is made, is separated out. The sulfite process had not been well understood by the people who built the mill, but he made the system work better by rearranging the equipment and fine-tuning its operation. He also invented a steel pressure cooker with an acid-resistant liner, which became known as the Little Digester. His modifications to the mill worked so well that Richmond Paper sent him to New Bern, North Carolina, to supervise the construction of a wood pulp mill there.

In 1886 Little left Richmond Paper, returned to Boston, and became partners with Roger B. Griffin in Griffin & Little, a chemical analysis and consulting firm. They quickly became the nation's foremost authorities on paper mill operations, and consulted for a variety of clients regarding plant construction and product and process analysis. Little also developed a way to convert cellulose into artificial silk, better known as rayon, as well as a way to tan hides by using chromium sulfate rather than tannin.

After Griffin died in 1893, Little embarked on several unsuccessful commercial ventures. In 1894 he formed the American Viscose Company, acquired a small pulp mill in Waltham, Massachusetts, and began making paper by the viscose method, whereby cellulose is mixed with caustic soda and carbon bisulfide and reduced to a viscous solution. Although the chemical process and the mill worked well enough, the company was undercapitalized and failed within a few years. In 1899 he tried to resuscitate it as the Cellulose

Products Company, but it failed within a year for the same reason. Having demonstrated his lack of ability as a businessman, by 1900 he was ready to revive his old consulting firm, becoming partners with William H. Walker and renaming it Little & Walker. This company branched out beyond paper mill operations and offered consulting services in the areas of analytical chemistry, coal, lubrication, biology, textiles, engineering, and forest products. The company thrived, and by 1905, when Walker left, it employed a staff of seven chemists and engineers. That same year Little renamed it the Arthur D. Little Company, and over the next 30 years he turned the company into the foremost industrial research company in the world.

Little's company developed a number of devices for industry, including a machine for converting bagasse, the waste fiber from sugarcane, into paper, as well as ways to make everything from dope for coating the wings of biplanes to charcoal for gas-mask filters. The company also played an important role in establishing research laboratories, including the U.S. Forest Products Laboratory in Madison, Wisconsin, in 1908, and the General Motors Research Laboratory in Detroit, Michigan, in 1921. Perhaps most important, Little himself designed a new approach to developing industrial chemical processes, called unit operations. When designing a new manufacturing or processing system, he espoused including all of the functions needed to bring about a particular physical or chemical change as one step, or unit. By 1930 unit operations had been adopted as standard operating procedure by virtually the entire American chemical industry.

Little was a tireless promoter of industrial research as being essential to improving a company's bottom line. To this end he once had his company make a silk purse out of a sow's ear. He rendered 100 pounds of sows' ears into glue, combined the glue with various chemicals, strained the gluey mass into gelatinous fibers, and then sewed the silklike fibers into two purses that he displayed at trade shows across the country. Needless to say, the industrial community was much impressed by this demonstration of what industrial research could do because, as the old saying goes, you can't make a silk purse out of a sow's ear. Ironically, in his own affairs he showed little interest in money.

He often refused to charge customers whom he failed to help, and until his death his company struggled to make ends meet. He once remarked that "a professional man starts to fail the moment he permits money to shape his career." In this, he reflected the ambivalence felt by much of the academic community, from which industrial researchers were drawn. Many were reluctant to use their training for what they perceived to be the crass pursuit of corporate profits, while others realized that the scientific method and scientific knowledge could be used to make life much easier for millions of people if they were properly harnessed with entrepreneurial activity. By his actions, he helped to overcome the reluctance of the former.

Little died on August 1, 1935, while vacationing in Northeast Harbor, Maine. In 1901 he had married Henriette Anthony, but they had no children, so he left the bulk of his estate to the Massachusetts Institute of Technology. His company survived his death, and by the end of the 20th century it employed more than 2,500 people in facilities around the globe.

Further Reading

Kahn, E. J., Jr. *The Problem Solvers: A History of Arthur D. Little, Inc.* Boston: Little Brown, 1986.

Magee, John F. *Arthur D. Little, Inc.: At the Moving Frontier.* New York: Newcomen Society in North America, 1986.

Report "On the Making of Silk Purses from Sows' Ears," MIT Institute Archives & Special Collections. Available online. URL: http://libraries.mit.edu/archives/exhibits/purse/. Downloaded on July 3, 2009.

Little, Royal
(1896–1989) *founder of Textron*

Royal Little is generally credited with starting the wave of conglomeration that swept American business beginning in the 1950s. Strictly speaking, ABRAM NICHOLAS PRITZKER beat him to it when he began acquiring diversified companies in the early 1940s. However, to this day Pritzker's operations remain shrouded in mystery, while Little's were out in the open for all to see. Consequently, it was Little and not Pritzker whose success as a conglomerateur was widely admired and copied by other American businesspeople.

Little was born on March 1, 1896, in Wakefield, Massachusetts. His father died when he was young, and his stepfather, an executive of a printing company, moved the family to Narragansett, Rhode Island, where he grew up. After graduating from high school, he enrolled in Harvard University and received his B.A. in 1919. At the suggestion of his uncle, ARTHUR DEHON LITTLE, he took a job with a synthetic fiber manufacturer in Boston, Massachusetts. In 1923 he borrowed $10,000, formed the Special Yarns Corporation in Boston, and began manufacturing rayon, a synthetic fiber. In 1932 he married Augusta Ellis with whom he had two children; they were divorced in 1959.

Unfortunately for Little, Special Yarns was grossly undercapitalized, and he fought off bankruptcy for more than 20 years. Finally, in 1944, he was able to recapitalize the company; he changed its name to Textron Corporation and began expanding its operations to include the manufacture of cloth and ready-to-wear garments as well as fibers. But by 1952 the company was in bad shape again, having that year lost $6 million despite doing sales of almost $100 million.

That same year Little had a brainstorm. He realized that, because his company's various divisions were all in the same basic business, when one had a bad year the others did, too. He further realized that the way to get around this dilemma was to diversify by buying companies in totally unrelated industries. That way, when one industry in which he owned a company was down, hopefully another industry in which he owned a company would be up; in essence, this is the same logic followed by managers of mutual funds. By shrewdly acquiring companies that already had good management teams in place, he hoped to be able to come out in the black every year.

Having had this idea, it remained for Little to convince Textron's stockholders of its wisdom. Perhaps not surprisingly, this was easily done, given the fact that the company was losing money. At the annual meeting in 1952, they voted to amend the articles of association to allow the executive board to acquire companies in unrelated businesses. Over the next eight years, Little got Textron into all sorts of businesses. His first

nontextile acquisition was the Burkart Manufacturing Company of St. Louis, Missouri, which made cushioning materials for automobiles. Other acquisitions included Bell Aerospace, which made helicopters and other defense-related items for the federal government; Camcar Screw, which manufactured metal fasteners; Dalmo Victor, which manufactured radar antennas; and E-Z-GO, which manufactured golf carts. By 1960 Little had acquired 40 companies in as many industries. Annual profits had risen to $14 million on annual sales of $383 million. Meanwhile, Little had been selling off Textron's textile-related divisions, and by 1963 it was no longer making fiber, cloth, or clothing.

In 1960 Little retired as Textron's chairman and chief executive. He spent his remaining years as chairman of the board of Narragansett Capital Corporation, a venture capital company that he had founded in 1959, and as chairman of Lonsdale Enterprises, a financial consulting firm in White Plains, New York. He divided his time between his homes in Narragansett and Nassau, the Bahamas. Other than business, his passion was golf, and he continued to shoot scores of less than 100 until the time of his death. He died on January 12, 1989, in Nassau. Meanwhile, Textron continued to diversify and thrive, and by the end of the 20th century it was a multibillion-dollar corporation.

Further Reading
Little, Royal. *How to Lose $100,000,000 and Other Valuable Advice.* Boston: Little, Brown, 1979.

"Textron Company Profile-History," Textron. Available online. URL: http://www.textron.com/about/company/company_history.jsp. Downloaded on July 3, 2009.

Lockheed, Malcolm
(Malcolm Loughead) (1887–1958), and
Allan Lockheed
(Allan Haines Loughead) (1889–1969)
founders of Lockheed Aviation

For many years, one of the most successful American aircraft companies was the Lockheed Corporation. Makers of huge commercial and military airplanes, the company had few rivals in the aviation industry. Ironically, the company did not achieve fame and fortune until after its founders, Malcolm and Allan Lockheed, had left the company.

The Lockheeds were born Malcolm and Allan Haines Loughead in 1887 (exact date unknown) and on January 20, 1889, respectively, in Niles, California. The last name is pronounced Lockheed, the spelling they both adopted legally around 1934. Their father, John, was a hardware store owner and truck farmer, and their mother, Flora, was a writer. At age 17 Malcolm moved to San Francisco and went to work as an auto mechanic, and he was joined two years later by Allan. In 1909 the brothers became interested in aviation when their brother Victor wrote a book about flying. Victor worked for James E. Plew, an automobile distributor in Chicago, Illinois, and in 1910 Plew hired Allan to be the mechanic for his two private airplanes. Allan quickly learned how to fly, and for the next year he supported himself by taking care of Plew's planes and flying them in aerial daredevil shows. In 1911 he married Dorothy Watts with whom he had two children. She died in 1922, and two years later he married Evelyn Starr. They divorced in 1936, and two years later he married Helen Kundert with whom he had one child.

In 1911 Plew sold his planes, leaving Allan without a job. Undaunted, he soon found work as a flight instructor with the International Aviation Company. He also began designing airplanes in his spare time, and in 1912 he returned to San Francisco and rejoined Malcolm in the garage. With Malcolm's help, he designed a seaplane; the Model G, as they called it, had a 30-foot fuselage and a 46-foot wingspan, making it one of the largest planes in the world. They built the plane at night after work, and in 1913 they took it on a test flight. For the next three years, they flew the Model G at air shows and supplemented their mechanics' wages by giving people rides over San Francisco Bay. During San Francisco's Panama-Pacific Exposition in 1915, they charged $10 for a 10-minute ride and made $6,000 in 50 days.

By 1916 the Lockheeds had attracted enough financial backers to open the Loughead Aircraft Manufacturing Company in a Santa Barbara garage, with Allan as vice president and Malcolm as secretary/treasurer. Two years later they demonstrated their first model, the F-1. This was another huge seaplane—its wingspan was 74 feet and it could carry 10 people while cruising at 70 miles per hour—and they hoped to sell it to the U.S. Navy for use during World War I. But the navy had already committed itself to buy seaplanes from GLENN HAMMOND CURTISS, so the Lockheeds retooled the F-1 into a land-based airplane. They tried to sell it to commercial aviation companies, but it was too big and too expensive for these companies to afford. In fact, the only people who could afford the F-1 were Hollywood film producers, who hired the plane for $150 per hour so they could get aerial shots for their movies. In 1919 Loughead Aircraft introduced a smaller plane called the S-1. This single-engine biplane featured the first single-shell fuselage and had wings that folded up to save on parking space. It was designed to appeal to the general aviating public, but by the time it came out World War I had ended and the government was selling surplus biplanes for almost nothing. Frustrated by Loughead Aircraft's failure to find its niche, Malcolm left the company and the industry, never to return. Allan held on until 1921, when the company officially went out of business.

Allan worked at various jobs until 1926, when he found new backers and formed the Lockheed Aircraft Company in Hollywood, with himself as vice president. This time the company had a new design, the Vega, which did well. A single-engine, enclosed-cabin, high-wing monoplane, the Vega closely resembled the Ryan NYP that Charles A. Lindbergh flew across the Atlantic Ocean in 1927. Following that historic flight, planes of that type became popular, and Lockheed Aircraft soon found itself swamped with orders from airlines and individuals alike. In 1928 the company upgraded the engine so the plane could cruise at 150 mph, thus making it highly attractive to commercial airlines. By 1929 Lockheed Aircraft was making so much money that it was targeted for acquisition by the Detroit Aircraft Corporation, a holding company that was trying to gain control of the aviation industry. Allan fought the takeover, but the stockholders insisted on the merger, which took place that same year. He immediately resigned from the company and sold all of his stock, just months before Detroit Aircraft went into receivership following the collapse of the stock market.

Having become a wealthy man as a result of the merger, Allan lived a life of relative luxury until 1937, when he got back into the aviation business. He formed the Alcor Aircraft Corporation to manufacture his new design, a twin-engine version of the Vega. Unfortunately, the plane crashed into San Francisco Bay on its test flight, and the company soon went out of business. Shortly thereafter he formed the Loughead Brothers Aircraft Corporation, but by World War II it had gone out of business also. After the war he moved to California's San Fernando Valley and became involved in real estate. He died on May 26, 1969, in Tucson, Arizona.

After leaving Loughead Aircraft, Malcolm moved to Detroit, Michigan. In 1917 he had patented a four-wheel hydraulic brake system for automobiles, and in Detroit he formed the Lockheed Hydraulic Brake Company. In 1929 he sold the company for $1 million just before the stock market crash and retired to Mokelumne Hill, California, where he died on August 13, 1958.

In 1932 Robert and Courtlandt Gross acquired Lockheed Aircraft and pumped new blood and money into it. The company made a fortune selling planes to the military during World War II. In 1960 Lockheed introduced the L-1011 TriStar jet airliner, which became popular with the airlines. The company also built the jumbo military transport plane, the C-5A, and after 1982 focused its efforts on building planes and missiles for the military.

Further Reading

Boyne, Walter J. *Beyond the Horizons: The Lockheed Story.* New York: St. Martin's Griffin, 1999.

The Lockheed Legend. Princeton, N.J.: Films for the Humanities & Sciences, 1990, videorecording.

Sanders, Richard Allen. *Revolution in the Sky: The Lockheeds of Aviation's Golden Age.* Atglen, Penn.: Schiffer, 1993.

Luce, Henry Robinson
(1898–1967) *entrepreneur in magazine publishing*

Henry Luce revolutionized American journalism by creating four of the most innovative and popular magazines in U.S. history. *Time* set the standard for the weekly newsmagazine, *Fortune* brought a witty but knowledgeable flare to business reporting, *Life* revolutionized the concept of the photojournal, and *Sports Illustrated* provided excellent photography and journalism to the sports fan.

Luce was born on April 3, 1898, in Tengchow, China, to American parents. His father, Henry, was a Presbyterian missionary, and his mother, Elizabeth, was a social worker. At age 15 he was sent to a private school in the United States to complete his secondary education. He then enrolled at Yale University where he served as coeditor of the student newspaper; he received his B.A. in 1920. For the next three years he studied briefly at Oxford University, then worked for newspapers in Chicago and Baltimore.

In 1921 Luce and Briton Hadden, a school chum from Yale, decided to publish their own newsmagazine. Bored with what they perceived to be the stuffy publications of the day, they conceived of a journal that would explain complex current events in colorful but concise writing that any educated person could understand. Over the next two years they recruited financial backers and subscribers, and in 1923 they formed Time Inc., and published the first issue of *Time* magazine.

Although *Time* was inspired in part by *Pathfinder*, a weekly magazine founded in 1894 that rewrote news stories for country folk, it was clearly different from other magazines. Where reporters for other publications researched and wrote their own stories, *Time* editors and reporters worked together in what the company called "group journalism." Also *Time* did not pride itself or even care about breaking a news story before the competition; indeed, its major sources were newspaper articles, wire reports from the major news agencies, and reference material from the public library. Instead of presenting the facts in a plain, disinterested fashion, *Time* articles were witty and irreverent, and they made no bones about sharing the values of the college-educated middle class: a profound disrespect for authority, an equally profound respect for success, and an unshakable belief in its own infallibility. But the biggest difference between *Time* and other publications was that while others focused on reporting who, what, where, when, and how, *Time* focused on explaining why. Despite the critics who thought *Time* was biased and inaccurate (which it was), people loved reading it. By 1929, the magazine had attracted a substantial base of loyal subscribers (sales would peak in the 1950s at around 2 million per issue), and Luce had become a millionaire.

In 1929 Hadden died, and Luce took over Time Inc. as editor in chief, a position he held for the next 35 years. In 1929 he also embarked on a new project, *Fortune* magazine. In essence, *Fortune* was *Time* for businesspeople; it sought to explain in terms they could understand how current events affected business. *Fortune* was meticulously researched, and its appearance in 1930, just after the stock market crash and in the early days of the Great Depression, made Luce a well-respected figure in the business community.

In 1935 Luce divorced his wife of 13 years, the former Lila Hotz, with whom he had had two children, to marry Clare Boothe Brokaw, a magazine editor and playwright. Meanwhile, he was about to initiate a third major magazine, *Life,* a journal featuring mostly photographs, which first appeared in 1936. Although it was modeled in part on popular European photojournals such as the *Berliner Illustrirte Zeitung,* in essence *Life* was *Readers' Digest* in pictures; it contained a mix of features ranging from horrific natural disasters to heartwarming human-interest stories. Indeed, *Life* seemed to capture everyday life in America on film better than any other publication.

Although the accompanying essays were often overly sentimental, *Life*'s photography was always excellent; in fact, Luce created the magazine around the photographs. He initially hired four of the finest photographers in the country, each famous for the sharpness and depth of their work, then encouraged them to let their cameras be guided by their minds rather than their eyes; in other words, he got them to think before they started shooting. He also equipped them with state-of-the-art cameras and flash equipment, so that they could capture people when they looked most natural instead of making them pose. *Life* photographers came back from shoots with rolls

and rolls of film so that editors had plenty of pictures to choose from. Then the editors created photo essays, in which the photographs told a story with a beginning, a middle, and an end. Only after the pictures were arranged was the text for the captions and essays written. Like *Time, Life* became a favorite with middle-class readers, and by the 1950s people were buying about 6 million copies of *Life* per week.

In the 1950s Luce began publishing two more major magazines. *House & Home* first appeared in 1952, but when it did not do as well as expected it was sold to the McGraw-Hill Publishing Company. In 1954 the highly successful *Sports Illustrated* appeared, a magazine that continues to feature amazing photographs of athletes in action as well as some of the best sports-related writing in the country.

Although Luce's work was his life, he played an active role in the Republican Party; his wife was appointed ambassador to Italy by President Dwight D. Eisenhower. He also served as an anticommunist advocate in China, and he contributed generously to charities and Christian colleges in the country of his birth. By 1964, the year Luce retired to Phoenix, Arizona, Time Inc. was earning more than $200 million per year. Luce remained nominally in charge of the company as editorial chairman until his death on February 28, 1967, in Phoenix.

Further Reading

Baughman, James L. *Henry R. Luce and the Rise of the American News Media.* Baltimore, Md.: Johns Hopkins University Press, 2001.

Griffith, Thomas. *Harry and Teddy: The Turbulent Friendship of Press Lord Henry R. Luce and His Favorite Reporter, Theodore H. White.* New York: Random House, 1995.

Herzstein, Robert E. *Henry R. Luce: A Political Portrait of the Man Who Created the American Century.* New York: C. Scribner's Sons, 1994.

Startt, James D., and W. David Sloan. *The Significance of the Media in American History.* Northport, Ala.: Vision Press, 1994.

M

Marriott, John Willard

(1900–1985) *founder of the Marriott Corporation*

Corporate travelers are certainly familiar with Marriott Hotels and Courtyard by Marriott, while many family diners know about the Roy Rogers chain of fast-food restaurants. All three operations are units of the Marriott Corporation, one of the largest hotel and restaurant organizations in the United States. The corporation was founded by J. Willard Marriott, whose first operation was a root-beer stand in downtown Washington, D.C.

Marriott was born John Willard Marriott on September 17, 1900, in Marriott, Utah, a town founded by his grandfather. His parents, Hyrum and Ellen, were farmers and ranchers. At age 19 he left home to serve for two years as a Mormon missionary in New England. Upon returning to Utah, he attended Wheeler State College and the University of Utah at Ogden on a part-time basis while also working as a salesman, receiving his A.B. in 1926.

While in college Marriott became interested in acquiring an A&W root-beer stand. The one in Salt Lake City seemed to be doing well, and his cousin in Fort Wayne, Indiana, was having great success with a franchise there. In 1927, the same year he married Alice Sheets with whom he had two children, he moved to Washington, D.C., where he and Hugh Colton, son of a Utah congressman, became partners in an A&W location downtown.

During the summer the nation's capital is a hot, muggy tourist trap, and the two partners made a lot of money selling root beer to thirsty sightseers. Trying to make ends meet during the winter, however, proved to be exceptionally difficult. In 1928 Marriott scraped together what little cash he could and bought out Colton, who wanted to go back to Utah. Marriott then got A&W's approval to sell sandwiches and other food items along with A&W beverages, and he renamed his little operation The Hot Shoppe. Business was so good that by 1932 he had six more stands around the city and had incorporated as Hot Shoppes Inc.

The Great Depression did little to slow the growth of Marriott's chain of eateries, which increasingly were sit-down restaurants instead of sandwich stands. Instead of borrowing heavily to expand, he paid most of the cost of opening new stores out of the profits from existing ones. Locating along major highways in Washington's Virginia and Maryland suburbs, he distinguished his operations from roadside diners that catered to a working-class clientele by offering a variety of dinner-type meals, installing air-conditioning, adding children's menus, providing table service by uniformed waitresses, and tastefully decorating inside and out, thus converting his eateries into family restaurants that greatly appealed to middle-class suburbanites.

After World War II Marriott built a number of new restaurants up and down the East Coast and in the Far West. He also broadened the appeal of his restaurants by adding drive-in service.

Instead of having to dress up to come inside, families (or, increasingly, teenagers "cruising the strip") could dine in their automobiles. Orders were called in to the kitchen on a speaker mounted next to a menu, and a carhop delivered the food on a tray that conveniently mounted to the driver's door once the window was rolled down. In addition to burgers, fries, and shakes, Hot Shoppes offered several specialty sandwiches, including the Mighty Mo, which consisted of two all-beef patties, special sauce, lettuce, cheese, onions, and pickles on a sesame-seed bun. This popular sandwich served as the inspiration for the Big Mac, which would become a world-famous product of the McDonald's Corporation. Between 1950 and 1970, Hot Shoppes and McDonald's were the fastest growing and most profitable restaurant chains in the country.

Marriott was more than just a successful restauranteur. In 1937 he won a contract to cater meals aboard airline flights originating at Washington National Airport. The huge institutional food preparation center he built at the airport to prepare and package hot meals served as a major profit center for years thereafter. The success of this operation also led him to establish cafeterias at a number of office buildings, both government and private. And in 1957 the company built its first motel, the Marriott Motor Inn in Arlington, Virginia. Located next to Arlington National Cemetery and just across the Potomac River from the Lincoln Memorial, this property quickly became one of the most popular places to stay for Washington visitors from around the country.

In 1964, the same year the company became known as the Marriott Corporation, Marriott retired from the active management of the company. Putting his eldest son in charge, he served as chairman of the board until his death, at which time the corporation and its franchisees operated more than 1,400 restaurants and 143 hotels and resorts. After his retirement, he remained involved in various Mormon charities and ministries and played an active role in the affairs of the Republican Party, serving as chairperson of President Richard Nixon's inaugural celebrations in 1969 and 1973. He died on August 13, 1985, at his summer home near Wolfeboro, New Hampshire.

Further Reading

"J. Willard Marriott, 1974," Horatio Alger Association of Distinguished Americans: Members. Available online. URL: http://www.horatioalger.com_info. CFM?memberid=mar74. Downloaded on July 3, 2009.

O'Brien, Robert. *Marriott: The J. Willard Marriott Story.* Salt Lake City, Utah: Deseret Book Co., 1995.

Marsh, Charles Wesley

(1834–1918) *inventor of the mechanical harvester*

CYRUS HALL MCCORMICK invented the mechanical reaper, thus revolutionizing American agriculture. However, his original machine did not gather or bind, features that most farmers found desirable. One farmer who improved on McCormick's original design was Charles Marsh, who converted the McCormick reaper into the world's first harvester.

Marsh was born on March 22, 1834, in Northumberland County, Ontario, Canada. His parents, Samuel and Tamar, were farmers. At age 15 he moved with his family to a farm near De Kalb, Illinois, and for the next 10 years he worked on his parents' farm. During this period the Marshes bought one of Cyrus McCormick's mechanical reaping machines. Although the McCormick reaper did a great job of cutting down wheat sheaves, it simply left them on the ground where they had been cut. The process of gathering, binding, and tying the sheaves had to be done later as a separate operation. Sometime between 1849 and 1858, Charles and his brother William developed a harvester that took McCormick's reaper one step further. In addition to cutting down the wheat, their machine swept the cut sheaves onto a canvas conveyor that carried them to a box where they could be bound by hand, thus combining two harvesting operations into one. In 1858 the Marsh brothers received a patent for their harvester.

In 1860 Marsh married Frances Wait with whom he had three children. That same year he tried to set up an operation to manufacture harvesters. However, by 1862 he had managed to build only one machine. In 1863 he entered into a partnership with Lewis Steward, and the two opened a factory in Plano, Illinois. The following year they made and sold 25 harvesters.

The partners prospered until 1869, when they sold their factory and went their separate ways. That same year Marsh organized the Sycamore Marsh Harvester Manufacturing Company in Sycamore, Illinois, and began building harvesters for export to Europe. Once again his business thrived, and in 1876 he sold the company to J. D. Easter and Company with the intention of retiring. Unfortunately, Easter went out of business after only one year, and Marsh was forced to take control of the company once again. Despite his entrepreneurial skill, the company had suffered under Easter's management; this fact, coupled with the expiration of his patent and manufacturing license, forced him out of business in 1881. That same year he married Sue Rogers, his first wife having died, with whom he had no children. He attempted to reenter the manufacturing business in 1881 by forming the Marsh Binder Manufacturing Company in Sycamore. He managed to run a profitable business for three years before he was forced to close down his operation in 1884.

In 1885 Marsh became editor of the *Farm Implement News,* a farm machinery trade journal. He later became president of the company that published the journal while continuing to serve as editor until 1908, when he retired. He died on November 9, 1918.

Further Reading

"History of Sycamore," Sycamore Chamber of Commerce. Available online. URL: http://www.sycamorechamber. com/history.html. Downloaded on November 20, 2001.

Schlebecker, John T. *Whereby We Thrive: A History of American Farming 1607–1972.* Ames: Iowa State University Press, 1986.

Masters, Sybilla Righton

(ca. 1670s–1720) *inventor of the corn refining machine*

The first patent holder in American history was Thomas Masters. However, the inventions for which he received his patents were invented by his wife, Sybilla. Sadly, little is known about "the mother of American inventors" other than the circumstances surrounding her inventions.

Masters was born Sybilla Righton. Nothing is known for sure about the circumstances of her birth, but evidence strongly suggests that she was born during the late 1670s on the island of Bermuda, from where her parents emigrated to the North American mainland. Her father, William, was a mariner and merchant, and her mother, Sarah, was a homemaker. In 1687 her family was living on a farm near Burlington in the British colony of West Jersey. Between 1693 and 1696 she married Thomas Masters, a Philadelphia merchant with whom she had four children.

Between the time of her marriage and 1712, Masters developed two patentable ideas. The first was a way for "Cleaning and Curing the Indian Corn Growing in the several Colonies in America." At the time, English settlers living in the New World ground their corn into meal by placing it between two millstones. One stone turned round and round while the other remained stationary, in the process grinding the corn into meal. Masters's process evidently imitated the Native American way of refining corn into what was known as Tuscarora rice by putting it into a tall bowl known as a mortar and pounding it with a long club known as a pestle. Masters modified the Indian process by making it mechanical. She mounted a row of pestles to a long cylinder that could be connected to either a waterwheel or a horse. As the cylinder rotated back and forth, it drove the pestles up and down in a row of mortars. Her other invention was a way to make hats and bonnets by weaving together straw and palmetto leaves, which grew plentifully throughout the Caribbean and the southernmost mainland colonies.

In 1712 Masters went to London, England, to obtain patents for her two inventions. Since all English patents at that time were granted personally by the English monarch, Masters spent several years convincing a seemingly endless stream of government officials to give her an audience with King George I. Another problem was that English law prohibited patents from being issued to women, but Masters got around this law by asking for the patents in her husband's name. She finally succeeded in 1715, when Thomas Masters was issued a patent for the corn refining machine; however, the patent clearly indicates that the refiner's inventor was Sybilla Masters. In 1716 Thomas Masters was issued another patent for the weaving process; this patent also acknowledges Sybilla Masters as the inventor. These two patents are the first ones known to have been issued to an inventor living in America.

Unlike many inventors, Sybilla Masters profited from her inventions. In 1714 her husband had purchased a mill in Philadelphia, and for years he processed cornmeal via his wife's process. He also obtained an English monopoly on the Caribbean palmetto-leaf trade, and before Sybilla Masters returned to Philadelphia, where she died on August 23, 1720, she opened a shop in London that sold straw-palmetto hats, bonnets, and baskets.

Further Reading

Blashfield, Jean F. *Women Inventors 4: Sybilla Masters, Mary Beatrice Davidson Kenner and Mildred Davidson Austin Smith, Stephanie Kwolek, Frances Gabe.* Minneapolis, Minn.: Capstone Press, 1996.

Vare, Ethlie Ann, and Greg Ptacek. *Mothers of Invention: From the Bra to the Bomb, Forgotten Women and Their Unforgettable Ideas.* New York: William Morrow and Co., 1988.

Matzeliger, Jan Ernst

(1852–1889) *inventor of the shoe lasting machine*

The invention of the shoe lasting machine was the last step in the total automation of shoe production. This machine was invented by Jan Matzeliger, a half-black, half-Dutch immigrant who died before he made any significant amount of money from his invention.

Matzeliger was born on September 15, 1852, in Paramaribo, Dutch Guiana (present-day Suriname). His father, Carl, was a Dutch engineer who supervised a machine works in Paramaribo, and his mother, whose name is not known, was a black Surinamese woman. At age 10 he became an apprentice in his father's machine works where he worked for nine years. At age 19 he joined the crew of a Dutch merchant vessel, and after a two-year voyage he landed in Philadelphia, Pennsylvania. He spent the next four years in Philadelphia, where he probably worked as a cobbler, then relocated in 1877 to Lynn, Massachusetts.

Matzeliger evidently hoped to break into Lynn's shoe manufacturing business as a mechanic, but racial prejudice seems to have kept him from being offered such a position. Instead, he was hired by the M. H. Harney Company to operate a McKay shoe-stitching machine. Invented by LYMAN REED BLAKE in the 1850s, the McKay machine sewed together the uppers, the various pieces of soft leather that form the upper part of the shoe, then sewed them to the sole. The machine was quite popular among New England shoe manufacturers, who by 1877 had produced more than 150 million pairs of shoes on it. However, the McKay machine was not perfect; although it did all the sewing by machine, it was still necessary to last, or shape, the uppers by hand around a last, a piece of wood shaped like a foot, before they could be stitched to the sole. This process of smoothing, pulling, and shaping the leather from which the uppers were cut was quite time consuming, and it was the last obstacle standing in the way of a fully automated shoe manufacturing process. Several people, including Blake, had already developed shoe lasting machines, but none of them worked satisfactorily.

After several years of operating his McKay machine, Matzeliger seems to have been inspired by the challenge to invent a shoe lasting machine that actually worked. Every night for six months, he retired to his room after work where he drew plans and built models of different designs. In 1883 he filed for and received a patent for a shoe lasting machine, but as yet the machine was not capable of out producing a skilled hand-laster. He continued to make improvements to the machine, and in 1885 he demonstrated its ability to last 75 pairs of shoes in one day, half again as many as a master hand-laster could do. By 1888 he had improved the machine to the point that it could last 700 pairs per day, thus making it capable of revolutionizing the shoe industry. At this point he took on two partners named Delsnow and Nichols who traded him $15,000 in stock in their manufacturing company (which eventually became part of the United

Shoe Machinery Corporation) in exchange for two-thirds of the rights to his invention.

Matzeliger's shoe lasting machine was dubbed "niggerhead" by unhappy hand-lasters who would soon be put out of work by it. Despite his mild manner and engaging personality, Matzeliger encountered racial prejudice in other ways while living in Lynn. A deeply religious man, he was denied membership in three local churches before the Christian Endeavor Society, the youth branch of the North Congregational Church, accepted him. Although he managed to make friends with several of the younger factory workers in Lynn, he never married. He died on August 24, 1889, in Lynn, before realizing any significant benefit from his invention.

Further Reading

James, Portia P. *The Real McCoy: African-American Invention and Innovation, 1619–1930.* Washington, D.C.: Smithsonian Institution Press, 1989.
"Jan Matzeliger," About Inventors. Available online. URL: http://www.blackinventor.com/pages/janmatzeliger. html. Downloaded on July 3, 2009.
Mitchell, Barbara. *Shoes for Everyone: A Story about Jan Matzeliger.* Minneapolis: Carolrhoda Books, 1986.

Mauchly, John William (1907–1980), and John Presper Eckert, Jr. (1919–1995)
inventors of first-generation computers

The computer revolution began in 1951 with the unveiling of UNIVAC I, the first all-electronic digital computer capable of handling alphanumeric input data. UNIVAC I proved that computers had a number of applications in the nonscientific world, and it stimulated the development of smaller, faster, more powerful machines for business and personal use. The two people responsible for the development of UNIVAC I were John Mauchly and John Presper Eckert, whose initial interest in computers was sparked in part by a desire to predict the weather.

Mauchly was born John William Mauchly on August 30, 1907, in Cincinnati, Ohio. His father, Sebastian, was a physics professor, and his mother, Rachel, was a homemaker. At age seven he moved

with his family to Chevy Chase, Maryland, where his father went to work for the Carnegie Institution of Washington, D.C. At age 18 he enrolled in Johns Hopkins University to study physics; he was such a brilliant student that he skipped his junior and senior years and went straight into the graduate physics program, receiving his Ph.D. in 1932. Two years earlier he had married Mary Augusta Walzl with whom he had two children. When she died in 1946, he married Kathleen McNulty with whom he had five children.

From 1933 to 1941 Mauchly taught physics at Ursinus College, where he became interested in developing a sophisticated mathematical model for forecasting the weather. This line of research required many calculations, which at the time were done by people known as "computers" who either did them by hand or used primitive mechanical calculators. While searching for a faster way to compute numbers, in 1941 Mauchly visited John V. Atanasoff, a professor of physics at Iowa State College. In 1939 Atanasoff had built a calculator he called "ABC," which was half-mechanical, half-electronic; this was the first known use of electronics for computing purposes. Inspired by Atanasoff's simple machine, that same year Mauchly took an electronics course at the University of Pennsylvania's Moore School of Electrical Engineering. The following year he became a professor of electrical engineering at the Moore School.

Eckert was born John Presper Eckert, Jr., on April 9, 1919, in Philadelphia, Pennsylvania. His father, John, was a wealthy businessman, and his mother, Ethel, was a socialite. In 1941 he received his B.S. in electrical engineering from the University of Pennsylvania, then became a graduate student at the Moore School, receiving his M.S. in 1943. In 1944 he married Hester Caldwell with whom he had two children. When she died in 1952, he married Judith Rewalt with whom he also had two children.

Mauchly and Eckert met in 1941 at the Moore School while working on a project for the U.S. Army. In order to determine the proper trajectory for a shell, artillery officers had to consider such factors as wind, humidity, distance, target elevation, and shell weight. Precalculated firing tables greatly simplified this process, and the army wanted to calculate these tables on the Moore School's differential analyzer. This machine was an electromechanical calculator similar to Atanasoff's ABC calculator and Howard Aiken's Mark I computer, which he built for the U.S. Navy at Harvard University in 1944. But Mauchly and Eckert decided that electronics, not mechanics, was the key to lightning-fast computation, so they proposed to the army that they build an all-electronic computer. Instead of using a combination of mechanical relays and vacuum tubes (glass-enclosed devices containing individual components for emitting and controlling the flow of electrons), they wanted to use vacuum tubes exclusively as the active logic elements. The army gave its approval in 1943, and in early 1946 Mauchly and Eckert officially dedicated ENIAC (Electronic Numerical Integrator and Computer).

By modern computer standards, ENIAC was a dinosaur. Built in the basement of the Moore School, it took up more than 1,900 cubic feet, weighed 30 tons, and contained approximately 10,000 capacitors, 18,000 vacuum tubes, 70,000 resistors, and 500,000 hand-soldered connections. To run a new program, programmers had to reroute wires, change switches, and move cables. If one of the vacuum tubes burned out, the whole machine might shut down in mid-calculation. But because it was all-electronic, ENIAC could execute almost 5,000 basic arithmetic operations per second, which was more than a thousand times faster than any electromechanical computer. Although it was completed too late to be used during World War II, ENIAC was used to check the calculations for the first hydrogen bomb in the early 1950s. ENIAC was later moved from the University of Pennsylvania to the army's Ballistics Research Laboratory at Aberdeen Proving Ground, Maryland, where it was used for a number of years to compute firing tables.

In 1947 Mauchly and Eckert left the Moore School to found the Electronic Control Company, later renamed the Eckert-Mauchly Computer Corporation. Unlike most scientists, Mauchly and Eckert realized that computers were not specialized pieces of equipment for use by the scientific community only, but that they also had an enormous range of applications for government, business,

and private use as well. With this in mind, they set out to build an all-purpose computer that could be used by people who did not have a scientific background. In 1949 they unveiled the BINAC (Binary Automatic Computer), which was one-tenth the size of ENIAC but had 25 times more memory. Originally designed for the Northrop Aviation Company to help airplanes navigate, BINAC was the first computer to use magnetic tape instead of punch cards for memory storage and a typewriter keyboard for memory access. Their most revolutionary product was UNIVAC I (Universal Automatic Computer), which was completed in 1951. Developed primarily for the U.S. Census Bureau, UNIVAC Is were also sold to the Department of Defense and General Electric. UNIVAC I was not successful financially, mostly because it was too expensive for most customers. However, it was the first computer that could handle both alphabetical and numerical information without difficulty, thus proving that computers could be built for nonscientific applications. For this reason, UNIVAC I is credited with starting the commercial computer boom.

Although Mauchly and Eckert were brilliant inventors, they were miserable businessmen. Having been brought up in the academic community, neither seemed to have the slightest clue how to run their company. The government gave Eckert-Mauchly a $300,000 deposit toward the construction of UNIVAC I, but this money ran out long before the computer was completed. Desperate to stave off bankruptcy and turn their attention to finishing UNIVAC I, in 1950 the two partners sold their company to Remington Rand, a manufacturing firm that made electric razors and typewriters. Both Mauchly and Eckert stayed to work for Remington Rand and Sperry Rand, which acquired the former company in 1955, although their working relationship changed; as director of special projects, Mauchly concentrated on developing software while Eckert continued to focus on hardware. Their most impressive achievement while with Remington/Sperry Rand was to encourage and support GRACE HOPPER's development of programming languages, which make it possible for virtually anyone to successfully operate a computer.

In 1959 Mauchly left Sperry Rand to form his own computer company, Mauchly Associates Inc. In 1962 his company released a suitcase-sized critical path computer for scheduling complicated projects. In 1969 he became president of Dynatrend Inc., a computer consulting firm, but in 1973 he returned to Sperry Rand as a consultant, a position he held until his death on January 8, 1980, in Abingdon, Pennsylvania. Meanwhile, Eckert finished his graduate work, and received his Ph.D. from Pennsylvania in 1964. He also continued to work as a computer designer at Sperry Rand (later renamed UNISYS Corporation) until 1989, when he retired to his home in Gladwyn, Pennsylvania, where he died on June 15, 1995.

Further Reading

Spencer, Donald D. *Great Men and Women of Computing.* Ormon Beach, Fla.: Camelot Pub., 1999.

Stern, Nancy B. *From ENIAC to UNIVAC: An Appraisal of the Eckert-Mauchly Computers.* Bedford, Mass.: Digital Press, 1981.

Zientara, Marguerite. *The History of Computing: A Biographical Portrait of the Visionaries Who Shaped the Destiny of the Computer Industry.* Framingham, Mass.: CW Communications, 1981.

Mayer, Louis B.

(1884–1957) *entrepreneur in motion picture industry*

The dominant figure of the dominant film studio throughout the first half of the 20th century, Louis B. Mayer rose from a poverty-ridden and harsh youth in Russia and Canada to become one of the wealthiest and influential Americans of his time. A complex man who was regularly described as tyrannical, fatherly, ambitious, ruthless, feisty, and brilliant, Mayer helped create and feed the desire for morally themed and glossy romantic film productions that backed his studio's motto, "More stars than there are in heaven."

Louis B. Mayer was born Lazar Meir in Minsk, Russia (now Belarus) in 1884. The exact date of his birth was unknown, so Mayer adopted July 4 as his birthday when he became an American citizen as an adult to honor his adopted country.

Fleeing poverty and persecution of Jews in late 1800s Russia, young Louis fled with his family to Canada. The Mayers settled in the province of New Brunswick on Canada's east coast. There, Mayer worked with his scrap metal and junk peddler father—whom he reportedly despised for his abusive treatment—in the family business. Mayer made regular trips to Boston to sell the scrap metal

Louis B. Mayer at the Oscars, November 1, 1930 *(AP)*

and at the age of 19 he moved to the city and—with the family business failing—he soon bought a 600-seat theater named the Gem in the neighboring town of Haverhill.

Mayer renamed the theater the Orpheum and signaled his future preference for what he considered wholesome entertainment by promising to show only "high class" films. The theater was successful, as was his foray into film distribution. In 1915, Mayer parlayed this success by joining with several partners to form the Metro Picture Corporation. Among the first films Metro acquired for distribution was the hugely popular *Birth of a Nation*. The financial success of that film helped Mayer move to Los Angeles, where he formed Louis B. Mayer Pictures, and began producing his own films. Mayer's early productions were successful and he emerged as a leading player in the burgeoning motion picture industry.

Explaining that he "will only make pictures that I won't be ashamed to have my children see," Mayer proceeded to enjoy nearly uninterrupted triumph at the box office with movies that were rich with the themes of honor, fidelity, and virtue. In 1924, Mayer consolidated his position as a major power broker by merging his company with the Metro Pictures company and the Goldwyn Company to form Metro Goldwyn Mayer (MGM). Mayer remained the head of MGM for 27 years, during which time his studio produced the most popular movies that were eagerly consumed by the growing motion picture–loving public in the United States and around the world. Included among these films are *Ben Hur, The Wizard of Oz,* and *Gone With the Wind*. The star system Mayer cultivated led to the rise to prominence of such legendary actors as Clark Gable, Katherine Hepburn, Greta Garbo, John Barrymore, Lana Turner, Buster Keaton, and the Marx brothers. At its height, MGM was producing an average of one film a week, helping Mayer become in 1936 the first business executive to make a salary of over $1 million.

Though Mayer portrayed the importance of values in his movies, his detractors claimed he did not always follow them in his personal or business dealings. Some, including actors whose requests for raises were routinely rejected by Mayer, felt he was phony, duplicitous, selfish, and capable of employing blackmail in order to maximize his and MGM's profit. However others revered the man known around Hollywood by his initials, L. B. To them, Mayer was a father figure who demanded and rewarded loyalty and punished insubordination. Reflective of the admiration among his vast stable of stars are the words of Katherine Hepburn, who noted of Mayer, "He was the most honest man I ever met in Hollywood. L. B. had a sense of romance about the movie business . . . he was really an entrepreneur in the old-fashioned sense . . . He believed. He adored the business and he understood it."

Mayer's place as the ruling mogul of the film industry began to weaken in the late 1940s. The emerging growth of television, changing public tastes, stars' increasing demands for a greater share of a film's profits, and legislation that restricted the connection between studios and their control over lucrative theater chains combined to marginalize Mayer's influence. Mayer lost an internal power struggle within MGM in 1951 and was forced to leave the studio. He remained out of active participation in the film industry over the next few years, before his death from leukemia on October 29, 1957.

In 1950, a year before being forced out at MGM, Mayer was given a special Academy Award for "distinguished service to the motion picture industry." In 1947, Mayer divorced his wife Margaret, to whom he had been married for 43 years and with whom he had two daughters. The following year Mayer married Lorena Danker, with whom he remained until his death. Mayer—a loyal supporter of the Republican Party throughout his adulthood who once counted President Herbert Hoover among his friends—disinherited his older daughter in his will because of the liberal political advocacy of her husband. His well-attended funeral service served as testimony to his enormous influence as well as the respect and fear he elicited among people in the film industry. Mayer's former business partner Samuel Goldwyn reportedly quipped that, "The reason so many people showed up at his funeral was because they wanted to make sure he was dead."

Further Reading

Eyamn, Scott. *Lion of Hollywood: The Life and Legend of Louis B. Mayer.* New York: Simon & Schuster, 2005.

Higham, Charles. *Merchant of Dreams: Louis B. Mayer, M.G.M., and the Secret Hollywood.* New York: Dutton, 1993.

Schulberg, Budd. "Louis B. Mayer" Time 100. Available online. URL: http://www.time.com/time/time100/builder/profile/mayer.html. Downloaded on August 27, 2009.

McCormick, Cyrus Hall

(1809–1884) *inventor of the mechanical reaper*

Cyrus McCormick's mechanical reaper revolutionized farming in the 19th century. In 1879 the French Academy of Sciences praised him for doing "more for the cause of agriculture than any other living man." The mechanical reaper permitted farmers to harvest as much grain in one day as they could harvest by hand in two weeks, thus greatly expanding the cultivation of wheat throughout the world. His primary motivation for inventing the reaper seems not to have been to make a fortune, but to succeed where his father had failed.

McCormick was born on February 15, 1809, in Walnut Grove, Rockbridge County, Virginia. His parents, Robert and Mary Ann, were farmers who also operated a blacksmith shop and a small iron foundry. For years Robert McCormick, who had invented several labor-saving farm tools, had tried to invent a mechanical reaper for harvesting grain. Most grains have to be harvested within two weeks of their ripening, so a farmer could not plant any more grain than could be harvested by hand in that time. If a labor shortage occurred during harvesting season, as it frequently did, the farmer stood to lose a significant portion of the crop. Like many others, Robert McCormick knew that speeding up the harvesting process would permit farmers to raise more grain and make more money, and whoever succeeded in inventing such a machine stood to make a fortune. Unfortunately for him, he was never able to do so.

In 1831, at age 22, McCormick picked up where his father had left off. To his family's amazement, within a year he developed a machine that worked well even if it looked a little strange; one critic remarked that it resembled a cross between a chariot, a wheelbarrow, and a flying machine.

What made it work was its relatively simple design; a divider separated the stalks to be cut, a reel pulled them against a reciprocating blade, and the blade cut and threw the stalks onto the ground where they could be bound by hand.

McCormick received a patent for his mechanical reaper in 1834, then promptly forgot about it, focusing instead on making a success of his father's iron foundry. But when the foundry failed three years later, leaving his family seriously in debt, McCormick was ready to make hay with his reaper. After making a number of improvements to his machine—the first model had clanked so loudly that horses were afraid to pull it—he started building reapers in his father's blacksmith shop. By the end of 1844 he had sold a total of 88 mechanical reapers. He probably would have sold more, except that the reaper did not operate well in the rolling hills of Virginia.

In 1844 McCormick visited the Midwest and the Great Plains, where he realized that the flat

Cyrus McCormick revolutionized farming by inventing the mechanical reaper. *(Library of Congress)*

terrain was perfectly suited for a mechanical reaper. After two false starts at opening a reaper factory, in 1847 he and William Ogden, the mayor of Chicago, Illinois, formed McCormick & Ogden in Chicago and began manufacturing reapers. In 1848 alone the company built and sold 800 machines, and in 1849, when sales approached 1,000, McCormick bought out Ogden and reorganized as the McCormick Reaper Company.

McCormick faced a major challenge to his success in 1848 when his original patent expired. Its renewal was challenged by Obed Hussey, who in 1833 had also patented a mechanical reaper; it differed from McCormick's machine in that it had no divider or reel. After a lengthy court battle, the renewal applications of both inventors were rejected, and their designs passed into the public domain. Almost overnight, dozens of reaper manufacturers sprang up to compete with McCormick and Hussey.

Undaunted, McCormick resolved to beat his competition by outselling them. Rather than waiting for orders to come to him, he toured the Great Plains, demonstrating his machine and soliciting orders. He brought the reaper to the attention of farmers he could not contact personally by advertising in catalogs and periodicals and by hiring a commissioned sales force. He overcame concerns about the machine's reliability by offering a warranty; he held down its price by mass-producing machines before they were sold; and he made the reaper more affordable by offering easy credit. By 1860, despite the heavy competition, McCormick's reaper was the most popular in the United States and the world. His machine won the Grand Medal at the 1851 Great Exposition in London, England, and the Grand Medal of Honor at the 1855 International Exposition in Paris, France. By 1860, two years after he married Nancy Fowler with whom he had five children, his company was selling 5,000 reapers a year.

After 1860 McCormick spent much time overseas promoting the reaper, leaving two of his brothers, Leander and William, in charge of day-to-day operations. His efforts paid off in the 1880s when large numbers of reapers were sold to farmers throughout the wheat-growing regions of the western world, including Argentina and Australia.

By 1884 his company was selling more than 50,000 reapers a year.

Next to selling reapers, McCormick was most interested in promoting the affairs of the Presbyterian Church. In 1859 he donated a large sum of money to a struggling Presbyterian seminary in New Albany, Indiana. After the seminary moved to Chicago and renamed itself the McCormick Theological Seminary, he continued to support it financially and took on an active role in hiring professors and shaping the curriculum. In 1872 he bought the *Interior,* a Presbyterian periodical, which he helped turn into the church's most respected publication. He also contributed generously to Presbyterian missions in this country and overseas, to the Union Theological Seminary, and to Washington and Lee College, which were near his family home in Rockbridge County, Virginia.

When McCormick died in Chicago on May 13, 1884, his fortune was estimated at $10 million. In 1902 McCormick's company was merged with several other farm implement manufacturers to form the International Harvester Company.

Further Reading

Brands, H. W. *Masters of Enterprise: Giants of American Business from John Jacob Astor and J. P. Morgan to Bill Gates and Oprah Winfrey.* New York: Free Press, 1999.

Casson, Herbert N. *Cyrus Hall McCormick: His Life and Work.* Freeport, N.Y.: Books for Libraries Press, 1971.

Noonan, Jon. *Nineteenth-Century Inventors.* New York: Facts On File, 1992.

Pursell, Carroll W. *Technology in America: A History of Individuals and Ideas.* Cambridge, Mass.: MIT Press, 1990.

Wren, Daniel A., and Ronald G. Greenwood. *Management Innovators: The People and Ideas that Have Shaped Modern Business.* New York: Oxford University Press, 1998.

McCoy, Elijah

(1844–1929) *inventor of the automatic lubricator*

Almost everyone has heard the phrase "the real McCoy," which means that the person or thing being referred to is genuine. Although some historians attribute this phrase to the handlers of Kid McCoy, an American boxer who was being confused with an inferior fighter of the same name, most attribute it to the railroads that purchased the automatic lubricator invented by Elijah McCoy.

McCoy was born on May 2, 1844, in Colchester, Canada West (present-day Ontario). His parents, George and Mildred, were farmers and former slaves who had run away from Kentucky. At age six he moved with his family to Ypsilanti, Michigan, and at age 15 he went to Edinburgh, Scotland, where he studied mechanical engineering as an apprentice for five years. He returned to Michigan in 1863 and tried to find work as an engineer, but racial prejudice kept him unemployed. He finally took a job with the Michigan Central Railroad as a fireman; at the time, trains were powered by steam locomotives, and the fireman kept the boiler fire burning and the moving parts lubricated.

Steam locomotives had thousands of moving parts, many of them hard to reach and most too hot to work around because of the steam and friction, and keeping them all oiled was really a job for more than one man. A particularly important but difficult job was keeping the pistons in the steam engine lubricated. Properly oiled, the pistons slid back and forth in their cylinders with great efficiency, but when they got dry they scraped against the cylinders' metal walls, causing the engine to drag, which required more steam (and hence more coal) to overcome. And once the locomotive was under way, there was no way to oil the pistons until the next whistle-stop; on a long run, they almost always needed lubricating before the fireman could oil them.

In the late 1860s McCoy began toying with the idea of inventing an automatic lubricator that could oil the pistons while the locomotive was en route. With this goal in mind, he began experimenting with an existing oiler for small, stationary steam engines then in use in factories. In 1872, the year before he married Mary Delaney with whom he had no children, he received his first patent for an improved lubricator, the rights to which he sold to William and S. C. Hamlin of Ypsilanti. He continued to build oilers for larger steam engines, and by 1882 he had finally developed a lubricator for a steam locomotive. This lubricator dripped oil into the stream of steam just as it entered the cylinder; valves controlled the rate of oil flow, and a sight gauge indicated the level of oil in the lubricator. Made mostly of brass, the lubricator was inexpensive yet sturdy enough to take the beating of hard railroad service.

McCoy sold the rights to this lubricator to Charles and Henry Hodges, who had them manufactured by the Detroit Railway Supply Company. The McCoy lubricator, as it became known, quickly established itself as the model of choice of discriminating railroads, and in time it became known as "the real McCoy" to distinguish itself from cheaper and less-effective imitations. In the mid-1880s the Michigan Central promoted McCoy from fireman to a supervisory position, and he spent the rest of this time with the railroad teaching mechanics and firemen how to install and operate his lubricator.

The introduction of superheated steam locomotives in the early 1900s posed a new problem for lubricators. The steam entering the cylinder was so hot that regular oil broke down and could no longer lubricate properly. In 1915 McCoy solved this problem by inventing a graphite lubricator. This model mixed graphite, a solid lubricant, with the oil, thus preserving the oil's integrity under intense heat. Independent testing showed that the graphite lubricator lubricated pistons so well that oil consumption was cut by one-third and coal consumption was reduced by approximately one ton per 1,000 miles.

In 1916 McCoy exchanged the patent rights to his latest invention for a minority stock holding in the Elijah McCoy Manufacturing Company, founded in Detroit to make graphite lubricators. The company was not well run and, despite the popularity of its product, it declared bankruptcy after a few years and the patent was acquired by another company. McCoy, who seems to have profited little from his inventions, retired to his home in Detroit where he died sometime in 1929.

Further Reading

"Elijah McCoy," Black Inventor. Available online. URL: http://www.blackinventor.com/pages/elijahmccoy.html. Downloaded on July 3, 2009.

James, Portia P. *The Real McCoy: African-American Invention and Innovation, 1619–1930.* Washington, D.C.: Smithsonian Institution Press, 1989.

Marshall, Albert P. *The "Real McCoy" of Ypsilanti.* Ypsilanti, Mich.: Marland Publishing, 1989.

McMahon, Vince
(Vincent Kennedy McMahon)
(1945–   ) *entrepreneur in wrestling*

One of the more interesting developments in entertainment during the late 20th century was the transformation of professional wrestling. In the 1950s and 1960s, it tried (and failed) to pass itself off as a legitimate sport, playing mostly before small crowds in small arenas. During the 1980s, however, professional wrestling became a glamour industry when it shucked the trappings of legitimacy and bedecked itself in the glittering rags of Hollywood. The individual most responsible for this turnabout is Vince McMahon, a third-generation wrestling promoter.

McMahon was born Vincent Kennedy McMahon on August 24, 1945, in Pinehurst, North Carolina. His father, Vincent James "Vince" McMahon, was a wrestling promoter. Shortly after his birth, his parents divorced, and McMahon moved to Greenwich, Connecticut, with his mother. At age 12 he met his father for the first time. McMahon Sr. owned the Capital Wrestling Federation, in essence the professional wrestling franchise for the northeastern United States, and as a teenager McMahon became interested in getting involved in the family business; his grandfather, Jess McMahon, had also been a wrestling and boxing promoter. At first, his father refused to let McMahon have anything to do with wrestling, insisting instead that his son take up a career like law or accounting.

McMahon received his B.S. in business administration from East Carolina University in 1968, the same year he married Linda Edwards with whom he has two children. Over the next three years, while working at various nondescript jobs, he continued to badger his father about letting him get involved with Capital Wrestling. Finally, in 1971, McMahon Sr. relented. He had just fired an announcer and was in desperate need of a new one, so he allowed McMahon to take the announcer's place. When McMahon did a creditable job, his father sent him to oversee the company's operations in Bangor, Maine, where Capital had been doing poorly. McMahon turned the operation around, and a few years later he was put in charge of Capital's operations throughout New England. In 1982 McMahon Sr. decided to retire and sold Capital Wrestling in its entirety to his son.

McMahon immediately set out to construct a worldwide wrestling empire. He began buying other regional wrestling federations and recruiting the top talent from the federations that would not sell out. Within a few years, he had created the Worldwide Wrestling Federation (later he shortened Worldwide to World), or the WWF, as it is more popularly known. McMahon then made two important moves. First, he recognized what an incredibly powerful vehicle television is for bringing wrestling into the homes of millions of fans. His father had televised weekly cards from small venues such as the Uline Arena in Washington, D.C., during the 1950s and 1960s, but these programs had been carried only by independent television stations in the larger regional markets. McMahon set his sights on getting his wrestlers on the major television networks. Second, he enhanced wrestling's credibility by publicly acknowledging what every thinking person in America already knew, that wrestling is fake. This admission freed him from being regulated by state athletic commissions and allowed him to showcase wrestling extravaganzas. In 1985 he put on the first Wrestlemania, an entertaining exercise in bombastic excess. Perhaps the most memorable of these annual events was Wrestlemania III, which pitted Hulk Hogan, the WWF's most popular star, against Andre the Giant, whose popularity had peaked during McMahon's father's tenure.

Calling wrestling "sports entertainment" rather than "sport," McMahon set out to turn wrestling into a soap opera for men. Wrestling had always had its good guys and bad guys, but McMahon took this idea several steps further. He introduced the complicated and ever-changing story lines characteristic of soap operas. In the WWF, friends became enemies, enemies became friends, alliances between and among wrestlers were made and broken, all at the drop of a hat. Just as important, he encouraged wrestlers to develop the most bizarre in-ring personalities they could think of. This sort of thinking led to the creation of one of the most popular wrestlers of the 1990s, Stone Cold Steve Austin, who patterned himself after several serial killers. And a major part of every wrestling program was the trash talking, whereby the various wrestlers attempted to out-shout and out-insult one another; indeed, an aspiring wrestling superstar had to be as good with a microphone outside the ring as he (or she, as McMahon also promoted female wrestlers) was at wrestling inside the ring.

In 1987 McMahon formed TitanSports Inc., a marketing and production company that also served as the WWF's parent company. In addition to putting on shows such as Wrestlemania, the company produced weekly cable television shows such as "Monday Night Raw" and "WWF Smackdown!" and broadcast WWF events in Australia, France, Germany, India, and Japan. It also licensed products, such as toys and T-shirts, bearing the likenesses of the most popular wrestlers, in the process making them as well known, if not more so, than athletes in legitimate sports. In the process, it also made itself one of the top merchandisers in the United States. By 2000 it was estimated that TitanSports, a privately held company, was grossing more than $250 million annually.

Although McMahon is a gifted wrestling promoter, his magic touch does not always work miracles. In 2001 he founded the ill-fated Xtreme Football League, or XFL, as a wrestling-type version of the National Football League. Despite the preseason hype, the league failed to live up to expectations and folded after one season with estimated losses of about $35 million.

In 2002, the WWF changed its name to World Wrestling Entertainment (WWE) following a long dispute with the World Wildlife Federation, another prominent organization with which it shared initials. McMahon remains the chairman of WWE and has been a focus of the still-popular storylines broadcast on highly rated television shows shown in over 100 countries. In 2008, McMahon— whose net worth is estimated to be close to $1 billion—was honored for his showmanship and iconic stature in business with the placement of a star in his name on the Hollywood Walk of Fame.

Further Reading
Alexander, Kyle. *Vince McMahon*. Philadelphia: Chelsea House Publishers, 2001.
"Vincent K. McMahon: Chairman/CEO." World Wrestling Entertainment. Available online. URL: http://corporate.wwe.com/company/bios/vk_mcmahon.jsp. Downloaded on October 19, 2009.

Mergenthaler, Ottmar
(1854–1899) *inventor of Linotype*

From about 1450 to 1884, the fastest way to set type for a printing press was by hand. Although Ottmar Mergenthaler did not invent mechanical typesetting, he made it practical by inventing the first mechanical typesetter that worked faster than hand setting. In the process, his Linotype machine revolutionized printing and remained the primary means of setting type between the 1880s and the 1970s, when photocomposition via computer became widespread.

Mergenthaler was born on May 11, 1854, in Hachtel, Wurttemberg, now part of Germany. His father, Johann, was a schoolteacher, and his mother, Rosina, was a homemaker. As a boy he earned the nickname "Cleverhead" when he figured out how to restart the village clock, which had not run for years. At age 14 he was apprenticed to his uncle, a clock maker in nearby Bietigheim. Four years later, in 1872, he emigrated to the United States and settled in Washington, D.C., where he went to work for his cousin, August Hahl, who made clocks, bells, and patent models. In 1874 Mergenthaler and Hahl formed a partnership and moved to Baltimore, Maryland. In 1878 Mergenthaler became an American citizen, and in 1881 he married Emma Lachenmayer with whom he had five children.

In 1876 Charles T. Moore, a local inventor, brought into the partners' shop a machine for typing letters for lithographic printing, whereby letters are etched into a flat stone or plate and then inked. Mergenthaler helped Moore improve the machine, but in the end it proved to be impractical. Meanwhile, Mergenthaler had been encouraged by James O. Clephane, Moore's financial backer, to think about mechanizing typesetting for the standard printing press. At the time, typesetters did their work by hand, in four steps: the type pieces, small blocks of metal with raised characters on one end, were taken, one at a time, from a typecase in which they were arranged alphabetically and numerically; the type pieces were arranged side by side in a composing stick, a wooden strip with corners on each end, to make one line of type; the line was justified, or made to the same length as the other lines, by inserting blank spacers between words; after printing, the type pieces were wiped off and put back into the typecase. Obviously, this was a time-consuming process—a good compositor could arrange about 5,000 type pieces per hour—and Clephane hoped to speed it up by producing type in complete lines rather than individual characters.

In 1878 Mergenthaler invented a rotary typing machine that could impress characters into strips of papier-mâché. He and Clephane hoped to make metal castings from the strips, but this proved to be impossible. After spending several fruitless years trying to solve this problem, in 1884 Mergenthaler took a different approach. First, he made type pieces from copper with indented, not raised, characters, and stored them in the machine as in a typecase. Then, he devised a keyboard system whereby pressing a key for a particular character released a type piece with that character on it and positioned it on a line of type. After all the type pieces had been positioned, the operator justified the line. Then a lead casting, called a slug, was made of the line, which was positioned on a frame from which a whole page would be printed. After printing, the slugs were melted down for reuse and the type pieces dumped in a channel; notches in the type pieces guided them back to their proper compartments. After some training, a compositor using Mergenthaler's machine could arrange the equivalent of about 7,000 type pieces per hour, a significant improvement over the handset method. In 1884 Mergenthaler completed a prototype of this machine and spent the next two years working out the basic kinks. Also in 1884, Clephane and a

group of investors formed what became known as the Mergenthaler Printing Company and opened a factory in Baltimore, with Mergenthaler as plant manager. In 1886 the factory's first machine was sold to the *New York Tribune;* the newspaper's publisher, Whitelaw Reid, named it the Linotype.

Shortly thereafter, Mergenthaler Printing took on new investors who wanted to speed up production faster than Mergenthaler thought was prudent for turning out a high-quality machine. In the ensuing brouhaha, the factory was moved to Brooklyn, New York, and he was forced out of the company that bore his name. In 1888 he opened a machine shop in Baltimore, and by 1891 he had perfected the Linotype so that it could justify lines. For the next three years he manufactured the Model 1 Linotype, the improved model of 1891, for Mergenthaler Printing. In 1894 he licensed his patents to Mergenthaler Printing and moved to Arizona Territory where he hoped to recover from tuberculosis. In 1898 a prairie fire destroyed his home and he returned to Baltimore, where he died on October 28, 1899.

Further Reading

Kahan, Basil C. *Ottmar Mergenthaler: The Man and His Machine: A Biographical Appreciation of the Inventor on His Centennial.* New Castle, Del.: Oak Knoll Press, 2000.

Romano, Frank J. *Machine Writing and Typesetting: The Story of Sholes and Mergenthaler and the Invention of the Typewriter and the Linotype.* Salem, N.H.: GAMA, 1986.

Schlesinger, Carl. *Biography of Ottmar Mergenthaler, Inventor of the Linotype.* New Castle, Del.: Oak Knoll Books, 1992.

Milken, Michael Robert
(1946–   ) *entrepreneur in junk bonds*

For American business, the 1980s was the decade of the corporate takeover. Countless numbers of companies changed hands, many of them ending up being owned by the management team that had made them profitable in the first place. The vehicle that fueled the bulk of these takeovers was junk bonds. Michael Milken did not invent junk bonds, but he did much to find several new and controversial uses for them. Ironically, junk bonds did not actually become "junk" until after Milken popularized them.

Milken was born Michael Robert Milken on July 4, 1946, in Los Angeles, California. His father, Bernard, was an accountant, and his mother, Ferne, was a homemaker. At age 10 he started helping his father by reconciling checks and filling out tax returns. In 1968 he graduated from the University of California at Berkeley and married Lori Hackel with whom he has three children. After graduation, he enrolled in the University of Pennsylvania's Wharton School of Business. He received his M.B.A. from Wharton in 1970 and went to work as a trader in the New York City office of Drexel Firestone (later known as Drexel Burnham Lambert).

As an undergraduate, Milken had become interested in so-called junk bonds. These securities were usually offered by small- to medium-sized companies that were in financial trouble or were attempting to engage in some sort of risky business venture; consequently, junk bonds paid a higher rate of interest that did other types of securities. Milken continued to study junk bonds at Wharton and with Drexel. He came to the surprising realization that, contrary to conventional wisdom, the default rate for junk bonds was only slightly higher than for higher-rated bonds. Thus, he concluded that junk bonds, since they offered such high rates of interest, actually offered a higher yield than all other types of securities that were supposedly more secure. He also concluded that, once this fact was properly understood by investors, small- to medium-sized companies could issue junk bonds and easily raise the capital they needed. In fact, junk bonds were particularly attractive to small companies; unlike raising money through venture capital firms, which often ended up owning a majority of the companies they financed, junk bonds allowed the principals of small companies to retain a greater degree of ownership.

Milken took it upon himself to begin educating investors about junk bonds, especially institutional money managers, who were constantly on the lookout for ways to increase the yields of the funds they managed. By 1978 Milken had sold millions of dollars worth of junk bonds to these highly sophisticated investors. In the process, he created and became head of Drexel's junk-bond division. In 1978 he realized that the companies that could profit the most from issuing junk bonds were being started on the West Coast, especially in California's Silicon Valley, so that same year he relocated Drexel's junk-bond division from Philadelphia to San Francisco. Over the next five years, junk bonds performed consistently with Milken's predictions for them. Their default rate remained tolerably low, and they looked as if they were the perfect vehicle for expanding the American economy to unprecedented heights.

The demise of junk bonds as an attractive investment tool began in 1983, when Milken discovered how to put them to a new use. He began touting junk bonds as the perfect way for corporate managers, who typically were long on managerial talent but short on capital, to take over their companies. Leveraged buyouts, or LBOs as these management-team takeovers became known, became popular on Wall Street. He also promoted LBOs as a way for major investors to gain control of major corporations such as Gulf Oil, Revlon, and Safeway Stores. By 1987, approximately $150 billion worth of junk bonds were in the hands of investors. Meanwhile, Milken had become known as the "junk bond king" and had acquired $1.5 billion in salary, commissions, and fees.

Junk bonds did not turn out to be the panacea that Milken had believed them to be. Many an LBO arranged by him and other bond dealers were based on the assumption that the company could carry an extraordinary amount of debt and remain profitable. In most cases, this proved to be true; however, by 1990 the economy was in a slump, corporate revenues were generally down across the board, and about 10 percent of all LBOs had defaulted on their loans. When the U.S. Congress passed a law forbidding savings and loan institutions from buying junk bonds, the bottom fell out of the junk-bond market, with some bonds declining in value by as much as 50 percent.

Meanwhile, Milken had encountered difficulties of a different nature. In 1988 Drexel was sued by Staley Continental on the grounds that Milken had threatened the company's top managers with a hostile takeover if they did not hire him to engineer an LBO on their behalf. That same year the Securities and Exchange Commission (SEC) began investigating Drexel after Ivan Boesky, a Wall Street entrepreneur convicted of insider trading, named Milken and several other Drexel employees as his accomplices. According to Boesky, he had been recruited by Milken to buy shares in the same companies that Drexel's clients were trying to take over, thus driving up the price of the LBO, increasing Drexel's profits, and contributing to higher fees for Milken. At first, Drexel denied having done anything wrong, but shortly thereafter the company confessed its guilt and paid a $650 million fine. In 1989 the SEC charged Milken with 98 counts of criminal racketeering, securities fraud, and other related crimes. In 1990 he pleaded guilty to six counts and agreed to pay a $600 million fine, the largest fine ever levied against an individual in American history. He also received a 10-year prison term, although he was freed after two years for good behavior.

Despite the record-setting fine, Milken remained a wealthy man. His experience with junk bonds, plus a bout with prostate cancer, seemed to have profoundly affected him. He had founded the Milken Family Foundation in 1982 as a means of funding medical research, and after getting out of jail he devoted the bulk of his time and fortune to this and other charitable causes, including the formation of the Prostate Cancer Federation, created by Milken after he was diagnosed with the disease soon after his release from prison. In 2004, Milken's extensive funding for medical research resulted in a cover feature about him in *Fortune* magazine entitled, "Mike Milken's Crusade: How It's Changing Medicine."

Milken sought presidential pardons for his criminal conviction from both Bill Clinton and George W. Bush, but was rejected each time. In 2007, *Forbes* magazine estimated his net worth as $2.1 billion, placing him among the 500 wealthiest people in the world. The father of three children and the grandfather of three, Milken lives outside Los Angeles with Lori, his wife of over 40 years.

Further Reading

Chancellor, Edward. *Devil Take the Hindmost: A History of Financial Speculation.* New York: Plume, 2000.

Kornbluth, Jesse. *Highly Confident: The Crime and Punishment of Michael Milken.* New York: William Morrow and Company, 1992.

Sobel, Robert. *Dangerous Dreamers: The Financial Innovators from Charles Merrill to Michael Milken.* Washington, D.C.: Beard Books, 2000.

Stewart, James B. *Den of Thieves.* New York: Simon & Schuster, 1991.

Monaghan, Tom
(Thomas Stephen Monaghan)
(1937–) *founder of Domino's Pizza*

As the two-breadwinner, no-homemaker family increasingly became the norm during the 1980s, many Americans began "subcontracting" the task of preparing the evening meal. Although many discovered that eating out was too expensive to do on a regular basis, they also discovered that Domino's Pizza was a relatively inexpensive and convenient place from which to get a dinner that their kids would eat. However, Domino's Pizza might never have been started if its founder, Tom Monaghan, had behaved himself with more decorum while preparing for the priesthood.

Monaghan was born Thomas Stephen Monaghan on March 25, 1937, in Ann Arbor, Michigan. His father, Francis, was a truck driver, and his mother, Anna, was a homemaker. At age four his father died, and his mother was forced to put Monaghan and his brother Jim in a foster home. Over the next 11 years, he lived variously with his mother or in a foster home or orphanage. At age 15 he entered the seminary with the intention of becoming a Catholic priest, but he was expelled within a year for excessive rambunctiousness. Shortly thereafter, he went to live with an aunt and uncle in Ann Arbor, where he barely graduated from high school. In 1955 he enrolled in Ferris State College, but dropped out after a year and joined the U.S. Marine Corps. Discharged in 1959, he invested all the money he had saved while in the service in a get-rich-quick oil scheme and lost it. He hitchhiked back to Ann Arbor, opened a downtown newsstand, and enrolled in the University of Michigan, but illness and lack of money for textbooks caused him to drop out the first semester.

In 1960 Monaghan became partners with his brother Jim in DomiNick's, a pizza parlor in Ypsilanti near the campus of Eastern Michigan University. They bought the business for less than $1,000, and after eight months Jim traded his share to Monaghan for a used car. At age 24, Monaghan found himself with no money, little education, and no partner. His only asset was a little pizza joint that nobody else wanted. Undaunted, he vowed to overcome his long streak of bad luck and failure and become the best pizza man in the world.

Dominick DiVarti, from whom Monaghan had bought the pizza parlor, had told him that the secret to good pizza is good sauce. Monaghan devoted himself tirelessly to perfecting his sauce, and then to perfecting the crust, the toppings, and the cheese. He also found a new partner, Jim Gilmore. By the end of 1961 they were doing enough business to open Pizza King, a store in Mount Pleasant, near the campus of Central Michigan University. Although their business continued to prosper and expand, in 1963 the partners agreed to part ways, with Monaghan retaining ownership of two stores in Ypsilanti and one in Ann Arbor, close to the campus of the University of Michigan. In 1962 he had married Marjorie Zybach, whom he met while delivering a pizza; they have four children.

Shortly after splitting with Gilmore, Monaghan came up with the name of Domino's for all his stores; the logo, three white dots on a red domino (one dot for each store), was developed by Sam Fine, an Ann Arbor ad executive. Monaghan also came up with the idea of selling nothing but pizza and eliminating sit-down service; instead, he decided to offer free delivery within 30 minutes or the pizza itself was free. He also decided to embark on a major expansion program, and by the end of 1968 there were 12 Domino's stores with 12 more getting ready to open. Flushed with success, Monaghan set the goal of opening one new store per week, and in 1969 32 new Domino's opened. Unfortunately, these new stores were located in residential areas, unlike his earlier ones, which were close to college campuses. They did so poorly that in 1970 he temporarily surrendered control of the chain in order to avoid bankruptcy. But by 1971 he had recovered from "The Crash," as he calls it, and vowed to continue to expand but at a slower rate.

Even so, Domino's continued to grow rapidly, in large part because Monaghan decided to begin franchising his proven concept. By 1975 there were 100 Domino's stores, a number that grew to 290 five years later. During the 1980s Domino's became a household name. The convenience of free delivery, coupled with the 30-minutes-or-free guarantee, enticed many customers into trying one of his pizzas, and once they did they were hooked. By 1989 there were more than 5,000 Domino's stores across America and another 250 or so in foreign countries. The company's annual sales had topped $2 billion, and Monaghan's personal fortune was estimated to be $480 million.

In addition to his enormous success in the pizza business, Monaghan also fulfilled a dream by purchasing his beloved Detroit Tigers baseball team in 1983 for a reported $53 million. In his first season as owner, the Tigers opened with a 35-5 record—the best 40-game start in Major League Baseball history—on their way to the 1984 World Series championship. Monaghan sold the team to fellow pizza magnate, Little Caesars owner Mike Ilitch in 1992 for $85 million.

In 1989 Monaghan stepped down as Domino's president to devote more time to charitable and church activities, although he stayed on as chairman of the board. In 1998 he sold all of his stock in Domino's Pizza for approximately $1 billion, and over the next several years he contributed millions to various Catholic charities and pro-life organizations.

Since his sale of Domino's, Monaghan has committed his career to a variety of endeavors related to his Catholic faith. In 1998, he established Ave Maria College in Ypsilanti, Michigan, and in 2003 he founded Ave Maria University in Ave Maria, Florida, near Naples. Monaghan is the chairman of the college's board of trustees, and he serves as the chancellor of the university.

Further Reading

Aaseng, Nathan. *Business Builders in Fast Food.* Minneapolis, Minn.: Oliver Press, 2000.

Landrum, Gene N. *Profiles of Genius: Thirteen Creative Men Who Changed the World.* Buffalo, N.Y.: Prometheus Books, 1993.

Monaghan, Tom. *Pizza Tiger.* New York: Random House, 1986.

Morgan, Garrett Augustus
(1877–1963) *inventor of safety devices*

Garrett Morgan is an excellent example of a creative inventor who also possessed strong entrepreneurial skills. His creativity was not confined to any one endeavor, as he developed three important but different inventions: a hair straightener, the safety hood, and an improved traffic signal. He also formed highly profitable companies to exploit the commercial possibilities afforded him by his inventive skill.

Morgan was born on March 4, 1877, in Paris, Kentucky. His parents, Sydney and Elizabeth, were farmers. At age 14 he left home and moved to Cincinnati, Ohio, where he found a job as a mechanic for a large landowner. Four years later, in 1895, he moved to Cleveland, and for the next 12 years he worked as a repairman for several sewing machine manufacturers. Meanwhile, he received his first patent, for a belt fastener for sewing machines, which in 1901 he sold to his employer for $50. He was a shrewd manager of his personal finances, and by 1907 he had saved enough money out of his wages to open his own sewing machine repair shop. The business thrived, and within two years he opened a garment factory that employed 32 people, moved his widowed mother to Cleveland, and married Mary Anne Hassek, with whom he had three children.

One of the problems Morgan faced in the factory was how to sew woolens without scorching the material due to friction from the rapid movement of the needle. One day, while trying to develop a lubricant for the needle that would not harm wool, he discovered that one solution had straightened the fibers in a wiry piece of cloth. Thinking that he may have discovered a way to straighten hair, which was in great demand among his fellow black people at the time, he applied the solution to a neighbor's Airedale dog. The dog's hair straightened out so much that its owner did not recognize it. Over the next several months, Morgan put more and more of the solution in his own hair, and when it straightened his hair, too, without making it fall out, he realized he had a marketable product. After adding a few ingredients to make the solution look, smell, and feel good, in 1913 he formed the G. A.

Morgan Hair Refining Cream Company. Morgan's hair straightener proved to be a popular product, and he made plenty of money from it for many years.

Meanwhile, Morgan had been experimenting with other useful apparatuses, and in 1912 he applied for a patent for a "breathing device," also known as a safety hood. Designed to prevent miners, excavators, and firemen from suffocating during the course of their duty, the safety hood consisted of a flexible headpiece to which two tubes were attached. A long tube hung down almost to the ground, and inside the tube near its lower end was a sponge. Morgan knew that smoke and noxious fumes generally rise upward, leaving a layer of breathable air close to the ground. By wetting the sponge, the wearer could breathe filtered air from this lower layer and be able to maneuver through a smoke-filled area without suffocating. Exhaled air was expelled from the hood through a short tube. In 1914 he received a patent for the safety hood, and that same year he formed the National Safety Device Company to manufacture it.

To boost sales, Morgan traveled across the northern United States demonstrating the device. His favorite demonstration was to build a big, smelly, smoky fire inside a large, closed canvas tent. Then, after a white spokesperson showed the crowd the fire and explained what was about to happen, Morgan—pretending to be a full-blooded Indian by the name of "Big Chief Mason"—donned the hood and entered the tent. Most prospective customers were convinced when "Big Chief" emerged after about 20 minutes without showing any ill effects from the smoke or the stench. A similar demonstration at the 1914 Second International Exposition of Sanitation and Safety in New York City earned the safety hood a First Grand Prize Gold Medal, and shortly thereafter fire departments across the North began ordering safety hoods.

The safety hood made national headlines in 1916 when Morgan used it to pull off a dramatic rescue. An underground explosion trapped two dozen excavators in a tunnel full of smoke and poisonous gases beneath the waters of Lake Erie. After the police and fire departments tried and failed to rescue the men, Morgan and his brother Frank were summoned to the scene, whereupon each put on a safety hood and began bringing the injured men to the surface. The brothers saved 20 lives that day and were rewarded by the city of Cleveland with diamond-studded gold medals and a citation calling them "our most honored and bravest citizen[s]." Almost immediately, fire departments and mining companies from around the country began ordering safety hoods, and the company's stock shot up from $10 per share to $250. A year later, KATHARINE BURR BLODGETT discovered how to provide the safety hood with a charcoal filter; thus modified, the safety hood became the first American-made gas mask and saved the lives of many American soldiers during World War I.

Morgan's last important invention was the traffic signal. As automobiles became more popular, the number of accidents at intersections increased. The traffic signals then in existence were hand-operated mechanical devices capable of telling motorists when to stop and go, but they could not warn drivers that the signal was about to change. This inability led to a number of accidents, since drivers could not always stop quickly enough to obey the signal. Morgan invented a polelike device with lights and arms that included a "caution" position, essentially the forerunner of the yellow light on the modern traffic signal. He received a patent for the traffic signal in 1923 and formed the G. A. Morgan Safety System Company to manufacture it; however, he soon felt overburdened by this enterprise, so he sold his patent to the General Electric Company for $40,000, a considerable sum of money at the time.

In the 1920s, Morgan began to focus his attention on other matters besides invention and business. By mid-decade he had founded the *Cleveland Call*, a newspaper that focused on the concerns of the city's black community. He served for a number of years as the treasurer of the Cleveland Association of Colored Men, helped found a black fraternity at Western Reserve University, and was an early member of the National Association for the Advancement of Colored People (NAACP). Throughout his career he earned and retained the respect of some of the country's most influential entrepreneurs, including J. P. MORGAN, after whom he named his first son. Although he lost 90 percent

of his vision to glaucoma in 1943, he continued to keep busy, and to hunt and fish, until a few years before his death on July 27, 1963, in Cleveland.

Further Reading

Amram, Fred M. B. *African-American Inventors.* Mankato, Minn.: Capstone Press, 1996.

Brodie, James M. *Created Equal: The Lives and Ideas of Black American Innovators.* New York: William Morrow, 1993.

James, Portia P. *The Real McCoy: African-American Invention and Innovation, 1619–1930.* Washington, D.C.: Smithsonian Institution Press, 1989.

Morgan, J. P.
(John Pierpont Morgan)
(1837–1913) *entrepreneur in high finance*

From the 1890s to the 1910s, J. P. Morgan was the most powerful financial figure in America. At a time when the Federal Reserve Board did not exist, Morgan came closest to being the chief regulator of the economy. Twice, in 1893 and 1907, he put together banking syndicates that effectively saved the country from financial chaos. He also emerged as the leading financier of his day, having backed the mergers that created the largest industrial and railroad combinations during an era when mergers were the order of the day.

Morgan was born John Pierpont Morgan on April 17, 1837, in Hartford, Connecticut. His father, Junius, was an investment banker, and his mother, Juliet, was a homemaker. After graduating from high school, he studied in Switzerland and at the University of Gottingen in Germany. In 1857 his father, who was head of George Peabody and Company, an American-owned bank in London, England, got him a job as an accountant with Duncan, Sherman and Company, Peabody's branch operation in New York City. In 1861 he married Amelia Sturges, who died five months later. Four years later he married Frances Tracy with whom he had four children.

In 1864 Morgan became a founding partner in Dabney, Morgan and Company; seven years later, at his father's urging, he merged this firm with one of Philadelphia's most prestigious investment banks to form Drexel, Morgan and Company. As an investment banker, Morgan's job was to put together syndicates to underwrite new stock issues. The underwriters bought the stock at a discount from the issuing corporation, then sold it to retail banks, insurance companies, and wealthy individuals. Over the years, Morgan developed a reputation as the foremost investment banker in the United States, primarily for two reasons. First, his connections with his father's bank gave him ready access to British investors who were looking for American investments. Second, he went to great lengths to make sure that the stocks he sold retained their value. Both factors ensured that a Morgan syndicate would be well-subscribed.

Railroad construction took off in the United States after the Civil War, so Morgan steered a number of his British clients into railroad stock. When CORNELIUS VANDERBILT died in 1879, his son William selected Drexel, Morgan and Company to sell his stock in the New York Central Railroad, which amounted to hundreds of thousands of shares. Six years later a cutthroat rate war between the New York Central and the Pennsylvania Railroad threatened to undermine the value of those shares, so Morgan personally arranged and moderated a meeting aboard his private yacht that brought the rate war to an end. This move greatly enhanced Morgan's prestige among the railroading fraternity, and in 1886 he was invited to refinance the other two major eastern railroads, the Chesapeake & Ohio and the Baltimore & Ohio. After the panic of 1893 caused hundreds of railroads across the country to fail, Morgan organized a number of bankrupt southern roads into the Southern Railway, which for many years dominated railroading in the southeastern United States. In 1901 he defused a major western railroad war between E. H. HARRIMAN's Union Pacific and JAMES JEROME HILL's Northern Pacific by forming the Northern Securities Company, which held the shares of both railroads as well as several others over which they were fighting to control. In each of these ventures, Morgan obtained for himself a seat

J. P. Morgan attempts to clear an intrusive photographer out of his path. *(Library of Congress)*

on the board of directors, and he used this position to ensure cooperation among potential rivals, thus avoiding the sort of competition that might have a negative effect on stock prices.

In the 1890s Morgan became the nation's leading financier for the federal government and private industry as well as the railroads. In 1891 he arranged the merger between two rival electrical manufacturing empires, Edison General Electric and Thomson-Houston Electric. The result was the General Electric Company, which dominated the electric-equipment manufacturing industry in the United States. During the panic of 1893, he put together a syndicate that provided the federal government with $62 million in gold, enough to prevent the collapse of the gold standard, thus saving the American economy from chaos. In 1898 he financed Elbert H. Gary's formation of Federal Steel in order to compete with ANDREW CARNEGIE's Carnegie Steel, which Morgan thought was ruining the steel business because it was selling its products at prices significantly below its competitors. When Federal proved unable to compete with Carnegie, Morgan financed the merger of the two rivals and several other steel manufacturers into the United States Steel Company, the world's first billion-dollar corporation. In 1902 he underwrote the merger of the McCormick Harvesting Machine Company and the Deering Harvester Company, thus creating International Harvester, for a number of years the largest manufacturer of farm equipment in the country.

In 1907 Morgan was called upon a second time to save the national economy. This time the occasion was the panic of 1907, which, like most panics, was brought on because widespread speculation had grossly inflated the stock prices of a number of companies that, because of financial mismanagement, could no longer pay their debts. To save as many of these companies from financial ruin as possible, Morgan put together a syndicate of major banks that used their assets as well as large government deposits to prop up those ailing companies, brokerage firms, and smaller banks that were deemed solvent enough to survive. Those companies deemed too shaky were either merged with larger companies or allowed to declare bankruptcy. For his reward in bringing about an end

to the panic, which subsided shortly after Morgan went into action, he obtained President Theodore Roosevelt's promise that the federal government would not prosecute United States Steel for acquiring controlling interest in the Tennessee Coal and Iron Company, a major southern producer of steel. Once the panic was over, both Morgan and Roosevelt received much criticism for the Tennessee Coal and Iron deal because it smacked of monopoly.

Morgan was a collector of ancient Egyptian relics, classical art, and all kinds of books. The books were eventually donated to the New York Public Library, while the art and relics found their way into New York City's Metropolitan Museum of Art. He died on March 31, 1913, in Rome, Italy, while returning from a trip to Egypt. At the time of his death, his fortune was estimated to be more than $68 million, a surprisingly small sum for a man who had exercised such financial clout.

Further Reading

Brands, H. W. *Masters of Enterprise: Giants of American Business from John Jacob Astor and J. P. Morgan to Bill Gates and Oprah Winfrey.* New York: Free Press, 1999.

Carosso, Vincent P. *The Morgans: Private International Bankers 1854–1913.* Cambridge, Mass.: Harvard University Press, 1987.

Chernow, Ron. *The House of Morgan: An American Banking Dynasty and the Rise of Modern Finance.* New York: Simon & Schuster, 1991.

Wren, Daniel A., and Ronald G. Greenwood. *Management Innovators: The People and Ideas That Have Shaped Modern Business.* New York: Oxford University Press, 1998.

Morris, Robert

(1734–1806) *entrepreneur in mercantile activity*

One of the most underrated heroes of the American Revolution is Robert Morris. Considered by many to be the wealthiest man in America during the Revolution, Morris used his personal fortune and mercantile connections to bail out the Continental Congress, and he played a major role in winning the ultimate victory against the British at Yorktown. Ironically, toward the end of his life Morris's financial genius failed him, and he spent several years in a debtor's prison in the city from which he successfully masterminded the financial details of the Revolution.

Morris was born on January 20, 1735, in Liverpool, England. His father, Robert, was an iron buyer and tobacco agent in Maryland, and his mother, Elizabeth, was a homemaker. At age 12 he joined his father in Maryland, and shortly thereafter he was apprenticed to Charles Willing, a merchant in Philadelphia, Pennsylvania. In 1757 Morris and Charles's son Thomas formed the mercantile firm of Willing and Morris, and over the next 16 years they acquired 10 ships that traded between the American colonies and Great Britain. They also traded with contacts in Portugal, Spain, and the West Indies, but because the Navigation Acts prohibited trade between the American colonies and everywhere other than Great Britain, this

Robert Morris used his skills as a merchant to help the United States win the American Revolution. *(Library of Congress)*

mercantile involvement was legally classified as smuggling. In 1767 he married Mary White with whom he had seven children.

During the American Revolution, Morris played an indispensible role in financing the American war effort and supplying the Continental Army with the necessary supplies. In 1775 he joined the Pennsylvania Council of Safety and was put in charge of procuring arms and ammunition for that state and serving as its banker. Later that year he was appointed chairman of the Continental Congress's Secret Committee of Trade, in essence the American department of defense. In this capacity he purchased commodities from American farmers and artisans for export, and he used the proceeds to buy war matériel from merchants and businesses. He made extensive use of his firm's commercial contacts in Europe and the West Indies, and he often used his firm's warehouses to store goods for the Continental army. Meanwhile, he continued to trade on his own behalf, often carrying his own goods in the same ships as the government's. Following the American evacuation of Philadelphia in 1778, Morris fled to Baltimore, Maryland, from where he sent money and supplies to General George Washington at Valley Forge, Pennsylvania. He also terminated his partnership with Willing, who remained in Philadelphia, and established an extensive network of commercial contacts throughout the 13 states and in Europe.

Having become, by 1781, the new nation's wealthiest man and its most successful merchant, Morris was appointed by Congress to the post of superintendent of finance. By this time Continental paper money was worthless; the American government was deeply in debt; it could no longer obtain anything on credit; and requisitions from the various states produced practically nothing in the way of money or supplies for the Continental army. Acting quickly, Morris obtained congressional approval to establish the Bank of North America, which solicited deposits from wealthy Americans and the French, then loaned the money to the national government. Meanwhile, the bank's notes began circulating as legal tender. To supplement these funds, Morris issued what became known as "Morris's notes," in essence personal

IOUs backed by his own fortune, which also circulated for a time as legal tender. Most important, he used his extensive mercantile connections to gather enough supplies and ships to feed and transport Washington's army from New York to Yorktown, Virginia, where it effectively ended the war by defeating a British army under General Lord Cornwallis. When Morris left office in 1783, his government accounts were in the black by $20,000, an incredible turnaround from two years earlier.

The war having freed American merchants from the strictures of the Navigation Acts, Morris moved boldly to expand his mercantile activities. He reconciled with Thomas Willing, and the two took on a new partner, John Swanwick, to form a new firm, Willing, Morris and Swanwick. In 1784 they dispatched the *Empress of China*, the first American ship to enter the China trade. Its success encouraged other Americans such as JOHN BROWN, THOMAS HANDASYD PERKINS, and JOHN JACOB ASTOR to get involved in trading with the Orient. In 1785 Morris's firm also became heavily involved in trading tobacco to the French, and it sold as many as 20,000 hogsheads of tobacco each year for the next three years.

By 1790 Morris had also become heavily involved in land speculation. At first, all went well; he bought 1 million acres from the state of Massachusetts, which he sold a year later for a 250 percent profit. This success led him into a partnership with John Nicholson and John Greenleaf that involved the acquisition of 6 million acres scattered across seven states. When the land did not sell as fast as they had hoped, the partners were unable to pay the debts they had incurred to buy the land and were forced into bankruptcy. In 1798 Morris was thrown into debtor's prison in Philadelphia, where he remained until passage of a new federal bankruptcy law outlawing imprisonment for debts set him free three years later. He spent his remaining years in Philadelphia, where he died on May 8, 1806.

Further Reading

"Morris, Robert," Signers of the Declaration of Independence. Available online. URL: http://www.ushistory.org/Declaration/signers/morris_r.htm. Downloaded on July 3, 2009.

Ver Steeg, Clarence L. *Robert Morris, Revolutionary Financier; with an Analysis of His Earlier Career*. New York: Octagon Books, 1976.

Morse, Samuel F. B.
(Samuel Finley Breese Morse)
(1791–1872) *inventor of the telegraph*

By the end of the 19th century, the United States had been crisscrossed by telegraph lines, thus creating a national communications system. This development facilitated the conduct of business on a national basis and the coordination of railroad traffic, to name just two benefits. The person most responsible for inventing the telegraph was Samuel F. B. Morse. Oddly, Morse had little mechanical aptitude and was in fact much more talented as a portrait painter.

Morse was born Samuel Finley Breese Morse on April 27, 1791, in Charlestown, Massachusetts. His father, Jedidiah, was a minister, and his mother, Elizabeth, was a homemaker. After graduating from Yale College in 1810, he worked briefly as a clerk for a Boston book publisher. In 1811 he went to London, England, to study painting. Upon returning to the United States in 1815, he began earning a living as a portrait painter, and for the next eight years he divided his time among Boston, New York City, and Charleston, South Carolina. In 1823 he established a studio in New York City, where he painted some of the finest portraits ever produced by an American painter. In 1818 he married Lucretia Walker with whom he had four children; she died in 1825.

In 1829 Morse went back to Europe and spent the next three years painting in France and Italy. On the return trip, he had several conversations with a fellow passenger about electricity, in particular the possibility of using it to transmit messages. In 1834, having secured a position as professor of sculpture and painting at what became known as New York University, he began experimenting with the telegraph. A year later he had invented a crude prototype, whereby electrical currents were transmitted via an electromagnet to a pencil that marked wavy lines on a strip of paper; the lines represented numbers, which in turn represented words.

Because Morse did not properly understand the operating principles of electromagnets, he could not get his telegraph to transmit messages for more than a few feet. But in 1836 he met Leonard D. Gale, a professor of chemistry at the university, and with Gale's help he was able to develop an electromagnet that could transmit messages for up to 10 miles. In 1837 Alfred Vail, one of Morse's art students who was also mechanically gifted, joined Morse and Gale. Vail was responsible for developing the telegraph key, a simple device that transmits a signal when a button is depressed, thus completing an electrical circuit, and the receiver, which eliminated the pencil and instead printed dots (for short signals) and dashes (for long signals) on a strip of paper. By 1838 Morse had also gotten rid of the idea to use numbers to represent words, and instead had developed Morse code, whereby the dots and dashes represented individual letters, numerals, and punctuation marks. Following dem-

Samuel F. B. Morse revolutionized the world of communications by inventing the telegraph. *(Library of Congress)*

onstrations in New York City, Philadelphia, and Washington, in 1840 Morse was issued a patent for the telegraph.

For the next three years, Morse petitioned Congress to adopt his telegraph for use in a national communications system. He enlisted a fourth partner, F. O. J. Smith, chairman of the House Committee of Commerce, to help out. In fact, in 1836 Congress had asked the secretary of the treasury to consider the feasibility of developing a national semaphore system such as that used throughout Europe, and Morse hoped that his telegraph system might be adopted instead. In 1843 Congress passed a $30,000 appropriations bill for a test telegraph system that had been introduced by Smith, after which Morse, Gale, and Vail began stringing wire between Washington and Baltimore, Maryland, a distance of 40 miles. At first, the wires for the system were to be placed underground, so the partners recruited EZRA CORNELL to dig the trench. After about 13 miles, however, it was discovered that the wires had shorted out, so they restrung the wires on poles. In 1844 the message "What hath God wrought" was successfully transmitted by telegraph between the two cities, and the telegraph era had begun.

In 1845 Morse and his partners formed the Morse Electromagnetic Telegraph Company for purposes of licensing the use of Morse's telegraph patent. Gale received a one-eighth interest, Vail and Smith each received one-quarter, while Morse retained the remaining three-eighths. From that moment on, Morse had little to do with the telegraph other than to spend the hundreds of thousands of dollars he received from licenses and fees. He gave much of his money to Vassar and Yale colleges as well as to a number of churches, theological seminaries, Bible, missionary, and temperance societies. He also contributed generously to the maintenance of starving artists. In 1847 he built a mansion on the Hudson River near Poughkeepsie, New York, and the following year he married Sarah Griswold with whom he had four children. He also took up painting once again, but by the 1850s he no longer possessed the artistic talent he once had. He spent the rest of his life between Poughkeepsie and New York City, surrounded by his children and grandchildren. He died on April 2, 1872, in New York City.

Further Reading

Crompton, Samuel W. *100 Americans Who Shaped American History.* San Mateo, Calif.: Bluewood Books, 1999.

Staiti, Paul J. *Samuel F. B. Morse.* New York: Cambridge University Press, 1989.

Wren, Daniel A., and Ronald G. Greenwood. *Management Innovators: The People and Ideas that Have Shaped Modern Business.* New York: Oxford University Press, 1998.

Muller, Gertrude Agnes

(1887–1954) *inventor of the child's toilet seat and car seat*

Two of the more perplexing challenges facing a young child in the 20th century were how to use the toilet without falling in, and how to see out of an automobile window. For inventing seats that make both tasks easier and safer, Gertrude Muller deserves the thanks of all present and former children. Ironically, Muller did not invent either seat for her own children—she never married—but in response to an embarrassing incident involving her sister.

Muller was born on June 9, 1887, in Leo, Indiana. Her father, Victor, owned several small businesses, and her mother, Catherine, was a homemaker. At age six her father died suddenly, and she moved with her remaining family to Fort Wayne, where her mother's family lived. To support her children, Catherine Muller took in boarders, baked doughnuts, and invested in property, all the while instilling in Muller a sense of what she might be able to do as a businesswoman. At age 17 she graduated from International Business College in Fort Wayne and went to work as a stenographer for the General Electric Company's local manufacturing facility. Six years later, in 1910, she became executive secretary to the president of the Van Arnam Manufacturing Company, which made wooden toilet seats. Four years later she was promoted to assistant manager of production.

Sometime during the late 1910s, Muller's sister went on a trip with her toddler. The child was in the process of being toilet trained, and the mother did not want to resort to diapers, thus throwing away all the hard-won progress that had been made. Instead, she developed a makeshift toilet seat that the child could sit upon without assistance. Unfortunately, as they were checking out of an upscale hotel, the covering concealing the modified seat fell to the floor, and the mother was left standing in full view of everyone in the lobby with what appeared to be one of the hotel's toilet seats in her hands. As the reactions of the onlooking guests and staff changed from shock to sniggering, the mother felt herself flush with embarrassment, and upon her return to Fort Wayne she related the whole sad incident to Muller.

Realizing that a golden business opportunity had just presented itself, Muller set out to invent a portable toilet seat just for children. With her sister's assistance, Muller designed what she called the "toidey seat," a child-sized, collapsible toilet seat that could be attached over a standard toilet bowl or used with its own basin and frame. She contracted with Van Arnam to manufacture her invention, which she tried to sell by recruiting plumbers as distributors. Not surprisingly, this sales strategy failed miserably, since no self-respecting mother would ever dream of buying a product for her child from a man covered in slime and sludge. Undaunted by her initial failure, in 1924 Muller formed the Juvenile Wood Products Company, with herself as president, to make and market the toidey seat. She recruited department stores and baby specialty shops to sell her product, and the toidey seat soon became a fast-selling item.

As her company prospered, Muller introduced new child-care products. "Toidey Two-Steps" was a junior stepladder that helped children climb up onto the adult-sized toilet or reach the wash basin. As more and more people began to drive automobiles, she invented the "Comfy-Safe Auto-Seat," a child's car seat that was hung from the front seat's upright cushion so that the child could see through the windows and be restrained to a certain degree from being thrown to the floor or into the dashboard if the car stopped suddenly. In addition to developing products and managing the office, Muller also wrote the company's promotional material and the directions for using the various products. In all of this material, she strove to inculcate in parents a sense that children should be encouraged to do as much for themselves as they are capable of doing, and that toilet training need not and should not be a herculean task conducted according to a strict timetable. Her best-known pamphlet was "Training the Baby"; first printed in 1930, it went through 26 printings over the next 20 years. In addition to being included with each toidey seat, it was also distributed by pediatricians and used in the public schools to teach home economics students about basic child care.

Muller's company progressed with the times by responding to changes in technology. In 1944 she switched from wood to plastic as the basic building material for her products, and she changed the company's name to the Toidey Company. As automobile speeds increased during the 1940s and 1950s, she began using auto crash studies to make the Comfy-Safe Auto-Seat safer. In recognition of her efforts in this regard, the National Safety Council made her a National Veteran of Safety, and in 1954 she was invited to the White House Conference on Highway Safety. She worked until her death on October 31, 1954, in Fort Wayne.

Further Reading

Sicherman, Barbara, and Carol Hurd Green. *Notable American Women: The Modern Period: A Biographical Dictionary.* Cambridge, Mass.: Belknap Press, 1980.

Stuber, Irene. "Gertrude Agnes Muller," Women of Achievement and Herstory. Available online. URL: http://www.thelizlibrary.org/collections/woa/woa06-09.html. Downloaded on March 15, 2010.

Munsey, Frank Andrew

(1854–1925) *entrepreneur in magazine and newspaper publishing*

Although the founding of magazine and newspaper chains predated him, Frank Munsey was the first to found one merely as a means of making money. Unlike Adolph Ochs, whose *New York Times* vowed to print "all the news that's fit to print," Munsey made no pretense at prizing journalistic excellence. In this sense, he was one of the first American businessmen in industries such as communications, entertainment, and sports to care

nothing at all about their industry except that it provide a high return on investment.

Munsey was born on August 21, 1854, in Mercer, Maine. His parents, Andrew and Mary Jane, were farmers. As a boy he moved to nearby Lisbon Falls where he worked for several years as a grocery clerk. In his spare time he taught himself how to operate a telegraph, and then he worked as a telegraph operator for a succession of hotels in New England. In the late 1870s he moved to Augusta, Maine, where he became manager of the Western Union telegraph office. Around 1880 he made the acquaintance of a publisher of several tabloid magazines. Despite their almost total lack of uplifting or informational content, people read the periodicals avidly, which led businesses to advertise heavily in them, thus making the tabloids surprisingly profitable. Munsey was so impressed with the money to be made from tabloids that he decided to become a publisher, too. In 1881 he moved to Poughkeepsie, New York, where he enrolled in a local business college. After taking a few courses, in 1882 he headed for New York City to begin publishing *Golden Argosy,* a magazine intended to appeal to young people.

When Munsey reached New York, he had $40 in his pocket and a handful of manuscripts under his arm. He soon found a printer who agreed to print the magazine for a portion of the profits rather than a flat rate, and Munsey was off and running on a shoestring. When he realized that authors would not write for the same consideration, he began writing his own material, including four serialized novels written in the style of Horatio Alger's highly popular rags-to-riches stories. When the printer went bankrupt in 1883, Munsey borrowed $300 from a banker in Augusta and bought the presses himself. By 1887 *Golden Argosy* was earning him a tidy profit of $1,500 per week.

In an effort to push his profits even higher, in 1887 Munsey decided to focus on the adult market. He changed his first magazine's name to *Argosy* and eliminated the youthful-appealing content in favor of more grown-up articles. In 1889 he founded *Munsey's Weekly,* an illustrated journal that he converted into the monthly *Munsey's Magazine* two years later. In 1891 he began dabbling with newspapers by acquiring the *New York Star,* converting it into a tabloid, changing its name to the *Daily Continent*, and then selling it, all within a period of about four months. And in 1893 he shocked the publishing world by lowering the price of *Munsey's Magazine* from 25¢ per issue, the standard price for illustrated magazines, to 10¢, thus making it the first low-priced illustrated monthly in the United States. When news distributors balked at the lowered fee they received for handling the magazine, Munsey formed *Red Star News* to distribute his own publications and to advertise them heavily across town. Within two years the circulation for *Munsey's Magazine* had tripled, and in 1895 Munsey opened a printing plant in New London, Connecticut. As circulation rose, advertisers lined up for the privilege of placing ads in *Munsey's Magazine,* which caused Munsey's profits to soar, even though the magazine's cover price did not cover the costs of printing and production. Munsey used the profits from *Munsey's Magazine* to enlarge his publishing empire. By 1919 he had founded or acquired an additional 13 magazines; some of them he nurtured into popular magazines of their own, some he merged with others to increase their popularity, and others he discontinued to keep them from competing with other popular magazines he controlled.

In 1901 Munsey reentered the newspaper business by buying the *New York Daily News* and the *Washington Times;* over the next 23 years he purchased 10 other major newspapers in Boston, Philadelphia, Baltimore, and New York with the intention of building a nationwide newspaper empire to rival those of WILLIAM RANDOLPH HEARST and Edward Scripps. But the newspaper business was not as kind to Munsey as the magazine business was; despite constant tinkering with graphics and format (but apparently not content) he was forced to fold the *Daily News* after three years and sell the *Times* in 1917. Meanwhile, he churned up the newspaper situation in New York City by founding, merging, and folding papers in an unsuccessful attempt to corner the city's press market. He acquired the *Sun* in 1916, only

to merge it with the *Press*, which he had founded in 1912. Having also acquired the *Evening Sun* in 1916, he renamed it the *Sun*, then merged it into the *Herald*, which he purchased in 1920. In 1923 he bought the *Globe*, which he also merged into the *Herald*. When his attempt to buy the *Tribune*, which he also intended to merge into the *Herald*, failed, in 1924 he sold the *Herald* to the *Tribune's* owners, who combined the two papers into the *Herald-Tribune*. He bought the *Evening Mail* in 1924, then closed it to keep it from competing with the *Press*.

Munsey seems to have cared not at all about the content of his publications. While their editorial policy was colorless and inoffensive, their coverage of news was sensational and, at times, scandalous. Munsey's sole interest in his publishing empire was that it make him wealthy, which it did. At the time of his death on December 22, 1925, in New York City, his fortune was estimated at $40 million. However, his money bought him little in the way of family or friendship. He never married, and most of his fortune was left to New York's Metropolitan Museum of Art. His tactics of closing and merging newspapers threw so many journalists and press people out of work that one writer, William Allen White, penned a scathing obituary in which he claimed that Munsey had "the talent of a meat packer, the morals of a money changer, and the manner of an undertaker." Before his death Munsey himself summed up his life this way: "I have no heirs. I am disappointed in my friendships. . . . I have forty million dollars, but what has it brought me? Not happiness."

Further Reading

Britt, George. *Forty Years—Forty Millions: The Career of Frank A. Munsey.* Port Washington, N.Y.: Kennikat Press, 1972.

"Munsey, Frank A. The founding of the Munsey Publishing House. Internet Archive. Available online. URL: http://www.archive.org/stream/foundingof munsey00munsoft#page/n1/mode/2up. Downloaded on October 19, 2009.

N

Naismith, James A.
(1861–1939) *inventor of basketball*

It is said that the only major sport strictly of U.S. origin is basketball. Although this may be true in that it was invented and popularized in the United States, its inventor, James Naismith, was a citizen of Canada at the time he invented it, and he did not become a naturalized U.S. citizen until 34 years later.

Naismith was born James Naismith on November 6, 1861, in Almonte, Ontario, Canada; he later adopted the middle initial "A." His father, John, was a carpenter and lumberjack, and his mother, Margaret, was a homemaker. At age nine Naismith's parents died during a typhoid epidemic, and he was raised successively by his grandmother and an unmarried uncle. At age 17 he went to work in a logging camp. Five years later he decided to become an ordained minister and enrolled in McGill University in Montreal. He received his A.B. in 1887, then studied theology for three years in a seminary associated with McGill. One of his seminarian duties his third year was to teach gymnastics classes at McGill, and as a result of this experience he lost his desire to preach and decided instead to devote his life to teaching physical education. In 1890 Naismith enrolled in the International Young Men's Christian Association (YMCA) Training School in Springfield, Massachusetts; today the school is known as Springfield College. He excelled on the football field and in the classroom, and after his first year, Luther Gulick, the head of the physical education department, invited him to become an instructor.

In 1891 American youths played two major sports, football in the fall and baseball in the spring. Students desiring to engage in organized physical activity could choose only between ice hockey and gymnastics. Believing that the former was too rough and the latter was too boring, Gulick asked his physical education instructors, Naismith included, to invent some kind of game that could be played during the winter that was both safe and fun to play. Naismith came up with a game called basketball that involved throwing a soccer ball into a peach basket suspended overhead. His game had 13 simple rules that prohibited personal contact, running with the ball (passing but not dribbling was allowed), and preventing another player from getting the ball. The first game of basketball was played by the 18 members of Naismith's physical education class playing nine to a side. After much running and passing, one player got off a lucky shot and the game ended 1-0, a seemingly inauspicious beginning. The players, however, loved the game because it was simple and fast, and its popularity quickly spread beyond Springfield to YMCAs all over the United States, Canada, France, and England. The game also became popular among college students, and the first college game was played in 1896 between the University of Chicago and the University of Iowa. In 1898 the National Basketball League, the first professional league, began play.

During the first 10 years of its existence, basketball underwent a number of rules changes. In

1895 the scoring was set at two points for a field goal and one for a free throw; also, a backboard was installed behind the hoop to keep fans from interfering with the ball. In 1897 the number of players per side was set at five. Equipment changed, too; the first basketball hoop was manufactured by the Narragansett Machinery Company in 1893; it had a hammock-type net that was finally opened at the bottom in 1912. In 1894 the first basketball was introduced; it was laced, measured 32 inches in circumference, and weighed less than 20 ounces, making it slightly bigger and lighter than the modern basketball.

Surprisingly, Naismith seems to have lost interest in basketball shortly after he invented it. Although he served on several of the early rules committees, he devoted most of his energy to teaching health and physical education as a means of instilling moral values. In 1894 he married Maude

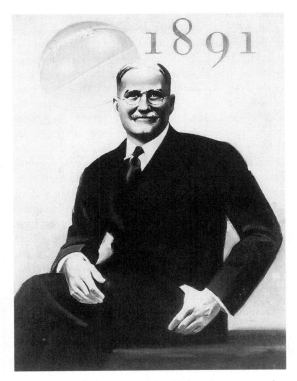

James Naismith, inventor of the all-American game of basketball, was born in Canada. *(Library of Congress)*

Sherman with whom he had five children. In 1895 he moved to Denver, Colorado, where he taught physical education at the Denver YMCA while studying medicine at the Gross Medical School. After receiving his M.D. in 1898, he became the first instructor of physical education at the University of Kansas, where he also coached the track and basketball teams until 1905. He continued to attend Kansas's home games after stepping down as head coach; however, he always insisted that basketball was a game that should be played for fun, and that coaches, players, and fans took it much too seriously.

In 1916 Naismith was ordained a Presbyterian minister, although he continued to teach at Kansas until he retired in 1937. In 1925 he became a naturalized citizen of the United States. In 1939 he married Florence Kincaid, his first wife having died two years earlier. He died on November 28, 1939, at his home in Lawrence, Kansas. In 1959 he was posthumously awarded a charter membership to the Naismith Memorial Basketball Hall of Fame in Springfield, Massachusetts, which was named in his honor.

Further Reading

Cosentino, Frank. *Almonte's Brothers of the Wind: R. Tait McKenzie and James Naismith.* Burnstown, Ontario: General Store Pub. House, 1996.

Webb, Bernice Larson. *The Basketball Man: James Naismith.* Lawrence, Kans.: Kappelman's Historic Collections, 1994.

Newmark, Craig

(1952–   ) *founder of Craigslist*

With the increasingly ubiquitous Web site Craigslist, Craig Newmark has created a conceptually and visually simple enterprise that has revolutionized the simple but lucrative field of classified advertisements.

Craig Alexander Newmark was born in Hillside, New Jersey, on December 6, 1952. His father, Lee, was a salesman who died of cancer a few months after Craig's bar mitzvah and his mother, Joyce, worked as a bookkeeper. Newmark grew up in Morristown, New Jersey, and graduated from

Morristown High School in 1971. He described himself as a teenager as a pocket-protector and taped-together–glasses wearing "nerd" with "marginal social skills." Newmark left New Jersey to attend Case Western Reserve University in Cleveland, where he earned bachelor's and master's degrees in computer science in 1975 and 1977 respectively.

Following graduate school, Newmark spent 17 years working for IBM in computer programming and software-related jobs in Detroit and Miami. In the mid-1990s Newmark moved to San Francisco and prospered as a freelance computer consultant, including contract work as a web developer for the brokerage company Charles Schwab. He discovered the widespread and largely untapped potential of the Internet, particularly as it related to social networking. In 1995, Newmark used his own time to organize and distribute information to friends about events taking place in and around San Francisco. His friends soon asked for more, and quickly Newmark's reputation as a tech-savvy information guru began spreading by word of mouth throughout the Bay Area. Within two years, Newmark's messages included even more useful information, such as apartment listings and job postings. As the site grew in popularity, Newmark wanted to name it SF-Events, but was persuaded by friends to give it a name that conveyed the personal, grassroots character of his endeavor, so he called it by the name many were already using to refer to it: Craigslist.

Founder of Craigslist, Craig Newmark *(Photo by Sierra Communications/Used under a Creative Commons license)*

Craigslist's popularity was greatly aided by software developed by Newmark that allowed users to automatically post e-mails to the site. The nature of these postings had a wide range similar to those of classified ads that had been placed in newspapers for decades. The main difference with Craigslist was that these postings were now free and were even more targeted to the technophile audience than newspapers. Craigslist's subsequent effect on newspapers has been significant. Though not solely responsible for the decline in ad sales and readership of newspapers across the United States, Craigslist has played a key role in intensifying the ills of the newspaper industry. By 2009, many long-standing and prominent newspapers were going out of business, in some measure because of the dramatic downturn in classified ad revenue spurred by Internet sites such as Craigslist.

Newmark repeatedly rejected enormously lucrative offers to sell all or part of his enterprise or even to accept advertising banners. In 2004, Newmark conceded that his repeated rejections of lucrative offers have led to conflicting feelings. However, he remains steadfastly committed to maintaining the integrity of Craigslist, saying, "I admit that when I think of the money one could make from all this, I get a little twinge. But I'm pretty happy with nerd values: Get yourself a comfortable living, then do a little something to change the world." For Newmark, changing the world has meant creating a site that "gives people a break" by helping them "get everyday stuff done" and meeting other people. Estimates of the revenue Craigslist could earn typically reach to approximately a half billion dollars a year, but Newmark has been content to keep his operation the way he likes it, which still generates about $20 million a year. Newmark has become a millionaire through Craigslist and has spent recent years increasing his efforts in advocating progressive political causes.

Newmark, who has never married and has no children, still resides in San Francisco and remains the head of Craigslist, which by 2009 had expanded into over 500 cities in 50 countries. He explains his resounding success in business by noting, "First, run and persist running a site that's a genuine community service, without specifically intending to get rich at it. Then, surround myself with people who are smarter than me . . . There's no genius to it. It's persistence and listening to people."

Further Reading

Cohen, Noam. "Craig (of the List) Looks Beyond the Web." *New York Times.* Available online. URL: http://www.nytimes.com/2008/05/12/technology/12craig.html. Downloaded on August 28, 2009.

"A conversation with Craigslist.com's Founder, Craig Newmark." Charlie Rose. Available online. URL: http://www.charlierose.com/view/interview/8605. Downloaded on August 28, 2009.

McHugh, Josh. "Mr. Craigslist, Master of the Nerdiverse." *Wired.* Available online. URL: http://www.wired.com/wired/archive/12.09/craigslist.html. Downloaded on August 28, 2009.

Noble, Edward John

(1882–1958) *founder of Life Savers candy and American Broadcasting Companies*

Few Americans are unfamiliar with either Life Savers, the fruit-flavored candy shaped like a miniature donut, or ABC, one of the country's biggest television networks. Even fewer Americans might know that Life Savers and ABC were both founded by the same man, Edward Noble, who almost went out of business because the first Life Savers he ever sold smelled like glue and tasted like cardboard.

Noble was born on August 8, 1882, in Gouverneur, a small town in upstate New York not far from the St. Lawrence River. His father, Harvey, was a merchant, and his mother, Edna, was a homemaker. In 1905 he received his B.A. from Yale University and went to work in the publishing department of an advertising firm in New York City. Two years later he became a salesman for a company that sold advertising in subways and elevated trains, a job he held for the next six years.

In 1913 Noble became partners with J. Roy Allen and went into the candy business. Clarence A. Crane, a candy manufacturer in Cleveland, Ohio, had developed a mint-flavored hard candy called Life Savers because it was white and donut-shaped like a life preserver. Life Savers were not selling in Cleveland as well as Crane would have liked, so in 1913 he sold his rights and his entire stock of Life Savers to Noble and Allen. The partners formed the Mint Products Company, with Noble as president, and began packaging and selling Life Savers in New York City, the candy being shipped to them from Cleveland in cardboard-lined tubes. Unfortunately, the cardboard absorbed all of the mint flavor and gave the candy a gluey odor and a cardboard taste. Needless to say, none of the partners' customers were tempted to buy a second pack of Life Savers.

At this point, Mint Products would have gone out of business, except that Noble came up with two brilliant ideas. The first was to wrap the Life Savers tightly in tinfoil to preserve the mint flavor. And since no professional salesman could be found to sell Life Savers because no store owner would buy them, he placed ads in publications catering to young people, and recruited boys and girls to sell the candy to their friends and neighbors. Noble developed a sales plan whereby children could either keep a portion of each sale for themselves or forward all the money to Mint Products in exchange for premium merchandise of their choice. The new strategies worked beautifully; sales rose to almost 1 million rolls in 1914, then to almost 7 million rolls the following year. In 1915 Noble and Allen established their own factory in New York City and did a booming business until the U.S. entry into World War I forced them temporarily to suspend operations; Noble spent the war in the U.S. Army Ordnance Corps. When their company reopened in 1920, the same year Noble married Ethel Tinkham with whom he had two children, it did so with a new plant in Port Arthur, New York, and another one in Australia. In 1923 the name of the company was changed to Life Savers Inc., and the following year the company produced its first fruit-flavored Life Savers. Over the next 30 years the company continued to grow by increasing sales and by acquiring competitors such as Beech-Nut Company, a Canadian firm that made chewing gum and fruit drops. Noble served as president until 1938 but continued as chairman of the board until his death 20 years later, at which time Beech-Nut Life Savers Inc. was doing annual sales of more than $120 million.

Having made a fortune selling Life Savers, Noble turned his attention to radio broadcasting. In 1940 he bought radio station WMCA in New York City, only to sell it three years later in order to become the major stockholder in the 140-station Blue Network Company, the broadcasting subsidiary of the Radio Corporation of America. As chairman of the board, Noble renamed the network the American Broadcasting Companies in 1945; under his direction, the network, which eventually became known as ABC, owned stations in New York City, Chicago, Los Angeles, San Francisco, and Detroit, and had more than 200 independent owned affiliates. In 1953 Noble engineered a merger between ABC and Paramount Theaters; the new company, American Broadcasting-Paramount Theaters Inc., with Noble as chairman of the board, either operated or was affiliated with 600 movie theaters, 350 radio stations, and 80 television stations. In 1955 he oversaw the purchase of a phonograph record company, which as the ABC Records Division established several prestigious record labels, including Dot and Impulse.

Although Noble continued to work until his death, he managed to find plenty of time for relaxation and philanthropy. He loved to fly, and in 1938–39 he served as chairman of the Civil Aeronautics Authority. He was also a speedboat enthusiast, sponsoring and winning the St. Lawrence River Inboard Speedboat Championships for a number of years. He contributed generously to charities in upstate New York, but his favorites were St. Lawrence University and the North Country Hospitals. He also created the Edward J. Noble Foundation for purposes of funding various educational, religious, and charitable programs. He died on December 28, 1958, in Greenwich, Connecticut.

Further Reading

Leipold, L. Edmond. *Founders of Fortunes*. Minneapolis, Minn.: T.S. Denison, 1967.
"Life Savers Candy," The Great Idea Finder. Available online. URL: http://www.ideafinder.com/history/inventions/lifesavers.htm. Downloaded on July 6, 2009.

Norton, Charles Hotchkiss

(1851–1942) *inventor of the cylindrical grinding machine*

Of all the machining processes for metal, grinding is the most accurate because it allows the removal of material in increments as small as 1/10,000 of an inch. Obtaining such tolerances on longer pieces of metal, however, was virtually impossible until Charles Norton invented a cylindrical grinding machine that was as long as the workpieces themselves. In so doing, he also made it possible for factories to do much of their own precision work rather than subcontract such work to independent machine shops.

Norton was born on November 23, 1851, in Plainville, Connecticut. His parents, John and Harriet, worked in a clock dial factory. At age 15 he went to work for the Seth Thomas Clock Company in nearby Thomaston. Over the next 20 years, he gradually worked his way up from general chore boy to manager of the department that made tower clocks, such as one might find in a town square. In 1873 he married Julia Bishop with whom he had two children.

In 1886 Norton moved to Providence, Rhode Island, to become the assistant plant engineer for the Brown and Sharpe Manufacturing Company, manufacturers of sewing machines. One of the firm's owners, Jacob R. Brown, had invented a small grinding machine that sharpened tools and removed excess metal with great precision via the rapid circular action of an abrasive wheel. Norton modified the machine and developed an abrasive spindle so that it could grind the hollow insides of tools and parts. Meanwhile, he had become well-acquainted with Henry M. Leland, Brown & Sharpe's superintendent. In 1890 Leland cofounded the Leland & Faulconer Manufacturing Company in Detroit, Michigan, to make parts for automobiles; that same year Norton moved to Detroit to design new machine tools for Leland's company. Five years later he returned to Brown and Sharpe, divorced his first wife, and in 1896 married Mary Tomlinson with whom he had no children. She died in 1915, and in 1917 he married Grace Harding.

While in Detroit, Norton had gotten the idea to expand the grinding machine's capabilities so that it could utilize a wider abrasive wheel. He was particularly interested in speeding up the process of grinding automobile crankshafts, whose length necessitated hours of careful grinding with standard equipment and wheels. Norton envisioned a machine that used a cylindrical "wheel" as long as the crankshaft itself, essentially a larger version of the abrasive spindle he had developed earlier, for greater precision, and that rotated the crankshaft as well as the wheel for greater speed. Doing this, however, meant making the grinding machine itself longer, heavier, and stronger so that it could power a larger wheel and stand up to the larger pieces of work it would be grinding.

At first Norton tried to get Brown and Sharpe to build his cylindrical grinder—in addition to manufacturing sewing machines, the company also made small grinding machines for other factories—but the company showed no interest in the project. Norton then turned to other manufacturers for backing, and by 1900 he had secured the financial support of an abrasive wheel manufacturer coincidentally named the Norton Emory Wheel Company. That same year he moved to Worcester, Massachusetts, where he founded the Norton Grinding Machine Company. Within a year he had developed a cylindrical grinder that was eight feet long and weighed more than six tons. It used a cylindrical wheel with a diameter of two feet, four times as big as the next largest wheel in existence, and was equipped with a feed mechanism that permitted a precision grind unmatched by any other machine.

Norton's first grinding machine was eventually sold to a manufacturer of newspaper printing presses, the automotive industry having shown no interest. Undaunted, Norton continued to make improvements to his invention, and in 1903 he demonstrated that the cylindrical grinder could grind a crankshaft in 15 minutes as opposed to five hours of grinding with a standard machine. Orders for crankshaft grinders began to flow in shortly thereafter, including an order for 35 machines for the Ford Motor Company's Model T factory. By 1919, when Norton Emory Wheel took over Norton's company,

renaming it the Grinding Division, his cylindrical grinding machine had become a standard machine tool in automotive plants across the country.

Norton continued to design bigger and better grinding machines for all sorts of workpieces until 1934, when he retired from the Grinding Division and returned to Plainville. He continued to consult, however, when not engaged in oil painting, a hobby he took up late in life. His machines worked so quickly and with such precision that they transformed the metalworking industry. Whereas before precision grinding had to be performed by master machinists, most of whom worked in independent machine shops, Norton's grinders made it possible for nonspecialists to obtain acceptable results in an assembly-line mode of production. He held more than 100 patents related to the manufacture of grinding machines, and in 1925 he was awarded the Franklin Institute's John Scott Medal. He died on October 27, 1942, in Plainville.

Further Reading

"Charles H. Norton," Machine Tool Hall of Fame. Available online. URL: http://www.americanprecision.org/option.com.easygallery/act,photos/cid,93/Itemid,76/. Downloaded on July, 6, 2009.

Tymeson, Mildred McClary. *The Norton Story.* Worcester, Mass.: Norton Co., 1953.

Noyce, Robert Norton
(1927–1990) *inventor of the computer chip*

The development of modern computers, microprocessors, and microcomputers would never have occurred without the development of the integrated circuit, more commonly known as the computer chip. The man most responsible for developing the chip into a usable tool for computers and other electronic devices was Robert Noyce.

Noyce was born on December 12, 1927, in Burlington, Iowa. His father, Ralph, was a Congregational minister, and his mother, Harriet, was a homemaker. At age 10 he moved with his family to Grinnell, Iowa, so that his father could accept a supervisory position with the Iowa Conference of Congregational Churches at Grinnell College.

At age 18 he enrolled at Grinnell, and in 1949 he received his B.S. in physics and mathematics.

When Noyce entered college, electron flow in electronic circuitry was controlled by vacuum tubes, glass tubes pumped free of air, which house the anodes and cathodes for emitting and amplifying electrons. Although these devices work well (some electronic applications today still use vacuum tubes), they are bulky yet fragile, take time to warm up, generate a considerable amount of heat, and burn out within a relatively short time. For these reasons, researchers at Bell Telephone Laboratories began looking for a replacement, and in 1947 they invented the transistor. Instead of a glass tube, transistors use a piece of semiconducting material for their housing; early transistors were made from germanium, a rare element, but today most of them are made from silicon, the second most abundant element on Earth. And unlike the vacuum tube, transistors are tiny, tough, cool, long lasting, and infinitely more flexible in what they can be made to do.

By a stroke of luck, Noyce was able to study these revolutionary new devices while they were still brand new and he was still in college. Grant Gale, one of his physics professors, was a personal friend of John Bardeen, one of the transistor's three coinventors. During Noyce's senior year, Gale obtained some transistors from Bardeen with which he and Noyce then experimented. Noyce was fascinated by transistors, and after graduation he enrolled at the Massachusetts Institute of Technology (MIT) to learn more about them. Upon his arrival, however, he discovered that transistors were so new that he knew as much about them as his professors did. He received his Ph.D. in physical electronics in 1953, the same year he married Elizabeth Bottomley, with whom he had four children, and went to work for Philco, a Philadelphia-based manufacturer of radios and televisions. At Philco he hoped to play an important role in the further development of transistors, but once again he was disappointed by his superiors' seeming lack of interest in transistor research.

In 1956 Noyce went to work for the Shockley Laboratory Division of Beckman Instruments in Mountain View, California, in the heart of what became known as Silicon Valley. The company had

just been founded by William Shockley, another coinventor of the transistor, to design and manufacture transistors. Although Shockley was a brilliant researcher, he was not a successful manager. He quickly alienated eight of his top researchers, one of whom was Noyce, and in 1957 they left Shockley and formed the Fairchild Semiconductor Company with SHERMAN FAIRCHILD, which was funded by the Fairchild Camera and Instrument Corporation with the assistance of ARTHUR ROCK, a New York investment banker. Noyce joined Fairchild Semiconductor as a full partner and served for two years as its director of research. In 1959 he was made the company's vice president and general manager.

Although the transistor was much smaller than the vacuum tube, it still had to be wired into a circuit with diodes, capacitors, and resistors before it would work properly. Meanwhile, the growing size of computers, which used hundreds of thousands of transistors, called for the development of a device even smaller than the transistor. Clearly, what was needed was some sort of integrated circuit whereby transistors and their related elements could be connected and combined in one tiny package.

In 1959 one of Fairchild's founders, Jean Hoerni, invented what he called the planar transistor, in essence several transistors mounted on a thin wafer or chip of silicon. Noyce figured out how to add the necessary diodes, capacitors, and resistors to the planar transistor, and then "wire" all of these elements together with a thin layer of conductive aluminum. Hoerni and Noyce received a patent for the integrated circuit, or computer chip as it is known today, in 1961. Their first chip, which was about one-eighth-inch square, contained 10 components.

Almost immediately Fairchild focused on customizing integrated circuits according to customer specifications. Electronic technicians no longer had to spend hours and days constructing their own circuits; instead, they had merely to specify what they wanted a chip to do and Fairchild would make it and ship it to them, ready to install. The result was a dramatic decrease in the size of computers and the amount of time required to build them, as well as a dramatic increase in their calculating speed and reliability. Meanwhile, it was discovered that in 1959 Jack Kilby of Texas Instruments had also figured out how to put together an integrated circuit. However, his method for connecting the various elements was not nearly as effective as Noyce's. After much debate within the semiconductor community and the U.S. Patent Office, it was decided that Kilby had invented the integrated circuit but that Noyce had made it work.

By 1968 Fairchild Camera had acquired all of the stock of Fairchild Semiconductor and had implemented a business plan that emphasized selling the company's existing products rather than developing more sophisticated ones. This left Noyce wealthy but frustrated. That same year he and two Fairchild colleagues formed N. M. Electronics, with Noyce as president and chief executive officer. Later renamed Intel Corporation, the company avoided competing with Fairchild by making memory chips using a process called large scale integration (LSI), by which thousands of transistors and other components can be fit onto a chip no larger than the first one developed by Noyce and Hoerni. In 1970 Intel introduced its first product, the Dynamic Random Access Memory (DRAM) chip. A year later it released a major innovation in computer technology, the microprocessor chip, which contains all the arithmetic, logic, and control circuitry required to interpret and execute instructions. By 1975 Noyce had helped establish Intel as one of the country's foremost companies in computer technology. A firm believer that profit-sharing encourages cost-cutting and discourages risk-taking, both of which are fatal to the development of a creative vision, he empowered company researchers to develop radically new products by giving them stock options, which rose in value every time Intel unveiled something new.

In 1975 Noyce decided to pursue industry-wide goals rather than to promote the interests of just one company. He stepped down as president of Intel to become chairman of the board, a position he resigned in 1979; he also married Ann Bowers with whom he had no children, having divorced his first wife the previous year. In 1977 he helped found the Semiconductor Industry Association, which promoted the interests of U.S. chip manufacturers in the face of serious competition from overseas, especially Japanese companies. He also helped found the Semiconductor Research Cooperative in 1981 and served on President Ronald Reagan's Committee on Competitiveness. For the last two years of his life he was the chief executive officer of Semiconductor Manufacturing Technology (SEMATECH) in Austin, Texas, a newly established research consortium of 14 leading electronics firms, the state of Texas, and the federal government. He died on June 3, 1990, in Austin.

Further Reading
Hansen, Dirk. *The New Alchemists.* New York: Avon Books, 1982.
Queisser, Hans. *The Conquest of the Microchip.* Cambridge, Mass.: Harvard University Press, 1988.
Reid, T. R. *The Chip: How Two Americans Invented the Microchip and Launched a Revolution.* New York: Random House, 2001.

O

Oakes, Ziba B.

(1806–1871) *entrepreneur in the slave trade*

Between 1820 and 1860, 750,000 slaves migrated out of Maryland, Virginia, and the Carolinas, where soil depletion was slowly killing the plantation system. Most of them ended up in the cotton-growing regions in Alabama, Arkansas, Mississippi, and Texas, or on sugar plantations in Louisiana. This mass migration was facilitated by a special type of slave trader known as the resident broker. These entrepreneurs bought excess slaves from local planters and farmers in the Upper South, then resold them to slave traders and auctioneers in the Deep South where the demand for slaves was high. Being a resident broker was a lucrative if risky business, and no one seems to have thrived at it any better than Ziba B. Oakes, the most successful resident broker in Charleston, South Carolina.

Oakes was born in 1806 in Sangersville, Maine. His father, Samuel, was a merchant, and his mother, Mary, was a homemaker. At age 11 he moved with his family to Charleston, where his father opened a grocery store. In 1829 his father, having closed that store, opened another that specialized in the sale of sugar. By 1831, the same year Oakes married Margaret Christie with whom he had four children, he had become his father's partner.

By 1846 Oakes had gotten out of the sugar business and become involved in the slave trade as a resident broker. He bought slaves mostly through trusted agents, such as A. J. McElveen in Sumter, whom he employed in at least six towns in South Carolina. In the mid-1850s McElveen alone sent Oakes between 20 and 40 slaves per year. Oakes also bought slaves from other brokers in Richmond, Virginia, and Savannah, Georgia, as well as at estate sales at Charleston's Slave Mart, where a deceased planter's slaves would be sold or auctioned to pay his debts or to divide his wealth among his heirs. One particularly memorable estate sale in which Oakes participated followed the death of James Gadsden in 1858, when the 235 slaves from Pimlico, his rice-growing plantation, were sold at auction over a two-day period (Oakes purchased five slaves for $3,880). Regardless of how they were acquired, some of Oakes's slaves, usually the ones best suited for domestic work, were resold at the slave mart or at his office and slave pen in downtown Charleston. The vast majority of the field hands, however, were sold to brokers in other states. Among Oakes's regular customers were Adams & Wicks in Natchez, Mississippi; Rees W. Porter in Nashville, Tennessee; and N. Vignie in New Orleans, Louisiana. However, Oakes maintained contacts with slave traders and resident brokers all over the South, from Virginia to Texas. During the 1850s Oakes's personal fortune increased by more than $100,000, a phenomenal increase for that 10-year period, and by 1860 he was the most prosperous of Charleston's approximately 40 slave traders.

In addition to providing him with slaves, Oakes's agents kept him well appraised of investment opportunities in their areas, especially farms and plantations that had been put on the market to satisfy debts. He invested a large part of the profits from slave brokering in farmland, and in 1860 the value of his real-estate holdings was estimated at more than $60,000, a substantial amount at the time. He also owned 16 slaves who worked as farm laborers, a considerable number given that most southerners did not own any slaves and that most slaveholders owned only one slave. By 1860 he had acquired enough stock in the Southwestern Railroad Bank to hold a seat on the board of directors. As a result of all his business dealings, in 1860 Oakes was one of the wealthiest men in Charleston.

Although Oakes lost his slaves as a result of the Civil War, he seems to have survived the conflict with the rest of his fortune intact. After the war, he became a real-estate speculator and a sales agent for three fire insurance companies; at the time of his death he was serving on the State Board of Underwriters. The notion that slave traders were looked down upon by the South's elite is contradicted by the prominent role Oakes played in Charleston society. He served as a city alderman from 1865 to 1868 as well as Commissioner of Markets and Commissioner of the Alms House. He was an officer in several benevolent organizations, including the International Order of Odd Fellows (treasurer) and the Knights Templar (generalissimo). He died on May 25, 1871, in Charleston.

Further Reading

Bancroft, Frederic. *Slave-Trading in the Old South.* Baltimore, Md.: J. H. Furst Co., 1931.

Drago, Edmund L., ed. *Broke by the War: Letters of a Slave Trader.* Columbia: University of South Carolina Press, 1991.

Tadman, Michael. *Speculators and Slaves: Masters, Traders, and Slaves in the Old South.* Madison: University of Wisconsin Press, 1996.

Ochoa, Esteban

(1831–1888) *entrepreneur in cartage and wholesale merchandise*

After the Mexican War, when the United States took formal control of the American Southwest, many Hispanic merchants and ranchers found themselves unable to compete, economically and politically, with the influx of Anglo businessmen and cattlemen. However, this fate did not befall all Mexican-American entrepreneurs. One, Esteban Ochoa, even managed to become one of the richest merchants and most prominent citizens in Arizona and New Mexico territories. Although Ochoa did eventually lose most of his business empire, the real culprit was not his Anglo rival but the railroad.

Ochoa was born on March 17, 1831, in Ambamen, Chihuahua, Mexico. His father, Jesus, was a rancher, and his mother, whose name is unknown, was a homemaker. As a boy he moved with his family to Santa Fe, Nuevo Mexico, where his father became engaged in the bustling trade along the Santa Fe Trail between northern Mexico and the United States. As a teenager he traveled frequently along the trail, spending much time in its eastern termini, Kansas City and Independence, Missouri. By 1848, when the United States had acquired Nuevo Mexico as part of the Mexican Cession, the teenaged Ochoa was a skillful merchant and capable speaker of English.

In the early 1850s Ochoa became partners in a cartage enterprise operating out of Las Cruces in New Mexico Territory. He used the profits from this business to open a flour mill in Las Cruces and a general store in nearby Mesilla, and by 1859 he owned a string of general stores in towns along the western extension of the Santa Fe Trail, which ran all the way to California via Tucson and Yuma. That same year he got out of the freight business and moved to Tucson, which was growing in importance as a trade center for the western part of the territory as well as the northern portion of the Mexican state of Sonora. By 1861 he was one of the most prominent businessmen in the territory.

The Civil War brought a temporary setback to Ochoa's prosperity. In 1861 a group of Confederate volunteers captured Tucson, confiscated Ochoa's property for refusing to swear allegiance to the Confederacy, and forced him to flee to Mesilla. However, a few months later the pro-Union Colorado Volunteers recaptured Tucson, and Ochoa was eventually reunited with most of his property. Almost immediately upon his return, he expanded his mercantile activities by importing grain, cattle, and sheep from the farms and ranches of Sonora and reselling them to U.S. Army units stationed in the territory as well as to the growing number of miners who began coming to New Mexico Territory to dig for copper and silver. In 1864 he and Pinckney R. Tully formed Tully, Ochoa and Company, a cartage and wholesale mercantile business. Operating out of Tucson, the company hauled freight to and from Santa Fe to the north, Guaymas, Sonora, to the south, and Yuma to the west in Arizona Territory. It also sold food and other supplies to the army, the mines, Indian reservations, and to a host of general stores such as the ones Ochoa continued to operate.

In the 1870s Ochoa expanded his commercial interests yet again by building the American Southwest's first woolen mill in Tucson. He also experimented with growing cotton, which eventually became an important crop in Arizona and New Mexico, and erected a windmill in order to pump groundwater to his plantings. By 1877, the year he married Altagracia Salazar with whom he had one child, he was one of the American Southwest's wealthiest people. He was also one of Arizona Territory's most prominent citizens. Two years earlier he had been elected mayor of Tucson, and he had already served two terms in the territorial legislature. He had also donated land in Tucson for the construction of Arizona's first public school.

In 1880 the Southern Pacific Railroad came to Tucson, an event that marked the beginning of the end of Ochoa's commercial empire. The railroad put an end to Tully, Ochoa's lucrative overland business, leaving it with only some local hauling to do. It also nullified the value of the firm's business contacts in Sonora, the firm having imported many of the goods it sold through the port of Guaymas, because now goods could be hauled from the United States faster and cheaper by train. And it also made it possible for local merchants to buy their goods cheaper from large eastern mercantile firms with which Tully, Ochoa could not compete. After valiantly hanging on for several years, in the mid-1880s Tully, Ochoa was forced into bankruptcy to satisfy its creditors. Although Ochoa himself continued to operate his mills and general stores, he was never able to reclaim his preeminent position in Arizona Territory's commercial community. He died on October 27, 1888, in Las Cruces.

Further Reading

Meier, Matt S. "Esteban Ochoa, Enterpriser," *Journal of the West* 25, no. 1 (January 1986): 15–21.

"Wells Fargo People." Wells Fargo. Available online URL: www.wellsfargohistory.com/resources/1852Book.pdf. Downloaded on July 6, 2009.

Olds, Ransom Eli
(1864–1950) *inventor of the Oldsmobile automobile*

Undoubtedly, the most famous American automobile manufacturer is HENRY FORD. Ford is remembered mostly for the Model T, an inexpensive runabout, and the assembly line, which he perfected. Few people, however, realize that both of these ideas had originated with Ransom Olds. Before the Model T, there was the Oldsmobile, the first commercially successful automobile manufactured in the United States. And before Ford's assembly line, Oldsmobiles were being built according to the American automobile industry's first successful attempt at mass production.

Olds was born on June 3, 1864, in Geneva, Ohio. His father, Pliny, was a blacksmith and machinist, and his mother, Sarah, was a homemaker. At age 16 he moved with his family to Lansing, Michigan, where his father and older brother formed P. F. Olds & Son, a machine shop. He dropped out of high school to work in the shop, and in 1885 he bought his brother's interest. In 1887 he convinced his father to shift the shop's focus away from repair work to building a steam engine with a gasoline burner. This engine was capable of building up pressure much faster than engines that burned either coal or wood. By 1890 the company had sold thousands of the engines, so P. F. Olds & Son incorporated in order to expand its production facilities. In 1895 he moved up from general manager to president when his father retired. In 1889 he had married Metta Woodward with whom he had at least three children.

By 1887 Olds had become interested in building a horseless carriage. That same year he built a three-wheeled, steam-powered vehicle, but the engine put out only one horsepower, which was hardly enough to get the vehicle to move. By

1892 he had built a more powerful steam-powered car, which he sold to a company in London, England. In 1893 he decided to replace the steam engine with a gasoline-powered internal combustion engine, having seen a display at the World's Columbian Exposition in Chicago, Illinois. Upon returning to Lansing, he and Madison F. Bates, a P. F. Olds & Son employee, began experimenting with various designs, and in 1896 they patented a one-cylinder, five-horsepower gasoline engine. P. F. Olds & Son began manufacturing the engine, and within a year it rivaled the steam engine as the company's best-selling product.

In 1896 Olds mounted one of his gasoline engines to the underside of a carriage and took the vehicle for a satisfactory spin. The following year he formed the Olds Motor Vehicle Company, but his partners failed to put up enough money to open a separate factory for building cars. In 1899 Samuel L. Smith, a Detroit millionaire, supplied the needed cash, but only in return for a controlling interest in Olds Motor Vehicle and P. F. Olds & Son. By 1901 Olds Motor Works, as the parent company was called, had opened a factory in Detroit where it built the Oldsmobile, a light automobile called a runabout with a distinctive curved-dash front. In its first year of operation, the factory produced slightly more than 400 Oldsmobiles, which it sold for $650 apiece.

As general manager, Olds's job was to increase factory production. He did this by implementing the first assembly line in Detroit's history. By modern standards, the line was crude. Oldsmobiles were built on wooden platforms mounted on casters, which were rolled from one workstation to the next during the manufacturing process. Rather than build one car from front to back, crews were trained to do one thing well, such as attach transmissions or upholster seats, and they performed their specialty on every vehicle. The parts they needed were kept close at hand in big bins. Although the system was primitive, it worked, and by 1904 Olds had increased production to 5,000 cars per year, making Olds Motor Works the largest auto manufacturer in the world.

Meanwhile, Olds had gotten into a power struggle within the company. Samuel Smith's son Fred had risen to a position of authority in the Detroit factory, and he wanted to abandon the runabout and make a larger car instead. By 1904 Fred Smith had gained the confidence of the company's board of directors, who voted to make the change. Angered by what he considered to be a bad decision, Olds sold his stock and left the company that bore his name. That same year he formed the REO Motor Car Company in Lansing; the name is derived from his initials. Although he took on additional investors, he had made enough from the sale of Olds stock that he was able to retain a majority interest in REO. The company made two cars: a runabout similar in design and price to the Oldsmobile, and a larger touring car that sold for about $1,250. By 1907 the touring car had become the fifth best-selling car in America. In 1911 REO expanded its product line by getting into the truck business.

After 1911, Olds seemed to lose interest in REO. He delegated more and more day-to-day decisions to subordinates while he experimented with gasoline-powered lawn mowers and invested in Florida real estate. He resigned as general manager in 1915, as president in 1923, and as chairman of the board in 1936. That same year, REO stopped making automobiles, although it continued to manufacture trucks well into the 1970s. He retired to his home in Lansing, where he died on August 26, 1950.

Further Reading

Heyden, Patricia E. *Metta and R. E. Olds, Loves, Lives, and Labors.* Lansing, Mich.: Stuart Pub., 1997.

May, George S. *R. E. Olds: Auto Industry Pioneer.* Grand Rapids, Mich.: Eerdmans, 1980.

Otis, Elisha Graves

(1811–1861) *inventor of the safety elevator*

Modern skyscrapers would not be practical were it not for the modern safety elevator. Although hoists and lifts had existed before the 1850s, it was not until Elisha Otis invented a safety device to keep them from falling unexpectedly that they became practical devices for hauling goods and people. Although he did not profit much from his invention, his two sons laid the foundation for the Otis

Elevator Company to become the world's preeminent manufacturer and installer of elevators.

Otis was born on August 3, 1811, in Halifax, Vermont. His parents, Stephen and Phoebe, were farmers. He left home at age 19, and over the next 22 years he restlessly changed addresses and professions on a regular basis. He worked for five years as a builder for his brother Chandler in Troy, New York, then spent three years as a wagoner hauling goods between Troy and Brattleboro, Vermont. In 1838 he moved to Brattleboro where he built a gristmill; it failed for lack of business, so he converted it into a sawmill and built wagons and carriages instead. In 1845 he moved to Albany, New York, where he became a mechanic with Otis Tingley & Company, a manufacturer of bedsteads, the frame that supports a bed's springs and mattress. Three years later he set up his own shop, called the Hudson Manufactory, and began manufacturing a machine of his own design, an automatic bedrail-turner he had invented while with Tingley. In 1851 he moved to Bergen, New Jersey, where he went to work in Josiah Maize's bedstead factory. When Maize moved his business to Yonkers, New York, the following year, Otis decided against moving to California to prospect for gold and moved to Yonkers with him. Meanwhile, in 1834 he married Susan Houghton with whom he had four children; she died in 1842, and three years later he married Elizabeth Boyd with whom he had no children.

Otis was put in charge of moving Maize's heavy equipment from Bergen to Yonkers, most of which could not be moved without a hoist. At the time this was a tricky operation; hoists made use of hemp rope, which often could not hold the weight of modern machinery, and many a manufacturer had lost an expensive piece of equipment due to a broken rope. To get around this problem, Otis used a platform hoist rigged with a safety feature of his own design; an automatic ratchet device locked the platform to its supporting frame in case the hoist rope broke, thus ensuring the safety of whoever or whatever was on the platform. Word of Otis's invention quickly spread, and he soon had three orders from other manufacturers wanting a "safety hoister," as his freight elevator became known.

Otis opened a shop in Yonkers where he built freight elevators when he was not working for

Maize. When Maize went out of business in 1854, Otis enlarged his operation and made it his full-time work. Business picked up considerably after he put on a dramatic demonstration at the American Institute Fair in New York City. He had himself elevated 30 feet into the air, then while the crowd gasped he had an employee cut the hoist rope. Instead of plummeting to his death, Otis remained standing placidly on his platform, tipping his hat and assuring everyone that he was perfectly safe. Within two and a half years of the demonstration, he had sold, built, delivered, and installed more than 40 elevators.

In 1857 Otis installed an enclosed, belt-driven elevator, the first elevator designed for passenger use, in the E. V. Haughwout & Company's five-story store in New York City. This elevator featured a more sophisticated safety device than the one on his freight elevators; the elevator car was designed to travel from floor to floor along toothed guide rails, to which a catching device would secure the car the moment the tension of the hoist rope became slack. In 1861 he introduced a steam-driven elevator capable of traveling up five stories in less than a minute. After his sons Charles and Norton reorganized the business as the Otis Brothers Elevator Company after their father's death, they made this model the standard of the elevator industry until the invention of the hydraulic-lift elevator.

Otis was a gifted inventor; in addition to his bedrail-turner and safety elevator, he received patents for a railcar brake, a steam plow, and a baking oven. However, as an entrepreneur he was less skilled. Although he kept busy over the last seven years of his life by building and installing elevators, when he died from diphtheria on April 8, 1861, in Yonkers, his company was more than $3,000 in debt.

Further Reading

"Elisha Otis," Lemuelson MIT Awards Program's Invention Dimension. Available online. URL: http://web.mit.edu/invent/iow/otis.html. Downloaded on July 6, 2009.

Jackson, Donald Dale. "Elevating Thoughts from Elisha Otis and Fellow Uplifters." *Smithsonian* 20 no. 8 (November 1989), p. 210.

P

Parker, Colonel Tom
(Andreas van Kujik)

(1909–1997) *entrepreneur in the management of Elvis Presley*

Elvis Presley is the most popular entertainer in American history. A talented singer and actor with plenty of charisma, Presley became one of the world's biggest stars. Next to Presley himself, the individual most responsible for his success was Colonel Tom Parker, the man who single-handedly masterminded Presley's rise to the top.

Parker was born Andreas van Kujik on June 28, 1909, in Breda, Holland. Little is known about his parents or early life, except that as a boy he ran errands for local shopkeepers. At age 16 he ran away from home, and a year later he stowed away aboard an ocean liner bound for the United States. He tried to legitimize his status in this country by lying about his age and citizenship to join the U.S. Army. Upon completing his enlistment around 1930, he changed his name to Tom Parker, in honor of an officer who had treated him kindly, and he went to work as an advance man for the Johnny J. Jones Exposition, a traveling carnival. Parker's job was to drum up business for the carnival, so he would go to the next town it planned to play and put on the most outlandish promotions he could think of. Two of his better ones were festooning an elephant (an exotic animal at the time) with signs and parading the enormous beast around town and arranging pie-eating contests in which he challenged locals to match appetites with "the

fattest man on earth," who traveled with the exposition. In 1935 he married Marie Mott with whom he had no children.

In 1940 Parker left the carnival and settled in Tampa, Florida. Shortly thereafter, he got elected dogcatcher and became director of the local humane society. Using the skills he had honed as a carnival promoter, he raised so much money that, for the first time in memory, the humane society began operating at a profit. Meanwhile, Parker used his positions to enrich himself. He opened a pet cemetery behind the society's animal shelter and sold miniature tombstones and a perpetual flower service to pet lovers. When people asked at the shelter for a small dog, he often gave them a Saint Bernard or a Great Dane puppy. When the dog became enormous after a few months, he counseled its owner to have it put to sleep—and buried in his pet cemetery. In 1948 he managed somehow—no one knows exactly how—to be made an honorary colonel in the Louisiana state militia by then-governor Jimmie Davis.

In the late 1940s Parker began promoting appearances in Tampa by nationally known country music stars. This allowed him to meet Eddy Arnold, a promising young singer. Before long, Parker had become Arnold's personal manager and moved to Nashville, Tennessee, so he could better manage Arnold's career. By 1953 Parker had gotten Arnold several roles in Hollywood movies as well as a number of gigs in the nightspots of Las Vegas, Nevada. For unknown reasons, in 1953 Arnold fired Parker, who became the personal manager of Hank Snow, another country music singer.

In 1955 Parker met Elvis Presley, who at the time was little known outside of his hometown of Memphis, Tennessee. Presley was under contract to Sam Phillips, a Memphis record producer, and to Bob Neal, his manager. Parker realized instantly that Presley's talent and sex appeal destined him for stardom, and he arranged for Presley to be the opening act for Snow's tour that same year. During the tour, Parker convinced Presley and his parents to take him on as an adviser. Shortly thereafter, Parker arranged for Phillips to sell Presley's contract to RCA Records for $35,000, at the time a huge amount for a relatively unknown performer. He also arranged for Presley to appear live on the CBS television network, thus gaining him national exposure. By the end of 1956 Parker had bought Neal's contract and sold Snow's. For the rest of Presley's career, Parker served as his dedicated and only official adviser and manager.

From an entrepreneurial point of view, Parker managed Presley almost perfectly. The songs he selected for Presley to record were well suited for the singer's range, style, and image, as well as for his audience; in all, 45 of Presley's records sold more than 1 million copies, and more than 500 million Elvis records were sold during the singer's lifetime. The Colonel, as Parker was known to everyone except Presley, who for some reason called him "Admiral," also steered Presley away from serious movie roles that might have compromised his image. Instead, he encouraged him to perform in a series of low-budget musical comedies—33 in all—that allowed the star to play himself while making a killing at the box office. He also introduced a line of "Elvis" products, such as clothing and cosmetics, that sold exceptionally well. After 1968 Parker transformed Presley into the quintessential Las Vegas act, in the process ensuring him access to the age group that had made him popular and would always adore him.

Under Parker's management, Presley grossed more than $1 billion. Parker has been criticized for taking 25 percent of Presley's share of that billion before 1968 (and 50 percent afterward) as his management fee, while most managers take only 10 percent. However, unlike other managers, Parker

had only one client, and he devoted himself tirelessly to grooming Presley's image and promoting his interests night and day, thus helping to make Presley a superstar and a multimillionaire. Nevertheless, some of Presley's family members and hangers-on tried unsuccessfully to convince the singer to fire Parker and hire someone who would work for less.

After Presley died in 1977 from a drug overdose, Parker continued to manage Presley's business affairs. Parker was eventually sued for fraud and mismanagement by Presley's heirs, and in 1982 a Memphis court ruled that Parker had no legal rights to the Presley estate. Following the ruling, Parker moved to Las Vegas, where he worked for the Hilton Hotel chain as an entertainment adviser. In 1980 his first wife died, and he later married Loanne (maiden name unknown). He died on January 21, 1997, in Las Vegas.

Further Reading

Dickerson, James. *Colonel Tom Parker: The Curious Life of Elvis Presley's Eccentric Manager.* New York: Cooper Square Press, 2001.

O'Neal, Sean. *My Boy Elvis: The Colonel Tom Parker Story.* New York: Barricade Books, 1998.

Perkins, Thomas Handasyd
(1764–1854) *entrepreneur in mercantile activity*

During the 18th century, most American entrepreneurs formed mercantile partnerships and entered the overseas trade. During the 19th century, entrepreneurs discovered that there was more money to be made in transportation and industrial activity, such as railroads and factories, than in trading. Thomas Perkins serves as an excellent model for the transition from one form of entrepreneurial activity to the other. Having made a fortune in the China trade in his early career, in his later career Perkins invested his money in railroads and textile mills.

Perkins was born on December 15, 1764, in Boston, Massachusetts. His parents, James and Elizabeth, were wine merchants. At age 15 he dropped out of Harvard College and, after working as an apprentice bookkeeper, became involved in the family business. In 1786 he and his brother James inherited enough money from their grandfather to become commercial brokers, and they began trading horses, flour, and dried fish to merchants in Haiti in exchange for slaves. In 1788 he married Sarah Elliott, with whom he had 11 children. That same year he became partners with Sarah's uncle, James Magee, in the mercantile firm of Magee & Perkins, while continuing to maintain the partnership with his brother. The partners specialized in a triangular trade whereby they bought iron and flour in New England, exchanged it in South Carolina for rice, exchanged the rice in Europe for wine and oil, and then sold the wine and oil in Boston. In 1789 Perkins accompanied the firm's first voyage to China via the Cape of Good Hope, trading iron goods for tea. The following year the partners sponsored their second voyage to China, this time exchanging a shipload of Oregon furs for tea. Eventually Magee & Perkins operated a fleet of ships in the China trade, exchanging furs and American manufactured goods for tea, silk, china, opium, and spices.

In 1792 the Haitian Revolution broke out, disrupting the mercantile activities of Perkins and his brother. That same year they formed J. & T. H. Perkins; James stayed in Boston and served as the firm's business manager, while Thomas did most of the traveling and deal making. Although the firm did business in France and the West Indies, it was primarily involved in the China trade, in which Perkins demonstrated great boldness. During the early 1810s he held his own against JOHN JACOB ASTOR, the fur magnate, in the trading of furs to China. Because Perkins bought his furs from the British, he was able to continue his involvement in this trade even after Astor lost his trading posts in the Pacific Northwest during the War of 1812. Perkins also competed with the British East India Company, which had its own private army and navy as well as the semiofficial backing of the British government, in the trading of opium from India to China. In 1822 the partnership was dissolved when James died, although Perkins nevertheless continued to trade in China. In 1830 he merged his interests with several others to form Perkins & Company, the dominant American mercantile firm in the China trade. He continued

to do business in China until 1838, shortly before he went blind.

Perkins formed no more mercantile partnerships after 1838. In fact, he had already turned his attention to other business endeavors. He built a railroad to haul granite from a quarry near Quincy to Boston, and he invested in a number of others, including the Michigan Central Railroad of which his nephew and protégé, John Murray Forbes, became president. He invested heavily in the cotton textile mills in Lowell, Massachusetts, and in 1828 was named president of the Appleton Mill Corporation. Meanwhile, he spent his money in ways that served as a model for other wealthy Bostonians. He was one of the first to build a home in suburban Brookline and a summer home in Nahant, thus helping to make both communities popular with the Boston elite. Perkins also financed a number of public improvements, such as the building of hospitals, libraries, and a school for blind children, and in 1823 he paid for the construction of the Bunker Hill Monument. He died on January 11, 1854, in Brookline.

Further Reading

"The China Traders: The House of Perkins." Encyclopedia of American Wealth. Available online. URL: http://www.raken.com/american_wealth/shipping_merchants/china_traders1.asp. Downloaded on November 21, 2001.

Seaburg, Carl, and Stanley Paterson. *Merchant Prince of Boston: Colonel T. H. Perkins, 1764–1854.* Cambridge, Mass.: Harvard University Press, 1971.

Perot, Ross
(Henry Ray Perot)
(1930–) *entrepreneur in data processing*

Twenty-first-century Americans have grown accustomed to seeing wealthy individuals with no political experience run for, and sometimes win, elected public office. This trend was started by Ross Perot, a self-made billionaire who won almost 20 percent of the popular vote in the presidential election of 1992.

Perot was born Henry Ray Perot on June 27, 1930, in Texarkana, Texas. His father, Gabriel, was a cotton broker, and his mother, Lulu, was a home-maker. At age 12 he legally changed his middle name to Ross, in memory of his older brother who had died. After graduating from high school in 1947, he spent two years at Texarkana Junior College, then won an appointment to the U.S. Naval Academy. He was commissioned in 1949 and spent the next eight years in the navy. In 1956 he married Margot Birmingham with whom he had five children.

Upon resigning from the navy, Perot moved to Dallas, Texas, where he took a job as a computer hardware salesman with IBM. He quickly became one of the company's top salesmen, but as his sales rose IBM reduced his commissions. Finally, in 1962 he determined to become his own boss by forming his own company, Electronic Data Systems (EDS). Perot's company focused less on selling computer hardware and more on taking care of its customers' total data management needs. To this end, EDS provided software and technical support in addition to hardware, and it even went so far as to lease time for its clients on other companies' computers rather than sell them new machines. Sales grew slowly over the next three years, but in 1965 they took off when the federal government implemented Medicare and Medicaid. These two national medical programs generated an incredible need for computerized handling of patients' claims, and EDS was perfectly poised to provide governments and physicians with the necessary services. By 1968 the company was earning profits of more than $2 million per year, and after taking EDS public that same year, Perot's share of the company was worth more than $1 billion.

By 1984 EDS had become one of the leading data management companies in the world, specializing in computerizing social security and health insurance programs for governments around the globe. That same year the company was acquired by General Motors, which hoped to modernize its data management system. Perot received from the sale $1 billion in cash and enough stock to make him GM's largest stockholder. He also remained as chairman of the board of EDS and joined the board of directors of GM. Although EDS did indeed improve the performance of GM's information system, Perot's overly zealous management style ruffled the egos of a number of GM officials, and two years later GM removed Perot from the equation by buying his shares for $700 million. After absenting himself from the world of data processing for 18 months, as required by his buyout clause, in 1988 he formed another data management company, Perot Systems Corporation, which quickly won a contract to computerize the U.S. Postal Service.

Since the late 1960s Perot had played a number of roles, both major and minor, in changing public policy at both the Texas and national level. In 1969 he founded United We Stand for purposes of bringing home the 1,420 American servicepeople who had been captured or were missing in action during the war in Vietnam. Perot's involvement in the cause is credited with winning improved treatment and an earlier release for about 350 POWs. He commissioned an alternative memorial for Vietnam veterans following the controversial response to the Vietnam Veterans' Memorial in Washington, D.C. In 1979 he engineered the release of two EDS employees held prisoner in Iran while President Jimmy Carter failed to free the Americans held hostage in the American embassy in that country. And in the 1980s Perot chaired the Select Committee on Public Education in Texas, and he succeeded in gaining passage of several measures to improve that state's school programs.

Despite his diminutive stature and his high-pitched voice, Perot was a powerful public speaker who was outspoken in his belief that he knew how to solve the problems associated with the national debt and the federal budget deficit. In 1987, following a powerful speech to the National Governors Association, he was encouraged by Bill Clinton, at the time governor of Arkansas, to run for president of the United States. Others urged Perot to run for the country's highest office as well, and in 1992 he declared his candidacy as an Independent. Perot ran a strong early campaign, which he paid for mostly out of his own pocket. However, in July he withdrew from the campaign without offering an explanation (he later claimed he had done so to prevent the Republican Party from disrupting the wedding of his daughter in August 1992), only to reenter it a month before the election. Had he not taken a hiatus, he surely would have polled more than the 19 percent of the popular vote he won, and he may have carried at least one state.

Perot ran for president again in 1996, but by then his popularity had slipped while Bill Clinton's had become strong enough to withstand Perot's challenge. Perot—who has remained largely out of the public eye in recent years, with the exception of occasional interviews near presidential elections—holds a unique place among the most prominent figures in the history of American business: a self-made man who became a billionaire and eventually a serious contender for the presidency.

Further Reading

Lamb, Brian. *Booknotes: Life Stories: Notable Biographers on the People Who Shaped America.* New York: Times Books, 1999.

Posner, Gerald L. *Citizen Perot: His Life and Times.* New York: Random House, 1996.

Wainer, Howard. *Visual Revelations: Graphical Tales of Fate and Deception from Napoleon Bonaparte to Ross Perot.* Mahwah, N.J.: Lawrence Erlbaum Associates, 2000.

Pickens, T. Boone

(1928–) *entrepreneur in oil and energy industry*

When T. Boone Pickens was 11 years old, he had a small paper route in the Texas town where he grew up. Over the next five years, Pickens expanded that route fivefold. Pickens later explained, "I did that not by getting new customers, but by merging with routes that were contiguous to me. That was my first introduction to expanding quickly by acquisition—a talent I would perfect in my later years." This aggressive business sense helped Pickens become a prosperous oilman, corporate raider, and financier, who in late 2008 was listed as the 131st richest American with a net worth of over $3 billion.

Thomas Boone Pickens, Jr., was born on May 22, 1928, in Holdenville, Oklahoma. Family lore holds that Pickens was the first baby delivered by Cesarean section in the history of Holdenville. His father, T. Boone, Sr., was an oilman and leaser of mineral rights and his mother, Grace, ran the regional Office of Price Administration, which was responsible for rationing such resources as gas, during World War II. Pickens would later credit both of his parents for their strong guidance, saying of his brash father and stoic mother, "The gambling instincts I inherited from my father were matched by my mother's gift for analysis." While a young teen, Pickens moved with his family to Amarillo, Texas, where his basketball skills earned him a scholarship to Texas A&M University. After one year Pickens transferred to Oklahoma A&M (now Oklahoma State), graduating with a degree in geology in 1951.

Following his graduation from college, Pickens went to work with Phillips Petroleum, where his father worked as a lease broker. Married by the age of 20 to his high school sweetheart, Pickens was unhappy at Phillips and remained in that job for only three years before taking large loans (mostly from his wife's uncle) and investors to start his own company, Petroleum Exploration, Inc., which focused on domestic development. His success with that company led Pickens to start another firm, Altair Oil & Gas to search in western Canada. He merged these companies and others into Mesa Petroleum, which he took public in 1964. Mesa was enormously prosperous, generating approximately 150 million barrels of oil and 3 trillion cubic feet of gas from 1964 to 1996. Reflective of Pickens's acumen and tireless work ethic was a 1959 Mesa investment of $35,000 in western Canada that was so rich in oil and gas that he sold it 20 years later for $600 million.

Early in the 1980s, Pickens seized on the volatility in the oil market to buy undervalued shares of oil company stocks, joking at the time that, "It has become cheaper to look for oil on the floor of the New York Stock Exchange than in the ground." Coupled with his smashing success in the oil and gas business, Pickens would become even more renowned for his activity as a corporate raider in the 1980s. Portraying him as a confident poker player with a high stack of chips next to the bold descriptor "The Takeover Game: Corporate Raider T. Boone Pickens," *Time* magazine featured Pickens on the cover of its March 4, 1985, issue. The cover article described Pickens by noting, "To many, he is a real-life J. R. Ewing, the ruthless but fascinating wheeler-dealer whom viewers of Dallas love to hate—and sometimes secretly admire. To his victims, mostly entrenched corporate executives, he is a dangerous upstart, a sneaky poker player, a veritable rattlesnake in the woodpile. To his fans, though, he is a modern David, a champion of the little guy who takes on the Goliaths of Big Oil and more often than not gives them a costly whupping. Whichever image he evokes, T. (for Thomas) Boone Pickens, 56, has swept up like a twister out of Amarillo, Texas, to become one of the most famous and controversial businessmen in the U.S. today."

The spread of mergers and acquisitions in the 1980s was quick, profound, and significantly influenced by Pickens. In a typical Pickens takeover attempt, he would buy a large percentage of a target firm's stock and offer to pay shareholders more than the current market level for their securities. He would then try to acquire 51 percent of the firm's share to win control of the company and run it, which often led to open warfare between Pickens and the firm's management as they sought to sway shareholders. Even if he did not take control of the company, the fear instilled in the management often led them to sell to a more friendly bidder at a high price, and Pickens was left with huge profits on the shares he had recently acquired. This aggressive approach has led many to criticize Pickens as shortsighted and ruthless, while many others praise him for his vision and brilliance.

Pickens, who has been divorced three times and has four children from his first marriage, is currently married to his fourth wife, Madeline. A lifelong Republican who never pursued political office despite rumors that he might, Pickens has attracted controversy by supporting the Swift Boat Veterans for Truth, which claimed that Democratic presidential candidate John Kerry had exaggerated or lied about the details of his military service during the Vietnam War. As he entered his 80s, Pickens has remained very active in public life, spending millions of dollars in advertisements for his Pickens Plan for energy independence that

is largely reliant on wind power. He has also been prominently featured as a philanthropist who has provided hundreds of millions of dollars for various causes, including health care initiatives and to his beloved alma mater, Oklahoma State University. He remains one of America's leading financiers and the chair of the BP Capital Management hedge fund.

Further Reading

"A Conversation with Texas Oil Mogul Boone Pickens." *Charlie Rose.* Available online. URL: http://www. charlierose.com/view/interview/354. Downloaded on August 31, 2009.

"High Times for T. Boone Pickens." *Time.* Available online. URL: http://www.time.com/time/magazine/article/0,9171,961946,00.html. Downloaded on October 5, 2009.

Pickens, T. Boone. *The First Billion Is the Hardest: Reflections on a Life of Comebacks and America's Energy Future.* New York: Crown Business, 2008.

"Thoughts on Leadership." T. Boone Pickens. Available online. URL: http://www.boonepickens.com/thoughts/default.asp. Downloaded on August 31, 2009.

Pinckney, Elizabeth Lucas
(1722–1793) *entrepreneur in indigo*

Elizabeth Pinckney was the first American to grow indigo successfully. Her success revitalized the economy of South Carolina during the last three decades of the colonial period. Her accomplishment is all the more remarkable when one considers that she began experimenting with indigo at age 17. Despite her youth, Pinckney possessed a true entrepreneurial spirit. Her efforts to cultivate indigo stemmed from a desire to serve her country and her region while providing a tangible financial benefit to herself and her family.

Pinckney was born Elizabeth Lucas on December 28, 1722, in the West Indies, probably on the island of Antigua. Her father, George, was a lieutenant colonel in the British army, and her mother, Anne, managed the family's sugar plantation overlooking Antigua's Willoughby Bay. As a young girl Eliza (as her family called her) spent several years in England obtaining the only formal education she would receive. In 1738 her family relocated to a 600-acre plantation on Wappoo Creek, six miles north of Charleston, South Carolina, to escape the disease-ridden environment of Antigua, where her mother had contracted an unknown illness that had severely incapacitated her. A year later her father was recalled to Antigua because of the outbreak of the War of Jenkins' Ear with Spain. Since her mother had not yet recovered, Pinckney soon found herself, at the time just 16 years old, managing Wappoo Plantation and two others her father owned in South Carolina.

With the encouragement of her father, Pinckney began experimenting with different crops, including indigo, cotton, and ginger. The one that seemed to her to offer the greatest promise as a cash crop was indigo, even though its cultivation had been tried and abandoned by South Carolinians shortly after the colony's settlement in 1660. Perhaps her hopes revolved around the fact that, in the early 18th century, indigo was highly prized in Europe as a source of blue dye for textiles. Other reasons may have been that indigo grew best on the high ground where rice, the colony's staple crop, grew poorest and that the growing season of the two crops was so different that one could be harvested while the other was still growing. Thus, indigo promised to serve as the perfect complement to rice. However, indigo grew only in warm climates such as the West Indies, and for some reason it seemed to grow best on the islands owned by France. Moreover, the steeping, beating, mixing, draining, drying, and packing required to produce top-quality dye was a tedious and painstaking process. Nevertheless, she believed that if indigo could be cultivated and processed in South Carolina, then British textile manufacturers would no longer be dependent on French dye; the colony's economy would surely take off; and her family's fortune would be ensured.

Despite her confidence in her ability to raise indigo, Pinckney knew little about its cultivation. She planted too late in 1739 to harvest enough seed to plant a second crop, so in 1740 she obtained some West Indian indigo seeds from her father, who also sent her a trained dye maker. Although she harvested a crop large enough to produce about 20 pounds of dye, an early frost damaged the seedpods so that only about 100 new bushes could be planted the next year. To make matters worse, the dye maker botched his job so badly that the dye was too light; according to one source, he hailed from the French West Indian island of Montserrat and deliberately tried to sabotage Eliza's efforts because he feared that if they succeeded they would supplant the indigo trade of his own island.

Undaunted, Pinckney persevered. In 1744, having obtained the services of a second dye maker, she was able to produce about 17 pounds of high-quality dye. In addition, she harvested enough seed to give some to several neighboring planters. As a direct result of her initiative and enthusiasm, the cultivation of indigo spread throughout the colony and quickly became a major export. After only two years, the colony's output of indigo dye was 40,000 pounds, and in 1747 it rose to almost 100,000 pounds. Encouraged by a generous cash bounty offered by Parliament in 1747, the cultivation of indigo continued to thrive for almost 30 years. The outbreak of the American Revolution effectively cut off South Carolina's indigo producers from the British textile industry, and the trade never recovered after the war. Instead, South Carolina's planters turned increasingly to the cultivation of cotton, especially after 1793 when ELI WHITNEY invented the cotton gin.

In 1744 Pinckney married Charles Pinckney, a wealthy South Carolina landowner with whom she had four children. Although she left Wappoo Plantation after her marriage, she continued to experiment with the cultivation of exotic crops. At their plantation on the Cooper River just outside Charleston, where she died on May 26, 1793, she attempted to raise silkworms. This experiment was never as successful as her efforts to cultivate indigo; however, she still managed to produce enough silk to make two fine dresses, one of which can be seen in the Smithsonian Institution in Washington, D.C.

Further Reading

Crompton, Samuel W. *100 Colonial Leaders Who Shaped North America.* San Mateo, Calif.: Bluewood Books, 1999.

Welden, Amelie. *Girls Who Rocked the World: Heroines from Sacajawea to Sheryl Swoopes*. New York: Scholastic, 1999.

Williams, Frances Leigh. *A Founding Family: The Pinckneys of South Carolina*. New York: Harcourt Brace Jovanovich, 1978.

Pinkerton, Allan

(1819–1884) *entrepreneur in private law enforcement*

Before there were FBI agents, there were Pinkertons. Prior to 1908, when the FBI was founded, national law enforcement was left in the hands of private detective agencies. The first, largest, and most successful of these agencies was the Pinkerton National Detective Agency. Founded by Allan Pinkerton, the agency established norms for private detectives and ushered in the new industry of private security services.

Pinkerton was born on August 25, 1819, in Glasgow, Scotland. His father, William, was a weaver, and his mother, Isabella, was a millworker. At age 15 he was apprenticed to a cooper, or barrel maker. Around 1840 he became affiliated with the Chartists, a militant labor group in Great Britain. In 1842 he married Joan Carfrae, with whom he had at least three children, and left Scotland to avoid being imprisoned by the authorities on account of his activities as a Chartist. After living for a year each in Canada and Chicago, Illinois, he settled in the small town of Dundee, about 40 miles northwest of Chicago, where he opened a cooper shop. In 1847, while on a deserted island searching for some likely trees to cut down and turn into barrel staves, he happened upon a gang of counterfeiters. Unseen by the gang, he quickly made his way back to town and summoned the sheriff, who then caught the counterfeiters red-handed. As a result, Pinkerton became a local hero, and the following year he was appointed deputy sheriff of Kane County. After several similar episodes, he sold his cooper business and moved to Chicago to pursue a career as a private detective.

For the next three years, Pinkerton's chief clients were various government agencies. The U.S. Treasury Department hired him to find other gangs of counterfeiters, the U.S. Post Office retained him to solve several cases involving mail theft, and the sheriff of Cook County recruited him to help out with his toughest cases. In 1853 he was appointed deputy sheriff of Cook County, although he continued to do private work.

In 1855 Pinkerton formed the North West Police Agency, the first private detective agency in the country. North West specialized in policing the railroads in Illinois, most of which ran through the countryside where law enforcement officials were unable to protect trains or to prevent employee theft. At the time, many trains consisted of both passenger and freight cars, so Pinkerton and his three men did their jobs disguised as passengers. Almost immediately, they caught a conductor pocketing ticket money as well as other railroad employees unloading merchandise in the middle of nowhere. Although railroad workers came to despise the North West, Illinois railroad owners came to rely on them more and

Allan Pinkerton established the first national private detective agency. *(Library of Congress)*

more. By 1861 Pinkerton's men had been employed to police railroads in other states, and Pinkerton himself escorted President-elect Abraham Lincoln aboard the train that carried him through Maryland to Washington, D.C. During the Civil War, Pinkerton's men operated a spy system in Virginia for General George McClellan's Army of the Potomac. Called the Secret Service, the system captured Rose Greenhow, a Confederate spy living in Washington, but lost Timothy Webster, who was hanged for spying by the Confederates. The Secret Service was disbanded in 1862 when McClellan was replaced by General Ambrose Burnside.

In 1862 Pinkerton returned to Chicago and formed the Pinkerton National Detective Agency. By 1866 the agency had become the first national detective agency in the country, with offices in New York City and Philadelphia, Pennsylvania. At first, the railroads remained the agency's main clients; in addition to policing trains, the Pinkertons, as the agency's men became known, were assigned to apprehend train robbers. During the 1870s the agency's 20 detectives were also recruited to hunt down bank robbers, and its 60 watchmen were employed to police strikes and to prevent vandalism of corporate property by disgruntled industrial workers. Between 1867 and 1877, Pinkerton agent James McParlan infiltrated the Molly Maguires, a group of militant Pennsylvania coal miners, and procured enough evidence for authorities to crush the organization. By 1884, the Pinkerton National Detective Agency had offices across the United States and was functioning as the country's first effective, if unofficial, police agency. It offered intelligence, counterintelligence, internal security, investigative, and law enforcement services to private businesses and government agencies alike.

Pinkerton died on July 1, 1884, in Chicago. His detective agency continued to serve as the nation's only national police service until 1908, when the Federal Bureau of Investigation was founded. As the FBI assumed responsibility for apprehending criminals, the Pinkerton National Detective Agency became more involved in providing a variety of security services to virtually every type of private enterprise.

Further Reading
Crompton, Samuel W. *100 Americans Who Shaped American History*. San Mateo, Calif.: Bluewood Books, 1999.

Mackay, James A. *Allan Pinkerton: The First Private Eye*. New York: J. Wiley & Sons, 1997.

Pinkham, Lydia Estes
(1819–1883) *inventor of patent medicine*

During the 19th century, most medical doctors knew practically nothing about gynecology, so women had to take matters into their own hands. One enterprising woman, Lydia Pinkham, invented a homemade elixir that purported to cure a number of gynecological problems. Whether it did or not, it sold well enough to stay on the market for more than 120 years.

Pinkham was born Lydia Estes on February 9, 1819, in Lynn, Massachusetts. Her father, William, was a land developer, and her mother, Rebecca, was a homemaker. After finishing her education, she taught school for several years. In 1843 she married Isaac Pinkham with whom she had five children.

By today's standards the practice of medicine at that time bordered on the barbaric. Many trained doctors believed that bloodletting and administering calomel, a powder whose main ingredient is mercury, were cure-alls for just about every ailment. To make matters worse for women, most doctors received no medical training in gynecology. Even if they had, it would have done little good because it was considered socially unacceptable for women to discuss matters related to sex with men, even doctors. Meanwhile, a growing number of people, led by SAMUEL THOMSON and other botanic physicians, rejected such harsh and potentially deadly treatments as bloodletting and calomel in favor of herbal-based medicines. Home remedies clearly fell into the latter category, and Pinkham concocted one of her own as a treatment for "female complaints." Called Vegetable Compound, Pinkham's elixir contained a number of ground herbs such as unicorn root, black cohosh, life root, pleurisy root, and fenugreek seed. They were boiled together in a kettle of water on the kitchen stove and then combined with a hefty dose of corn liquor, which served as a solvent and preservative. The resulting brew was about 18 percent alcohol, and it was believed to provide relief from such conditions as menstrual cramps, nervous prostration (general physical or nervous exhaustion), and prolapsed uterus (a condition in which the uterus dislocates downward; in some cases, the cervix protrudes out of the vaginal orifice).

For years, Pinkham made and distributed Vegetable Compound to her female neighbors free of charge. But when her husband, a real-estate speculator, lost their money during the panic of 1873, she could no longer afford to do so. She and her children began making and bottling Vegetable Compound and selling it for $1 a bottle. By 1876 the family had gotten into the business full time. That same year she patented the medicine as Lydia E. Pinkham's Vegetable Compound. Her sons distributed handbills, written by her, that proclaimed "Only a woman can understand a woman's ills." They also sold bottles door-to-door in a number of communities in northeastern Massachusetts.

In 1879 Pinkham's son Daniel suggested that she use her picture in newspaper advertisements so that customers would know that Vegetable Compound was a true home remedy and not some snake-oil elixir concocted by an impersonal corporation or an incompetent doctor. She took his advice, and soon a massive national advertising campaign proclaimed "the savior of her sex" under a picture of her plain but honest-looking visage. The ads also invited women to write to her to receive free advice about their particular conditions. To this end, she established a Department of Advice with an all-female staff to answer the letters, sometimes as many as 100 a day, from women who were clearly ignorant about how their bodies worked. This discovery prompted her to write a facts-of-life manual describing the female reproductive system, from puberty through the childbearing years to menopause, which she distributed free of charge.

Although no scientific evidence existed to prove that Pinkham's elixir actually cured all the ills it claimed to cure, none existed to prove that it did not. Before long, thousands of women were swearing by the bracing effects of Pinkham's tonic.

By 1883 she and her family were selling almost 300,000 bottles per year, and the bottling operation had moved out of the kitchen and into a laboratory.

Pinkham died on May 17, 1883, in Lynn. Undaunted by her demise, her family members continued to make and sell Lydia E. Pinkham's Vegetable Compound, to use her picture in advertisements, and to invite customers to write to Mrs. Pinkham. By 1925 the Lydia E. Pinkham Medicine Company's annual sales topped the $3 million mark. At about that same time, the federal government began investigating the company, and by 1930 much of the alcohol content and the claims for what the product could do had been reduced. Still, sales remained healthy. In 1968 her heirs sold the company, which was acquired by Numark Laboratories in 1987. Although the name and the formula have been changed, Lydia Pinkham's Herbal Compound remained a big seller at the end of the 20th century.

Further Reading

Burton, Jean. *Lydia Pinkham is Her Name*. New York: Farrar, Strauss, 1959.

Helfand, William H. *"Let Us Sing of Lydia Pinkham" and Other Proprietary Medicines*. Madison, Wis.: American Institute of the History of Pharmacy, 1994.

Twitchell, James B. *20 Ads that Shook the World: The Century's Most Groundbreaking Advertising and How It Changed Us All*. New York: Crown Publishers, 2000.

Pittman, Robert Warren

(1953–) *inventor of Music Television (MTV)*

Perhaps the most culturally significant development in American entertainment since 1980 was the creation of Music Television, or MTV. At some point in their lives, virtually every child and most adults in America have spent time watching music videos or other programming on MTV. The person most responsible for creating MTV is Robert Pittman, who went on to become president and chief executive officer of one of the largest entertainment companies in the United States.

Pittman was born on December 28, 1953, in Jackson, Mississippi; his parents' names were

Warren and Lanita. At age 15 he became a disc jockey at a radio station in Jackson. He graduated from high school in 1971 and enrolled in nearby Millsaps College while continuing to work as a broadcaster. After a year at Millsaps, he spent the summer at a radio station in Milwaukee, Wisconsin, then transferred to Oakland University near Detroit, Michigan, where he also worked as research director at a radio station. He completed two semesters at Oakland, then transferred to the University of Pittsburgh in Pennsylvania. While still a student, he became the program director of radio station WPEZ-FM. Within a year he had made the station the most popular in Pittsburgh with high school and college students by playing a lot of hard rock music and recruiting deejays with a hard rock attitude.

By the end of his junior year, Pittman had come to the attention of officials at the National Broadcasting Company (NBC). The company was desperately seeking to turn around WMAQ-AM, a country music station in Chicago, Illinois, that was rated 22nd in its market. When NBC offered the position of program director to Pittman in 1974, he dropped out of school and moved to Chicago. Although he kept the country music format, he completely revamped the playlist and the on-air personalities. Within three years he had made WMAQ the third most popular radio station in the Windy City, and resuscitated its sister station, WKRX-FM, by converting it to a hard rock format. These two amazing feats earned Pittman the nickname "Boy Wonder."

In 1977 NBC asked Pittman to move to New York City to revitalize its flagship station, WNBC-AM. Once again, Boy Wonder came through. Using his trademark techniques of targeting a specific listener demographic, then playing music and hiring deejays who appealed directly to that demographic, within two years he had converted WNBC into a contemporary music station and made it a major player in the New York market. By age 26, Pittman had achieved national renown as a program director, having used three different music formats to regenerate three different radio stations in three different cities. Many radio analysts consider him to have been the most successful program director in the history of American radio. In 1979 he married Sandra Hill with whom he had one child.

While reviving WNBC's fortunes, Pittman also served as executive producer for Album Tracks, a late-night weekend video program on the NBC television network. At the time, video clips were seen as little more than an interesting way to boost record sales, and at first they were mostly shown only late at night, when audiences will watch anything. But in 1979, John Lack, the executive vice president of Warner Amex Satellite Entertainment Company (WASEC), began toying with the idea of a cable channel that broadcast nothing but music 24 hours a day. Later that year Lack hired Pittman, ostensibly to work as a programmer for The Movie Channel (TMC), but in reality to lay the foundation for a music channel. As he had done three times before in radio, Pittman carefully researched the target demographic, this time the under-30 television generation, and developed concepts for programming, logos, and "veejays" (video disc jockeys) that would clearly mark the new channel as antiestablishment and antiauthoritarian. The result was Music Television (MTV), which first aired on August 1, 1981.

Part of Pittman's genius was to broadcast nothing but music videos. This meant that MTV would get its content for virtually nothing, since videos were provided free of charge, just like records were provided gratis to radio stations. In its early years, MTV's programming was simply a constant stream of music videos; commercials and chatter were virtually nonexistent. The three- to five-minute clips were shown one after the other in a furious and mind-numbing progression that viewers found mesmerizing. By 1983, MTV had become a cultural touchstone for the so-called Generation X, the offspring of Baby Boomers. Its overwhelming success made it the first profitable cable channel in American television history.

In 1983 Pittman became executive vice president of WASEC, now known as MTV Networks Inc., and was put in charge of MTV and related cable channels. In this capacity he retooled Nickelodeon, the first cable channel just for kids; created VH-1, a video hits channel that mostly appealed to a slightly older viewer than MTV's target audience; created Nick at Nite, an extension of Nickelodeon that showed reruns of popular television programs from the 1950s, '60s, and '70s; and created European,

Japanese, and Australian versions of MTV. All of these endeavors were hugely successful.

In 1987 Pittman left MTV to cofound Quantum Media, a television production company. Two years later Quantum was acquired by Time-Warner Enterprises, a division of Time Warner Inc. and the new parent company of MTV Networks, and he became an executive adviser to the parent company's president. In 1990 he was made president and chief executive officer of Time-Warner Enterprises. In 1995 he became chief executive officer of Century 21 Real Estate, but left in 1996 to take over as president of AOL Networks. In 1998 he became president and chief operating officer of AOL. When the company merged with Time Warner in 2000, he became co-chief operating officer of the new company, AOL Time Warner.

Pittman stayed with AOL Time Warner only until 2002. He then joined with several former colleagues to form Pilot Group, LLC, an investment firm in New York City that specializes in late-stage and turnaround investments in privately owned companies, primarily in the areas of media and branded consumer products. Pittman and Hill divorced in 1997, and he married Veronique Choa later that same year. Together they have two children.

Further Reading

"Pittman, Robert W.," Museum of Broadcast Communications. Available online. URL: http://www.museum.tv/archives/etv/P/htmlP/pittmanrobe/pittmanrobe.htm. Downloaded on July 6, 2009.

Powers, Ron. *The Beast, the Eunuch, and the Glass-Eyed Child: Television in the '80s.* New York: Harcourt Brace Jovanovich, 1990.

Schultz, Ron. *Unconventional Wisdom: Twelve Remarkable Innovators Tell How Intuition Can Revolutionize Decision Making.* New York: Harper Business, 1994.

Polese, Kim

(1961–) *entrepreneur in the Java computer programming language*

The most significant business development in the 1990s was the emergence of the Internet as a commercial medium. The potential of e-business, or shopping done over the Internet, was so great that the so-called dot-coms, businesses that specialized in e-business, became the darlings of Wall Street investors. In large part, e-business is possible because of Java, a computer language that allows users to interact with Web sites. The person most responsible for the popularization of Java is Kim Polese, who eventually cofounded a company that specializes in building tools to further facilitate e-business.

Polese was born on November 13, 1961, in Berkeley, California. Her father, Angelo, was a civilian engineer with the U.S. Navy, and her mother, Inge, was a homemaker. After graduating from the University of California at Berkeley in 1984 with a B.S. in biophysics, she studied computer science for a year at the University of Washington in Seattle. In 1985 she went to work as an applications engineer for IntelliCorp, and she researched ways to "teach" computers and robots how to "think" like humans. Four years later she moved to Burlingame, a suburb of San Francisco, California, to join Sun Microsystems as a product manager for C++, a new programming language. In 1993 she transferred to FirstPerson, a Sun subsidiary, to become product manager for Oak, a programming language that was still in the developmental stages. Unlike C++, which was an operating system language like FORTRAN or BASIC and was intended for use in computers, Oak was originally intended for use in devices such as interactive televisions and hand-held remote controls.

As product manager, Polese's duties were essentially those of a marketer. While the programmers developed the language, she figured out how to sell it to the world at large. This involved working with the programmers to make Oak more user-friendly and developing relationships with computer hardware companies that were building devices that could use Oak. After a few months, however, she realized that Oak's designers were blind to their product's enormous potential. When she had first been introduced to Oak, she marveled that it could do so many things in such a small package and that it could run on multiple operating systems. This last feature was particularly important, because it meant that a device using Oak could interact with virtually any computer, whether its operating system ran on software developed by Microsoft, Apple, or any of their competitors.

After a series of talks with Patrick Naughton, FirstPerson's chief technologist, Polese and Naughton developed a marketing plan that proposed to retool Oak as a language that personal computers could use to access the Internet. At the time, Web surfers could not interact with Web site; they could access information by staring at a page, but they could not get the page to do anything. Nor could Web pages be loaded with special effects like animation or real-time information. But Oak would allow users and programmers to do all these things. At first, the marketing plan elicited little enthusiasm, mostly because FirstPerson had been founded to focus on developing products for interactive television. By mid-1994, however, the company had made a commitment to Polese and Naughton's plan, and to the new name for Oak that Polese had devised, Java.

To create a buzz about Java, Polese got First-Person's engineering department to create a Web browser. Called HotJava, the browser contained software applications written entirely in Java, and she gave away one to every Web site developer and programmer she could find so that they could experience firsthand what Java could do. Java was released to the public in mid-1995, and immediately became a hit with the computer industry. At the time, most personal computers ran on software whose rights were controlled by Microsoft or Apple. Web applications designed to run on machines using either company's software had to communicate with the computer via its operating system program, which meant that licensing fees and royalties had to be paid either to Microsoft or Apple. The beauty of Java is that it communicates directly with a computer's microchips without accessing operating system software. By using Java, programmers could write programs capable of running on any operating system without having to pay royalties to Microsoft, Apple, or anyone else. By 2000, Java had become the language of choice for building Internet applications.

Although Java was perfect for downloading text and graphics, it was incredibly slow at downloading programs. Polese decided to solve this problem by forming her own company to develop products that would expand even further the capabilities of Java. In late 1995, she formed a partnership with Arthur van Hoff, Jonathan Payne, and Sami Shaio—three engineers who had helped design Java—and in 1996 they opened for business in Palo Alto as Marimba, Inc., with Polese as president and chief executive officer. Later that year, the company announced the development of Castanet, a technology similar to cable television by which software could be transmitted over the Internet. Users received a Castanet tuner, which picked up a number of channels of information. By subscribing to a particular channel, they could download whatever programs or software that channel had available. Castanet allowed users to have the information they wanted sent directly to their personal computers, rather than searching the Internet to find that information. Unfortunately, Castanet was ahead of its time, and it never achieved the acceptance by channel providers or users it needed to survive.

Undaunted, Polese refocused Marimba's efforts to building an infrastructure for the Internet. Polese played a key role in helping Marimba become profitable and in brokering its 2004 sale to BMC Software for $239 million. Later in 2004 Polese became the chief executive officer of northern California–based SpikeSource, a leading provider of business-ready open-source solutions.

Further Reading

"Archive/Kim Polese," Wired. Available online. URL: http://www.wired.com/wired/archive/people/kim_polese/. Downloaded on November 21, 2001.

Carlassare, Elizabeth. DotCom.Divas: E-Business Insights from the Visionary Women Founders of 20 Net Ventures. New York: McGraw-Hill, 2001.

Reid, Robert. Architects of the Web: 1,000 Days that Built the Future of Business. New York: John Wiley & Sons, 1997.

Post, C. W.
(Charles William Post)
(1854–1914) *inventor of breakfast cereal*

C. W. Post was a man of many interests, the pursuit of which tended to wear him out. Following one collapse, he developed the idea that would bring him fame as the first manufacturer of a breakfast cereal. His two most popular cereals, Grape-Nuts and Post Toasties, helped change what Americans ate for breakfast.

Post was born Charles William Post on October 26, 1854, in Springfield, Illinois. His father, Charles, was a farm implements salesman, and his mother, Caroline, was a homemaker. At age 14 he entered the Illinois Industrial University where he studied mechanical engineering for a year. He spent the next four years as a state militiaman in Illinois and a cowboy in Kansas and Indian Territory (present-day Oklahoma). In 1873 he and a friend opened a hardware store in Independence, Kansas. The following year he sold his share of the store, returned to Springfield, and married Ella Merriweather with whom he had at least two children. They divorced in 1904, and that same year he married Leila Young.

After returning to Springfield, Post spent the next six years selling farm equipment throughout the Great Plains states. In 1881 he and several family members opened a plow factory in Springfield, but after four years of working as the factory's general manager, he suffered a nervous breakdown. By 1887 he had recovered and moved to Fort Worth, Texas, where he managed a woolen mill and a paper plant that he and his family had acquired. Once again, the strain proved to be too much for him, and in 1891 he had another nervous breakdown. That same year he was admitted to the Battle Creek Sanitarium in Battle Creek, Michigan, which was run by JOHN HARVEY KELLOGG.

At Battle Creek, Post was introduced to the first of Kellogg's innovative health foods. Kellogg was a great believer in the nutritive value of cereal grains, and by the time Post had arrived at the sanitarium Kellogg had developed "Granola," a biscuit about ½-inch thick made from the meal of wheat, oats, and corn. Kellogg was also opposed, for health reasons, to stimulants such as coffee, and he had experimented unsuccessfully with several grain-beverage substitutes. Post was greatly impressed with Kellogg's ideas about nutrition, especially after they contributed to his complete recovery. After his discharge from the sanitarium in 1892, he opened the La Vita Inn in Battle Creek as a sort of rival to the Battle Creek Sanitarium

and developed a grain beverage of his own. Called Postum, it was made from wheat, bran, and molasses, and before long the residents of the inn as well as Battle Creek locals in general began clamoring for more.

In 1896 Post formed the Postum Cereal Company and began promoting Postum by advertising in national newspapers. In 1897 he introduced the company's first cold cereal product, Grape-Nuts (despite the name, it contained neither grapes nor nuts, but the blend of grains and molasses made it taste as if it did). Grape-Nuts was made by using the wheat-flaking process patented by John Harvey and W. K. KELLOGG several years earlier, but which they had yet to put to commercial use. Heavy newspaper advertising, the copy written by Post, promoted the use of Postum in the winter and Grape-Nuts in the summer as part of a healthy year-round diet. Post was especially vociferous in attacking the traditional American breakfast of

C. W. Post played a major role in popularizing breakfast cereals. *(Library of Congress)*

eggs, pork, and coffee, which he declared to be unhealthy in the extreme and a horrible way to start the day. Much better, he proclaimed, to consume a breakfast of healthy grains that produced plenty of energy to get one through the morning without unnecessarily burdening one's digestive system. Not content to rely solely on the power of his persuasion, Post also introduced trial-size boxes of his cereals, recruited celebrity endorsements, and put prizes in a number of packages. By 1902 Postum was thriving, and Post found it necessary to build a large factory in Battle Creek, complete with company housing for his hundreds of employees.

Although Post moved to Washington, D.C., that same year, he continued to play an important role in the management of Postum Cereal for several more years. In 1904 he introduced the first cold cereal made from flaked corn. Called Elijah's Manna, the product elicited anguished howls of protest from religious groups across America for its blasphemous use of Holy Scripture to promote a secular product. Meanwhile, the general public took little note of its name and bought it off the shelves as fast as Postum could make it. In 1908 the product was renamed Post Toasties; despite the name change, it continued to sell well. By 1914, Postum Cereal's annual sales had topped $50 million.

By 1906 Post had embarked on yet another new venture. That same year he bought more than 200,000 acres of land in Texas and founded a model farming and ranching community. Named Post City in 1907, the community quickly ran into the problem of too little rain on the Texas prairie. From 1910 to 1913 he sponsored a series of highly innovative experiments designed to make rain, but none of them worked and the community suffered as a result. He also served as president of the National Association of American Advertisers for four years. In 1914 he suffered an attack of appendicitis; while recovering from the appendectomy, he was seized with a bout of severe depression and committed suicide. He died on May 9, 1914, at his winter home in Santa Barbara, California. Postum Cereal survived his death, and in 1929 it became the nucleus of the General Foods Corporation, which thrived well into the 21st century.

Further Reading

Butler, Mary, et al. *Walking the Road to Wellville: C. W. Post and the Postum Cereal Company*. Battle Creek, Mich.: Heritage Publications, 1995.

Major, Nettie L. *C. W. Post—The Hour and the Man: A Biography with Genealogical Supplement*. Washington: Judd & Detweiler, 1963.

Paxson, Peyton John. *Charles William Post: The Mass Marketing of Health and Welfare*. Ann Arbor, Mich.: University Microfilms International, 1993.

Pritzker, Abram Nicholas
(1896–1986) *founder of the Marmon Group*

Billionaires are rare creatures in the United States, but obscure billionaires are rarer still. Perhaps the most obscure American billionaire during the 20th century was Abram Pritzker, a Chicago real-estate speculator who eventually acquired more than 200 major companies. Although CHARLES G. BLUHDORN and ROYAL LITTLE brought the practice to the attention of the general public, Pritzker created the first conglomerate in American history, which eventually became known as the Marmon Group.

Pritzker was born on January 6, 1896, in Chicago, Illinois. His father, Nicholas, was a lawyer, and his mother, Annie, was a homemaker. At age 20 he received his B.A. from the University of Chicago, then went to study law at Harvard University. He left school to serve in the U.S. Navy during World War I, but returned to graduate in 1920. That same year he joined his father's law firm in Chicago, and in 1921 he married Fanny Doppelt with whom he had three children. After practicing law for a year, Pritzker decided it was not the career for him. He resigned from the firm and began dabbling in real estate instead. After making some money buying and selling properties in and around Chicago, he invested heavily in the Florida land boom of the 1920s and lost everything. Undaunted, he refocused his attention on the Chicago real estate market, and by 1940 he had amassed a modest fortune.

In 1942 Pritzker embarked on a new venture, buying failing companies and rejuvenating them. The first company he acquired was Cory Corporation, a manufacturer of small appliances, which he and his partner, James W. Alsdorf, purchased for only $100,000. Alsdorf took over the day-to-day management of Cory and made it profitable again, and in the late 1960s the partners sold it to Hershey Corporation for more than $22 million. Meanwhile Pritzker had continued to buy companies that were short on cash but long on potential. After 1950 he was ably assisted by his children; Jay Pritzker had a keen talent for spotting ailing companies with a future, Robert Pritzker was particularly skilled at getting the industrial companies Jay bought to operate profitably, and Donald Pritzker was a brilliant resuscitator of hotels and related businesses.

Pritzker's empire was a bewildering compendium of holding companies, operating companies, and corporate shells that were intertwined in such a complicated way that it took one accountant three years of doing nothing else to figure out how it all worked. Most of the companies that Pritzker controlled were organized in the Marmon Group, which in 1984 included approximately 65 domestic companies and 16 affiliated foreign companies. In 1984 it was estimated that the Marmon Group had taken in more than $3 billion in revenue that year alone. Several of his holdings, however, remained independent of the Marmon Group. In 1957, Pritzker bought the Hyatt Hotel in Los Angeles, California, and 15 years later, Donald Pritzker had made it the flagship property of the highly successful Hyatt Hotel chain and the most profitable unit in Pritzker's H Group Holdings. Other units in the H Group were Braniff Airlines and the Elsinore Corporation, which operated casinos in Las Vegas, Nevada, and Atlantic City, New Jersey. The rest of Pritzker's companies were held independently of these two groups, including *McCall's* magazine, travel agencies, cable television systems, and part-ownership of Levitz Furniture and the company that managed the Louisiana Superdome in New Orleans. But regardless of how they were organized, Pritzker followed the same strategy with each company he acquired: build it up, put it in the hands of a competent manager, and then keep tabs on it without stifling the manager's ability to run it.

In 1970 Pritzker's wife died; two years later, he married Lorraine Colantonio. By this time he had relinquished day-to-day control of his companies and real-estate holdings to his children, and he spent his remaining years giving away more than $4 million per year to various charities in Chicago. Major recipients included the University of Chicago School of Medicine, the Illinois Institute of Technology, the Michael Reese Hospital, the Museum of Science and Industry, the Chicago Symphony, the Art Institute of Chicago, the Pritzker Center for Disturbed Youth, the Pritzker Youth Foundation, and the Hyatt Foundation. But his favorite charity was Wicker Park Elementary School, which he had attended as a youth. Of all the gifts he gave the school and its students, the most memorable one was when he hired the Harlem Globetrotters, perhaps the world's most famous professional basketball team, to play Wicker Park and lose. At the time of his death on February 8, 1986, in Chicago, it was estimated that Pritzker's empire was worth $1.5 billion. Most of it had been assigned to more than 1,000 trusts that he had set up and managed for the maintenance of his family.

Further Reading

"Abram Nicholas Pritzker." Infoplease.Com. Available online. URL: http://www.infoplease.com/ipa/A0771986.html. Downloaded on July 6, 2009.

Pritzker, Lee. *The Pritzker Book: Honoring the Past, Bringing Togetherness to the Present, Lighting a Path for the Future.* Baltimore: n.p., 1962.

Pulitzer, Joseph

(1847–1911) *entrepreneur in newspaper publishing*

By 1880 many American big-city newspapers had achieved reputations for editorial independence and accurate reporting. After 1880 Joseph Pulitzer's *St. Louis Post-Dispatch* and the *New York World* developed into the first modern newspapers by also being idealistic, entertaining, and at times sensationalistic. For these reasons Pulitzer is often regarded as the father of the modern newspaper.

Pulitzer was born on April 10, 1847, in Mako, Hungary. His father, Philip, was a grain and produce dealer, and his mother, Louise, was a homemaker. Having grown up in Budapest, at age 17 he left home and made his way to Hamburg, Germany, where he was recruited to join the Union army. He arrived in the United States in time to serve during the last eight months of the Civil War. Unable to find work in New York City after his discharge, he went to St. Louis, Missouri, where he worked successively as a waiter, stevedore, and mule handler.

In 1868 Pulitzer met Carl Schurz, a former Union army general who was part-owner of the *Westliche Post,* St. Louis's leading German-language daily newspaper. Schurz offered him a job as a reporter, and he quickly developed into a first-class journalist. He exulted in exposing the corruption in the city's government and the unethical behavior of many of its prominent businesspeople. Thrilled with his work, in 1869 Schurz made Pulitzer the paper's correspondent in Jefferson City, the state capital. In 1871 he returned to St. Louis to become a part-owner of the *Westliche Post,* although he continued to write.

In 1873 Pulitzer sold his interest in the paper and focused his attention on law and politics. He became a popular stump speaker for Democratic

Along with William Randolph Hearst, Joseph Pulitzer popularized what became known as yellow journalism. *(Library of Congress)*

Party candidates and was admitted to the Missouri bar in 1876. Meanwhile, he had kept his hand in publishing by buying and then selling the *Staats-Zeitung,* another German-language daily. In 1878 he married Kate Davis with whom he had seven children. That same year he returned to newspaper publishing full time when he bought the *St. Louis Evening Dispatch* at a sheriff's sale for $2,500. Almost immediately he merged his paper with the rival *Evening Post* to form the *St. Louis Post-Dispatch,* and the following year he became its sole owner. Under his editorship, the *Post-Dispatch* exposed crime and shady dealings, offered insightful glimpses into the workings of the city's economic affairs, gossiped about local celebrities, and preached the Democratic gospel of "power to the people" rather than rule by the wealthy.

In 1883 Pulitzer expanded his newspaper publishing horizons by moving to New York City and buying the *New York World* with the profits he had made with the *Post-Dispatch.* Founded in 1860, the *World* was a religious daily with a circulation of about 15,000, but within three years he had increased circulation to 250,000 by making extensive use of illustrations, banner headlines, and color, and by creating what one critic called "the first modern newspaper." In florid language, the *World* crusaded against crime and privilege, uncovered scandal, campaigned for the commonweal, covered sports and women's fashion, and included comic strips. Its editorial page developed into a strong voice for democratic institutions in general and the Democratic Party in particular. Best of all, a copy cost only one penny. Moreover, the *World* had "hobbies," as Pulitzer called them; in 1885 the paper raised $100,000, mostly in small change, to build a pedestal for the Statue of Liberty, which the citizens of France had just donated to the United States. Its most spectacular hobby was to send star reporter Nellie Bly around the world in 1889–90 to see if she could make it in less than 80 days, the time taken by Phileas Fogg in Jules Verne's epic novel *Around the World in Eighty Days.* Bly's trip was chronicled on a daily basis by the *World,* which promised a free trip to Europe to whomever came closest to guessing her time; more than 1 million entries were sent in by enthralled readers. After traveling on ships, trains, horses, donkeys, rickshaws, and sampans, Bly made the last leg from San Francisco, California, on a special train and arrived back in New York City after 72 days, 6 hours, 11 minutes, and 14 seconds.

By 1895 Pulitzer had built the *World* into New York City's leading newspaper. But that same year he encountered a strong challenger in the form of the *New York Journal*. Newly acquired by millionaire WILLIAM RANDOLPH HEARST, the *Journal* initiated a bidding war for the *World's* top people that the *World* could scarcely afford. Then the *Journal* adopted a highly sensational style of reporting that attracted many former readers of the *World*. Within a short time the *World* was forced to respond with sensationalistic coverage of its own. The result was yellow journalism; the name derives from a cartoon character, the Yellow Kid, that appeared in both papers. Yellow journalism reached its peak in 1898 during the Spanish-American War, which both papers zealously supported, but subsided shortly thereafter when Pulitzer ordered his editors to take on a more restrained tone.

Pulitzer was gradually forced to relinquish day-to-day control of his newspapers after 1887, when a ruptured blood vessel in his eye caused his vision to deteriorate; by 1892 he could barely see. He continued to supervise the *World* and the *Post-Dispatch* until his death, although in 1904 he made Frank I. Cobb editor of the *World* and in 1906 gave control of the *Post-Dispatch* to his son Joseph II. During his final years, he donated $2 million to establish a graduate school of journalism at Columbia University and established an endowment to fund the Pulitzer Prizes, which are awarded annually for excellence in journalism and literature. He died on October 29, 1911, aboard his yacht in the harbor of Charleston, South Carolina.

Further Reading

Brian, Denis. *Pulitzer: A Life.* New York: J. Wiley, 2001.
Whitelaw, Nancy. *Joseph Pulitzer and the New York World.* Greensboro, N.C.: Morgan Reynolds, 2000.

Pullman, George Mortimer

(1831–1897) *inventor of the Pullman sleeping car*

One of the more interesting social experiments of the 19th century was the creation of Pullman, a model company town outside Chicago, Illinois. The man responsible for the town's existence, George Pullman, was the inventor of the Pullman sleeping car and was a wealthy railroad entrepreneur.

Pullman was born on March 3, 1831, in Brocton, New York. His father, James, was a carpenter and mechanic, and his mother, Emily, was a homemaker. At age 14 he left school to go to work as a clerk in his uncle's store in nearby Westfield. After a year he moved back with his family, who by now had relocated to Albion, New York. For the next five years he worked in his brothers' cabinet shop and helped his father, who moved buildings via a wheeled machine he had invented. After his father died in 1853, he took over the business, which in 1855 he moved to Chicago, Illinois.

Pullman's business required him to travel by train, and he often spent the night in a sleeping car. Designed and manufactured by Theodore T. Woodruff, the first sleeping cars were little more than rolling dormitories with bunk beds, and they were uncomfortable and cramped. After one particularly bad night's sleep, Pullman realized that the situation presented a business opportunity. In 1858 he contacted Benjamin C. Field, a friend of his in the railcar business, and together they convinced the Chicago & Alton Railroad to let them convert three day coaches into sleeping cars. The cars were outfitted with retractable berths, which Pullman had designed, that could be raised to the ceiling when not in use. Although the cars proved to be popular with travelers, the railroad decided that three such cars were all it needed. When no other railroad expressed an interest in retractable berths, in 1860 Pullman temporarily abandoned the sleeping car business and headed for Colorado.

Gold had just been discovered near Pike's Peak, and Pullman profited from the resulting gold rush by opening a stamping mill for crushing ore into powder, a general store, and a wagon line. Three years later he returned to Chicago a wealthy man and threw himself with renewed vigor into the sleeping-car business. By 1865 he and Field had designed, patented, and built the Pioneer, a luxury sleeping car with individual compartments featuring a personal washstand, a fold-down upper berth, and two plush seats that folded out to make

George Pullman invented the Pullman sleeping car so passengers on overnight train trips could get a good night's sleep. *(Library of Congress)*

a lower berth. The Pioneer was so expensive that most railroads preferred either to lease them or to let Pullman and Field operate them under contract; within a year the partners were operating 40 Pioneers on six different railroads. In 1867 the partners split, and Pullman incorporated as the Pullman Palace Car Company, with himself as president and general manager. That same year he married Harriet Sanger with whom he had four children.

At the time the only real competition Pullman's company had was the Central Transportation Company, builders of the Woodruff sleeping car. But the Pioneer was so superior to the Woodruff in terms of comfort and amenities that by 1870 Pullman had dominated the marketplace and acquired Central Transportation. One of the reasons for Pullman's success was the support he received from ANDREW CARNEGIE, the millionaire steel manufacturer. Carnegie had been a director of Central Transportation for years, but he much preferred Pullman's product and business sense, so he helped Pullman win a major contract from the newly completed Union Pacific/Central Pacific transcontinental line as well as gain control of Central Transportation. Another reason was the way Pullman operated his sleeping cars. He staffed them with courteous porters who conducted their

business according to strict company guidelines, and after every run he had each car cleaned thoroughly and disinfected. After 1868 he also began producing parlor cars and dining cars; his first diner, the Delmonico, featured a kitchen in mid-car with a luxurious dining area on each end. By 1880 Pullman Palace Car was building more than 100 cars per year and operating more than 1,000 cars over most of the nation's railroads.

The 1880s was a time of growing labor unrest, and Pullman decided that the best way to ensure his workers' continued loyalty was to build a company town. That same year he initiated construction of the community of Pullman, located on Lake Calumet just south of Chicago. Within five years the town was home to more than 8,000 people, all of them Pullman employees or their families. In addition to almost 1,500 townhouses and single-family homes, all of them owned by the company and rented out to employees, the town included parks, churches, schools, a shopping arcade, and a hotel. Although the company charged rents that were a bit higher than rents in neighboring communities, it also kept the town clean and safe, thus making it a model community. Pullman Palace Car's central shops were relocated to Pullman from Detroit, and by 1890 the company was building thousands of freight cars and streetcars in addition to sleeping, dining, and parlor cars. Meanwhile, Pullman himself had acquired substantial interests in several railroads, including New York City's elevated passenger line.

Pullman's fortunes took a turn for the worse during the 1890s. The panic of 1893 resulted in the bankruptcy of almost 200 railroads, and proceeds from the sale and operation of railcars slumped precipitously. Pullman reacted by laying off one-third of his employees and reducing the wages of the ones remaining by up to 30 percent. However, he did not reduce their rents, nor did he reduce the salaries of corporate officials or the dividends paid to stockholders. Incensed by Pullman's seeming indifference to their plight, many Pullman workers joined the American Railway Union, the very thing Pullman had hoped to avoid by building the town of Pullman. When the union went on strike in 1894, its members refused to handle Pullman cars on any line in the nation, and violence broke out in Chicago. Although the strike was broken quickly by federal troops who took the places of striking union members, Pullman himself was heavily criticized in the media for having caused the strike in the first place. His image as a paternalistic employer, which he had worked hard to achieve, was forever shattered.

The strike seemed to affect Pullman's health, and a few years later, on October 19, 1897, he died at his home in Chicago. His estate was estimated to be worth well over $40 million. As a final attempt to fix his tarnished reputation as a kindly employer, he left in his will more than $1 million for the construction and operation of a free vocational education school for the residents of Pullman. By 1939 Pullman had been annexed by Chicago, and Pullman's social experiment came to an end.

Further Reading

Knoll, Charles M. *Go Pullman: Life and Times: The Man, the Company, Products, Services and Contemporaries.* Rochester, N.Y.: Rochester Chapter, National Railway Historical Society, 1995.

Leyendecker, Liston E. *Palace Car Prince: A Biography of George Mortimer Pullman.* Niwot: University Press of Colorado, 1992.

Papke, David R. *The Pullman Case: The Clash of Labor and Capital in Industrial America.* Lawrence: University Press of Kansas, 1999.

Pupin, Michael Idvorsky

(1858–1935) *inventor of the inductance coil*

Calling long distance on the telephone would be impossible if a way to amplify one's voice over hundreds and thousands of miles of telephone cable did not exist. In 1899 Michael Pupin figured out how to do exactly that when he invented the inductance coil.

Pupin was born on October 4, 1858, in Idvor, Banat, Austria-Hungary. His parents, Konstantin and Olympiada, were farmers. At age 15 he went to Prague to further his education, and the following year he emigrated to the United States. For the next five years he worked a succession of farm and factory jobs in Maryland, New Jersey, and

New York City. At age 21 he won a scholarship to Columbia University and received his B.A. in 1883, the same year he became an American citizen. He then went to the University of Berlin where he received his Ph.D. in physics in 1889. The year before he had married Sarah Jackson with whom he had one child; his wife died in 1896 and he never remarried.

After graduation Pupin returned to Columbia as a professor of mathematical physics in the Department of Electrical Engineering. He began experimenting with electromagnetism, and in the mid-1890s he developed an electrical resonator that increased the volume of radio waves. In 1903 Pupin sold his patent to the device to the Marconi Company of America, which used the electrical resonator to improve its ability to send and receive radio signals between Europe and the United States.

Pupin next turned his attention to the transmission of sound via wires over long distances. By the late 1890s telephone companies had solved the electrical problems associated with transmitting telephone messages over short distances. However, long distance transmission remained a problem because of the need to amplify a signal over a long stretch of telephone line. But by 1899 Pupin had solved the problem. To give the signal a boost while it was in transit, he invented the inductance coil. This device is essentially a transformer consisting of a primary coil with a few windings of heavy wire and a secondary coil with many windings of fine wire, both of which are wrapped around a single soft-iron core. When low-voltage alternating current passes through the primary coil, it induces high-voltage alternating current in the secondary coil. The high voltage can then be used to boost, or amplify, a signal traveling along a wire. By spacing inductance coils at mathematically determined points along a telephone cable, a signal can be boosted repeatedly over a virtually infinite distance so that the signal is as strong on the receiving end as it was on the transmitting end.

Pupin received a U.S. patent for his inductance coil in December 1899, just four months before George Campbell and Edwin Colpitts, two telephone engineers with American Bell, filed for a patent on a similar device. In 1901 American Telephone & Telegraph bought Pupin's U.S. patent; he later assigned his European patent to the inductance coil to a German firm, Siemens & Halske. The sale of these rights made Pupin a relatively wealthy man, although he continued to teach and to conduct research at Columbia until his retirement in 1931. Pupin received a number of awards for his inventions, including the American Institute of Electrical Engineers' Edison Prize in 1921 and the Institute of Radio Engineers' Gold Medal of Honor in 1924.

Later in life Pupin developed an interest in the mystical aspects of scientific inquiry, which he explored in *The New Reformation: From Physical to Spiritual Realities* (1927). As he put it, "The physical facts of science are not cold, unless your soul and your heart are cold." He also wrote several other books about a wide range of topics, and he received a Pulitzer Prize for his autobiography, *From Immigrant to Inventor* (1922). He died on March 12, 1935, in New York City.

Further Reading

Markey, Dorothy. *Explorer of Sound: Michael Pupin*. New York: J. Messner, 1964.

Pupin, Michael I. *From Immigrant to Inventor*. New York: Arno Press, 1980.

Reynolds, Terry S. *The Engineer in America: A Historical Anthology from Technology and Culture*. Chicago: University of Chicago Press, 1991.

R

Reuther, Walter

(1907–1970) *entrepreneur in organized labor*

Lists of the wealthiest Americans never include his name, but few people made as large an impact on American industry as Walter Reuther. During his nearly quarter-century tenure as head of the United Auto Workers (UAW), Reuther steadfastly and successfully advocated for improved working conditions and benefits packages for members of his union, helping to create the largest and most prosperous middle class in the world.

Walter Philip Reuther was born in Wheeling, West Virginia, on September 1, 1907. Reuther's childhood was filled with several strong influences from within his own family that would inspire his life's work of labor organizing. His grandfather Jacob Reuther, an immigrant from Germany who conducted Lutheran Sunday services at his home in rural Illinois, argued that some churches, "do too much for God and not enough for man." His father, Valentine, was a union organizer in Wheeling who took young Walter with him to visit Eugene Debs, who was sentenced to 10 years in prison in nearby Moundsville under the Espionage Act for his resistance to World War I. The Reuther parents encouraged lively debate of the leading topics of the time among Walter, his two brothers, and one sister, but the compact, red-headed young Reuther was not enchanted by school, so he dropped out at the age of 16. Reuther worked as a tool and die maker's apprentice until getting fired for trying to organize a union. Reuther then moved to Detroit in 1927 for greater employment opportunities.

In Detroit, Reuther got a job as a mechanic in Ford Motor Company's River Rouge plant, and he quickly established a reputation as one of the factory's top workers. He worked nights while taking classes to graduate from high school and at Detroit City College (now Wayne State University). In the early stages of the Great Depression, Reuther organized soup kitchens and socialist advocacy groups in Detroit and, in 1932, he supported the presidential campaign of socialist candidate Norman Thomas. Following that year's election to the presidency of Franklin D. Roosevelt, Reuther traveled to Europe with his younger brother, Victor, with the goal of what he called "studying life." For two years, Reuther visited European nations, spending the most time in the Soviet Union, where he worked at an American-built automobile factory.

Reuther returned to Detroit in 1935 and married a physical education teacher May Wolf the following year. He immersed himself in labor organizing for the fledgling UAW and quickly rose in its ranks. In 1936, he was elected to serve as a delegate from the Michigan delegation at the UAW national convention where his dynamic presence and eloquent speaking led to his being named to the UAW's national executive board. Soon Reuther became president of UAW Local 174, which counted over 30,000 members. He played a key role in the renowned 1937 Sit-Down Strike at a General Motors plant in Flint, Michigan, and he gained national attention and sympathy for the cause of organized labor when he was pictured beaten and bloody after being attacked by Ford security while passing out leaflets in front of the River Rouge plant.

A 1955 cover story in *Time* magazine captured the story of Reuther's rise during the mid to late 1930s and noted, "Reuther has displayed the winner-take-all talents of a Commando leader in his strike strategy." Reuther continued his rise in importance and influence into the 1940s, suggesting to President Roosevelt that some of Detroit's plants should be converted to wartime capacity over a year before the attack on Pearl Harbor drew the United States into World War II. In 1946, Reuther was elected to the presidency of the UAW, where he would serve for the remainder of his life.

Prior to accepting this post and throughout his tenure, Reuther doggedly, and usually successfully, pursued advancements for workers that are now often taken for granted. Among the provisions fought for by Reuther were wage increases (including a breakthrough 1948 concession for an annual wage increase tied to a quarterly cost of living adjustment), improved benefits and protections for retirees and those laid off from their jobs, health care and tuition reimbursement programs, life insurance, profit sharing, severance pay, and jury duty and bereavement pay.

Reuther accomplished so many of his goals because he was able to weather much of the cold war fear of communist influence in unions due to his consistent opposition to communism dating back to his return from the Soviet Union. He referred to the Soviets as "colonial agents of foreign power." Also critical to his success was his tireless work ethic that typically included 12 to 18 hour days. Though feisty and charismatic, Reuther was well known for living a rather quiet lifestyle, eschewing vacations and rarely consuming alcohol.

In addition to his long service as head of a union with over a million members, Reuther was also an important civil rights advocate, which often ran counter to the sentiment of many within trade unions at the time. Reuther enjoyed sharing an anecdote that centered on his being one of the few whites invited to speak at the 1963 March on Washington, famous for Martin Luther King's "I have a dream" speech. Standing close to

the podium were two elderly African-American women. As he was introduced, one of the women asked, "Who is Walter Reuther?" Replied her friend, "Walter Reuther? He's the white Martin Luther King."

Walter Reuther died on May 9, 1970, when the small commuter airplane he was traveling in crashed as it was approaching landing in a small airfield about 250 miles northwest of Detroit. The crash also claimed the life of his wife of 34 years, May, as well as two others. Reuther's impact on the labor movement is still strongly felt four decades after his death and is reflected in the philosophy of life he fondly and regularly referenced: "There is no greater calling than to serve your fellow men. There is no greater contribution than to help the weak. There is no greater satisfaction than to have done it well."

Further Reading

Bluestone, Irving. "Walter Reuther." Time 100. Available online. URL: http://www.time.com/time/time100/builder/profile/reuther.html. Downloaded on September 1, 2009.

Dickmeyer, Elizabeth Reuther. *Putting the World Together: My Father Walter Reuther, the Liberal Warrior.* Lake Orion, Mich.: LivingForce Publishing, 2004.

Lichtenstein, Nelson. *Walter Reuther: The Most Dangerous Man in Detroit.* Champagne: University of Illinois Press, 1997.

"Walter Reuther (1907–1970.) AFL-CIO. Available online. URL: http://www.aflcio.org/aboutus/history/history/reuther.cfm. Downloaded on September 1, 2009.

Rock, Arthur
(1926–) *founder of Silicon Valley*

Arthur Rock did not invent venture capital; according to him, that honor probably belongs to the Medicis, the medieval Italian banking family. He did, however, coin the term and become one of the most successful venture capitalists in the United States. Rock played a major role in the creation of Silicon Valley, California's monument to technological innovation. In the process, he originated the idea, at least in this country, of forming a partnership for the sole purpose of raising and investing money in other people's companies. Ironically, Rock became involved with financing high-tech ventures largely as a result of a letter that was not addressed to him.

Rock was born on August 19, 1926, in Rochester, New York; his parents' names were Hyman and Reva. After graduating from Syracuse University in 1948, he enrolled in Harvard Business School and received his M.B.A. three years later. In 1951 he joined Hayden, Stone, a New York City investment banking firm that specialized in arranging financing for new companies. Over the next six years, he became particularly adept at raising capital for small- to medium-sized companies via small public offerings of stock and by getting wealthy individuals to invest. A good example of his success with the former method was General Transistor, the first publicly held, independent manufacturer of transistors, the tiny electronic circuits that replaced vacuum tubes.

In 1957 one of Hayden, Stone's stockbrokers received an interesting letter from seven California scientists, one of whom was the son of one of his clients. The seven all worked for Shockley Laboratory Division of Beckman Instruments, an electronics manufacturer, but were planning to leave the company because of their differences with the owner, William Shockley. At first, the seven simply wanted to know if Hayden Stone knew of one company where all seven could get jobs. The stockbroker showed the letter to Rock, who decided to find out if the seven wanted to start their own company. After two trips to California, Rock and the scientists (who now numbered eight, having been joined by ROBERT NORTON NOYCE) formed a company. Each scientist received 10 percent of the stock, while Hayden Stone would receive 20 percent on condition that it raise the $1.5 million needed to start manufacturing transistors.

Rock decided that the best way to raise the money was to find a bigger company to finance the venture, the same way that Shockley had financed his venture. Rock approached 35 different companies, each of which wanted to expand its technology, and was turned down by all 35. Finally, he convinced SHERMAN FAIRCHILD to finance the California venture as a subsidiary of his own company,

Fairchild Camera and Instrument. With the money in hand, the eight scientists formed Fairchild Semiconductor in Mountain View, just down the road from Shockley Laboratory, thus forming the foundation from which Silicon Valley would grow.

By 1961 Rock had realized that most of U.S. innovative technology was being developed on the West Coast, while most of the country's major financiers were on the East Coast. That same year he moved to San Francisco and became partners with Thomas J. Davis, Jr., who had been vice president of a California land investment company, to form Davis & Rock, one of the country's first venture capital firms. The two partners raised $5 million, mostly from contacts Rock had back East, which they invested in up-and-coming technology companies such as Teledyne and Scientific Data Systems (SDS). The two partners served on the boards of directors of many of these companies in an effort to provide some much-needed management guidance to the company founders, who generally were strong on technical know-how but weak on managerial skills. Rock served as SDS's chairman of the board, and he masterminded its sale to Xerox in 1969 for $9 million, a far cry from the $257,000 he and Davis had invested in it. In 1968 Davis and Rock terminated their partnership amicably, mostly for reasons having to do with the pending sale of SDS. In 1969 Rock formed a new partnership, Arthur Rock & Associates. In 1975 he married Toni Rembe with whom he has no children. When Arthur Rock & Associates expired in 1980, he established his own venture capital firm, Arthur Rock & Company, which he was still managing as of his 75th birthday.

Rock's financial acumen and management oversight helped some of the biggest names in computer technology get started. In 1968, while he was between partnerships, he played a major role in financing Intel, which eventually became the largest manufacturer of microprocessors in the world. Two of Fairchild Semiconductor's founders, Robert Noyce and Gordon Moore, had decided to form their own company. Rock was impressed with Noyce's management skills and Moore's technical wizardry, so he invested heavily in the new company. Rock provided some managerial oversight as chairman of the board and other director-type positions for more than 30 years. This association proved to be a lucrative one for Rock; as of 1998, he owned more than 10 million shares of Intel stock. In 1980, having just dissolved his second partnership, Rock played a major role in helping STEPHEN GARY WOZNIAK and STEVEN PAUL JOBS establish Apple Computer, then served as a director for the next 13 years.

Now in his 70s, Rock remains among the most successful and respected American venture capitalists. He works in San Francisco and is an active member of several corporate and nonprofit boards. Regarding his work of providing critically needed support for burgeoning companies, Rock has expressed his personal philosophy: "If you're interested in building a business to make money, forget it. You won't. If you're interested in building a business to make a contribution to society, then let's talk."

Further Reading

Gupta, Udayan. *Done Deals: Venture Capitalists Tell Their Stories.* Boston: Harvard Business School Press, 2000.

Sigismund, Charles G. *Champions of Silicon Valley: Visionary Thinking from Today's Technology Pioneers.* New York: John Wiley, 2000.

Rockefeller, John Davison

(1839–1937) *founder of Standard Oil Company and Trust*

John D. Rockefeller was one of the most controversial entrepreneurs in American history. He is considered by many to be one of the robber barons, ruthless 19th-century capitalists who crushed their competitors without compunction and manipulated markets without regard to the effect on consumers. Certainly, Rockefeller resorted to illegal tactics while creating the Standard Oil Trust, perhaps the largest monopoly in U.S. history. However, this action must be balanced by the facts that Standard Oil frequently reduced prices and improved services for many customers, and that Rockefeller himself gave away more than a half billion dollars to charity.

Rockefeller was born John Davison Rockefeller on July 8, 1839, in Richford, New York. His father, William, was a traveling salesman who sold, at various times in his career, horses, lumber, salt, and patent and herbal medicines; his mother, Eliza, was a homemaker. As a boy he lived with his family in a succession of towns in New York and Ohio, and in 1853 he went off to high school in Cleveland, where he settled. After graduating in 1855, he briefly attended a local business college, then went to work as a clerk and bookkeeper for Isaac Hewitt and Henry Tuttle, produce wholesalers. Four years later, at age 20, he borrowed $1,000 from his father and formed a wholesale produce firm of his own, Clark & Rockefeller, with Maurice Clark.

In 1863, the year before he married Laura Spelman with whom he had four children, Rockefeller became partners with Clark and Samuel Andrews in Andrews, Clark & Company, which refined crude oil shipped from Pennsylvania to Cleveland into kerosene for lamps. With Andrews managing the refinery, and Rockefeller and Clark managing the office, in two years the partners developed the company into the biggest kerosene business in Cleveland. But when Rockefeller proposed expanding the business even further, Clark balked, and in 1865 Rockefeller bought him out; later that year they dissolved their produce business as well. Now doing business as Rockefeller & Andrews, the company built a second refinery and opened a sales office in New York City. Two years later Rockefeller and Andrews took on two new partners, HENRY MORRISON FLAGLER and Stephen Harkness, and in 1870 the four founded Standard Oil Company as a joint stock company, with Rockefeller as largest stockholder and president.

During the late 1860s, prices for petroleum products had been falling, mostly because refiners were producing more than consumers demanded. Meanwhile, railroads began competing for the hauling of crude from the Pennsylvania oil fields, as well as for the shipment of refined oil from refineries all over the Northeast, by offering lower rates to oil producers and refiners who guaranteed to ship large quantities on a regular schedule. By 1870 these situations had caused the prices of crude and refined oil to fluctuate wildly from day to day, thus throwing the petroleum industry into a chaotic state, and Rockefeller and his partners began thinking of ways to rationalize the market so that oil producers, refiners, and railroads could all make a decent profit. His efforts would ultimately revolve around two strategies: regulate the quantity of oil being refined, and secure low, fixed rates from the railroads.

Rockefeller's first two attempts to achieve these ends resulted in frustration. In 1872 he and his associates chartered the South Improvement Company in Pennsylvania for purposes of guaranteeing lower rates from the three major oil-hauling railroads: the Erie, the New York Central, and the Pennsylvania. Refiners who joined the company by exchanging some of their stock for Standard Oil's would receive rates as much as 50 percent lower than nonmembers; in addition, they would share rebates of up to 25 percent of the higher rates charged nonmembers. But when the Pennsylvania oil producers found out about the plan, they feared South Improvement might become so strong that it could negotiate a lower price for crude oil, and they refused to sell to any refiner involved in the scheme. Almost immediately Standard Oil's supplies of crude oil were cut off, and the South Improvement Company was disbanded. Later in 1872, Rockefeller formed the National Refiners' Association. Its purpose was to reduce the quantity and increase prices for refined oil by allocating crude oil among its members. But this arrangement quickly proved to be impossible to regulate without some form of coercive control exercised from above.

Meanwhile, Rockefeller had found a way to bring order to the market that also brought it under his personal control. By 1873 Standard Oil was the largest oil refiner in the United States, and the company's profits for that year alone exceeded a half million dollars. Having branched out into the refining of lubricants as well as kerosene, the company was able to obtain lower rates from railroads in exchange for guaranteed minimum daily shipments from his own refineries. Rockefeller then offered to share these rates with any refinery that would secretly exchange a majority of its stock for shares in Standard Oil. He soon discovered that, in order to gain control of the petroleum industry, all he had to do was increase the capitalization of Standard Oil so that it could issue additional shares, which could then be exchanged for

shares in rival companies, provided that none of his machinations became public knowledge. By the end of 1872 Standard Oil controlled all refining in Cleveland and was gaining control over refining in New York City. By 1876 it had acquired controlling interest in most refineries in Ohio, Pennsylvania, New York, and West Virginia. By 1877 it had arranged major rate reductions in return for guaranteed daily minimum shipments with the Erie and New York Central railroads. By 1879 it had acquired controlling interest in 90 percent of the nation's oil refineries, and it exercised significant control over the shipping of crude and refined oil. In the span of seven years, Rockefeller had secretly created one of the largest monopolies the United States had ever seen.

Unfortunately for Rockefeller, the method by which he created this monopoly was illegal. As a company chartered in Ohio, Standard Oil was forbidden from owning stock in companies chartered in other states. To get around the law, Rockefeller designated certain company officials as trustees of the stocks of companies in particular states. But this system tended to decentralize Standard Oil, which was precisely the problem the conglomerate was formed to eliminate in the first place. In 1882, Rockefeller created the Standard Oil Trust. The trust combined Standard Oil and its affiliates, more than 40 corporations in all, and placed them under the control of nine trustees. These trustees, who met weekly, had the power to dictate each company's operating policy as well as to sell, merge, or dissolve any of the companies.

Standard Oil Trust did indeed make the petroleum industry more profitable for producers, refiners, and railroads. It also reduced prices and regulated the delivery of refined oil to most of the markets it served. However, the possibility that it could raise prices or restrict the supply of oil at its whim terrified many Americans as they learned of its existence, and its legality was questioned in a number of states. In 1892 the Ohio Supreme Court declared it an illegal monopoly and ordered it to be dissolved, but the trust simply transferred its operations from Cleveland to New York City. To avoid a similar ruling from the New York supreme court, in 1899 the trust was incorporated as a holding company under New Jersey law (the trust's name was changed to Standard Oil Company of New Jersey), thus making itself completely legal for the first time. But when the Sherman Antitrust Act was passed by the U.S. Congress the following year, Standard Oil was once again on shaky legal ground. In 1906 the federal government brought suit against Standard Oil under the Sherman Act, and in 1911 the company was forced to divest itself of its holdings, some 33 companies in all. From the wreckage of Standard Oil were formed many of the major oil companies of the early 21st century, including Mobil, Amoco, Chevron, Exxon, Atlantic Richfield, and Pennzoil.

But by the time Standard Oil was broken up, Rockefeller had ceased to be involved in its day-to-day affairs. Having created the trust, in 1897 he left it to others to run while he devoted the rest of his life to giving away money. Exactly how much money he had at his disposal to give away has never been determined, but his fortune was estimated to be as high as $900 million. Among his countless gifts were the funds necessary to found the University of Chicago, at one time one of the leading institutions of higher learning in the United States; the Rockefeller Institute for Medical Research, later renamed Rockefeller University, best known for playing a major role in finding vaccines for deadly diseases such as yellow fever; the General Education Board, best known for greatly improving education at all levels throughout the South; and the Rockefeller Foundation, which contributed money to hundreds of worthy causes around the world. Over the course of his lifetime, Rockefeller gave away $540 million to charitable organizations.

Rockefeller spent his retirement in his palatial homes in Cleveland; Forest Hills, New York; Lakewood, New Jersey; and Ormond Beach, Florida. He died on May 23, 1937, in Ormond Beach.

Further Reading

Chernow, Ron. *Titan: The Life of John D. Rockefeller, Sr.* New York: Vintage Books, 1999.

Crompton, Samuel W. *100 Americans Who Shaped American History.* San Mateo, Calif.: Bluewood Books, 1999.

Ernst, Joseph W., ed. *Dear Father/Dear Son: Correspondence of John D. Rockefeller and John D. Rockefeller, Jr.* New York: Fordham University Press, 1994.

Olien, Roger M., and Diana D. Olien. *Oil and Ideology: The Cultural Creation of the American Petroleum Industry.* Chapel Hill: University of North Carolina Press, 2000.

Smith, George D., and Frederick Dalzell. *Wisdom from the Robber Barons: Enduring Business Lessons from Rockefeller, Morgan, and the First Industrialists.* Cambridge, Mass.: Perseus Pub., 2000.

Rosenthal, Ida
(Ida Kaganovich, Ida Cohen)
(1886–1973) *inventor of the Maidenform bra*

Many inventors and entrepreneurs change the shape of their respective industries, but few change the shape of their customers in the process. One who did is Ida Rosenthal, inventor and promoter of the modern brassiere.

Rosenthal was born Ida Kaganovich on January 9, 1886, in Rakov, Russia. Her father, Abraham, was a scholar and her mother, Sarah, owned a small general store. As a young teenager Rosenthal was apprenticed to a local seamstress, and at age 16 she went to Warsaw, at the time a part of Russia, to attend high school. In 1904 she emigrated to the United States, settled in Hoboken, New Jersey, changed her last name to Cohen, and opened a dressmaking shop. Two years later she married William Rosenthal, who had left Rakov for the United States a few months before her; they eventually had two children. With her husband as a business partner, Rosenthal built a thriving dressmaking business. By 1918, the same year they relocated their business to upper Manhattan in New York City, the shop employed 15 seamstresses.

Shortly after this move, Rosenthal also began making dresses for Enid Bissett, proprietor of Enid Frocks, an upscale dress shop on New York City's West 57th Street. In 1921 Rosenthal left her upper Manhattan shop in the hands of her husband to become Bissett's partner. The Roaring Twenties had just begun, and women were beginning to feel less constrained than they had in the past. Previously women had shaped their figures by wearing corsets, tight-fitting inner garments that were painfully uncomfortable to wear. But after World War I they insisted on wearing tight-fitting dresses that could not possibly be worn over corsets. This so-called flapper look worked well on women with slim figures, but fuller-figured women needed bust support or their dresses simply did not fit right. The backless brassiere, invented in 1914 by Mary Phelps Jacobs (who later changed her name to Caresse Crosby) was no help, either, as it was basically two handkerchiefs sewn to ribbons. This bra merely flattened the breasts without supporting them, thus making the job of fitting most women into a form-hugging dress almost impossible.

Rosenthal and Bissett solved this problem by adding shoulder straps and a few tucks and folds to the Crosby to create cups, thus supporting and shaping the breasts without using a corset. At first they gave away their modified bras because they were inexpensive to make and they helped sell dresses, but when customers came back to buy the giveaways they realized they had a moneymaking idea on their hands. In 1923 Rosenthal, Bissett, and William Rosenthal founded the Maiden Form Brassiere Company (later known as Maidenform Inc.), with Rosenthal in charge of sales, finance, and public relations.

The company was tremendously successful from the start. In 1924, after one year in business, the company had outgrown its production facilities on West 57th Street and moved to a new factory in Bayonne, New Jersey. Rosenthal quickly realized that making a bra was not the same as making a dress. Whereas a dress was an individual creation best left in the hands of one seamstress, a bra was a more basic garment that could easily be made on an assembly line. Rosenthal convinced her husband, who was in charge of production, to implement a production system whereby each employee made a part of the brassiere, then passed it to another employee who added another part. As the flapper look faded in popularity and women wanted a more feminine look, Maidenform came out with bras in different cup sizes that would accentuate virtually any woman's figure. By 1938 the company was grossing more than $4 million yearly, and the Rosenthals moved into an 18-room mansion on Long Island. When Bissett's health failed in the 1940s, the Rosenthals bought her shares and assumed total control of the company.

In addition to being a skilled seamstress and fashion designer, Rosenthal was also an astute entrepreneur. During World War II she convinced government officials to make the production of bras a priority because they increased comfort and reduced fatigue for women working on assembly lines. In 1949 Maidenform began one of the most memorable, and successful, advertising campaigns in U.S. history. Rosenthal and Mary Filius, a copywriter for a New York advertising agency, created the "dream" series that ran for almost 20 years. Each ad pictured a young woman, clad from the waist up in nothing but a bra, with the caption "I dreamed I —— in my Maidenform bra." The ads pictured these women doing everything from dancing all night to putting out fires, and they immediately captured the attention of women across the country.

In 1958 Rosenthal became president of the company following the death of her husband. In 1959 she became chairman of the board and relinquished the presidency to her son-in-law. An untiring salesperson, she continued to tour the nation and the world, personally promoting Maidenform bras wherever she went. A stroke in 1966 forced her to quit traveling and to give up her business responsibilities. At the time of her stroke, the company employed 4,000 people, operated nine factories, and grossed $40 million in annual sales. She died on March 28, 1973, in New York City.

Further Reading

Altman, Linda Jacobs. *Women Inventors*. New York: Facts On File, 1997.

Vare, Ethlie Ann, and Greg Ptacek. *Mothers of Invention: From the Bra to the Bomb, Forgotten Women and Their Unforgettable Ideas*. New York: William Morrow and Co., 1988.

Rozelle, Pete

(1926–1996) *Entrepreneur in professional football*

In January of 1960, 33-year-old Pete Rozelle became commissioner of the National Football League (NFL). Particularly for his time, he was an unusually young man in a position of such prominence.

After almost 30 years in this role, however, Rozelle would eclipse even the most optimistic hopes of those who supported his selection as head of the NFL, having invented the Super Bowl, created *Monday Night Football* (the second longest-running prime time show in American television), and serving as a model for how to run a profitable professional sports league.

Alvin Ray Rozelle was born on March 1, 1926, in South Gate, California. Nicknamed "Pete" by one of his uncles, he grew up in the nearby towns of Lynwood and Compton southeast of Los Angeles, an avid fan of sports and the outdoors. Rozelle played basketball and tennis at Compton High School, served as the sports editor of the school's newspaper, and worked weekends for the *Long Beach Press Telegram.*

Following his graduation from high school, Rozelle served in the navy on a tanker in the Pacific Ocean during World War II. He returned from the war, attended Compton Junior College, and took a part-time job with the publicity department of the Los Angeles Rams football team, which had recently relocated from Cleveland and trained at the college. Rozelle transferred to the University of San Francisco where he worked as the athletic news director. Following his graduation from college, Rozelle was hired as the publicity director for the Rams. Rozelle remained with the Rams throughout the 1950s and eventually became the team's general manager, with the exception of a one-year stint working with a public relations firm that promoted the 1956 Olympics in Melbourne.

Rozelle's meteoric rise to becoming the lead executive of the NFL was sparked by the unexpected death of league commissioner Bert Bell in 1959. Team owners were unable to reach consensus on Bell's replacement until Rozelle was suggested as a compromise choice. Rozelle accepted the job at the remarkably young age of 33 and quickly set about expanding the position beyond its traditional role of mediating disputes among the league's notoriously headstrong owners. When he became commissioner, the NFL had only 12 teams and generated about $20 million in revenue. Each team negotiated its own television deal, and disparity between the league's large-market (New York Giants) and small-market teams (Green Bay Packers) was growing. This financial trouble—combined with competition from the newly formed American Football League (AFL)—threatened the survival of the NFL.

To strengthen the stability and competitiveness of the NFL and raise its prominence in the sports world, Rozelle led the drive to expand into new markets, such as Minneapolis and Dallas, and he successfully lobbied the U.S. Congress and President John F. Kennedy to receive an antitrust exemption that allowed the league to directly negotiate contracts with the major television networks. The NFL soon agreed to a $9.3 million, two-year deal with CBS to broadcast the league's games, with the revenue shared equally with each of the league's teams. Rozelle further burnished his reputation as a diplomatic but determined steward of the NFL in 1963 by suspending league stars Paul Hourning of the Green Bay Packers and Alex Karras of the Detroit Lions for a year when it was discovered that they had bet on football games, even though they did not wager on games involving their teams.

In 1966, Rozelle agreed to a merger with the rival AFL. Although the NFL still attracted greater crowds, television revenue, and player talent, Rozelle viewed the continuing and growing competition with the AFL as potentially debilitating for the NFL. The merger was fully implemented in 1970 under the NFL name, with the former leagues constituting separate National and American Conferences. Before the full implementation, Rozelle created a championship game between the champions of the two leagues, which came to be called the Super Bowl (Rozelle reportedly disliked the name, which was suggested by AFL commissioner Lamar Hunt). Although Super Bowl I failed to sell out, it was broadcast on both CBS and NBC, which led to increased promotion of professional football. Within a few years, the Super Bowl had become the most watched sports event of the year and a national institution.

Always seeking ways to more fully and effectively promote the NFL, Rozelle introduced the concept of a weeknight football game. The foundering ABC television network added what became known as *Monday Night Football* to its prime-time lineup in 1970, and it remained a money-making staple of the network for over three decades, before moving to ESPN, which like ABC, is owned by the Walt Disney Company. Largely as a result of the revolution in negotiating television contracts and the Super Bowl, the NFL under Rozelle became the leading professional sports league, with regular season games typically attracting more viewers than playoff games in other sports. When Rozelle—who was inducted into the Pro Football Hall of Fame in 1985—arrived as commissioner, the NFL had 12 teams averaging about $1 million in value. When he left office, there were 28 teams averaging about $100 million in value. The 1960 NFL total revenue of approximately $20 million rose to over $3 billion just a few years after he retired.

Rozelle's successful reign as NFL commissioner did include some high-profile setbacks. When President Kennedy was assassinated on November 22, 1963, NFL teams were only two days away from playing their scheduled games. After much consultation and debate, Rozelle gave the go-ahead to play the games, despite criticism that the games should have been postponed or cancelled due to the mourning of the nation. He later said of this, "It was the most regrettable decision I ever made." Rozelle also endured strained relationships with some owners, none more so than with Al Davis of the Raiders, who successfully battled with Rozelle to move his team from Oakland to Los Angeles.

Rozelle's profound influence on the NFL and professional sports in the United States was recognized during his tenure as commissioner. *Sports Illustrated* named Rozelle its 1963 "Sportsman of the Year," explaining, "Perfectly cast in the role of the modern executive, Rozelle is a man who hardly ever raises his voice . . . Rozelle's aptitude for conciliation no longer deceives people into thinking he is a bootlicker, the puppet of string-pulling owners who have been described as 'the most contrary bunch of individualists you ever saw.'" In a *Time* magazine article on the 100 most influential people of the 20th century, the writer Michael Lewis echoed this sentiment 35 years later, noting of his vision and skill, "Each year that Rozelle presided over the NFL, another owner published his autobiography explaining how he was the visionary behind the rise of pro football. Each year Rozelle

laughed and let him enjoy his press. Rozelle seems to have been the sort of spectral tycoon who took his satisfaction in managing other people without their knowing it."

After nearly 30 years as commissioner of the NFL, Pete Rozelle retired in 1989 and moved to southern California with his second wife, Carrie. He died of brain cancer at the age of 70 on December 6, 1996. Three years later, Rozelle was named the 20th century's most powerful person in sports by the *Sporting News*.

Further Reading

Carter, Bob. "Rozelle Made NFL What It Is Today." ESPN Classic. Available online. URL: http://espn.go.com/classic/biography/s/rozelle_pete.html. Downloaded on September 1, 2009.

Fortunato, John. *Commissioner: The Legacy of Pete Rozelle.* Lanham, Md.: Taylor Trade Publishing, 2006.

Lewis, Michael. "Pete Rozelle." Time 100. Available online. URL: http://www.time.com/time/time100/builder/profile/rozelle.html. Downloaded on September 1, 2009.

"Pete Rozelle." Academy of Achievement. Available online. URL: http://www.achievement.org/autodoc/page/roz0bio-1. Downloaded on September 1, 2009. Available online. URL: Downloaded on September 1, 2009.

Rudkin, Margaret Fogarty
(1897–1967) *founder of Pepperidge Farm*

By the early 20th century, store-bought bread was readily available in cities and towns across the United States. The mass production techniques that commercial bakers used to bake thousands of loaves per day, however, left bread tasting rather plain. One of the first companies to make commercially baked bread tastier was Pepperidge Farm. The woman responsible for making Pepperidge Farm a commercial success, Margaret Rudkin, was a former New York City socialite who took up baking bread as a way to make ends meet during the Great Depression.

Rudkin was born Margaret Fogarty on September 14, 1897, in New York City. The occupations of her parents, Joseph and Margaret, are unknown, but their economic situation seems to have bordered on poverty, because for the first 12 years of her life she lived with her parents and four siblings in her grandmother's townhouse in Manhattan. When her grandmother died in 1909, she moved with her family to Flatbush in Brooklyn, New York. Six years later she graduated from high school and was hired as a bookkeeper for a Long Island bank. In 1919 she went to work as a receptionist for McClure, Jones & Company, a stock brokerage firm in Manhattan. Four years later, she married Henry Rudkin, a partner in the firm, with whom she had three children. Several years later the Rudkins bought 125 acres in Fairfield, Connecticut, and built a mansion on the estate they named Pepperidge Farm. During the late 1920s, they were members of the New York "horsey set," and they occasionally hosted hunts, horse shows, and polo matches at their estate.

Although Henry Rudkin's business soared during the stock market boom of the Roaring Twenties, it crashed with the onset of the Great Depression. This downturn, coupled with a serious polo accident that left him unable to work for six months, almost resulted in the Rudkins' economic ruin. It fell to Margaret Rudkin to dismiss the servants, sell the polo ponies and other extravagances, and make ends meet by turning the estate into a moneymaking proposition. At first she tried raising apples (a commodity in great demand with street-corner peddlers during the Great Depression) and turkeys. In 1937 she hit upon the idea of starting a bakery. Although her first few experiments failed miserably, one day she finally baked four loaves of stone-ground whole wheat bread that were truly delicious.

Rudkin's first customer was her own grocer in Fairfield. Because she used fresh ingredients like real butter and whole milk, her bread tasted much better (and cost far more) than other store-bought bread, and despite its high price, demand increased to the point that she had to move her operation out of the kitchen and into the garage.

At this point she also began baking white bread made from unbleached flour. She eventually convinced Charles & Company, a specialty food store in New York City, to buy 24 loaves of white bread every day. This brought Pepperidge Farm, as she called her business, to the attention of the New York newspapers, which praised the bread's delicious taste. After *Reader's Digest,* a worldwide magazine with a circulation in the millions, ran a favorable article in 1939 about Rudkin's "bread de luxe," orders began pouring in from all over the United States and Canada. In 1940 she took out a loan and moved the bakery from the garage to a former auto salesroom in Norwalk, Connecticut, and within a year Pepperidge Farm was baking almost 1,000 loaves per week. Seven years later, Pepperidge Farm moved into a state-of-the-art facility in Norwalk, then added another one in Pennsylvania in 1949 and a third bakery in Illinois in 1953. In the 1950s the company began running advertisements on national television, with Rudkin playing herself in the ads. By 1960 the company also sold frozen pastries and cookies, employed more than 1,000 workers, and did an annual business of $32 million.

In 1960 Rudkin sold Pepperidge Farm to the Campbell Soup Company for $28 million in Campbell stock. She also became a director of Campbell Soup and stayed on as president of Pepperidge Farm. In 1962 she relinquished this position to her son William and became chairwoman of the board. One of her first accomplishments in this role was to write a best-selling cookbook, which included a history of the business; the book first came out in 1963 and was reprinted seven years later. She retired in 1966 and died on June 1, 1967, in New Haven, Connecticut.

Further Reading
Gill, Brendan. *Late Bloomers.* New York: Artisan, 1996.

Lavine, Sigmund A. *Famous Merchants.* New York: Dodd, Mead, 1965.

Rudkin, Margaret. *The Margaret Rudkin Pepperidge Farm Cookbook.* New York: Galahad Books, 1992, reprint.

S

Sanders, Harland David (Colonel Sanders)
(1890–1980) *founder of Kentucky Fried Chicken*

Few people would be surprised to hear that, by the late 1970s, the most recognized figure in the world was Mickey Mouse. Most people might be shocked to learn, however, that the second-most recognized figure was Colonel Sanders, the inventor and enthusiastic spokesman for Kentucky Fried Chicken. And although Mickey embarked on his career as a world figure at a relatively young age, the colonel did not begin his until after retiring from a long career as a restaurateur.

Sanders was born on September 9, 1890, in Henryville, Indiana. His parents, Wilbert and Margaret, were farmers. His father died when he was young, and at age 10 he went to work as a farmhand for $2 per month. When his mother remarried two years later, he left home for good. From 1902 to 1929 he worked successively as a farmhand and streetcar conductor in Indiana, a soldier in Cuba, a railroad section hand and fireman in Alabama, a lawyer in a justice of the peace court in Arkansas, a ferryboat operator on the Ohio River, a traveling salesman of insurance and tires, and a service station manager in Kentucky. In 1908 he married Josephine King with whom he had three children.

In 1930 Sanders bought a Shell service station on the outskirts of Corbin, Kentucky. The station was situated on U.S. Highway 25, the main route connecting the Midwest and Florida, and he did a booming business. In addition to servicing automobiles, he also served hot lunches to hungry customers on the dining table in his own living quarters adjacent to the service station. His lunches became so popular that he purchased the 143-seat restaurant and motel across the highway from his service station, renaming the restaurant Sanders' Cafe. The café's specialty and most popular menu item was fried chicken seasoned with a mix of herbs and spices that Sanders had developed himself. In 1935 the governor of Kentucky commissioned him an honorary colonel for his contributions to the state's cuisine.

In 1939 Sanders discovered that preparing his fried chicken in a pressure cooker greatly reduced cooking time while also making the chicken more flavorful and moist. He continued to experiment with the blend of seasonings until 1952, when he finally hit upon a combination of eleven herbs and spices that made the chicken, in Sanders's words, "finger lickin' good." Meanwhile, in 1949 he married Claudia Ledington, his most trusted manager, having divorced his first wife two years earlier.

In 1955 Sanders discovered that the construction of Interstate 75 around Corbin would put his café and motel several miles from an exit. Realizing that this meant the end of his profitable business, he auctioned off the café and motel; unfortunately, he received just enough to pay all his bills, leaving him with little more than a monthly Social Security check for income. Undaunted, the 65-year-old Sanders decided to franchise his fried chicken recipe. Having already licensed one franchise the year before—to a friend who operated a restaurant in Salt Lake City, Utah—in 1955 he set off in his white Cadillac with a pressure cooker and a big bag of his secret spice mix. Nattily attired in a white double-breasted suit and a black string tie, and sporting white hair and a white goatee, he began calling on restaurant owners across the country. He took his pressure cooker and spices into the restaurant, fried up a batch of "Colonel Sanders' Kentucky Fried Chicken," and served it to the owner and employees. If the owner liked the taste, and most of them did, Sanders offered a handshake deal: Pay me four cents per chicken you sell and buy your spices from me, and the franchise is yours. The going was slow at first; it took him two years to establish five franchises. But three years later that number had grown to 200, and three years after that to 600.

By then Sanders was in his seventies and ready to retire, so in 1964 he sold his business to John Y. Brown, Jr., and Jack Massey for $2 million. He also agreed to make public appearances for the new owners for $40,000 per year. Brown and Massey turned the loosely scattered franchises into the Kentucky Fried Chicken (KFC) chain, using Sanders's alter ego, "the Colonel," to boost the chain's recognition. Sanders relished his new role; the greatest joy of his later years was to appear in public, whether for pay or for charity, as "the Colonel." He logged almost 4 million miles over the next 16 years, making appearances at new KFC restaurants around the country and the world and visiting established ones to check up on how things were tasting. By the time of his death on December 16, 1980, in Louisville, Kentucky, he had become one of the most recognized celebrities in the world.

Although Sanders went to great lengths to portray "the Colonel" as the very soul of southern hospitality, he himself had a quick temper and a penchant for violence. While a justice of the peace court lawyer, he had once gotten into a fistfight in the courtroom with a client over nonpayment of Sanders's fee, and in the early 1930s he became involved in an argument with a rival service station owner that led to a shootout in which one person died. On the other hand, Sanders was a generous man who throughout his life contributed unselfishly of his time and money to a number of charities, especially those that benefited children and alcoholics.

Further Reading

Gill, Brendan. *Late Bloomers*. New York: Artisan, 1996.

Pearce, John. *The Colonel: The Captivating Biography of the Dynamic Founder of a Fast-Food Empire*. Garden City, N.Y.: Doubleday, 1982.

Sanders, Harland. *Life as I Have Known It Has Been Finger Lickin' Good*. Carol Stream, Ill.: Creation House, 1974.

Sanders, Margaret. *The Colonel's Secret: Eleven Herbs and a Spicy Daughter*. Wellington, Fla.: Royal Book Mfg., 1996.

Sarnoff, David

(1891–1971) *entrepreneur in broadcast communication*

As a boy in a poor village in Russia, David Sarnoff spent countless hours preparing to become a rabbi. But soon after immigrating to the United States, he began venturing into the virgin world of telecommunications, and he would eventually become credited as the leading visionary and pioneer in both radio and television industries. When Sarnoff died in 1971, his obituary took up nearly the entire front page of the *New York Times*, which noted of his remarkable contribution to American business and culture, "He was not an inventor, nor was he a scientist. But he was a man of astounding vision who was able to see with remarkable clarity the possibilities of harnessing the electron."

David Sarnoff was born in the village of Uzlian, near Minsk, Russia, on February 27, 1891. His father was a trader and his mother was the daughter of a rabbi who came from a long line of scholars. Sarnoff recalled of his boyhood that prestige was not based on money but on the "possession of knowledge." When Sarnoff was four years old, his father left for the United States in hopes of earning enough money to help the rest of the family join him. Young Sarnoff spent the next five years living with his mother's uncle, who schooled David in study of the Talmud—the Jewish book

President of RCA and chairman of the board of NBC, David Sarnoff *(New York Harris & Ewing Collection/Library of Congress)*

of law, ethics, customs, and history—for 15 hours a day. Though he disliked the rigor and loneliness of this study, Sarnoff credited it with strengthening his intellect and ability to analyze.

At the age of nine, Sarnoff left with his mother to join his father in the United States. Sarnoff's mother was concerned that they would not be able to observe strict kosher dietary laws on the long journey, so she prepared a large amount of food. When Sarnoff noticed the food being stowed in the ship's hold, he became afraid that he would never see it again. He took a dangerous jump down to retrieve it before a Russian sailor rescued Sarnoff from danger, praising the boy's intrepid determination and foreshadowing the boy's future in his new country, saying, "You'll do all right in America." But once reunited in New York City, the Sarnoff family struggled because Abraham Sarnoff was suffering from tuberculosis. Sarnoff worked selling newspapers and singing in synagogues to aid the

family, and by his early teens he was working full time as an office boy for the American Marconi communications company.

Sarnoff worked his way up the Marconi ladder quickly, working as a telegraph operator, assistant engineer, and becoming at age 18 the youngest manager in the entire company. In 1912, Sarnoff was among the few wireless operators who reported the news of the *Titanic's* sinking to the people across the United States, though many historians dismiss as false self-promotion his claim that he did so by working three consecutive sleepless days, and some dispute his claim that he worked as a wireless operator at that time in his career. In 1919, Marconi's assets were taken over by General Electric (GE), which used them to create the Radio Corporation of America (RCA). Demonstrating his ease and ability working with both the scientific and business operations of communications industry, Sarnoff quickly ascended in RCA, helping develop the plans, technology, and programming for radio before becoming general manager and playing a key role in the 1926 formation of RCA's National Broadcast Company (NBC).

In 1927, Sarnoff joined the board of RCA, beginning a tenure that would continue until his retirement more than 40 years later. At the age of 39—remarkably young by the standards of the time—Sarnoff became president of RCA. Over the next two years, Sarnoff fought tirelessly and largely successfully to counter U.S. government lawsuits against GE and RCA on monopoly and restraint of trade charges that many viewed could have destroyed RCA. The result of this conflict was the divestiture of RCA from GE and the licensing of RCA's patents to competitors.

Prior to becoming president of RCA and throughout the first decade in this role, Sarnoff was deeply involved in developing television. He was intrigued by the theoretical concept of television dating back to 1910, but once in a position of authority with RCA he pursued what he believed was an exciting and potentially transformative invention. In 1928, he met with the engineer Vladimir Zwyorkin, who worked at Westinghouse on television technology on his own time. Sarnoff agreed to underwrite a research and development team led by Zwyorkin. Though the project took much more time and money than Sarnoff anticipated—and was delayed by patent disputes, particularly with television research pioneer Philo Farnsworth—the technology to create a primitive form of television broadcasting was available by the end of the 1930s.

Sarnoff debuted the first television broadcast at the 1939 World's Fair in New York City. Introducing the broadcast, Sarnoff presciently announced, "Now we add sight to sound . . . It is with a feeling of humbleness that I come to this moment of announcing the birth in this country of a new art so important in its implications that it is bound to affect all society. It is an art, which shines like a torch of hope in the troubled world. It is a creative force, which we must learn to utilize for the benefit of all mankind. This miracle of engineering skill which one day will bring the world to the home also brings a new American industry to serve man's material welfare . . . [Television] will

become an important factor in American economic life."

Although the race to advance television would be slowed during the 1940s by World War II, Sarnoff continued to play a pivotal role in American life. During World War II, Sarnoff turned his attention to radar, sonar, and other technologies that would help the United States fight and win the war. He served as a consultant to General Dwight Eisenhower and was named by Eisenhower as a brigadier general. This was enormously gratifying to Sarnoff, who had been refused commission in naval communications during World War I ostensibly because his role as a wireless operator was critical to the war effort, though Sarnoff suspected the rejection was based on anti-Semitism. Sarnoff's appointment by Eisenhower earned him the nickname, "The General," which he was proudly and regularly referred to for the rest of his life.

Television and other technology, such as FM radio, satellites, rocketry, and computers, remained a central passion for the remainder of Sarnoff's career at RCA. Often his desire to succeed resulted in long-standing legal battles over patents (such as with the development of color television and FM radio), ruined relationships, and a personal reputation among many rivals as a ruthless businessman. Sarnoff reflected this sentiment, explaining, "Competition brings out the best in products and the worst in men."

Sarnoff retired as chairman of the board of RCA in 1970, and he died of cardiac arrest on December 12, 1971. He was survived by his wife of 54 years, Lizette, and their three children. The recipient of 27 honorary degrees, including doctorates from Columbia University and New York University, Sarnoff is buried in Valhalla, New York.

Further Reading

"Big Dream, Small Screen." PBS. Available online. URL: http://www.pbs.org/wgbh/amex/technology/bigdream/masarnoff.html. Downloaded on September 1, 2009.

"David Sarnoff." Time 100. Available online. URL: http://www.time.com/time/time100/builder/profile/sarnoff.html. Downloaded on September 1, 2009.

"Sarnoff, David." Museum of Broadcast Communications. Available online. URL: http://www.museum.

tv/archives/etv/S/htmlS/sarnoffdavi/sarnoffdavi.htm. Downloaded on September 1, 2009.

Stashower, Daniel. *The Boy Genius and the Mogul: The Untold Story of Television.* New York: Broadway Books, 2002.

Schwab, Charles

(1937–   ) *entrepreneur in investment services*

The dramatic increase in the number of people involved in owning stock that occurred in the last portion of the 20th century was due to many factors, including the development of brokerage houses and the advancement of online trading. Few contributed more to these factors than Charles Schwab, the founder and chief executive officer of the discount brokerage Charles Schwab Corporation.

Charles Robert Schwab, Jr., was born in Sacramento, California, on July 29, 1937. He grew up in Sacramento and Santa Barbara, California. His father, Robert, was a lawyer, who Charles later recalled, often led family discussions "about how limited resources were." Schwab had many jobs as a youth, including raising chickens, selling ice cream from a pushcart, bagging walnuts, and working on a beet farm. He attended Catholic schools and excelled in math and science but struggled with reading and writing as a result of having dyslexia, which was not diagnosed until he was an adult. He graduated with a degree in economics from Stanford in 1959 and earned his MBA from Stanford Graduate School of Business two years later.

In 1963 Schwab and two partners launched an investment newsletter called *Investment Indicator.* Over the next few years, the newsletter attracted over 3,000 subscribers and helped Schwab strengthen his reputation as a mutual fund manager. The success of the newsletter and the firm Mitchell, Morse, and Schwab led to the creation of the Investment Indicators mutual fund, which was soon the largest mutual fund in California. However, Schwab occasionally overlooked administrative details that led to problems and even legal trouble. In addition, other professional endeavors, including a wild animal drive-through park called Congoland and a San Francisco music festival that failed to connect to contemporary musical tastes, were failures.

Frustrated with his setbacks and under strain from the breakup of his first marriage (which produced three children), Schwab used $100,000 borrowed from his uncle Bill in the early 1970s to start First Commander Corporation, a brokerage firm in San Francisco. In 1974, he changed its name to Charles Schwab & Company and it became the first discount brokerage firm, based on the belief—soon to become very popular—that stock market investing should be accessible to everyone.

In 1977, Schwab opened a branch in Seattle, which started a nationwide expansion of Charles Schwab offices beyond California's borders. He also started offering client information seminars and soon began implementing advanced systems of automated transaction and record-keeping that helped spur growth and encourage transitions into further technological efficiency of upcoming years. Schwab enjoyed even more dramatic growth in the 1980s and into the 1990s, raising the total number of accounts from 500,000 in 1983 to over 2 million in 1992. His reputation for providing straight, sound, and understandable advice was boosted with the 1985 publication of his book *How to Be Your Own Stock Broker.*

Schwab sold the company to Bank of America for $57 million in 1983 and purchased it back in 1987 for $280 million. Schwab continued remarkable growth and prosperity spurred by the deregulation of brokerage commissions and the online investment craze of the 1990s. Still crafting the image of the investment everyman with frequent personal appearances in advertisements and a "Talk to Chuck" slogan, Schwab's company managed over $1 trillion in assets by 2008. Late in 2008, Schwab was ranked by *Forbes* magazine as the 55th richest American, with a net worth of over $6.2 billion.

In 2008, Schwab stepped down as chief executive officer of his firm, though he remains its chair. He lives with his second wife, Helen, with whom he has two children, in Atherton, California.

Further Reading

Fishman, Charles. "Face Time with Charles Schwab." *Fast Company.* Available online. URL: http://www.

fastcompany.com/magazine/48/facetime.html. Downloaded on September 1, 2009.

Kador, John. *Charles Schwab: How One Company Beat Wall Street and Reinvented the Brokerage Industry.* New York: Wiley, 2005.

Zweig, Jason. "We Talked to Chuck." *Money* magazine. Available online. URL: http://money.cnn.com/magazines/moneymag/moneymag_archive/2007/01/01/8397411/index.htm. Downloaded on September 1, 2009.

Sears, Richard Warren

(1864–1914) *founder of Sears, Roebuck and Company*

At the end of the 20th century, Sears, Roebuck & Company was the largest retailer of general merchandise in the world. In addition to hundreds of department stores throughout North and South America, Sears, Roebuck owned Allstate Insurance, the brokerage firm of Dean Witter Reynolds, the real-estate firm Coldwell Banker, and Discover Card. The company has grown tremendously since its founding by Richard Sears, who got his start in retailing by selling surplus watches by mail.

Sears was born on December 7, 1864, in Stewartville, Minnesota. His father, James, was a blacksmith, and his mother, Eliza, was a homemaker. When Sears was 14 years old, his parents bought a nearby farm, but that same year his father became too ill to work and the task of running the farm fell to Sears. When his father died two years later, Sears went to work for the St. Paul and Duluth Railroad, and over the next six years he worked successively as a station agent, auditor, and freight depot manager.

In 1886 Sears got into the watch business. A merchant in North Redwood, Minnesota, where Sears was stationed, received a shipment of gold watches he had not ordered from a manufacturer who wanted the merchant to sell them on a commission basis. When the merchant tried to send them back, Sears took them instead and sold the watches to his fellow freight agents, making a significant profit. He was so enamored by this success that he quit the railroad, moved to Minneapolis, and started the R. W. Sears Watch Company, a mail-order company. By buying surplus watches and selling them at a discount, he made enough money in two years to be able to retire. He sold his company for $100,000 to an employee, Alvah Curtis Roebuck, and bought some land in rural Iowa where he hoped to live quietly. But at age 28 Sears was too young to retire, and within a year he was buying and selling farm mortgages. Then he started a mail-order watch and jewelry company, which he also sold to Roebuck. Finally, in 1891, he moved to Chicago, Illinois, where he and Roebuck formed Sears, Roebuck & Company.

At its founding Sears, Roebuck did all of its business by mail order. At the time Montgomery Ward had been in the business for almost 20 years and was doing more than $2 million in sales annually. Undaunted, Sears set out to beat the mail-order giant at its own game. Rather than grow slowly like Montgomery Ward did, after only three years (and in the middle of the panic of 1893, the

Along with Montgomery Ward, Richard Sears (shown here) helped popularize catalog shopping. *(Library of Congress)*

second-worst depression in U.S. history) Sears was putting out a catalog with more than 500 pages and thousands of items. He took business away from Montgomery Ward by undercutting the giant's prices, but he was selling at such a low profit margin that he had to scramble to pay his bills. In 1895 he married Anna Meckstroth with whom he had four children; that same year Roebuck, fearing that the company was about to collapse, sold his interest to Sears. Roebuck's departure was a temporary blessing in disguise; Sears soon became partners with Julius Rosenwald, a successful clothier and administrative genius, and Rosenwald's brother-in-law Aaron Nusbaum, who would sell out to Sears and Rosenwald in 1901.

While Rosenwald concentrated on daily operations, Sears focused on marketing. He eventually filled the catalog, which he wrote mostly by himself, with more than 100,000 items, then promoted it as the "Nation's Wishbook." Writing his own copy, he placed advertisements in every publication he could buy space in, from national magazines to church bulletins. He offered rebates, held sweepstakes, and started a pyramid scheme in an effort to get customers to recruit their neighbors and friends. He established a "send no money" policy whereby customers could examine a product in their homes without obligation, then return it if they were not completely satisfied. He even allowed customers to order merchandise without filling out an order form; all they had to do was write him a letter, telling him in their own words what they wanted to buy, in much the same way that a child writes to Santa Claus. It all added up to success; by 1900, Sears, Roebuck was selling more than $10 million in merchandise annually and had overtaken Montgomery Ward as the number-one mail-order firm in the United States.

In 1907 the country entered another economic downturn, and although it was not as serious as the panic of 1893, it cost Sears his position in his company. Characteristically, he hoped to weather the storm by expanding, as he had in 1894, but Rosenwald insisted on cutting back on expenses, especially advertising. In the ensuing power struggle, Sears was forced to resign the presidency in 1908. He sold his interest in the company for $10 million and retired to his farm in Waukesha, Wisconsin, where he died on September 28, 1914.

Further Reading

Asher, Frederick. *Richard Warren Sears, Icon of Inspiration: Fable and Fact About the Founder and Spiritual Genius of Sears, Roebuck & Company.* New York: Vantage Press, 1997.

Sears, Roebuck and Company. *The 1902 Edition of the Sears, Roebuck Catalogue.* New York: Gramercy Books, 2000, reprint.

Wren, Daniel A., and Ronald G. Greenwood. *Management Innovators: The People and Ideas that Have Shaped Modern Business.* New York: Oxford University Press, 1998.

Sholes, Christopher Latham
(1819–1890) *inventor of the typewriter*

Between 1860 and 1890, a number of devices were invented that greatly enhanced communications and business practices. One of these devices was the typewriter, invented by Christopher Sholes. Not only did the typewriter make business letters faster to produce and easier to read, but also it opened the doors for women to gain employment in the commercial world as typists and secretaries.

Sholes was born on February 14, 1819, in Mooresburg, Pennsylvania. His father, Orrin, was a cabinetmaker, and his mother, whose name is not known, was a homemaker. As a young boy he moved with his family to nearby Danville where he grew up. At age 14 he became an apprentice printer for the Danville newspaper. Four years later he moved to Green Bay, Wisconsin, to join the staff of the Wisconsin Territory's legislative newspaper. Two years after that be became editor of the *Wisconsin Inquirer* in Madison, and a year later, in 1841, he moved to Southport (modern Kenosha) where he and Michael Frank started the *Southport Telegraph.* In 1851 he married Mary Jane McKinney with whom he had 10 children. In 1860 he moved to Milwaukee to become editor of the *Milwaukee Sentinel.* Meanwhile, he had become an important voice for the Democratic Party in Wisconsin as both a journalist and a state legislator, and in 1861 President Abraham Lincoln appointed him customs collector for the port of Milwaukee.

Sholes had always been an inventive sort, but his newspaper positions left him with little time to invent. As customs collector, however, he suddenly had both the time and the money to pursue his avocation. He became partners in a machine shop with Samuel W. Soule, and they began tinkering with various mechanical devices for printing. One such device printed page numbers on books, which they patented in 1864. When a third inventor, Carlos Glidden, saw the page-numbering machine, he suggested to Sholes that it could be converted to produce letters as well as numbers, and he told him about an article in *Scientific American* magazine that described a "pterotype," a letter-printing machine devised by the Englishman John Pratt. In fact, other hand-typing machines had been invented before Pratt's pterotype, but none of them, including Pratt's, could type faster than a person could write by hand.

Using the information in the article as a starting point, by 1867 Sholes had invented a "typewriter," as he called it, that produced letters much faster than a person could by hand. He received a patent the following year. By modern standards, Sholes's machine was rather primitive; it was made out of wood, used piano keys for the keyboard, and could produce only capital letters. However, it did include several devices that for many years were standard features on typewriters: typebars, arranged in a carriage so that the letters strike the paper at dead center; an inked ribbon, for making a carbon impression of the letter on the paper; the escapement, which spaces letters by moving the carriage after a letter is struck; and the cylinder, with separate mechanisms for spacing lines and returning the carriage at the end of a line. And instead of arranging the letters in alphabetical order on the keyboard, which jammed the typebars together when the keys were struck rapidly, Sholes's keyboard arranged them in the order in which they now appear on a modern keyboard; for example, instead of having the top row read "ABCDEFGHIJ," Sholes's top row read "QWERTYUIOP." Although inventors have devised arrangements of letters that they claim lead to faster typing speeds and greater accuracy, Sholes's arrangement became standard on American English typewriters, word processors, and computer keyboards and remained that way into the 21st century.

Unfortunately, Sholes lacked the capital and the entrepreneurial expertise to mass-produce and market the typewriter. Five years after receiving the patent, he had manufactured only 50 machines, most of which were given away for publicity purposes. In 1873 he sold his patent rights to the Remington Arms Company, a manufacturer of firearms, for $12,000; the company later marketed Sholes's invention as the Remington Typewriter. However, for the rest of his life he made and patented improvements to his original invention; the most important improvement came in 1878, when he added a shift key so that both upper and lower case letters could be produced. He died on February 17, 1890, in Milwaukee.

Further Reading

"Christopher Sholes," National Inventors Hall of Fame. Available online. URL:http://www.invent.org/hall_of_fame/68.html. Downloaded on July 6, 2009.

Foulke, Arthur Toye. *Mr. Typewriter: A Biography of Christopher Latham Sholes.* Boston: Christopher Publishing House, 1961.

Romano, Frank J. *Machine Writing and Typesetting: The Story of Sholes and Mergenthaler and the Invention of the Typewriter and the Linotype.* Salem, N.H.: GAMA, 1986.

Siebert, Muriel

(1932–   ) *entrepreneur in high finance*

Not only was Muriel Siebert the first woman to own a seat on the New York Stock Exchange, but she was also the only woman member of the exchange for 10 years. She has made shrewd use of various unrelated developments, such as government deregulation of brokerage commissions and the incredible popularity of online trading, to position her firm as one of the top three online discount brokers between 1998 and 2000.

Siebert was born in 1932, in Cleveland, Ohio. Her father, Irwin, was a dentist, and her mother, Margaret, was a homemaker. In 1949 she enrolled in Western Reserve University (known today as Case Western University) with the intention of becoming an accountant, but she was forced to drop out after three years when her father became too ill to work. In 1954 she moved to New York City where she eventually landed a job with Bache & Company as a trainee research analyst. Three years later she took a job with the Utilities and Industries Management Corporation, but she left in 1958 to return to stock analysis. In 1961 she became a partner at Stearns & Company, a position she held at two other firms over the next six years.

By 1967 Siebert had proven to herself that she was ready to do business on Wall Street on her own. At the time, there were no women members of the New York Stock Exchange, so in addition to coming up with the $445,000 it cost to purchase a seat on the exchange, she had to find a male member to sponsor her. The first nine she approached turned her down, but the tenth agreed, and in 1967 she became the first woman to own a seat on the exchange. Two years later she formed her own firm, Muriel Siebert & Company. When the Securities and Exchange Commission deregulated brokerage commissions in 1975, Siebert's was one of the first firms to offer discount rates to the general public. The reaction to this move angered a number of old-guard Wall Streeters, who were particularly incensed by a full-page ad featuring her cutting a $100 bill in half. The public, however, loved it, and within two years Siebert's company was doing a booming business in discount trading.

In 1977 Siebert put her company in a blind trust to become the superintendent of banking for the state of New York. She took this position at a time when the nation was mired in stagflation, rising interest rates in a downward-spiraling economy. To prevent New York's banks from going under during this difficult period, she forced banks on the brink of insolvency to merge or reorganize. New York bankers learned to resent her heavy-handed tactics, but they had to admit she had kept them all out of bankruptcy, thus preserving the integrity of the New York banking system.

In 1983 Siebert returned to the active management of her firm. She was a vocal opponent of junk bonds, which had been made popular by MICHAEL ROBERT MILKEN, among others, and she kept her firm from trading in them at a time when they were popular in the investment community. Consequently, when the bottom began falling out of the junk bond market in the late 1980s,

Siebert's firm escaped from the resulting financial debacle relatively unscathed while some of her tonier competitors went under. She also benefited from government regulations that made it easier for businesses owned by women or minorities to thrive. By 1990, Muriel Siebert & Company was doing so well that she formed the Siebert Entrepreneurial Philanthropic Plan (SEPP); using some of the commissions from deals made possible by this government-enforced affirmative action climate, she contributed more than $5 million to charity through SEPP.

In 1996 Siebert began taking her firm in several new directions. The most unusual move came that same year, when she merged her firm with J. Michaels, a chain of furniture stores, to form Siebert Financial Corporation, a public company. She liquidated J. Michaels' assets, then used the proceeds to form a partnership with Napoleon Brandford and Suzanne Shanks, called Siebert Brandford Shanks & Company, as a division of Siebert Financial. This division specialized in trading municipal bonds, an area in which Muriel Siebert & Company had been weak. And in 2001 she launched the Women's Financial Network at Siebert, an attempt to capture a greater share of the business generated by the growing number of women investors. The online program is geared toward educating women about how to better manage their finances, which investment products are right for them, and how to manage the financial issues related to marriage, divorce, and the care of children and the elderly.

In recent years Siebert, dubbed the "First Lady of Finance," has continued the active leadership of her firm. A 1994 inductee into the National Women's Hall of Fame, Siebert has also been the recipient of 18 honorary doctorate degrees. She is a frequent public speaker whose belief in the value of inclusiveness in business is reflected in her statement, "The men at the top of industry and government should be more willing to risk sharing leadership with women and minority members who are not merely clones of their white male buddies. In these fast-changing times we need the different viewpoints and experiences, we need the enlarged talent bank. The real risk lies in continuing to do things the way they've always been done."

Further Reading

MacLean, Barbara Hutmacher. *I Can't Do What? Voices of Pathfinding Women.* Ventura, Calif.: Pathfinder Publishing, 1997.

"Muriel Siebert, Wall Street's "First Woman of Finance" Named to U.S. Business Hall of Fame by Junior Achievement." Reuters. Available online. URL: http://www.reuters.com/article/pressRelease/idUS155811+04-Mar-2009+BW20090304. Downloaded on July 6, 2009.

Simmons, Russell

(1957–   ) *entrepreneur in music recording industry*

The emergence of hip-hop as a musical, fashion, and cultural force in the United States has been among the most significant aspects of youth and urban life over the past few decades. In the center of this profound change in American society has been Russell Simmons, who was described in a 2004 profile on *60 Minutes* as, "the businessman who took hip-hop music from the inner city streets of New York to the shopping malls of Middle America."

Russell Wendell Simmons was born in the Queens section of New York City on October 4, 1957. He grew up in the predominantly black, working-class Hollis neighborhood, the second of three sons born to his parents, Daniel and Evelyn, who both worked for New York City, his father as a teacher and his mother as a recreation director. He later explained that he dabbled in some street hustling activity, including selling marijuana, but he was able to avoid serious violence or arrest. Simmons graduated from high school and attended the City College of New York, where he studied sociology.

While still in college, Simmons began promoting music shows at clubs throughout the Harlem and Queens sections of New York City. Though these efforts met with mixed results, Simmons was encouraged to continue by his mother and his promotion partner, Curtis Walker, an early rap performer who later gained renown as Kurtis Blow. Simmons served as his manager and soon dropped out of college to establish Rush Produc-

tions. In 1982, Simmons began representing his younger brother Joseph, who was an aspiring rapper in a group Simmons branded as Run DMC. Within three years, Run DMC was among the most popular rap acts in the world. Energized by his success, Simmons partnered with young music aficionado Rick Rubin in 1984 to form Def Jam Records. With Run DMC, as well as other enormously successful artists, including LL Cool J, the Beastie Boys, and Public Enemy as part of the label, Def Jam—which derived its name from the hip-hop slang meaning cool, freewheeling music—became very lucrative and the most important record company in the exploding field of rap and hip-hop.

In 1985 Simmons took an key step in what would become his expansive entertainment empire by producing the film *Krush Groove*. Though the

Russell Simmons at Emory University *(Photo by Brett Weinstein/Used under a Creative Commons license)*

movie was nearly unanimously panned by critics, it was a popular success. Made for only $3 million, it grossed over $20 million and helped launch the careers of the Def Jam acts featured in it. Simmons followed on this triumph in 1991 with the creation of HBO's "Def Comedy Jam" television specials, which sparked the popularity of black standup comedians such as Chris Rock, Martin Lawrence, Jamie Foxx, and Bernie Mac. Known almost exclusively within the black community at the time, these comedians and others spotlighted on "Def Comedy Jam" would soon rank among the most popular comedians and television and movie stars in the United States.

Simmons extended his remarkable run of success in 1992 with the rollout of the Phat Farm men's clothing line, describing the name by explaining, "Phat means like cool. Like def is cool . . . Farm is a place where you make cool things. They grow." Later he started a women's line of clothing, Baby Phat, which was eventually run by the model Kimora Lee Simmons, whom he married in 1998. Meanwhile, Def Jam continued to produce huge hits, and Simmons became widely recognized as a leading black entrepreneur and among the most influential business figures of his time.

In 1999, Simmons sold his share of Def Jam to Universal Music Group for a reported $100 million. He remained as the company's chairman and retained his reputation as the person most responsible for mainstreaming rap and hip-hop music and culture. Simmons elaborated on his relationship with corporate America and particularly his success in bringing what had previously been perceived as black culture to wider and receptive audiences of white people, particularly young, middle-class whites, explaining, "They're [corporate America] getting an entrée in a world that they don't know enough about. So they want a gateway to selling their clothes and their phones, their movies, whatever it is they want to see, to America."

In recent years, Simmons has become more active in philanthropy and speaking out on issues, including calling for the elimination of racist and sexist terms from rap music. In 2008, he wrote *Do You!: 12 Laws to Access the Power in You to Achieve Happiness and Success*, and the following year he became the editor in chief of the Web site Global Grind, which describes itself as "the premier social media platform developed by and for the hip-hop community." Simmons has an estimated worth of over $350 million and lives on a 30,000-square-foot estate in Upper Saddle River, New Jersey. Divorced from Kimora Lee Simmons in 2009, Simmons is the father of two daughters.

Further Reading

"Russell Simmons." VH1. Available online. URL: http://www.vh1.com/artists/az/simmons_russell/bio.jhtml. Downloaded on September 1, 2009.

Simmons, Russell, and Chris Morrow. *Do You!: 12 Laws to Access the Power in You to Achieve Happiness and Success*. New York: Gotham, 2008.

Stark, Jeff. "Brilliant Careers: Russell Simmons." *Salon.* Available online. URL: http://www.salon.com/people/bc/1999/07/06/simmons/. Downloaded on September 1, 2009.

Singer, Isaac Merritt

(1811–1875) *inventor of the modern sewing machine*

One of the most amazing inventors in American history was Isaac Singer. Barely able to read and write, and possessed with the ability, temperament, and charm of a professional actor, Singer had the ability to look at a machine and figure out almost instantly how to make it work better. He might have become as great an inventor as THOMAS ALVA EDISON had he not frittered away so much of his energy on five different women by whom he sired two dozen children.

Singer was born on October 27, 1811, in Pittstown, New York. His father, Adam, was a cooper (barrel maker), and his mother, Ruth, was a homemaker. At age 12 he moved to Rochester to live with an older brother, and for the next seven years he worked as a machinist and at various odd jobs. In 1830, at age 19, he became fascinated with the theater and joined a traveling troupe. That same year he married Catherine Haley with whom he had two children. He abandoned her a few years later, and around 1835 he began living with Mary Ann Sponsler with whom he had 10 children.

From 1830 to 1839 he traveled the country as an actor whenever he could find work with a troupe, and he worked as a machinist between gigs. In 1839 he invented a rock drill, sold the patent for $2,000, started his own acting troupe, and toured the Midwest as head of the Merritt Players for five years until the money ran out in Fredricksburg, Ohio.

Having been rejected by the theatergoing public, Singer returned to being a machinist. By 1849 he had patented another device, this time a machine for carving wooden type for printing presses. In the process of finding financial backers for manufacturing the machine, that same year he moved to New York City. An inveterate ladies' man, Singer immediately acquired two new mistresses, Mary Walters with whom he had one child and Mary McGonigal with whom he had five children. He also managed to find enough time to meet George Zieber, a book publisher from Boston, Massachusetts, who offered to back Singer. Zieber paid for Singer to move to Boston and rented manufacturing space for him in the machine shop of Orson Phelps, who held a license to build sewing machines for the Lerow & Blodgett Company.

Unfortunately, Singer's machine for carving wooden type never caught on, probably because most printers had switched to metal type. Meanwhile, Phelps, on the other side of the room, seemed to have plenty of work. One day he asked Singer to help him fix a Lerow & Blodgett sewing machine; having nothing better to do, Singer agreed. While working on it, he immediately saw several things that could be improved to make it a better machine. Eleven days later he had developed a sewing machine that was significantly better than the Lerow & Blodgett machine. His most important change was to redesign the machine so that it could stitch continuously and in curved lines. He did this by mounting the needle bar on an arm that hung over the table on which the work was stitched. Then he replaced the hand crank with a foot-operated pedal, thus freeing both hands for manipulating the work on the table. He immediately formed a partnership with Zieber, Phelps, and Barzillan Ransom, called I. M. Singer & Company, and filed for a patent, which he received in 1851.

Quite often, inventors are bamboozled by their financial backers. In Singer's case, perhaps because of his acting background, it worked the other way around. He filed the patent claim in his name only, a blatant violation of the partnership agreement. When Zieber fell deathly ill, Singer convinced him to sell his share of the company for only $6,000, then refused to sell it back when Zieber recovered. Through an exaggerated and prolonged display of irascible behavior, Singer also got rid of Phelps and Ransom. To take their places, in 1851 Singer became partners with Edward Clark, a lawyer. By then, a number of sewing machine inventors, including ELIAS HOWE, had filed suit against one another, and the entire sewing machine industry was threatened with implosion. Largely as a result of Clark's skillful machinations, a patent pool was developed in 1856 by which all contestants were able to profit, but since Singer's machine was by far the best, Singer's company profited the most. By 1860 it was the best-selling sewing machine in the world, partly because of the quality of the machine itself and partly because Singer offered liberal credit terms to whoever wanted to buy one.

In 1860 Singer finally got around to divorcing his wife. The resulting publicity led two of his other three families to somehow meet each other, and in the ensuing brouhaha Singer skipped off to England. While there he met Isabella Boyer, whom he married in 1863 and with whom he had six children. That same year he and Clark incorporated I. M. Singer & Company and changed the name to the Singer Manufacturing Company. From that point on, Singer had nothing to do with the company except to cash his checks, and in 1867 he moved permanently to England, settling in a mansion in Torquay, Devonshire. He died on July 23, 1875, in Torquay. At the time of his death, his estate was valued at more than $13 million.

Further Reading

Bissell, Don. *The First Conglomerate: 145 Years of the Singer Sewing Machine Company*. Brunswick, Me.: Audenreed Press, 1999.

Brandon, Ruth. *Singer and the Sewing Machine: A Capitalist Romance*. New York: Kodansha International, 1996.

Slater, Samuel

(1768–1835) *inventor of the water-powered textile mill*

Even though OLIVER EVANS opened a fully automated gristmill in 1785, the Industrial Revolution did not begin in the United States until five years later. In 1790 Samuel Slater built the first water-powered textile mill, thus revolutionizing the way cotton and woolen goods were produced.

Slater was born on June 9, 1768, in Belper, Derbyshire, England. His parents, William and Elizabeth, were farmers. At age 14 he apprenticed himself to Jedediah Strutt, who operated one of the first cotton mills in England to use water-powered machinery. Seven years later, in 1789, he completed his apprenticeship and emigrated to the United States, where several states were offering bounties to skilled English machine operators who would settle in their state. He had to disguise himself in order to leave the country, because British law prohibited the emigration of skilled machine operators and the exportation of spinning machinery.

After landing in New York City, Slater went to work for an association of merchants who had organized to manufacture textiles. In 1790, he was contacted by William Almy and Moses Brown, the proprietors of Almy & Brown, a mercantile firm in Providence, Rhode Island. The partners wanted to get into the manufacture of textiles also, and they were paying top dollar to mechanics who could replicate English textile machinery. Brown had managed somehow to obtain several textile machines, but none of them actually worked, mostly because they had either broken or missing parts. Slater convinced him that, having worked in Strutt's mill for seven years, he carried in his head enough information to build operable machines for carding (combing and straightening the cotton fibers for spinning), roving (twisting the straightened fibers), and spinning (turning the twisted fibers into yarn) cotton fibers. In return, he convinced Brown to give him half-ownership, with Almy & Brown holding the other half, in a partnership to build a cotton mill fully equipped with water-driven machines. In 1791 Slater married Hannah Wilkinson with whom he had nine children. She died in 1812, and in 1817 he married Esther Parkinson.

Slater did not have any blueprints or diagrams from which to work, although he did have Brown's machines, which he either rebuilt or used for parts. He also had the services of several skilled ironworkers and woodworkers, who made the individual parts for the machines Brown lacked to whatever dimensions Slater remembered them being. By the end of 1790 Slater and his workmen had produced three machines for carding, two for roving, and three for spinning. They set up this equipment in an old mill in Pawtucket, Rhode Island, hooked up the machines to the mill's water-wheel via a system of shafts, gears, and leather belts, and began operating the first water-powered textile mill in the United States.

Unable to procure the services of adults to work in their mill, the three partners hired children between the ages of seven and 12 to run the equipment. Within a few years the mill was producing enough cotton yarn to keep 100 hand-weavers busy. Between the machines and the child labor, the mill's labor costs were much lower than at competing mills, which made the mill hugely profitable. In 1793 the three partners moved their yarn-making equipment into a new building, which later became known as the Old Slater Mill. In 1798 Slater branched out on his own, forming Samuel Slater & Company and opening a water-powered mill in Rehoboth, Massachusetts. In 1807 the three partners plus Slater's brother John opened a third mill on the Blackstone River, just outside Pawtucket. A mill community sprang up around this mill that was later named Slatersville. Around 1812 Slater opened a fourth mill in Oxford, Massachusetts, which he later renamed Webster in honor of Daniel Webster, the famous orator and statesman. In 1827 he opened a steam-powered mill in Providence. By the time of his death, Slater had played a major role in the establishment of 13 textile mills. Many of the people who worked in his mills went on to start mills of their own, thus spreading the Industrial Revolution throughout New England and the rest of the country. He died on April 20, 1835, in Webster.

Further Reading

Cutliffe, Stephen H., and Terry S. Reynolds. *Technology & American History: A Historical Anthology from*

Technology & Culture. Chicago: University of Chicago Press, 1997.

Rivard, Paul E. *Samuel Slater: a Short Interpretive Essay on Samuel Slater's Role in the Birth of the American Textile Industry.* Pawtucket, R.I.: Slater Mill Historic Site, 1974.

Tucker, Barbara M. *Samuel Slater and the Origins of the American Textile Industry, 1790–1860.* Ithaca, N.Y.: Cornell University Press, 1984.

Smith, Frederick
(1944–   ) *founder of Federal Express*

In 1973, Frederick Smith—a graduate of Yale and veteran of the Vietnam War—launched an ambitious business called Federal Express. His goal of greatly accelerating the pace at which commercial delivery could be conducted was reflected in the new company's now iconic slogan, "When it absolutely, positively has to be there overnight." Overcoming initial struggles, Smith's company—now called simply FedEx—has a vast fleet of trucks and planes that deliver a variety of goods around the world, leading the history devotee Smith to note, "We are the clipper ships of the information age."

Frederick Wallace Smith was born in Marks, Mississippi, on August 11, 1944. He grew up with two half-brothers, a half-sister, and an adopted sister in Memphis. Smith's father, who became a wealthy entrepreneur by starting a bus company that was later sold to the Greyhound Bus Company and a chain of southern-cooking restaurants throughout the United States, died when Smith was only four years old. He was raised by his mother and would later describe his youth as "autonomous . . . I had a lovely mother, but not having a father influence, I learned a lot of things on my own." Smith overcame hip arthritis that required him to wear braces for much of his young boyhood and became an amateur pilot, accomplished athlete, and outstanding student at Memphis Prep before enrolling at Yale University.

Smith graduated with a degree in economics from Yale in 1966. While still an undergraduate, he wrote a paper for a business course in which he described the impact the emerging computerization would have on commerce, particularly the distribution of goods, and he outlined the idea for the company that would later become Federal Express. Though Smith would later recall that the paper failed to receive a high grade, he maintained interest in the concept of a business that would guarantee the overnight delivery of small, time-sensitive goods, such as replacement parts and medical supplies, even after enlisting in the U.S. Marine Corps following his graduation from college.

In the marines, Smith rose to the rank of second lieutenant and eventually served as a pilot on over 200 ground support missions in Southeast Asia during the Vietnam War. His experience in Vietnam helped develop his dream of creating the trailblazing delivery service that he had first expressed in that paper at Yale. He explains, "[During] the Vietnam War . . . I spent four and a half years in the Marine Corps. That's when I sort of crystallized the idea for FedEx on the supply side, how to solve the problem that had been identified in that paper . . . In the military there's a tremendous amount of waste. The supplies were sort of pushed forward, like you push food onto a table. And invariably, all of the supplies were in the wrong place for where they were needed. Observing that and trying to think about ways to have a different type of a distribution system is what crystallized the idea." He added, "I wanted to do something productive after blowing so many things up."

Smith was granted an honorable discharge from the marines in July 1969 after earning the Silver Star and two Purple Hearts. A month later, Smith married his first wife, Linda (they had two children together before divorcing in 1977). Back in the United States, Smith used $4 million of his inheritance as well as tens of millions in venture capital to form Federal Express in 1973. Smith based the company's operations in Memphis, not only because it was his hometown, but also because of the city's central location and mild climate that would make weather delays less likely. Initially, Federal Express had only 14 jets and delivered goods to 25 cities. Within three months, Smith's new company had lost about a third of its startup money. The ensuing months brought additional challenges, including the skyrocketing cost of fuel, outdated aviation regulations, and even legal challenges brought by Smith's sisters, who claimed that he had misappropriated funds from their trust (Smith was acquitted on these charges at trial).

However, Smith's tireless efforts and clear vision for Federal Express helped the company turn a profit by 1976 as individuals, businesses, and government agencies discovered the benefits of affordable, dependable, and remarkably faster delivery services. By 1984, after Smith's emphasis on national expansion and prominent and inventive advertising had taken hold, Federal Express had over $1 billion in revenue. Always seeking ways to extend the reach of his company (which was renamed FedEx in 1998), Smith sought to gain a strong presence in international markets and to become stronger through the adaptation of emerging e-commerce technology. In each of these endeavors, Smith had some setbacks but overall was enormously successful. By the end of the 1990s, FedEx had over 120,000 employees and handled an average of over 2.5 million deliveries a day.

In recent years, Smith has remained the prominent and influential leader of the company he envisioned in college and started soon after returning home from service in the Vietnam War. In 2003, Smith led FedEx's purchase of the office and print store chain, Kinko's, for $2.4 billion. This acquisition greatly expanded FedEx's already prolific shipping services and increased the company's share of the profitable express documentation and delivery business. In 2009, Smith was listed by *Forbes* magazine as the 559th wealthiest person in the world, with a net worth of over $1.3 billion.

The foundation for these and other FedEx accomplishments—as well as an often-stated source of pride for Smith—is the company's culture, particularly its emphasis on PSP: People-Service-Profit, which expresses the belief that taking care of FedEx's people will lead to impeccable service, which will result in profits that will secure the future of all involved with FedEx. Smith has gained renown for making FedEx a workplace with generous wages and benefits, and he has rewarded employees with perks, such as special bonuses given to those who worked extra hours to process hundreds of thousands of additional orders during a UPS strike and taking out 11 full-page thank you ads in newspapers across the United States.

Smith has been married to his second wife, Dianne, for over 30 years and together they have eight children. He remains the chief executive officer, president, and chairman of the board of FedEx, a company described on its Web site and by millions of customers around the world as one that has "revolutionized global business practices and now defines speed and reliability."

Further Reading

"Fedex Chief Takes Cues from Leaders in History." *USA Today.* Available online. URL: http://www.usatoday.com/money/companies/management/2005-06-19-fedex-advice_x.htm. Downloaded on September 1, 2009.

"Frederick W. Smith." Academy of Achievement. Available online. URL: http://www.achievement.org/autodoc/page/smi0bio-1. Downloaded on September 1, 2009.

Frock, Roger. *Changing How the World Does Business: Fedex's Incredible Journey to Success—The Inside Story.* San Francisco: Berrett-Koehler Publishers, 2006.

Smith, Willi
(Willie Donnell Smith)
(1948–1987) *entrepreneur in fashion design*

The civil rights movement of the 1960s had a far-ranging effect on American society, and one of its more unlikely results was the impact it had on the world of fashion. Beginning in the late 1960s, African-American fashion—derived in part from African patterns and designs as reflected in dashikis and other ethnic garments and in part on the adaptation of black people to American and Caribbean culture—began to have a major influence on the large design houses. One result of this influence was the rise of young black fashion designers to positions of power and prestige they could scarcely have imagined possible in the 1950s. One of the most popular of these black designers was Willi Smith, whose brilliant career came to a tragic end.

Smith was born Willie Donnell Smith on February 29, 1948, in Philadelphia, Pennsylvania. His father, Willie, was an ironworker, and his mother,

June, was a homemaker. His parents divorced when he was young, and he was raised in large part by his grandmother, Gladys Bush. As a young boy, he loved to draw and to spend his free time at the Philadelphia Museum of Art, and at age 14 he enrolled in the Philadelphia College of Art. Over the next four years, he developed a strong interest in fashion design, and upon graduation in 1965 he won a scholarship to study at the Parsons School of Design in New York City. Shortly after graduation he also got his first job as a fashion designer; his grandmother did housework for a client of Arnold Scaasi, a noted New York City designer, and she convinced the client to help Smith get a summer job with Scaasi.

After graduating from Parsons in 1969, Smith spent a few months as a sketcher of women's sportswear for Bobbie Brooks, then went to work as a sportswear designer for Digits, Inc. His early designs incorporated many of the features that would make his later work so distinctive: relaxed, free-flowing, colorful, and oversized in a way that combined functionality with fun. Smith drew on several disparate sources for inspiration; he had a particular interest in African, Asian, and contemporary artwork, and many of his designs reflected that interest, while others simply reflected what he had seen on the streets of Manhattan while walking to work that day. By 1974 he had gained a reputation in the sportswear industry as a rising star, and he decided to strike out on his own, forming his own studio with his sister Toukie and a friend as partners.

Although Smith was a good designer, he turned out to be a poor businessman, and his company floundered financially almost from the beginning. He eventually found several partners with experience in the New York fashion game who funded his struggling enterprise in exchange for the rights to his name. He soon discovered that this arrangement also meant that his partners enjoyed considerable control over his designs, and he found himself pressured to design sportswear in expensive fabrics and outrageous styles that struck him as being overpriced and functionally absurd. By 1976 he had successfully sued for the right to use his own name, and he was doing freelance work for large sportswear companies.

In 1976 Smith's luck took a turn for the better, largely as a result of a chance meeting with a former classmate named Laurie Mallet. She was importing cotton leisure shirts from India, and she convinced Smith to accompany her on a trip to Bombay to visit the factory where they were made and perhaps get involved in their design. He accepted, and their trip led to the formation of WilliWear Limited, with Mallet as president and Smith as vice president and designer. Their first year in business, he designed what would soon become a popular style of pants, in essence a pair of baggy fatigues with a high, wrapped waist that was similar to the pants his father had favored. Each year's collection outsold the one from the year before, and in 1978 he made a successful foray into men's fashion with the introduction of WilliWear Men, a line of formal and casual male clothing. By 1982 WilliWear Limited was grossing more than $5 million in annual sales from men's and women's clothing. Much of the company's success had to do with the fact that it featured separates—skirts, tops, pants, shirts, and blazers—that not only reflected the latest street-smart style but also mixed and matched well with pieces from previous years' collections, so that none of his work ever seemed dated. Other reasons were that Smith had a natural flair for combining plaids, stripes, and bright colors in the same garment in a way that was stylish without being garish, and that he insisted on using natural fibers, especially cotton, and on keeping his clothes within the price range of the stylishly hip but financially challenged consumer.

By 1986 WilliWear was being sold in more than 1,000 stores in the United States, and the company was doing more than $25 million in annual sales. Unfortunately, that same year, while on one of his many trips to India, Smith came down with shigellosis, a deadly form of dysentery caused by bacteria in untreated drinking water. He apparently did not seek treatment until after returning to New York City, but by then it was too late. He died on April 17, 1987, in New York City.

Further Reading
Obituary, *New York Times*, April 19, 1987, p. I, 34.
Videofashion Men New Attitudes. New York: Videofashion, Inc., 1988, videorecording.

Sperry, Elmer Ambrose
(1860–1930) *inventor of gyroscope applications*

Elmer Sperry was one of the most prolific American inventors of all time. Inspired by the research methods of THOMAS ALVA EDISON, Sperry went on to receive more than 400 patents and form eight manufacturing firms. His fame, however, rests on his use of the gyroscope as a means of guiding and stabilizing airplanes and ships.

Sperry was born on October 12, 1860, in Cortland, New York. His parents, Stephen and Mary, were farmers. Lacking the funds to continue his education beyond high school, he arranged with several professors at Cornell University to let him audit their classes. He was encouraged by physics professor William A. Anthony to invent a current regulator for arc lighting, which he did at age 20. He obtained financial backing from the Cortland Wagon Company and designed a new and improved arc light lamp and system. In 1883 he formed the Sperry Electric Light, Motor and Car Brake Company in Chicago, Illinois, and began manufacturing his system. Although the company enjoyed some small successes in Chicago, overall it did not fare well against the rising popularity of incandescent lighting, which was being made more practical and affordable by Edison and his associates. In 1887, the same year he married Zula Goodman with whom he had four children, Sperry Electric Light went out of business.

Undaunted, in 1888 Sperry formed the Elmer A. Sperry Company, an experimental laboratory similar to Edison's. The basic idea was to invent things that operated on electricity, then either form separate companies to manufacture them or sell the patents to other companies. In 1889 he formed the Sperry Electric Mining Machine Company to manufacture and market an electric pick and a small electric locomotive. In 1892 he formed the Sperry Electric Railway Company to manufacture brakes, transmissions, and speed controls for electric streetcars, but three years later he sold the company to the General Electric Company. He also developed an electric car, a battery, and steering and braking mechanisms for the automobile, then sold the electric car patent to the Cleveland Machine Screw Company and the other patents to the American Bicycle Company. After inventing ways to produce chlorine and caustic soda via electrolysis, he sold the patents to Elon H. Hooker, who in 1909 formed the Hooker Chemical Company.

In 1907 Sperry began experimenting with the gyroscope. This simple device consists of a rapidly spinning wheel set in a framework of two or three rings; although the rings tilt as the base to which the gyroscope is mounted tilts, the wheel itself never tilts. Until then, the gyroscope had been considered a child's plaything, but Sperry realized that its ability to maintain its orientation meant it could be used as a navigational aid and vehicle stabilizer. At first, he tried to incorporate the gyroscope into a sort of shock absorber for automobile, but when auto manufacturers were not impressed, he focused on using it to stabilize ships. He connected the gyroscope to a set of stabilizing fins on the ship's hull; the exact degree of tilt in each ring was transmitted to the fins, which were raised or lowered to compensate for the change. Although commercial shippers showed little interest in the device, the U.S. Navy expressed great interest. One of its biggest problems at the time was stabilizing a ship while it was firing its guns, and Sperry's invention seemed to be the perfect solution.

Working with the navy enlightened Sperry to the need for a new type of compass. Since warships of the day were made out of ferrous metal, they affected the way a magnetic compass worked. Also, a magnetic compass pointed the way to magnetic north and not true north, which was a significant problem for ships operating in the North Atlantic Ocean. Although the gyrocompass had been invented a few years earlier by Hermann Anschutz-Kaempfe, a German entrepreneur, Sperry improved on it by aligning the wheel's axis with the earth's axis, and by developing a feedback system that compensated for changes in the ship's acceleration and latitude. By 1910 he had perfected the gyrocompass, and that same year he formed the Sperry Gyroscope Company in Brooklyn, New York, to manufacture gyrocompasses and gyrostabilizers for the navy. The outbreak of World War I was a tremendous boost to the company's fortunes, as it received orders from the British and Russian navies as well.

In 1914, Sperry Gyroscope adapted the gyro-stabilizer for use on airplanes. After the war, it adapted its gyrocompass and gyrostabilizers for commercial shipping and aircraft as well. By 1922 Sperry had figured out how to combine a gyro-compass, a gyrostabilizer, and an accelerometer to make an automatic pilot system for ships and airplanes. Although primitive by modern standards, it served as a jumping-off point for future developments in this area.

Sperry died on June 16, 1930, in Brooklyn. His company survived his death, and in 1955 it became the Sperry Corporation. It remained a leader in the building of automatic guidance systems and also got involved in the manufacture of computers. In 1986 it became part of the Unisys Corporation.

Further Reading

"Elmer Ambrose Sperry: The Gyroscopic Compass," Lemuelson-MIT Awards Program's Invention Dimension. Available online. URL: http://web.mit.edu/invent/iow/sperry.html. Downloaded on July 6, 2009.

Hughes, Thomas P. *Elmer Sperry: Inventor and Engineer.* Baltimore, Md.: Johns Hopkins University Press, 1993.

Stanley, Francis Edgar (1849–1918), and Freelan Oscar Stanley (1849–1940)
inventors of the Stanley Steamer automobile

Many people are interested in automobiles that run on so-called alternative fuels. Much attention has been given to cars that use electricity or natural gas instead of petroleum. About 100 years ago, another alternative fuel for autos existed: steam. Although impractical in today's world for any number of reasons, between 1900 and 1925 it was possible to buy a steam-powered vehicle. For most of those years, the only steam-powered car on the American market was the Stanley Steamer, which was invented by Francis and Freelan Stanley.

The Stanley twins were born on June 1, 1849, in Kingfield, Maine. Their parents, Solomon and Apphia, were farmers. In 1871, the year after Francis married Augusta Walker with whom he had three children, they graduated from Farm-

ington State Normal and Training School and began teaching school in Maine. Francis eventually became a high-school principal in Mechanic Falls, while Freelan gave up teaching in 1874 and moved to Lewiston where he worked as an artist and photographer; in 1876 he married Flora Tileston. In 1885 they left their separate careers and opened a shop in Lewiston to manufacture dry plates for photographers. Four years later they sold the shop, moved to Watertown, Massachusetts, and formed the Stanley Dry Plate Company, which they sold to Eastman Kodak in 1904.

Meanwhile, the Stanleys had become interested in building an automobile. At the time, auto designers had yet to decide on the internal combustion engine as the sole source of power for the automobile, and some designers were still experimenting with steam and electricity as feasible alternatives. The Stanleys chose steam, and they set out to make a functional steamer. By 1898 they had developed a steam-powered car that weighed just 600 pounds, a major accomplishment given that other steam-powered cars weighed about twice as much. The car featured a two-cylinder, 3.5 horsepower steam engine with a gasoline burner, and had a top speed of about 27 miles per hour. The water tank held 14 gallons, or just enough to make a round trip of 15 miles. In 1899 they bought an old bicycle factory in the building next to their dry plate shop in Watertown and began building steamers. Meanwhile, their car had attracted a great deal of media attention, and a month later, they sold the company for $250,000 to John B. Walker and A. Lorenzo Barber.

Walker and Barber soon moved the operation to larger facilities in other towns, and in 1901 the Stanleys re-bought the old bicycle factory for just $20,000, formed the Stanley Motor Carriage Company, and started making a car that came to be known as the Stanley Steamer. The Steamer was attractive to the motoring public for several reasons. Instead of having a transmission with a lot of complicated moving parts, the Steamer was driven by a simple chain-and-sprocket mechanism similar to that used in a bicycle. Its engine made no noise, other than a little hissing from time to time, and its only emission was an odorless and harmless plume of water vapor. Perhaps most important, it sold for $650, which was $300 less than the Ford Model T. Unfortunately, the Steamer had many drawbacks as well. Although it ran on water, which is free, the burner consumed more gasoline per mile than did a car with a gasoline engine. In order to make it light enough to be powered by a steam engine, the Stanleys had to build it out of light-weight parts, which could not take the wear and tear of primitive turn-of-the-century roads. Since it got poor water mileage—slightly more than one mile per gallon—the driver had to stop for water every 10 miles or so. Firing the boiler on a cold day was a difficult chore, and even on a warm day it took almost 30 minutes for enough pressure to build up to power the car. Worst of all, the gasoline burner occasionally would backfire, and sometimes this set the car on fire.

Despite all these problems, enough people—about 14,000—bought Stanley Steamers to keep the company in business until the mid-1920s. But by then the Stanleys had moved on, having sold the company in 1917 and retired. Francis died the following year on July 31 in Wenham, Massachusetts, while driving a Stanley Steamer. Freelan spent most of his retirement in Colorado, and he died on October 2, 1940, in Newton, Massachusetts.

Further Reading

Davis, Susan. *The Stanleys: Renaissance Yankees: Innovation in Industry and the Arts.* New York: Newcomen Society of the United States, 1997.

Griffin, Nancy. *The Remarkable Stanley Brothers and Their Amazing Cars.* Portland, Me.: Guy Gannett Pub., 1987.

Stern, David

(1942–) *entrepreneur in professional basketball*

The history of the National Basketball Association (NBA) is rich in legendary names, including Bill Russell, Jerry West, Magic Johnson, Larry Bird, and Michael Jordan. Though he did not make his impact on the court, David Stern—the commissioner of the NBA since 1984—has also become one of the most important men in the history of the league, by helping to lead it out of serious financial difficulty by expanding marketing opportunities and encouraging the popularity of American basketball throughout the world.

David Joel Stern was born in New York City on September 22, 1942. He lived in Manhattan until he was 12, occasionally working at the delicatessen owned by his father. The Sterns then moved to Teaneck, New Jersey, where David—a solid but unspectacular student—graduated from high school. He earned a degree in political science from Rutgers University in 1963 and a law degree from Columbia University in 1966 before going to work in New York City with the law firm Proskauer Rose. As a young lawyer, Stern—a lifelong New York Knicks fan—was assigned as outside counsel to the NBA and he impressed many league executives with his diligence and intelligence. In 1978, Stern left the law firm to take a job as general counsel with the NBA.

By 1980 Stern was promoted to executive vice president of the NBA and in 1984 he replaced Larry O'Brien—for whom the league championship trophy is named—to become the fourth commissioner in the history of the NBA. He took over leadership of a league that faced significant challenges. Attendance and television ratings were lagging in most cities. Evidence of weak public interest was seen just three years earlier, when the NBA Finals were broadcast on tape delay because the CBS television network determined their regular prime-time lineup was likely to attract more viewers and advertising dollars. In addition, high-profile incidents of drug use and fighting by NBA players created the sense among many that the league lacked institutional discipline.

Stern quickly moved to address the NBA's problems. In addition to his initiatives, Stern was aided by an influx of the legendary talents and personalities of players such as Magic Johnson, Larry Bird, Isiah Thomas, and especially Michael Jordan. These superstars were able to reinvigorate the fan base through their outstanding play and intense marketing campaigns to highlight the excitement they brought to basketball arenas across the United States. During what many consider this Golden Era of the NBA, Stern led negotiations that resulted in labor-management peace, record levels of television broadcast revenue and marketing agreements, stadium construction, and franchise expansion. During Stern's tenure, 28 new stadiums have been built for NBA teams and seven new franchises have been added, including two in Canada (the Toronto Raptors and the Vancouver Grizzlies, which relocated to Memphis in 2001). League revenues during this time have increased twelvefold.

Two of Stern's greatest and most imitated successes have been the league's drug policy and salary cap. Though both of these initiatives were created while Stern was an executive vice president for the NBA, he was influential in their conception and instrumental in their implementation in his role as commissioner. The drug policy allowed players to receive treatment without penalty if they came forward with a drug dependency problem while setting up punishments including suspension from participation and loss of pay for those caught using illegal substances. The salary cap helped corral rapidly rising and likely unsustainable player salaries, while providing flexibility for lucrative contracts and financial incentives for players to remain with their current teams.

Stern has also been active in pursuing opportunities to link the NBA to nations around the world, which has led to dramatic increases in broadcast, merchandising, and marketing revenue and has been credited with helping lead the booming global popularity of basketball over the past few decades. NBA teams regularly play preseason games overseas and the influx of international players during Stern's tenure, such as German Dirk Nowitzki, Argentinian Manu Ginobili, Spaniard Pau Gasol, and Chinese star Yao Ming, has profoundly and positively affected the NBA and the sport of basketball. Along with this international outreach, Stern consistently expresses pride in the NBA's public service activities, such as the Read to Achieve and NBA Cares programs that receive a great deal of publicity during NBA broadcasts.

Despite what even critics concede has been his great success as commissioner, Stern has been the object of criticism, particularly during what many viewed as his hardline, though successful, stance during the 1999 lockout that suspended NBA play in the middle of the season. He instituted a dress code for players sitting on the bench during games, which some described as unnecessary and disrespectful.

Protective of his privacy and rarely accessible for interviews unless they focus on the NBA, Stern has been described by some as imperious, though most league fans and observers subscribe with respect and admiration to the description of him made by *ESPN The Magazine* writer Bill Simmons in 2008, who noted, "Hanging with Stern is like watching a performance from beginning to end. He talks deliberately and dramatically, measuring each word. He's not against banging a table to make a point . . . When I asked about his leadership style, Stern joked, 'I delegate . . . and then I episodically micromanage.' . . . he was the one who cleaned up drugs and fighting, fought for a salary cap, urged networks to market players over teams and turned franchises into minicorporations."

Stern married his wife Dianne during his last year in law school and together they have two sons. Now commissioner of the NBA for over a quarter of a century, Stern lives in Scarsdale, New York.

Further Reading

Araton, Harvey. "Sports of the Times: For Commissioner Stern, a Battle Is Won but an Image Is Changed." *New York Times.* Available online. URL: http://www.nytimes.com/1999/01/07/sports/sports-times-for-commissioner-stern-battle-won-but-image-changed.html. Downloaded on September 1, 2009.

"A Conversation with David Stern." Charlie Rose. Available online. URL: http://www.charlierose.com/view/interview/9772. Downloaded on September 1, 2009.

McCallum, Jack. "The World According to David Stern." *Sports Illustrated.* Available online. URL: http://sportsillustrated.cnn.com/vault/article/magazine/MAG1104424/index/index.htm. Downloaded on October 8, 2009.

Simmons, Bill. "Curious Guy: David Stern." ESPN. Available online. URL: http://sports.espn.go.com/espn/page2/story?page=simmons/stern/060216. Downloaded on September 1, 2009.

Stevens, Robert Livingston
(1787–1856) *inventor of the T-rail for railroads*

One of the most important developments in American railroading was the invention of the T-rail. Because of its design, the T-rail can be easily attached to crossties which, when covered with gravel, provide a sturdy roadbed for trains. The T-rail was invented by Robert Stevens, who spent most of his life designing improvements to steamboats and yachts as well as to railroads.

Stevens was born on October 18, 1787, in Hoboken, New Jersey. His father, John, was a wealthy businessman and inventor, and his mother, Rachel, was a homemaker. At age 17 he dropped out of Columbia College and went to work in a Hoboken machine shop. The following year he became involved in his father's work with steamboats, and he personally operated the *Little Juliana*, the first steam ferryboat to cross the Hudson River. Four years later, in 1809, he moved to Trenton, New Jersey, to oversee the operations of the *Phoenix*, another one of his father's steamboats, which plied the Delaware River between Philadelphia and Trenton. Over the next 30-plus years he invented a number of improvements that made the steamboat's engine safer and its hull sturdier. By 1823 the Stevenses were providing regular steamboat service between New York City and Perth Amboy, New Jersey, and between Philadelphia and Trenton, while connecting the two lines via regular stagecoach service between Perth Amboy and Trenton.

John Stevens's plan to replace the stagecoach line with a railroad became a reality in 1830, when Stevens, his brother Edward, and Robert F. Stockton received a charter from the New Jersey legislature to form the Camden & Amboy Railroad and Transportation Company, with Stevens as president and chief engineer. At the time, the American railroad industry was in its infancy, and although railroad people had made a commitment to running trains on wrought-iron rails, they had yet to agree on a standard design for rails. That same year, Stevens began experimenting with various configurations for rail and roadbed, and he determined that the sturdiest roadway consisted of rail anchored to wooden crossties that were themselves anchored by ballast, either crushed stone or gravel. To this end he invented the T-rail, which remains to this day the standard configuration for railroad rail. In essence, the T-rail is an I-beam with a wide bottom flange, so that when the rail is laid on the ground it gives the appearance of an upside-down "T," hence the name. Stevens gave his rail a wide bottom so that it could be fastened

more easily to the crossties. He also invented the hook-headed railroad spike for nailing rail to crossties, and the fish plate, the iron fitting used to bolt two sections of rail together. Under Steven's direction, Camden & Amboy perfected the modern system for laying rail: Survey and clear the line of brush and tress, grade a right-of-way, distribute the crossties, lay the rail and fasten it to the ties, and fill in the gaps between the crossties with ballast.

Stevens made other contributions to railroading. He invented the pilot, or cowcatcher, for clearing objects—such as cows—from the path of the locomotive, and he increased the number of drive wheels on the locomotive from four to eight to provide better traction. He also designed several different locomotives and steam boilers, and he invented the double-slide cutoff valve. Meanwhile, under his direction the Camden & Amboy prospered. It eventually merged with a Philadelphia-to-Trenton railroad and made connection with another line running from Jersey City to New Brunswick. These connections gave it a monopoly on rail traffic between New York City and Philadelphia, the nation's two largest cities, and made the Stevenses even wealthier. In the late 19th century, the Camden & Amboy became part of the Pennsylvania Railroad.

Next to steamboats and railroading, Stevens's passion was yachting. In 1845 he designed a 92-foot centerboard sloop called the *Maria;* until his death the *Maria* was one of the fastest yachts in the world. He died on April 20, 1856, in Hoboken.

Further Reading

"Robert Livingston Stevens," Stevens Institute of Technology. Available online. URL: http://www.stevens.edu/sit/about/robert_stevens.cfm. Downloaded on July 6, 2009.

Turnbull, A. D. *John Stevens, an American Record.* Freeport, N. Y.: Books for Libraries Press, 1972.

Stewart, Martha
(Martha Kostyra)
(1941–) *entrepreneur in home furnishings and home entertaining*

Few American entrepreneurs have marketed themselves as effectively as has Martha Stewart.

Photogenic in a casual sort of way, by 2000 Stewart had emerged as the mistress of gracious but casual living. It is a mark of her genius that she was able to translate her own persona and lifestyle into a model for millions of others to emulate—and in the process become a millionaire.

Stewart was born Martha Kostyra on August 3, 1941, in Jersey City, New Jersey. Her father, Edward, was a pharmaceuticals salesman, and her mother, Martha, was a teacher. At age three, she moved with her family to nearby Nutley. As a child she showed a great deal of interest in gardening, cooking, and organizing parties, and while still in high school she catered her first affair, a big breakfast for her school's football team. In 1959 she enrolled in Barnard College where she studied art and architectural history while working part time as a model. In 1961 she married Alexander Stewart with whom she had one child; they were divorced in 1989. In 1963 she received her B.A. from Barnard.

Stewart continued to model until 1965, when she became pregnant. Shortly after giving birth, she went to work as a stockbroker, her father-in-law's profession, for the Wall Street brokerage firm of Monness, Williams, and Sidel. By 1973 she was earning six figures annually. Then a recession hit, after which the brokerage business ceased to be fun for her, so she quit.

In 1973 the Stewarts moved into an old farmhouse in Westport, Connecticut. Instead of looking for a new job, Stewart decided to remodel the farmhouse herself. She and her husband also gave over a good deal of the property that came with the farmhouse to raising chickens and growing fruits, vegetables, and herbs. Meanwhile, she taught herself how to cook French cuisine, using much of the homegrown produce and herbs in her dishes. By 1976 she had developed into a talented chef, so she opened a catering service and was immediately deluged with customers. Over the next 10 years she developed this enterprise into a million-dollar-per-year business. She also opened a store in Westport that sold homemade food and accessories for entertaining.

In 1980 Stewart was catering an affair in New York City when she was invited by Alan Mirken, president of Crown Publishers, to write a book about hosting home parties. The result was *Entertaining* (1982), which she wrote with Elizabeth Hawes. The book contains suggestions for throwing 35 different parties, ranging in size and degree of difficulty from a Sunday omelet brunch for 10 to an Italian feast for 50. Well-illustrated with color photographs of every detail, the book sold more than 600,000 copies, an astronomical amount for a first-time author. To be sure, the parties themselves were creative and fun, and the book presented the details in such a way that anyone who could follow a recipe in a cookbook could probably throw any one of the book's parties with a considerable amount of success. However, what really made the book so popular was that it highlighted Stewart's message that gracious living should be done casually. She had managed to roll the glamour of a model, the professionalism of a stockbroker, and the informality of a gardener into one persona, and she made it work with what seemed to be negligible effort. It was this persona, which Stewart projected so well through her work, that made her message so appealing to her audience and so lucrative to her.

Other books followed over the next seven years, all of them similar in message and presentation, if not content, to *Entertaining*. Perhaps the one that most successfully captures the Stewart message is *Martha Stewart's Quick Cook: 200 Easy and Elegant Recipes* (1983). Other books outlined the how-to of making hors d'oeuvres, pies and tarts, producing a wedding, and celebrating Christmas. The success of the books led to two television specials and a series of home videos about home entertaining. *Dinner Classics* (1989), for example, is an ingenious set of recipes and compact discs; one prepares the food according to the recipe, then listens to the appropriate music while eating the food with one's family and guests. In 1991 she departed from the basic theme of home entertaining to write a book about gardening.

Obviously, Stewart's expertise at home decorating and entertaining could be exploited to sell related merchandise, and in 1987 K-Mart signed her to a five-year, $5-million contract to serve as a company spokesperson and consultant for home furnishings. In 1997 Stewart and K-Mart introduced Martha Stewart Everyday, a collection of housewares. She began appearing in television, magazine, and newspaper ads, touting the linens and tableware she had designed as well as the merits of the company's other products. She also began lecturing across the country, speaking to packed houses everywhere, and giving weekend lifestyle seminars at her home in Westport. In 1990 she signed a 10-year, $15-million contract with Time Warner to become editor in chief of *Martha Stewart Living,* a bimonthly lifestyle magazine that features her ideas about fixing and furnishing a home as well as living in that home graciously yet casually; by 1993 circulation was hovering around 750,000.

In 1997 she became the chief executive officer of Martha Stewart Living and Omnimedia, the Time Warner division that publishes the magazine and produces Stewart's videos. In 1999 she took Martha Stewart Living public; by the end of the first day of trading, the stock had doubled in price and Stewart was a billionaire. (In February 2002 when K-Mart announced its bankruptcy, Stewart issued a statement saying that she would continue to have K-Mart sell the products in her Martha Stewart Everyday line.)

In 2002 Stewart again drew the attention of the business world, but this time she was the focus of an intensely followed scandal rather than widely held admiration. The U.S. Securities and Exchange Commission (SEC) charged that Stewart had used insider-trading information related to the stock of the biopharmaceutical company ImClone to avoid a loss of almost $50,000. Stewart was indicted on nine counts of securities fraud and obstruction of justice in 2003, and she was found guilty following a five-week trial in March 2004. She served a five-month prison sentence at a federal facility in West Virginia and was released in early 2005.

Stewart immediately returned to prominence as the head of Martha Stewart Living Omnimedia. Very quickly, Stewart had resumed her place among the top lifestyle businesspeople in the world, leading her new television show, satellite radio program, and several other corporate partnerships to great financial success.

Further Reading

Byron, Christopher. *Martha Inc.: Incredible Story of Martha Stewart Living Omnimedia.* New York: Wiley, 2002.

Leavitt, Sarah A. *From Catherine Beecher to Martha Stewart: A Cultural History of Domestic Advice.* Chapel Hill: University of North Carolina Press, 2002.

Oppenheimer, Jerry. *Martha Stewart—Just Desserts: The Unauthorized Biography.* New York: William Morrow and Co., 1997.

"SEC Charges Martha Stewart, Broker Peter Bacanovic with Illegal Insider Trading," Securities and Exchange Commission. Available online. URL: http://www.sec.gov/news/press/2003-69.htm. Downloaded on July 6, 2009.

Strauss, Levi
(Loeb Strauss)
(1829–1902) *inventor of Levi's jeans*

The largest manufacturer of pants in the world is Levi Strauss & Company, makers of Levi's jeans. Levi's became popular as work pants among cowboys and miners in the 1870s, and after World War II denim jeans in general and Levi's in particular became the most popular leisure pants for men and women around the world. However, none of this ever would have happened if Levi Strauss, the inventor of Levi's jeans, had bought the right kind of canvas for his brother-in-law's store.

Strauss was born Loeb Strauss on February 26, 1829, in Buttenheim, Bavaria (part of present-day Germany). His father, Hirsch, was an itinerant dry-goods salesman, and his mother, Rebecca, was a homemaker. At age 18 he left Bavaria with his mother and three sisters to join his two brothers in New York City. Almost immediately he changed his name to Levi because most Americans could not pronounce Loeb. He then went on the road with his brothers who, like their deceased father, peddled dry goods (bolts of fabric and sewing notions such as needles and thread) to rural homemakers. After a year, his brothers had made enough money to open a dry-goods store in New York City, and in 1849, Strauss moved to Louisville, Kentucky, to peddle merchandise from their store in the surrounding countryside.

In 1850 Strauss's sister Fanny married a dry-goods peddler named David Stern. Hoping to cash in on California's tremendous demand for all types of items that had been sparked by the gold rush of

1849, the newlyweds moved to San Francisco and opened a dry-goods store. By 1852 business had prospered to the point that Stern needed a capable partner, so he made an offer that Strauss accepted. In 1853 Strauss left New York City with a considerable supply of merchandise from his brothers' store, most of which he sold to his fellow passengers on the ship. By the time he reached California, all he had left were some bolts of canvas that he intended to sell to tent and wagon cover makers. But when none of them would buy his canvas because it was too thin, he began searching for another use for the material.

Strauss soon noticed that the work trousers worn by miners and ranch hands were not sturdy enough to stand up to the daily wear and tear of the workers. Having learned a little about garments during his peddler days, he guessed that a pair of pants made from canvas might last longer, so he got a tailor to make him some canvas trousers. These work pants proved to be much sturdier than the thin trousers working people had been wearing, and they quickly became popular among the working class, so when Strauss ran out of canvas he asked his brothers to send him more. Instead, they sent him denim, which is just as tough as canvas but a lot easier to sew. The denim jeans sold so well that in 1856 Strauss was able to open his own store, Levi Strauss & Company, with his brothers and brother-in-law as partners. The store sold a variety of dry goods, but the most popular item was Strauss's denim jeans.

The only problem with Strauss's jeans was that the pockets tended to tear off long before the pants had worn out. In 1872 Jacob W. Davis, a Nevada tailor who was one of Strauss's customers, proposed that Strauss reinforce the pocket stitching with copper rivets, thus giving them added strength as well as the distinctive look they retained into the 21st century. The following year Strauss and Davis formed a partnership, patented the new design of the jeans, and copyrighted the name "Levi's" and the world-famous double-arch logo stitched on the hip pocket. The demand for Levi's was so great that in 1874 Strauss and Davis bought an old woolen mill and started making their own denim. By 1880 the partners had opened two jeans factories in San Francisco just to keep up with the demand. By 1900 Levi Strauss & Company had closed its retail store to focus on manufacturing and wholesaling Levi's.

Strauss was a benevolent employer as well as an intelligent entrepreneur. He insisted on being called Levi by his workers, whom he paid well and provided with safer working conditions than could be found in most textile mills at the time. Toward the end of his life he devoted most of his time, energy, and money to charitable activities. He contributed generously to the University of California at Berkeley and at least three orphanages, and he served as a board member for various organizations serving immigrants and the deaf. At the time of his death on September 26, 1902, in San Francisco, his fortune was estimated at $6 million. Having never married, he left his money to his favorite charities and his company to the children of Fanny and David Stern.

Further Reading

Shapiro, Michael. *The Jewish 100: A Ranking of the Most Influential Jews of All Time.* New York: Citadel Press, 2000.

Van Steenwyck, Elizabeth. *Levi Strauss: The Blue Jeans Man.* New York: Walker, 1988.

Strong, Harriett
(Harriet Williams Russell)
(1844–1926) *entrepreneur in walnuts and pampas grass*

Harriett Strong was a woman of many talents. She played such an instrumental role in the cultivation of walnuts in California that she became known as "the walnut queen," and her efforts to cultivate pampas grass for decorative purposes led her to become known as "the pampas queen." While looking for ways to keep her walnuts and pampas grass well watered, she invented a unique system of converting canyons into reservoirs. Her achievements are all the more impressive when one considers that at one point Strong was a semi-invalid with four small children and a mountain of debt so steep that it drove her husband to suicide.

Strong was born Harriet Williams Russell on July 23, 1844, in Buffalo, New York. Her father,

Henry, was a mining engineer, and her mother, Mary, was a homemaker. In the early 1850s she moved with her family to San Francisco, California, where her father became involved in the California gold rush. At age 17 she moved with her family to Carson City, Nevada, when her father became engaged in that state's silver rush. Two years later she married Charles Strong, superintendent and part-owner of a silver mine near Nevada City, California, with whom she had four children.

In 1864 Charles Strong had a nervous breakdown, and the Strongs bought a 220-acre ranch in southern California's San Gabriel Valley near present-day Whittier where he could recuperate. When he recovered, he returned to Nevada City while Harriett remained on the ranch, and they saw each other sporadically during the rest of their marriage. By 1883 her health had deteriorated to the point that she had been a semi-invalid for a number of years. That same year her husband, who was deeply in debt, killed himself, and his partners sued for control of his portion of the mine and the ranch. In a display of tremendous courage and inner strength, Strong declared herself cured and set out to save her ranch.

Regaining her vitality, Strong decided to give up ranching and become an orchard farmer. Within a year she had planted walnut trees, which she had seen growing wild throughout California, on 150 acres of her ranch, thus making it the largest walnut grove in the world. Since walnut trees mature slowly, she also planted some groves of oranges and lemons, and in between the walnut trees she planted pomegranates and pampas grass, faster-growing crops that flourish in Southern California's semiarid climate. The silvery plumes of the pampas grass were prized for decorative purposes by fashionable middle-class hostesses, especially when they were colored and given a silky finish. After spending the first year mastering the curing and dyeing process, the second year she realized a profit of $4,000 from the pampas grass alone, more than enough to save the ranch.

Strong next turned her attention to making sure her now-thriving orchards had plenty of water. Watercourses in southern California tend to run dry in the summer but flood in the spring, so she devised a water-storage system whereby the region's many canyons could be used to store water and control floods. The technology and engineering know-how that permitted the building of a huge dam like the Hoover Dam in the 1930s had yet to be developed, so she conceived of a system of short, stair-step dams for use in canyons or wherever a watercourse fell steeply over a short distance. The dams would be located so that their foundations were submerged by the water from the next dam downstream, the pressure of the water thus helping to support the base of the dam. The steep walls of the canyons would serve as the reservoirs' retaining walls, thus allowing the storing of spring floodwater until it was needed during the summer.

Strong built such a reservoir in a canyon on her land, then applied for and received a patent for her dam idea in 1887. In 1893 she exhibited a model of her dam-and-reservoir system at the World's Columbian Exposition in Chicago, Illinois, where it received considerable attention from professional engineers. However, local officials in California refused to spend the money required to implement Strong's idea, so it was never implemented on a statewide basis.

Meanwhile, Strong had continued to expand her business operations. She used the profits from walnuts and pampas grass to buy more land, on which she planted vegetables for truck farming as well as more walnuts and pampas grass. She also formed a water company, as well as an oil company that drilled three gushers. In the 1893 exposition she also exhibited her orchard crops and the impressive Isabella Pampas Palace, a 20-foot-square building made entirely out of pampas plumes. She served as president of the American Walnut Growers' Association and was the first women to serve on the Los Angeles, California, Chamber of Commerce. She died on September 16, 1926, in a car accident while returning to her ranch from Los Angeles.

Further Reading

Macdonald, Anne L. *Feminine Ingenuity: Women and Invention in America.* New York: Ballantine Books, 1994.

Vare, Ethlie Ann, and Greg Ptacek. *Mothers of Invention: From the Bra to the Bomb, Forgotten Women and Their Unforgettable Ideas.* New York: Quill, 1989.

Sutter, John
(Johann Augustus Suter)
(1803–1880) *entrepreneur in mercantile activity*

One of the most interesting figures in the history of the American West is John Sutter. Called the "Father of California" by many, Sutter has been hailed for many years as a paragon of enterprise and hospitality who failed because he had the incredibly bad luck to discover gold in his backyard. In fact, Sutter failed because he was one of the worst entrepreneurs in the history of American business.

Sutter was born Johann Augustus Suter on February 15, 1803, in Kandern, Baden, today part of Germany. His father, Johann, managed a small paper mill, and his mother, Christine, was a homemaker. As a teenager he was apprenticed to a publishing company in Basel, Switzerland, and eventually became a clerk. In 1826 he married Annette Dubeld, with whom he had five children, and opened a dry-goods store. He quickly proved to be a poor merchant, and after eight years in business he had amassed a pile of bills. To avoid being thrown into debtor's prison, in 1834 he emigrated to the United States and settled in St. Louis, Missouri. The following year he started trading with merchants in New Mexico and points west via the Santa Fe Trail. By 1838 he had amassed another pile of bills and decided to head farther west. Over the next year he visited Fort Vancouver in British-held Oregon Country, Honolulu in the kingdom of Hawaii, and Sitka in Russian-held Alaska before finally settling along the American River near the site of present-day Sacramento in Mexican-held California.

By 1841 the Mexican governor of California had granted Sutter almost 50,000 acres in the heart of the Sacramento Valley. Calling his little empire Nueva Helvetia, or New Switzerland, Sutter began employing Hawaiians, American Indians, mountain men, and drifters of every background. By 1844 he had built up several profitable enterprises, including wheat fields, orchards, vineyards, a cattle ranch, a blacksmith shop, a tannery, a distillery, a beaver-trapping operation, and a riverboat service to San Francisco. At its center was Sutter's Fort, its thick adobe walls serving as a symbol of Western civilization, enterprise, and hospitality. In fact, Sutter lived like a feudal lord. He maintained a standing militia of about 1,000 Indians outfitted in hand-me-down Russian uniforms (obtained from a Russian fort in northern California), and his home became a fount of free-flowing hospitality to whatever weary traveler happened to set foot in it. As a result, he found himself buried under yet another pile of bills.

For a while, Sutter's efforts to hold his creditors at bay succeeded, mostly because his land holdings were situated beyond the pale of civilized California, where he was the de facto upholder of law and order. But his world began to crumble in 1848, when John W. Marshall, a carpenter he had hired to build a sawmill, discovered gold on the American River about 35 miles northeast of the fort. Sutter tried to suppress news of the find, but within a year Nueva Helvetia had become the center of the California gold rush.

Unfortunately, Sutter failed to seize the several opportunities the discovery afforded him. He could have worked the claim himself, using his multinational labor force to mine gold while his Indian militia kept out claim jumpers. Or he could have established some sort of land office to sell claims to would-be miners, then make his money as the primary purveyor of goods and supplies to thousand of miners. Instead, he vacillated, reacting only when it was too late to take effective action. Once the gold rush shifted into high gear, he was unable to prevent the '49ers from trampling his fields and shooting his cattle. When he appealed to the newly established U.S. courts for redress, they denied the validity of one of his Mexican land grants. Having sold most of the land in the denied grant, he had to make the sales good by giving his buyers land in his other grant, which left him virtually landless and bankrupt. By 1853 he had fled Nueva Helvetia and taken up residence on Hock Farm on the Feather River. In 1865 a disgruntled employee set the farm on fire, and the financially ruined Sutter moved to Lititz, Pennsylvania. He survived for his remaining years on a meager pension paid to him by the state of California, in partial compensation for his lost empire. He also tried in vain to get a pension from the federal government. He died on June 18, 1880, in Washington, D.C.

Further Reading

Limerick, Patricia N. *Something in the Soil: Legacies and Reckonings in the New West*. New York: W. W. Norton, 2000.

Owens, Kenneth, ed. *John Sutter and a Wider West*. Lincoln: University of Nebraska Press, 1999.

Swift, Gustavus Franklin

(1839–1903) *inventor of packaged meat*

Before 1880 most urban Americans ate meat that had been slaughtered and butchered in their own city or town just a few days before. By 1900 they were eating meat that had been slaughtered and dressed (prepared for butchery) a week or two earlier in the Midwest and then shipped by refrigerated railcar to their local butcher. This revolutionary change was largely the result of the vision of one man, Gustavus Swift.

Swift was born on June 24, 1839, in Sandwich, Massachusetts. His parents, William and Sally, were farmers. After struggling through eight years of school, at age 14 he went to work in his older brother's butcher shop. Two years later he went into business for himself as a livestock driver; he bought cattle, hogs, and sheep at the regional livestock market in Brighton and then herded them to Eastham on Cape Cod, where he sold them to a slaughterhouse that killed and dressed the meat before selling it to local butchers. In 1861 he married Annie Higgins with whom he had 11 children. From 1862 to 1872 he operated a slaughterhouse and butcher shop, first in Barnstable and later in Brighton. In 1872 he and James A. Hathaway, a meat wholesaler in Boston, formed Hathaway & Swift; Hathaway handled the slaughtering and wholesaling aspects of the business, and Swift bought the livestock and supervised their shipment to Boston. At first Swift made his purchases from the regional stockyards in Albany and Buffalo, New York. But rail service between the East and the Midwest improved dramatically during the early 1870s, so in 1875 he decided to move his office to Chicago, Illinois, home of the nation's biggest livestock market.

In Chicago, Swift realized that the national distribution system for meat was entirely too inefficient. Live animals were being herded onto railcars in Chicago, then shipped all over the country. During the trip most animals lost weight and many died. Once they arrived and were slaughtered, more than 60 percent of their carcasses was thrown away. But he soon developed a better way. He concluded that killing and dressing the animals in large packing houses in Chicago, then shipping the dressed meat via refrigerated railcars to keep it from spoiling, would be much cheaper than handling and transporting live animals. It would also result in a substantial profit from the conversion of animal bone, hide, and internal organs into various by-products. He hired Andrew J. Chase, a well-known refrigeration engineer, who designed an insulated railcar that chilled air by constantly circulating it over ice. In 1877 Swift successfully shipped his first carload of dressed meat from Chicago to Boston.

In 1878 Swift and Hathaway parted company, and Swift and his brother Edwin formed Swift Brothers and Company, with Gustavus Swift as president. By now he realized that refrigerated railcars were not enough; he also had to have refrigerated storage space for the railcars to deliver to, as well as a sales force to sell the dressed meat quickly. To this end he began establishing branch offices in each city he wanted to do business in, as well as "car lines" by which dressed meat was sold straight off the railcar to butchers in towns and villages along the line. Concentrating first on establishing his company in New England, by 1900 Swift had created a national delivery and sales network that included almost 200 branch offices and almost 6,000 railcars. To keep up with the demand, he built six packing houses west of the Mississippi River, and by 1903 these plants were killing and dressing 8 million cattle, hogs, and sheep per year. Meanwhile, Swift and Company (the name was changed in 1885 when the company incorporated) had started making products such as glue, soap, and fertilizer from the remains of slaughtered animals.

Swift had to overcome several other obstacles to make his business successful. Hauling cattle was a lucrative enterprise for railroads, and they refused to build Swift's refrigerated cars. When he had them built on his own, the railroads refused to haul the cars until after he convinced a line on the verge of bankruptcy to do so. Slaughtering and dressing meat was a lucrative enterprise for local meat wholesalers, who in 1886 formed the National Butchers' Protective Association, which organized boycotts of dressed meat. And consumers had to be taught that dressed meat was just as tasty, wholesome, and safe to eat as fresh meat. These last two problems were solved partly by advertising but mostly by the fact that Swift's dressed meat tasted better and cost less than fresh meat. By 1900 the shipment of live animals east of Chicago had virtually ceased, and the dressed meat industry consisted of Swift and five competitors.

Toward the end of his life, Swift became a philanthropist, donating generously to the Methodist Episcopal Church, the University of Chicago, and the Young Mens' Christian Association (YMCA). At the time of his death on March 29, 1903, at his home in Lake Forest, a suburb of Chicago, his company was estimated to be worth $50 million.

Further Reading

Chandler, Alfred D. *The Visible Hand: The Managerial Revolution in American Business.* Cambridge, Mass.: Belknap Press, 1977.

Swift, Louis Franklin. *The Yankee of the Yards: The Biography of Gustavus Franklin Swift.* New York: AMS Press, 1970.

T

Tesla, Nikola

(1856–1943) *inventor of the alternating-current electric motor*

One of the most important inventions of the industrial era was the alternating-current electric motor. Because of its simple construction, efficiency, ruggedness, and low cost, this motor found a wide range of applications as a constant-speed device in factories all over the world. The inventor of the alternating-current electric motor, Nikola Tesla, was a scientific genius whose experiments with a number of physical phenomena continue to serve as a source of wonder and inspiration for scientists. He was also an eccentric who died broke and alone.

Tesla was born on July 10, 1856, in Smiljan, Croatia, at the time part of the Austro-Hungarian Empire. His father, Milutin, was a priest, and his mother, Djouka, was a homemaker. At age seven he moved with his family to Gospic, where he grew up. In 1875 he enrolled in the polytechnical college at Graz, Austria, where he studied physics, mathematics, and mechanics. In 1879 he enrolled in the University of Prague but had to drop out after two years when his father died. He went to work at the central telephone office in Budapest, Hungary, and in 1882 he moved to Paris, France, taking a job as an engineer with the Continental Edison Telephone Company.

While working in Budapest, Tesla had envisioned the possibility of devising an electric motor that would run on alternating current. At the time, the only available electric motors ran on direct current. Although these motors worked fine, they were limited in their usefulness because direct current required too much voltage to transmit electricity safely for any distance at all. Consequently, any industry wishing to use electric motors had to build its own power generating station, which was expensive. On the other hand, the long-distance transmission of alternating current was easy and safe, and it was already being used to light homes and offices in the United States and Europe.

Tesla had concluded that making an alternating-current motor was a simple matter of using two alternating-current sources of different phases to create a rotating magnetic field, which could then be used to drive a motor. He built a crude prototype of an alternating-current motor while working for Continental Edison, and in 1884 he emigrated to the United States to promote it. He arrived in New York City with 4¢ and a letter of introduction to THOMAS ALVA EDISON. Although by this time Edison had committed himself to making direct current the standard for the country, he was impressed with Tesla's motor and gave him a job with the Edison Machine Works redesigning direct-current dynamos, or generators. The following year Tesla and Edison formed a company to develop and market industrial arc lighting, but they had a falling-out, probably over the relative merits of direct current versus alternating current, and parted ways. After two years of odd jobs, in 1887 Tesla set up a laboratory of his own and resumed his experiments with alternating current. Within a year he had obtained patents for alternating-current motors, dynamos, and transformers.

Unlike Edison, GEORGE WESTINGHOUSE was committed to making alternating current the standard for the country. Seeing the value of Tesla's work, in 1888 Westinghouse bought all of Tesla's alternating-current patents for more than $200,000. Tesla's inventions essentially removed the last objections that opponents had to alternating current because they made it possible to harness the tremendous hydroelectric power potential of Niagara Falls. When this happened in 1895, two years after Westinghouse lit up the World's Columbian Exposition in Chicago, Illinois, by using Tesla's dynamos and transformers, it was clear that alternating current, and not direct current, would become the standard electric current in the United States and the world.

After 1888 Tesla withdrew to his laboratory and conducted a wide-ranging number of experiments with all sorts of physical phenomena. In 1891, the same year he became an American citizen, he invented the Tesla coil, an air-core transformer that is used extensively in radio and television equipment today. He also experimented with lightning, and at a tower he built in Colorado he produced artificial lightning spikes of millions of volts up to 135 feet long. Toward the end of his life he became somewhat eccentric. He claimed to have communicated via high-frequency waves with beings from another planet, and to have created a "death ray" that could destroy 10,000 airplanes at a range of 250 miles, but offered no proof to substantiate either claim. He continued to invent, but because he rarely filed for patents, he made little money from his inventions. He spent the last 30 years of his life living in a series of cheap New York hotel rooms and associated with few people, preferring instead the company of the pigeons in the park. He died on January 7, 1943, in New York City.

Further Reading

Cheney, Margaret. *Tesla: Man Out of Time.* New York: Simon and Schuster, 2001.

Floyd, E. Randall. *The Good, the Bad & the Mad: Weird People in American History.* Augusta, Ga.: Harbor House, 1999.

Lomas, Robert. *The Man Who Invented the Twentieth Century: Nikola Tesla, Forgotten Genius of Electricity.* London: Headline, 2000.

Thompson, J. Walter

(1847–1928) *entrepreneur in magazine advertising*

Magazine readers in the 21st century will not be surprised to know that from one-half to two-thirds of their favorite magazine consists of advertisements. But they might be shocked to know that in the 19th century magazines contained little or no advertising. The person most responsible for this dramatic change is J. Walter Thompson, whom some have called the father of American magazine advertising.

Thompson was born on October 28, 1847, in Pittsfield, Massachusetts. His father, Alonzo, was a bridge builder, and his mother, Cornelia, was a homemaker. As a young boy he moved with his family to Freeport, Ohio, where he grew up. At age 19 he joined the U.S. Marine Corps and served a two-year hitch. He was discharged in New York City, where in 1868 he found a job as a bookkeeper for Carlton & Smith, one of the nation's first advertising agencies.

Advertising in the 1860s was a far cry from the slick salesmanship of the 21st century. The most popular forms of advertising were storefront displays, and signs and billboards on the sides of buildings that advertised local businesses to local people. Although most newspapers accepted advertising, the ads looked and read more like modern classified ads, and like the classifieds they were usually jammed together in the back of the paper. Since national brands did not yet exist, about the only businesses that bothered to advertise in the newspaper were local retailers and wholesalers that sold dry goods, hardware, and groceries. The few national magazines that existed were reluctant to accept advertising because they thought it cheapened the tone of their publications, so they preferred to support themselves almost exclusively on the money received from subscriptions and newsstand sales. In fact, the first advertising agencies were not founded to create ads but to sell space.

In essence, all Carlton & Smith did was convince publishers to sell the agency blocks of space in their publications, then resell the space to advertisers at a profit. Although the agency did write some ad copy, mostly this writing was done by either the customer or the publication's editorial staff.

After a short stint as a bookkeeper, Thompson convinced William J. Carlton, the agency's managing partner, to let him try his hand at selling. He enjoyed some success buying and selling space in several small religious publications, but he realized that he could make more money selling space in magazines with a national appeal and reputation. He was especially interested in the potential offered by women's magazines such as *Godey's Lady's Book,* which since 1837 had been filled with features on fashion, shopping, and homemaking. Unlike most of his contemporaries, Thompson foresaw the birth of America's consumer society after the Civil War. Industries were on the rise in the East, farmers were cultivating the Midwest and the West, and railroads were being built all over the country. All of this commercial activity created a national economy with capabilities and needs that were different from the regional and local economies of antebellum days. Manufacturers were beginning to produce for the entire country, and they had a need to present their wares to the nation's consumers. Consumers had more money to spend, and they had a need to know what new things were available and from whom to buy them.

Thompson set out to convince the publishers of the national magazines that it was in their best interest to accept advertising. He succeeded in part by convincing them that they were offering their readers a valuable service by informing them of particularly useful goods now available in the marketplace. This pitch was made more effective over the years by the growing popularity of Montgomery Ward's mail-order catalog; first appearing in 1872, it proved that consumers would eagerly pore over reading matter that contained a lot of advertising. Thompson also succeeded in buying space by offering to pay high rates for it. By 1890 magazine publishers had realized that the proceeds from advertising far exceeded the amount of money that subscriptions and newsstand sales could bring in, and they dedicated more and more of their space to advertising. By 1900 several publishers had discovered they could maximize profits by selling their publications at cover prices below their costs of production in order to boost circulation, thus permitting them to charge more for advertising space.

Having acquired space in quality magazines, Thompson simply resold it to eager advertisers at an even higher rate. By 1877 he was making enough money to buy Carlton & Smith when Carlton retired that same year, and the following year he renamed it the J. Walter Thompson Company. In 1879 he married Margaret Bogle with whom he had one child. As national magazines became more interested in selling space to advertisers, the number of advertising agencies grew. Thompson managed to avoid ruinous competition by securing exclusive contracts from the magazines he represented. In the 1880s he created the "List of Thirty Select Magazines," all of them nationally respected publications represented by his agency, and he sold space in these magazines to advertisers on a block basis. This meant that advertisers could negotiate at one sitting for space in all 30 magazines. As advertising dollars contributed more and more to a publication's profitability, magazines vied with one another to be included on Thompson's list, which further enhanced the prestige of his agency.

Thompson's next step was to sell advertising in the United States to foreign manufacturers. In 1889 he published *Advertising in America,* a thick book in French and English that explained the American advertising system to foreign manufacturers, and in 1899 he opened a sales office in London, England. After 1900 Thompson oversaw the evolution of his company from a sales office to a full-service agency that not only secured space but also designed the ad, wrote the copy, and provided the necessary illustrations and photographs. In 1911 he further enhanced the prestige of his agency by publishing *Things to Know about Trade-Marks,* a handy guide concerning the ins and outs of brand names and logos and explaining what legal rights trademarks confer. By 1916, when Thompson retired, his agency had offices throughout the Northeast and Midwest serving 300 advertisers and doing an annual business of about $3 million. He died on October 16, 1928, in New York City.

Further Reading

Fox, Stephen R. *The Mirror Makers: A History of American Advertising and Its Creators.* Urbana: University of Illinois Press, 1997.

"J. Walter Thompson Company (JWT) History," James W. Hartman Centery for Sales, Advertising & Marketing History. Available online. URL: http://library.duke.edu/specialcollections/hartman/guides/jwt-history.html. Downloaded on July 6, 2009.

Thomson, Samuel

(1769–1843) *entrepreneur in botanic medicine*

Although doctors typically make a lot of money, most entrepreneurs do not consider making a career out of medicine. One who did was Samuel Thomson, a semiliterate farmer who patented a system of home medical treatment that could have made him a millionaire.

Thomson was born on February 9, 1769, in Alstead, New Hampshire. His parents, John and Hannah, were farmers. His entire formal education consisted of one month of elementary school, although he later taught himself how to read and write. An elderly herb and root doctor took a liking to him when he was young and taught him much about the medicinal uses of plants. In 1790 he married Susan Allen with whom he had eight children, and he settled down to a life of farming.

Medical doctors of the day relied primarily on two techniques, regardless of the patient's illness or condition: bloodletting and the administration of calomel, a powder whose main ingredient is mercury. These two treatments often caused more harm than they did good. Thomson was particularly disgusted after physicians using these treatments killed his mother and almost killed his wife. On the other hand, two herb and root doctors once saved his wife's life after six physicians had declared they could do nothing for her. Following this last episode, he determined to learn all he could about botanic medicine and use what he learned to treat his family himself.

Over the next several years, Thomson developed a system for treating illness that seemed to work much better than bloodletting and calomel. His basic idea was to purge the body of whatever was making it sick by inducing vomiting and sweating, and then restore it to health by administering healthful herbal remedies. First, he administered a hefty dose of lobelia, or Indian tobacco, which initiates intense vomiting and sweating but is followed by a feeling of invigoration. Next, he administered successive doses of cayenne pepper, herbal teas and tonics, and brandy or wine mixed with herbs. In some cases, he also had the patient take a steam bath after ingesting the lobelia. The system seems unorthodox by modern medical standards, and yet he used it on his relatives and neighbors with such great effectiveness that he became known as a healer. He was hounded throughout his life by medical doctors for being a fraud, but he followed the same basic theory they did: out with the bad, in with the good. The differences were that Thomson used medicines made from vegetables rather than from minerals, and he substituted vomiting and sweating for bloodletting. Although he may not have done his patients any good, he at least did not do them as much harm as many a medical doctor would have done.

In 1805 Thomson moved to Boston, Massachusetts, became what he called a botanic physician, and began treating people from Boston to Bangor, Maine. Six years later he established in Eastport, Maine, a medical mutual aid society, and in 1813 he patented his system and began selling pamphlets that described how it worked. In 1823 he renewed his patent and began selling a book (ghostwritten by a friend who was a minister) called *New Guide to Health, or Botanic Family Physician.* The book was an extended version of his pamphlet, and it basically taught heads of households everything Thomson thought they needed to know about treating their own families. In addition to selling the book himself, he established a network of agents throughout the United States. Over the next 10 years, the network grew to include 167 agents, mostly in Ohio, Tennessee, and Alabama. The book sold for $20, an enormous sum of money for the day, and it gave the purchaser the right to use Thomson's patented botanic system for curing illness and disease. It also gave the purchaser the right to join a local Friendly Botanical Society, which was similar to the group he had founded in Eastport.

By 1839 Thomson had sold more than 100,000 copies of his book. Unfortunately, he never collected anything close to the $2 million, minus commissions, he should have received from its sale. Many copies were sold on credit, and thus were never paid for, and many of his agents turned out to be dishonest. Thomson seemed less bothered by this than by those who misused his methods for gain, believing firmly that each man should be his own family's physician. And although the botanic system never made him wealthy, it did force the medical profession to address the efficacy of his and their methods, and it led ultimately to changes in the way medical doctors treated patients. Thomson died on October 4, 1843, in Boston.

Further Reading

Gevitz, Norman. *Other Healers: Unorthodox Medicine in America.* Baltimore, Md.: Johns Hopkins University Press, 1988.

Haller, John S. *The People's Doctors: Samuel Thomson and the American Botanical Movement, 1790–1860.* Carbondale: Southern Illinois University Press, 2000.

Thorp, John

(1784–1848) *inventor of the ring spinning frame*

One of the more obscure heroes of the Industrial Revolution in America is John Thorp. By inventing the ring spinning frame, Thorp made it possible for the textile industry in the United States to employ a large percentage of unskilled workers, thus leading to its tremendous expansion during the 19th century. However, Thorp's contribution to the rise of American textiles remained virtually unrecognized until 80 years after his death.

Surprisingly little is known about Thorp's life. He was born in 1784 in Rehoboth, Massachusetts. His father, Reuben, was a wheelwright and coach builder, and his mother, Hannah, was a homemaker. In 1812 he filed for a patent for an improved power loom, a device that weaves fabric mechanically rather than by hand. In 1813 Thorp's older brother David began selling power looms made to Thorp's design, and they became popular in the textile factories in and around Pawtucket, Rhode Island. By 1816 Thorp had moved to Taunton, Massachusetts where he became partners with Silas Shepard. They applied for a patent for further improvements to the power loom that same year, and they did a brisk business making and selling them to mills along the Blackstone River in Massachusetts and Rhode Island. In 1817 he married Eliza Williams with whom he had no children.

Between 1817 and 1828, during which period Thorp moved to Providence, Rhode Island, he invented other devices for use in textile manufacturing, most notably machines for making braiding and netting from cotton yarn. By far the most important of his inventions was the ring spinning frame for the making, or spinning, of yarn. This machine stretched, or drew, cotton fibers heaped up on spindles through rollers, then passed the drawn fibers through small wire devices called travelers. The travelers twisted the fibers by moving rapidly around steel raceways, or rings, mounted on plates, which wound the drawn and twisted fibers, or yarn, onto revolving wooden bobbins by moving up and down.

In 1828, when Thorp received a patent for the ring spinning frame, most yarn was spun on a machine known as a mule. This device consisted of multiple spindles mounted on a carriage; as the carriage traveled down a five-foot track, the cotton fibers were drawn by rollers revolving at different speeds so that the fibers were also twisted. Then, when the carriage returned to its original position, the yarn was wound by hand onto a bobbin. This method only permitted the intermittent spinning of the yarn; while the carriage was returning to its starting place, it was not spinning. It also required skilled laborers to carefully wind the yarn onto the bobbin in the required conical pattern. Thorp's machine was an improvement over the mule because it spun yarn continuously and because it could be operated more easily by unskilled laborers. This latter factor was particularly important in the United States, where few skilled textile workers lived but where large numbers of unskilled workers, especially young women and children, could be employed in the textile mills.

Thorp's ring spinning frame was imperfect and therefore did not begin to catch on in a widespread way until the 1840s, when improvements to it had been made; not surprisingly, Thorp was one of the inventors who made such adjustments, receiving a patent in 1844 for improvements in ring and traveler spinning. By 1870 ring spinning had virtually replaced mule spinning in the United States.

During the early 1830s Thorp designed machines for manufacturing braid for Thomas and William Fletcher. In 1832 he opened his own machine shop. He died on November 15, 1848, an obscure man of modest means in Providence, having failed to make a reputation or a fortune from his inventions. In 1928, on the 100th anniversary of the invention of the ring spinning frame, the National Association of Cotton Manufacturers erected a plaque in his honor at the Slater Mill Historic Site in Pawtucket, Rhode Island.

Further Reading

Clark, C. H. "John Thorp—Inventor of Ring Spinning," *Transactions of the National Association of Cotton Manufacturers* (1929), 72–94.

Reynolds, Douglas M., and Marjory Myers, eds. *Working in the Blackstone River Valley: Exploring the Heritage of Industrialization.* Woonsocket: Rhode Island Labor History Society, 1991.

Tilghman, Benjamin Chew (1821–1901), and Richard Albert Tilghman (1824–1899)
inventors of sandblasting

Candle making, wood pulping, and sandblasting are three endeavors that have little in common. What links them together is that at one time the Tilghman brothers, Benjamin and Richard, devoted their collective energies to making improvements in each area. Although they were not always successful commercially, they always managed to come up with something new.

Benjamin and Richard Tilghman were born on October 26, 1821, and May 24, 1824, respectively, in Philadelphia, Pennsylvania. Their father, Benjamin, was a lawyer, and their mother, Anna Maria, was a homemaker. Benjamin received his B.A. from Bristol College in New Jersey in 1839, then studied law for two years; Richard received his B.A. from the University of Pennsylvania in 1841. Having developed an interest in chemistry and physics while in college, from 1841 to 1844 the brothers traveled throughout Europe where they studied the procedures and problems of various laboratories, chemical works, factories, and mills.

In 1844 the Tilghmans became business partners, and for the rest of their lives they engaged in a succession of innovative enterprises. First, they perfected a process, originally invented by Richard, for breaking down animal fat into glycerine and fatty acid by "cooking" it in a high-temperature pressure cooker. They succeeded in extracting a fatty acid of such high quality that in 1847 they were able to sell their method to the Price Patent Candle Company of London, England. Next, they devoted themselves to the development of hardened steel shot, an endeavor in which Benjamin led the way, for use in sawing, grinding, and polishing stone, as well as for providing the abrasive edge on rock drills. Then, they tried their hands at breaking down wood into pulp by using sulfuric acid; although they succeeded in doing so in 1857, the Civil War broke out before they could make this discovery profitable. In 1860 Richard married Susan Toland with whom he had five children; Benjamin never married.

The brothers' collaborations were halted temporarily by the Civil War, during which Benjamin served as an officer in the Union army. Upon his return to Philadelphia, they resumed their papermaking experiments. In 1867 they received patents for making paper pulp out of vegetable material by "cooking" wood pulp in a high-temperature pressure cooker, and for preventing the paper pulp from becoming burned or discolored by adding calcium to the mix. Despite the novelty and usefulness of this approach, the Tilghmans were unable to translate the making of paper via the sulfite process, as it later became known, into economic success. By the time the sulfite process for making paper pulp did become popular, their patents had lapsed without being renewed; meanwhile, other inventors had figured out independently how to make the sulfite process commercially viable.

In 1870 the Tilghmans invented the sandblasting business. Having already developed hardened steel shot, Benjamin figured out how to project shot and sand with great force via steam pressure. The brothers then perfected the process, later substituting compressed air for steam, so that it could be used to cut and shape stone, inscribe limestone and granite, reface grinding wheels, remove dirt from the exterior walls of buildings, etch glass, depolish china and porcelain, smooth armor plate, sharpen files, remove rust and scale from iron forgings and castings, and remove paint from the hulls of ships, among other tasks. The brothers formed two sandblasting companies, which proved to be lucrative enterprises; Benjamin managed the affairs of the Tilghman Patent Sand Blasting Company, Ltd., in England, while Richard directed the operations of the B. C. & R. A. Tilghman Company in the United States. By the late 1890s both Tilghmans had retired to Philadelphia where they died, Richard on March 24, 1899, and Benjamin on July 3, 1901. Their business holdings were left in the hands of Richard's two sons.

Further Reading

Iles, George. *Leading American Inventors*. New York: H. Holt, 1912.

"Sand Blasting," *Illustrated Glass Dictionary*. Available online. URL: http://www.glassonline.com/infoserv/dictionary/353.html. Downloaded on July 6, 2009.

Trippe, Juan Terry
(1899–1981) *founder of Pan American Airways*

Pan American Airways was the world's first international airline, and until 1970 it was also its best. The man most responsible for the success of Pan American was Juan Trippe, who also played a significant role in the development of the world's first successful commercial jet airliners.

Trippe was born on June 27, 1899, in Sea Bright, New Jersey. His father, Charles, was a stockbroker and banker, and his mother, Lucy, was a real-estate speculator; he was named in honor of his great-aunt, Juanita Terry. At age 10 he watched a barnstorming exhibition over New York City harbor, and from that moment on his main interest in life was aviation. He attended private schools in New York City and Philadelphia, and at age 18 he enrolled in Yale University. He left school during World War I to become a pilot in the U.S. Navy, but the war ended before he saw combat. After receiving his B.A. from Yale in 1921, he went to work selling bonds for a Wall Street firm, but after two years he had become so bored with this line of work that he decided to become a professional aviator.

In 1923 Trippe and several friends bought some government surplus biplanes and started Long Island Airways, an air taxi service in and around New York City. When the Kelly Act of 1925 forced the federal government to get out of the airmail business, he and his friends and several other investors formed Colonial Air Transport and won a contract to deliver the mail between New York City and Boston, Massachusetts. Almost immediately, he turned his attention to establishing an airmail route between Florida and Cuba, but the other investors refused to go along with his plan and so he resigned. He then formed Pan American Airways, negotiated successfully with Cuba's leader, Gerardo Machado, for landing rights in Havana, and in 1927 won a contract to deliver mail between Key West, Florida, and Havana.

Juan Trippe, founder of Pan-American Airways, the world's first international airline *(Library of Congress)*

In 1928, the same year Trippe married Elizabeth Stettinius with whom he had four children, Pan American inaugurated air passenger service between Key West and Havana.

Over the next four years Trippe continued to expand his airline's routes in Latin America. He purchased a fleet of S-38 twin-engine amphibians from the U.S. company of Igor Sikorsky, the noted Russian-born aircraft designer; employed Charles A. Lindbergh, the first pilot to fly across the Atlantic Ocean, as a surveyor; and established a 12,000-mile mail and passenger circuit connecting the United States, Cuba, Puerto Rico, Haiti, the Dominican Republic, Colombia, Panama, British Honduras, and Mexico. By 1932 Trippe had secured the U.S. government's contracts for mail delivery to every country in Central and South America, as well as most of the mail route contracts between those countries and the United States. At this point Pan American was flying more route miles than any other airline in the world.

Trippe then turned his attention to establishing air routes among the United States, Asia, and Europe. By 1935 Pan American was providing air service between San Francisco, California, and Honolulu, Hawaii, via the Martin M-130 "flying boat." In 1936 the company introduced the S-42, a four-engine amphibian which became known as the "China Clipper," and extended its run to Manila, the Philippines, that same year and to Hong Kong the following year. Meanwhile, Pan American's expansion across the Atlantic Ocean was held up while a suitable aircraft could be built and landing rights could be negotiated. In 1939 the Boeing 314 or "Yankee Clipper," at the time the world's largest airliner, initiated commercial air service between New York and London, England. In 1947 Pan American became the first airline to offer around-the-world service.

The invention of jet aircraft during World War II attracted the attention of many commercial aviation executives, especially Trippe. By 1947 Pan American had lost its monopoly on U.S. international air routes without being able to obtain domestic routes, and Trippe reasoned that the best way to dominate the new competition was to provide faster air travel via jet airliners. A British firm, the De Havilland Aircraft Company, was the first to develop a commercial jet airplane, the De Havilland Comet, which was introduced in 1949. Unfortunately, the Comet suffered from structural defects that forced it to be grounded. Eager to employ jets in his international flights, Trippe strongly encouraged the Boeing Airplane Company to build an American jet airliner, and in 1958 the Boeing 707 began flying nonstop transatlantic flights for Pan American. As air travel became increasingly popular, Trippe pushed for the development of a wide-bodied, tri-engine jet. Again Boeing complied, this time with the Boeing 747, which entered service in 1970. Meanwhile, Trippe had retired two years earlier to his home in New York City, where he lived a quiet life until his death on April 3, 1981.

Further Reading

Bender, Marylin. *The Chosen Instrument: Pan Am, Juan Trippe, the Rise and Fall of an American Entrepreneur.* New York: Simon & Schuster, 1982.

Daley, Robert. *An American Saga: Juan Trippe and His PanAm Empire.* New York: Random House, 1980.

Josephson, Matthew. *Empire of the Air: Juan Trippe and the Struggle for World Airways.* North Stratford, Mass.: Ayer Co. Publishers, 1999, reprint.

Tupper, Earl Silas

(1907–1983) *inventor of Tupperware*

Most households in the United States own at least one piece of Tupperware. The most innovative products in the line, the plastic food storage containers, are a reliable, convenient way to preserve leftovers, and the company's other plastic home products are colorful, durable, and easy to care for. Oddly enough, these revolutionary plastic products were invented by a man, Earl Tupper, who had no formal training as a chemical engineer and whose original goal was to make a million dollars as a tree surgeon.

Tupper was born on July 28, 1907, in Berlin, New Hampshire. His parents, Earnest and Lulu, were farmers. As a young boy he moved with his family to a farm in Shirley, Massachusetts, and at age 10 he helped supplement the family finances by selling door-to-door some of the chickens and produce his parents raised. After graduating from high school in 1925, he stayed on the farm for two years, then went to work as a mail clerk and a railroad laborer. In 1928 he took a course in tree surgery and opened Tupper Tree Doctors, which also did landscaping work. Unfortunately, the Great Depression held down the demand for his services, and in 1936 he was forced to declare bankruptcy. One of his customers had been Bernard Doyle, the general manager of Viscoloid, a Du Pont plastics division facility in nearby Leominster, and in 1937 Doyle offered him a job. For the next year Tupper gained valuable experience in plastics manufacturing and design, and he came to see plastics as the materials of the future.

In 1938 Tupper left Viscoloid and formed the Earl S. Tupper Company in Leominster. Although Tupper advertised that his company designed and engineered industrial plastics, most of his work was subcontracted to him by Viscoloid. At the outbreak of World War II, Tupper won government contracts to mold parts for gas masks for the U.S. Army and signal lamps for the U.S. Navy that enabled him to open a factory in 1942 in nearby Farnumsville. To hold down costs, he contracted with Viscoloid to buy their scrap plastic. Called polyethylene slag, this material was black, smelly, and hard as a rock, but Tupper figured out how to convert it into a usable plastic, which he called "Poly-T," that was flexible, tough, nonporous, nongreasy, translucent, and odorless. He also invented an injection molding machine to convert Poly-T into such products as bathroom tumblers, cigarette cases, and novelty cups, which he sold mostly to companies that gave them away as premiums for buying something else. In 1945 he began making dishes, bowls, and cups that were resistant to hot and cold temperatures as well as to cracking, thus making them perfect for kitchen use. At first the plasticware was sold in hardware and department stores, and in 1946 he started putting out a catalog.

In 1947 Tupper turned his attention to making plastic food storage containers. To ensure that food stored in the containers would stay fresh, he invented a special seal that was airtight and watertight; in fact, the seal copied the sealing principle employed by the lid on a can of paint. Called Tupperware, these containers were a vast improvement over glass canning jars and tinfoil because they were easier to use and worked better. The general public, however, was comfortable with glass canning jars and tinfoil, did not understand plastics at the time, and could not figure out in the store how to make the seal work; consequently, not much Tupperware was sold.

Meanwhile, two independent sales representatives for Stanley Home Products, Brownie Wise of Florida and Thomas Damigella of Massachusetts, had "discovered" Tupperware. They began buying it in bulk from local plastics distributors and selling it via Stanley home parties, wherein the hostess invites several of her friends and coworkers to her house, and the sales representative entertains them while demonstrating useful home products. By 1948 Wise and Damigella were selling so much Tupperware that Tupper contacted them to find out how they were doing it. That same year he, Wise, Damigella, and several local Stanley distributors met at a hotel in Worcester, Massachusetts, to work out a new distribution plan for Tupperware. Essentially, the group decided to retain the basic Stanley home party plan with certain modifications as worked out by Wise; independent distributors bought the products directly from Tupper, and Wise developed a plan for demonstrating the many different styles and colors and, most important, showing customers how the seal worked. The new marketing strategy worked so well that in 1951 Tupper took his products out of stores, changed the name of the company to Tupperware Home Parties, moved the company headquarters to Kissimmee, Florida, and made Wise a vice president. Within a few years, annual sales exceeded $100 million.

In 1958 Tupper sold Tupperware Home Parties to the Rexall Drug Company for $16 million. That same year he divorced his wife of 27 years (name not known) with whom he had five children. He stayed on as chairman of the board until 1973, when he retired to San Jose, Costa Rica. He died on October 3, 1983, in San Jose.

Further Reading

Clarke, Alison J. *Tupperware: The Promise of Plastic in 1950s America.* Washington, D.C.: Smithsonian Institution Press, 1999.

Gershman, Michael. *Getting It Right the Second Time: How American Ingenuity Transformed Forty-Nine Marketing Failures into Some of Our Most Successful Products.* Reading, Mass.: Addison-Wesley Publishing Co., 1990.

Turner, Ted
(Robert Edward Turner III)
(1938–) *entrepreneur in cable television*

Ted Turner is one of the most colorful figures of the late 20th century. He built an outdoor advertising company into one of the nation's biggest media and sports empires, in the process changing the way people watch the news and making it possible for them to watch thousands of classic movies without leaving their living rooms.

Turner was born Robert Edward Turner III on November 19, 1938, in Cincinnati, Ohio. His father, Robert Edward Jr., owned an outdoor advertising company, and his mother, Florence, was a homemaker. He was educated at boarding schools in Ohio, Georgia, and Tennessee, where he gained a reputation for being a disciplinary problem. As a student at Brown University, he was suspended for excessive drinking and expelled for having a woman in his dorm room. After serving briefly with the U.S. Coast Guard, in 1960 he joined his father's company, Turner Advertising.

In 1962 Turner Advertising bought a number of billboards from a competitor, including many of the best locations in Atlanta, Georgia. The acquisition placed an enormous debt burden on the company, and shortly after the deal was struck Turner's father decided he had made a horrible mistake. Over the vehement objections of Turner, he tried to sell the newly acquired billboards to another competitor. Six months later the new billboards remained unsold, and the elder Turner committed suicide. Turner took over the company, canceled the sale, and went to Atlanta where he personally saw to it that the company's billboards in that town began generating income for Turner Advertising. His actions saved the company, and over the next seven years the company became profitable.

In 1970 Turner decided to diversify his holdings by buying television stations in Atlanta and Charlotte, North Carolina. Both stations were losing money, but Turner turned them around by advertising them heavily on his billboards and by showing a number of black-and-white films and reruns of sitcoms that had been popular 20 years earlier. (This is the same strategy that JOHN WERNER KLUGE had used when trying to rejuvenate a television station he had bought 11 years earlier.) He also mixed in a heavy dosage of professional wrestling matches and live games played by Atlanta's professional baseball, basketball, and hockey teams, the rights to which he outbid the major networks. He bought baseball's National League Atlanta Braves in 1976 and the National Basketball Association Atlanta Hawks in 1977, thus ensuring that his stations would enjoy exclusive rights to future broadcasts of their games.

By 1976 satellite communications had become a reality with the successful launchings of several Intelsats and Satcom, all of which were capable of transmitting color television programs. Although the equipment for beaming programs up to the satellites was expensive, Turner reasoned that broadcasting by satellite to cable systems around the country would greatly increase the size of his potential audience, and therefore his advertising revenues from national accounts. In 1976 he renamed his Atlanta station Superstation TBS (for Turner Broadcasting System) and began beaming its signal to cable systems all across America.

Although his stations devoted little attention to broadcasting the news, in 1980 Turner implemented what is perhaps the most revolutionary development in television news since the television itself. The Cable News Network, better known as CNN, became the first 24-hour, live news program in the world. The experts scoffed at the idea, saying that no one would watch it for more than 30 minutes at a time, the length of the major networks' nightly news programs. What they failed to realize was that CNN would change the nature of broadcast journalism. Instead of telling people what had happened earlier in the day, as the major networks did, CNN told them what was happening while it was happening. Over the course of a day, CNN updated its stories every time there was something new to report, thus making the news much more dynamic than it had ever been before. Turner further expanded this concept in 1982 when he created Headline News, a 30-minute encapsulation of the world news that was updated every 30 minutes. Over the years, new CNNs were added; CNNfn focused on financial news, CNN/SI focused on sports, and CNN International is shown overseas as the foreign version of CNN.

In 1986 Turner made another monumental move when he bought MGM's entire inventory of more than 3,000 classic movies for more than $1 billion. The move almost cost him control of Turner Broadcasting, but once the movies began playing on Superstation TBS, that station became one of the most popular cable channels in the country. Moreover, the movies allowed him to create two more channels devoted entirely to movies, Turner Network Television (TNT) and Turner Classic Movies (TCM). In 1991 he bought all of the cartoons ever made by Hanna-Barbera, one of the greatest cartoon studios of all time, and began showing them 24 hours a day on a new channel, the Cartoon Network. And in 1994 he merged with New Line Cinema, one of the country's largest independent movie production and distribution companies, so that occasionally he could show something new on TBS and TNT.

By 1996 Turner's entertainment empire had grown so large that it rivaled Time Warner, the industry's giant. That same year Turner merged his operations into Time Warner, in the process becoming vice chairman and gaining access to the old Warner Bros. library of films and cartoons. When Time Warner merged with AOL in 2000 to create AOL Time Warner, the largest Internet and media company in the world, Turner became vice chairman and senior adviser of the new company.

Turner has been married three times: to Judy Hallisey (1960–1962) with whom he had two children, to Jane Smith (1964–1988) with whom he had two children, and to Jane Fonda (1991–2001). He has a passion for yachting, and in 1977 his crew won the America's Cup, the world's most prestigious yachting trophy. In 1986, he began sponsoring the Goodwill Games, an off-year version of the Olympics. Turner continued to support the games until their demise in 2001, despite losing more than $100 million on the games. In 1997, he pledged to provide $1 billion to the United Nations to help fund its various charities and in 2006 delivered on that pledge with $600 million from his foundation and $400 million from other sources raised by Turner. A confirmed environmentalist, Turner has purchased more than 1 million acres of land in Montana, New Mexico, and Nebraska that he says will never be developed.

Further Reading

Bibb, Porter. *Ted Turner: It Ain't As Easy As It Looks.* Boulder, Colo.: Johnson Books, 1997.

Chethik, Neil. *Fatherloss: How Sons of All Ages Come to Terms with the Deaths of Their Dads.* New York: Hyperion, 2001.

Lowe, Janet. *Ted Turner Speaks: Insight from the World's Greatest Maverick.* New York: Chicester, Wiley, 1999.

Schonfeld, Reese. *Me and Ted against the World: The Unauthorized Story of the Founding of CNN.* New York: Cliff Street, 2001.

Turner, Ted, and Bill Burke. *Call Me Ted.* New York: Grand Central Publishing, 2008.

V

Van Andel, Jay (1924–2008), and
Rich DeVos (**Richard Marvin DeVos**)
(1926–   )
founders of Amway

Few adult Americans have never heard of Amway. Today this multilevel direct sales company sells billions of dollars of products and services across the country and around the world. Ironically, its founders, Jay Van Andel and Rich DeVos, started Amway as a means of saving another business of theirs.

Van Andel was born on June 3, 1924, in Grand Rapids, Michigan. His father, James, owned an automobile dealership, and his mother, Nella, was a homemaker. At age 18 he enrolled in nearby Calvin College; shortly thereafter, he joined the U.S. Army Air Reserve Corps and fought in World War II as a lieutenant. DeVos was born Richard Marvin DeVos on March 4, 1926, in Grand Rapids, Michigan. His father, Simon, was an electrician, and his mother, Ethel, was a homemaker. After graduating from high school in 1944, he enlisted in the U.S. Army and served in the Army Air Force until the end of World War II.

Van Andel and DeVos had met in high school, when Van Andel offered to give DeVos a ride to school each day in exchange for 25¢ per week for gasoline. By 1942, when Van Andel graduated, they were fast friends. In 1946 they were both discharged from the service and returned to Grand Rapids, where they decided to go into business together. That same year they opened the Wolverine Air Service, which gave flying lessons and offered charter passenger service, while taking business courses at Calvin College. In 1947 they dropped out of school and invested some of the profits from Wolverine in a drive-in restaurant that they built at the airfield and operated themselves. In 1948 they sold their businesses, bought a sailboat, and toured the Caribbean and South America.

Upon returning to Grand Rapids in 1949, Van Andel and DeVos were ready to start another business together. That same year they formed the Ja-Ri Corporation, an umbrella company for various enterprises such as importing items made from Haitian mahogany, making and selling wooden rocking horses, and distributing organic baked goods. They also became distributors for Nutrilite, a dietary supplement in pill form. Nutrilite Products Inc. consisted of two divisions; one did the product research, grew the ingredients that went into its all-natural vitamins, processed the pills, packaged them, and shipped them, while the other managed a nationwide direct sales network of independent distributors who sold the products and kept a share of the proceeds for themselves. In addition to selling the products, distributors could recruit new distributors whom they trained and supported in exchange for a small share of the profits. By the end of their first full year as Nutrilite distributors, the two partners had abandoned all of their other moneymaking schemes, mostly because they and their distributors had sold about $85,000 worth of vitamins. In 1952 Van Andel married

Betty Hoekstra with whom he has four children, and in 1953 DeVos married Helen Van Wesep with whom he has four children.

By 1958 Van Andel and DeVos had recruited, directly or indirectly, about 5,000 Nutrilite distributors. Meanwhile, Nutrilite had come under attack from two directions. First, the Federal Drug Administration took exception to some of the claims the company was making for its vitamins, and it enjoined Nutrilite from using testimonials as a selling tool. This ruling greatly affected their distributors' sales, because most of them had relied on customer testimonials to close sales with prospects. Second, internal disputes between the manufacturing and distributing branches of the company were seriously eroding distributor faith in the entire company. In 1958 Van Andel and DeVos were afraid that their sales organization was about to fall apart unless they took decisive action. Later that year they called a meeting in Charlevoix, Michigan, of everyone in their organization and suggested to them that they should diversify the Ja-Ri product line. When their distributors agreed, the two partners worked up a plan to sell cleaning products, which were easy to sell and which the government showed no interest in regulating, in addition to Nutrilite vitamins. They also modified the Nutrilite distribution plan so that the internal problems that had plagued Nutrilite would not plague their new endeavor. They sold the cleaning products via a new division of Ja-Ri called the American Way Association, which was incorporated in 1959 as Amway. Over the years, Van Andel became chairman of the board with primary responsibility for manufacturing and other internal operations, while DeVos became president with primary responsibility for building and training the distributor network.

At first, Van Andel and DeVos operated Amway out of the basements of their homes in Ada, Michigan, a suburb of Grand Rapids. Their first product was a concentrated biodegradable cleaner called Frisk bought ready-made from various suppliers; it was later known as Liquid Organic Concentrate, LOC All-Purpose Cleaner, and LOC. By mid-1960 the company had sold more than $500,000 worth of LOC, thus forcing the two partners to move Amway out of their basements and

into a converted gas station. Also in 1960, they bought a 50-percent interest in the Atco Manufacturing Company in Detroit, then convinced the other owners to rename the business Amway Manufacturing Company and move its facilities to Ada. By 1970 the company was manufacturing a complete line of cleaning, laundry, and aerosol products in a 450,000-square-foot facility, with annual sales of more than $100 million.

In the 1970s Amway introduced a personal shopper's catalog that included hundreds of brand-name products. It also expanded its operations into Australia, Great Britain, Hong Kong, and Malaysia. In 1980 annual sales topped $1 billion. By 1992 Amway was doing business in 45 countries, employed more than 14,000 people, manufactured more than 450 products, and sold another 6,500 brand-name products via catalogs. Its global distribution network included more than 2 million distributors whose combined annual sales approximated $6 billion.

In 1992 Van Andel stepped down as chairman of the board in favor of his son, Steve, while DeVos turned over the presidency to his son, Rich Jr. In the mid-1990s, DeVos founded RDV Sports, which owns several professional sports teams in Orlando, Florida, including the Magic of the National Basketball Association. The partners and longtime friends continued to be active philanthropists, particularly in their native Grand Rapids, and they were among the largest contributors to conservative political candidates and causes in the country. DeVos—who was the recipient of a heart transplant in 1997—remains active in running the Magic. Van Andel died of Parkinson's disease in 2004.

Further Reading

Bernstein, Adam, "Amway Co-founder Jay Van Andel Dies at 80." *Washington Post.* Available online. URL: http://www.washingtonpost.com/wp-dyn/articles/A45577-2004Dec7.html. Downloaded on July 6, 2009.

Cross, Wilbur. *Amway: The True Story of the Company That Transformed the Lives of Millions.* New York: Berkley Books, 1999.

Van Andel, Jay. *An Enterprising Life.* New York: HarperCollins, 1998.

Vanderbilt, Cornelius

(1794–1877) *entrepreneur in steamships and railroads*

Ask the typical student of American history how Cornelius Vanderbilt made his millions, and the reply will probably be "railroads." In fact, "Commodore" Vanderbilt made his first fortune as a steamship operator, hence the nickname, and it was this fortune that enabled him to become the railroad magnate of the history books.

Vanderbilt was born on May 27, 1794, in Port Richmond, New York. His parents, Cornelius and Phebe, were farmers. As a baby he moved with his family to nearby Stapleton, where his father supplemented the farm income by hauling people and produce from Staten Island to Manhattan by boat. He dropped out of school at age 11 to help his father in the boat business. At age 16 he borrowed $100 from his father, bought a sailboat, and established a regular ferry service between Staten Island and Manhattan. In 1813 he married Sophia Johnson with whom he had 13 children. She died in 1868, and that same year he married a woman named Frank Crawford.

During the War of 1812, Vanderbilt won a contract from the federal government to supply the various forts in and around New York harbor. By the end of the war he had amassed a fleet of sailing vessels and was trading up and down the Hudson River as well as all along the coast from Boston, Massachusetts, to Charleston, South Carolina. By 1818, however, he was being outdone by his rivals with steamships, so that same year he sold his entire fleet, took a job as captain of a steam ferry serving New York City and New Brunswick, New Jersey, and moved his family to New Brunswick where his wife opened a tavern.

By 1829 Vanderbilt felt satisfied that he had learned everything he could about the steamboat business and started a line of his own. At first, he tried competing with ROBERT LIVINGSTON STEVENS in the New York-to-Philadelphia corridor, but he gave up after a year when Stevens replaced his trans-Jersey stagecoach line, which connected his steamboats, with a railroad. Next, Vanderbilt turned his attention to the New York-to-Albany corridor, with much better results. He took customers away from preexisting rival lines by cutting the prices so low that his rivals eventually paid him $100,000 and an annual bonus to take his steamboats somewhere else. "Somewhere else" turned out to be the Atlantic coast, although the ocean trade demanded a sturdier steamboat than was required on the Hudson. Undaunted, he purchased a new fleet of steamships, and by 1838 he controlled most of the steamship traffic between New York City and Portland, Maine, and was a strong competitor on the Washington-to-Charleston route.

In the wake of the California gold rush in 1849, Vanderbilt became involved in the carrying trade between the East and West coasts. His Accessory Transit Company established steamship service from New York City to Nicaragua, traversed Nicaragua via riverboat and stagecoach, and established steamship service from Nicaragua to San Francisco. Once again, he took business away from his rivals, in this case a similar operation that traversed Central America in Panama,

Cornelius Vanderbilt, railroad magnate, got the nickname "Commodore" because he made his first fortune in the steamship business. *(Library of Congress)*

by cutting rates to the point that they paid him almost $700,000 per year to abandon his operation. Before that happened, however, Vanderbilt had to deal with William Walker. Walker was an American adventurer who in 1856 had set himself up as dictator of Nicaragua and then tried to seize control of Accessory Transit. Although the United States recognized Walker's regime, Vanderbilt organized a coalition of Central American states to overthrow Walker, who was forced to surrender in 1857. Although an attempt in the mid-1850s to compete with the British for the transatlantic carrying trade was aborted, the "Commodore," as he was widely known, had become the preeminent shipping magnate in America, and his mansions on Staten Island and Manhattan were among the finest in the country.

Having made more than $30 million from his steamship operations by the mid-1850s, Vanderbilt began investing some of it in railroad stock. His first investment was in the New York & Harlem Railroad, which connected New York City and Albany. By 1863 he had acquired controlling interest in the line and become its president. By 1867 he had gained control of the Hudson River and New York Central railroads as well, and in 1873 he merged all three lines into one. Meanwhile, he had gotten involved in a struggle with JAY GOULD over control of the Erie Railroad, which competed with the New York Central west of Albany. Gould emerged victorious from this contest, but in 1873 Vanderbilt acquired the Lake Shore & Michigan Southern, which he merged with the New York Central in order to provide uninterrupted service between New York City and Chicago, Illinois, via Buffalo, Cleveland, and Detroit. Within a few years the New York Central was the preeminent railroad in the New-York-to-Chicago corridor.

Vanderbilt was a domineering individual who intimidated his family as much as he did his business rivals. He devoted most of his energy to making money, although he did indulge himself from time to time by racing horses, playing cards, and vacationing at Saratoga Springs, New York. He died on January 4, 1877, at his home in New York City. At the time of his death, his estate was valued at more than $100 million. He left nine-tenths of it to his son, William Henry Vanderbilt, and divided the rest among his wife, other children, grandchildren, and Central University in Nashville, Tennessee, which was later renamed Vanderbilt University in his honor. William Henry Vanderbilt proved to be an apt administrator of his father's fortune, using it to gain control of several important railroads in the Midwest. As a result, he left his heirs an estate worth twice what his father had left him. His children, however, seemed to be quite content to cash their dividend checks and indulge themselves with such expensive hobbies as breeding show horses and yachting.

Further Reading

Brands, H. W. *Masters of Enterprise: Giants of American Business from John Jacob Astor and J. P. Morgan to Bill Gates and Oprah Winfrey.* New York: Free Press, 1999.

Crompton, Samuel W. *100 Americans Who Shaped American History.* San Mateo, Calif.: Bluewood Books, 1999.

Gordon, John Steele. *The Scarlet Woman of Wall Street: Jay Gould, Jim Fiske, Cornelius Vanderbilt, the Erie Railway Wars, and the Birth of Wall Street.* New York: Weidenfeld & Nicolson, 1988.

Perkins, Jack, et al. *The Vanderbilts: An American Dynasty.* New York: A&E Home Video, 1995, videorecording.

W

Wachner, Linda Joy

(1946–) *entrepreneur in contract apparel manufacturing*

The first woman to become the head of a Fortune 500 company was Linda Wachner. As chairman of the board and president of the Warnaco Group, a contract apparel manufacturer for major brand-name designers, she became one of the most powerful businesswomen in the United States.

Wachner was born Linda Joy Wachner on February 3, 1946, in New York City. Her father, Herman, was a fur salesman, and her mother, Shirley, was a homemaker. After receiving a B.A. in economics and business administration from the State University of New York at Buffalo in 1966, she went to work as a buyer's assistant for the Associated Merchandising Corporation, a buying agency for several department store chains. Two years later, she moved to Houston, Texas, to become a junior buyer for Foley's Federated Department Stores, and a year later she returned to New York City to be the buyer of bras and girdles for Macy's Department Store. In 1973 she married Seymour Applebaum with whom she has no children.

In 1974 Wachner became a buyer with the Warnaco Group, a major manufacturer and marketer of men's and women's clothing. The following year at the age of 29, she became the company's first female vice president and was put in charge of Warner's, the company's lingerie division. At the time, bras were sold and displayed in boxes, so that the only way a customer could tell what she was buying was to look at the picture on the box. Wachner came up with the novel idea that bras would sell better if women could actually see what they looked like, so she convinced the stores she sold to to take the bras out of the boxes and hang them on hangers. The result was a dramatic rise in bra sales, and since that time the open display of bras and other lingerie items has become a standard practice in stores.

Wachner's ambition and drive, coupled with her brusque manner with subordinates (and sometimes superiors) who did not share her goals, made it impossible for her to settle into a vice presidency for life, which she could easily have done at Warnaco. In 1977, she was on the move again, this time to be a vice president at Caron International, a yarn manufacturer. Two years later she became president of Max Factor's U.S. division, a cosmetics manufacturer that was losing millions of dollars each year. By 1984 she had turned the division around so it was profitable again. Having proved that she could run a company on her own, in 1984 Wachner set out to acquire one. She arranged with a New York investment firm to loan her $280 million to buy the Max Factor division, but Beatrice Companies, the parent company, refused her offer. Then she arranged financing totaling more than $900 million in an effort to buy the cosmetics division of Revlon, but at the last minute someone else offered a few million more. Finally, in 1986 she and Andrew Galef, a venture capitalist from California, arranged a deal whereby they bought Warnaco, her old employer, for $480 million.

As president and chief executive officer, Wachner began transforming the way Warnaco did business. Her biggest move was to become a licensed manufacturer and marketer of brand-name apparel such as Calvin Klein jeans, Ralph Lauren menswear, and Speedo swimwear. She also added a number of high-margin items to the company's mix while eliminating slow-selling merchandise. Under her management, sales continued to grow until 2000, when they peaked at roughly $2.2 billion.

The bottom began falling out for Warnaco and Wachner, however, as early as 1998. That year the company lost more than $32 million, thanks to the softening of the American retail industry. Another blow hit when the company became embroiled in an expensive and highly publicized lawsuit with Calvin Klein, which charged Warnaco with selling Calvin Klein jeans at discount outlets without authorization and with manufacturing Calvin Klein jeans of inferior quality. At the time, the jeans represented approximately 40 percent of Warnaco's total sales. Although the suit was settled in 2001, the damage had been done; sales of the jeans had dropped by more than 25 percent and no other product line had taken its place. When sales of Fruit of the Loom bras, another Warnaco mainstay, plummeted precipitously, the company found itself in extreme trouble, posting a loss of more than $344 million in 2000.

Throughout 2001, Wachner struggled to turn things around by reducing the company's debt, which totaled $1.5 billion, and trying to sell some of its assets. These measures did not work, however, and by the end of the year Warnaco had filed for bankruptcy and ousted Wachner from the company. Her troubles were not through. Wachner—who still lives in New York City—was under investigation for accounting fraud by the Securities and Exchange Commission until 2003, when she and two other former Warnaco executives agreed to pay almost $13 million in fines without any admission of wrongdoing.

Further Reading

Kaufman, Leslie, "On the Defensive, Warnaco's Chief Executive Plays Aggressively." *New York Times.* Available online. URL: http://www.nytimes.com/2000/06/07/business/markets-market-place-defensive-warnaco-s-chief-executive-plays-aggressively.html. Downloaded on July 6, 2009.

———. "After 15 Years, Executive's Short Goodbye." *New York Times.* Available online. URL: http://www.nytimes.com/2001/11/17/business/after-15-years-executive-s-short-goodbye.html. Downloaded on July 6, 2009.

Walker, Madame C. J.
(Sarah Breedlove, Sarah McWilliams)
(1867–1919) *entrepreneur in beauty aids*

Madame C. J. Walker was the first black woman in the United States to become a millionaire. This achievement is even more impressive when one considers that she was once an illiterate, unskilled, 20-year-old single mother living in the Deep South during the heyday of racial segregation.

Walker was born Sarah Breedlove on December 23, 1867, in Delta, Louisiana. Her parents, Owen and Minerva, were sharecroppers and former slaves, and her earliest memories were of helping her parents pick cotton. When she was six years old, her parents died in a yellow fever epidemic and she went to live in Vicksburg, Mississippi, with her older sister. Five years later her sister married a man who took an intense dislike to Walker. After three years of enduring his cruel insults, at age 14 she married Moses "Jeff" McWilliams with whom she had one child. In 1887 McWilliams was murdered, possibly in a race riot, and she and her child moved to St. Louis, Missouri.

The best job Walker could find in St. Louis was washing clothes for well-to-do white people for about $1.50 per week. Doing laundry in the late 19th century was an arduous task. After filling a large wooden tub with steaming water, one threw in the soiled garments and stirred them with a broom handle. Once the clothes were saturated, one pulled them out of the tub and scrubbed them against a corrugated washboard with a bar of lye soap made from boiled animal fat and potash (wood ashes). Then one put the clothes back in the tub and stirred some more. Clean garments were then rinsed in more hot water, treated with blueing to eliminate dingy yellow stains, hung on a line to dry, starched, and ironed. The constant exposure to harsh chemicals and steam caused most washer-women of the day to suffer from irritated skin and hair loss.

After a few years of doing laundry, Walker discovered that her hair had begun to thin and fall out in places. Determined to reverse this process, she began experimenting with various homemade concoctions but had little success. In 1904 she attended a speech by Margaret Washington, the wife of Booker T. Washington, the eminent black educator. Walker was particularly impressed with Mrs. Washington's elegant appearance, and she redoubled her own efforts to do something about her own hair. By 1905 she had developed a dressing that restored much of the life to abused hair, even if it did not make it grow back (as Walker insisted it would do). She never divulged the formula for the hair dressing; some believed that its "secret ingredient" was sulfur, while others believed she had simply figured out how to duplicate a hair-care product sold by the Poro Company. Walker herself claimed to have gotten the formula in a dream from "a big black man." He told her to get a variety of ingredients, some of which could be found only in Africa, and mix them together in a certain way. Whatever the source of the formula, her dressing quickly became popular among Walker's black female acquaintances because it also helped remove kinks from nappy hair, thus making it straighter and easier to style.

Suddenly, Walker knew she had a money-making idea on her hands, and she decided to go into business selling "Wonderful Hair Grower," as she called the dressing. Realizing that St. Louis's segregated and racist Jim Crow atmosphere would surely prevent her from becoming too successful, in 1905 she moved to Denver, Colorado, where her brother's widow and daughters lived. Until her business got off the ground, she worked full time as a cook. She spent the rest of her time making and selling her complete hair care system. In addition to Wonderful Hair Grower, this system included "Vegetable Shampoo" for washing hair, "Glossine" for giving hair a glossy shine, and a steel comb with wide-gapped teeth; when heated and pulled through a head of hair that had been treated with Wonderful Hair Grower, the comb straightened curls and made hair more manageable. Dressed in

a white blouse and a long black skirt, she sold her products door-to-door in Denver's black neighborhoods. One look at Walker's own gorgeous head of hair was frequently all it took to get a prospect to buy the entire system.

In 1906 Walker married Charles J. Walker, a newspaper publisher. A skilled advertiser, he convinced her to do business under the name Madame C. J. Walker. He also urged her to expand her business by advertising in black newspapers across the United States, which resulted in a huge volume of mail orders. As her products became increasingly popular, she built the Walker Manufacturing Company's first factory in Denver, then recruited black women as sales agents and trained them to sell door-to-door the Walker Hair Care System. In 1908 she opened another factory in Pittsburgh, Pennsylvania, which included a sales office and the first Walker School of Beauty Culture; from the school would grow a national chain of beauty schools, all of them using the Walker Hair Care System. That same year she began touring the eastern and southern states, recruiting sales agents by giving demonstrations at black churches and women's clubs. Black women eagerly lined up to become Walker sales agents because, for most of them, it was their only chance to work without being someone else's servant. In 1910 she moved her entire Denver operation to Indianapolis, Indiana, where she established the company's national headquarters so she could be more centrally located to her sales agents. The move caused an irreparable breach between her and her husband, and in 1912 they divorced.

In 1913 Walker began organizing her sales agents into "Walker Clubs," which served as community service agencies in black neighborhoods as well as sales organizations. In 1917 the Madame C. J. Walker Hair Culturists Union of America held a national convention in Philadelphia, Pennsylvania, so that club members could inspire and learn from one another. That same year her company employed more than 2,000 sales agents and grossed $500,000, a large amount for the day, from sales of its line of 14 personal care products, which by then included dental cream, vegetable oil soap, "Wonder Pomade for Men," and "Tan Off."

Walker never had any formal education and did not learn to read and write until well into adulthood, and yet by 1917 she had become a millionaire. She gave much of her money to civil rights groups and black schools, including the National Association of Colored Women, the National Association for the Advancement of Colored People (NAACP), the National Conference on Lynching, Bethune-Cookman College, and Tuskegee and Palmer Memorial institutes. In 1913 she moved to New York City; four years later she built a mansion on four acres in nearby Irvington overlooking the Hudson River. By the time her new home was completed, she was suffering from high blood pressure and weak kidneys. She ignored her doctor's advice to slow down and died shortly thereafter, on May 25, 1919. In a tribute to her memory, some of her employees wrote these words: "She did not gain her wealth by overworking or underpaying her employees. She was devoted to her helpers and so were they to her."

Further Reading

Alexander, Amy. *Fifty Black Women Who Changed America.* New York: Citadel Press, 1999.

Gates, Henry L., and Cornel West. *The African-American Century: How Black Americans Have Shaped Our Country.* New York: Free Press, 2000.

Salley, Columbus. *The Black 100: A Ranking of the Most Influential African-Americans, Past and Present.* Secaucus, N.J.: Carol Pub. Group, 1999.

Smith, Jessie C. *Black Heroes of the 20th Century.* Detroit: Visible Ink Press, 1998.

Stone, Deborah. *Madame C. J. Walker.* Englewood Cliffs, N.J.: Quercus, 1990.

Walker, Maggie Lena
(Maggie Mitchell)
(1867–1934) *entrepreneur in banking*

The first woman bank president in the United States was Maggie Walker, one of the most unlikely candidates for such a position. Unlike some bank presidents who are born with silver spoons in their mouths, Walker was born "with a laundry basket practically on my head," an allusion to the fact that as a young child she delivered laundry. Known as "the Lame Lioness" because of her energetic attitude and a knee injury that left her crippled for

the last six years of her life, she was an ardent supporter of black entrepreneurialism as a means of helping black people overcome racial segregation.

Walker was born Maggie Lena on July 15, 1867, in Richmond, Virginia. Her father, Eccles Cuthbert, was a newspaperman, and her mother, Elizabeth Draper, was a house servant. She was given the last name of Mitchell shortly after her birth, when her mother married William Mitchell, a butler with whom she worked. In 1876 William Mitchell died, and her mother was forced to supplement her income by taking in laundry; the nine-year-old Walker helped out by picking up the dirty clothes and delivering the clean ones. Despite their financial difficulties, Walker finished her high-school education in 1883 and became a teacher. She left teaching three years later to marry Armstead Walker; they had three children and adopted a fourth.

Instead of working outside the home for a salary, Walker got involved in volunteer work with the Independent Order of St. Luke, a black fraternal and mutual aid organization. Like many similar organizations, the order offered black people an opportunity to obtain life insurance, burial benefits, and financial assistance during times of illness and unemployment. In 1895 she played an important role in creating a juvenile division for purposes of providing special assistance to members' children. Four years later, she was elected secretary-treasurer of the order, which at the time had about 3,400 members. Since the order paid for services out of the dues it received from members, as well as from modest cash reserves it maintained for emergencies, Walker reasoned that a larger order meant expanded services and better benefits at cheaper rates. With this thought in mind, she embarked on a nationwide membership recruitment drive, which resulted in the admission of almost 100,000 new members in 22 states.

Having greatly increased the order's size, Walker next sought to harness its burgeoning economic power in new ways. Rather than continue to provide mutual aid benefits only, she envisioned the order as a source of capital from which enterprising blacks could borrow the funds required to start small businesses of their own, which in turn would cater to the needs of the black community at large and free blacks as much as possible from being economically dependent on whites. To this end she convinced the leadership of the order to build and to operate a department store and a newspaper, both of which were operated by blacks with the unique needs of the black community in mind. After several years of persuading her fellow leaders to take further action, in 1903 they agreed to the formation of the St. Luke Penny Savings Bank, with Walker as president, thus making her the first woman to head a bank in the United States. Part of the order's reluctance to form a bank was that no blacks had any experience in running one, so Walker became an astute observer of a local white-owned bank, and by the time the order's bank opened she was reasonably well-versed in banking operations.

Under Walker's direction, the St. Luke Penny Savings Bank thrived; it got its name because it accepted deposits as small as one penny, so as to encourage everyone in the black community to save. It loaned money to a rising black middle class for home mortgages and business loans, and it helped to create a bustling black business community in Richmond whereby black consumers patronized black merchants. The bank also became one of the first banks to collect payments of utility bills and city taxes. St. Luke Penny Savings Bank thrived until the Great Depression in the 1930s, which forced the closing of thousands of banks across America. However, the bank survived by merging with several other black-owned banks to form the Consolidated Bank and Trust Company, which continues to do business today.

In 1907 Walker suffered a debilitating injury to her knees that got progressively worse until she was confined to a wheelchair after 1928. Nevertheless, she did not let this stop her from running the bank or from participating in civil rights organizations such as the National Association for the Advancement of Colored People (NAACP) and the National Urban League. She died on December 15, 1934, at her home in Richmond; many years after her death, a high school and a street in Richmond were named in her honor.

Further Reading

Branch, Muriel, and Dorothy Rice. *Miss Maggie: A Biography of Maggie Lena Walker*. Richmond, Va.: Marlborough House Publishing, 1984.

Malson, Micheline R. *Black Women in America: Social Science Perspectives*. Chicago: University of Chicago Press, 1990.

Waller, Frederic
(1886–1954) *inventor of Cinerama*

Before there were Imax, Omnimax, and Surround-Sound, there was Cinerama. The first wide-screen technology to be shown in movie theaters, Cinerama was the brainchild of Fred Waller, who used his background as an inventor, movie producer, and aircraft instrument manufacturer to inspire the movie industry to make movies that were more visually and auditorily realistic.

Waller was born Frederic Waller on March 10, 1886, in Brooklyn, New York. His father, Frederic, was a commercial photographer, and his mother, Katherine, was a homemaker. At age 14 he dropped out of school to work in his father's photography studio, and in 1905 he became president of the company, which he renamed the Fred Waller Company. That same year he married Irene Seymour with whom he had two children. They divorced in 1919, and in 1920 he married Grace Hubbard. She died in 1941, and in 1942 he married Doris Caron.

In 1905 Waller got involved with the movie industry when his company began making large photographs of motion picture advertisements for display in movie theater lobbies. In 1918 he opened an illustrating studio to make title and caption frames for silent movies. Four years later he opened his own movie studio, the Film Guild Inc., which shot five features and three short historical films before it went out of business two years later; the movies were a critical hit but a box office flop. In 1924 he went to work for Paramount Pictures as head of the special effects department. In 1929 he became production manager for the company's short films, and by 1936 he had formed a department for making commercial films. Meanwhile, he had patented several pieces of photographic equipment, including an automatic printer and timer, a still camera that could take 360-degree pictures, and an optical printer.

In 1936 Waller left Paramount to take charge of special productions for the upcoming New York

World's Fair. His pet project was to produce the necessary components for showing panoramic movies with more depth to them than could be shown via the narrow-screen film system of the day. It was his belief that human depth perception resulted from peripheral vision, not from having two eyes, a hypothesis that was later proven by the Dartmouth Eye Institute. To this end, he wanted to make movies, design camera equipment, and build theaters that projected a wider movie image on the screen. In 1938 he and Ralph Walker, an architect, formed the Vitarama Corporation to develop a wide-screen system for the World's Fair. The basis of the system would be a concave screen designed by Walker that would be wide enough and tall enough to fill a viewer's peripheral vision, with images projected onto the screen by 11 movie projectors. Although they were unable to complete the project before the fair opened in 1939, they did create a scaled-down version of the project, called Perisphere, which played to rave reviews.

Between 1936 and 1942, Waller had also served as president of the Kenyon Instrument Company, which manufactured instruments for airplanes. In 1942, when the United States got involved in World War II, he combined his knowledge of wide-screen movies and aircraft instruments to invent the Waller Flexible Gunnery Trainer. This device simulated aerial combat for would-be fighter pilots by projecting dogfights onto a wide, concave screen via five movie projectors. Vitarama received contracts to build Trainers from the U.S. and British air forces, and the company used these contracts as opportunities to fund and conduct further research into a wide-screen movie system.

By 1946 Waller had designed the basic components for building the system of his dreams. Called Cinerama, it used three synchronized movie projectors to project images onto a wide, concave screen that filled almost 90 percent of the eye's horizontal range and more than 90 percent of its vertical range. He enhanced the visual reality of Cinerama by recruiting Hazard Reeves, a sound engineer, to create a stereo system that surrounded the audience with sound. By 1949 he was giving private demonstrations of the system to movie executives on an enclosed tennis court in Oyster Bay, New York. At first, the executives showed

little enthusiasm for Cinerama because it required extensive renovation of a theater before it could be used. But by 1952 they were showing more interest, primarily because the new medium of television was taking away their audience and they were desperate to do anything that might bring that audience back into the theaters. That same year Waller formed Cinerama Inc., with himself as chairman of the board; by the end of the year the company was ready to show its first movie, *This Is Cinerama*, at the Broadway Theatre in New York City. The film was shown from the viewer's perspective, placing the viewer in the front seat of a roller coaster and in the cockpit of a small plane flying through the Grand Canyon, among other scenarios. By 1954 22 theaters had been renovated to show Cinerama, and *This Is Cinerama*, which had cost only $1 million to produce, had grossed $32 million. That same year Waller received an Academy Award for developing Cinerama.

Unfortunately, Waller died shortly thereafter, on May 18, 1954, at his home in Huntington, New York. Despite its initial popularity, Cinerama was abandoned around 1962, partly because of the expense involved in renovating theaters and partly because of the emergence of cheaper (and less effective) wide-screen technologies such as CinemaScope. But Cinerama had shown movie executives and audiences what could be done to enhance the realism of going to the movies, thus contributing to the development of Imax and Omnimax.

Further Reading

Belton, John. *Widescreen Cinema*. Cambridge, Mass.: Harvard University Press, 1992.

"Cinerama," Widescreen Museum. Available online. URL: http://www.widescreenmuseum.com/widescreen/wingcr1.htm. Downloaded on July 6, 2009.

Walton, Sam
(Samuel Moore Walton)
(1918–1992) *founder of Wal-Mart*

Before 1970, many of America's top retail executives would have been surprised to discover that country people have a lot of money to spend. Sam

Walton impressed this fact upon them when he opened hundreds of large stores in small communities and made billions of dollars as a result. In the process, he created stores that, perhaps more than any others, returned a significant portion of their profits to the local community and generated a real sense of pride and loyalty among its workforce.

Walton was born Samuel Moore Walton on March 29, 1918, in Kingfisher, Oklahoma. His father, Thomas, was a farm mortgage broker, and his mother, Nancy, was a homemaker. Between the ages of five and 12, Walton and his family moved often as his father's business took them to a number of rural Missouri communities before finally settling in Columbia, Missouri, where he grew up. He graduated from high school in 1936, then enrolled in the University of Missouri where he received a B.A. in economics four years later. He spent the next two years working as a manager trainee at a J. C. Penney department store in Des Moines, Iowa. In 1943 he married Helen Robson with whom he had four children.

After serving in the U.S. Army during World War II, in 1945 Walton bought a Ben Franklin five-and-ten franchise in Newport, Arkansas. Popularized by F. W. WOOLWORTH, the typical five-and-ten store carried items that, for the most part, sold for either five cents or ten cents. At the time, Ben Franklin was one of the more prosperous chains, operating almost 1,600 stores across the United States. In 1950 Walton lost his lease and had to close his store, but then he and his brother James acquired the Ben Franklin franchise in Bentonville in the far northwest corner of the state. By 1962 the two brothers were operating Ben Franklins in 15 towns in Missouri and Arkansas.

Meanwhile, Walton had gotten the idea that the large retail chains were overlooking an untapped source of customer demand, rural America. This was particularly true for the South, where in 1960 more than 40 percent of the population lived in communities that had fewer than 5,000 residents; in Arkansas, Walton's base of operations, almost 60 percent lived in the country. His upbringing in rural Missouri had taught him that country folks had plenty of money to spend, and yet the major chains persisted in locating their stores in large communities. After trying in vain

for several years to get Ben Franklin officials to let him open a large store in a small town, he finally decided just to do it himself. In 1962 he opened what he called Wal-Mart Discount City on the outskirts of Rogers, Arkansas, a small community just down the road from Bentonville. He changed the name to Wal-Mart Stores in 1970, the year he took the company public. In 1972, 10 years after the first Wal-Mart opened, there were 64 Wal-Marts, most of them within 300 miles of company headquarters in Bentonville. That same year the chain's annual sales were $125 million, or almost $2 million per small-town store. Ten years later, in 1982, there were 642 Wal-Marts doing total annual sales of more than $4 billion.

The key to Wal-Mart's phenomenal success was really quite simple. Since the stores did business in rural communities, they had to become part of those communities and run themselves like small-town communities. In this regard, Walton's genius shone through. Best described as a "good ole boy," he spent four days per week visiting stores; before he had so many, he managed to visit each store at least once a year. He would usually arrive before the store opened so he could help the janitors and stockers get ready for another day. Then, wearing a Wal-Mart baseball cap and a name tag that simply read "Sam," he would visit with customers and employees alike, using a portable tape recorder to record how they thought their store ought to be run and what it should sell. Around noon, he would take a bunch of employees out to lunch. After lunch, he would lead a pep rally, then chat some more until it was time to climb back into his private plane and fly to the next store. At all times, Wal-Mart employees had the right to examine their store's profit and loss statements, and they could see for themselves how much any given item cost, how much it sold for, and how much it cost to light, heat, and otherwise operate the store. Each Wal-Mart also contributed generously to local charities and let local groups like the Girl Scouts, Little League, and church youth groups hold fundraisers on its sidewalk. Not surprisingly, many Wal-Mart employees developed a strong sense of pride in their jobs and loyalty to their stores.

After 1982 Walton began putting Wal-Marts in larger southern communities like Little Rock,

Dallas, and Shreveport. In 1983 he opened the first Sam's Wholesale Club, which catered at first to small businesspeople to whom it sold merchandise in bulk at about 10 percent above cost. By 1988 he had also opened the first Wal-Mart Supercenter, which combined a Wal-Mart and a supermarket.

In 1988 Walton stepped down as Wal-Mart's chief executive officer, although he remained chairman of the board until his death. At the time there were more than 1,300 Wal-Marts doing total annual sales of $26 billion. Walton's personal fortune was estimated at $18.5 billion. Despite his wealth, he remained a down-to-earth man, living in a modest home in Bentonville and driving a pick-up truck. He died on April 5, 1992, in Little Rock, Arkansas.

Further Reading

Brands, H. W. *Masters of Enterprise: Giants of American Business from John Jacob Astor and J. P. Morgan to Bill Gates and Oprah Winfrey.* New York: Free Press, 1999.

Krass, Peter. *The Book of Management Wisdom: Classic Writings by Legendary Managers.* New York: Chichester, Wiley, 2000.

Ortega, Bob. *In Sam We Trust: The Untold Story of Sam Walton and Wal-Mart, the World's Most Powerful Retailer.* New York: Times Business, 2000.

Teutsch, Austin. *The Sam Walton Story: An Inside Look at the Man and His Empire.* New York: Berkley Books, 1992.

Trimble, Vance H. *Sam Walton: The Inside Story of America's Richest Man.* New York: Penguin Books, 1991.

Wanamaker, John

(1838–1922) *entrepreneur in retail merchandising*

Anyone who has ever worked in a department store knows that "the customer is always right." This phrase was coined by John Wanamaker, one of the pioneers of American retail merchandising.

Wanamaker was born on July 11, 1838, in Philadelphia, Pennsylvania. His father, Nelson, was a brick maker, and his mother, Elizabeth, was a homemaker. At age 11 Wanamaker moved with his family to Leesburg, Indiana, where they remained

two years before returning to Philadelphia. His formal education consisted of three years of grammar school.

Upon his return in 1851, Wanamaker went to work as an errand boy, first for the Troutman and Hayes Bookstore, then for Barclay Lippincott's Clothing Store, and finally for Tower Hall, one of the premier clothing stores in Philadelphia. In 1853 he was promoted to salesman, a position he held for four years until his health failed. For a year afterward he traveled around the country, and at some point he seems to have had a faith experience. When he returned to work in Philadelphia in 1858, it was not as a retail salesman but as the secretary of the Young Mens' Christian Association (YMCA).

For two years Wanamaker threw himself into lay ministry. Under his direction, the YMCA's membership grew from 57 to more than 200. The organization won many young men for the temperance movement and trained 40 to be Sunday school teachers. Then, in 1860, he married Mary Brown; later that year the first of their six children was born. These two events apparently led him to the realization that he could not support a family on a YMCA secretary's salary. For a year he searched his soul, then decided to return to retailing full time and devote his spare time to the lay ministry.

In 1861 Wanamaker and his brother-in-law, Nathan Brown, opened Oak Hall, a clothing store for men and boys in downtown Philadelphia. Despite fierce competition, the store prospered by holding frequent sales, a relatively new marketing technique, and by selling uniforms to the Union army. In 1869, the year after Brown's death, Wanamaker opened another men's clothing store, John Wanamaker & Company. In 1876 Wanamaker opened a third store, this one in the Pennsylvania Railroad's old freight depot. At first it specialized in men's and boys' clothing, but soon after opening it began selling women's clothing and dry goods as well. Thus the Grand Depot, as Wanamaker called it, became the first department store in Philadelphia and one of the first in the United States.

Wanamaker was greatly influenced by Alexander T. Stewart, the retailing pioneer who in 1862 built the world's largest retail store in New York City; in fact, Wanamaker bought this store in 1896, 20 years after Stewart's death. Unlike other retailers who haggled with customers over prices, Stewart and Wanamaker charged every customer the same price for the same item. However, Wanamaker was a retailing pioneer in his own right. He was the first retailer to offer a money-back guarantee. He also pioneered the full-page newspaper advertisement, the plastering of ads on horse-drawn carriages, and the placing of ad poster boards on sandwich men who walked up and down the sidewalks. His stores were the first to offer restaurant service, to send merchandise buyers overseas, to be illuminated with electric lighting, to hold a white sale on household items such as bedsheets and towels, to offer free in-store musical concerts, and to sponsor children's drawing contests.

In terms of employee relations, Wanamaker and Stewart were opposites. While Stewart paid his employees low wages and fined them for making mistakes, Wanamaker offered his employees a host of fringe benefits. These included a free education at the John Wanamaker Commercial Institute, which taught bookkeeping and finance in addition to reading, writing, and arithmetic; two-weeks summer vacations for employees' children at Camp Wanamaker in Island Heights, New Jersey; membership in an insurance association; and inexpensive lodging for single female employees at the Hotel Walton.

Wanamaker stayed active in the lay ministry in Philadelphia throughout his life. He served as president of the local YMCA and founded three Presbyterian churches as well as the Bethany Brotherhood, which offered religious instruction and fellowship. He also enjoyed a brief political career. From 1889 to 1893 he was U.S. postmaster general; later he ran unsuccessfully for governor and U.S. senator. After his death on December 12, 1922, in Philadelphia, a statue was erected in his memory in front of city hall.

Further Reading

Applegate, Edd. *Personalities and Products: A Historical Perspective on Advertising in America.* Westport, Conn.: Greenwood Press, 1998.

Ershkowitz, Herbert. *John Wanamaker: Philadelphia Merchant.* Conshohocken, Penn.: Combined Publishing, 1999.

Zulker, William A. *John Wanamaker: King of Merchants.* Wayne, Penn.: Eaglecrest Press, 1993.

Wang, An
(1920–1990) *inventor of data processing devices*

Three important developments in data processing can be directly attributed to the genius of one man, An Wang. First, he invented magnetic core memory, which greatly speeded up the computational abilities of mainframe computers. Second, he invented the hand-held calculator, thus making life easier for millions of engineers and math students. Third, he invented the word processor, thus making life easier for millions of nontechnical workers. As a result of these three inventions, it is safe to say that An Wang has invented something that just about everyone in America has used at one time or another.

Wang was born on February 7, 1920, in Shanghai, China. His father, Yin Lu, was a teacher, and his mother, Zen Wan, was a homemaker. In 1940 he received a B.S. in electrical engineering from Chiaot'ung University in Shanghai and went to work as an engineer at the Central Radio Works in Kuei-lin. In 1945 the Chinese government sent him to Harvard University to study physics, and he received an M.Sc. in 1946 and a Ph.D. in 1948. In 1949 he married Lorraine Chiu with whom he had three children, and in 1955 he became an American citizen.

After graduation Wang became a research fellow with the Harvard Computation Laboratory, developer of the Mark I, II, and III electronic computers. The laboratory was working on the Mark IV computer, and he was assigned to develop a memory system that worked faster than the Mark III's magnetic drum memory, which provided relatively large storage capacity but relatively slow access. In 1949 he developed magnetic core memory. Rather than store memory on a magnetized rotating drum, he stacked pieces of magnetized metal shaped like tiny washers, called cores, into memory arrays, with each core storing one bit of memory. This system proved to be so easy to build and to expand that it quickly became the memory system of choice, and remained that way until ROBERT NORTON NOYCE perfected the integrated circuit in the 1960s.

In 1951 Wang left Harvard and started Wang Laboratories in a Boston garage. He built and sold magnetic core memory arrays to various computer builders as well as several devices of his own design that used magnetic core memory, such as Weditrol, a digital machine tool controller, and Linasec, an automated typesetting machine. He also licensed magnetic core memory to several companies, including the International Business Machines Corporation (IBM). When Wang received a patent for magnetic core memory in 1955, IBM bought the exclusive U.S. patent rights for $400,000.

With money in hand, Wang went looking for something else to invent. He realized that a huge gap existed between the available tools for making mathematical computations; a civil engineer designing a bridge, for example, could choose to make the necessary calculations on either a computer the size of a small room or on a slide rule. Wang set out to develop a tool that fit somewhere in between, and by 1964 he had invented the desktop, or hand-held, digital calculator. Despite costing hundreds of dollars, the Model 300 LOCI, as Wang called it, quickly caught on with engineers, students, and office workers, and Wang Laboratories sold more than $8 million worth in three years. When Wang took the company public in 1967, the initial stock offering rose in price on the first day it was publicly traded from $12 to $40 per share. By the end of the day, Wang's holding in the corporation was worth about $40 million.

Shortly thereafter, however, other competitors began entering the digital calculator field, and the price of such devices plummeted. Rather than get involved in a price war over what was rapidly becoming a household item, Wang went looking for something else electronic to invent. After studying the marketplace once again, he realized that data processing focused around the manipulation of numbers, not words. He concluded that a great demand existed for an electronic word processor. His first foray in this direction was to acquire Philip Hankins Inc., a data processing company, so that Wang Laboratories could learn how to develop the software required to operate a word processor. By 1971 the lessons had been learned, and Wang came out with its first model, in essence an editing typewriter with computerized memory. Unbeknownst to Wang, however, IBM had also decided to get into the word processing business, and at about the same time it released a model of its own

that was similar to Wang's. Owing to IBM's greater name recognition, sales of Wang's offering suffered, so Wang went back to the drawing board.

In 1976 Wang Laboratories demonstrated the first modern word processor. This new model, called the Word Processing System, or WPS, featured a built-in cathode ray tube (CRT) monitor that permitted the viewing and editing of text, as well as an easy-to-use menu of control commands so that someone with no knowledge whatsoever about computers could be using WPS with confidence in a matter of hours. WPS was exactly what millions of secretaries and students had been looking for, and its sales skyrocketed. By 1981 Wang's sales topped the $1 billion mark, and throughout the decade annual sales remained between $1 billion and $2 billion.

Although Wang was a brilliant inventor, he was not a good business administrator. At its peak, Wang Laboratories remained a one-man show, with Wang himself directing virtually every detail in product development and sales. Although this strategy worked well enough in the company's early days, by the mid-1980s it was hardly working at all. Wang had developed throat cancer, and he could no longer play the dominant role he had played before. To make matters worse, he insisted that his son, Frederick, become his successor, even though Frederick showed none of Wang's genius for developing new products or for doing much of anything related to the company's business. Meanwhile, IBM and other competitors were closing the gap between their word-processor offerings and WPS. In 1989 the company lost more than $400 million, and its stock had fallen to about $5 per share. That same year Wang appointed Richard W. Miller, a former General Electric executive, to run Wang Laboratories and then retired. He died on March 24, 1990, in Boston. Although Wang Laboratories declared bankruptcy shortly thereafter, in 1994 it emerged from the ordeal a much smaller but stronger company.

Further Reading

Kenney, Charles C. *Riding the Runaway Horse: The Rise and Decline of Wang Laboratories*. Boston: Little, Brown, 1992.

Wang, An. *Lessons: An Autobiography*. Reading, Mass.: Addison-Wesley, 1988.

Ward, Montgomery
(Aaron Montgomery Ward)
(1844–1913) *entrepreneur in mail-order merchandising*

Nearly everyone has purchased something at one time or another from a catalog mailed to their home. The man who had the idea for the first mail-order catalog was Montgomery Ward. His ideas about how merchandise could be sold revolutionized the way many American businesses operated.

Ward was born Aaron Montgomery Ward on February 17, 1844, in Chatham, New Jersey. His parents, Sylvester and Julia, were farmers. At age nine he moved with his family to Niles, Michigan, where his father had bought a general store and its entire inventory; in fact, the store was run-down and completely empty. Having no money left with which to buy goods, the Wards turned the store into a house and Sylvester Ward found work as a clerk in another store. At age 14 Ward left school to help support the family, and for the next three years he worked in factories that made barrel staves and bricks. In 1861 he moved to nearby St. Joseph to be a clerk in a general store, and three years later he had worked his way up to manager. In 1865 he moved to Chicago, Illinois, where he worked for two years as a salesclerk for MARSHALL FIELD, the retailing pioneer.

In 1867 Ward became a traveling salesman for a Chicago-based dry-goods wholesaler, calling on general stores in Illinois, Missouri, and Kansas. He quickly found out that many rural customers were unhappy with the selection and price of goods in most general stores. This realization led him to the idea of developing a mail-order business, whereby customers could make their selections from a catalog mailed to their home, then mail their orders to a wholesaler who would ship the merchandise by railroad, thus eliminating the middleman and his profit. He figured he could hold prices down by buying in bulk from manufacturers, paying them cash, and shipping all customer orders COD (cash on delivery), thus making the U.S. Post Office his collection service.

Around 1870 Ward became a buyer for C. W. & E. Pardridge Company, a Chicago wholesaler and retailer. In addition to buying for Pardridge, he also bought merchandise that he planned to sell via mail order. He experienced a major setback in 1871, when the great fire that destroyed much of Chicago also burned up all of the inventory he had accumulated. However, Ward was a determined man with a sure-fire plan, and so he refused to give up. Instead, he took on as partners two fellow employees at Pardridge's, George Drake and Robert Caulfield. In 1872, the same year he married Elizabeth Cobb with whom he had no children, one of his wife's uncles helped arrange for Ward's company to become a preferred supplier to the National Grange. The Grange was an organization of thousands of farmers and small businessmen that operated cooperatives and retail stores across the rural Midwest. In 1872 the Original Grange Supply House, as Ward's company was first called, issued its first catalog, a single sheet of paper with about 150 items on it. By 1875 Ward had bought out Drake and Caulfield, taken on a new partner, his brother-in-law George Thorne, and quit his job at Pardridge's.

Ward had gauged the temperament of rural consumers perfectly. Grange members eagerly bought from Ward, especially after he offered a 10-day money-back guarantee on any item that failed to meet the customer's expectations. Although he was not the first merchant to offer a money-back guarantee, he did coin the phrase "satisfaction guaranteed or your money back." Soon, non-Grange members were becoming enthusiastic customers as well. By 1889, when the company changed its name to Montgomery Ward & Company, it was grossing more than $2 million annually.

Ward's success was predicated on several factors. First, Ward offered a wide variety of good-quality merchandise at reasonable prices; his 1884 catalog featured 10,000 items. Second, he developed efficient methods for buying, warehousing, and shipping goods. Third, he included in his catalog testimonials from satisfied customers and Grange officials. These endorsements helped alleviate suspicion on the part of rural consumers, thus making them more likely to buy. Fourth and most important, he transformed his one-page catalog into a "dream book," as it became known. Ward's catalog featured pictures and descriptions of items that many rural consumers did not know existed. Mailed free of charge to millions of people every year, it brought these marvelous things right into their homes where they could peruse it at their leisure without being pressured by a salesman. In the days before radio and television, rural folk spent many a spare moment gleefully thumbing through Ward's catalog while trying to decide what to buy next. The mail-order catalog revolutionized business in America by drawing millions of rural consumers into the rising tide of consumption that had already engulfed the nation's cities.

Ward's success inspired a host of imitators. The most successful was Sears, Roebuck & Company, which was founded in 1891 and eventually relegated Montgomery Ward to second place in the mail-order business. But by that time Ward had exited from the company he founded. In 1893 he sold his interest in Montgomery Ward to Thorne. Although he retained the title of president, he no longer drew a salary or played any role in the company's operations. Under the management of Thorne and his five sons, Montgomery Ward continued to thrive. At the time of Ward's death, the company was grossing $40 million annually and employed 6,000 workers. In 1921 the Thornes relinquished control of the company, and five years later the new management began opening retail outlets across the country. Meanwhile, Montgomery Ward continued its mail-order business until 1985. By this time rural America had been transformed by the automobile and the paved highway to such an extent that virtually everyone living in the country had easy access to large stores in neighboring towns and malls.

Ward lived a luxurious retirement. In addition to his large home in Highland Park on the outskirts of Chicago, he bought La Belle Knoll, a sprawling estate in Oconomowoc, Wisconsin, where he raised Thoroughbred horses, and a winter home in Pasadena, California, where he played golf. But he also used his fortune—estimated at more than $15 million at his death—to do good. He successfully fought many long and expensive legal battles to keep Chicago's Grant Park from being developed, and he contributed millions of dollars to charity. He died on December 7, 1913, in Highland Park.

Further Reading

Baker, Nina B. *Big Catalogue: The Life of Aaron Montgomery Ward.* New York: Harcourt Brace, 1956.

Hucke, Matt. "Aaron Montgomery Ward," Graveyards of Chicago. Available online. URL: http://www.graveyards.com/rosehill/ward.html. Downloaded on July 6, 2009.

Latham, Frank B. *1872–1972: A Century of Serving Consumers; the Story of Montgomery Ward.* Chicago: Montgomery Ward, 1972.

Watson, Jr., Thomas J.
(1914–1993) *CEO and president of IBM*

The history of American business features many examples of children taking over an enterprise founded by their parent. Rarely are such businesses already as large and successful as International Business Machines (IBM) was when son Thomas Watson, Jr., took the reins from his father, Thomas Watson, Sr., in 1951. Despite his enormous trepidation that he could not live up to his father's example of leadership, few, if any, steered their parent's creation more prosperously than Watson, Jr., during his almost 20-year reign at IBM.

Thomas John Watson, Jr., was born in Dayton, Ohio, on January 14, 1914. He grew up in Short Hills, New Jersey, the oldest of four children. Watson was immersed in the work of IBM from an early age, accompanying his father on plant inspections as early as five years old. Of his close but complex relationship with his father, Watson would later recall, "I was so intimately entwined with my father. I had a compelling desire, maybe out of honor for the old gentleman, maybe out of sheer cussedness, to prove to the world that I could excel in the same way that he did." Watson was an indifferent and rebellious student, earning him the nickname "Terrible Tommy," who attended several private schools before graduating from the Hun School in Princeton, New Jersey. He then enrolled at Brown University, where his disdain for studies and penchant for pursuing a good time threatened to prevent him from graduating until a friendly school administrator helped Watson obtain a degree.

In 1940, Watson joined IBM as a salesman. He showed little interest in sales but was soon relieved of this drudgery by enlisting in the U.S. Army as a pilot in the army's air force. Watson spent the next five years serving as a trusted aide to Major General Follett Bradley and flying throughout Asia, Africa, and the Pacific, demonstrating bravery, skill, and a great aptitude for planning and execution of missions. Late in his military service, Watson was set to pursue a postwar career as a pilot, but on the advice of Bradley and brimming with newfound confidence, chose instead to work for IBM.

IBM in 1946 was a flourishing company, but Watson quickly determined that it needed to evolve quickly and decisively in order to remain that way. He consistently advocated that the company increase its research and development of computer technology and move away from its lucrative manufacturing of older technology, such as the punchcard tabulators that had helped make IBM one of the world's most successful companies but that Watson viewed as having dwindling prospects. Many within IBM were skeptical of Watson's view of the future, most notably his father, with whom Watson had many heated arguments related to IBM's business strategy. Watson persevered with his vision, and in 1952 he became the president of IBM.

The handsome, prematurely gray 41-year-old Watson was featured on the cover of *Time* magazine in March 1955. In an article in that issue, he explained what proved to be the prescient vision of IBM, saying, "Our job is to make automatic a lot of things now done by slow and laborious human drudgery. A hundred years ago there was an industrial revolution in which seven to ten horsepower was put behind each pair of industrial hands in America. Today we're beginning to put horsepower behind office hands, electric energy in the place of brain power." By this time he had already moved IBM in his desired direction by hiring top electronics and computer experts.

A critically important development in IBM's ascendance as a leading company in computer technology resulted from Watson's early 1960s proposal to create a line of computers that could fill every data processing need. He called the line of computers System 360 (after 360 degrees in a circle) and designed plans that allowed users to move up to a more sophisticated model as their needs changed. The project cost $5 billion, which was three times IBM's revenues at the time. The System 360 project encountered significant struggles early in development, leading Watson to fire his younger brother who was head of engineering and manufacturing. Eventually, Watson's vision was vindicated. By 1963, IBM had an eight to one lead in revenues over major competitor Sperry Rand, which had manufactured Univac, the first commercial computer, years before IBM began commercial computer development. From 1964 to 1975, IBM increased its total number of computer installations from 11,000 to 35,000 and its revenues doubled to $7.5 billion.

Much of Watson's success grew out of his personal style, which shared certain aspects of his father's formality but embraced other traits that were typically admired by IBM employees. Watson regularly worked 12 to 15 hour days and traveled around the country and world (often piloting the plane) to personally inspect IBM factories and products. He preferred to be called Tom and, though considered combative and intense in competition, he was known to treat colleagues, particularly IBM's rank and file, in quiet, respectful tones, though he could be harsh on top aides and would himself recall "savage, primal, unstoppable" conflicts with his own father. Watson implemented what he called a "contention system" that encouraged managers to challenge one another, allowing almost anyone within the company to challenge the decisions of other managers, even superiors, and force them to explain their reasoning.

In 1971, the 57-year-old Watson suffered a severe heart attack that led him to retire his leadership of IBM. He spent the next two decades enjoying his favorite pursuits of flying and sailing and served two years as the U.S. ambassador to the Soviet Union (1979–81), where he strongly advocated the reduction of nuclear arms.

Watson died on December 31, 1993, in Greenwich, Connecticut, due to complications from a stroke suffered earlier that month. He was survived by his wife of 52 years, Olive, a son, and five daughters. At a memorial service, Watson—earlier described by *Fortune* magazine as "the most successful capitalist who ever lived"—was recalled by family and friends as a passionate man of great instinct, skill, and accomplishment. They remembered him for his remarkable success leading IBM, where he emerged from his father's formidable shadow to become one of the greatest American corporate leaders in history, as well as a skilled yachtsman, skier, and pilot. Capturing the essence of Watson's personal and professional endeavors, Watson's grandson said of him, "He always tried to get places he wasn't supposed to go."

Further Reading

"Corporations: The Brain Builders." *Time*. Available online. URL: http://www.time.com/time/magazine/article/0,9171,937187,00.html. Downloaded on September 1, 2009.

Greenwald, John. "Thomas Watson, Jr." *Time* 100. Available online. URL: http://www.time.com/time100/builder/profile/watson.html. Downloaded on September 1, 2009.

"Thomas Watson, Jr., Reference Room." IBM. Available online. URL: http://www-03.ibm.com/ibm/history/exhibits/watsonjr/watsonjr_reference.html. Downloaded on September 1, 2009.

Watson, Thomas J. *Father, Son & Co.: My Life at IBM and Beyond*. New York: Bantam, 2000.

Wells, Henry

(1805–1878) *founder of American Express and Wells Fargo*

At the end of the 20th century, American Express and Wells Fargo were two of the most prominent financial services companies in the world. The man most responsible for their initial success was Henry Wells. However, this pioneer expressman founded both companies to deliver mail and freight, and they served as the 19th-century forerunners to such companies as United Parcel Service (UPS) and FedEx.

Wells was born on December 12, 1805, in Thetford, Vermont. His father, Shipley, was a Presbyterian minister, and his mother, Dolly, was a homemaker. As a young boy Wells moved with his parents to Fayette, New York, where he grew up on a farm. Leaving home at age 16, he worked successively over the next 20 years as a tanner, cobbler, store clerk, and freight clerk, including a brief stint with the Pennsylvania Railroad. Sometime during this 20-year period he married Sarah Daggett with whom he had three children.

In 1840 the process of shipping freight by rail was in its infancy in the United States. Businesses lacking their own rail spurs shipped and received freight via the team track at the local freight station. This track was usually the scene of mass confusion, as dozens of wagons lined up either to drop off or to pick up a shipment. Since small shippers did not ship enough freight to fill an entire railcar, their shipments were combined with other small shipments, in much the same way that luggage is loaded onto an airplane. This arrangement frequently resulted in individual packages being damaged, delayed, or lost.

By 1840 express transportation companies had begun offering specialized services to small businesses. They picked up a shipper's load at his place of business in a company wagon, shipped it via rail in the company's private railcar, and delivered it to the customer in another company wagon. Express companies offered faster delivery and more careful handling of fragile and valuable shipments than any railroad. They also delivered mail faster and cheaper than the federal government, although for a time this was against the law. Rather than attempt to run express companies out of business, railroad companies worked with them because they greatly simplified the task of handling freight and dealing with customers.

Wells's experience with the Pennsylvania Railroad acquainted him with the tremendous profit potential in express transportation. In 1841 he cofounded Livingston, Wells & Pomeroy, which provided express service between Albany and Buffalo. He was arrested several times for delivering mail for 5¢ per letter, about one-fourth the government rate. In 1844 he cofounded Wells & Company, which connected Buffalo to Cleveland and Detroit, thus making it the first company to offer express service west of Buffalo. By 1850 Wells & Company had extended its services to Chicago and St. Louis, thus becoming the first express company to serve these cities. In 1850 Wells engineered a merger—combining Wells & Company and Livingston, Wells & Pomeroy with a third company that provided service between Albany and New York City—into the American Express Company, with himself as president. By offering a direct connection between New York City and most points west, and by establishing offices in London, England, and Paris, France, American Express quickly became the nation's major express company.

The California gold rush of 1849 created an urgent need for secure shipments of gold dust and bullion from the gold fields to the East. In 1852 Wells cofounded Wells Fargo & Company to transport gold via steamship from San Francisco to New York City. At the time the Panama Canal did not exist, so the company hauled gold across the Isthmus of Panama in wagons with armed escorts. Wells Fargo also provided banking and stagecoach services to a number of California mining communities. In 1855 the company began offering express service via stagecoach from St. Louis westward, eventually establishing a stage line all the way to California. By 1866 Wells Fargo had acquired virtually every rival stage line west of the Mississippi River and held the federal contract to deliver the overland mail from St. Louis to San Francisco.

In 1868 Wells effected two important mergers, one between American Express and Merchants Union Express in the East and the other between Wells Fargo and Pacific Union Express in the West. The two mergers enabled American Express and Wells Fargo to dominate their regions until 1918, when the federal government consolidated all express companies into the American Railway Express. After 1918 American Express specialized in financial services such as credit cards and travelers checks, while Wells Fargo specialized in banking and armored car services.

In 1868 Wells retired to his home in Aurora, New York, with his second wife, Mary Prentice, with whom he had no children. He died on December 10, 1878, while visiting Glasgow, Scotland.

Further Reading

Massengill, Reed. *Becoming American Express: 150 Years of Reinvention and Customer Service.* New York: American Express Co., 1999.

Wells Fargo Since 1852. San Francisco: Wells, Fargo & Co., 2000.

Westinghouse, George

(1846–1914) *inventor of railroad and electrical components*

Although railroads and electric power companies have little in common, they both owe a debt to George Westinghouse. By inventing the modern air brake and signal system, and by perfecting the transmission of electrical power via alternating current, Westinghouse contributed greatly to the expansion and the safety of both industries.

Westinghouse was born on October 6, 1846, in Central Bridge, New York. His parents, George and Emeline, were farmers. At age nine he moved with his family to Schenectady, where his father opened a farm-tool factory. Westinghouse was given the run of the machine shop, and by age 15 he had invented a rather impractical rotary steam engine. That same year he ran away to join the Union army, but his parents made him come home. However, when he turned 16, he convinced them to let him serve, and he spent one year in the Union army and one year in the Union navy.

After the Civil War, Westinghouse returned to his father's machine shop; in 1867 he married Marguerite Walker with whom he had one child. Having developed an interest in railroading, he invented one device for setting derailed freight cars back on the track and another to extend the service life of railroad switches. However, the partnerships he set up to market these devices both fell through, and in 1868 he moved to Pittsburgh, Pennsylvania. In 1869 he invented a vastly improved air brake for railcars. Whereas previous models took a long time to engage the wheels and could be operated only by the engineer, Westinghouse's model worked much faster and could be operated by either the engineer or the conductor. By stopping railcars faster, his air brake permitted trains to travel faster and safer. That same year he organized the Westinghouse Air Brake Company to manufacture and market his air brake. He continued to improve its design over the years, and he eventually was awarded more than 20 patents for the air brake and its modifications. When the U.S. Railroad Safety Appliance Act of 1893 made air brakes a required feature on all railcars, Westinghouse's fortune was assured.

Meanwhile, Westinghouse had turned his attention to the communications aspects of railroading. In 1880 he began buying patents for devices that permitted the remote control of signals and switches. He combined the best devices with ones of his own invention and produced an innovative system that made use of both electricity and compressed air. In 1881 he formed the Union Signal & Switch Company to manufacture and market this system, which quickly gained acceptance in the railroad industry.

Westinghouse's entry into the world of electrical components led him next into the debate concerning the best means of transferring electrical

George Westinghouse was a major contributor to the growth of both the railroad and electrical industries. *(Courtesy of Westinghouse Electric Company)*

current for commercial purposes. THOMAS ALVA EDISON, the famous American inventor, preferred direct current (DC), and many people fell under his influence. However, Westinghouse knew from designing his signal and switch systems that direct current required too much voltage to transmit electricity safely for any distance at all, and for this reason he preferred alternating current (AC). In 1882 he found out that Lucien Gaulard and John D. Gibbs had designed a transformer that could regulate the voltage of alternating current as it traveled along a wire. Over the next four years he acquired a Gaulard-Gibbs transformer and an alternating current generator, hired several electrical engineers to help him perfect these devices for long-distance power transmission, and set up an electrical system using alternating current in Pittsburgh. In 1886, convinced that alternating current was a safer and more economical means of transmitting electrical current than direct current, he formed the Westinghouse Electric Company and began manufacturing electrical components for use with alternating current.

For seven years the battle raged between the two camps. The opponents of alternating current claimed that it was too dangerous for in-home use, despite Westinghouse's invention of an induction meter and other devices to regulate the amount of current entering a home. Meanwhile, Westinghouse was proving to most people the advantages of low-voltage alternating current, especially after he acquired the patent rights to NIKOLA TESLA's AC motor and hired Tesla to make the motor suitable for use in a commercial AC power system. And at the 1893 World's Columbian Exposition in Chicago, Westinghouse put on a magnificent display that proved alternating current's ability to provide large amounts of light and power safely. This display won his company a contract to build three 5,000-horsepower AC generators at Niagara Falls, New York, thus silencing the opponents of alternating current forever.

Despite these successes, Westinghouse Electric struggled financially in its early days. In addition to the struggle with the proponents of direct current, the company also fought many expensive legal battles over patent infringement suits. In 1889 Westinghouse was forced to sell stock to Pittsburgh investors, and in 1891 the company was almost forced to declare bankruptcy. The company skidded along until 1907 when it went into receivership and Westinghouse was forced out as chairman of the board. He regained control of the company in 1908, but resigned three years later. He spent the remaining years of his life concentrating on the affairs of his other two companies. He died on March 12, 1914, in New York City.

Further Reading

Frey, Robert L. *Railroads in the Nineteenth Century.* New York: Facts On File, 1988.

Norman, Jon. *Nineteenth-Century Inventors.* New York: Facts On File, 1992.

Ravage, Barbara. *George Westinghouse: a Genius for Invention.* Austin, Tex.: Raintree Steck-Vaughn, 1997.

Weyerhaeuser, Frederick
(Friedrich Weyerhaeuser)

(1834–1914) *entrepreneur in the lumber industry*

One of the more interesting entrepreneurs in American history is Frederick Weyerhaeuser. Most people who corner the market in a particular industry, like JOHN DAVISON ROCKEFELLER or BILL GATES, become household names. Weyerhaeuser was different; although at the time of his death he had for many years controlled the production of commercial timber in the United States, his name was virtually unknown to the average American. For whatever reasons, Weyerhaeuser was content to amass his wealth and live a quiet, unpretentious life at home with his family and a few friends.

Weyerhaeuser was born Friedrich Weyerhaeuser on November 21, 1843, in Nieder Saulheim, Hesse (present-day Germany). His parents, Johann and Katerina, were farmers. When Weyerhaeuser was 12 years old, his father died, so for the next four years he worked on the farm to help support his family. At age 18 Weyerhaeuser emigrated with his mother and sister to Erie, Pennsylvania, where he spent the next four years working in a brewery and on a farm. In 1856 he moved to Coal Valley, Illinois, and over the next four years

he worked for a grain dealer, a coal merchant, and a lumberman. In 1857 he married Elizabeth Bloedel with whom he had seven children.

In 1860 Weyerhaeuser and Frank Denkmann, his brother-in-law, bought at a foreclosure sale a sawmill on the Mississippi River near Rock Island, Illinois. The partners agreed that Denkmann would manage the sawmill while Weyerhaeuser journeyed up the Mississippi to Wisconsin to buy stands of timber along the Chippewa River. In this way the partners could cut the timber, float it approximately 250 miles downriver, and mill it at their sawmill without having to erect a new mill farther north.

Weyerhaeuser traveled back and forth to Wisconsin over the next 15 years. In addition to buying timber for his own mill, he used his share of the profits from that mill to buy percentages of other milling operations along the tributaries of the Mississippi. By 1870 he owned three mills outright and had controlling interest in a number of others. By 1872 his influence in the northern timber industry was such that he was elected president of the Mississippi River Boom and Logging Company, a cartel of 16 lumber companies that controlled the milling of virtually every tree cut down on the northern reaches of the Mississippi.

After 1872 Weyerhaeuser continued to expand his holdings, both directly and indirectly, in lumbering operations in all parts of the country. In 1879 he helped organize and became president of the Chippewa Lumber and Boom Company in Chippewa Falls, Wisconsin, which for many years operated the largest lumber mill in the world. He formed groups of investors to acquire timber stands and milling operations in upstate Minnesota, which by 1896 had been consolidated as the Northern Lumber Company, and in Arkansas and Louisiana, which by 1902 had been consolidated as the Southern Lumber Company. In 1891 he moved to St. Paul, Minnesota, to be closer to his growing holdings in the north. In 1900 he personally bought 900,000 acres of timber in the Pacific Northwest from the Northern Pacific Railroad for $6 per acre. This purchase formed the basis of the Weyerhaeuser Timber Company, founded in 1901 with headquarters in Tacoma, Washington. He also became the unofficial head of the so-called

Weyerhaeuser Syndicate, an association of approximately 100 lumbermen with extensive holdings across the country. Under his direction, the syndicate bought controlling interests in existing mills and smaller land companies; at its peak, the syndicate controlled more than 2 million acres containing more than 15 billion standing feet of timber.

At the time of his death on April 4, 1914, in Pasadena, California, Weyerhaeuser was president of 16 different lumber companies and the major stockholder in countless others. The stock value of Weyerhaeuser Timber was more than $150 million, almost four times the value of its four closest rivals combined, and his personal wealth was estimated at $30 million. Although he was known within the timber industry as the "Lumber King," he attracted scant attention from the general public. He seems to have had no interests outside his family and his work.

Further Reading

Hidy, Ralph W., et al. *Timber and Men: The Weyerhaeuser Story.* New York: Macmillan, 1963.

Sensel, Joni. *Traditions through the Trees: Weyerhaeuser's First 100 Years.* Seattle, Wash.: Documentary Book Publishers, 1999.

Twining, Charles E. *F. K. Weyerhaeuser: A Biography.* St. Paul, Minn.: Minnesota Historical Society Press, 1997.

White, Eartha Mary Magdalene

(1876–1974) *entrepreneur in community-based businesses*

Most successful entrepreneurs donate considerable sums of money to charitable organizations. However, few entrepreneurs go into business with the idea of donating the bulk of their profits to charity. One entrepreneur who did exactly that was Eartha White.

White was born on November 8, 1876, in Jacksonville, Florida. Her mother, Mollie Chapman, was a prostitute, and her father's name is unknown. As a baby she was adopted and named by Lafayette and Clara White; he was a drayman and she was a domestic and cook. When White was five, Lafayette White died. Clara White was

a strong, God-fearing woman who worked hard to make Jacksonville's black community a better place to live, and she convinced White that God had a special plan for her in this world. At age 17 White went to New York City to study hairdressing and music. She was a cast member of the 1895–96 world tour of the Oriental-American Opera Company, the first black opera company in the United States. On a trip home she became engaged, but her fiancé died before they could be wed. At this point White, who was 19 years old, decided to give up her musical career, return to Jacksonville, and do everything in her power to help its black community.

In 1897 White graduated from the Florida Baptist Academy with the intention of becoming a teacher. This plan was postponed by the Spanish-American War, during which she served as a volunteer nurse. Upon returning to the United States in 1899, she began teaching in a rural black school outside Jacksonville and working as a clerk for the Afro-American Life Insurance Company, a black-owned concern that offered blacks a variety of life and disability insurance benefits at affordable prices. The following year she attended the National Negro Business League convention in Boston, Massachusetts, where she met and befriended Booker T. Washington, the unofficial leader of American blacks.

Washington was an avid proponent of black self-help. He firmly believed that blacks could best gain civil and social equality with whites by first gaining economic equality. To this end he counseled blacks to learn crafts, develop industrial skills, and practice the virtues of enterprise and thrift. This was a message that White took to heart, and for the rest of her life she practiced what he preached.

In 1901 White began teaching at a school in one of Jacksonville's black neighborhoods. By 1905 she had saved enough money to open a small department store; the store was staffed with blacks and catered to blacks. Once the store began turning a profit, she sold it to black investors and used part of the proceeds to open another business run by and for blacks. When this business became profitable, she sold it and opened another. By 1930, in addition to the department store, she had opened and sold a taxi service, an employment agency, a janitorial service, and a steam laundry. After 1930 she obtained a realtor's license so that she could promote economic growth in black neighborhoods by buying and selling business property.

White also used her profits to fund a variety of community services such as a maternity home, a child placement center, a community center, and a rest home for patients with tuberculosis. Two of her most important services were the Clara White Mission, a combination homeless shelter and job training center named for her adoptive mother, and the Eartha M. White Nursing Home, a 120-bed facility providing physical and occupational therapy that was funded partly by her and partly by federal grants. At the time of her death on January 18, 1974, "Jacksonville's Angel of Mercy" was still using her money and talents to help people.

Further Reading

Neyland, L. W. *Twelve Black Floridians.* Tallahassee: Florida Agricultural and Mechanical University Foundation, 1970.

"Eartha M. M. White Collection," Thomas G. Carpenter Library, University of North Florida, Jacksonville. Available online. URL: http://www.unf.edu/library/per/earhome.html. Downloaded on November 23, 2001.

Whitney, Eli

(1765–1825) *inventor of the cotton gin*

One of the most revolutionary inventions in American history was the cotton gin. This simple device transformed the South by encouraging the cultivation of cotton just about everywhere. It also transformed New England by stimulating the construction and operation of cotton mills. Ironically, Whitney made less money from the invention that made him famous than he did at making guns; however, his process for manufacturing firearms led to substantial developments in manufacturing by encouraging the production of interchangeable parts.

Whitney was born on December 8, 1765, in Westboro, Massachusetts. His parents, Eli and Elizabeth, were farmers. As a boy he demonstrated

an aptitude for making items, such as nails and hat pins, from metal. After teaching school for several years to raise enough money for tuition, he enrolled in Yale College where he studied science and the applied arts. He graduated in 1792 and accepted a position as a tutor in Charleston, South Carolina, but upon arriving there he discovered that the position no longer existed. En route he had met Catherine Greene, owner of a cotton plantation near Savannah, Georgia. Upon learning of Whitney's predicament, Greene invited the destitute and distraught young Whitney to stay at her plantation for as long as he liked.

Whitney demonstrated his gratitude by fixing things around the plantation. Impressed with his mechanical aptitude, Greene teasingly challenged him to invent a machine for removing the seeds from short-staple cotton. At the time, Greene was growing long-staple cotton, whose long fibers were

Eli Whitney spent most of the money he made from inventing the cotton gin on suing patent infringers. *(Library of Congress)*

relatively easy to clean, or remove the seeds from. Short-staple cotton, however, because it had such short fibers, was difficult to clean, and it took one slave all day to clean just one pound of it. Since long-staple grew only along the coast of South Carolina and Georgia, the key to growing cotton inland, which Greene wanted to do, was to find a way to clean short-staple cotton faster. Within days Whitney had invented a device to do exactly that. Called the cotton gin, short for "engine," this boxlike device forced raw cotton through a series of slits, while a revolving wire-studded cylinder separated the seeds from the fibers. A slave using Whitney's invention could clean about 50 pounds of cotton per day.

In 1793 Whitney and Phineas Miller, Greene's overseer, formed Whitney & Miller for purposes of manufacturing cotton gins. Unfortunately, the partners hardly profited at all from their venture, because the cotton gin was so easy to make that dozens of imitators had made gins of their own. Although Whitney obtained a federal patent in 1794, it proved to be virtually worthless in the South, largely because southern courts simply refused to honor it. In 1797 the two partners closed their business, and Whitney returned to New England. In 1802 Whitney received a token payment for his patent rights from the state of South Carolina, as well as similar payments in later years from three other southern states. Altogether, these payments totaled about $100,000, about what he had paid out in legal fees.

The cotton gin revolutionized the production of cotton in the South. In 1790, the United States had grown about 2 million pounds of cotton; 10 years later, that figure had increased to 18 million pounds. By the time of Whitney's death in 1825, cotton production had spread throughout the Deep South all the way to Texas and increased to about 250 million pounds. Much of this cotton found its way to New England, where cotton textile mills sprang up to compete with their counterparts in England. By 1825 cotton plantations dominated the economy of the South while cotton mills dominated the economy of New England, all thanks to the cotton gin.

In 1798 Whitney got involved with the manufacture of firearms. That same year he secured a

government contract to produce 10,000 muskets in two years, even though he had no experience as a gunsmith and lacked a factory or a workforce. But by early 1799 he had built a factory complex on the outskirts of New Haven, Connecticut, which eventually became known as Whitneyville, and had recruited about 50 skilled gunsmiths from Massachusetts. Whitney realized that the successful completion of the contract hinged upon his ability to mechanize the gunmaking process. Making a firearm requires a great deal of metalworking, especially cutting and grinding, and at the time all of this was done by hand. Moreover, each firearm was made by one gunsmith, who crafted all of its parts himself. Consequently, a part that fit one weapon would not necessarily fit on another, not even one made by the same gunsmith. Whitney had conceived of using water-powered machinery operated by unskilled laborers to do the cutting and grinding, while the skilled laborers concentrated on those tasks that could not be done by machines. In this way, interchangeable parts could be produced in record time, which could then be put together to make the finished musket.

Whitney discovered that perfecting this system required far more time than he had imagined, and by 1800 he had produced only about 500 of the 10,000 muskets. Still, Whitney's operation turned out muskets faster than the government's other contractors. Moreover, the government's inspectors were impressed by the fact that Whitney was producing firearms with interchangeable parts, which meant that in the future his muskets could be more readily repaired, so they gave Whitney all the time he needed. Finally, in 1809, he delivered the last of the 10,000 muskets. In 1812 he received another contract for 15,000 muskets, and at the time of his death in 1825 his factory was working to complete a third government order for 15,000 more. Although Whitney may not have been the first to come up with the idea of interchangeable parts—in 1785 Thomas Jefferson, at the time the American minister to France, wrote home about Honore Blanc, whose gunshop made interchangeable parts—he was certainly the first to do so on a large scale.

In 1817 Whitney married Henrietta Edwards, with whom he had one child. When he died on

January 8, 1825, in New Haven, Connecticut, his estate was worth $130,000, a considerable amount of money for that day.

Further Reading

Crompton, Samuel W. *100 Americans Who Shaped American History*. San Mateo, Calif.: Bluewood Books, 1999.

Gaines, Ann. *Eli Whitney*. Vero Beach, Fla.: Rourke Books, 2001.

Mirsky, Jeanette, and Allan Nevins. *The World of Eli Whitney*. New York: Collier Books, 1962.

Pursell, Carroll W. *Technology in America: A History of Individuals and Ideas*. Cambridge, Mass.: MIT Press, 1990.

Wren, Daniel A., and Ronald G. Greenwood. *Management Innovators: The People and Ideas that Have Shaped Modern Business*. New York: Oxford University Press, 1998.

Wilson, Kemmons
(Charles Kemmons Wilson, Jr.)
(1913–2003) *founder of Holiday Inn*

Holiday Inn was not the first chain of motels in the United States. That honor goes to Alamo Plaza Courts, a loosely organized chain of motels that was established across the Southeast after 1929 by Lee Torrance. Holiday Inn, however, was the first referral chain to rise to national prominence, and thus to dictate standards of excellence to other chains and independent motels. The Holiday Inn concept was so successful that the changes the chain began implementing almost 50 years ago condition the expectations of the present-day traveler. The founder of Holiday Inn was Kemmons Wilson, a home builder who was inspired to create the chain after suffering through a motoring vacation with his five young children.

Wilson was born Charles Kemmons Wilson, Jr., on January 5, 1913, in Osceola, Arkansas. His father, Charles, was a life insurance salesman, and his mother, Ruby, was a homemaker. Shortly after Wilson's birth, his father died and he moved with his mother to Memphis, Tennessee, where she worked a succession of low-paying jobs. Living on the edge of poverty, he was forced to grow up fast.

At age six he began selling newspapers, and over the next 11 years he worked at a long procession of odd jobs at night while sleeping at school during the day. At age 17 he dropped out of school to open his own business when his mother lost her job. Having purchased a popcorn machine on credit, he bought the rights to sell popcorn outside the lobby of a Memphis movie theater. He was soon making more money selling popcorn than the theater's manager, who revoked Wilson's rights and bought the popcorn machine. Undaunted, Wilson used the proceeds from the sale of the popcorn machine to buy five pinball machines, which he placed in local businesses. He also began purchasing and placing cigarette machines as well as buying and reopening old movie theaters. By 1933 he had made enough money to pay cash for a modest house for himself and his mother. A year later he used the house as collateral to buy a jukebox company, and in 1935 he used the profits from this company to become a home builder. In 1945 he opened his own real-estate company, and by 1950 he had established himself as one of Memphis's largest tract-housing developers.

In 1941 Wilson had married Dorothy Lee, and within 10 years they had five children. In 1951 they decided to drive to Washington, D.C., to vacation. For Wilson, the most memorable part of the trip was the motels. At the time, the vast majority of roadside lodging establishments were family-run motels with fewer than 20 rooms, and they were inconsistent in terms of the services they offered and the prices they charged. Few offered all of the amenities modern travelers have come to expect: restaurant, air-conditioning, swimming pool, in-room telephone, and free ice. Wilson was particularly outraged at having to pay extra for each of his five children, even though three of them spent the night in sleeping bags on the floor. Halfway through the trip, he vowed to build a chain of 400 motels that would provide all of these amenities free of charge. Upon returning to Memphis, he hired Eddie Bluestein, a draftsman who had done work for him before, to draw up the blueprints based on ideas Wilson had sketched out during the trip. Bluestein whimsically dubbed the building in his renditions the Holiday Inn, after the title of a 1942 movie starring Bing Crosby and Fred Astaire. In 1952 the first Holiday Inn Hotel Court opened on the site of an old lumberyard that Wilson owned on the outskirts of Memphis. This property did so well that within 18 months Wilson had built three more, all of them along major highways leading into Memphis.

In 1954 Wilson founded Holiday Inns of America, a franchise operation that would do for the lodging industry what McDonald's would do for the restaurant industry. The early going, however, was slow; at first, Wilson tried to interest other home builders in becoming Holiday Inn franchisees for a one-time payment of $500 and a royalty of 7¢ per room per night. When only three builders accepted his offer, he began seeking franchisees among doctors, lawyers, and other professionals with money to invest. He also took the company public in 1957 to attract investor attention and to provide the company with the operating capital it desperately needed. Both tactics worked brilliantly, and by 1959 there were 105 Holiday Inns. Ten years later that number had grown to more than 1,100, and in 1969 the company's annual revenues topped $500 million. This success was built upon several factors. First, Wilson insisted that all franchisees build their properties according to the same general design concept—the classic two-story, U- or L-shaped structure made of concrete, steel, and glass—and operate them according to the same general standards for service and cleanliness. Soon, the traveling public began looking for Holiday Inns because they knew they would provide a decent night's lodging at a reasonable price. Second, the company was successful at purchasing land adjacent to interchanges along the growing interstate highway system, thereby positioning its properties where future travelers would be sure to drive. Third, in 1965 Wilson spent millions of dollars to create a nationwide, computerized reservations system. Known as Holidex, this system allowed guests to make reservations at other Holiday Inns, thus keeping many travelers as guests somewhere in the system for several days at a time.

Holiday Inn continued to grow during the 1970s, to more than 1,700 properties and annual revenues of more than $1 billion by 1979. However, the problems associated with the constant threat of an oil shortage during the 1970s, coupled with the rise of several competing chains during this decade, forced Wilson to share power with an expanded management team. In 1979 he lost the confidence of the board of directors and retired, at age 66, as chairman of the board.

Despite his wealth and poor health—he had suffered a heart attack—Wilson refused to stay retired. After a few months of rest and recuperation, he began developing Orange Lake Country Club in Orlando, Florida, a time-share community not far from Disney World. Shortly thereafter, he founded two new lodging companies, Wilson World Hotels and Wilson Inns and Suites, with about 20 properties scattered throughout the Southeast. In addition, he acquired or started more than 60 companies, including an oil well, a coal mine, an insurance agency, a property management company, lumberyards, a commercial printing operation, a candy and snack food manufacturer, and a construction company, all of them managed under the umbrella group known as Kemmons Wilson Companies.

Wilson died at his home in Memphis on February 12, 2003, at the age of 90. He was survived by his five children, 14 grandchildren, and four great-grandchildren. Ten years earlier, Wilson's legacy was captured by historian David Halberstam in his book *The Fifties,* who described the Wilson family trip that led to the creation of Holiday Inn as "the vacation that changed the face of the American road."

Further Reading

Halberstam, David. *The Fifties.* New York: Ballantine, 1994.

Martin, Douglas, "Kemmons Wilson, 90, Dies; Was Holiday Inn Founder." *New York Times.* Available online. URL: http://www.nytimes.com/2003/02/14/business/kemmons-wilson-90-dies-was-holiday-inn-founder.html. Downloaded on July 6, 2009.

Wilson, Kemmons, with Robert Kerr. *Half Luck and Half Brains: The Kemmons Wilson, Holiday Inn Story.* Nashville, Tenn.: Hambleton-Hill Publishing, 1996.

Winfrey, Oprah
(Orpah Gail Winfrey)
(1954–) *entrepreneur in television production*

Oprah Winfrey emerged during the late 20th century to claim the undisputed title of "Queen of Talk." A brilliant talk show host, she became the first black woman to host a regularly broadcast, nationally syndicated television program. She also became one of the wealthiest people in the United States by becoming the first black woman to own her own television and film production studios.

Winfrey was born Orpah Gail Winfrey on January 29, 1954, in Kosciusko, Mississippi; she was called Oprah from the time she was a little girl. Her father, Vernon Winfrey, was a barber and a grocery store owner, and her mother, Vernita Lee, was a house cleaner. At the time of her birth, her father was in the military, and her mother left town shortly thereafter, so Winfrey spent the first six years of her life on a farm with her mother's parents. At age six she went to Milwaukee, Wisconsin, to live with her mother. This arrangement did not work well, mostly because Winfrey's mother was too busy to spend much time with her precocious daughter. After eight years of little parental supervision, at age 14 Winfrey moved to Nashville, Tennessee, to live with her father and his wife, Zelma, who refocused Oprah's life and impressed upon her the importance of reading books and getting an education. Three years later she enrolled in Tennessee State University, receiving her B.A. in 1976.

Winfrey embarked on her show business career in 1971, at age 17, when she took a part-time job as a newscaster for a Nashville radio station. Two years later, while still in college, she began working as a reporter and weekend anchorperson for WVTF-TV in Nashville. After graduation, she moved to Baltimore, Maryland, to be an anchorperson for WJZ-TV, an ABC affiliate, but she lacked the maturity and experience to do a creditable job and was fired after only a few months. However, she had demonstrated repeatedly that she had a true gift for gab, so the station offered her a position as cohost of a morning talk show, *People Are Talking.* This switch proved to be a blessing in disguise; she quickly developed the ability to relate to guests of all backgrounds, and she began learning how to get the audience to participate in the show. With each passing year, her ratings increased until she became one of the brightest stars of Baltimore television. In 1984, after seven years in Baltimore, she moved to Chicago, Illinois, to host AM *Chicago* on WLS-TV. By now an accomplished host, she displayed an instinctive flair for comedy

and a folksy, down-home style of interviewing. Within a year she had become the most popular television personality in Chicago, and her program was renamed *The Oprah Winfrey Show.*

Winfrey began her acting career in 1985, when she was invited to play the role of Sofia in the hit movie *The Color Purple.* Her performance earned her an Academy Award nomination for best supporting actress, which greatly increased her nationwide visibility and led indirectly to the national syndication of her television show. In 1986 *The Oprah Winfrey Show* aired in more than 120 cities across the country. Oprah, as she was known to admiring fans everywhere, became a favorite of women, many of whom gave up watching their favorite soap operas in order to tune in to her show. Her popularity stemmed in part from the fact that she paid special attention to the problems, both mundane and catastrophic, faced by women and children. A typical program might begin with several ordinary women discussing their experiences with the topic of the day and then conclude with one or more experts offering advice to the guests and to the audience. In between, Oprah encouraged the studio audience to interact with the guests in such a way that the program quite frequently took on the trappings of a community forum. This format was simple yet powerful, and it worked all the better due to Oprah's ability to relate to all sides of the discussion while interjecting just the right amount of lightheartedness into the proceedings. By 1987 *The Oprah Winfrey Show* was the most popular syndicated talk show in the country, and it was viewed by more than 9 million people every day in almost 200 cities. During the 1990s the show went into international syndication, and by 2001 it was seen daily by 22 million American viewers as well as an unknown number of viewers in 119 foreign countries.

In 1988 Winfrey expanded her horizons by becoming an entrepreneur as well as a media personality. That same year she formed Harpo Productions (Harpo is Oprah spelled backward, as well as a lighthearted jibe at herself; Harpo Marx was a popular movie star who never said anything), which assumed ownership of *The Oprah Winfrey Show* from WLS-TV. As chairwoman of Harpo Productions, this move gave Winfrey total control of the show's content as well as its revenue, which was estimated to be more than $50 million in 1988–89 alone. However, Winfrey succumbed to bad advice during the early 1990s, when she allowed her program to descend to the level of such trash-talking programs as *The Jerry Springer Show*. Although Oprah never tolerated fistfights the way that Springer did, she did foster an atmosphere of confrontation that was remarkably different from the cooperative tone of her earlier days. After a few years of hosting shows that were virtually indistinguishable from every other talk show on television, she discarded the format to return to the quasi-educational yet entertaining tone that had made her show so enjoyable to watch and so financially successful. In 1994 she was inducted into the Television Hall of Fame, and in 1997 she won *TV Guide's* Television Performer of the Year award.

In 1989 Harpo Productions made its first television miniseries, *The Women of Brewster Place*, a television adaptation of a novel about black women who live in the ghetto, featuring Winfrey as coproducer and star. In the 1990s Harpo Productions produced a number of made-for-television movies, most of them based on award-winning books that Winfrey had read and enjoyed. By 2000 Winfrey's company had been renamed Harpo Entertainment Group; in addition to the production company, the group included divisions that produced films for movie theaters and home videos. That same year her personal fortune was estimated at well over $80 million, making her one of the wealthiest women in America.

Winfrey capitalized upon her success as a talk show host in other ways. In 1996 she launched Oprah's Book Club, and the club's choice of the month is featured on her show. Having developed a love of reading as a teenager, she wanted to encourage her viewers to do more than just watch television. To date, virtually every monthly choice of the book club has become an overnight best-seller, thus demonstrating Winfrey's ability to influence her viewers. In 1998 she became a partner in Oxygen, a women's cable network with associated Internet Web sites, and in 2000 she began publishing *O, The Oprah Magazine*, which features a mixture of uplifting messages, self-help tips, and personal management and household advice.

Winfrey has maintained her run of phenomenal business success and increased cultural influence in recent years. She signed a lucrative contract to continue her *Oprah* show through the 2010–11 season. The program remains a ratings stalwart and is now broadcast on over 200 television stations in the United States and in over 100 countries around the world. In addition, Winfrey has extended her media empire with endeavors into the internet and satellite radio. Her already iconic status in American culture—she was named by *Newsweek* magazine in 2001 as the Woman of the Century—has strengthened largely through her expansive philanthropy, including the creation in 1998 of Oprah's Angel Network, which has raised over $70 million for a variety of causes, including relief for victims of 2005's Hurricane Katrina that struck the Gulf Coast and the founding in 2007 of the Oprah Winfrey Leadership Academy for Girls in South Africa.

In 2008, Winfrey ventured into the realm of elective politics for the first time by appearing at several campaign functions in support of presidential candidate, fellow Chicagoan, and eventual 44th president of the United States, Barack Obama. Winfrey—whose net worth was estimated in 2008 by *Forbes* magazine at almost $3 billion—has never married, though she has been in a relationship with public relations executive Stedman Graham since 1992. She owns several homes but lives mainly in Chicago and outside Santa Barbara, California.

Further Reading

Brands, H. W. *Masters of Enterprise: Giants of American Business from John Jacob Astor and J. P. Morgan to Bill Gates and Oprah Winfrey.* New York: Free Press, 1999.

Gates, Henry Louis, and Cornel West. *The African-American Century: How Black Americans Have Shaped Our Country.* New York: Free Press, 2002.

"Oprah's Angel Network Fact Sheet." Oprah. Available online. URL: http://www.oprah.com/article/pressroom/fastfacts/20080621_orig_charityfaq. Downloaded on July 6, 2009.

Raatma, Lucia. *Oprah Winfrey: Entertainer, Producer, and Businesswoman.* Chicago: Ferguson Publishing, 2001.

Woods, Granville T.

(1856–1910) *inventor of various electrical components*

"The black Edison," "the greatest electrician in the world," and "the best known of all the inventors whose achievements . . . credit [his] race"—these words have all been used to describe Granville Woods, one of the most prolific black American inventors. At the time of his death, Woods had received approximately 60 patents, most of them relating to electricity. But unlike THOMAS ALVA EDISON, who died a wealthy man, Woods always struggled financially and died broke.

Woods was born on April 23, 1856, in Columbus, Ohio. The occupations of his parents, Tailer and Martha, are unknown. At age 10 he was apprenticed to a local machine shop, and for the next six years he learned the trades of machinist and blacksmith. At age 16 he left Columbus, and for the next 12 years he worked successively as a fireman on the Iron Mountain Railroad in Missouri, as a laborer in a rolling mill in Springfield, Illinois, as a machinist in a shop in New York City, as an engineer on the British steamship *Ironsides,* and as a locomotive engineer for the Danville & Southern Railroad operating out of Cincinnati, Ohio. During this period he also studied electrical and mechanical engineering in night school for two years in New York City and tried his hand at inventing new apparatuses. In 1884 he received his first patent, for an improved furnace for a steam boiler.

That same year Woods became partners with his brother Lyates in Woods Electric Company in Cincinnati. The business's primary purpose was to develop, manufacture, and sell inventions that used electricity, and over the next six years Woods produced a number of innovations. The company's first success came in 1884 when Woods invented an improved telephone transmitter for projecting the human voice more distinctly over a long distance. The following year he followed up this success by inventing what he called a "telegraphony." This device combined the telephone and the telegraph; the operator could send a message either by tapping out Morse code on a key or by speaking near the sending key, in which case the voice would be heard at the other end. Although Woods Electric tried to market both devices, in each case the brothers lacked the capital to bring their product successfully to market, so the patents were sold to the American Bell Telephone Company.

The most important invention developed by Woods Electric was the induction telegraph system, also known as the synchronous multiplex railway telegraph. The system was an attempt to improve communications between train crews and dispatchers via a simple but ingenious application of the law of electromagnetic induction. Woods simply passed an electric current through a coiled cable suspended from the underside of a train, thereby generating a magnetic field around the train. As the train traveled along the tracks, the magnetic field moved with it, thus inducing a similar current in the telegraph lines running along the tracks, even though the train and the telegraph lines were not in contact with each other. This phenomenon allowed dispatchers to note the locations of all trains in their jurisdiction at any moment. It also allowed train crews and dispatchers to communicate with each other via telegraph, thus making it much easier for crews to avoid such hazards as washed-out bridges and oncoming trains.

Although Woods received a patent for the induction telegraph system in 1887, his patent was challenged in court by two other inventors, one of them the legendary Thomas Edison. In both cases, Woods was declared to be the rightful patent holder, thus enabling him to sell his patent to the Westinghouse Air Brake Company, which also specialized in electrical signaling. Unfortunately for Woods, much of what he made from the sale went to pay legal fees, rather than going into research and development. In fact, much of what the brothers earned was spent on legal fees, and in 1890 they closed their business.

That same year Woods moved to New York City where, once again, he tried to make a living as a self-employed inventor. And, once again, he developed some ingenious devices. Probably the most important one was an improved method for routing electricity to trolley cars. Previously, trolleys were powered electrically by attaching a pole known as a troller to an overhead transmission line. The troller made contact with the line by means of a pad, which was dragged along the line as the trolley progressed. To reduce the friction caused by this pad, Woods substituted a grooved wheel that rode along the wire. As before, Woods lacked the capital to bring this idea to market, so he sold it to the American Engineering Company. Other inventions from his New York era include a regulator for an electric motor, a dynamotor (an electric generator for trolleys), an egg incubator, and an automatic air brake. Although these inventions were sold to major companies like General Electric and Westinghouse, Woods was forced to defend many of his patents in court, and as a result most of his earnings were frittered away on legal fees. He died, having never married, in poverty in January 30, 1910, in New York City.

Further Reading

Beckner, Chrisanne. *100 African-Americans Who Shaped American History*. San Francisco: Bluewood Books, 1995.

Brodie, James M. *Created Equal: The Lives and Ideas of Black American Innovators*. New York: William Morrow, 1993.

James, Portia P. *The Real McCoy: African-American Invention and Innovation, 1619–1930*. Washington, D.C.: Smithsonian Institution Press, 1989.

Jenkins, Edward S. *To Fathom More: African American Scientists and Inventors*. Lanham, Md.: University Press of America, 1996.

Woolworth, F. W.
(Frank Winfield Woolworth)
(1852–1919) *inventor of five-and-ten stores*

One would have to sell a lot of items for five cents or ten cents apiece to amass $65 million, and yet that is exactly what F. W. Woolworth did. For 40 years, his stores sold no item of merchandise for more than a dime. In the process, he popularized the five-and-ten store, the forerunner of the late 20th century's dollar store.

Woolworth was born Frank Winfield Woolworth on April 13, 1852, in Rodman, New York. His parents, John and Fanny, were farmers. At age seven he moved with his family to nearby Great Bend, where he grew up. At age 16 he briefly

attended a commercial college in Watertown. In 1872, having learned to despise farmwork, he took a job as a store clerk in Watertown. Over the next seven years he worked successively for Augsbury & Moore, A. Bushnell and Company, and Moore & Smith. In 1876 he married Jennie Creighton with whom he had three children.

While with Moore & Smith, Woolworth was introduced to the sales technique that would make him rich and famous. A traveling salesman had told William H. Moore, the store's senior proprietor, about a store in Michigan that had gotten rid of excess merchandise by putting it on a table with a sign that read, "Any Article on This Counter, 5¢." Before long, the table was empty and the store's cash register was full of nickels. Moore had some old inventory that he wanted to move, so he had Woolworth set up a nickel counter; sure enough, the merchandise moved just like in Michigan. Woolworth was so impressed that he decided to open a store of his own that sold nothing but nickel items, and in 1879 he opened the "Great 5¢ Store" in nearby Utica. Moore loaned him $315.41 with which to purchase merchandise and to pay rent. The store was poorly located on a back street where it received little pedestrian traffic, and it closed after three months. Undaunted, that same year Woolworth opened a second 5¢ store in Lancaster, Pennsylvania, on a busy street corner; business was so good that he added a line of items that sold for a dime, thus making it the first five-and-ten store in the country. In 1880 he opened two more Pennsylvania stores, in York and Harrisburg; neither of them prospered and soon were closed. However, a third new store, in Scranton, did exceptionally well. By the end of the year Woolworth had paid off his debt to Moore and still had $2,000 and two profitable stores, proving to Woolworth that his concept would work on a grand scale.

Woolworth's concept grew slowly over the next six years; Woolworth preferred to raise money for his new stores by taking on partners rather than by borrowing money. By 1886 he had opened four more stores in Pennsylvania, New York, and New Jersey in partnership with his brother Charles, his cousin Seymour Knox, Moore, and Fred M. Kirby. Meanwhile, Woolworth and Moore had converted Moore & Smith into a five-and-ten store. That same year Woolworth moved to Brooklyn, New York, and opened a central purchasing and administration office in Manhattan, the center of American commercial activity. By 1888 he had made so much money that he decided to sever his partnerships, with each of the partners forming his own five-and-ten chain. From that time on, he would finance everything he bought or built with his own money.

In order to remain competitive in the retail trade, Woolworth had to have reliable sources of good quality but inexpensive merchandise that he could sell for a nickel or dime and still turn a profit. In 1890, acting on a tip from a New York retail executive, he made his first trip to Europe in search of such merchandise. In Germany he found bargains on dolls, glass marbles, and Christmas ornaments; in Austria and Bohemia, on vases and glassware; and in France, on all sorts of things. He immediately began importing all of these items, and by 1900 he employed seven buyers in Europe and Asia to acquire such things as china and lace, in addition to more mundane items. He held down costs by eliminating high-priced clerks and putting items on counters where customers could serve themselves. Attractive displays with big signs calling the customer's attention to the spectacular bargains at hand greatly boosted sales volume.

By 1893 Woolworth's stores were sporting a new logo, a diamond with a red "W" in the center. The economic downturn that began that year and ran for several years was a godsend for him. While most businesses were closing or contracting during the panic of 1893, the sales volume in Woolworth's stores increased significantly. As a result, he was able to finance further expansion into New England as well as to locate stores in larger trading centers of the Northeast such as Boston, Brooklyn, New York, Philadelphia, and Washington. By 1905, when he formed F. W. Woolworth & Company, he was the sole owner of 120 stores in 21 states. Over the next five years, he built stores in Canada and Great Britain, and he introduced his first lunch counter, where shoppers could sit and relax while consuming inexpensive malted milks and grilled cheese sandwiches, among other nutritious but low-priced fare. In 1912 he merged Woolworth's with the chains of his four former partners and with

that of Earle P. Charlton, who owned a number of stores in the West, thus creating a retail empire of almost 600 stores from coast to coast with an annual sales volume of more than $50 million. By the time of his death seven years later, the number of Woolworth's stores in the United States and Canada had grown to almost 1,100.

One of Woolworth's more memorable accomplishments was the construction in 1913 of the Woolworth Building in lower Manhattan. This 60-story skyscraper cost $13.5 million to build, a significant amount of money at the time, yet he paid for the entire project in cash. In one of the lobby's upper corners, there is a gargoyle depicting him with his hands full of nickels and dimes. He died on August 8, 1919, in New York City. At the time of his death, his estate was estimated at $65 million.

Further Reading

Baker, Nina Brown. *Nickels and Dimes: The Story of F. W. Woolworth.* New York: Scholastic Book Services, 1975.

Gustaitis, Joseph. "The Nickel & Dime Empire." *American History,* March 1998: 40–46.

Winkler, John K. *Five and Ten: The Fabulous Life of F. W. Woolworth.* Freeport, N.Y.: Books for Libraries Press, 1970.

Wright, Wilbur (1867–1912), and Orville Wright (1871–1948)
inventors of the airplane

The airplane is one of the few major inventions whose inventors are agreed upon by virtually everyone. Wilbur and Orville Wright became the fathers of the airplane largely because they approached its development in a totally different way from their predecessors. Rather than build a machine that worked in theory and then try to make it fly, the Wright Brothers mastered the science of flying and then built a machine that conformed to that science.

Wilbur Wright was born on April 16, 1867, in Dayton, Ohio. Orville Wright was born on August 19, 1871, near Millville, Indiana. Their father, Milton, was a clergyman, and their mother, Susan, was a homemaker. They both grew up in Dayton, where they attended high school without graduating, and in 1889 they became partners in a printing shop. Three years later they also opened a bicycle shop, and by 1896 they were manufacturing bicycles as well as fixing and selling them.

As boys, the Wrights had become interested in manned flight. This interest was rekindled in 1896 when they learned of the death of Otto Lilienthal, the German inventor of several successful gliders. Shortly thereafter, they began gathering data about other fliers and their aircraft from the local public library and the Smithsonian Institution in the hope of building the first successful airplane. In 1899 they built their first flying device, a biplane kite. While they were building it, Wilbur, who had

Wilbur (left) and Orville Wright invented the world's first self-propelled airplane. *(Library of Congress)*

been watching buzzards fly, realized that a successful airplane had to duplicate a bird in flight; that is, it had to be able to bank to either side, climb or descend, and turn left or right, sometimes all three simultaneously. At the time, no aviator had developed a steering mechanism that gave a pilot the ability to maneuver in all three axes at once. The first two motions were easy to duplicate; an elevator on the front would allow the plane to go up or down, and a rudder on the tail would make it turn from side to side. The key to banking came when Wilbur discovered that a buzzard banks by twisting its wings in an asymmetrical fashion, which meant that an airplane's wings somehow had to be made so that one could turn upward while the other turned downward.

In 1899 the Wrights began experimenting with various control mechanisms on a series of biplane kites. By 1900 they had developed a satisfactory triple-axis steering mechanism, which controlled the moving parts via lever-operated wires. That same year they installed it on a biplane glider, which they tested at Kitty Hawk, a fishing village on North Carolina's Outer Banks. They chose the site because it had huge sand dunes from which the glider could be flown, and the wind blew strongly there year-round. When the glider's wings failed to generate as much lift as they had thought they would, the Wrights returned to Dayton and built a glider with almost twice as much wing area, which they tested the following year at Kill Devil Hills, just south of Kitty Hawk. Its wings also failed to lift satisfactorily, so the brothers returned to Dayton and built a crude wind tunnel in the back of their bicycle shop. After extensive testing of a variety of wing configurations and areas in the wind tunnel, in 1902 they returned to Kill Devil Hills, and this time the glider's wings and steering mechanism performed perfectly.

Having solved the problems of steering and lift, the Wrights' next task was to make their airplane self-propelled. This step turned out to be more complicated than they had thought. At first they tried mounting two push propellers on the back of the plane, but the propellers' flat blades simply sliced through the air without generating any forward thrust. They eventually learned that twisting the blades enabled the propeller to grab hold of the air and force the plane forward. Next came the design of a lightweight gasoline engine, since automotive engines were far too heavy for an airplane that weighed about 300 pounds. After some experimentation, they and Charles Taylor, a mechanic in their bicycle shop, designed a four-cylinder engine light enough and powerful enough to do the job. In 1903 the Wrights returned to Kill Devil Hills with their first powered airplane, the *Flyer I*, later known as the *Kitty Hawk*. Its best flight lasted almost one full minute and covered less than 900 feet. The following year they flew longer and further in the *Flyer II*, which had an improved engine, at Huffman Prairie near Dayton. In 1905 they developed the *Flyer III*, the world's first practical airplane; on its best flight it took off from level ground and then turned, banked, climbed, and dove for almost 40 minutes before making a smooth landing.

Fearful that further flying would only alert potential competitors who would steal their design, the Wrights warehoused *Flyer III* and began looking for buyers in the United States and abroad. By 1908 they had sold the French rights to the airplane to a group of French investors. They also reached an agreement with the U.S. Army, whereby it would pay $25,000 for the Wrights' airplane if it could stay aloft with a pilot and passenger for at least one hour and travel at a speed of at least 40 miles per hour. That same year Wilbur made the first public demonstration of the Wrights' airplane on a racecourse near Le Mans, France. By the end of the year he had flown hundreds of flights, including one that lasted more than two hours. Meanwhile, Orville was duplicating Wilbur's feats at Fort Myer, Virginia, on the outskirts of Washington, D.C., and in 1909 the American government took delivery of the world's first military airplane.

In 1909 the Wrights formed the Wright Company, with offices in New York City and a factory in Dayton. While Orville concentrated on training exhibition pilots, in essence the company's marketing team, Wilbur battled the company's rivals in court over patent infringements. In 1912 Wilbur developed a case of typhoid fever and died on May 30 in Dayton. In 1915 Orville sold his and Wilbur's shares in the Wright Company. He served

as a consultant through the end of World War I and then spent most of the next 30 years serving in volunteer groups, such as the National Advisory Committee for Aeronautics and the Guggenheim Fund for the Promotion of Aeronautics, and tinkering in his laboratory. He died on January 30, 1948, in Dayton.

Further Reading
Brady, Tim. *The American Aviation Experience: A History.* Carbondale: Southern Illinois University Press, 2000.

Crompton, Samuel W. *100 Americans Who Shaped American History.* San Mateo, Calif.: Bluewood Books, 1999.

Crouch, Tom D. *The Bishop's Boys: A Life of Wilbur and Orville Wright.* New York: W. W. Norton, 1990.

Culick, F., and Spencer Dunmore. *On Great White Wings: The Wright Brothers and the Race for Flight.* New York: Hyperion, 2001.

Howard, Fred. *Wilbur and Orville Wright: A Biography of the Wright Brothers.* Mineola, N.Y.: Dover Publications, 1998.

Wrigley, William, Jr.
(1861–1932) *entrepreneur in chewing gum*

Just about every kid in America, and a large number of the adults as well, loves chewing gum. Although he did not invent it, William Wrigley, Jr., is the man most responsible for making chewing gum the popular pastime that it is today. His aggressive advertising campaigns (at one time his company had one of the largest advertising budgets in the United States) and personal creation of several still-popular flavors made chewing gum a fashionable activity in the United States and around the globe.

Wrigley was born on September 30, 1861, in Philadelphia, Pennsylvania. His father, William, was a soap maker, and his mother, Mary, was a homemaker. At age 10 he began helping his father by selling soap on the street corner outside the soap factory on Saturdays. The following year he dropped out of school and went to work in his father's factory. At age 13 he became a full-time salesman, and for the next 17 years he covered

Pennsylvania, New York, and New England for his father's company. In 1885 he married Ada Foote with whom he had two children.

In 1891 Wrigley borrowed $5,000 from his uncle, William Scatchard, and moved to Chicago, Illinois, to start his own soap business. To get store owners to handle his products, he offered them premiums such as knives, coffee grinders, and fishing tackle, and to get customers to buy his products he included a packet of baking powder in each box of soap. The baking powder proved to be more popular than the soap, so in 1892 he quit making soap to make baking powder instead. A firm believer in giving premiums to customers as an inducement to buy his product, even though the baking powder was already a popular item, he started putting a stick of chewing gum, a relatively new novelty, in each box.

Wrigley did not invent chewing gum, nor was he the first to manufacture it. For centuries, American Indians had been chewing the sweet, gummy resin of the spruce tree to clean their teeth and freshen their breath, and the first European settlers adopted the practice. By the mid-19th century, Americans had given up chewing spruce resin in favor of sweetened paraffin, a waxy petroleum by-product. In the latter half of the 19th century, it was discovered that chicle, the chewy resin of

William Wrigley was a great baseball fan; here he watches his beloved Chicago Cubs. *(Library of Congress)*

Yucatán's sapodilla tree, could be flavored, and that it held its flavor much longer than paraffin. This discovery led to the beginning of the chewing gum business. One of the first gum makers was the Zeno Manufacturing Company, which supplied Wrigley with his gum.

Before long, Wrigley discovered that the stick of gum was more popular than the baking powder, so he focused his attention on selling gum. In 1893 he closed down his own business and used Zeno as his manufacturer. By 1899 he had introduced "Spearmint," a flavor of his own invention, which was later joined by "Doublemint" and "Juicy Fruit"; all three remained popular flavors through the end of the 20th century. To boost the sales of his chewing gum, he relied heavily on advertising, spending more than $250,000 in 1907 alone. But his efforts paid off, and by 1908 annual sales topped the $1 million mark. In 1911 he purchased Zeno and renamed it the William Wrigley, Jr., Company. Within a few years he had opened factories in New York City as well as in Canada, England, Germany, and Australia. By 1925 Wrigley Gum was advertised around the globe in 30 languages, and Wrigley's company was the largest chewing gum manufacturer in the world with annual sales of $35 million. Much of this money was contributed to Chicago charities, and the company commissioned the construction of a new headquarters, the Wrigley Building, whose distinctive clock tower became a landmark in downtown Chicago.

Wrigley's two favorite hobbies were the Chicago Cubs and California's Santa Catalina Island. Between 1916 and 1921 he acquired a majority interest in the Cubs, a National League baseball team, and eventually built idyllic Wrigley Field on Chicago's North Side as the team's home ballpark. In 1921 he bought Santa Catalina, a semi-deserted island 22 miles off the California coast in Los Angeles County. Over the years he developed the island commercially by quarrying sand and gravel, starting a pottery and tile factory that used the island's superior grade of clay, and mining silver, copper, and zinc. He also turned the island into one of the country's most famous resorts by building a casino, several hotels, and a ballpark where the Cubs trained in the spring.

In 1925 Wrigley relinquished the presidency of his company to his son, Philip, but continued to serve as chairman of the board. He spent his summers on his estate in Lake Geneva, Wisconsin, and his winters on Santa Catalina. He also bought a winter resort in Phoenix, Arizona, where he died on January 26, 1932. He was buried on Santa Catalina Island.

Further Reading

"William Wrigley Jr." Available online. URL: http://www. wrigley.com/global/about-us/william-wrigley-jr.aspx. Downloaded on March 15, 2010.

Zimmerman, William Jr. *William Wrigley, Jr., the Man and His Business, 1861–1932.* Chicago: R. R. Donnelly and Sons, 1935.

Y

Yale, Linus, Jr.
(1821–1868) *inventor of the Yale lock*

Perhaps the most common type of lock today is the Yale lock. This lock, which is used in most house and automobile doors as well as most small padlocks, is unlocked by means of a flat, serrated key. The inventor of the Yale lock, Linus Yale, Jr., modeled his design after a lock first used in ancient Egypt.

Yale was born on April 4, 1821, in Salisbury, New York. His father, Linus, Sr., was a metalworker and a general repairman, and his mother, Chlotilda, was a homemaker. Around 1840 he became a traveling portrait painter and spent the next several years plying his trade in New York and New England. In 1844 he married Catherine Brooks with whom he had three children. In 1847 he went to work full time for his father, who had just opened the Yale Lock Shop in Newport, New York. The shop specialized in the design and manufacture of bank locks, a type of heavy-duty lock used to secure the contents of a safe or strong room.

In 1851 Yale invented the Infallible Bank Lock, the first lock for which he received a patent. Most bank locks of the day secured the lock's bolt, or locking mechanism, by means of one or more tumblers, a lever or large pin that engages a slot in the bolt, thus keeping the bolt from sliding to the open position. To open the lock, the tumbler had to be lifted out of the slot to exactly the right height by turning what is known as a skeleton key, which then would slide the bolt. A skilled lock picker, however, had little trouble getting past such locks because the tumblers were located just inside the keyhole and could be lifted easily with a picking tool. The Infallible simply moved the tumblers further toward the interior of the lock, thus making it more difficult (but not impossible) to pick.

Having received a patent for the Infallible in 1855, that same year Yale moved to Philadelphia, Pennsylvania, where he established a facility to manufacture it. Four years later, he took on Halbert Greenleaf as a partner, and in 1861 they moved the business to Shelburne Falls, Massachusetts, the hometown of both Greenleaf and Yale's wife. Although the partnership was dissolved in 1865, Yale remained in Shelburne Falls where his facility eventually employed about 30 people. By 1865 he had developed several more improved bank locks, including the Magic, the Double Treasury, and the Monitor; this last one was a combination lock that did not require a key.

By 1865 Yale had perceived that the market for bank locks was maturing, while the demand for a simple household lock was growing. That same year he received a patent for the cylinder pin tumbler lock, better known today as the Yale lock. It was an improvement on a lock invented by his father in 1848, which was itself patterned after a lock first used by the ancient Egyptians. In a pin tumbler lock, the tumblers are pins, usually five in number, that hang down inside of the lock. In the Egyptian version, a large wooden key that resembled a toothbrush was inserted into the lock and lifted up, which lifted the pins and allowed the bolt to slide open. In the Yale version, a small metal key is inserted into a cylinder; turning the key rotates the cylinder, which slides the bolt. To make the lock more secure, Yale cut the pins into two pieces, called bottom pins and drivers; the joint where a bottom pin and a driver meet is called the breaking point. When the correct key is inserted into the cylinder, it lifts the bottom pins and drivers so that all the breaking points are aligned with the edge of the cylinder, thus allowing the cylinder to rotate. Since the breaking points must be aligned to within a fraction of a millimeter, the Yale cylinder lock makes possible a virtually infinite number of pin tumbler arrangements. Although it is not as secure as a bank lock, the Yale lock is sufficient for most door locks and padlocks, which are designed to keep out petty thieves.

The Yale lock was different enough from bank locks to necessitate the establishment of a new facility for its manufacture. In 1868 Yale went to Philadelphia in search of a partner, and there he met Henry R. Towne. Towne was a skilled mechanical engineer and operations manager whose father, John Henry Towne, was wealthy. With John Towne putting up 60 percent of the capital, Yale and Henry Towne formed the Yale Lock Manufacturing Company in Stamford, Connecticut. Before the new factory was completed, however, Yale had a heart attack in New York City where he died on Christmas Day, 1868. His son, John B. Yale, took his place, and in conjunction with Henry Towne built the company into one of the world's foremost lock manufacturers.

Further Reading

Hennessy, Thomas F. *Locks and Lockmakers of America.* Park Ridge, Ill.: Locksmith Publishing Co., 1997.

"Linus Yale," Infoplease. Available online. URL: http://www.infoplease.com/ipa/A0772017.html. Downloaded on July 6, 2009.

Yerkes, Charles Tyson

(1837–1905) *entrepreneur in public transportation*

One of the more colorful characters in American business history is Charles Yerkes. Jailed on felony charges stemming from the misappropriation of municipal funds in Philadelphia, he rose to be the king of streetcars in Chicago, then lost his fortune while expanding the subways in London. His life was the stuff of novels, and it inspired the famous American author Theodore Dreiser to write three: *The Financier* (1912), *The Titan* (1914), and *The Stoic* (1947).

Yerkes was born on June 25, 1837, in Philadelphia, Pennsylvania. His father, Charles, was a bank president, and his mother, Elizabeth, was a homemaker. After graduating from high school he went to work as a clerk for James P. Perot Brothers, a commission brokerage house. In 1859 he married Susanna Gamble with whom he had six children. By 1862 he had learned enough about the ins and outs of the financial marketplace to start his own investment bank. Unlike a savings bank, an investment bank buys, at a discount, stocks and bonds when they are first issued, then resells them at face value to stockbrokers, banks, and wealthy individuals. He specialized in high-risk investments, the equivalent of late-20th-century junk bonds, and made a fortune. Around 1871 he was entrusted with a sizable sum of money by the Philadelphia municipal government to invest on its behalf, but instead he invested it for his own benefit. When the city demanded the money's return, his financial position was not liquid enough to allow him to comply. In 1871 he was convicted of embezzlement, sentenced to 21 months in jail, and pardoned after serving seven. He recouped his fortune and prestige during the panic of 1873 by buying distressed stocks, but he lost his social standing around 1880 when his wife filed suit against him for adultery. By 1882 he had divorced her, married Mary Moore, and moved to Chicago, Illinois, where he opened a brokerage firm.

Not long after his arrival in Chicago, Yerkes bought the North Chicago Street Railway, which operated horse-drawn streetcars. Using his stock position in the railway as leverage, he acquired another street railway, then another, until eventually he owned almost all of Chicago's public transportation. Although he was criticized loudly and often by the streetcar-riding public, Yerkes did a lot to make its riding experience more comfortable and convenient. He converted the power of most of the streetcars from horse to cable and, in many cases, to electricity, thereby greatly decreasing travel times. He had tunnels dug under the Chicago River for his lines on the north and west sides of town so that his riders would not have to wait at any of the river's many drawbridges. He extended his lines into the suburbs, adding hundreds of miles of public transportation to the existing system, and had about half of it electrified. Most important, he built the system of elevated electric trains that have become a distinctive part of north and downtown Chicago and that have resulted in the Windy City's central business district being nicknamed "the Loop." In the process of doing all this, Yerkes may have invested as much as $25 million, much of which he obtained from a group of investors headed by Peter A. B. Widener, a street-railway magnate in Philadelphia. In return, Yerkes may have taken in as much as a half million dollars in profit each year.

One of the things that complicated the operation of Yerkes's transportation empire was the fact that his street railways ran down the middle of the streets, which were owned by the various municipalities. Obtaining franchises from these municipalities meant applying to boards controlled by poorly paid aldermen, who expected gifts and money in exchange for their votes. Yerkes was successful in large part because, in the 1880s, he cheerfully accepted the realities of doing business in such an environment. In addition to bribing municipal officials, he also allowed party bosses to nominate people for job openings with his operating and construction companies,

thus furthering the bosses' prestige among their constituents.

By 1890, however, Yerkes had determined to free himself from this situation by securing long-term leases for all his operating companies. This entailed getting the state legislature to take responsibility for regulating street railways away from the municipalities, then bribing the legislators to vote him his leases. In 1899 these efforts seemed to pay off handsomely, when the legislature generously awarded him 100-year leases at no charge, a potential loss to the various municipalities (and therefore, to Yerkes, a potential savings) of $150 million. Outraged, the citizens voted out the legislators who supported such legislation, and it seemed as if Yerkes would be forced to deal with mendacious aldermen after all. Instead, in 1901 he sold his empire for $15 million to a group of investors headed by Widener and moved to London, England. Although Yerkes greatly expanded London's subway system, the project proved to be too much for him to handle financially. At the time of his death on December 29, 1905, in New York City, he was on the verge of declaring bankruptcy.

Further Reading

"Charles Tyson Yerkes (1837–1905)," Chicago "L." Available online. URL: http://www.chicago-l.org/figures/yerkes/. Downloaded on July 6, 2009.

Krambles, George, and Art Peterson. *CTA at 45: A History of the First 45 Years of the Chicago Transit Authority*. Oak Park, Ill.: George Krambles Transit Scholarship Fund, 1993.

Z

Zuckerberg, Mark
(1984–) *founder of Facebook*

In February 2004, a still teenage Mark Zuckerberg and friends hanging out in his Harvard dorm room developed a social networking Web site that eventually became known as Facebook. Seemingly moving with the incomparable speed of the Internet itself, the site soon spread to other colleges, then across the United States, then around the world. By 2009, Facebook would claim 200 million users and Zuckerberg—at the age of 24—was listed by *Forbes* as the youngest person to ever place on the magazine's annual ranking of the 400 wealthiest Americans.

Mark Elliot Zuckerberg was born on May 14, 1984, in Dobbs Ferry, New York. He grew up in this small, upper-middle-class suburb 20 miles north of New York City the second child of four and the only son of his dentist father and psychiatrist mother. Zuckerberg was an incredibly bright child and demonstrated great aptitude in programming from the time he received his first computer in sixth grade. Zuckerberg attended Ardsley High School before transferring to prep school at Phillips Exeter Academy in New Hampshire, because it offered more advanced math and computer courses. While at Exeter, Zuckerberg and a friend developed Synapse, a computer application that designed a music playlist based on the listener's musical tastes. Major corporations including Microsoft and America Online offered to purchase the program, reportedly offering as much as $2 million for it, but Zuckerberg and his friend declined. Two years later, the teenaged inventors sought to make a deal but found that companies were no longer interested.

Zuckerberg's excellent academic record earned him acceptance into Harvard, where he continued to pursue programming in his spare time, explaining in 2004, "I'm just like a little kid. I get bored easily and computers excite me." His main programming project was to create an online face book, which is a college student directory with photos and basic information. Harvard did not offer a face book and rejected Zuckerberg's requests to accumulate the information in order to create one himself. Saying, "I just wanted to show that it could be done," Zuckerberg then hacked into the university's student records and created a site called Facemash, which randomly paired photos of undergraduates and invited visitors to determine which one was "hotter." Four hours (and 450 visitors later), Harvard blocked Zuckerberg's Internet connection.

After a brief conflict with Harvard, Zuckerberg apologized and was not punished. He soon launched Thefacebook.com in February 2004 and invited Harvard students to voluntarily post their information on the site. Within two weeks, approximately half of Harvard's undergraduates had signed up. By May, Zuckerberg expanded the site to 30 colleges and banner ads on the sites were beginning to bring in thousands of dollars. That summer between his sophomore and junior years at Harvard, Zuckerberg went to Palo Alto, California, where he met with several of Silicon Valley's top venture capitalists and computer programmers.

Remembering a speech by famous Harvard dropout Bill Gates, who left college before graduation to start Microsoft, Zuckerberg decided to stop attending school in order to pursue his entrepreneurial dreams.

With the support of large amounts of capital, an influx of top talent, and an idea of social networking that precisely aligned to the desires of users, Zuckerberg's site, now known as Facebook, was immediately successful. By November 2004, Facebook had 1 million registered users, by fall 2005 it reached 5 million. In 2007, Facebook grew to 25 million users and by mid-2009 that number reached the astounding and growing figure of 250 million.

Individuals and groups use Facebook for all possible social networking purposes, from posting

Mark Zuckerberg in Paris, France *(Photo by Raphaël Labbé/Used under a Creative Commons license)*

daily status updates and family vacation photos for friends to view (by mid-2009 there were over 20 billion photos posted) to promoting professional endeavors of all kinds. Key to making Facebook the leading social networking site in the world has been Zuckerberg's focus on developing support for it in languages used by over 97 percent of the world's population. Zuckerberg, who still typically wears his sweatshirts and jeans to work, noted of the Facebook phenomenon, "I think Facebook is who people really are. We use this term the social graph, and the verb we use is mapping it out. We think the social graph exists in the world. We try to give people the ability to map out as much of their real identity as possible. We're far from the real result. But we have a start."

With Zuckerberg's enormous success has come controversy. As a pioneering Web site with global popularity, Facebook has been criticized for possible violation of privacy issues. Outraged users protested in February 2009 when Facebook updated its terms, deleting a provision that said users could remove their content at any time, at which time the license would expire. It also added new language that said Facebook would retain users' content and licenses after an account was terminated. Zuckerberg responded to these protests by reversing course on these changes in terms. Zuckerberg has also been accused by former Harvard students of stealing the original idea for Facebook, which they claim was conceptualized by them and only included Zuckerberg once he was asked to write computer code for it. Zuckerberg has denied these allegations and a lawsuit is pending.

Zuckerberg answers critics who claim that Facebook is simply a fleeting fad by explaining that his vision in creating the site is matched by his long-term commitment to it. In 2009, Zuckerberg expanded on this idea by noting, "Two hundred million in a world of six billion is tiny. It's a cool milestone. It's great that we reached that, especially in such a short amount of time. But there is so much more to do."

Further Reading

McGirt, Ellen. "Facebook's Mark Zuckerberg: Hacker. Dropout. CEO." *Fast Company*. Available online. URL: http://www.fastcompany.com/magazine/115/

open_features-hacker-dropout-ceo.html. Downloaded on September 1, 2009.

Stone, Brad. "Is Facebook Growing Up Too Fast?" *New York Times.* Available online. URL: http://www.nytimes.com/2009/03/29/technology/internet/29face.html. Downloaded on September 1, 2009.

Vogelstein, Fred. "The Wired Interview: Facebook's Mark Zuckerberg." *Wired.* Available online. URL: http://www.wired.com/epicenter/2009/06/mark-zuckerberg-speaks/. Downloaded on September 1, 2009.

Zworykin, Vladimir Kosma
(1889–1982) *inventor of the electronic picture tube*

Vladimir Zworykin was not the first person to imagine sending pictures over the airwaves, but he was the first to perfect a system for doing so electronically. For this reason he warrants the title of the "father of television." Although the iconoscope, Zworykin's first transmission tube, has long since been replaced by more sophisticated devices, the basic design of his kinescope remains the model for the modern television picture tube.

Zworykin was born on July 30, 1889, in Murom, Russia. His father, Kosma, was a wealthy businessman, and his mother, Elaine, was a homemaker. In 1912 he received the equivalent of a B.A. in physics from the St. Petersburg Institute of Technology, and he then spent two years in the graduate physics program at the College de France in Paris. When World War I broke out in 1914, he joined the Russian army and served as an officer in the signal corps. Two years later he married Tatiana Vasilieff with whom he had two children. Fearing what might happen to his family during the Russian Revolution, in 1919 he emigrated to the United States. He worked for a year as an adding machine operator at the Russian embassy in New York City, then found a job with the Westinghouse Electric Company in Pittsburgh, Pennsylvania, building cathodes for radios and working on photoelectric cells. In 1924 he became a naturalized citizen, and in 1926 he received a Ph.D. in physics from the University of Pittsburgh.

In the early 1920s, great interest was being demonstrated in the electromechanical transmission of pictures, and in his spare time Zworykin conducted experiments along such lines. However, like PHILO TAYLOR FARNSWORTH, he believed that mechanical scanners, which all existing television systems used at the time, would never be able to transmit a sharp image because they were so much slower than light, and that pictures would have to be converted into electronic waves in order to reproduce them clearly.

In 1923 Zworykin developed an electronic scanning and storage device he called the iconoscope. This device is a dipper-shaped, vacuum-tight glass envelope. Inside the envelope is a sheet of mica that has been coated with millions of tiny beads of silver oxide. When light strikes the beads, electrons are released via the photoelectric effect, giving each bead a positive charge whose strength

Along with Philo Farnsworth, Vladimir Zworykin (shown here) invented the electronic technology necessary to transmit and to receive television pictures. *(Library of Congress)*

is determined by the amount of light striking it. When an electron scanning beam strikes the sheet of mica, the positive charges are transferred to a signal plate behind the sheet, which are amplified and transmitted to a receiver. The following year he invented an electronic picture tube called the kinescope. This device feeds the positive charges it receives from the iconoscope into an electron gun, thus regulating the flow of electrons that are scanned onto the magnetically coated fluorescent screen of a cathode ray tube where the original shades of light and darkness are reproduced.

Westinghouse showed no interest in Zworykin's inventions, which at first were rather crude. Undaunted, he continued to improve his all-electronic television system, and in 1929 he made a presentation of the kinescope to the Institute of Radio Engineers. David Sarnoff, a vice president of the Radio Corporation of America (RCA), was so impressed with the presentation that he offered Zworykin a job with RCA in Camden, New Jersey. By 1934 Zworykin had perfected his system—except for the addition of the ability to project color pictures, the modern picture tube has changed little from the kinescope—and he received a patent in 1938.

Meanwhile, Farnsworth had also developed an all-electronic television. His oscillite was no match for the kinescope; however, when the light was bright, his image dissector produced a sharper image than Zworykin's iconoscope, so RCA began making a transmission tube that was a cross between Zworykin's and Farnsworth's. When Farnsworth sued RCA for patent infringement in 1934, the U.S. Patent Office conducted a hearing and found in his favor. In 1939, having failed to invent a transmission tube that worked better in bright light than the image dissector, RCA entered into a licensing arrangement with Farnsworth for the rights to use the image dissector in their televisions.

Surprisingly, the remainder of Zworykin's career had little to do with television. He conducted some of the first experiments involving the development of the electron microscope, and during World War II he helped develop night-vision equipment for the U.S. military. After the war he played a role in the development of missile guidance systems. In 1947 he became a vice president of RCA, and after his retirement in 1954 he served for a number of years as director of the Medical Electronics Center at the Rockefeller Institute. In 1951 he divorced his first wife and married Katherine Polevitsky. He died on July 29, 1982, in Princeton, New Jersey.

Further Reading

Abramson, Albert. *Zworykin: Pioneer of Television.* Urbana: University of Illinois Press, 1995.

Aaseng, Nathan. *Twentieth-Century Inventors.* New York: Facts On File, 1991.

"Vladimir Kosma Zworykin," National Inventors Hall of Fame. Available online. URL: http://www.invent.org/hall_of_fame/158.html. Downloaded on July 9, 2009.

BIBLIOGRAPHY AND RECOMMENDED SOURCES

Aaseng, Nathan. *Black Inventors*. New York: Facts On File, 1997.

———. *Business Builders in Computers*. Minneapolis: Oliver Press, 2000.

———. *Business Builders in Fast Food*. Minneapolis: Oliver Press, 2001.

———. *Business Builders in Oil*. Minneapolis: Oliver Press, 2000.

———. *Business Builders in Real Estate*. Minneapolis: Oliver Press, 2001.

———. *Twentieth-Century Inventors*. New York: Facts On File, 1991.

Abbott, David. *The Biographical Dictionary of Scientists, Engineers and Inventors*. New York: P. Bedrick Books, 1986.

Bowman, John S. *The Cambridge Dictionary of American Biography*. New York: Cambridge University Press, 1995.

Brands, H. W. *Masters of Enterprise: Giants of American Business from John Jacob Astor and J. P. Morgan to Bill Gates and Oprah Winfrey*. New York: Free Press, 1999.

Brown, Kenneth A. *Inventors at Work: Interviews with 16 Notable American Inventors*. Redmond, Wash.: Tempus Books of Microsoft Press, 1988.

Concise Dictionary of American Biography. New York: Scribner; Simon & Schuster and Prentice Hall International, 1997.

Contemporary Black Biography, Profiles from the International Black Community. Detroit: Gale Group, 2001.

Current Biography. New York: H. W. Wilson, 1940–.

Day, Lance, and Ian McNeil, eds. *Biographical Dictionary of the History of Technology*. Lawrence, Kans.: Routledge, 1998.

Dictionary of American Biography. New York: Charles Scribner's Sons, 1996.

Dow, Sheila M., ed. *Business Leader Profiles for Students*. Detroit, Mich.: Gale Research, 1998.

Garraty, John A., and Mark C. Carnes. *American National Biography*. New York: Oxford University Press, 1999.

Hallett, Anthony, and Diana Hallett. *Encyclopedia of Entrepreneurs*. New York: John Wiley and Sons, 1997.

Hamilton, Neil A. *American Business Leaders: From Colonial Times to the Present*. Santa Barbara, Calif.: ABC-Clio, 2001.

Haskins, James. *African American Entrepreneurs*. New York: J. Wiley and Sons, 1998.

Hooper, Roger B. *Who's Who of American Inventors*. Baton Rouge, La.: Hooper Group Publishing, 1990.

Ingham, John N. *Biographical Dictionary of American Business Leaders*. Westport, Conn.: Greenwood, 1983.

Jeffrey, Laura S. *American Inventors of the 20th Century*. Berkeley Heights, N.J.: Enslow, 1996.

Logan, Rayford W., and Michael R. Winston. *Dictionary of American Negro Biography*. New York: Norton, 1982.

McCluskey, Krista. *Entrepreneurs*. New York: Crabtree, 1999.

National Cyclopedia of American Biography. Clifton, N.J.: James T. White, 1984.

Oppedisano, Jeannette M. *Historical Encyclopedia of American Women Entrepreneurs: 1776 to the Present.* Westport, Conn.: Greenwood Press, 2000.

Pilato, Denise E. *The Retrieval of a Legacy: Nineteenth-Century American Women Inventors.* Westport, Conn.: Praeger, 2000.

Sicherman, Barbara, and Carol Hurd Green. *Notable American Women: The Modern Period: A Biographical Dictionary.* Cambridge, Mass.: Belknap Press, 1980.

Smith, Jessie Carney. *Notable Black American Women.* Detroit: Gale Research, 1992.

Sullivan, Otha R., and James Haskins. *African American Inventors.* New York: Wiley, 1998.

Tycoons and Entrepreneurs. New York: Macmillan Library Reference USA, 1998.

Vare, Ethlie Ann, andzek. *Mothers of Invention: From the Bra to the Bomb: Forgotten Women and Their Unforgettable Ideas.* New York: Morrow, 1998.

———. *Patently Female: From AZT to TV Dinners: Stories of Women Inventors and Their Breakthrough Ideas.* New York: Wiley, 2001.

———. *Women Inventors and Their Discoveries.* Minneapolis: Oliver Press, 1993.

Entries by Invention/Business Type

Advertising
Burnett, Leo
Thompson, J. Walter

Agriculture
Ellison, William
Grandin, Temple
Keith, Minor Cooper
King, Richard
Masters, Sybilla
Pinckney, Elizabeth Lucas
Strong, Harriett
Whitney, Eli

Air-Conditioning
Carrier, Willis Haviland
Gorrie, John

Airplanes
Curtiss, Glenn Hammond
Hughes, Howard Robard, Jr.
Lear, William Powell
Lockheed, Malcolm and Allan
Trippe, Juan Terry
Wright, Wilbur and Orville

Architecture
Bogardus, James
Fuller, R. Buckminster

Automobiles
Buick, David Dunbar
Durant, William Crapo

Duryea, Charles Edgar and
　　James Frank
Ford, Henry
Olds, Ransom Eli
Stanley, Francis Edgar and
　　Freelan Oscar

Automotive Parts
Anderson, Mary
Bendix, Vincent Hugo
Kettering, Charles Franklin

Business Equipment and
　　Supplies
Burroughs, William Seward
Carlson, Chester Floyd
Drew, Richard Gurley
Graham, Bette Nesmith
Gregg, John Robert
Sholes, Christopher Latham
Yale, Linus, Jr.

Chemicals and Chemical
　　Processes
du Pont de Nemours,
　　Éleuthère Irénée
Frasch, Herman
Hall, Charles Martin
Julian, Percy Lavon
Little, Arthur Dehon

Communications
Bell, Alexander Graham

Cornell, Ezra
Coston, Martha Hunt
Field, Cyrus West
Gray, Elisha
House, Royal Earl
Morse, Samuel F. B.

Computers
Dell, Michael
Eckert, John Presper, Jr.
Ellison, Larry
Gates, Bill
Grove, Andrew
Hewlett, William
Hollerith, Herman
Hopper, Grace
Jobs, Steven Paul
Mauchly, John William
Noyce, Robert Norton
Packard, David
Perot, Ross
Polese, Kim
Wang, An
Watson, Thomas J.
Wozniak, Stephen Gary

Conglomerates
Bluhdorn, Charles G.
Icahn, Carl Celian
Little, Royal
Pritzker, Abram Nicholas

Drew, Richard Gurley
Franklin, Benjamin
Gabe, Frances
Gillette, King Camp
Howe, Elias
Jacuzzi, Candido
Joyner, Marjorie Stewart
Muller, Gertrude Agnes
Singer, Isaac Merritt
Stewart, Martha
Tupper, Earl Silas
Walker, Madame C. J.
Yale, Linus, Jr.

IRON AND STEEL
Anderson, Joseph Reid
Bogardus, James
Carnegie, Andrew
Gates, John Warne
Gayley, James
Kelly, William

INTERNET
Bezos, Jeffrey
Brin, Sergey
Case, Steve
Clark, James H.
Filo, David
Newmark, Craig
Page, Larry
Yang, Jerry
Zuckerberg, Mark

LUMBER
Weyerhaeuser, Frederick

MACHINERY AND MACHINE TOOLS
Blanchard, Thomas
Evans, Oliver
Hughes, Howard Robard, Sr.
Knight, Margaret
Norton, Charles Hotchkiss
Slater, Samuel
Thorp, John
Tilghman, Benjamin Chew
    and Richard Albert
Whitney, Eli

MEDICINE
Pinkham, Lydia Estes
Thomson, Samuel

MERCANTILE ACTIVITY
Bloomingdale,
    Alfred Schiffer
Brown, John
DeVos, Rich
Field, Marshall
Fuller, Alfred Carl
Goldman, Sylvan Nathan
Henry, Vickie Lea
Hunt, John Wesley
Morris, Robert
Oakes, Ziba B.
Ochoa, Esteban
Perkins, Thomas Handasyd
Sears, Richard Warren
Sutter, John
Van Andel, Jay
Walton, Sam
Wanamaker, John
Ward, Montgomery
White, Eartha Mary Magdalene
Woolworth, F. W.

MINING
Daly, Marcus

NAVIGATION EQUIPMENT
Godfrey, Thomas
Sperry, Elmer Ambrose

ORGANIZED LABOR
Reuther, Walter

PETROLEUM
Bissell, George Henry
Drake, Edwin Laurentide
Flagler, Henry Morrison
Getty, J. Paul
Hammer, Armand
Houdry, Eugene Jules
Hunt, H. L.
Pickens, T. Boone
Rockefeller, John Davison

PHARMACEUTICALS
Brown, Rachel Fuller
Hazen, Elizabeth Lee
Elion, Gertrude Belle

PHOTOGRAPHY
Eastman, George
Edgerton, Harold Eugene
Land, Edwin Herbert

PUBLISHING
Beach, Alfred Ely
Bok, Edward William
Brown, Marie Dutton
Cooper, Kent
Davis, Benjamin Jefferson
Day, Benjamin Henry
Forbes, Malcolm Stevenson
Franklin, Benjamin
Gernsback, Hugo
Graham, Katherine
Hearst, William Randolph
Hefner, Hugh Marston and
    Christie Ann
Leslie, Miriam
Luce, Henry Robinson
Mergenthaler, Ottmar
Munsey, Frank Andrew
Pulitzer, Joseph

RADIO/TELEVISION
Armstrong, Edwin Howard
De Forest, Lee
Farnsworth, Philo Taylor
Gernsback, Hugo
Goldmark, Peter Carl
Griffin, Merv
Kluge, John Werner
Noble, Edward John
Pittman, Robert
Pupin, Michael Idvorsky
Sarnoff, David
Turner, Ted
Winfrey, Oprah
Zworykin, Vladimir Kosma

Entries by Year of Birth

INDEX

Boldface locators indicate main entries. *Italic* locators indicate photographs.

mL   は～り